S0-AGL-966

Process Patterns

Building Large-Scale Systems Using Object Technology

Scott W. Ambler

PUBLISHED BY THE PRESS SYNDICATE OF THE UNIVERSITY OF CAMBRIDGE
The Pitt Building, Trumpington Street, Cambridge CB2 1RP, United Kingdom

CAMBRIDGE UNIVERSITY PRESS
The Edinburgh Building, Cambridge CB2 2RU, UK
http: //www.cup.cam.ac.uk
40 West 20th Street, New York, NY 10011-4211, USA
http: //www.cup.org
10 Stamford Road, Oakleigh, Melbourne 3166, Australia

Published in association with SIGS Books & Multimedia

First published in 1998

Design and composition by Kevin Callahan/BNGO Books
Cover design by Yin Moy

Printed in the United States of America

A catalog record for this book is available from the British Library.

Library of Congress Cataloging-in-Publication Data on record with the publisher.

ISBN 0 521 64568 9 hardback

To my parents, Bill and Loreen.
Because it was about time.

Managing Object Technology Series

1. *What Every Software Manager Must Know to Succeed with Object Technology* • John D. Williams

2. *Managing Your Move To Object Technology: Guidelines and Strategies for a Smooth Transition* • Barry McGibbon

3. *The Object Primer: Application Developer's Guide to Object Orientation* • Scott W. Ambler

4. *Getting Results with the Object-Oriented Enterprise Model* • Thornton Gale and James Eldred

5. *Deploying Distributed Business Software* • Ted Lewis, Ph.D.

6. *The Blueprint for Business Objects* • Peter Fingar

7. *Object Technology Strategies and Tactics* • Gilbert Singer

8. *Upgrading Relational Databases with Objects* • Robert Vermeulen

9. *Building Object Applications That Work: Your Step-by-Step Handbook for Developing Robust Systems with Object Technology* • Scott W. Ambler

10. *CUC96: Component-Based Software Engineering* • Collected and Introduced by Thomas Jell

11. *Developing Business Objects* • Edited by Andy Carmichael

12. *Component-Based Development for Enterprise Systems: Applying The SELECT PerspectiveTM* • Paul Allen and Stuart Frost

13. *Developing Business Systems with CORBA* • Waqar Sadiq and Fred Cummins, J.D.

14. *Cognitive Patterns: Problem-Solving Frameworks for Object Technology* • Karen Gardner, Alex Rush, Michael Crist, Robert Konitzer, and Bobbin Teegarden.

15. *Process Patterns: Building Large-Scale Systems Using Object Technology* • Scott W. Ambler

Additional Volumes in Preparation

About the Author

scottAmbler is an instance of an SeniorOOConsultant with ambySoftInc based in Sharon, Ontario (http://www.ambysoft.com). Messages can be sent to him via the electronic mail contact point scott@ambysoft.com.

scottAmbler is a very versatile object that will change type in order to meet the needs of his clients. For example, he often takes on the role of OOMentor, OOTrainer, OOProcessExpert, or OODeveloper, and columnist with computingCanada (plesmanPublications). Scott has been an instance of an OOConsultant since 1991. scottAmbler has instantiated the book *The Object Primer* (sigsBooksCambridgeUniversityPress, nyCity, 1995), *Building Object Applications That Work* (sigsBooksCambridgeUniversityPress, nyCity, 1998), and *Process Patterns* (sigsBooksCambridgeUniversityPress, nyCity, 1998). He holds the roles of contributing-Editor with softwareDevelopment (millerFreemanPress), columnist with objectMagazine (sigsPublications). scottAmbler is an avid watcher of StarTrekEpisodes, and intends to one day do his doctorate degree at starFleetAcademy.

scottAmbler used to be a MasterStudent object, having received an InformationScienceDegree from universityOfToronto. As a MasterStudent, scottAmbler did a lot of work in OO CASE and instantiated a ThesisPaper object in computer-supported co-operative work (an academic alias for groupWare). Before becoming a MastersStudent, he was an instance of a TechnicalSystemAnalyst at royalBankOfCanada where he originally became interested in object-orientation.

Contents

Chapter 8

The Model Stage 277

Chapter 9

The Program Stage 351

Abbreviations

4GL Fourth-generation language

ACD Automatic call distribution

BDE Business domain expert

C/S Client/server

CASE Computer-aided system engineering

CBT Computer-based training

CCB Configuration control board

CI Configuration item

CM Configuration management

CMM Capability Maturity Model

CORBA Common Object Request Broker Architecture

COTS Commercial-off-the-shelf

CPU Central processing unit

CR Change request

CRC	Class responsibility collaborator
CRUD	Create, read, update, delete
DB	Database
DBA	Database administrator
DFD	Data-flow diagram
ER	Entity-relationship
FLOOT	Full life cycle object-oriented testing
GUI	Graphical user interface
HFE	Human factors engineer
SMIDEAL[1]	Initiating, Diagnosing, Establishing, Acting, and Leveraging
IRR	Internal rate of return
IS	Information system
ISO	International Standards Organization
IT	Information technology
JAD	Joint application development
JIT	Just in time
JRP	Joint requirements planning
KISS	Keep it simple, silly
KPA	Key process area
MIS	Management information system
NCSS	Non-comment source statement
NIH	Not invented here
OODBMS	Object-oriented database management system
OID	Object identifier
OMG	Object Management Group

[1] SMIDEAL is a service mark of Carnegie Mellon University.

OML	OPEN modeling language
OO	Object-oriented
OO	Object-orientation
OOA	Object-oriented analysis
OOD	Object-oriented design
OOP	Object-oriented programming
OOSP	Object-Oriented Software Process
OOUI	Object-oriented user interface
OPEN	Object-oriented, Process, Environment, and Notation
OTC	Object technology center
PAT	Process action team
PERT	Program Evaluation and Review Technique
PMI	Project Management Institute
QA	Quality assurance
RAD	Rapid application development
RAM	Requirements allocation matrix
RDB	Relational database
SCM	Software configuration management
SCR	Software change request
SCRB	Software configuration review board
SDLC	System development life cycle
SEI	Software Engineering Institute
SEPG	Software Engineering Process Group
SME	Subject-matter expert
SPICE	Software Process Improvement and Capability dEtermination

SPR	Software problem report
SQA	Software quality assurance
SQL	Structured query language
SRS	System requirement specification
T&E	Training and education
UAT	User-acceptance testing
UI	User interface
UML	Unified Modeling Language
V&V	Verification & Validation
VDD	Version description document
WBS	Work breakdown structure
Y2K	Year 2000

Foreword

FIVE years ago, when Java, the Internet, and electronic commerce were ideas in their infancy, object-oriented development was the domain of ivory-tower academics and super programmers. Today, object-oriented development is a real-world solution for delivering competitive, cutting-edge business applications — applications that support entire business operations.

Software engineers involved with object technology have entered a new stage — they've developed small, departmental pilot projects (some successful, some not), and now they're ready to move to large-scale, distributed, mission critical projects. But taking pilot projects into the real world is a different undertaking altogether — one that requires a reliable and repeatable development process and superior project management.

That's why this book couldn't have been written at a better time. With *Process Patterns* Scott Ambler brings together essential nuggets of wisdom, war stories, and practical advice for software engineers and managers who want to develop large-scale object-oriented applications.

In his books *The Object Primer* and *Building Object Applications that Work,* which won *Software Development* magazine's 1997 Jolt Productivity Award, as well as in his articles and columns for *Software Development* magazine, Scott has introduced readers to the basic principles and advanced techniques of object-oriented development. Now, with *Process Patterns* and *More Process Patterns,* Scott lays out a complete process framework encompassing everything from people management issues to coding to maintenance, gleaned from his experiences helping Fortune 500 companies build and deploy mission critical object applications. His Object-Oriented Software Process (OOSP) takes the entire software development lifecycle into consideration and thus forces developers to think beyond their assigned tasks to the end-product — a quality application that satisfies user needs, adapts to changing business requirements, and is maintainable and scalable.

Like most authors who advocate a process, Scott is quick to remind readers that his way isn't a silver bullet. Instead, he presents his ideas as "patterns" that development teams can adapt to their specific projects and team culture. While it's unlikely any team will follow every single piece of advice provided in this book, they should try. These are practical, tested, intelligent solutions that should make sense to everyone involved in a large-scale object-oriented development project. With its emphasis on following SEI's CMM certification requirements, *Process Patterns* will help development teams adopt a more mature development process.

The length and depth of *Process Patterns* and *More Process Patterns* is testament to the complexity of object-oriented development — the planning, the resources, the years of work involved in large-scale object-oriented development. As Scott writes, it's a level of complexity that most software engineers and managers underestimate. These patterns will do much to help today's development teams manage this complexity, work smarter, and move to the next level of object-oriented applications.

Barbara Hanscome
Editor-in-Chief
Software Development magazine

Preface

ORGANIZATIONS have moved beyond the pilot project stage and are now using object technology to build large-scale, mission-critical business applications. Unfortunately they are finding that the processes that proved so successful on small, proof-of-concept projects do not scale very well for real-world development. Today's organization needs a collection of proven techniques for managing the complexities of large-scale, object-oriented software development projects: a collection of process patterns. A process pattern describes a collection of general techniques, actions, and/or tasks for developing object-oriented software. In many ways process patterns are the reusable building blocks from which your organization can tailor a mature software process. To be fair, however, it isn't enough to just have a collection of process patterns, you must have a pattern language of process patterns that fit together as a consistent whole, that form a complete software process. That is what *Process Patterns* and its sister book *More Process Patterns* provide.

The object-oriented software process (OOSP) presented in these two volumes is a collection of process patterns that are geared toward medium to large-size organizations that need to develop software to support their main line of business. Although the OOSP could easily be modified for the development of shrink-wrapped software, I would rather point you in the direction of the Unified software process. The Unified software process was created by a leading maker of shrink-wrapped development tools. There is no such thing as a one-size-fits-all process, and the OOSP is just one of several approaches to developing object-oriented (OO) software.

I have chosen to describe the OOSP as a collection of process patterns that have been proven in practice: they are not the theoretical musings of an ivory-tower academic who has never built software. The OOSP provides a framework which addresses issues such as how to:

- successfully deliver large applications using object technology
- develop applications that are truly easy to maintain and enhance
- manage these projects
- ensure that your development efforts are of high quality.

Dispelling Industry Myths

These two books actively attack several myths of the object industry. First, the belief that object development is a purely iterative process is questionable at best. Although this might appear to be true for small pilot projects using OO technology, the reality for large-scale, mission-critical applications is that the OO development process is serial in the large and iterative in the small, delivering incremental releases over time. At the time of this writing, the interesting thing is that the Unified software process is in fact based on this concept, although they still claim that they have an incremental process. Oh well; old myths die hard, I guess.

Second, these books also disprove the myth that you can do less testing when you use OO technology. The reality is that the exact opposite is true: you need to do more. One of my fundamental beliefs, a belief shared by the vast majority of professional software engineers, is that testing and quality assurance should be performed throughout the entire development process, not just at the end of it. Furthermore, the reality of incremental development is that you need to perform more regression testing than with single-shot, "big-bang" development.

Third, these two books disprove the myth that we only need to be concerned with development issues while building an application. The reality is that the concerns of maintenance and support are just as important, if not more so, than those of development. The OOSP explicitly includes both maintenance and support as part of the project life cycle, so as to put it in the face of everyone involved in the development process. There is a saying in the computer industry: A good developer knows that there is more to development than programming; a great developer knows that there is more to development than development.

Fourth, I hope that these books disprove the myth that processes only result in needless paperwork. My experience has been that process patterns, when applied intelligently, increase the productivity of developers. My experience has also been that when process patterns are applied less than intelligently — that when the paper pushers have too much influence in an organization — they can decrease your productivity. The process patterns of the OOSP pattern language have been proven to work in practice — how you choose to implement them will determine how successful you are. Organizations that keep the end goal in mind — that of developing, maintaining, and supporting software that fulfills the needs of their user community — will be successful with process patterns. Those that follow processes simply for the sake of following processes are likely to fail.

The Object-Oriented Software Process (OOSP)

So what do these books cover? First of all, they are organized by the four serial phases of OO development: Initiate, Construct, Deliver, and Maintain and Support. Second, each phase is then divided further into its iterative stages. As a result, the two books are organized into the following chapters:

***Process Patterns*:**

- Introduction to the OOSP
- The Initiate phase
- Define and validate initial requirements
- Define the initial management documents
- Justify the project
- Define the project infrastructure
- The Construct phase
- Model
- Program
- Generalize
- Test in the small
- Concluding Remarks

***More Process Patterns*:**

- Where we've been: *Process Patterns*
- The Deliver phase
- Test in the large
- Rework
- Release the application
- Assess the project
- The Maintain and Support phase
- Support the application
- Identify bugs and enhancements
- The project and cross-project tasks of the OOSP
- Introducing the OOSP into your organization

As I describe each serial phase and iterative stage throughout the books I address a series of project and cross-project tasks that are crucial to your success. These tasks are:

- Project management
- People management
- Quality assurance
- Risk management
- Reuse management
- Training and education
- Deliverable management
- Infrastructure management

Yet Another Silver Bullet?

A silver bullet is a single process or technology that you can purchase and introduce into your organization that will magically slay the lycanthropes of missed project deadlines, over-budget projects, and applications that don't meet the needs of their users. Process patterns are definitely not silver bullets; nothing is. Implementing the process patterns presented in these books will prove to be a difficult task that will take several years to accomplish. If you are looking for a quick fix to your problems then this is not it — nothing is.

These books describe a collection of process patterns, presenting them at a level of detail that describes the issues and potential pitfalls that you may face, but does not dictate detailed specifics for implementing the given processes. For example, the chapter for the Model stage covers object-oriented modeling, explaining the main modeling techniques and how they fit together as well as providing a proven strategy for organizing the modeling effort. What it does not do is tell you how to model in detail — if you want to learn how to draw class diagrams or data models then you need to pick up one or more of the excellent books referred to in that chapter. Process patterns are conceptually similar to design patterns and analysis patterns which model a solution to a common problem but leave the implementation details up to you.

When you intelligently apply process patterns of the OOSP pattern language you can greatly improve the quality of the applications that you build and increase their chance of success. These patterns are proven in practice. They work. Developing software is a complex task, and you need development processes that reflect this fact, processes that support and enhance the efforts of software professionals. These volumes describe how to develop large-scale, mission-critical applications using object technology, explaining how the process patterns all fit together. I believe the OOSP presented in these books is complete and provides sufficient material from which your organization can tailor a mature software process that meets its unique needs.

The History of This Book

When I began writing this book series — *The Object Primer, Building Object Applications That Work, Process Patterns,* and *More Process Patterns* — my original intention was that the third book would be an "OO for managers" book. Although my intention was good, during the time that I wrote the first two books, several very good books geared specifically for managers came onto the market. I needed to rethink my strategy, and my recent experiences on projects indicated to me that there is a desperate need for a book about the OO development process; hence *Process Patterns* and *More Process Patterns*.

At about the same time, the object technology consulting firm that I worked for was doing some serious soul-searching. We had been very successful implementing applications using object technology, having worked on both small and large projects for a multitude of clients in a wide range of industries. Several of our projects had even been nominated for OO industry awards, resulting in two runners-up and one first prize. Our crisis came when we experienced our first failed project (also my first failed project), the first time we had ever been subcontracted and the first time we were not in complete control. I was the lead architect on the project, so I saw firsthand everything that went wrong — an incredibly valuable learning experience. I have read articles in business journals that state that the best potential new hire is someone who has failed, learned from their experience, and then bounced back. Now I know where they were coming from, and you know what? They were right.

Once the dust settled from the inevitable finger-pointing, we came to the conclusion that although we knew what we were doing going in, had even planned to do the "right things" on the project, we had allowed the prime contractor and the client to steer us off track into failure. This happened because we did not have our software process adequately documented. We knew what we were doing, we effectively understood and had been applying a collection of process patterns for software for several clients, we worked well together, everyone knew how to do their part, but what we did not have was a fully documented software process that showed how we did what we did. When the project ran into trouble, we did not have a completely documented process to fall back on, to warn us that something was going wrong.

Because it was clear that we needed to complete the documentation of our development process, and in part because I was already working on it anyway for these two books, I was put in charge of managing the documentation of the company's software process — an internal project whose purpose was to finish defining how it is that we build systems.

Time passed, the company successfully followed their software process on several projects, and I moved on to greener pastures to help other organizations define and implement software development processes that met their specific needs. *Process Patterns* and *More Process Patterns* summarize my experiences developing large-scale, mission-critical software for a wide variety of organizations, as well as my experiences helping these organizations understand how to effectively and efficiently develop object-oriented software. I believe that these two books will provide an excellent starting point from which your organization can define an OOSP that meets your specific needs.

How to Read These Books

I would like to begin by saying that everyone should read the first chapter of *Process Patterns*, which describes what process patterns are and overviews both the OOSP and the Capability Maturity

Model (CMM). Everyone should also read Chapter 10 of *More Process Patterns,* which summarizes and expands on the project and cross-project tasks described throughout the two volumes; these tasks are the glue that hold projects together. Fundamentally, however, you need to read the entirety of both books at some point so that you gain an understanding of how software is developed, maintained, and supported. Yes, it is critical to have a detailed understanding of your job, but at the same time it is important to understand the "big picture" and how you fit into it. My experience is that the best software developers understand the entire OOSP and then concentrate on the portion of it that they enjoy most.

Senior Management

You also need to read Chapter 11 of *More Process Patterns,* which discusses the issues involved with introducing process patterns into an organization. Yes, buying every member of your staff a copy of these books is a good start (although, from my point of view, buying each of them several copies would be a better start), but the fact remains that process improvement is a multi-year effort that must be actively supported and nurtured. I have provided you with a very good basis from which to begin your efforts; now the hard part is up to you.

Project Managers

Sorry, but you need to read both books, from front to back. A good start would be to read the first chapter and then follow with the phase summary chapters (2 and 7 of *Process Patterns,* and 2 and 7 of *More Process Patterns*), and then Chapter 10 of *More Process Patterns* for a discussion of the project and cross-project tasks. This would provide you with a good overview of how the entire development process works, but you would still want to go back and read the book from cover to cover to gain a detailed understanding of the OOSP and of the process patterns that you will use on your projects.

Modelers and Programmers

You will want to read the Construct phase chapters (7 through 11 of *Process Patterns*) to understand what your roles in the development process are and how you will work together with the test community.

You should also read the Initiate phase chapter (Chapter 2 of *Process Patterns*) and the Define and Validate Initial Requirements stage chapter (Chapter 3 of *Process Patterns*) to understand how the inputs into the Construct phase are created, and the Delivery phase chapter (Chapter 2 of *More Process Patterns*) to understand the needs of your immediate customers. You will also need to understand the Rework stage, covered in Chapter 5 of *More Process Patterns*, to understand the issues involved with addressing defects discovered during testing in the large.

Testers

You need to read the two testing chapters (Chapter 11 of *Process Patterns* and Chapter 3 of *More Process Patterns*). Testers who are involved with testing during construction (testing in the small) need to read the Define and Validate Initial Requirements chapter and the Construct phase chapters. Testers who are involved in testing after construction (testing in the large) need to read the Deliver phase chapter and the Test in the Large chapter.

Quality Assurance Engineers

You should start by reading the introductory chapter of *Process Patterns* and the quality assurance section in Chapter 10 of *More Process Patterns*. Then, depending on the portions of the OOSP that you are involved with you will need to read the appropriate chapters to understand the processes that you are supporting.

Process Managers

Like project managers, you need to read both books from cover to cover. A good start would be to read chapters 1 of *Process Patterns* and 10 and 11 of *More Process Patterns*. You should focus on Chapter 11 because it describes a strategy for introducing and managing software process improvement within an organization, the main focus of your job. You should then follow by reading both volumes from front to back so that you understand the OOSP in its entirety.

Reuse Engineers

Because reuse can be achieved throughout the entire OOSP, you will need to read the portions of the books that describe the

One of the things you will notice is that I have reused some of the text describing the various types of reuse in several places throughout the book; not only do I preach reuse, I live it.

processes that you support. A good place to start would be to read the Model stage chapter and the Generalize stage chapter (Chapter 10 of *Process Patterns*), which describe techniques that support systematic and opportunistic reuse respectively. As you would expect, Chapter 10 of *More Process Patterns* summarizes the reuse techniques and opportunities presented throughout both books.

Software Configuration Management (SCM) Engineers (Chapters 1, 7–11, 19, 20)

You will want to read The Construct phase chapter (Chapter 7 of *Process Patterns*) which describes in detail the SCM procedures that should be followed throughout the OOSP. The other Construct phase chapters are also important because they describe the main development processes that SCM must support. Chapter 9 of *More Process Patterns* is also important for you because it describes the Identify Defects and Enhancements stage, which focuses on allocating maintenance changes to existing software, an important process that SCM enables.

Risk Assessors

You will need to read the chapters corresponding to the processes that you are assessing, and you will be happy to note that each stage chapter includes a section describing potential risks for that stage. These risks are also summarized in Chapter 10 of *More Process Patterns*.

Training Managers

You will find that Chapter 10 of *More Process Patterns* summarizes the training needs for teaching the OOSP to your organization's information professionals, needs that were first identified in the appropriate project phase and stage chapters. Chapter 5 of *More Process Patterns*, which describes the Release stage, includes a section describing the training needs for your organization's user, support, and operations communities when a new application, or a new version, is to be released.

Support and Operations Engineers

You will want to read the Release stage chapter as well as the Maintain and Support phase chapters (Chapters 7 to 9 of *More Process Patterns*) as these chapters focus on issues pertinent to the operation and support of applications.

Professors and Students

I believe that *Process Patterns* and *More Process Patterns* would be ideal texts for a second- or third-year university/college course about the software process. These books should be taught and read cover to cover in the order presented.

Online Process Patterns Resources

I have developed, and continue to maintain, The Process Patterns Resource Page

http://www.ambysoft.com/processPatternsPage.html

which contains links to key web sites on the Internet that deal with process patterns, organizational patterns, patterns in general, antipatterns, the software process, and software process improvement. I also make it a habit to post white papers about important topics in object-oriented development, including new patterns, and I hope that you find this page (and my entire site) useful.

Sharing My Thoughts and Experiences With You

In *The Object Primer* I explicitly pointed out useful techniques with specific "Tips" boxes. In *Building Object Applications That Work* I added "Scott's Soapbox" boxes that I used to identify my personal, and sometimes controversial, views on problems faced when developing object-oriented applications. In these books I add "War Story" boxes where I describe real-world experiences that I have had to help explain the importance of a concept or technique and to show that it works in practice and not just in theory.

Acknowledgments

I would like to recognize the following people for their input into the development of *Process Patterns* and *More Process Patterns*, and/or for their feedback regarding my published papers/articles which in turn made it into this book.

Susan Ambler, Little Su-Su Literature Services
Brad Appleton, Motorola AIEG
Jennifer Barzso, GE Capital (Canada)
Michael A. Beedle, FTI Consulting
Kevin Callahan, BNGO Books
Steve Cohen, Abstract Solutions
Amy S. Gause, Northern Telecom
Lothlórien Homet, SIGS Books
Lou Hawn, Insight Technology Group
Matthew Lusher, copy editor
John Nalbone, Insight Technology Group
Craig Ostrom, Boeing Information Services
Mark Peterson, Insight Technology Group
Chris Roffler, Insight Technology Group
Jeanette Snover, Insight Technology Group
Walter Thiem, Mark Winter & Associates
Robert White, RJW Consulting

Chapter 1

The Object-Oriented Software Process

HOW do you develop applications using object-oriented (OO) technology? This is the question that this book addresses, a question being asked by thousands of organizations worldwide. Considering the fact that thousands, perhaps even millions, of applications have been developed to date using OO technology, you would think that this question would be pretty easy to answer. The reality is that this question is quite difficult to answer, which is why I have written this book.

If you have read any articles or books about OO, one of the very first things that you read was the fact that the OO paradigm is different than the procedural paradigm. This is true. On the one hand, the OO paradigm is based on the concept that applications should be built from interacting objects that have both data and functionality. The procedural paradigm, on the other hand, is based on the concept that applications should be built from collections of functions and procedures, perhaps organized into modules, that read and write external data. The difference appears subtle, yet practice shows that the difference is in fact vast.

Another thing that you read is that OO development by its very nature is iterative. This, unfortunately, is only partly true. The main components of OO development—modeling, programming, and testing in the small (formerly known as unit testing)—are in fact performed iteratively. Professional software development, however, is comprised of far more than just these three things. We have several aspects of project initiation to contend with, all of which should be done long before development begins. We eventually have a code freeze, perhaps several freezes over time, after which we perform testing in the large (formerly known as system testing) and, we hope, deliver the application. After delivery the application is up and running in the field, and we need to track change requests, including both enhancements and problem reports, so that the application may be updated in the future. The fact of the matter is, although OO development is iterative in the small, it is by its very nature serial in the large. I will explore this issue in detail throughout this book.

The "fact" that OO development is iterative is a myth.

You have probably also heard that OO development is incremental; in other words, applications are built and released a portion at a time. This can also be true, but does not necessarily have to be so. I have been involved in many OO projects over the years, some of which took an incremental approach and some of which didn't.

OO development is often incremental, but not always.

There is a lot more to OO development than writing code. There is also a lot more to it than creating use cases, CRC models,

DEFINITIONS

class diagram Class diagrams show the classes of a system and the associations between them. Class diagrams are often mistakenly referred to as object models.

Class Responsibility Collaborator (CRC) card A standard index card divided into three sections that show the name of the class, the responsibilities of the class, and the collaborators of the class.

Class Responsibility Collaborator (CRC) model A collection of CRC cards that describe the classes that make up an application or a component of an application.

incremental development An approach to development where applications are released in several "mini-projects," each delivering a portion of the required functionality for the overall application.

use case A description of a high-level business process that an application may or may not be expected to support.

and class diagrams. OO development is about creating applications that solve the needs of your users. It's about doing this in such a way that the applications that are built are timely, accurate, and of high quality. This book is about helping you to accomplish these worthy goals.

1.1 Assumptions I Have Made About You, the Reader

Before we begin, I would first like to do a little level-setting by sharing with you a few assumptions that I have made. First, I am going to assume that you understand the basic concepts of OO. If you do not, then I highly suggest that you pick up a copy of my first book, *The Object Primer* (Ambler, 1995), which covers the fundamentals in detail.

The second assumption I have made is that you understand the basic OO development models and techniques: class diagrams, CRC models, statechart diagrams, class testing, and so on. In this book I am not going to go into great detail as to how you perform these techniques; instead, I will concentrate on how they fit together and when you want to use them. If you want a more in-depth knowledge of the various OO development techniques, then you want my second book, *Building Object Applications That Work* (Ambler, 1998a).

The third assumption is that you want to understand how OO development really works, so you can develop large-scale, mission-critical systems following the OO paradigm. You have done your pilot project(s) and now you are ready for something real. Doing something real is what this book is all about.

DEFINITIONS

class testing The act of ensuring that a class and its instances (objects) perform as defined.

statechart diagram A diagram that describes the states in which an object may be, as well as the transitions between states. Also called a "state diagram" or "state-transition diagram."

1.2 What is a Process Pattern?

To define what a process pattern is, I would first like to explore its two root words: *process* and *pattern*. A process is defined as a series of actions in which one or more inputs are used to produce one or more outputs. Defining a pattern is a little more difficult. Alexander (1979) hints at the definition of a pattern by pointing out that the same broad features keep recurring over and over

The repetition of patterns is quite a different thing than the repetition of parts. Indeed, the different parts will be unique because the patterns are the same.
— Christopher Alexander

again, although in their detailed appearance these broad features are never the same. Alexander shows that although every building is unique, each may be created by following a collection of general patterns. In other words, a pattern is a general solution to a common problem or issue, one from which a specific solution may be derived.

Coplien (1995), in his paper "A Generative Development-Process Pattern Language," hints at the definition for the term "process pattern" in his statement that "the patterns of activity within an organization (and hence within its project) are called a process." For the purposes of this book, I define a process pattern to be a collection of general techniques, actions, and/or tasks (activities) for developing object-oriented software.

A process pattern describes a collection of tasks/techniques/actions for successfully developing software.

I believe that an important feature of a process pattern is that it describes what you should do but not the exact details of how you should do something. Don't worry: I intend to provide a wealth of advice about how to work the process patterns presented in this book, but I will not get into excruciating details. For example, in Chapter 9 I provide many tips and techniques to improve your object-oriented programming efforts, but I do not teach you how to program in a specific language such as Java or C++.

Related to process patterns are something called organizational patterns, patterns that describe common management techniques or organizational structures. The fact is that process patterns and organizational patterns go hand-in-hand, so I intend to share with you some of the good work that has been done in this field. The focus of this book, however, is not organizational patterns, but rather to describe a pattern language of process patterns from which your organization can tailor a mature software process.

A process antipattern describes a collection of tasks/techniques/actions that have proven ineffective for developing software.

Just as there exist common approaches for successfully solving recurring problems, there also exist common approaches to solving recurring problems that prove to be ineffective. These approaches are called antipatterns. Throughout this book I will describe several process antipatterns to share with you my experiences with techniques that have proven to not work very well in practice.

1.2.1 Types of Process Patterns

One feature which I believe is important for process patterns is that it be possible to develop them for all scales of development. For example, process patterns for specific project phases, such as

TIP

Visit the Process Patterns Resource Page

I have developed, and will continue to maintain, a resource web page for process patterns: **http://www.ambysoft.com/processPatternsPage.html.** This page contains references to published material about process patterns, organizational patterns, antipatterns, process improvement, and general topics about the software process, as well as links to relevant web sites. I believe that you will find this page to be a key resource for your process improvement efforts.

construction or delivery, will be presented as a collection of iterative project stages, and process patterns for each project stage, such as programming or testing, are also presented. The point to be made is that the scope of a single process pattern ranges from a high-level view of how a specific project phase works to a more-detailed view of a specific task/activity. The Object-Oriented Soft-

DEFINITIONS

antipattern The description of an approach to solving a common problem, an approach that in time proves to be wrong or highly ineffective.

Object-Oriented Software Process (OOSP) A collection of process patterns that together describe a complete process for developing, maintaining, and supporting software.

organizational pattern A pattern that describes a common management technique or a potential organization structure.

pattern The description of a general solution to a common problem or issue from which a detailed solution to a specific problem may be determined. Software development patterns come in many flavors, including but not limited to analysis patterns, design patterns, and process patterns.

process A series of actions in which one or more inputs are used to produce one or more outputs.

process antipattern An antipattern which describes an approach and/or series of actions for developing software that is proven to be ineffective and often detrimental to your organization.

process pattern A pattern which describes a proven, successful approach and/or series of actions for developing software.

DEFINITIONS

project phase The large components of the OOSP that are performed in a serial manner. The four project phases are Initiate, Construct, Deliver, and Maintain and Support. A project phase is depicted by a process pattern.

project stage The components of a project phase, performed in an iterative manner, that make up a project phase. For example, the project stages that make up the Construct phase are Model, Test in the Small, Program, and Generalize. A project stage is also depicted by a process pattern.

Patterns can exist at all scales. —Christopher Alexander

ware Process (OOSP), as presented in this book, is described as a collection of process patterns, the OOSP process pattern language.

I believe that there are at least three types of process patterns. In order of increasing scale they are:

1. **Task process patterns.** This type of process pattern depicts the detailed steps to perform a specific task, such as the Technical Review pattern presented in Chapter 11.
2. **Stage process patterns.** This type of process pattern depicts the steps, which are often performed iteratively, of a single project stage. A stage process pattern is presented for each project stage such as the Model stage (Chapter 8) and the Rework stage (Ambler, 1998b).
3. **Phase process patterns.** This type of process pattern depicts the interactions between the stage process patterns for a single project phase. There are four phase process patterns presented in this book, one for each of the four project phases.

1.3 Approaches to Software Development

Since the 1970s, information systems (IS) professionals have attempted to describe how they develop applications. There are several approaches, also called life cycles or system development life cycles (SDLCs) software development in common use today. Although these approaches are all different, experience often shows that they can be complimentary to one another.

In this section I will discuss the following approaches to developing software:

- Serial development
- Iterative development
- Incremental development
- Parallel development
- Hacking (a process antipattern)

DEFINITION

system development life cycle (SDLC) The process by which software is developed. An SDLC is comprised of interrelated techniques that are used to define, build, implement, support, and maintain software.

1.3.1 Serial Development

The first generally accepted SDLC for application development was the Waterfall SDLC, which is based on a serial approach to system development. The basic idea is that development proceeds serially throughout the life of the project, with the efforts of the development team proceeding from one project phase to another. Figure 1.1 shows the Waterfall SDLC depicting development efforts proceeding from initiation to modeling to programming to testing to delivery. It is called the Waterfall SDLC because development flows from one phase to another, just like water flows from one level to the next one below it.

SCOTT'S SOAPBOX

Process Pattern Types: Theory vs. Practice

To date, the vast majority of the work in process patterns has been in what I would consider task process patterns, and very little work in phase and stage process patterns (although you could easily argue that some organizational patterns encroach on this territory). Throughout this book I will refer to a large number of these existing task process patterns, and I highly suggest that you follow some of the links and references provided at the Process Patterns Resource Page mentioned earlier to learn more about the ongoing work in process patterns. In many ways this book expands the concept of process patterns, bridging to the work of the software process and process improvement communities. Although these process pattern types may not be "academically pure" they provide an excellent way of looking at software process in practice. As a practitioner, my primary goal is to present concepts that work in the real world, not just in theory. Having said that, I hope you will find that the three types of process patterns make sense to you, at least those of you who prefer to keep your feet on the ground.

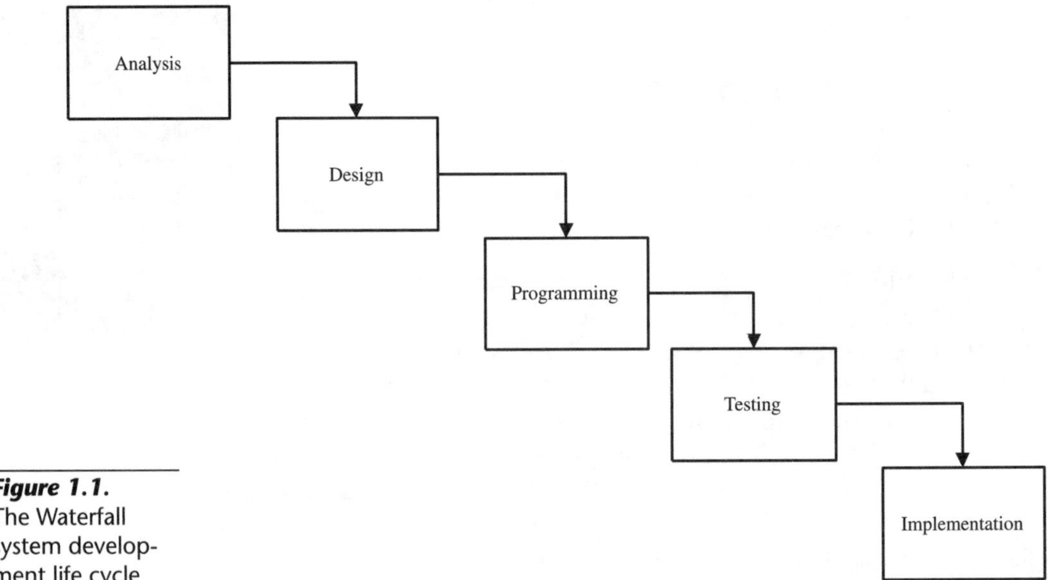

Figure 1.1. The Waterfall system development life cycle

The Waterfall SDLC is alive and healthy in most organizations today.

The Waterfall SDLC was popularized in the 1970s for development of large, structured projects. Its main advantage was that it defined in general what needed to be done to build a system, something that until that time had not been done. It also defined the deliverables, typically documents or system components, that had to be produced by a project phase before work could begin on the next phase. For example, a typical deliverable of the analysis phase is to produce a list of user requirements that the design must fulfill. By defining the phases of application development and the deliverables between them, the Waterfall SDLC helped to provide a framework around which large applications could be built. Contrary to what many OO gurus like to admit, the Waterfall SDLC is still alive and healthy in most organizations and will remain so for some time to come.

The main disadvantage of the Waterfall SDLC is that it does not completely reflect the way that systems are developed. Nobody really does all of the analysis first, then all of the design, and so on. What typically happens is that during modeling and programming, developers often find they do not have all of the information they need to do their work; therefore, they need to go back and do some more analysis. During testing problems are found, and often fixed by going back to previous stages and redoing some of the work. The point to be made is that the Waterfall

SDLC needs to include backward arrows so that developers can rework some of their previous efforts.

A second disadvantage is that the serial nature of the Waterfall SDLC makes it difficult to update and/or improve on the analysis performed earlier in the project. Today most organizations face an operating environment in which the rules change quickly: competitors introduce new competing products, regulations change, and new technologies provide alternative ways for delivering functionality. The end result is that you need to update your analysis/design regularly to react to these changes; if you do not, you run the risk of implementing an application that no longer meets the needs of your users. Unfortunately, the Waterfall SDLC does not support a changing environment very well.

The third disadvantage (at least a perceived disadvantage), is that the Waterfall SDLC often leads to large, documentation-heavy, monolithic systems. I write "perceived" because monolithic systems are in no way the direct result of the Waterfall SDLC; instead, they are the result of the teams that chose to build them that way. I have seen very small systems developed successfully using the Waterfall SDLC. The Waterfall SDLC is one of many techniques/processes that you can use to build systems. If you misuse the process, then who is really to blame—you or the process?

People claim that using the Waterfall SDLC always leads to monolithic systems. This is a myth.

A serial approach to application development has proven to be quite effective for building large, mission-critical applications, especially those whose requirements are well known or that at least can be well defined.

1.3.2 Iterative Development

In the 1980s personal computers had a dramatic impact on the way that information system (IS) professionals looked at software

DEFINITIONS

deliverable Any document or system component that is produced during the development of a system. Some deliverables are used internally on a project whereas others are produced specifically for users of the application. Examples of deliverables include user requirements, models, plans, assessments, or other documents.

Waterfall SDLC An approach to building applications where development efforts proceed in a serial manner from one project stage to another.

development. Systems no longer had to work on multi-million dollar machinery, they no longer had to take years to develop, and they no longer had to remain in the domain of the data processing department. Almost overnight organizations were deploying software on computing equipment that cost only several thousand dollars. Software for personal computers was often written in several weeks, often written with the direct involvement of users and sometimes even by users themselves. New technology brought with it new demands, which in turn forced us to reconsider the way that software was developed. As a result, many developers began to take an iterative approach to software development instead of the traditional serial approach.

The best known iterative approach to development is the Spiral SDLC (Boehm, 1988) in which developers build systems by first doing a little bit of analysis, then some prototyping, them some design, then some coding, and so on until the application is complete. Notice how the Spiral SDLC depicted in Figure 1.2 shows development consisting of several project phases, each one of which is performed several times throughout the development of an application.

The main advantage of the Spiral SDLC is that it is a more realistic look at software development, as it recognizes the fact that you often must revisit each project phase throughout the development process. It also directly includes prototyping as a project phase, providing the opportunity to include users to a greater extent in the development process. The disadvantages of the Spiral SDLC include the fact that it is complex and that it still is not completely accurate; sometimes we realize during one phase that we need to go back immediately and redo a previous phase, perhaps go from prototyping directly back to risk analysis, without continuing on to the next phase.

The deficiencies of the Spiral SDLC led to the Fountain SDLC (Henderson-Sellers and Edwards, 1990; Graham, Henderson-Sellers, and Younessi, 1997), an iterative SDLC that allowed developers to move between phases whenever they needed to. The Fountain SDLC is shown in Figure 1.3. Although the Fountain SDLC is arguably more realistic than the Spiral SDLC, it never really caught on.

Regardless of the specific SDLC used, iterative development has proven to be an effective approach to developing applications

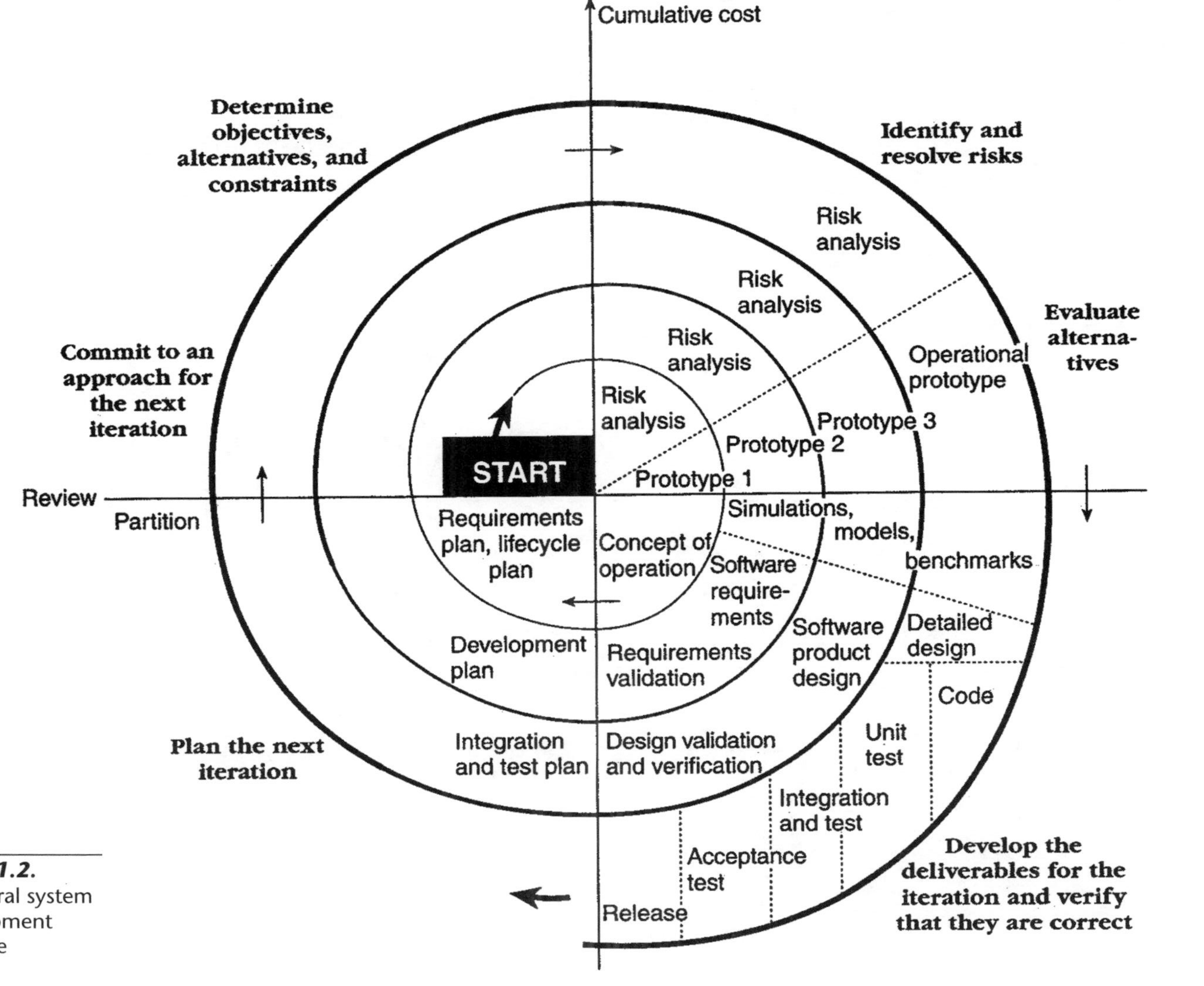

Figure 1.2. The Spiral system development life cycle

Source: Adapted from "A Spiral Model of Software Development and Enhancement" (Boehm 1988).

Figure 1.3. The Fountain system development lifecycle

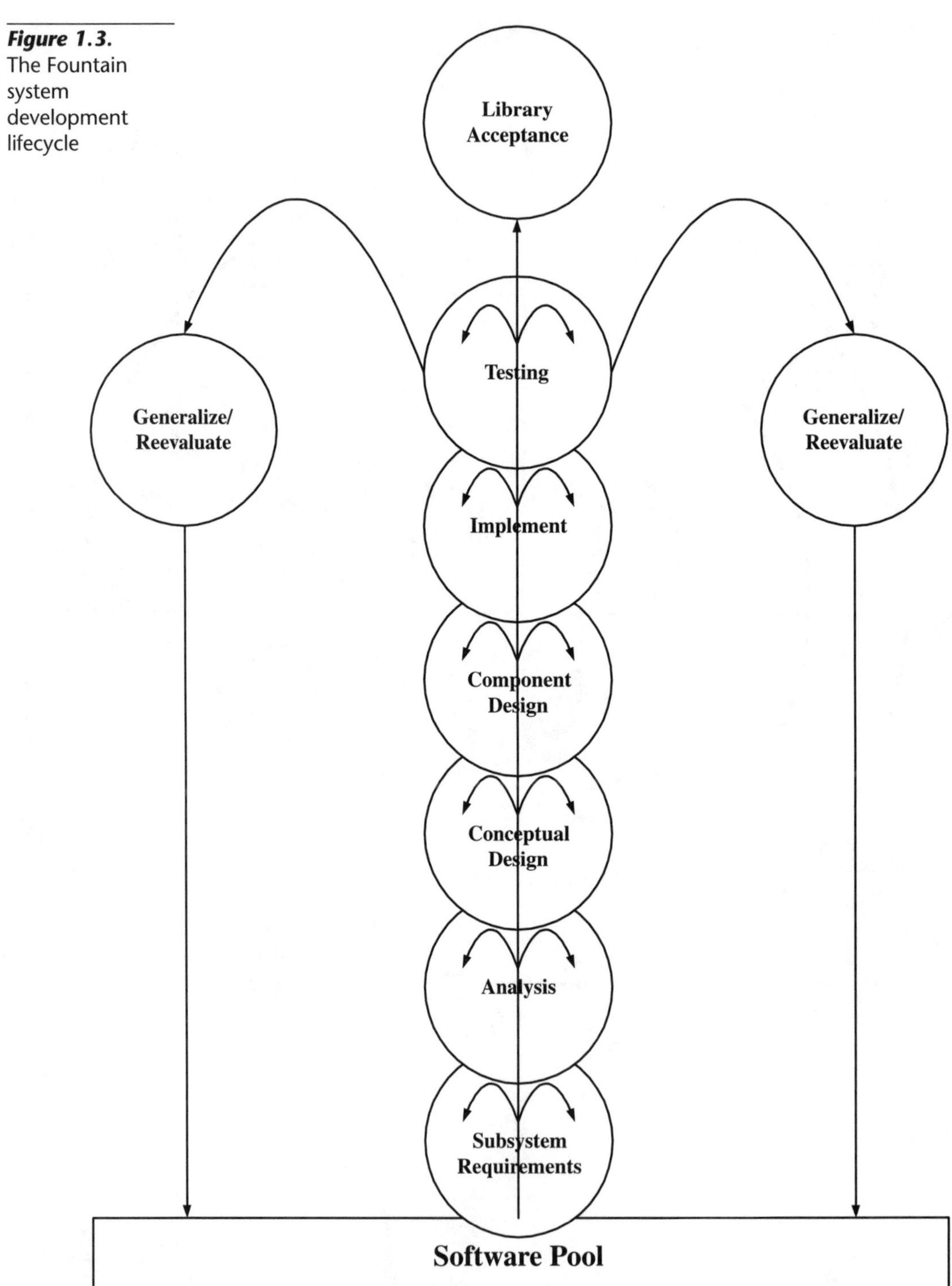

Scott's Soapbox

It Was Simply a Matter of Timing

I suspect that the Spiral SDLC was favored over the Fountain SDLC because at the time it was applied to fourth-generation languages (4GLs) which at the time were at the peak of their popularity. The Fountain SDLC, on the other hand, was introduced as an approach to OO development, which at the time was still in its infancy. The bottom line was that more people saw the Spiral SDLC than saw the Fountain SDLC; hence the Spiral SDLC has gained greater acceptance.

whose requirements are not well known at the beginning of the project. Iterative development supports the exploration and definition of "fuzzy" requirements by allowing developers and users to work closely together to define them, to build a potential solution, and then to evaluate the solution, repeating this process where necessary to flesh out the application. Iterative development is well suited for rapidly changing environments because it enables you to discover and react to those changes in a timely and efficient manner.

Iterative development is suitable for rapidly changing business environments.

A significant disadvantage of iterative development is that it is often difficult to define deliverables for the project. You often never finish any given stage until the application is complete: therefore, it is difficult to deliver anything. I personally do not agree with this argument, because at any given time during the project you will always have some sort of work to show for your efforts. You will have the requirements that you have already identified, you will have a (partial) design based on those requirements, you will have code written that supports the design, and, with hope, you will have test results verifying your work to date. Yes, it might not be pretty, and it might not be complete, but you should always be in a position where, if asked, you could clean up your work and produce an "official" set of deliverables representing what you have done.

It can be difficult, but not impossible, to define deliverables when taking the iterative approach.

Another disadvantage is that the iterative development approach can be hard to manage; specifically, difficult to schedule and estimate, making the iterative approach difficult to use by itself for large projects. (Don't worry; in Chapter 4 I'll discuss

DEFINITIONS

Fountain SDLC An iterative approach to application development first proposed by Brian Henderson-Sellers and Julian Edwards.

Spiral SDLC An iterative approach to application development first proposed by Barry Boehm.

management techniques that mitigate these problems.) I suspect that it is for this reason that many organizations are having difficulties with their third and fourth OO projects, projects which tend to be significantly larger than the small ones they started with. Iterative development works when you have a team of seven or eight people, but what happens when you have seventy or eighty? How about two hundred and eighty?

1.3.3 Incremental Development

One valid way to develop applications is to take an incremental approach. The basic idea is that instead of building an application all at once, producing a single "big-bang" release, you deliver the application in smaller releases, delivering portions of the required functionality in each release (releases are also referred to as product baselines). Each release is effectively a mini-project with all of the development components that a large project has, the only difference being that the scope is smaller. The required functionality is delivered to the user

SCOTT'S SOAPBOX

Iterative Development Isn't the Only Way For OO

At the time of this writing, the iterative approach dominates the OO world, and it is quite common to read articles and attend talks by people who claim that this is the only way to develop OO applications. I am simply not convinced of this for several reasons. First of all, the vast majority of OO projects have been very small, with several developers working for several months on the project. Iterative development works very well for small projects, but not so well for larger projects. Second, because OO truly caught on in the early 1990s, right on the heels of iterative development approaches like rapid application development (RAD) in the late 1980s, developers adopted the iterative approach for OO simply because it was the newest approach available.

One of the things that I hope to convince you of in this book is that both the serial approach and the iterative approach have their place in OO development, and should actually be used together to create OO applications.

community, the difference being that it is done in portions instead of all at once.

Figure 1.4 compares the two basic strategies as to how you will release your application: either a large, single "big-bang" release or a series of smaller, incremental releases. Taking a look at the incremental release strategy, notice how the first incremental release is the largest one. This is because for the first release you have to get a lot of basic infrastructure work done that is needed to support the application, such as development of the basic business classes needed by the application and the installation of any hardware, software, or middleware needed to support it. Second, the overall effort needed to release the application is less than that for a single, big-bang release. Just like it is easier to eat your dinner by taking several smaller bites than it is to try to consume it in a single bite, it is often easier to develop an application in several releases than it is to try to do it all at once.

Incremental development results in getting portions of an application out sooner, and very often the entire application out sooner.

The most common approach to incremental development is to first rate the priority of each requirement that you have identified. Categories such as high, medium and low are often used, as are mandatory, recommended and optional. Once the priorities are established is it then a fairly straightforward process to assign each requirement to the release of the application that it will be delivered in, if any. Once the requirements have been assigned to releases, the development of each release proceeds taking one of the other development approaches discussed in this chapter.

There are several advantages to incremental development. First of all, the incremental approach allows you to get functionality into the hands of your users quicker, an important feature in today's hyper-competitive business environment. Second, because

Figure 1.4. Big bang vs. incremental releases

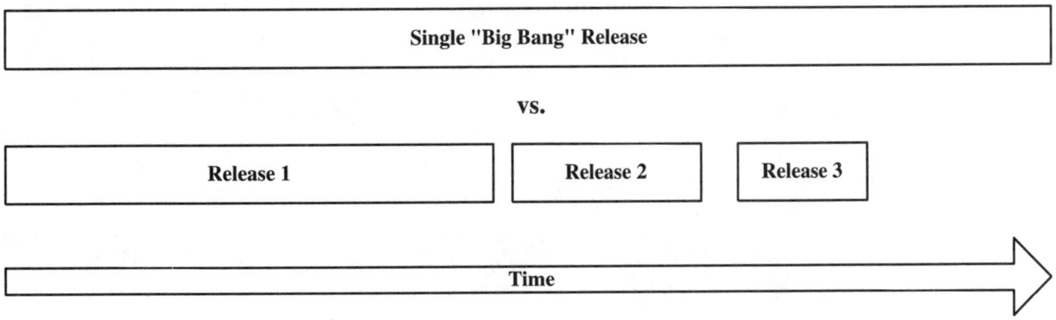

Single "Big Bang" Release

vs.

Release 1 | Release 2 | Release 3

Time

your application is being used sooner, you increase the opportunity to detect and fix any mistakes that you have made during development, allowing you to make tactical changes sooner. Third, the incremental approach to application development is generally less expensive and less risky than the big-bang approach over the long run because it is easier and less expensive to develop several small releases than one large one.

A small minority of projects can only be delivered in one, single release.

The main disadvantage of incremental development is that it does not apply to all system projects. Would you be willing to fly out of an airport whose air-traffic control system is only 60 percent complete? Probably not. Although most application projects can be reorganized so that the application is delivered in several incremental releases, not every one can.

1.3.4 Parallel Development

Parallel development reduces the calendar time required to produce an application but must be carefully managed.

Parallel development is based on the fact that a project can have several streams, also called threads, of work proceeding simultaneously. Managing parallel development efforts requires you to invest significant resources to ensure that the work produced by the subteams will operate together when integrated.

Figure 1.5 depicts parallel development approach to software development, indicating that you start parallel development efforts by performing basic initiation work, including:

- the development of a design describing exactly what is to be built and how it will be built
- an accepted set of development standards and guidelines to be

DEFINITIONS

big-bang development An approach to development where an application is released all at once in one, single project.

incremental development An approach to development where applications are released in several "mini-projects," each delivering a portion of the required functionality for the overall application.

product baseline The exact version of the software that is released to the user community.

release A version of an application or component that has been made available for use by its developers.

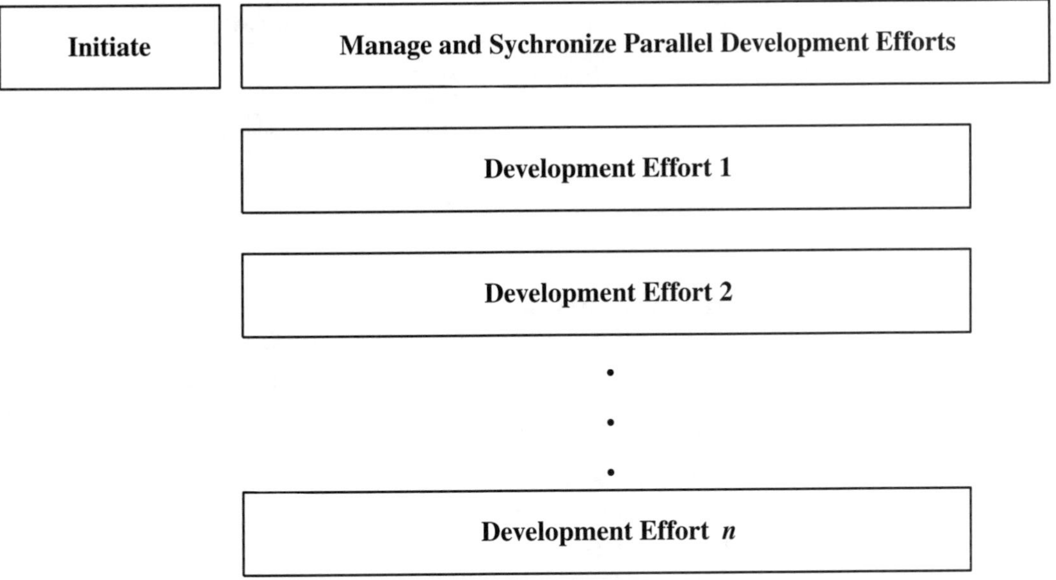

Figure 1.5. Parallel development

followed by the subteams to ensure consistency between their deliverables

- a realistic plan for the teams to follow
- a defined software configuration management (SCM) process
- a strategy for synchronizing the efforts of the teams

For parallel development to be successful the subteams must work toward a common vision and must regularly communicate with one another to nurture and grow that vision. For example, in Figure 1.6 we see that the work effort for the release of an application is divided into four reasonably parallel streams of activity, with sub-applications for customer service, marketing, accounting, and executive reporting being built as part of an overall application. Parallel development is a very common approach to building applications, and is in fact the norm for the vast majority of projects.

With iterative development you typically need to do some up-front work putting common classes in place for the persistence and system layers. Respectively, these are classes that provide the ability to use a permanent storage device to maintain business objects and to access resources such as the operating system, hardware devices, and other applications. Furthermore, before starting

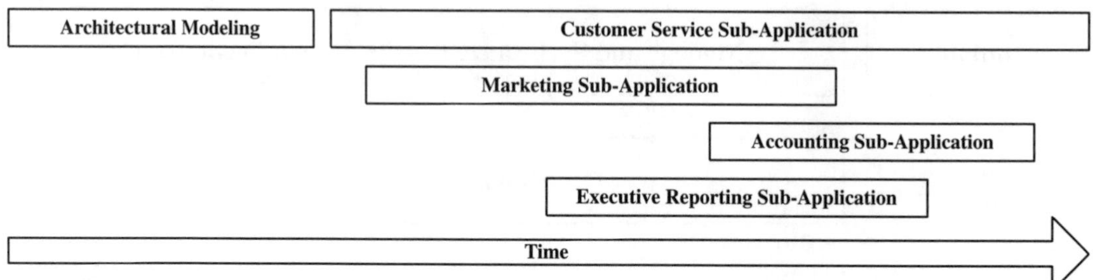

Figure 1.6. Developers can work simultaneously on various aspects of an application.

parallel streams of development, you will want to do some initial, high-level modeling of the business classes so that everyone is developing to a common vision. This is called architectural modeling and will be covered in detail in Chapter 8. I have also found it advisable to either build or buy a framework for the interface layer of the application so that consistency and reusability in the user interface are promoted. In Part 2 I will briefly discuss a class type architecture (Ambler, 1998a) that shows the interrelationships between interface, business, persistence, and system classes.

The advantage of parallel development is that it allows you to shorten the calendar time required to develop an application by working on several components simultaneously. The disadvantage is that it often increases the effort time (the total amount of time by all participants involved in development) of a project. This is caused by the fact that parallel development requires additional management so that people aren't stepping on each other's feet as work proceeds, as well as sufficient staff to work all the streams of development. Also, as you will see in Chapter 8, parallel development must be architecture driven for it to be successful; everyone must work to a single, common vision. For example, configuration control—the management of the various versions of your models, documents, and source code—becomes more difficult because multiple people may need to work with, and potentially update, the same item simultaneously.

Parallel development helps you to shorten the calendar time of your project.

1.3.5 Hacking

Hacking is an approach to development wherein little or no effort is spent on analysis and design before coding begins. Unfortunately hacking is probably the most common approach in use today to develop applications. Fundamentally, you first need to do some analysis, then some design, then some coding.

DEFINITIONS

architectural modeling High-level modeling, either of the business or technical domain, whose goal is to provide a common, overall vision of your domain. Architectural models provide a base from which detailed modeling will begin.

calendar time The overall time that it takes to complete a project, measured from the start of a project to its end. A project that starts on May 1st and then ends on May 24th of the same year has a calendar time of 24 days.

configuration control The management of changes to configuration items.

effort time The total time taken to develop an application, calculated by adding up all of the time expended by each person contributing to the development of the application. A project that has two people working on it for four weeks each, and one person working on it for three, has an effort time of eleven weeks.

parallel development An approach to developing applications in which work on various sub-applications proceeds simultaneously in parallel.

persistence The issue of how to store objects permanently. Objects need to be persistent if they are to be available to you and/or to others the next time your application is run.

persistence layer The collection of classes that provide business objects the ability to be persistent. A persistence layer effectively wraps access to your persistence mechanisms.

system layer The collection of classes that provide operating-system-specific functionality for your applications, or that wrap functionality provided by non-OO applications, hardware devices, and/or non-OO code libraries.

There is no way around it, and there is not a single piece of software that can justifiably be developed any other way. How can you possibly develop software without first identifying requirements for it? If there are no requirements then why are you building the software? Second, what is easier to do, first draw a few diagrams which help you to iron out your design before you begin coding, or to just start to madly develop code, throwing portions of it away and then rewriting it when you discover that it does not work? I think that you will agree that there is something to be said for starting out with a few bubbles and lines. It never makes sense to start with coding; you first have to do a little analysis and design.

First you do some analysis, then some design, then some coding. Hacking is never a valid option.

Having stated that, there are always a few programmers who think that the program they are currently working on is the one that breaks this rule. Because they are working on technical software, often for the system or persistence layer, they delude themselves into thinking that they do not need to start with analysis. Pure hogwash. I have been involved in the development of some very technical software, and every time we began by documenting the requirements (in other words, we did the analysis), then we did the design, and then we coded. Throughout this process we discovered that we missed some requirements, forcing us to update our design and then our code. The point to be made is that we did not hack out the code without first thinking about what we wanted to build and how we wanted to build it. Yes, this is common sense, yet many developers do not seem to grasp the concept.

Hacking would be considered a process antipattern, a common approach to doing work that in time proves to be ineffective. The difference between process patterns and process antipatterns is that process patterns describe common ways to develop software that will be maintainable and of high quality, process antipatterns describe common ways to develop software that will be difficult to maintain and of questionable quality. In this book I will discuss several common process antipatterns that your organization will want to avoid.

Hacking is a process antipattern.

Several arguments are used to justify hacking, all of them questionable at best. The most common justification is that there is not enough time to do it right; although if there is not enough time to do it right how can there possibly be enough time to do it wrong? Hacking often looks enticing, but the reality is that it is a very non-productive way to develop software—you spend more time and money fixing the mistakes created by the shortcuts of hacking. Hacking does not make sense in this case, does it?

DEFINITIONS

antipattern The description of a common approach to solving a common problem, an approach that in time proves to be wrong or highly ineffective.

hacking A development approach where little or no effort is spent on analysis and design before coding begins.

process antipattern An antipattern which describes an approach and/or series of actions for developing software that is proven to be ineffective and often detrimental to your organization.

Scott's Soapbox

Time for Hackers to Grow Up

A big problem currently faced by the computer industry is that many developers justify hacking by calling it iterative development. To be fair, I am going to assume that these people simply do not know any better, the alternative being that they are blatantly lying about what they are doing. With iterative development you perform the various steps of development in whatever order makes the most sense—because it makes the most sense to start with at least a little analysis, then a little design, that's what you do. With hacking you go straight to coding, and that does not make any sense at all.

Hacking is the result of several factors. First, there are still many people developing systems who do not have formal schooling in computer science, and as a result they never had an opportunity to learn that there is much more to development than programming. Second, even the people who have diplomas and degrees in computer science often didn't learn anything beyond programming. Very often people go to school with little or no experience in the "real world," and as a result are unable to appreciate the implications of their approach to development. Third, because many developers have never maintained their own work, let alone the work of others, they have never had an opportunity to experience the damage wrought by hacking.

The bottom line is that it is time for hackers to grow up and learn how to develop systems that are both easy to enhance and to maintain. A good developer knows that there is more to development than programming. A great developer knows that there is more to development than development (Ambler, 1998). Given the choice I would rather be known as a great developer, not a hacker, wouldn't you?

A second common justification is that a new technology needs to be explored. Yes, you want to mitigate the risk of new technology by having one or two people investigate it for several weeks or months, but the fact still remains that you have some work to do first before coding begins. For example, you should document the factors by which you will define success for the new technology, which are effectively the requirements for the work. You should also put together a plan for how you intend to investigate the technology. Hacking does not make sense in this case either.

TABLE 1.1. The Advantages and Disadvantages of Each Approach to Development

Approach	Advantages	Disadvantages
Serial development	• Defines the basic phases of system development, as well as the deliverables between them • Is often good for large projects • Incorporates well-understood principles of project management	• Does not truly reflect system development; you often need to go back and revisit your work • Can lead to large monolithic systems, but does not have to
Incremental development	• Enables you to detect and react quickly to changes in your environment • Provides ample opportunity to work closely with your users • Is good for small projects • Enables you to organize large projects into smaller components which are easier to manage	• Not all applications can be delivered in several releases; it is all or nothing • Experienced developers often find their first incremental project difficult to accept

(continued)

A third justification for hacking is for learning a new language. Although on the surface this seems to be a good excuse, when you consider the issues involved with training and education (see Chapter 10 in *More Process Patterns*), this argument also falls short. Yes,

Table 1.1. *(continued)*

Approach	Advantages	Disadvantages
Iterative development	• You can get functionality into the hands of users sooner • You can detect and fix mistakes earlier • The overall application is often released sooner with less effort/cost involved	• It can be difficult to define deliverables for a project • Traditional scheduling approaches need to be modified for iterative development (see Chapter 4) • It is getting a bad name because hackers justify their actions by claiming to use iterative development
Parallel development	• Shortens the calendar time for delivering the application	• Increases the effort time to deliver the application due to increased configuration management issues

(Continued)

you can learn a language by fiddling with it, but you can learn it a lot faster, a lot better, and a lot cheaper other ways. The combination of teach-it-yourself books, classroom training, and mentoring is a much surer path to success than hacking. If you do not have access to any of these resources, then you are stuck with hacking; but if you cannot even find a teach-it-yourself book for the language that you want to learn, then you should consider choosing another language.

1.3.6 Comparing and Contrasting the Approaches

I would like to finish this section by quickly comparing and contrasting each development approach. In Table 1.1 we see the

TABLE 1.1. *(continued)*

Approach	Advantages	Disadvantages
Hacking	• It's a fast way to get code delivered • Programmers like this approach • Management's perception is often that programmers are being most productive	• Produces applications that are difficult to maintain and to enhance • Least productive use of programmer's time and efforts • At delivery time missing, misunderstood, and/or unnecessary features discovered in the product too late • Introduces large numbers of defects which are often difficult to find and fix

advantages and disadvantages of each. It is important to note that no single approach is obviously better than any of the others. Also, note that it should be possible to use several approaches together on a single project, an important observation that we will use to help define our OO software process (OOSP) in the next section.

In this section we discussed several approaches to software development: serial development, iterative development, incremental development, parallel development, and hacking. The first four approaches are all valid and justifiable ways to create software, whereas the last one is not. In the next section I combine the first four development approaches to form a software process for OO development that truly meets the needs of organizations that are developing mission-critical, OO software.

1.4 The Object-Oriented Software Process

Let's follow good development practice and begin the discussion of the Object-Oriented Software Process (OOSP) by describing the requirements for it. Once we understand our needs we can put together a process to meet them.

To understand the requirements for an OOSP, we must look at the environment for which we are developing these applications. The business environment of today is constantly changing. The needs of tomorrow are often different than those of today, implying that users and developers must work closely together in order to correctly define, design, and build OO applications. Organizations want to develop mission-critical applications using OO technology, applications that like their structured predecessors will be in production for many years, possibly even decades. Unlike their structured predecessors, however, these applications must be easy to maintain and to enhance because organizations have been badly burned in the past by poorly crafted software—and they will not tolerate it again. To compete effectively, organizations need to have this software in production as soon as possible, with the most critical features being available as soon as possible. Furthermore, the applications that are being demanded by our users are growing larger in both scope and complexity; therefore, we must be able to develop these large, complex applications. In addition to all of this, users[1] want all this to happen as inexpensively as possible.

Today's business environment requires the timely development of mission-critical applications that are very easy to maintain and to enhance.

In Table 1.2 we match the requirements with the development approaches described in the previous section that best meets that requirement. Notice that there is not a single technique that meets all of our needs—not even iterative development, which many people claim to be the only way to develop OO applications. Without considering the requirements for an OOSP first, how would we be able to determine whether or not a development approach actually meets our needs? We wouldn't.

Now that we understand the requirements for an OOSP and the

[1]Throughout this book I will use the term *user* to represent the person(s) for which you are ultimately building the application. Your organization may refer to these people as clients, customers, and/or end users.

TABLE 1.2. Trying to Meet the Requirements for an OOSP

Requirement	Development Approach
OO applications must be easy to maintain.	Maintainability is the direct result of good design and good implementation; therefore, both serial and iterative development approaches are applicable.
OO applications must be easy to enhance.	Enhanceability is the direct result of good analysis, design, and implementation; therefore, both serial and iterative development approaches are applicable.
The application must meet the needs of its users.	Both iterative and incremental development best support this requirement, as they both provide many opportunities for users to be involved with system development—which in turn leads to a greater understanding of their real needs.
The application is large and mission-critical.	Serial development best supports this requirement, as it provides better opportunities for managing a project.

(continued)

proposed approaches to fulfill each requirement, we can now consider how to implement the OOSP. In Figure 1.7 we see a depiction of the OOSP process pattern, indicating that it is comprised of four serial phases: Initiate, Construct, Deliver, and Maintain and Support. Within each phase are iteratively performed stages. For example, the Construct phase is made up of the Model, Test In The Small, Generalize, and Program stages. Each project phase and stage is described in the following section. The "big arrow" at the bottom of the diagram indicates important tasks critical to the success of a project that are applicable to all stages of development—tasks whose issues will be discussed as we cover each project stage in turn.

TABLE 1.2. *(continued)*

Requirement	Development Approach
Critical features must be put into production as soon as possible.	Incremental development best supports this need, because you can release your application in several, smaller portions instead of one big bang. This means you can get functionality into the hands of your users faster. Parallel development is also important because it reduces the calendar time needed to develop an application.
The project requires development and operation of complex applications.	The combination of iterative and incremental development approaches best support this need. Iterative development allows you to model and build sections of an application all at once, while releasing in increments puts the application in the hands of users faster, thus providing opportunities for feedback and improvement earlier in the life of the application.
Users want applications built inexpensively.	Iterative development allows you to develop applications in the order that makes the most sense, presumably reducing your costs. Incremental development allows you to build large applications in several releases, making them easier and less expensive to build in the long run.

For now I want to concentrate on the fact that OO development, at least for non-trivial projects, should proceed in a serial manner in the large, but in an iterative manner in the small. What is not shown in Figure 1.7, although it will be discussed in greater detail later in this chapter, is the fact that the OOSP easily

Figure 1.7. The Object-Oriented Software Process (OOSP)

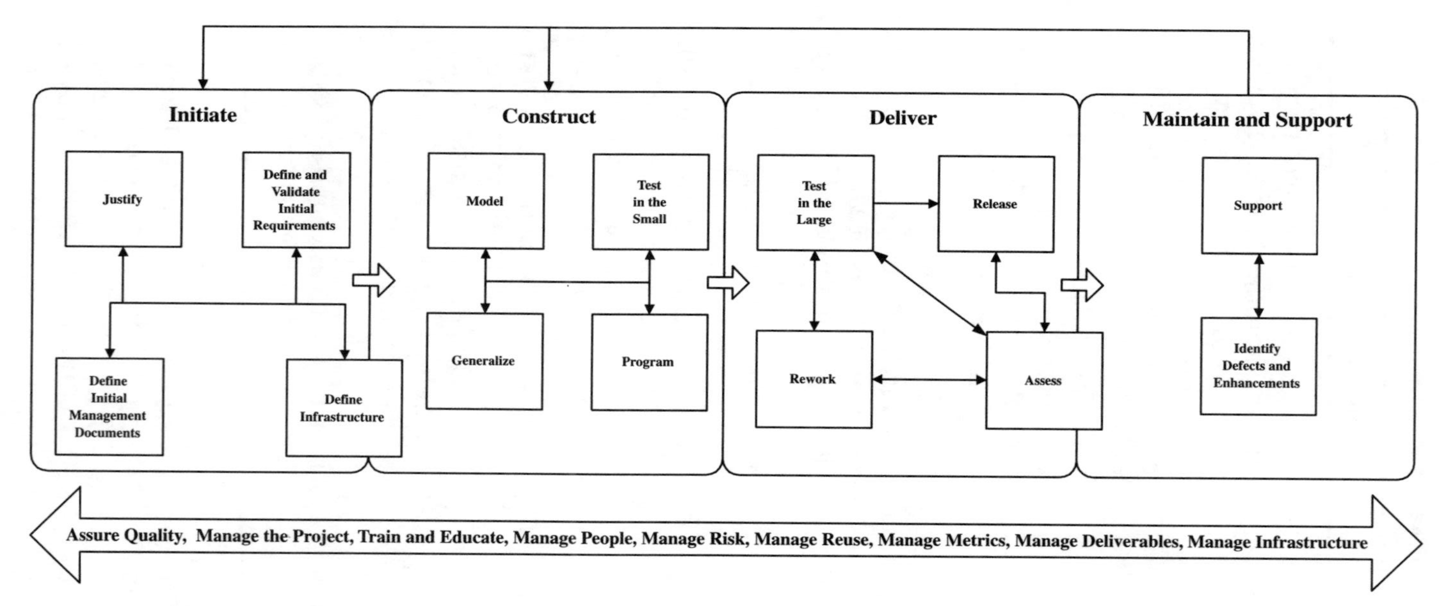

supports the delivery of incremental releases of an application as well as parallel development activities. OO development is fundamentally serial in the large, iterative in the small, and should deliver incremental releases whenever possible. In the following sections we will discuss in detail the features of the OOSP, as well as compare and contrast it to competing software processes.

The OOSP is serial in the large and iterative in the small, delivering incremental releases over time.

1.4.1 Serial in the Large

From a 50,000 foot level, the OOSP is fundamentally serial in nature. You must first get the project started by identifying the initial requirements, justifying that the project is viable, and determining the tools and techniques that you will use to deliver your application. Once these tasks are more or less complete, you actually begin to build the application by developing models, writing code, generalizing your work, and testing it in units. Once construction is complete, you will freeze your code so you can test the entire application and release it to your users. Once the application is released, you maintain and support the application.

The OOSP is serial in the large, and is comprised of four serial project phases:

- Initiate
- Construct
- Deliver
- Maintain and Support

1.4.1.1 Initiate

The main goal of the Initiate phase, covered in detail in Chapters 2 through 6, is to lay the foundation for a successful project. It is made up of the definition and validation of the initial require-

DEFINITIONS

project phase The large components of the OOSP that are performed in a serial manner. The four project phases are Initiate, Construct, Deliver, and Maintain and Support. A project phase is depicted by a process pattern.

project stage The components of a project phase, performed in an iterative manner, that make up a project phase. For example, the project stages that make up the Construct phase are Model, Test in the Small, Generalize, and Program. A project stage is depicted by a process pattern.

ments and management documents, the project justification, and the definition of the project infrastructure. The initial requirements give the project team somewhere to start when construction begins, and the initial management documents provide a basis for managing the project throughout the entire development process. The project justification effort produces a feasibility study that shows whether the project is expected to be successful. (If it shows that the project does not make sense then you should not continue.) The project infrastructure effort puts in place a collection of documents that describe the tools that the project team will use, how they will use them, the standards that the team will follow, how their work will be evaluated, and the deliverables that they must produce during the project.

1.4.1.2 Construct

The main goal of the Construct phase, covered in detail in Chapters 7 through 11, is to build the application in such a way that it is easy to maintain and to enhance. This includes modeling the application via traditional OO techniques such as CRC modeling, use cases, class diagrams, sequence diagrams, and so on—techniques that I will discuss in Chapter 8. Programming is performed using leading-edge OO languages like Java, Smalltalk, C++, and ObjectCOBOL that support the OO development paradigm. Your modeling and programming efforts are verified using testing-in-the-small techniques such as use-case scenario testing, design walkthroughs, class testing, and inheritance regression testing. During the Construct phase you also want to take the time to generalize your work so that it can be reused successfully; without a distinct generalization stage, this work rarely gets done. By the way, do not forget that modeling, programming, testing in the small, and generalization are all occurring iteratively.

1.4.1.3 Deliver

The main goal of the Deliver phase, covered in detail in *More Process Patterns* (Ambler, 1998b), is to put a working, high-quality, well-documented application in the hands of your users. This means that you need to perform testing in the large on the application by using techniques such as system testing, installation testing, stress testing, and user acceptance testing. Because your testing efforts will find some problems with your application, you will need to do some rework, effectively more construction, to fix these problems. Once the application has been tested and fixed, you release the application by making it available to users and by training them. Finally, during this phase take the opportunity to improve your development process and to identify training opportunities for your staff by doing a project review, also called a project postmortem, to learn what you did right and wrong on the project.

1.4.1.4 Maintain and Support

The main goal of the Maintain and Support phase, covered in detail in *More Process Patterns* (Ambler, 1998b), is to keep the application running and as up-to-date as possible. This means that you need to support the needs of users by providing training, answering their questions, and by fixing any problems that they may encounter. You also need to have a change-control process in place so you can identify any possible defects or enhancements for the application, prioritize those changes, and then address the changes in a future release. Change control is an integral part of the OOSP and is put in place during the Initiate phase.

1.4.2 Iterative in the Small

We've seen that the OOSP is fundamentally serial in the large, so now let's explore the idea that it is iterative in the small by considering the iterative stages of each project phase.

1.4.2.1 Initiate

The first serial phase of the OOSP is Initiate, which is comprised of four iterative project stages:

- Define and validate initial requirements
- Define initial management documents
- Justify
- Define infrastructure

1.4.2.1.1 Define and Validate Initial Requirements

During this stage, also known as requirements engineering, you want to determine accurately what you are going to deliver to the end user, at least at a high level. Chapter 3 describes several techniques that you can employ to do so, including CRC cards, use cases, use-case scenario testing, traditional interviews, and joint application development (JAD) sessions (also known as Joint Requirements Planning (JRP) sessions). There are several ways to gather and validate the initial requirements for your application. Furthermore, it is also possible to get your users actively involved in the project during this stage; they will potentially do the majority of the work of gathering the initial requirements. After all, who knows the user requirements better than the users? The key deliverable of this stage is a definition of the project scope based on validated, high-level requirements.

All projects, even the most technical ones, must have a high-level set of requirements defined for them at the beginning of the project.

1.4.2.1.2 Define Initial Management Documents

Chapter 4 explores the fact that during a project, many critical management documents are started early in a project. Documents like the risk assessment, the project schedule, the project estimate, and the team definition are all started at this time. These documents are not only crucial to the management of the entire project itself, but are also valuable input into the process of justifying the project. Key deliverables of this phase are the management documents themselves, which often have titles such as "Initial Risk Assessment" and "Initial Project Plan."

Key project management documents are started during the Initiate phase.

1.4.2.1.3 Justify the Project

The Justify stage, covered in Chapter 5, is probably the most important part of the Initiate phase, yet it is usually the most poorly done. Because upwards of eighty-five percent of all large projects fail[2] (Jones, 1996), for various reasons, if you do a good job in this stage then most projects should end here before a large investment has been made in them. The key deliverable of this stage is a feasibility study that addresses the project's economic feasibility (does the project make financial sense?), technical feasibility (can it actually be built?), and operational maintainability (can you support and maintain the application?).

You should justify your project on technical, economic, and operational factors.

---

[2]This figure has two components: 65 percent of large projects are absolute failures (canceled) and 21.33 percent are relative failures (delayed). In The Object Primer (Ambler, 1995) I take a much harder stance on project failure: any project that is late, over budget, or does not meet the needs of its users should be considered a failure. With this definition, few projects succeed.

1.4.2.1.4 Define the Project Infrastructure

For a project to be successful, you need to define the team, the tools that you will use, the quality standards to which you will adhere, and the deliverables that you will produce. This naturally needs to be done as soon as possible in the project so that construction can get underway, although sometimes you will start construction before getting the infrastructure completely in place. (That's why this stage overlaps into the Construct phase.) In many ways this stage, described in Chapter 6, helps to define how the members of the development team will interact internally with each other and externally with their users. The key deliverables include an indication of the team members and their roles and responsibilities on the project, a description of the development toolset, and a collection of standards and guidelines for construction and testing. This project stage will require a lot of effort the first couple of times that you do it, but will proceed quite quickly on subsequent projects because you can reuse your infrastructure efforts from previous projects.

You need to define the tools that you will use, the environment that you will develop for, and the standards and guidelines that you will follow as early in the project as possible.

1.4.2.2 Construct

The second serial phase of the OOSP is the Construct phase, which is comprised of four iterative project stages:

- Model
- Program
- Generalize
- Test in the Small

1.4.2.2.1 Model

The Model stage, described in Chapter 8, is composed of analysis, which defines what the application does and does not do; and design, which defines how the application will be built. In the structured world, analysis and design were considered two separate stages of the software process, but with the OOSP we really need to consider them as one stage. With OO development the line between analysis and design is blurred, so blurred in fact that both of them share many techniques in common. The bottom line is that the real difference between analysis and design is what you are modeling and who is doing the modeling—not how you are modeling. One way to think about it is that modeling is mostly analysis when users dominate the modeling effort, and mostly design when developers dominate the modeling effort. A better way to think about it, I believe, is that it is just modeling. The key deliverable is a collection of interrelated models/diagrams, which potentially include: class diagrams (object model), interface-flow diagrams, prototypes, CRC models, use cases, use-case diagrams, state diagrams, activity models,collaboration diagrams, deployment diagrams, data diagrams, activity diagrams, and sequence diagrams. These modeling techniques are discussed in Chapters 3 and 8.

Modeling is a highly iterative process involving different mixes of people for different types of models.

Figure 1.8 shows a task process pattern called Detailed Modeling; the figure depicts many of the common OO modeling techniques and diagrams and indicates the relationships between them. The arrows show the relationships between each technique, with the arrow heads indicating an "input into" relationship; for example, we see that an activity model is an input into a class diagram. In the bottom right-hand corner of each box is a series of one or more letters that indicate who is involved in working on that technique/diagram. The underlined letter indicates which group of people performs the majority of the work for that diagram; for example, we see that users form the majority of the people involved in developing a CRC model, but designers form the majority of those creating state diagrams.

1.4.2.2.2 Program

Object-oriented coding, covered in Chapter 9, is different than procedural/structured coding. First, you are working with classes, methods, and attributes, rather than functions, procedures, and data. Second, your program code should flow right out of your models because they too are based on the same concepts as OO coding. The key deliverable in this project stage is the source code itself and the accompanying documentation, both having undergone testing in the small.

1.4.2.2.3 Generalize

Chapter 10 describes the Generalize stage, a stage that is critical to your organization's reuse efforts (Meyer, 1995) because it forces project managers to account for the time that it takes to make your work reusable. If you do not invest the time during a

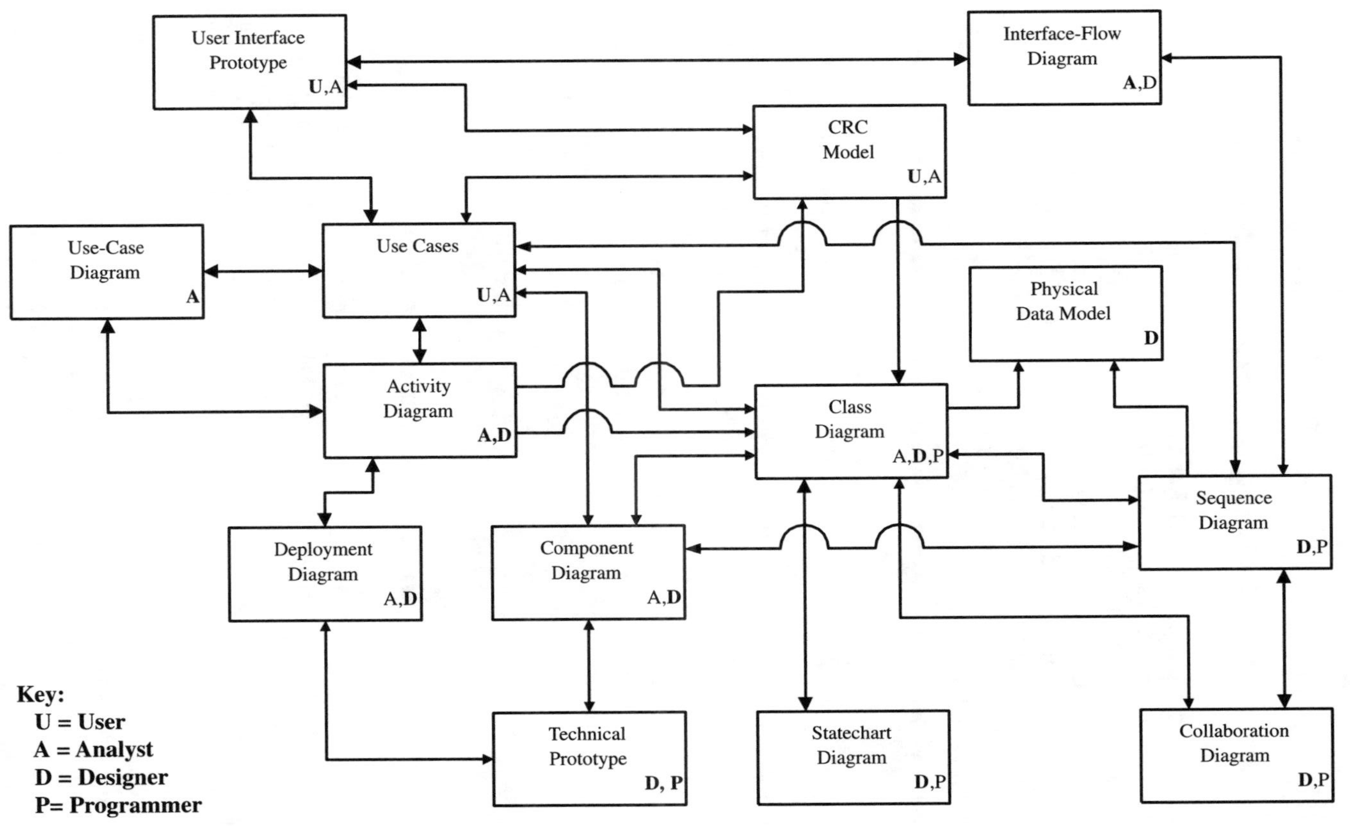

Figure 1.8.
The Detailed Modeling process pattern

SCOTT'S SOAPBOX

OO Modeling is Iterative in Nature

You can see from Figure 1.8 that OO modeling by its very nature is an iterative process. I suspect that because many of the leading methodologies have concentrated on OO analysis and design, instead of the entire OOSP, and that because OO modeling is iterative in nature, many people have concluded that OO development is also iterative in nature. When we step back and think about it, however, we know that this statement is not completely true: OO development is actually serial in the large and iterative in the small.

project to look for opportunities for reuse, and take the time then to make what you find reusable, then chances are very good that you never will. When a project ends, people always want to go on to the next project; they generally do not want to go through their old work trying to make it reusable. The key deliverable of the Generalize stage is a reusable component, be it model or code, that can be used either on the current project or on future projects.

Take the time to actually make your development efforts reusable.

JENNIFER BARZSO'S SOAPBOX

Include Technical Writers

To ensure that your application code is properly documented, you should have technical writers working side by side with developers. For some reason information technology (IT) departments think that it is easy to write good documentation and that anyone can do it. Nothing could be further from the truth, so hire an expert who knows how to do it properly.

Note from Scott: Jennifer is a long-time friend and coworker who has provided valuable input into all three of my books, so I felt it was about time that she had an opportunity to directly share some of her thoughts with you. Also, I'm proud to point out that Jennifer has stumbled onto Coplien's (1995) Mercenary Analyst organizational pattern.

1.4.2.2.4 Test in the Small

This project stage, explored in Chapter 11, was traditionally referred to as unit testing in the structured world but has been extended to include the testing of your modeling efforts as well. Because OO modeling and coding are iterative efforts, testing in the small is iterative as well because the best time to test your work is immediately after you finish it. If you have developed a new model, walk through it. If you have programmed a new class, or even a new method, test it. You do not want to wait until the end of your project to find out that something does not work; it is far better to find out right away while it is still easy to fix. Object-oriented testing is both similar to, yet at the same time significantly different from, structured testing. This can prove frustrating and confusing to experienced developers who are new to OO. Testing in the small techniques combined with testing in the large techniques make up the Full Life Cycle Object-Oriented Testing (FLOOT) methodology (Ambler, 1998) which we will discuss later in this chapter. The key deliverable from testing in the small is a working, verified, high-quality portion of the work required to complete an application.

Testing in the small addresses the testing of your construction efforts as they proceed, in order to find and fix any problems as early in the life cycle as possible.

1.4.2.3 Deliver

The third serial phase of the OOSP is Deliver, covered in detail in *More Process Patterns* (1998b), which is comprised of four iterative project stages:

- Test in the Large
- Rework
- Release
- Assess

1.4.2.3.1 Test in the Large

The Test in the Large stage is the traditional testing phase from structured development, with the caveat that we are now testing an OO application instead of a structured one. Testing in the large, consists of testing techniques such as function testing, system testing, user acceptance testing (UAT), stress testing, operations testing, and alpha/beta/pilot testing. The key deliverables of this stage are a tested application and test results indicating whether or not the application can be released to the user community. Note that if the test results show that the application

You need to freeze the code and test your application before putting it into production.

should not be released, then that release of the application must be reworked and then retested.

1.4.2.3.2 Rework

Very often testing in the large shows that portions of an application need to be improved, or reworked, before it can be released to its users. Although you hope that something like this will not happen, it is unfortunately one of the realities of life—we aren't perfect and we cannot always do a perfect job. Another reality is that we are typically blind to the fact that we aren't perfect and that we make mistakes, the end result being that we forget that we often need to invest time reworking our applications before they can be released to our users. The OOSP includes an explicit Rework stage so that we do not forget to include the need to rework our applications in our schedules and estimates.

We almost always need to rework an application before it can be released.

1.4.2.3.3 Release

The Release stage is the point at which you put the application and its corresponding documentation into the hands of your users. It is also at this point that you train the users, operations staff, and support staff in the application. The key deliverable of

Scott's Soapbox

Release No Application Before Its Time

In the 1970s an American wine company promised to "sell no wine before its time," words of wisdom that should be applied to the release of applications. If you do not have enough time to test, or if testing tells you that you need to rework portions of your application, then it is foolish to release your application. Experience tells us that software does not work the first time that you try to run it, so if you have not tested adequately, then you can safely assume that your application does not work. If your application has failed testing, then you know for certain that it does not work. Releasing an application that does not work is a recipe for disaster, so *don't do it.* If your users are putting pressure on you to release your application, you have to have the fortitude to not release it until it is ready. Yes, this is often difficult to do, but it is far more difficult and far more expensive to clean up the mess that your defective application will create.

this stage is the provision of an application that successfully supports users doing their work.

1.4.2.3.4 Assess

Part of the Delivery phase is to review the project to determine what went right as well as what went wrong. The main goal of the Assess stage is to learn from your experiences so that you may improve the development practices of your organization. The key deliverable here is a report indicating both best and worst practices that occurred on the project, as well as an action plan to improve your development efforts next time. In addition to assessing the project, you should also assess the people who worked on the project, rewarding them appropriately and defining a training plan for them to help them address any skills gap that they may have.

By assessing the project you can improve your development efforts the next time.

1.4.2.4 Maintain and Support

The fourth serial phase of the OOSP is Maintain and Support, covered in more detail in *More Process Patterns* (1998b), which is composed of two iterative project stages:

- Support
- Identify Defects and Enhancements

1.4.2.4.1 Support

Because the OOSP is concerned with the entire life of an application, including efforts beyond development, the Support stage is included in the OOSP. We are concerned with different levels of support: direct support for users of the application by the support desk (who may in fact be one of the application's developers), as well as technical support for the support people by the developers to help answer difficult questions. The key deliverable of this stage is the summary of collected metrics, such as the number of support calls taken and the average length of time to respond to a support call.

1.4.2.4.2 Identify Defects and Enhancements

Because no application works perfectly or meets 100 percent of the needs of its users, we need a project stage that handles the identification of defects within the application, as well as desired enhancements for it. A change control process is needed to track and verify these requests. This process should distinguish the differences between something that does not work, something that could work better, and something that simply is not there. If you do not have a process in place to actively manage the identification of defects and enhancements, then the quality of the application will degrade over time because you are making changes to it on an ad hoc basis. The key deliverable of this stage is a series of verified and prioritized requirements for subsequent releases of the application.

This stage defines and prioritizes new requirements for future releases of your application.

I have briefly discussed the serial phases, as well as their iterative stages, of the OOSP. Now it is time to discuss how to deliver incremental releases of an application with the OOSP.

1.4.3 Delivering Incremental Releases Over Time

There are two keys to incremental development: first, you need to be able to organize the functionality of your application into several distinct packages that you can release one at a time. It is typical that each "functionality package" will build on the previous ones, although this is not always the case. Second, you want to organize your development efforts so that the project teams for each release do not step on the toes of the project teams for the other releases.

Let's consider three approaches to incremental development using the OOSP. In Figure 1.9 you see the aggressive approach for using the incremental development approach with our OOSP, indicating that the work on the second release starts while development of the first release is still underway, that development of the third release starts while development of the second release occurs, and so on. Although this approach may appear to speed up the development process, chances are very good that it will actually slow it down. The problem is one of version control: having two teams work on the same code simultaneously is very difficult to manage. Note that it is reasonably easy to manage parallel development, however, assuming of course that the parallel components are reasonably uncoupled. With incremental releases, however, release *n* usually builds on release *n-1,* hence they are highly coupled. Another issue is that of staffing: To develop releases in parallel, you need to have enough people to staff each project team.

A less risky approach to incremental development is shown in Figure 1.10, and a safer one yet, the conservative approach to incremental development in Figure 1.11. At a minimum, you really shouldn't start your next release until the code is frozen

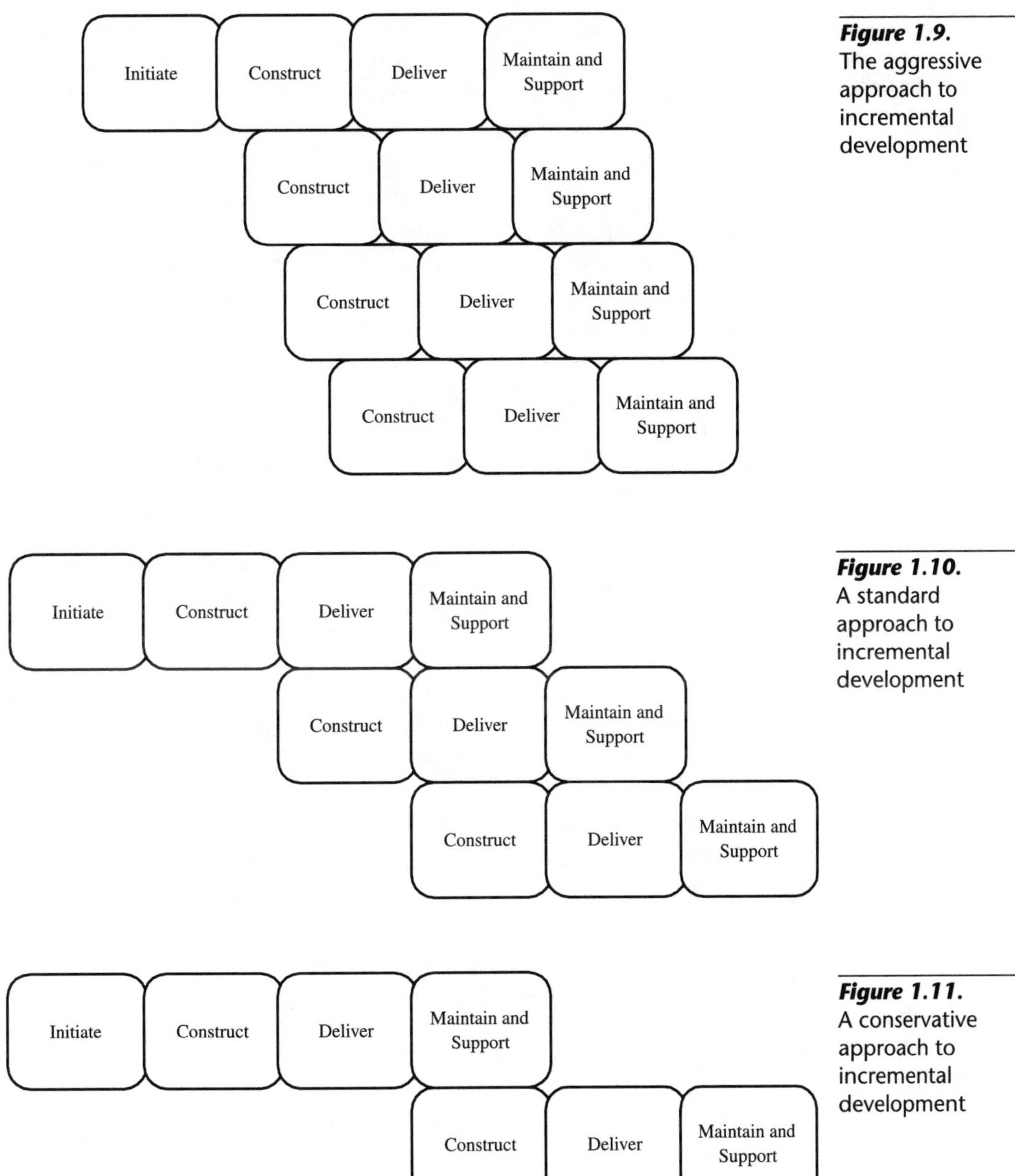

Figure 1.9. The aggressive approach to incremental development

Figure 1.10. A standard approach to incremental development

Figure 1.11. A conservative approach to incremental development

Don't start your next release until after the code is frozen on your current one, and preferably after the code has been tested and fixed.

from the previous release, as shown in Figure 1.10; but ideally, you want to wait until the previous release has been fully tested and put into production. This ensures that you have a solid, versioned base of code to work from, and it also provides an opportunity for developers to catch their breath between releases. Furthermore, if you wait until the previous release is in the Maintenance and Support phase, you have an opportunity to act on the input of the people who are using the previous release, as well as to put into place any recommendations made in the previous release's Assess stage.

Notice how in Figures 1.9, 1.10, and 1.11 that only the first release has a project initiation phase. This probably is not completely true, due to the fact that at the start of a new release you really should revisit your project infrastructure based on the results of the project review of the previous release. Furthermore, you also need to justify, or perhaps rejustify, the requirements for the new release as many of them may be the result of change requests from the user community. The reason why we do not show the project initiation phase for subsequent releases is because of the fact that the change in infrastructure is usually made as part of the recommendations of the review stage, and that justification of any new requirements are made as part of the change control process during the maintenance and support phase.

1.4.3.1 Incremental vs. Parallel Development

Incremental and parallel development are complementary approaches, not competing ones.

Incremental development is based on the concept that an application can be delivered in multiple releases—releases which often build on the functionality of previous releases. Parallel development is based on the concept that you can work on portions of an application simultaneously. For parallel development to work smoothly, these portions should have as little overlap as possible; otherwise version control quickly overwhelms you. The basic issue is that it is easier to have two programmers working on different pieces of code simultaneously than it is to have them work on the same piece of code. The good news is that incremental development and parallel development are complementary approaches, not competing ones. In other words, you can have multiple, parallel efforts going on during a single release of an application.

1.4.4 With a Little Bit of Glue to Hold It All Together

It is not enough to identify the discrete phases and stages of the OOSP, because frankly they aren't enough. There are tasks, or perhaps overriding concerns, that are applicable throughout your project and across projects. Without these tasks being performed, your project will fail, regardless of how good your developers are. The following project and cross-project tasks make up the glue that hold projects together, helping to increase your chance of success:

- Quality assurance
- Project management
- People management
- Risk management
- Reuse management
- Training and education
- Metrics management
- Deliverable management
- Infrastructure management

Throughout this book I will explore these project/cross-project tasks where appropriate and will even present several task process patterns that are applicable to them. In *More Process Patterns* (1998b) I will summarize in detail the issues involved with each task; for now I present a brief overview of each.

1.4.4.1 Quality Assurance

Quality assurance is the process of ensuring that the efforts of a project meet or exceed the standards expected of them by the organization. Fundamentally, quality assurance attempts to answer the following questions: "Are you building the right thing?" and "Are you building it the right way?" Quality assurance is critical to the success of a project, and should be an integral part of all project stages. At all points in the OOSP you should be reviewing your work to ensure its quality.

1.4.4.2 Project Management

Project management is the process of organizing, monitoring, and directing a project. Project management is planning. Project man-

DEFINITIONS

deliverable Any document or system component that is produced during the development of a system. Some deliverables are used internally on a project whereas others are produced specifically for users of the application. Examples of deliverables include user requirements, models, plans, assessments, or other documents.

deliverable management The process of organizing, monitoring, and directing the deliverables of a project.

education The process by which people gain knowledge and understanding.

infrastructure management A cross-project effort which includes your organization's architectural and enterprise modeling efforts, as well as the definition and support of your organization's processes, standards, guidelines, and chosen toolsets.

metric A measurement.

metrics management The process of collecting, summarizing, and acting on measurements (metrics) to potentially improve both quality of the software that your organization develops and the actual software process of your organization.

project management The process of organizing, monitoring, and directing a project.

quality assurance (QA) The process of ensuring that the efforts of a project meet or exceed the standards expected of them.

reuse management The process of organizing, monitoring, and directing the efforts of a project team that lead to reuse on a project, either reuse of existing or purchased items.

risk management The process of identifying, monitoring, and mitigating the risks faced by a project team. These risks may typically be strategic, technical, and/or political.

training The process by which people gain tangible skills.

agement is scheduling. Project management is estimating. Project management is people. As you will see throughout this book, projects must be skillfully managed if they are to be successful.

1.4.4.3 People Management

People management is the process of organizing, monitoring, coaching, and motivating people in such a manner to ensure that they work together effectively and contribute to a project/organization positively. People develop software; therefore, managing people must be part of the software development process.

1.4.4.4 Risk Management

Risk management is the process of identifying, monitoring, and mitigating the risks faced by a project team. These risks may come from a range of sources and may be strategic, technical, and/or political. The key concept of risk management is that you want to identify and deal with risks as soon as possible, and if you are unable to deal with them, or at least unwilling to deal with them, then you should at least keep an eye on them to ensure that they do not harm your project (at least not too badly). Risk management is one of the keys of success for system development projects, a task which must be performed throughout the project.

Risk management is a key factor in the success of an OO project.

1.4.4.5 Reuse Management

Reuse management is the process of organizing, monitoring, and directing the efforts of a project team that lead to reuse on project (or on subsequent projects); either reuse of existing or of purchased items. It is possible to achieve reuse throughout the entire OOSP, but it is not free and it is not automatic. You have to work at it. Furthermore, although we have a project stage called Generalize (Chapter 10) that is dedicated specifically to building reusable components during the Construct phase, this is only a start. You can reuse your project plans, your estimates, your risk analysis, your test strategies, your construction standards, and your documentation templates—but only if you put in the effort. Reuse management is key to reducing the overall cost of application development.

Reuse is not free and it is not automatic. You need to manage the process.

Table 1.3 describes several approaches to reuse; Figure 1.12 compares their effectiveness. For example, component reuse is generally more effective than template reuse. An interesting point that Figure 1.12 shows is that the least productive type of reuse is code reuse, in fact code reuse can even provide a negative productivity rate when buggy code is copied several times. Figure 1.12 also shows that domain-component reuse is the most productive form of reuse, although because it is based on an architecture-driven approach to modeling (Chapter 8) it is also the most difficult approach to reuse to successfully achieve.

Table 1.3. The Various Approaches to Reuse

Reuse Strategy	Description
Artifact reuse	The reuse of previously created development artifacts—use cases, standards documents, domain-specific models, procedures and guidelines, and other applications—to give you a kick start on a new project.
Code reuse	The reuse of source code within sections of an application and potentially across multiple applications.
Component reuse	The reuse of pre-built, fully encapsulated components in the development of your application.
Domain-component reuse	The reuse of pre-built, large-scale domain components that encapsulate cohesive portions of your business domain.
Framework reuse	The reuse of collections of classes that together implement the basic functionality of a common technical or business domain.
Inheritance reuse	The use of inheritance in your application to take advantage of behavior implemented in existing classes.
Pattern reuse	The reuse of publicly documented approaches, called patterns, to solving common problems.
Template reuse	The reuse of a common set of layouts for key development artifacts—documents, models, and source code—within your organization.

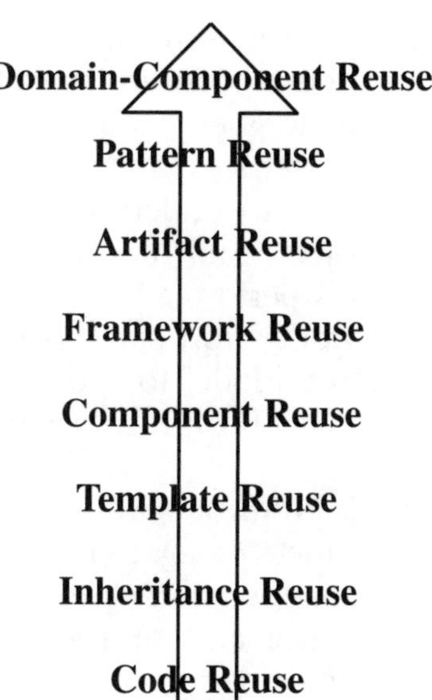

Figure 1.12. The effectiveness of the various approaches to reuse

1.4.4.6 Training and Education

Training and education (T&E) are important to the success of a project. Training gives people the skills that they need to do their jobs, whereas education provides them with the knowledge that they need to understand their jobs. For example, people may take a course that teaches them the fundamentals of application development. This is education because it provides them with knowledge. The same people may attend a five-day course to learn how to program in Java. This is training because it teaches them a specific skill. Education generally deals with knowledge that is useful for a long period of time, whereas training often has a much shorter shelf life, often on the order of months or years. You want to distinguish between training and education because in many ways training is an investment that needs to pay for itself in the short term, perhaps over one or two projects, whereas education pays for itself over the long term, typically the employment of an individual. At some point most projects require the training and/or education of both developers and users; therefore T&E is an important part of the OOSP.

1.4.4.7 Metrics Management

Metrics management is the process of collecting, summarizing, and acting on measurements (metrics) to potentially improve both the quality of the software that your organization develops and the actual software process of your organization. As the old saying goes, "You cannot improve it if you cannot measure it." Metrics management provides the information that is critical to understanding the quality of the work that your project team has performed and how effectively that work was performed. Metrics range from simple measurements of work effort such as the number of hours invested to develop a model to code quality measurements such as the percentage of comments within your code.

DEFINITIONS

guideline A description, ideally with an example provided, of how something should be done. It is recommended, but not required, that you follow guidelines (unlike standards which are mandatory).

standard A description, ideally with an example provided, of how something must be done. It is required that you follow standards (unlike guidelines which are optional).

1.4.4.8 Deliverable Management

Deliverable management is key to the management of a project, to the successful operation of an application, and to the successful maintenance and support of an application. A deliverable is any information, either printed or electronic, that describes all or part of an application or system such as models, documents, and plans. Deliverables may be internal, used only by members of the project team; or external, delivered as part of the application. Deliverables may be for developers, for users, for support staff, or for operations staff. The review and update of deliverables is a fundamental part of quality assurance, and the existence of accurate and complete documentation is a fundamental part of risk management. Deliverables are created and updated by all members of a project team throughout the entire project.

1.4.4.9 Infrastructure Management

Infrastructure management is a cross-project effort which includes the architectural and enterprise modeling efforts of the Model stage (Chapter 8), and the definition and support of your organization's processes, standards, guidelines, and chosen toolsets. The Define Infrastructure stage (Chapter 6) is a key function of infrastructure management because it defines and/or selects the infrastructure for a single project. However, from the point of view of your organization, the Define Infrastructure stage is not sufficient to promote a common infrastructure between projects; hence the need for infrastructure management.

1.5 Comparing the OOSP to Other Software Processes

The OOSP, presented in this book as a collection of process patterns called the OOSP pattern language, is not the only approach to developing OO applications. Let's spend a few minutes discussing the alternatives.

1.5.1 "Traditional" Iterative OO Development

Iterative development definitely has its place, but it is only part of the solution. When your project is small, or just a proof of concept, the initiate and delivery efforts become very small. The end result is that you spend most of your time in the Construct phase, which internally is an iterative process. Because the vast majority of OO projects were reasonably small in the late 1980s and early 1990s, everybody was doing iterative OO development and became convinced that this was the way that OO development is done. Well, bitter experience on large OO projects has shown that this is simply not so, and that OO development is serial in the large and iterative in the small.

Imagine an eighteen-month project with a team of one hundred developers. Would you tell them to just start working, or would you first invest the time to put a plan in place, procedures in place, standards in place, and a common set of tools in place? Of course you would. Once you are organized, then you would start building the application; you would eventually have a code freeze; then the application would be tested. Once it passes testing, you would put it in production and start supporting its users. In other words, you would first initiate the project, then you would construct it, then you would deliver it, and finally maintain and support it—a serial development process.

1.5.2 SOMA

The OOSP is actually very similar in concept to the Semantic Object Modeling Approach (SOMA) process (Graham, 1995) shown in Figure 1.13. The SOMA software process has three main stages—propose, build, and implement—which align nicely with our Initiate, Construct, and Deliver phases. The big difference

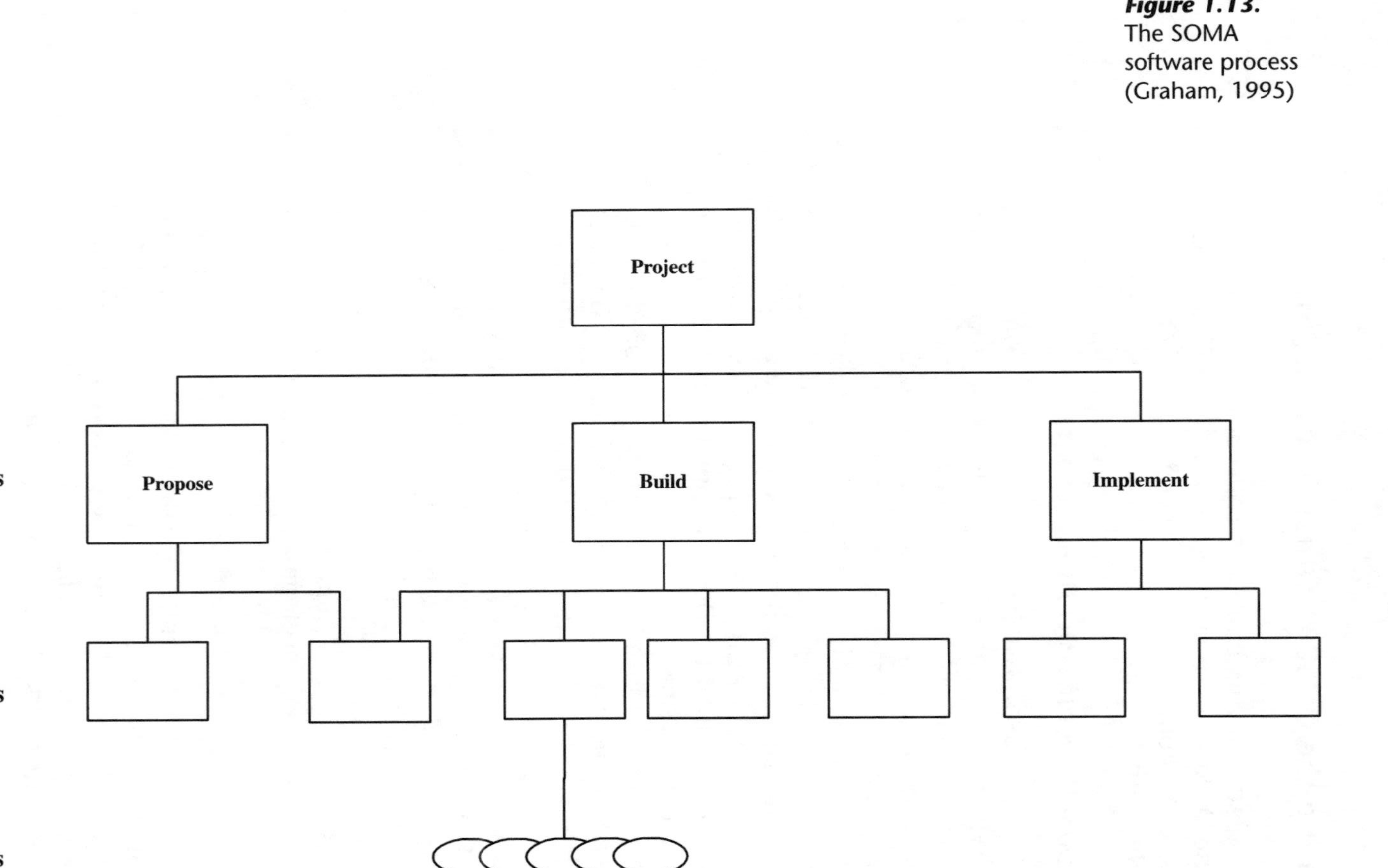

Figure 1.13. The SOMA software process (Graham, 1995)

between the OOSP and the SOMA process is that the OOSP includes the Maintain and Support phase, making it a complete process. Like the OOSP, SOMA stages (what we call phases) break down into activities (what we call stages), which in turn break down into tasks. One thing that I do not like about the SOMA process is the way that it is drawn: in a top-down, almost structured approach. Yuck. SOMA did, however, get the fundamental concepts correct: OO development is fundamentally serial in the large, iterative in the small, with iterative releases. It could just have been communicated a little better.

1.5.3 The Objectory Software Process

The Objectory software process is drawn differently but is in fact very similar to the OOSP, although not as complete.

The Objectory software process (Rational, 1996), tentatively called the Unified Process, shown in Figure 1.14, is another attempt at defining the OO development process. Although it is drawn differently from the OOSP, it is based on similar principles. The Inception phase is similar to our Initiate phase; the combination of Elaboration and Construction phases are similar to our Construct phase, and the Transition phase is similar to our Deliver phase. An iteration in the Objectory software process maps directly to our concept of a build, which we'll cover in detail in coming chapters. As with SOMA, the Objectory software process is missing a Maintain and Support phase (at the time of this writing). Risk manage-

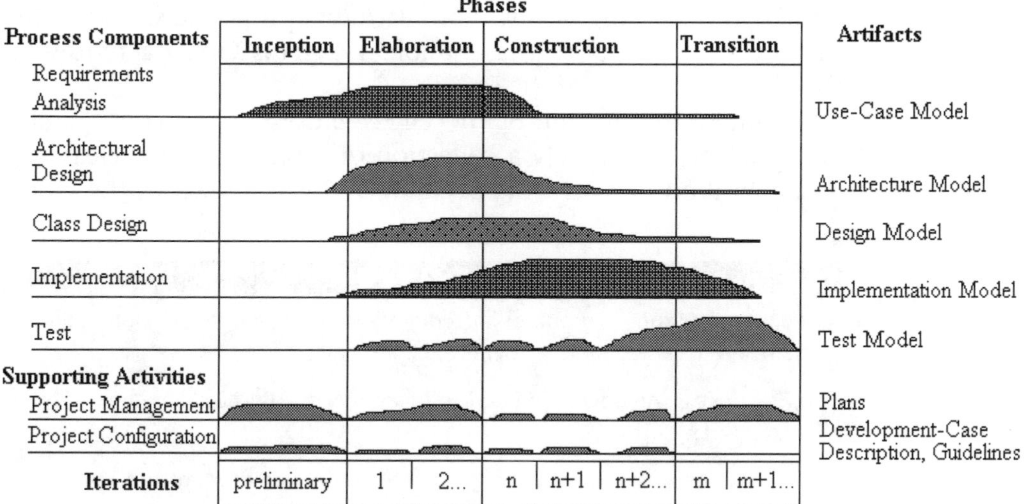

Figure 1.14. The Objectory software process (Rational, 1996)

ment is built into the development of iterations, as is project management, and people management appears to be assumed.

The Objectory software process claims to be based on an iterative development approach with incremental releases, although it is clear that their process is really serial in the large, just like the OOSP. The Objectory software process appears to be fairly solid, however, I suspect that it leans toward the needs of tool builders, not application builders. This is because of the nature of the software that Rational Software Corporation develops—tools, not applications. I also question any process that does not directly address the issue of maintenance and support. History shows that applications spend 80 percent of their lifetimes in maintenance, so it makes a lot of sense to include maintenance in the process.

1.5.4 The OPEN Process

The contract-driven life cycle of the OPEN process (Graham, Henderson-Sellers, and Younessi, 1997), shown in Figure 1.15, represents an approach similar to the OOSP, albeit one illustrated differently. Each OPEN activity is shown as a rectangle, with unbounded activities shown as rounded rectangles and tightly bound activities as simple rectangles. The left-hand side of the diagram represents the activities for a single project, whereas the activities in the right-hand side represent cross-project activities. In other words, the left-hand side generally maps to the first three project phases of the OOSP and the right-hand side to the combination of the "big arrow" project/cross-project tasks and the Maintain and Support phase. Table 1.4 maps OPEN activities to the process patterns of the OOSP.

An interesting feature of the OPEN process is the concept of a "programme," effectively a collection of projects and/or releases of an application or suite of applications. This is shown in the OPEN

DEFINITIONS

OPEN Consortium A group of individuals and organizations promoting and enhancing the use of object-oriented technology.

OPEN process An object-oriented software process promoted by the OPEN Consortium.

programme A collection of projects or releases of one or more applications.

Table 1.4 Mapping the OPEN Software Process to the OOSP

OPEN Activity	OOSP
Analysis and Model Refinement	Define and Validate Initial Requirements stage
Model stage	
Bug Fixing	Rework stage
Consolidation	Program stage (Integrate and package)
Domain Modeling	Model stage (Architectural modeling)
Evaluation	Assess stage
Implementation Planning	Release stage
Object-oriented analysis (OOA) and object-oriented design (OOD)	Model stage
Object-oriented programming (OOP)	Program stage
Programme Planning	Project Management task Infrastructure Management task
Project Initiation	Initiate phase
Project Planning	Project Management task
Requirements Elicitation	Define and Validate Initial Requirements stage
Resource Planning	Define Infrastructure stage
Use of System	Maintain and Support phase
User review	Test in the Small stage Test in the Large stage Quality Assurance task
Verification and validation	Test in the Small stage
(V&V)	Test in the Large stage Quality Assurance task

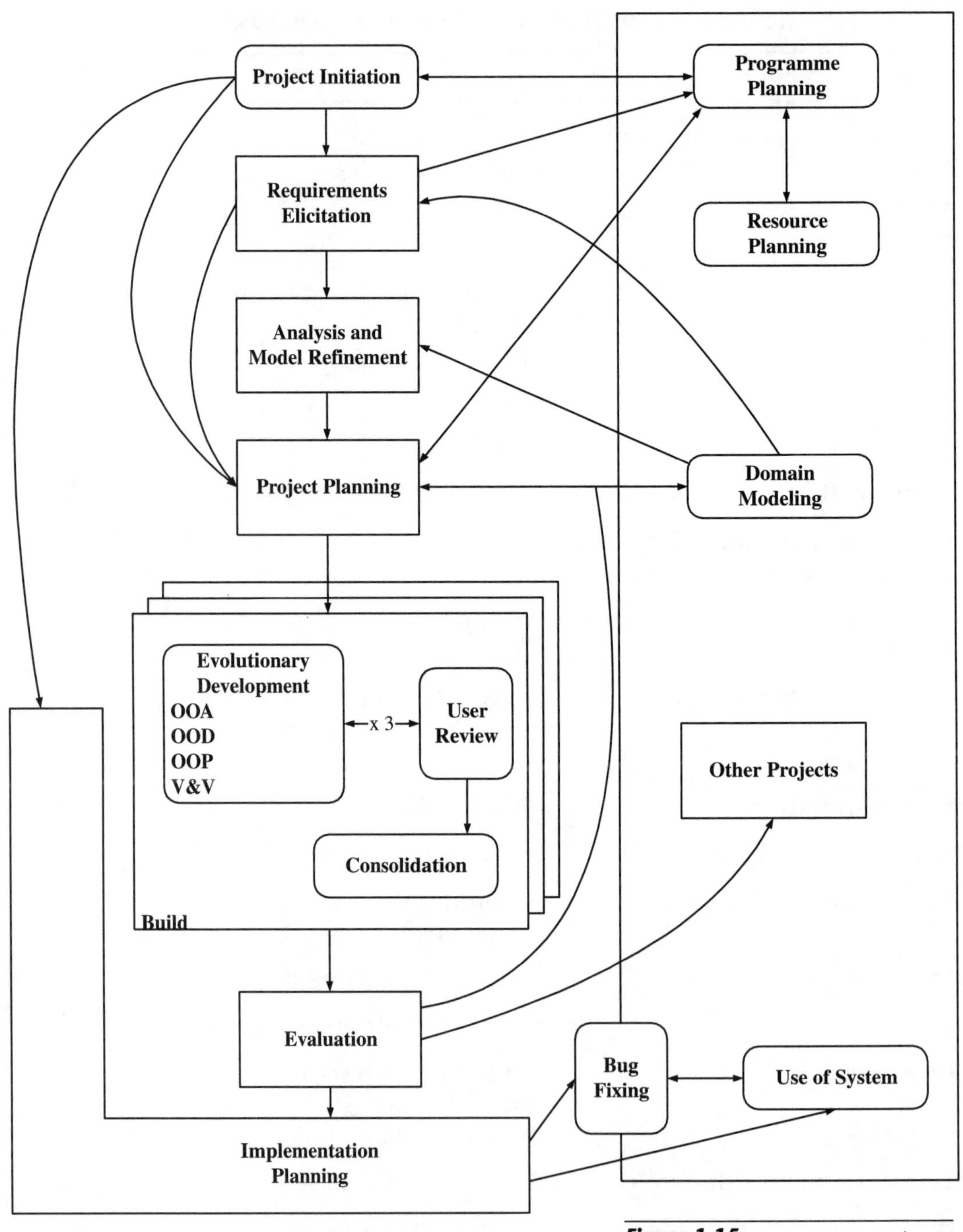

Figure 1.15.
The OPEN Contract-Driven Life Cycle (Graham, Henderson-Sellers, and Younessi, 1997)

process by the Programme Planning and Other Projects activities. The OOSP does not call out programmes, due to the potential confusion with the term "software program," although, as you have seen, it obviously includes the concept of multiple projects and releases of an application. In all, the OPEN process is an interesting alternative and I highly suggest referring to it for a second opinion as to how to develop large-scale applications using object technology.

1.6 The OOSP and Full Life Cycle Object-Oriented Testing (FLOOT)

Testing and QA are key components throughout the entire OOSP.

Full Life Cycle Object-Oriented Testing (FLOOT) techniques (Ambler, 1998a), including quality assurance techniques, are key components of the OOSP. In the OOSP, testing is explicitly represented by two stages, Testing in the Small and Testing in the Large; and implicitly by the Assure Quality task. In Figure 1.16 we see a depiction of the FLOOT techniques for testing and quality assurance, indicating techniques that can be used at various stages throughout the OOSP. Later in this book I will discuss two process patterns based on FLOOT, one for the Test in the Small stage (Chapter 11) and one for the Test in the Large stage (Ambler, 1998b)

Figure 1.16. Full Life cycle Object-Oriented Testing (FLOOT)

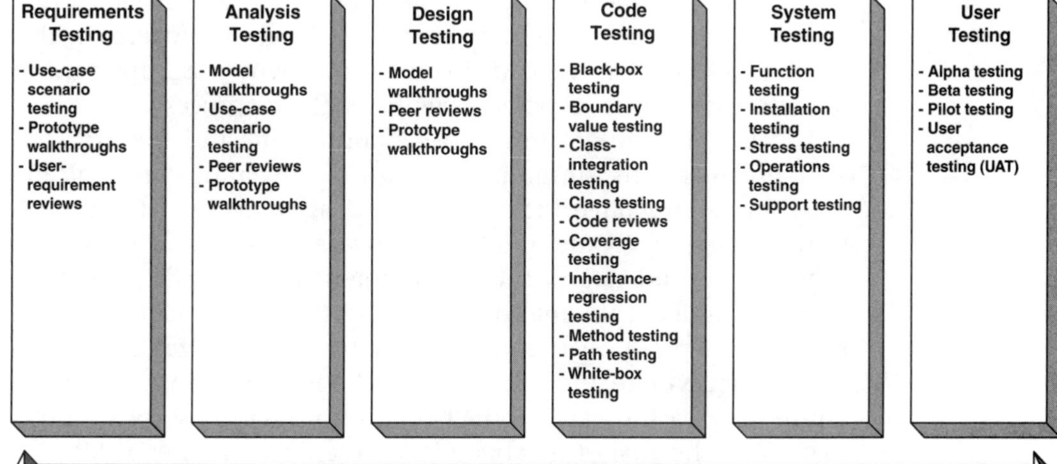

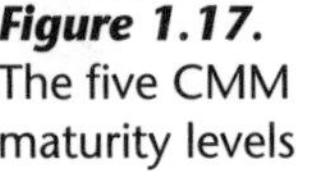

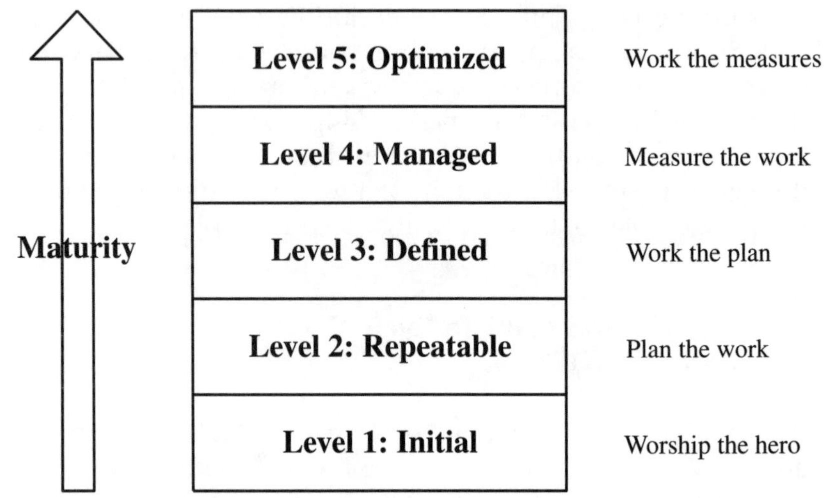

Figure 1.17. The five CMM maturity levels

1.7 Toward a Mature Object-Oriented Software Process: The SEI CMM

The Software Engineering Institute (SEI) at Carnegie Mellon University has proposed the Capability Maturity Model (CMM), which provides a framework from which a process for large, complex software efforts can be defined (Software Engineering Institute, 1995). Sponsored by the United States Department of Defense (DoD), the CMM has been adopted by hundreds of organizations worldwide who want to improve the way that they develop software. In this section I will discuss the CMM and discover why it is important to our efforts to define an object-oriented software process.

The CMM distinguishes between immature and mature software organizations. Immature software organizations are typically reactionary and have little understanding as to how to successfully develop software. Mature software organizations, on the other hand, understand the development process, which enables them to judge the quality of the software products and the process that produces them. Mature software organizations have a higher success rate and a lower overall cost of software across the entire life of a software product than do immature software organizations. The goal of this book is to describe a mature OOSP.

DEFINITIONS

baseline A tested and certified version of a deliverable representing a conceptual milestone which thereafter serves as the basis for further development and that can be modified only through formal change control procedures. A particular version becomes a baseline when a responsible group decides to designate it as such.

Capability Maturity Model (CMM) A strategy defined by the Software Engineering Institute (SEI) that describes the key elements of an effective software process.

immature software organization A software organization that is reactionary: its managers are usually focused on solving immediate crises. There is no objective basis for judging product quality or for solving product or process problems. There is little understanding of how the steps of the software process affect quality, and product quality is difficult to predict.

key process area (KPA) An issue that must be addressed to achieve a specific Capability Maturity Model (CMM) maturity level.

mature software organization A software organization wherein the managers monitor the quality of the software products and the process that produces them. There is an objective, quantitative basis for judging product quality and analyzing problems with the product and process.

maturity level A well-defined evolutionary plateau toward achieving a mature software process. According to the Capability Maturity Model (CMM), for an organization to achieve a specific maturity level, it must satisfy and institutionalize all of the key process areas (KPAs) for that level and the levels below.

Software Engineering Institute (SEI) An organization within Carnegie Mellon University whose goal is to provide leadership in advancing the state of the practice of software engineering so as to improve the quality of systems that depend on software.

software process A set of project phases, stages, methods, techniques, and practices that people employ to develop and maintain software and its associated products (plans, documents, models, code, test cases, and manuals).

1.7.1 The Five CMM Maturity Levels

The CMM defines five maturity levels, evolutionary plateaus toward achieving a mature software process, that an organization can attain with respect to the software process. The five maturity levels of the CMM are shown in Figure 1.17[3] and described in

[3]The descriptions of the right side are taken from (Whittington, 1996).

Table 1.5 The Five CMM Maturity Levels

Level	Description	Characteristics
1. Initial	The software process is ad hoc, and occasionally even chaotic. Few processes are defined, and success depends on individual effort and heroics.	• Overcommitment is common. • During a crisis, planned procedures are abandoned and project teams revert to coding and testing. • Success depends on having an exceptional manager and a seasoned and effective software team. • The software process is effectively a black box to the user community. Resources go in and software potentially comes out.
2. Repeatable	Basic project management processes are established to track cost, schedule, and functionality. The necessary process discipline is in place to repeat earlier successes on projects with similar applications.	• The planning and management of new projects is based on experience with similar projects. • Process capability is enhanced at the project level by establishing basic process management techniques. • Software requirements and deliverables are baselined. • Processes often differ between projects, reducing opportunities for teamwork and reuse. • The user community is provided visibility into the project at defined occasions, typically via the review and acceptance of major project deliverables, allowing limited management control.

3. Defined	The software process for both management and development activities is documented, standardized, and integrated into a standard software process for the entire organization. All projects use an approved, tailored version of the organization's standard software process for developing and maintaining software.	• A standard process is used, with possible tailoring, on all projects. • Management has good insight into technical progress on the project. • Defined processes allow the user community greater visibility into the project and enable accurate and rapid status updates.
4. Managed	Detailed measures, called metrics, of the software process and product quality are collected. Both the software process and products are quantitatively understood and controlled.	• Productivity and quality are measured for important software process activities across all projects. • The user community can establish an accurate, quantitative understanding of the software process capability of your organization/team and the project risk before the project begins.
5. Optimized	Continuous process improvement is enabled by quantitative feedback from the software process and from piloting innovative ideas and technologies.	• Innovations that exploit the best software engineering practices are identified and shared throughout the organization. • The software process is improved by changing common causes of inefficiency. • Disciplined change is the norm, not the exception. • The user community and the software organization work together to establish a strong and successful relationship.

Table 1.5. All organizations are at least at the Initial Level, the lowest level of software process maturity, by definition.

As you can see, each maturity level builds upon aspects and features of the previous levels. This implies that for your organization to achieve CMM Level 4, it must satisfy the requirements for CMM Levels 2 and 3 as well as those for CMM Level 4. The goal of this book is to define an OOSP that meets the needs of a mature software organization, one that aims for CMM Level 5. For our purposes the important thing is to identify the issues, called key process areas, for each maturity level so that you can determine which aspects of the software process you should concentrate on.

1.7.2 Key Process Areas (KPAs)

The true value of the SEI CMM is that it defines the issues that must be addressed by a software process to achieve each maturity level. These issues are called key process areas (KPAs) and are shown by maturity level in Figure 1.18. In this section we will describe each KPA in detail, and throughout the book we will indicate the applicable KPAs as we describe the phases, stages, and tasks of the OOSP.

1.7.2.1 KPAs for CMM Level 2, Repeatable

The KPAs of CMM Level 2 focus on establishing basic project management controls.

1. **Requirements management.** This is the process of establishing, documenting, and maintaining an agreement with the user community regarding the requirements for the project.
2. **Software project planning.** This involves developing and negotiating estimates for the work to be performed, establishing the necessary commitments, and defining the plan to perform the work.
3. **Software project tracking and oversight.** This is the act of providing visibility into the actual progress of a project so that management can take effective action whenever the performance on the project deviates from the plan.
4. **Software subcontract management.** This involves selecting and effectively managing qualified software subcontractors.
5. **Software quality assurance.** This is the act of reviewing and auditing the project deliverables and activities to verify that they comply with the applicable standards, guidelines, and processes adopted by your organization.

6. **Software configuration management.** This involves establishing and maintaining the integrity of the project deliverables throughout the entire life cycle.

1.7.2.2 KPAs for CMM Level 3, Defined

The KPAs of CMM Level 3 address both project and organizational issues that establish an infrastructure to institutionalize effective software engineering and management processes across all projects.

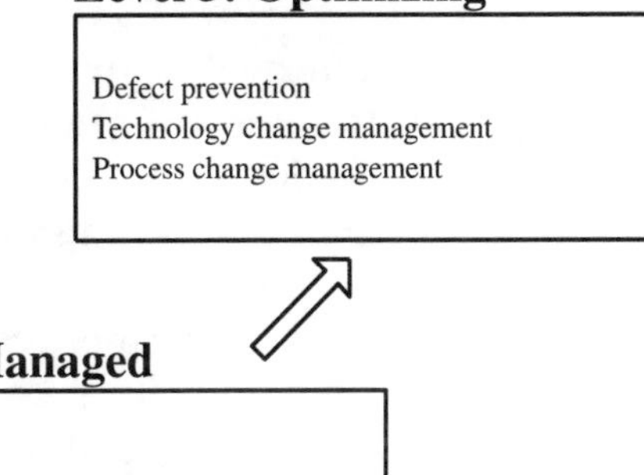

Figure 1.18. The key process areas of the SEI CMM (SEI, 1995)

1. **Organization process focus.** This involves developing and maintaining an understanding of your organization's and project's software processes and coordinating the activities to assess, develop, maintain, and improve these processes. This responsibility should be assigned to a permanent team within your organization.
2. **Organization process definition.** This involves developing and maintaining your organization's standard software process, along with related process assets such as descriptions of software life cycles, process tailoring guidelines and criteria, your organization's software process database, and a library of software process-related documentation.
3. **Training program.** This involves identifying of the training needed by your organization, projects, and individuals, and then developing or procuring training to address the identified needs.
4. **Integrated software management.** This is the act of integrating both software engineering and management activities into a coherent, defined process for each project that is tailored from the standard software process of your organization. This involves developing the project's defined software process and managing the software project based on this process.
5. **Software product engineering.** This is the act of performing the engineering tasks to build and maintain the software in accordance with the project's defined software process and appropriate methods and tools.
6. **Intergroup coordination.** This involves the participation of a project team with other teams and groups throughout your organization to address the requirements, objectives, and issues that are applicable to your entire organization.
7. **Peer reviews.** This is the methodical examination of deliverables by the developer's peers to identify potential defects and areas where changes are needed.

1.7.2.3 KPAs for CMM Level 4, Managed

The KPAs of CMM Level 4 focus on the establishment of a quantitative understanding of both the software process and the software products being built by your organization.

1. **Quantitative process management.** This is the act of estab-

lishing goals for, and then measuring, the performance of a project's defined software process. It is critical that the performance of individuals are measured, to aid in their professional development, but that the information not be used to their detriment.

2. **Software quality management.** This is the definition of quality goals for software products and the establishment of plans to achieve these goals. It also involves the monitoring and adjustment of the software plans, software work products, activities, and quality goals to satisfy the needs and desires of the user community for high-quality products.

1.7.2.4 KPAs for CMM Level 5, Optimized

The KPAs of Level 5 cover the issues that both your organization and projects must address to implement continuous and measurable software process improvement.

The OOSP presented in the book supports and exceeds the requirements defined by the CMM.

1. **Defect prevention.** This is the analyzing of defects that were encountered in the past and taking specific actions to prevent the occurrence of those types of defects in the future.
2. **Technology change management.** This involves identifying, selecting, and evaluating new technologies and incorporating effective technologies into the organization.
3. **Process change management.** This involves defining process improvement goals and proactively and systematically identifying, evaluating, and implementing improvements to your organization's software process on a continuous basis.

1.7.2.5 Mapping the Key Process Areas to the OOSP

As mention previously, the CMM KPAs define the issues that must be addressed by a mature software process. Table 1.6 shows where the KPAs are implemented by the Object-Oriented Software Process (OOSP). Note that some KPAs are implemented by project stages, some by project phases, some by project tasks, and some by combinations of the three. The important thing to note is that the OOSP presented in this book supports, and often exceeds, the requirements defined by the CMM.

Figure 1.19. Quality rises and risk decreases as your software process matures

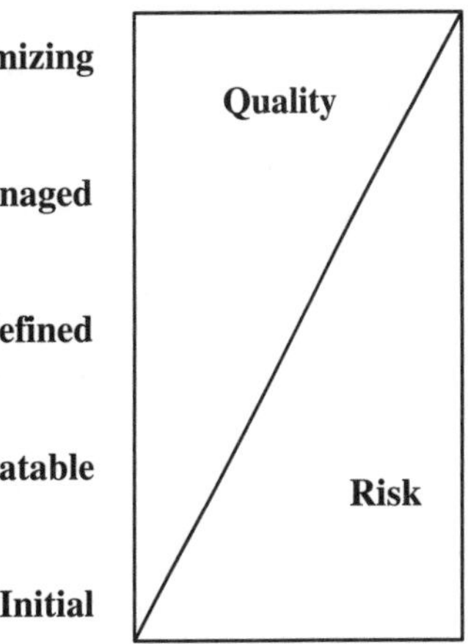

TABLE 1.6 Mapping the CMM Key Process Areas (KPAs) to the OOSP

Key Process Area	Level	OOSP
Defect Prevention	5	Define and Validate Initial Requirements stage Test in the Small stage Test in the Large stage Quality Assurance
Integrated Software Management	3	Define Infrastructure stage—Process Tailoring Project Management
Intergroup Coordination	3	Define Initial Management Documents stage—Management Define Infrastructure stage—Management Justify stage—Management Construct phase—Management Project Management
Organization Process Definition	3	Define Infrastructure stage—Process Tailoring Infrastructure Management
Organization Process Focus	3	Infrastructure Management
Peer Reviews	3	Define and Validate Initial Requirements stage—Walkthrough Requirements and Walkthrough prototypes Test in the Small stage—Validating Your Models, Code Inspections Quality Assurance

(continued)

Table 1.6 *(continued)*

Key Process Area	Level	OOSP
Process Change Management	5	Define Infrastructure stage—Creating a Group Memory Initiate phase—Exit Criteria Construct phase—Exit Criteria Test in the Large stage—Defect Source Metrics Assess stage Support stage—Escalation Assessments
Quantitative Process Management	4	Assess stage—Assessing Individuals Infrastructure Management
Requirements Management	2	Define and Validate Initial Requirements stage Rework stage Identify Defects and Enhancements stage
Software Configuration Management	2	Construct phase Rework stage Release stage Identify Defects and Enhancements stage Deliverable Management
Software Product Engineering	3	Construct phase Rework stage
Software Project Planning	2	Define Initial Management Documents stage Construct phase Project Management
Software Project Tracking And Oversight	2	Project Management

(continued)

TABLE 1.6 *(continued)*

Key Process Area	Level	OOSP
Software Quality Assurance	2	Define and Validate Initial Requirements stage—Walkthrough Requirements and Walkthrough prototypes Quality Assurance Test in the Small stage—Validating Your Models, Code Inspections
Software Quality Management	4	Define Initial Management Documents stage Project Management Quality Assurance
Software Subcontract Management	2	Define Infrastructure —Define team
Technology Change Management	5	Model Stage — Technical Architecture Modeling
Training Program	3	Define and Validate Initial Requirements stage Define Infrastructure stage Release stage

1.7.3 Why Software Maturity?

Why should your organization strive to increase its software maturity? The answer, shown in Figure 1.19, is two-fold: first, the greater the software maturity of your organization, the greater the quality of the software products that it produces. This is a direct result of the increased focus on management and project deliverables as the maturity of your organization increases. Second, as the software maturity of your organization grows, there is a corresponding reduction of risk on your software development projects, the result of increased management control and use of measurements (metrics) to understand and manage the software process and the products that you produce.

Although the SEI CMM defines what an organization must do to have a mature software process, it does not describe how to actually develop, maintain and support software. Because the SEI CMM is a generic look at the software process, it does not describe techniques that are specific to object-orientation md nor should it. That's where this book comes in: it describes a mature software process for the object-oriented paradigm. To relate the various CMM KPAs to the techniques employed during the phases, stages, and project tasks of the OOSP the following symbols will be used to demarcate the CMM KPAs:

1.8 The Advantages and Disadvantages of the OOSP

The OOSP, and the OOSP pattern language, presented in this book has many advantages:

- The emphasis on quality assurance, testing, and working closely with users leads to greater quality in your applications and helps to promote the traceability of requirements throughout an application.
- The OOSP defines how applications are built and shows the interrelationships between development processes, promoting understanding and teamwork within and between project teams.
- The emphasis on project management and risk management reduces the risks associated with development, increasing your chances of success.
- The OOSP provides a consistent, proven approach to OO development, based on real-world experience and not the musings of ivory-tower academics.

- The OOSP provides insight into how developers, users, managers, and external vendors interact with one another to build an OO application.
- The OOSP helps to define staffing requirements for projects, as well as the deliverables.
- The emphasis on reuse management and generalization increases the chance that you actually will achieve reuse within your organization.
- By explicitly defining how you do things you have the opportunity to measure and reflect on the development process, allowing you to improve it over time.
- The OOSP promotes a mature approach to development and creates an environment that is inhospitable to hacking.
- The OOSP is mapped to the Software Engineering Institute's Capability Maturity Model, and industry-standard framework for improving the software maturity of an organization.
- The OOSP pattern language shows how to apply process patterns in a consistent and comprehensive manner, providing a framework within which other process patterns may be added later.

There are also a few disadvantages:

- You still need to fill in the details: for example, Chapter 8 covers the modeling process in general, reviewing the various modeling techniques and how they fit together, as well as providing a modeling strategy for large projects but what it does not do is teach you how to model. (There is a plenitude of good books on this subject, including a few written by myself.)
- It becomes difficult to underestimate the effort required for developing OO applications, making it harder to justify pet projects and to ram through emergency projects that have little chance for success.

TIP

Spread the Costs Over Several Projects

Implementing an OOSP such as this within your organization is only possible if you spread the costs of it over several projects. A process is an investment made by your organization, not just by a single project.

1.9 How the Rest of This Book Is Organized

Chapters 2 through 11 describe the Initiate and Construct phases of the OOSP, presenting many applicable process patterns. These chapters are organized into four parts, one for each project phase and its associated stages.

Each "phase overview" chapter, describing a single phase process pattern, is organized into the following sections:

- Overview
- Initial context: Entry conditions to begin the phase
- Solution: How work proceeds during the phase
- Solution: Project task issues
- Resulting context: Exit conditions to end the phase
- Secrets of success
- Phase process checklist
- What you have learned in this chapter
- References and suggested reading

Each "stage" chapter, describing a single stage process pattern, is organized into the following sections:

- Overview
- Initial Context: Entry conditions to enter the stage
- Solution: How work proceeds during the stage
- Solution: Project tasks (quality assurance, risk management, reuse, metrics)
- Resulting context: Exit conditions to leave the stage
- Secrets of success
- Stage process checklist
- What you have learned in this chapter
- References and suggested reading

The approach that I will take throughout this book is to present the phase and stage process patterns as templated patterns, patterns that follow a consistent documentation format. I've stuck as close as possible to the generally accepted format, albeit reworking it a bit to move away from its reference-oriented nature to what I consider a more readable format. I suspect that this decision will cause heartburn for some of the theoreticians in the patterns com-

DEFINITIONS

degenerate pattern A pattern that has been described without the use of a pattern template.

process checklist An indication of the tasks that should be completed while working a defined process.

templated pattern A pattern that has been documented using a pattern template.

munity, sorry about that. Task process patterns, on the other hand, are presented as degenerate patterns, patterns that are described without using a template (personally, I feel the term "untemplated pattern" would have been a little more forgiving than degenerate pattern). Yes, at some point I should document each of these patterns using a common, "standard" template, but for the sake of readability I have chosen to simply present task process patterns as simple prose, not as structured reference material.

The overview section for each project phase and stage describes the pertinent issues and forces applicable to the process pattern being described by the chapter. The next section describes the initial context, the situation before the process pattern is worked, focusing on the entry conditions that should be met for the process to begin. The solution to resolving the issues of the process pattern is described in two parts, one describing the mechanical tasks/activities to be performed and one describing project task-related issues (the "big arrow" of the OOSP). The resulting context, the situation after the process pattern is worked, is described in the following section via a focus on the exit conditions for the process. The chapters end with a summary of the secrets of success for the process, many of which hint at possible task process patterns for those of you interested in extending the OOSP pattern language, and a process checklist that you can tailor to meet the unique needs of your organization. Process checklists should be used as part of your software process improvement efforts as they provide a feedback mechanism about your internal processes. I highly suggest adding standard questions at the end of each checklist that investigate needed improvements to the process.

1.10 What You Have Learned in This Chapter

The OOSP is serial in the large and iterative in the small, delivering incremental releases over time.

In this chapter I discussed several common approaches to application development—serial, iterative, incremental, parallel, and hacking—and discussed their advantages and disadvantages. I covered the requirements that the Object-Oriented Software Process (OOSP) must support. The OOSP is serial in the large, iterative in the small, delivering incremental releases over time, taking a more realistic approach to OO development than the "traditional" iterative-only approach. I also introduced you to the concept of the OOSP pattern language, a collection of process patterns that describe the OOSP. I compared the OOSP to other similar approaches—SOMA, the Objectory software process, and the OPEN Process—and that the OOSP was either more robust or at least the equal of the other approaches. I ended the chapter with a discussion of the Capability Maturity Model (CMM) and the advantages and disadvantages of the OOSP.

There is no reason why good cannot triumph as often as evil. The triumph of anything is a matter of organization.
—Kurt Vonnegut, Jr.

1.11 References and Recommended Reading

Alexander, C. 1979. *The Timeless Way of Building*. New York: Oxford University Press.

Ambler, S. W. 1995. *The Object Primer: The Application Developer's Guide to Object Orientation*. New York: SIGS Books/Cambridge University Press.

Ambler, S. W. 1998. *Building Object Applications That Work—Your Step-by-Step Handbook for Developing Robust Systems with Object Technology*. New York: SIGS Books/Cambridge University Press.

Ambler, S. W. 1998b. *More Process Patterns: Delivering Large-Scale Systems Using Object Technology*. New York: SIGS Books/Cambridge University Press.

Baudoin, C., and Hollowell, G. 1996. *Realizing the Object-Oriented Life Cycle*. Upper Saddle River, New Jersey: Prentice-Hall, Inc.

Boehm, B.W. 1988. A Spiral Model of Software Development and Enhancement. *IEEE Computer* 21(5), 61-72.

Coplien, J.O. (1995). *A Generative Development-Process Pattern Language*. Pattern Languages of Program Design, eds. Coplien, J.O. and Schmidt, D.C., Addison Wesley Longman, Inc., pp. 183-237.

Emam, K. E.; Drouin J.; and Melo, W. 1998. *SPICE: The Theory and Practice of Software Process Improvement and Capability Determination*. Los Alamitos, California: IEEE Computer Society Press.

Fowler, M. 1997. *Analysis Patterns: Reusable Object Models*. Menlo Park, California: Addison Wesley Longman, Inc..

Gamma, E.; Helm, R.; Johnson, R.; and Vlissides, J. 1995. *Design Patterns: Elements of Reusable Object-Oriented Software*. Reading, Massachusetts: Addison-Wesley Publishing Company.

Graham, I. 1995. *Migrating to Object Technology*. Reading, Massachusetts: Addison-Wesley Publishers Ltd.

Graham, I.; Henderson-Sellers, B.; and Younessi, H. 1997. *The OPEN Process Specification*. New York: ACM Press Books.

Henderson-Sellers, B., and Edwards, J. M. 1990. The Object Oriented Systems Life Cycle. *Communications of the ACM*, 33(9), pp.142–159.

Jones, C. 1996. *Patterns of Software Systems Failure and Success*. Boston, Massachusetts: International Thomson Computer Press.

Meyer, B. 1995. *Object Success: A Manager's Guide to Object Orientation, Its Impact on the Corporation and Its Use for Engineering the Software Process*. Englewood Cliffs, New Jersey: Prentice Hall, Inc.

Rational. 1996. *Rational Rose: A Rational Approach to Software Development Using Rational Rose*. Santa Clara, California: Rational Software Corporation.

Software Engineering Institute. 1995. *The Capability Maturity Model: Guidelines for Improving the Software Process*. Reading Massachusetts: Addison-Wesley Publishing Company, Inc.

Whittington, L. W. 1996. *The SEI Software Capability Maturity Model*. http://home.earthlink.net/~rpr-online/LW-CMM.htm

Part 1

Initiate

THE FIRST SERIAL PROJECT phase of the OOSP is the Initiate phase, commonly referred to as the project initiation phase in the structured world.

Chapter 2

The Initiate Phase

THE main goal of the Initiate phase, the first serial phase of the object-oriented software process (OOSP), is to lay the foundation for a successful project. Unfortunately, this is often easier said than done due to pressures by senior management and developers to start "the real work," the Construct Phase, as soon as possible and by a lack of understanding of why the Initiate Phase is critical to your project.

The main goal of the Initiate phase is to lay the foundation for a successful project.

As you can see in the process pattern depicted in Figure 2.1, it is made up of the definition and validation of the initial requirements and management documents, the project justification, and the definition of the project infrastructure. The deliverables of the Initiate phase include project management documents such as the project plan and project schedule, initial requirements which will form the basis of the modeling efforts, standards and guidelines to be used on the project, and adequate funding for the project.

The main input into the Initiate phase is maintenance changes allocated to your application by the Maintain and Support phase (Ambler, 1998b). Remember that object-oriented development is incremental—previous releases of your application may already be in production; and as a result, maintenance changes, either fixes or new features applicable to/for the previous versions may have been assigned to your project team by the Identify Defects and Enhancements stage (Ambler, 1998b). These allocated maintenance changes will be used as input for identifying requirements

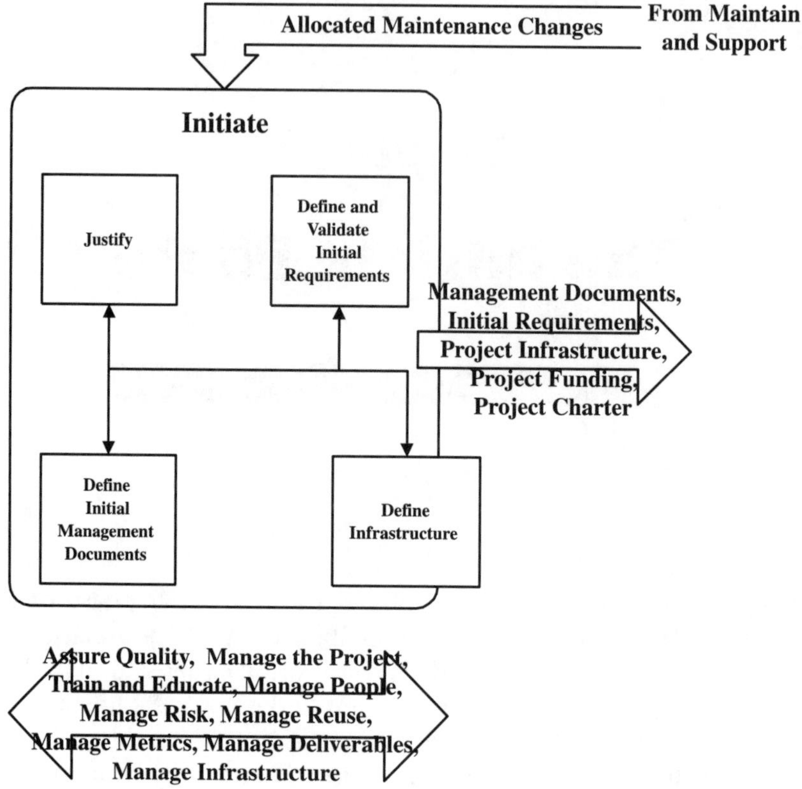

Figure 2.1. The Initiate process pattern

for the release of your application that your team will develop.

Because OO development is incremental, you will likely need to address maintenance changes from previous versions of your application in your new release.

The four iterative stages of the Initiate phase are highly interrelated, and in many SDLCs are simply considered one single stage called "project initiation." It is my experience, however, that the Initiate phase is made up of four distinct stages, as we see in Figure 2.1—each stage having its own set of deliverables. By defining the initial requirements during the Initiate phase, the project team is given somewhere to start when construction begins. Management documents, such as the project estimate and risk assessment, are started during the Initiate phase and provide a basis for managing the project throughout the entire development process. The project justification effort shows that the project is expected to be successful (if it shows that the project does not make sense then you shouldn't continue on) and is the basis on which project funding is obtained. The project infrastructure is put in place so

DEFINITIONS

feasibility study A document that addresses three main issues: can the system be built, can you afford to build the system, and once the system is in place can you maintain and support it. In other words, is the system technically feasible, is it economically feasible, and is it operationally feasible? Feasibility studies are a deliverable of the Justify stage.

maintenance change A description of a modification to be made to one or more existing configuration items (CIs).

project estimate An appraisal of how long a project will take and how much it will cost, given a specific environment and a specific team. Change the environment and/or change the team and your estimate should change. Project estimates are a deliverable of the Initiate phase and are updated regularly throughout a project.

project infrastructure The team, tools, and processes that will be used on a given project.

project plan A project plan is a collection of several project management deliverables, including, but not limited to, a project overview, a project schedule, a project estimate, a team definition, and a risk assessment. Project plans are a deliverable of the Initiate phase and are updated regularly throughout a project.

project schedule A project schedule indicates what will be done, when things will be done, and who will do them. A major component of a project schedule is a Gantt chart with its corresponding descriptions of tasks and resources. Project schedules are a deliverable of the Initiate phase and are updated regularly throughout a project.

risk assessment A document indicating potential factors, called risks, that if they were to occur would harm the project. A risk assessment is used to identify risks so that they may be dealt with appropriately. Risk assessments are a deliverable of the Initiate phase and are updated regularly throughout a project.

that the project team knows what tools they will use, how they will use them, how their work will be evaluated, and what deliverables they must produce during the project.

2.1 Initial Context: Entry Conditions to the Initiate Phase

Because the Initiate phase is the first phase in the OOSP, the entry conditions for it are fairly light. First, you must be in a situation in

DEFINITIONS

infrastructure artifact An item, such as your organization's software process, a standard, a guideline, or a chosen tool that is common between project teams to build applications to support your organization.

software change request (SCR) A description of a potential improvement to a software deliverable, often identified by users of that deliverable.

software problem report (SPR) A description of a potential software defect identified by someone who is not directly responsible for a given software deliverable.

which your organization wants to develop an application, and if it proves feasible they must intend to support its development. In other words, someone has demonstrated the need for a development project. Second, maintenance changes to address the repair of defects or the enhancement of a previous release of your application may have been assigned to your project team. These maintenance changes will be accompanied by the original software change request (SCR) or software problem report (SPR) that initiated the required change to provide your team with the information required to identify new and/or updated requirements for your application. Third, your organization's existing infrastructure is available to you, comprised of a collection of infrastructure items such as programming standards and a development toolset.

2.2 Solution: How Work Typically Proceeds During the Initiate Phase

What typically happens during the Initiate phase is that a project plan gets put in place (at least a schedule and a team definition) and the initial requirements may or may not get defined properly. The justification process is usually "Mr. Bigwig wants it, so let's do it" and the project infrastructure is defined by going out and purchasing a few development tools based on whatever magazine articles or Web sites your top programmers have been reading lately. A recipe for disaster.

As you can see in Figure 2.2 what you need to do is put a serious effort into three parallel activities: one, defining and validating the initial requirements, the topic of Chapter 3; two, beginning the initial project management documents and justifying the project,

Scott's Soapbox

Upper Management Is Not Always the Best Source for Defining Your Project Infrastructure

Very often you will find that senior management has already done some of the project infrastructure work for you because they will often define the platform that you will be developing for and the development language that you will be using. More often than not this is more harmful than it is beneficial, especially when their decision has been guided more by what they've read in a recent article in their favorite business magazine instead of what makes the most sense for your organizational environment. If they've made a poorly informed choice you will need to show this in your feasibility study, which is easy to say but often hard to

the topics of Chapters 4 and 5 respectively; and, three, defining the project infrastructure, the topic of Chapter 6. Note that the feasibility study and several of the project management documents, specifically the schedule and the estimate, are highly related to one another and are typically written at the same time by the same person(s). For a larger project it is quite reasonable to expect a small team of people to be given the task of defining and validating the initial requirements and one or two people to define the project infrastructure. In short, the potential exists for running three streams of effort in parallel during the Initiate phase. In the bottom right-hand corner of each activity box is an estimate of the percentage of time within the Initiate phase each activity will typically take.

Work often proceeds in three parallel streams during the Initiate phase.

Notice how the greatest range of effort lies in defining the project infrastructure. This is because your first OO project will need to spend a lot of effort in researching and experimenting with tools, standards, and methodologies. Later projects will be able to reuse the infrastructure work of earlier projects and should therefore have much less to do. The other two streams generally take the same amount of effort, which can often be frustrating because most developers prefer requirements work over project management work (actually, they would rather do construction work but that is a completely different issue).

Figure 2.3 shows a detailed look at how work proceeds during the Initiate phase. Each box represents the development of a

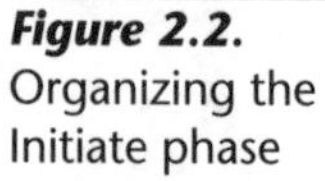

Figure 2.2. Organizing the Initiate phase

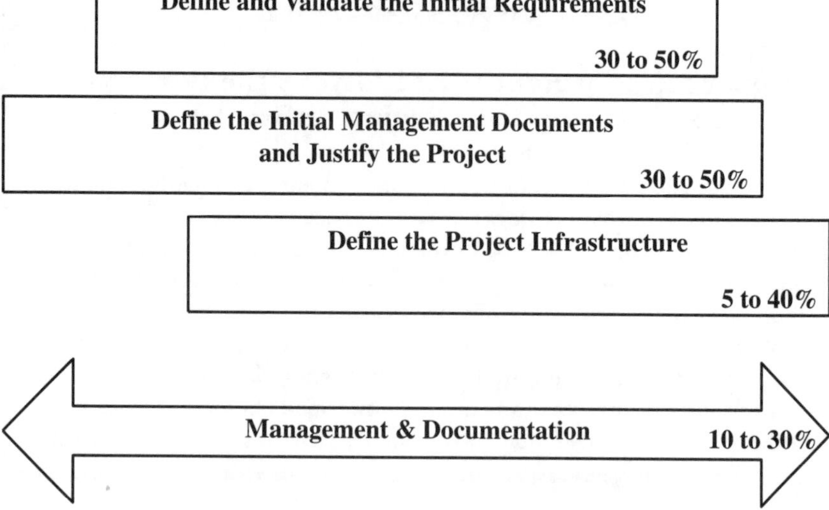

major deliverable, showing when the work generally starts. The first thing that must occur is the definition of the project. Once this effort is underway, planning activities, justification activities, and infrastructure definition activities may begin. Many of the decisions must be finalized, such as the team definition, before the project estimate and schedule may be completed. The final deliverable, ignoring tool selection which often goes into the Construct phase (Chapters 7 through 11), is the project charter which indicates that the project team has the support and funding that it needs to continue with the project.

DEFINITIONS

group memory A record of what your project team accomplished, decisions made by your team and the reasoning behind them, deferred decisions, and the lessons learned on your project. A group memory provides a mechanism to record this information when it is first recognized so that it isn't lost.

master test/quality assurance(QA) plan A document that describes your testing and quality assurance policies and procedures, as well as the detailed test plans for each portion of your application.

project charter A document issued by senior management that provides the project manager with the authority to apply organizational resources to project activities.

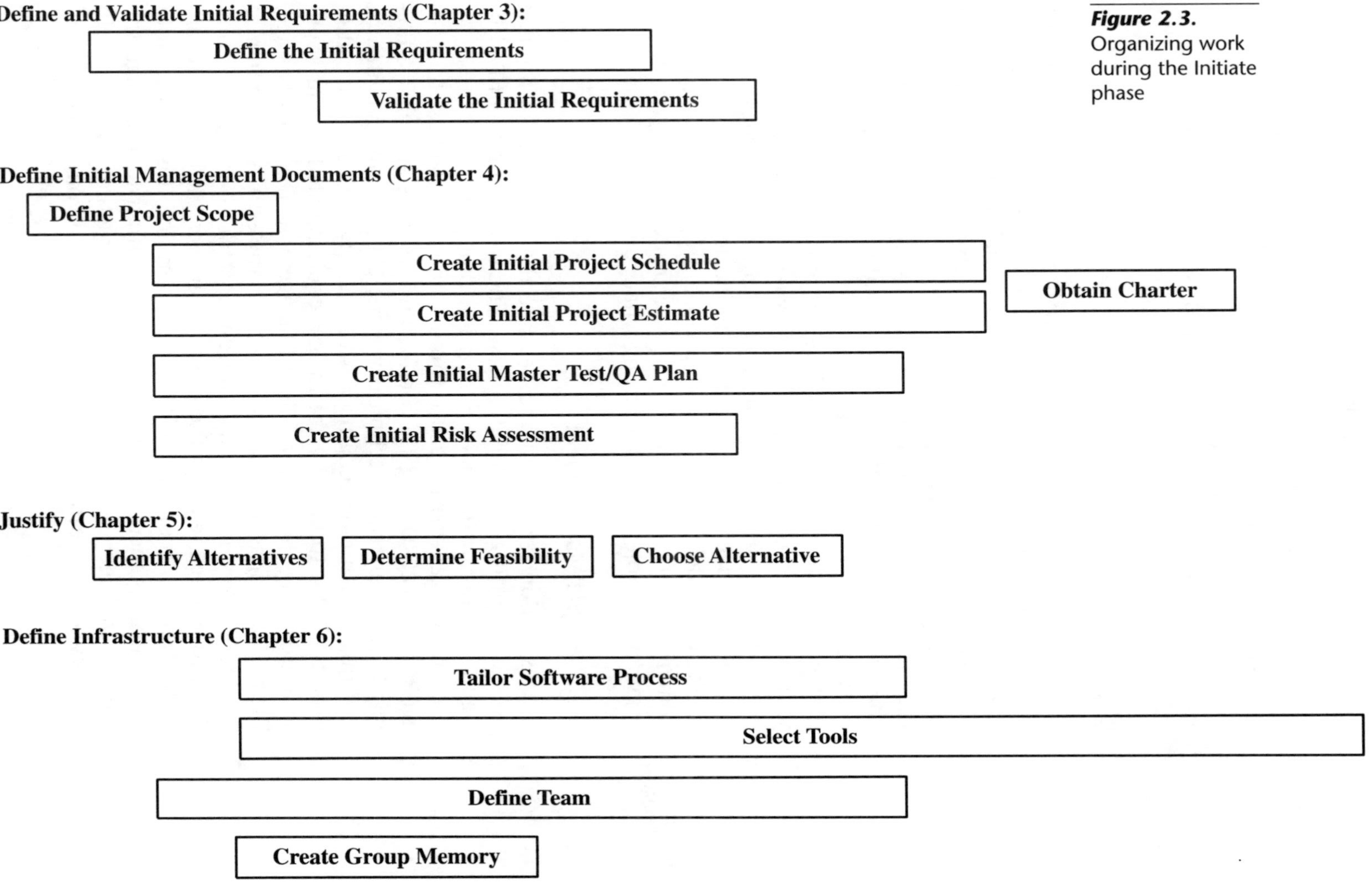

Define and Validate Initial Requirements (Chapter 3):
Define the Initial Requirements
Validate the Initial Requirements
Define Initial Management Documents (Chapter 4):
Define Project Scope
Create Initial Project Schedule
Create Initial Project Estimate
Obtain Charter
Create Initial Master Test/QA Plan
Create Initial Risk Assessment
Justify (Chapter 5):
Identify Alternatives
Determine Feasibility
Choose Alternative
Define Infrastructure (Chapter 6):
Tailor Software Process
Select Tools
Define Team
Create Group Memory

Figure 2.3. Organizing work during the Initiate phase

2.3 Solution: Project Tasks

In this section I will discuss project task issues pertinent to the Initiate phase.

2.3.1 Managing the Initiate Phase

This is the easiest phase to manage, simply because it is mostly project management tasks to begin with. The team is typically made up of the project manager and an analyst or two, and for a very large project the manager may also require an assistant. The overriding project management goal during this phase is to get the support of senior management because they have to believe in your project and be willing to support it if it is to succeed.

Start your project by determining what you can reuse from previous efforts.

Another important goal of the Initiate phase is to identify items that your team may reuse to develop your application. Perhaps someone else has built a portion of what you need, or perhaps you can purchase part of your application. Throughout this book you will see that you are able to reuse documentation templates, source code, deliverables from previous projects, and large-scale domain components. The point to be made is that you should begin every project by determining what you can first reuse.

2.3.2 People Management

In this section I would like to describe the various roles fulfilled by people during the Initiate phase. These roles are identified in Figure 2.4 and are described in detail in Table 2.1.

A project manager is needed through the Initiate phase to manage the project. During the Define and Validate Initial Requirements stage, analysts, technical writers, JAD/meeting facilitators, and quality assurance engineers work closely with subject matter experts (SMEs) to identify the initial requirements for your application. During the Define Initial Management Documents stage, the project manager works together with the estimator/planner to initiate the key management documents for your project team. The Justify stage requires the project manager, likely with the aid of the project sponsor, to garner support for the project from senior management. Finally, during the Infrastructure stage the project manager works with the infrastructure engineers to define/select the infrastructure to be used by your project team.

Project Manager	Analyst	Subject Matter Expert	Quality Assurance Engineer
Estimator/ Planner	Process Specialist	Standards Specialist	Tools Specialist
Project Sponsor	JAD/ Meeting Facilitator	Technical Writer	Infrastructure Engineer

Figure 2.4. Potential roles during the Initiate phase

2.3.3 Potential Risks During the Initiate Phase

Several common risks are endemic to the Initiate phase:

1. **Senior management pressures you to start construction too early.** Senior management always wants new applications yesterday; they want to see immediate progress and that means code. Most project managers are pressured into starting construction too early, before the project infrastructure is in place and before the team members are trained properly.
2. **You are pressured to bring people on the project too early.** A related problem is that you are given far too many people at the start of the project, but not during construction when you really need them, usually for the simple reason that they are available now. Unless you need to train your developers in object technology and want to get this done before construction begins, do not bring them on during the Initiate phase—it is too tempting to start coding, and if you have developers sitting around looking for something to do that's exactly what is going to happen. You also want to ensure, by defining the project infrastructure, that the tools you have chosen actually work before construction begins. If your tools do not work, or if they do not work together, your project is in serious trouble.
3. **Beware the new toy/fad syndrome.** In far too many organizations an executive will read an article in their favorite business magazine telling them about a new product or management

fad, so they instantly have to implement it in your organization. The Justify stage should help you to avoid this problem, butÖ

4. **Resistance to change.** The desire of people to protect their existing turf will quickly motivate them to undermine your efforts. Not everyone is your friend, even the people who

TABLE 2.1. Common Roles Held During the Initiate Phase

Role	Description
Analyst	The person(s) responsible for defining and validating the initial requirements for the application by working closely with subject matter experts.
Estimator/planner	The person(s) responsible for activities such as initial project estimating, scheduling, and planning.
Infrastructure engineer	A person who is responsible for defining and supporting the project infrastructure.
JAD/meeting facilitator	The person(s) responsible for organizing, running, and summarizing the results of joint application design (JAD) sessions in which requirement definition and validation is performed.
Process specialist	The person(s) responsible for choosing/defining the development processes to be used on the project and may act as an infrastructure consultant during later phases.
Project manager	The person responsible for obtaining funding and authorization for the project from senior management.
Project sponsor	The person(s) who take responsibility for supporting, nurturing, and protecting the project throughout its life and is crucial for successfully starting the project.

(continued)

claim to be. If you do not get everyone on your side at the beginning of a project you will be constantly having to watch your back for people who want to see you fail. Now is the time to start dealing with resistance to change, not when you are trying to put your application into production.

TABLE 2.1. *(continued)*

Role	Description
Quality assurance engineer	The person responsible for validating that the deliverables produced by the development team meet or exceed the agreed to standards and guidelines for the project.
Risk assessor	The person(s) responsible for identifying and potentially addressing the initial risks associated with the project.
Standards specialist	The person(s) responsible for choosing/defining the development standards to be used on a project, and may act as an infrastructure engineer/consultant during later phases.
Subject matter expert (SME)	The person(s) responsible for providing pertinent information about the problem and/or technical domain either from personal knowledge or from research.
Technical writer	The person responsible for writing, updating, and/or improving the technical documentation produced on the project, potentially including the requirements, models, standards, guidelines, and project plans.
Tools specialist	The person(s) responsible for evaluating and selecting the development tools to be used on the project, and may act as an infrastructure engineer/consultant during later phases.

Scott's Soapbox

Do Not Just Get Tool Training

Although it is important to get training in the tools that you use to manage a project, this isn't enough. Too many people make the mistake of taking a three day training course in their chosen tool without first obtaining an education in project management. Just like taking a training course in using a specific word processor doesn't automatically make you a good writer, taking a training course in a specific project management tool doesn't automatically make you a good project manager.

2.3.4 Training and Education Issues

For the people involved in this stage of the project, it is project management skills that they need the most. A good project management course should include topics such as the fundamentals of project management, scheduling, estimating, and feasibility studies. If your local college or university has a computer science program they should have a course in this, otherwise you will need to go to a training company with courses in computer technology.

As indicated earlier, you might need to provide senior management training in the fundamentals of OO development and OO technology. There are a lot of consultants offering half-day and full-day overview courses in OO for managers, and a few of the courses are actually quite good. Look for an instructor with real-world experience, someone who has gotten their hands dirty writing code, done some modeling, done some testing, and has managed a few OO projects. People like this are few and far between, but they are worth their weight in gold if you can find them.

2.4 Resulting Context: Exit Conditions from the Initiate Phase

Because this phase effectively builds the foundation for the project, meeting the exit conditions is fairly important. Six basic exit conditions should be met before construction can begin on a project.

1. **Initial version of key project management documents are approved.** The initial project management documents—the project plan, estimate, schedule, and risk assessment—are started during this phase. Furthermore, although they are not complete they must still be verified and approved by senior management before construction can begin.
2. **The project is justifiable.** The feasibility study should honestly show that the project makes sense at technical, operational, and economic levels.
3. **The project infrastructure is defined.** The project infrastructure—team definition, standards and guidelines, methods, tools, and processes—should be either completely defined or very close to it. Defining the infrastructure for the Deliver and Maintain and Support phases can be put off for a short while as those phases do not immediately follow the Initiate phase. If all components of the infrastructure are not in place then a schedule to do so must be defined.
4. **High-level requirements are in place.** The requirements document should document most or all high-level requirements, with the project scope identified and agreed to by all appropriate parties. Furthermore, the high-level requirements should be validated and approved before construction begins.
5. **Funding has been obtained for the project.** Management must approve and fund the project, or at least the initial release of the project, otherwise work cannot proceed. Note that some projects do not receive official funding, but are instead financed out of "slush" funds.
6. **The project charter is in place.** A project charter summarizes many of the key project management documents, but more importantly indicates that that the project is funded and given the support of senior management.

7. **Lessons learned have been identified.** At the end of the Initiate phase you should take the time to consider the processes that could be improved, what processes need to be added, and what processes could be removed. By identifying lessons learned at the end of the phase you discover opportunities to improve your software process, and provide valuable input for the Assess stage (Ambler, 1998b).

2.5 Process Checklist

The following process checklist can be used to verify that you have completed the Initiate phase.

INITIATE PHASE PROCESS CHECKLIST

Fulfillment of Entrance Conditions:

- ✔ Senior management support exists to initiate a new project.
- ✔ Maintenance changes pertaining to previous versions (if any) are identified.
- ✔ Your organization's existing infrastructure is available.

Processes Performed:

- ✔ The initial requirements have been defined and validated.
- ✔ The initial management documents have been defined.
- ✔ The project has been technically, economically, and operationally justified.
- ✔ The project infrastructure has been defined.
- ✔ Potential artifacts to be reused have been identified.
- ✔ The project team has been identified and trained where appropriate.

Fulfillment of Exit Conditions:

- ✔ The project plan has been accepted by senior management.
- ✔ The project schedule has been accepted by senior management.
- ✔ The initial risk assessment has been performed.
- ✔ The initial requirements have been accepted by senior management.
- ✔ Appropriate standards and guidelines have been identified.
- ✔ The software process has been tailored to meet the specific needs for your project.
- ✔ The appropriate tools have been identified, purchased if necessary, and installed.

- ✔ Funding for the project, at least the next portion of it, has been obtained.
- ✔ The project charter has been defined and accepted.
- ✔ Potential improvements to the Initiate phase processes have been identified.
- ✔ The project team has been assembled.

2.6 What You Have Learned in This Chapter

The main goal of the Initiate phase is to lay the foundation for a successful project. The Initiate phase is made up of four iterative stages: Define and Validate the Initial Requirements, Define the Initial Management Documents, Justify, and Define Infrastructure. The deliverables of the Initiate phase include project management documents such as the project plan, schedule, estimate, and risk assessment; the initial requirements, standards, guidelines, tools, and procedures to be used on the project; and adequate funding and management support for the project.

2.7 References and Recommended Reading

Ambler, S. W. 1998a. *Building Object Applications That Work—Your Step-by-Step Handbook for Developing Robust Systems with Object Technology*. New York: SIGS Books/Cambridge University Press.

Ambler, S. W. 1998b. *More Process Patterns—Delivering Large-Scale Systems Using Object Technology*. New York: SIGS Books/Cambridge University Press.

Blum, B. I. 1992. *Software Engineering: A Holistic View*. Oxford: Oxford University Press.

Booch, G. 1996. *Object Solutions: Managing the Object-Oriented Project*. Menlo Park, California: Addison-Wesley Publishing Company, Inc.

Due, R. T. , and Henderson-Sellers, B. 1995. The Changing Paradigm for Object Project Management. *Object Magazine* 5 (July–August): 54–60,78.

Jones, C. 1996. *Patterns of Software Systems Failure and Success*. Boston: Thomson International Press.

Chapter 3

The Define and Validate Initial Requirements Stage

FUNDAMENTALLY, you cannot build something until you know what it is that you're building. That's what this stage is all about: determining what needs to be built, at least from a high-level perspective. By defining and then validating the initial requirements for an application you help to build a solid foundation from which modeling can begin. Without this foundation, without knowing what requirements your application must fulfill, you will not be able to build an application that fully meets the needs of its users. The definition and validation of requirements is known as *requirements engineering*.

You need to determine what you're going to build before you actually build it.

Figure 3.1 shows that there are several important inputs into this stage: a vision, commitment to the project, a feasibility study, and knowledge of the existing applications (if any) that this application will replace or enhance. Because of the iterative nature of the Initiate phase, these deliverables will probably not be complete when you begin defining and validating the initial requirements for an application. They will, however, have at least been started. The key deliverables of this stage are a requirements document, also referred to as a System Requirements Specification

Figure 3.1.
The Define and Validate Initial Requirements stage

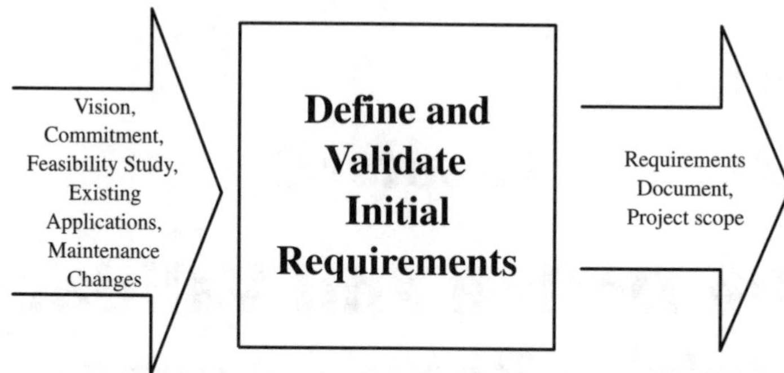

(SRS), and a definition of the project scope based upon the validated requirements document. Note that other stages within the Initiate phase will use these deliverables as input long before they are finished, just as this stage uses their deliverables long before they are finished. Quid pro quo.

A very important point to note about this stage is that you often need to collect more than just user requirements. There are usually very important technical requirements to define and validate, such as the response time of the application and the target delivery platform. Environmental requirements, ranging in topic from the political environment to ergonomic considerations, also need to be collected during this stage. Regulatory requirements, the result of specific laws, must also be identified and validated. Although this chapter concentrates on user requirements, never forget that there are other kinds of requirements to take into consideration.

3.1 Initial Context: Entry Conditions for Defining and Validating the Initial Requirements

There are several important entry conditions that must be met for work to proceed during this stage. Some of these conditions center on people issues such as commitment to the project, whereas others are physical deliverables that you need as input into defining the requirements.

1. **A vision.** The most important input to defining and validating the initial requirements is a vision for what the application should do, as well as a corporate vision in general. A

DEFINITIONS

environmental requirement A non-functional requirement that deals with the environment in which the application will be used. This may be a politically motivated requirement, an ergonomic requirement, a requirement to follow specific standards or guidelines, or a requirement generated by the external business environment in which your firm operates.

feasibility study A document that addresses three main issues: can the system be built, can you afford to build the system, and once the system is in place can you maintain and support it. In other words, is the system technically feasible, is it economically feasible, and is it operationally feasible? Feasibility studies are a deliverable of the Justify stage.

maintenance change A description of a modification to be made to one or more existing configuration items (CIs).

regulatory requirement A requirement that you must fulfill by law. Regulatory requirements include the need to provide specific information to the government, perhaps for taxation or environmental reasons, or the use of a specific programming language or technique in the case of government contracts.

requirement Something that is essential, or perceived to be essential.

requirements document A document, also called a System Requirements Specification (SRS), that describes the user, technical, and environmental requirements for an application. This document potentially contains the major use cases for the application, detailed use-case scenarios for the application, and traditional requirements for the application as well. Requirements documents are a deliverable of the Initiate phase and are updated regularly during modeling. Requirements documents are also updated during the Maintain and Support phase as bugs and enhancements are identified.

vision provides guidance to everyone involved in this process by providing initial boundaries to the scope of the project. Note that the vision of the project will be refined during this stage as the requirements are better understood.

2. **Commitment.** You need the commitment of several groups of people if you want to define and validate requirements successfully. First, you need the commitment of the users and technical experts with whom you will work. If these people are not committed to the project, they will not be willing to find and then invest the substantial amounts of

The surest way to project failure is for senior management to insist that construction begins before the initial requirements are understood.

time that it takes to define and validate requirements. Second, you need the commitment of the systems professionals involved in the project. They must be willing to invest the time to gather, validate, and understand the initial requirements for the application before construction begins. Third, the commitment of senior management is important to your project. They must be willing to both support the project and not put unreasonable demands and pressures to begin construction too early.

3. **An understanding of the existing applications being replaced extended.** It is quite common to find that a new application is developed to replace and/or extend one or more existing legacy applications. This existing application already fulfills a myriad of requirements, many of which will need to be supported by the new application. Furthermore, because the two applications may need to coexist for a period of time, you need to determine how they will do so; therefore, you will need to understand the existing application. Be aware that it is often difficult to get people to think out of the box, to see beyond their existing way of doing things. Although you would often prefer to forget the past and start fresh, you usually cannot do so; you need to understand the existing application(s) and the perspectives of your user community.
4. **A feasibility study.** Before you start defining and validating user requirements, the work on the project justification should have begun. This work might be something as simple as initial research into the problem, just to get an understanding for whether or not to proceed with the project, or it might be a full-fledged feasibility study. The reason this is important is that a feasibility study indicates whether or not the project makes sense, and this helps to both verify the vision and increase the commitment to the project, assuming of course that the project does make sense. In Chapter 6 we will cover how to perform feasibility studies in greater detail.
5. **Maintenance changes allocated to your application's release are identified.** Maintenance changes to address the repair of defects or the enhancement of a previous release of your application may have been assigned to your pro-

TIP

Do Not Forget that Work Proceeds Iteratively

Because work during the Initiate phase proceeds iteratively, you do not need to have all of these conditions completely met; in fact, most these conditions will still be a "work in progress." The important thing is that for a stage to be successful, all of the conditions are met before the final work of the stage is completed. This can often be a difficult concept for experienced developers to grasp at first, especially those whose experience is on traditional waterfall life cycle projects. During a phase the deliverables of its stages are in a constant state of flux and are not complete until the phase is declared finished.

ject team. Depending on your organizational policy and how far along in the project you are, these changes will either be assigned to the release of your application during the Initiate phase where they are used to drive initial requirements, or during the Construct phase (Chapter 7) where they are incorporated into the design of your application. These maintenance changes will be accompanied by the original software change request (SCR) or software problem report (SPR) that initiated the required change to provide your team with the information required to make the given change.

DEFINITIONS

software change request (SCR) A description of a potential improvement to a software deliverable, often identified by users of that deliverable.

software problem report (SPR) A description of a potential software defect identified by someone who is not directly responsible for a given software deliverable.

An important thing to remember while defining and validating the initial requirements for an application is that as the stage progresses, the inputs into the stage will be improved. The project vision will be better understood and defined as requirements are gathered. Commitment will grow as more people are involved in the project, and a better understanding of the existing environment will be gained as your project defines how it will be improved. Finally, because work on the feasibility study often occurs in parallel to defining and validating initial requirements you will have a better understanding of what will and will not be included in each release of your application. Remember, object-oriented applications are often delivered incrementally to the user community.

3.2 Solution: Defining and Validating the Initial Requirements for an Application

The definition of requirements is an iterative process made up of one or more modeling techniques, and the validation of those requirements can be accomplished via various analysis testing techniques. Figure 3.2 depicts the process pattern for this stage, demonstrating the iterative nature of the techniques for defining and validating initial requirements. It is important to note is that there are many options to choose from, and that you do not need to perform all of them to get the job done. Experience shows that no single technique is right for all jobs, so it is important to have several options available to you to define and validate user requirements. In this section we will discuss each technique in general, explaining their strengths and weaknesses.

You want to accomplish several things when you are defining and validating the initial requirements for an application. First, you want to identify the goals and success factors of the applica-

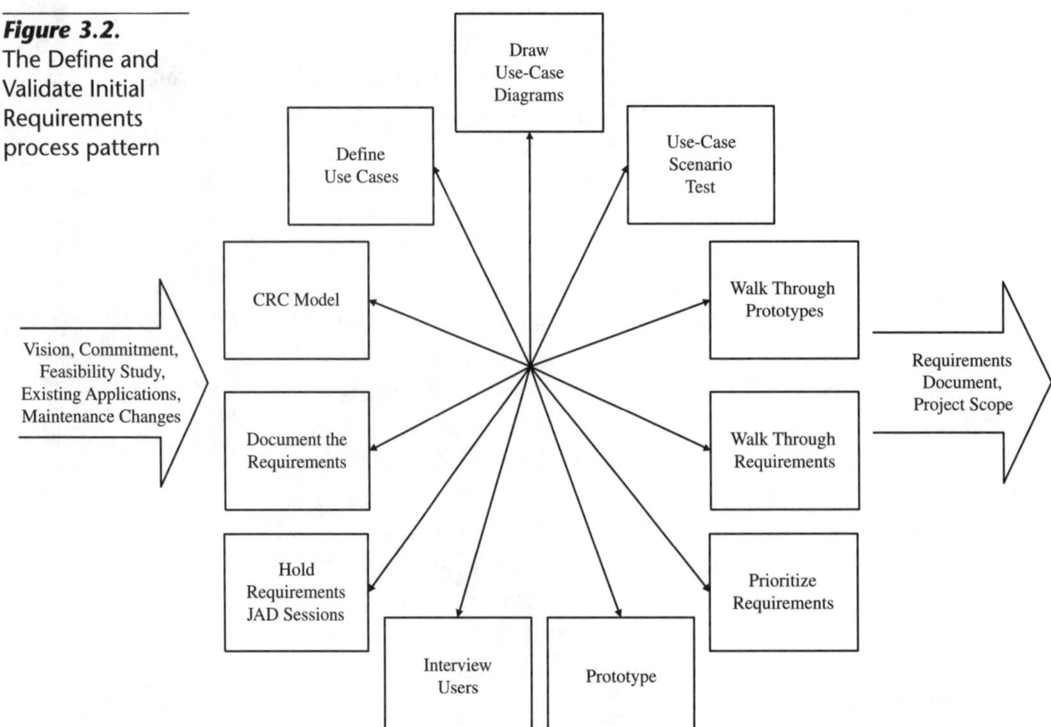

Figure 3.2. The Define and Validate Initial Requirements process pattern

tion to provide high-level guidance to its developers. Second, you want to define the scope of the project, indicating what characteristics will be delivered in the application and those that will not. The only way to avoid scope/feature creep—the addition of unplanned features—during development is to define exactly what will be delivered and exactly what will not be. The requirements that are in scope—the ones that you intend to implement—will naturally be documented far more thoroughly than those that are out of scope.

To avoid scope/feature creep, you must define both the features that you will and will not deliver.

DEFINITION

Feature creep The addition, as development proceeds, of new features to an application that are above and beyond what the original specification described. This is also called scope creep.

3.2.1 Defining Initial Requirements

When defining the initial requirements for an application, it is important to get them from expert sources. To define user requirements, work with your user community; for technical requirements, work with technical experts; for environmental requirements, work with people who understand the internal environment of your organization and the external business environment in which your organization operates. It is possible to get these experts actively involved in the project during this stage, and depending on the techniques used, they will potentially do the majority the work of gathering the initial requirements.

Do not forget that if you are replacing or extending an existing application, you will often find that you need to reverse-engineer requirements from the existing code *and* identify new requirements. Luckily the techniques that we discuss below are applicable to achieving both of these goals. The techniques that we cover in this section are:

TIP

Create a Business Glossary

If your organization has not already done so, it is critical that you define a glossary of common terms that are in use within your organization. Often your industry will already have a specialized dictionary describing common terms used by organizations within it, a dictionary that you should have so that you have a basic idea of what your users are talking about, but that's only a start. Every company has its own specialized jargon, and you need to understand it if you want to communicate effectively with the experts with which you working.

- Interviewing
- CRC modeling
- Use cases
- User-interface prototyping
- Joint application development (JAD) sessions

3.2.1.1 Interviewing

Interviewing is a key part of defining initial requirements.

You almost always start defining requirements by interviewing experts, either potential users of the application or people with expertise in either the problem domain or the technical domain. When interviewing these experts you have several potential goals to accomplish: you might want to broaden your understanding of the application, you might want to determine who to invite to JADs and/or CRC modeling sessions, or you might want to directly identify new or existing requirements for your application. The point to be made is that you need to sit down and talk with other people about your application.

Interviewing is a skill that takes years to master, one that cannot possibly be taught in a few paragraphs. Here are a few helpful pointers, however, to help you to improve your interviewing skills:

1. Send ahead an agenda so as to set expectations and allow your interviewee to prepare for the interview.
2. Verify a few hours ahead of time that the interview is still on, because people's schedules can change.
3. When you first meet the person, thank them for taking time out of their busy day.

TIP

Observe Your Users

I make it a habit to spend a day or two with my users and simply sit and observe what they do. One of the problems with interview people is that they will leave out important details, details that you likely won't know to ask about, because they know their jobs so well. Another advantage of observing your users is that you see the tools that they use to do their jobs—perhaps they use a key reference manual or use a notepad to write reminder notes for themselves and/or their coworkers. The point to be made is that taking the time to observe your users doing their work will give you insight into the requirements for the application that you are building.

4. Tell the interviewee what the project is about and how they fit into the overall process. This lets them know that their input is important.
5. Summarize the issues that you want to discuss, and verify how long the interview will go. This helps to set their expectations and they will help you to manage the time taken during the interview.
6. Ask the critical questions as soon as possible; if the interview is cut short, you have gotten the important information.
7. Ask them if you have missed anything, or if they'd like to add something. This gives them a chance to voice their concerns and will often open new avenues of questioning.
8. Do not assume that you know everything, especially if you think you have already heard it before. Your users will rarely have a consistent view of the world, and part of the requirements definition process is to understand where everyone is coming from. If everyone has the same view on everything, that's great; but it's incredibly rare, so do not shut down your users with a comment like "I've already heard this before."
9. End the interview by summarizing the main points. This lets you review your notes and ensure that you understood everything.
10. Thank the person again at the end of the interview.
11. Inform the interviewee when you will summarize the interview notes (hopefully immediately after the interview when it's still fresh in your mind) and tell them that you will send them a copy for their review. This helps to put them at ease because they know that their input wasn't taken out of context, and it also helps to improve the quality of your notes because they review them and give you feedback.
12. Remember, there's more to interviewing people than just talking to them.

TIP

Send Analysts to Journalism School

The best place to get training in interviewing is at journalism school. Because interviewing is recognized as a key skill needed by journalists, journalism schools tend to have top-notch interviewing courses. Although interviewing is also a key skill needed by computer professionals, very few computer science programs teach it. Interesting.

3.2.1.2 CRC Modeling

CRC (class responsibility collaborator) modeling (Beck & Cunningham, 1989; Wirfs-Brock, Wilkerson, and Wiener, 1990; Jacobson, Christerson, Jonsson, and Overgaard, 1992; Ambler, 1995) provides a simple yet effective technique for working with users to determine their needs. CRC modeling is a process in which a group of subject matter experts analyze their own needs for a system. CRC modeling sessions typically start with brainstorming, a technique in which people suggest whatever ideas they come up with about the application. Brainstorming allows people to get loosened up, as well as to gain a better understanding of where the other SMEs are coming from. After the brainstorming is finished, the group produces a CRC model, which describes the requirements for th

CRC modeling is an analysis technique in which users form most of the modeling team.

A CRC model is a collection CRC cards, standard index cards (usually 5″x7″) that have been divided into three sections as shown in Figure 3.3. A class is any person, place, thing, event, concept, screen or report. The responsibilities of a class are the things that it knows and does, its attributes and methods. The collaborators of a class are the other classes that it works with to fulfill its responsibilities. CRC cards are a simple, easy to explain, low-tech approach to working with users to define the requirements for an application.

Experience shows that CRC modeling works best with frontline employees, whereas techniques such as use cases, discussed in the next section, are more effective with senior management. CRC modeling originated as a training tool (Beck & Cunningham,

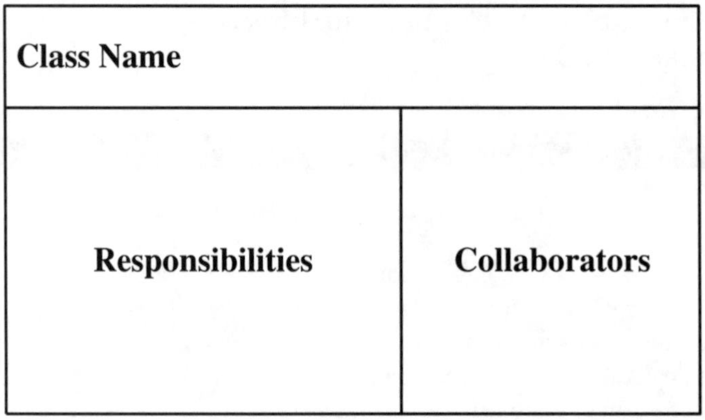

Figure 3.3. The layout of a CRC card

Class Name	
Responsibilities	**Collaborators**

1989) to teach experienced developers OO concepts, and is also used as a design brainstorming technique that leads directly to class diagramming (object modeling). Because CRC models approach requirements definition from a different direction than do use cases, they are often used to validate the information gathered by use cases (and vice versa).

3.2.1.3 Defining Use Cases, Use-Case Scenarios, and Use-Case Diagrams

A use case (Jacobson, Christerson, Jonsson, Overgaard, 1992; Ambler, 1995) is a description, typically written in structured Eng-

TIP

Make Your Subject Matter Experts Feel at Home

Large organizations often find that they need to bring SMEs in from other areas of the company, often requiring them to come from other parts of the world. If this is the case, the chances are good that some of your SMEs have never visited your office before and may hope to get in some sightseeing while they are working on your project. Whenever I have people traveling to come work with me, I always try to make sure that:

- Their hotel and rental car have been arranged.
- They have a map of the city and outlying area, as well as directions to get to the office.
- Security arrangements have been made (i.e. security badges have been arranged).
- A draft schedule for the work that we are doing has been prepared.
- They've been informed of what they need to bring (manuals, documentation, forms, and so on).
- A letter welcoming them to the project that defines their role and the expectations of them has been sent ahead of their joining the project.
- Important contact information, such as surface addresses, email IDs, and phone numbers have been provided in case they run into trouble while traveling to your site.
- A description of the process, at least at a high level, has been sent ahead for their perusal.

DEFINITIONS

class A person, place, thing, event, concept, screen, or report.

Class Responsibility Collaborator (CRC) card A standard index card divided into three sections that show the name of the class, the responsibilities of the class, and the collaborators of the class.

Class Responsibility Collaborator (CRC) model A collection of CRC cards that describe the classes that make up an application or a component of an application.

collaborator On a CRC card, a collaborator of a class is another class with which it interacts to fulfill one or more or its responsibilities.

joint application development (JAD) A structured, facilitated meeting in which modeling is performed by both users and developers together. JADs are often held for gathering user requirements.

responsibility Behavior that a class is expected to be able to perform, either for its own use or in response to a request from another class. A responsibility may be for a class to know something, to have data, or to do something, to perform a function.

lish or point/bulleted form, of a potential business situation that an application may or may not be able to handle. You can also say that a use case describes a way in which a real-world actor—a person, organization, or external system—interacts with the application. For example, the following would be considered use-cases for a university information system:

Use cases describe the basic business logic of an application.

- Enroll students in courses.
- Output seminar enrollment lists.
- Remove students from courses.
- Produce student tr

A use-case scenario is a specific example of a use case, and in many ways could be considered an instance of a use case. Potential use-case scenarios for the use case "Enroll students in courses" are:

- A student wants to enroll in a course, but they are missing a prerequisite.
- A students wants to enroll in a course, but the course is overbooked for the term.

- A student wants to enroll in a course, they have the prerequisites and there is still

Use-case scenarios are instances of use cases.

To put our use cases into context, we will draw a use-case diagram (Booch, Jacobson, Rumbaugh, 1996; Jacobson, Christerson, Jonsson, Overgaard, 1992; Ambler, 1998), an example of which is shown in Figure 3.4. Use-case diagrams are straightforward, showing the actors, the use cases they are involved with, and the system itself. An actor is a role played by any person, organization, or system that interacts with the application but is external to it. Actors are shown as stick figures; use cases are shown as ovals; and the system is shown as a box. The arrows indicate which actor is involved in which use cases, and the direction of the arrow indicates flow of information (in the Unified Modeling Language (UML), indicating the flow is optional, although I highly recommend it). In this example, students are enrolling in courses via the help of registrars. Professors input and read marks, and registrars authorize the sending out of transcripts (report cards) to students. Note how for some use cases there is more than one actor involved, and that sometimes the flow of information is in only one direction. The act of capturing requirements with use cases is sometimes referred to as the Scenarios Define Problem (Coplien, 1995) task process pattern.

Use-case diagrams put use cases into context.

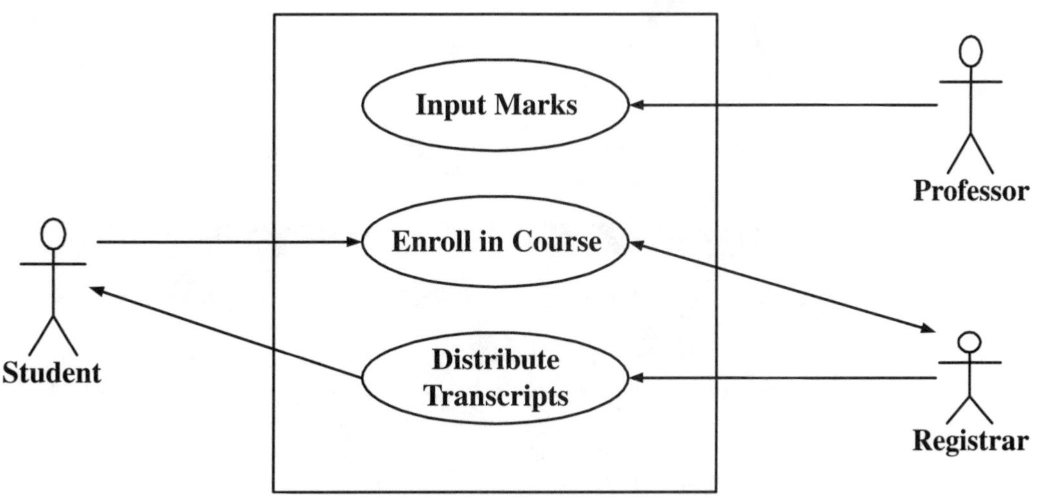

Figure 3.4. An example of a use-case diagram

DEFINITIONS

actor A role played by any person, organization, or system that interacts with an application but is external to it. Actors are modeled on use-case diagrams.

instance Another word for object. We say that an object is an instance of a class.

Unified Modeling Language (UML) The industry-standard OO modeling notation proposed by Rational Software Corporation of Santa Clara, California. The UML has been accepted by the Object Management Group (OMG) to make it the industry standard.

use case A description of a high-level business process that an application may or may not be expected to support.

use-case diagram A diagram that shows the use cases and actors for the application that you are developing.

3.2.1.4 User Interface Prototyping

User interface prototyping (Ambler, 1998) is an iterative analysis technique in which users are actively involved in the mocking-up of screens and reports. The purpose of a prototype is to clarify requirements by showing people the possible design(s) for the user interface of an application. There are four steps to the user-interface prototyping process:

1. Determine the needs of your users.
2. Build the prototype.
3. Evaluate the prototype.
4. Determine whether or not the prototype is complete.

TIP

Make Someone Responsible for Obtaining Information

During the definition of requirements you will need to access various sources of information—written documentation, existing forms, existing procedures, books, and web sites to name a few—to support and enhance the requirements defined by your subject matter experts. One person on your team, often an SME, should be held responsible for obtaining this information as quickly as possible so that you have it in a timely manner.

Prototyping allows you to model the user interface of an application early in the development process.

User interface prototyping, described by the Prototype (Coplien, 1995) task process pattern, is best done by one technical person working closely with one or two users; when there are too many people working simultaneously on the prototype, it is incredibly difficult to come to a consensus.

User interface prototyping is often a key component of defining the initial requirements for an application because, to most people, the application is the screens and reports, the very things that prototyping is excellent at exploring. Because prototypes look like the real application, but do not provide its full functionality, users often have difficulty understanding why you simply cannot install the prototype tomorrow and let them work with it. This means that prototypers need to communicate the prototyping process to their users, explaining to them that a prototype only simulates the functionality of the real application. Another important thing to do during prototyping is to allow people to sit down and work with the prototype, to pretend to use it to do their work. Just as you can take a car for a test drive to see if it meets your needs, you should also be able to take a prototype for a test drive. By working with a prototype, people quickly get a feel for what needs to be reworked—information that is critical for the success of your project.

Your user interface prototyping efforts can be enhanced via the use of the use of reusable user interface (UI) components and UI frameworks. UI components (also known as widgets) and frame-

TIP

Create an OO Glossary

CRC cards. Use cases. JADs. Important concepts, but to your users, just more jargon used by the computer geeks from the systems department. To gain the respect and trust of your users, you should take the time to explain to them what these concepts are and why they're important. This will help them understand the process, which in turn should make them more willing to work with you and more productive because they'll have a better idea of what they need to do.

A glossary that includes both the relevant technical and business terminology goes a long way to improving the communications between developers and users. If you do not understand each other's language, you cannot communicate effectively.

TIP

Prototyping Reduces Risk

Prototyping is a reasonably fast and inexpensive way to increase your understanding of an issue—perhaps a new technology or a business requirement that you do not completely understand. Increasing your understanding in turn reduces the risk associated with your project.

User interface components and frameworks can be used to increase the productivity of your prototypers.

works encapsulate common behaviors required to build the user interface of an application. By using UI components and frameworks in your prototypes, you increase the productivity of your p

User interface prototypes have several advantages. First, they are an excellent mechanism to explore requirements because they make the application seem real to the users. Second, they are useful to demonstrate upcoming features to users or to potential clients at trade shows. The one drawback with prototypes is that they're artificial—they're not the real application. Because of this, it is quite common that users will set their expectations too high and think that the application is almost finished.

3.2.1.5 Joint Application Development (JAD) Sessions

JAD sessions are basically structured meetings led by a trained facilitator. JADs are often held to gather requirements, to design part of or the whole of an application, or to perform walkthroughs of a project deliverable. In a requirements JAD, the facilitator will often lead the group through CRC modeling, prototyping, and/or the definition of use cases. There are three steps to a JAD:

DEFINITIONS

components Small-scale, cohesive items such as user interface widgets that programmers reuse when building applications.

framework A reusable, almost-complete application that can be extended to produce custom applications.

prototyping An iterative analysis technique in which users are actively involved in the mocking-up of the user interface for an application.

1. **Plan the JAD:** The facilitator, with the help of the project manager and project sponsor, determines who will attend the JAD (in this case, key users and one or two developers with intimate knowledge of the existing system), defines the agenda, sets the location and date of the session, and distributes the agenda to the JAD participants. Note that some of the participants at a JAD will be there simply to observe the JAD. These people might by key developers on the project, other project managers who will be involved in JADs in the near future, or JAD-facilitator trainees.
2. **Hold the JAD:** JADs should be held in large meeting rooms with a U-shaped table that faces a whiteboard and/or projection screen that the facilitator uses during the session. The observers do not participate directly in the JAD, whereas the other attendees follow a set of structured meeting rules: everyone is allowed to speak and share their ideas, everyone at the table is equal, and ideas are to be shared but not judged. There are usually one or two people who act as scribes so that the generated information is recorded.
3. **Follow-up:** The facilitator prepares the minutes of the JAD session, a summary of the information that was generated as well as the details. The minutes are distributed to all attendees so that they may review the minutes and add any comments or corrections to ensure that the minutes are

DEFINITION

JAD/meeting facilitator The person(s) responsible for organizing, running, and summarizing the results of joint application development (JAD) sessions in which requirement definition and validation is performed. This is a key role during the Define and Validate Initial Requirements stage.

Facilitators are key to the success of JADs.

The main advantage of JADs is that they provide a structured environment in which people can work together as a team to accurately define and document requirements for an application. Furthermore, they provide an opportunity for disparate users of your application, who may have never met before, to hear the needs and priorities from each other—needs and priorities that may conflict directly with one another. The main disadvantages are that they require a trained meeting facilitator to run properly, and that they require a lot of preparation and follow-up if you want to do them right.

3.2.2 Documenting Initial Requirements

Once you have defined the initial requirements for an application via one of the techniques mentioned above, you need to docu-

TIP

Do Not Expect to Obtain All Information That You Need

Although you will often identify the need for information to support and/or enhance a requirement, you may not always be able to obtain the information you need. For example, you might identify the requirement to interface with an existing legacy system, but not be able to obtain the system documentation for it due to political reasons (often, the documentation doesn't exist or is known to be out of date and the people responsible for the system do not want this fact revealed). The point to be made is that you can ask for information, but you will not necessarily get it.

CRC modeling, use cases, JADs, user-interface prototyping, and interviews provide the input that you need to document the requirements of an application.

ment those requirements. CRC modeling is great for defining requirements, but few people would expect to present a stack of index cards as their only documentation. User interface prototypes are also very useful for defining requirements, and obviously defining what screens and reports look like, but they leave too much room for interpretation for what actual requirements they fulfill. A prototype reflects the requirements, but it does not explicitly describe them. Use cases are a good start at documenting behavioral requirements, but can lack detail. Interview notes and the notes taken during JAD sessions have the detail that you need, but are not organized enough in their raw form. You need to go further and document the requirements for your application in a form that developers can use.

Depending on how far you want to take your definition of the initial requirements, any work that you do not do now will need to be done during modeling; your requirements document, also commonly referred to as a System Requirement Specification (SRS), will at least include the high-level use cases for your application. If you decide to go deeper than this, and you probably should, then you will also want to document the high-level requirements for the application, at least the ones implied by the use cases. For each requirement you want to:

- Describe it.
- Assign it a unique number so that it can be traced later through the development deliverables.
- Indicate its priority.

TIP

Minimize the Number of Purely Technical Requirements

Technology changes very quickly, and very often requirements that are based on technology change just as quickly. An example of a pure technical requirement is that an application be written in Java, or must run on the XYZ computer. Whenever you have a requirement based purely on technology, try to determine the real underlying business need being expressed. To do this, keeping asking why your application must meet a requirement. For example, when asked why your application must be written in Java, the reply was that it has to run on the Internet. When asked why it must run on the Internet, the reply was that your organization wants to take orders for its products and services on the Internet. The real requirement is to sell things on the Internet; one technical solution to this need (and a very good one) is to write that component in Java. There's a big difference between having to write the entire application in Java and having to support the sales of some products and services over the Internet.

- Describe the source of the requirement (a person, a document, or other source).
- Include any issues, concerns, and/or risks with the requirement.
- Document any further sources of information for it.

An initial cut of a requirements document includes high-level use cases and potentially a collection of well-documented requirements.

The important thing is that each requirement can be understood by the developers who will create the models and the code to fulfill it.

One thing that use cases do not document well, nor do CRC models and prototypes, are technical requirements. Technical requirements include descriptions of the computing platform that the application must operate on, performance requirements such as the response time of your persistence mechanism, and operational requirements such as the need to operate 7 days a week, 24 hours a day. These requirements are typically documented in their own section of your requirements document.

3.2.3 Validating Initial Requirements

If you miss or misunderstand a user requirement, you automatically ensure that the system will not completely meet the needs of

WAR STORY

Do Not Forget the Needs of Operations

Several years ago I worked on the redevelopment, using object technology, of a legacy billing system. The existing system had been in place for years, and although it functioned properly, it wasn't very flexible. The team that I was on developed a new design for the billing statement, changing everything from the layout of the statement to the paper that it was printed on. A graphics design company designed new letterhead for the statement with a new envelope design to match it. The new billing application was designed and coding had begun. Then we talked to operations.

One of the things that we didn't find out during modeling, because we didn't bother to talk to operations, was that this company ordered envelopes in batches large enough to last them an entire year. By ordering them in such large quantities, they were able to obtain a very good price for them; plus, it meant that they only had to worry about envelopes once a year. The problem was twofold: nobody had told them that we were redesigning the envelopes, and we had assumed that we could switch a new set of envelopes in at any time. The point to be made is that the requirements of your operations department need to be taken into account: that you need to have a firm understanding of the operations procedures associated with your application.

DEFINITIONS

performance requirement A requirement defining the speed at which a software feature is to operate.

requirements document A document, also called a System Requirements Specification (SRS), which describes the user, technical, and environmental requirements for an application. This document potentially contains the major use cases for the application, detailed use-case scenarios for the application, and traditional requirements for the application as well. Requirements documents are a deliverable of the Initiate phase and are updated regularly during modeling. Requirements documents are also updated during the Maintain and Support phase as bugs and enhancements are identified.

technical requirement A description of a non-behavioral feature, such as the required time in which something must run or the operating system in which an application must work.

your users, either because it is missing a feature or because a feature is implemented incorrectly. Analysis errors such as this often result in project failure, or at least in serious cost overruns to fix the problem.

DEFINITION

analysis error An error caused by a missed or misunderstood requirement.

Figure 3.5 depicts the Full Life Cycle Object-Oriented Testing (FLOOT) process pattern, which indicates that there are three techniques that you may employ to validate your initial requirements:

- Use-case scenario testing
- Prototype walkthroughs
- User-requirements reviews

3.2.3.1 Use-Case Scenario Testing

Use-case scenario testing (Ambler, 1995; Ambler, 1998) is a testing process in which users are actively involved with ensuring that user requirements are accurate. The basic idea is that a group of users, with the aid of a facilitator, step through a series of defined use cases to verify that the CRC model (use-case scenario testing can also be used to verify other models, including class diagrams) they created reflects accurately the requirements defined by the use cases. In Figure 3.6 you see a process pattern, shown as a flow chart, representing the steps of use-case scenario testing. The participants, typically the people who worked on the CRC model, work through each scenario one at a time and update the CRC model where appropriate. The advantage is that once the use-case scenario testing is finished, they will be assured that their model is complete and accurate.

3.2.3.2 Prototype Walkthroughs

During analysis it is quite common to create a user interface prototype, a mock-up of the user interface, for your application. User interface prototyping, discussed in section 3.2.1.4, is an iterative

DEFINITIONS

flow chart A diagram depicting the logic flow of a single process.

use-case scenario testing A testing process in which users work through use cases with the aid of a facilitator to verify that the user requirements are accurate.

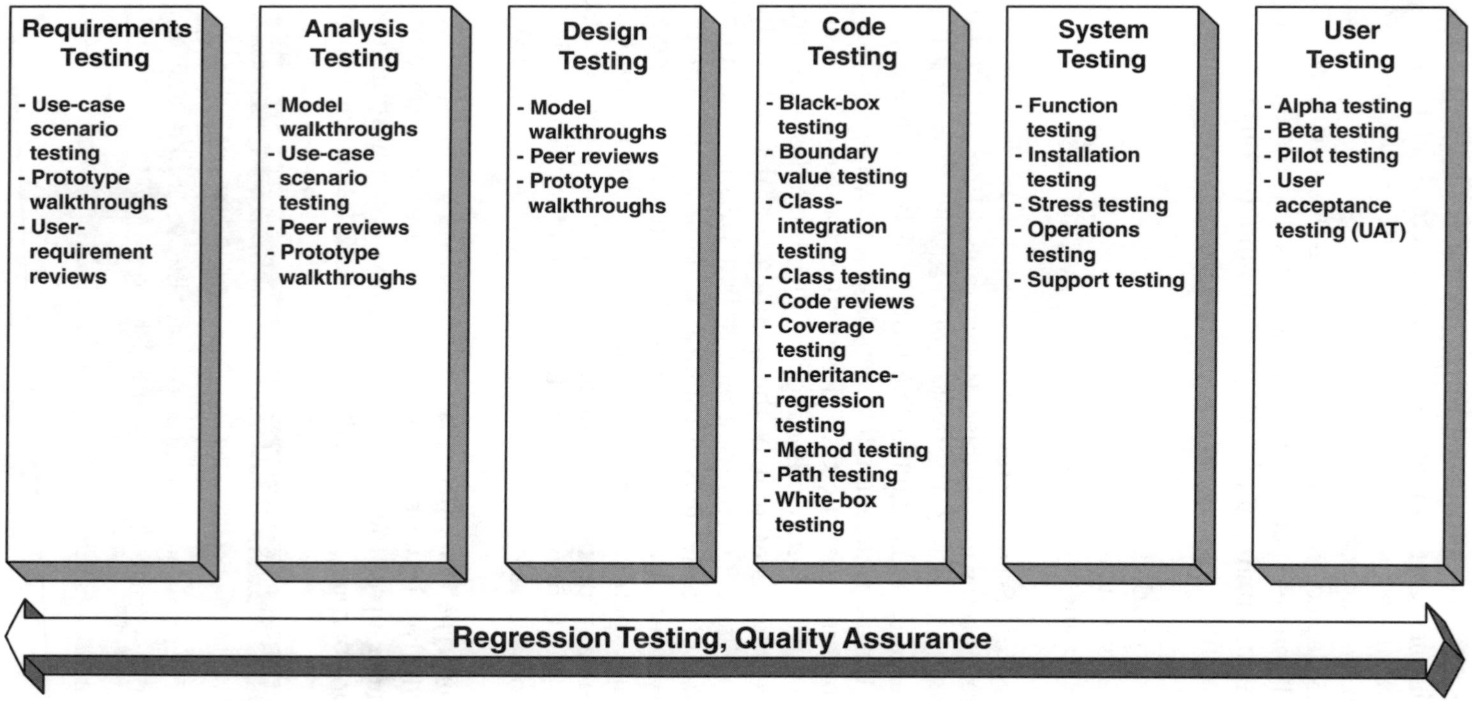

Requirements Testing
- Use-case scenario testing
- Prototype walkthroughs
- User-requirement reviews

Analysis Testing
- Model walkthroughs
- Use-case scenario testing
- Peer reviews
- Prototype walkthroughs

Design Testing
- Model walkthroughs
- Peer reviews
- Prototype walkthroughs

Code Testing
- Black-box testing
- Boundary value testing
- Class-integration testing
- Class testing
- Code reviews
- Coverage testing
- Inheritance-regression testing
- Method testing
- Path testing
- White-box testing

System Testing
- Function testing
- Installation testing
- Stress testing
- Operations testing
- Support testing

User Testing
- Alpha testing
- Beta testing
- Pilot testing
- User acceptance testing (UAT)

Regression Testing, Quality Assurance

Figure 3.5. The FLOOT process pattern

process in which you work closely with your users to clarify the design of the user interface for the application that you are developing. Although you will eventually create an interface design that your users like (one hopes) the question of whether or not the interface will actually work still remains. This is why you need to do a prototype walkthrough.

A prototype walkthrough is an analysis-testing process in which your users work through a collection of use cases to verify that the design of a prototype meets their needs. The basic idea is that they pretend the prototype is the real application and they try to use it to solve real business problems described by the scenarios. Granted, they will need to use their imaginations to fill in the functionality that the application is missing (such as reading and writing objects to/from permanent storage), but for the most part this is a fairly straightforward process. Your users simply sit down at the computer and begin to work through the use cases. Although they do this, it is your job to sit there and observe them, looking for places where the system is difficult to use or is just plain missing some features. In a lot of ways, prototype walkthroughs are a lot like user acceptance tests, discussed in detail in Chapter 3 in *More Process Patterns*; the only difference is that you are working with the prototype instead of the real system.

Prototype walkthroughs quickly verify that your prototype meets the needs of your users.

3.2.3.3 User-Requirement Reviews

After you have gathered user requirements you need to document and present them to your users to both verify that they are accurate and to prioritize them. A User-Requirement Review (Ambler, 1998) is a formal process in which a facilitator puts together a group of users with the authority to confirm and prioritize the user requirements gathered by a development team. This process

DEFINITIONS

analysis testing The testing of your analysis modeling efforts.

prototype walkthrough A process by which your users work through a collection of use cases using a prototype as if it was the real thing. The main goal is to test whether or not the design of the prototype meets their needs.

user-acceptance testing (UAT) A testing technique in which users verify that an application meets their needs.

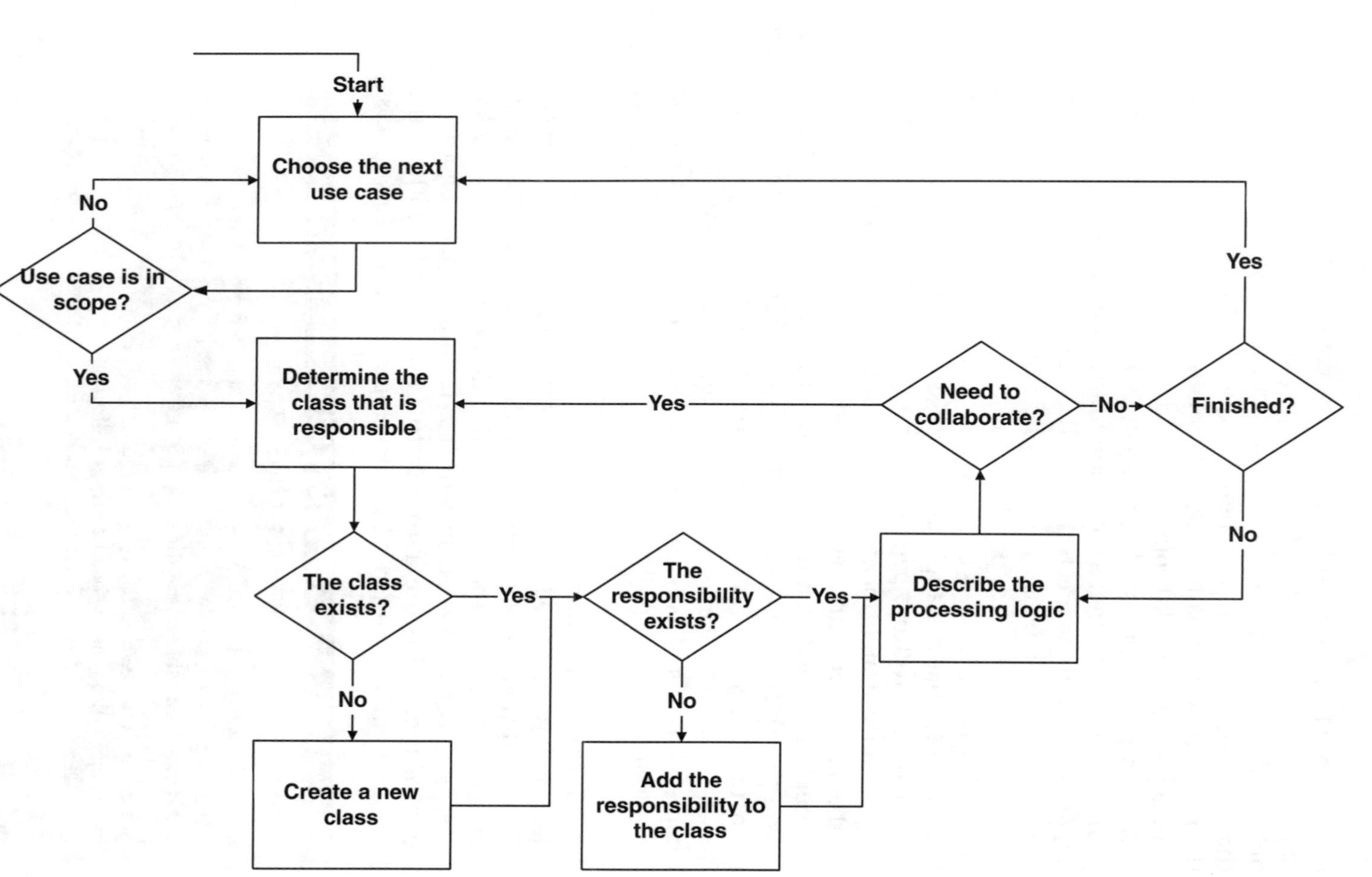

Figure 3.6. The Use-Case Scenario Testing process pattern

could take from several hours to several days, depending on the size of the project.

It is important to document, review, and prioritize user requirements so as to verify that what you are building will meet the needs of your users and to define the scope of your project. Part of the prioritization process should be to provide an indication as to which release of the application a specific feature will appear. User requirement reviews follow the Technical Review process pattern, depicted in Figure 3.7 and described in detail in Chapter 11, with the exception that business experts instead of technical experts review the work of the development team. The Validation by Teams (Harrison, 1996), Review (Coplien, 1995), Creator-Reviewer (Weir, 1998), and Group Validation (Coplien, 1995) task process patterns are all variations of the same process pattern theme. User requirement reviews are often used in addition to use-case scenario testing and prototype walkt

DEFINITION

user requirement review A testing process in which a facilitated group of users verify and prioritize the user requirements gathered by a development team.

User requirement reviews are used to verify that your application will meet the needs of your users and to define the scope of your project.

3.2.4 Prioritizing Initial Requirements

One of the harsh realities of software development is that there is never enough time to do everything, because resources such as developers, time, and money are scarce. Although we all know this to be true, it is still the norm for project managers to commit to delivering every single requirement identified for an application. Later in the project, when it becomes obvious that the project team is not going to be able to deliver the world, the project manager must then renegotiate the scope of the project to a realistic set of requirements. Ed Yourdon (1997) refers to this as triage, and anybody who has ever had to do this knows how difficult and uncomfortable a process this turns out to be, with more than one project manager losing their job as a result.

Recognizing the fact that at some point in the project you will need to restrict yourself to a realistic set of requirements that you can actually deliver, doesn't it make sense to do so earlier in the project rather than later? Of course it does. Part of defining and validating user requirements is to perform requirements triage on them—the act of prioritizing requirements into the categories "must haves," "nice to haves," and "nonessentials." This is a negotiation process that must be done with the development team and subject matter experts

DEFINITION

Requirements triage The act of prioritizing requirements—for example, "must have," "nice to have," and "non-essential"—to aid in the definition of an application that can be delivered with the limited resources at hand.

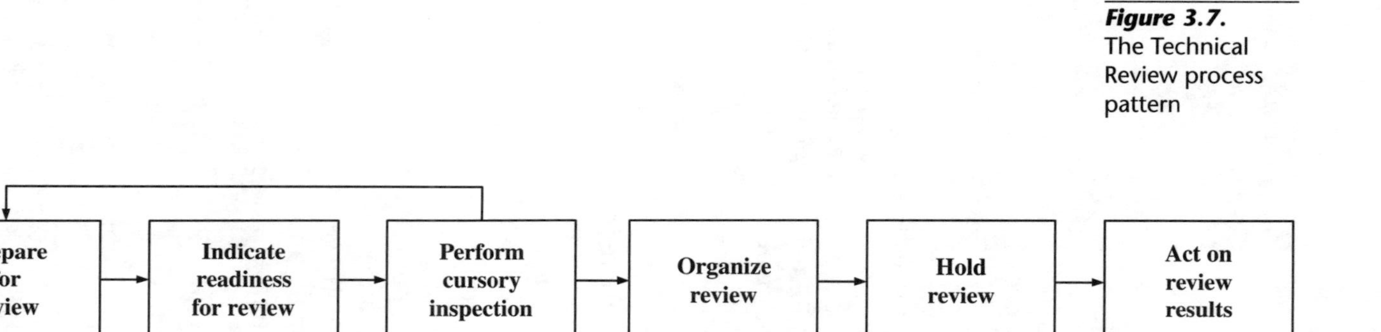

Figure 3.7. The Technical Review process pattern

so that everyone accepts the assigned priorities. The end result is that your user community is not going to get everything that they want, and when you include them in the requirements triage process they will understand why they're not going to get it. At some point in your project you're going to have to perform triage, and it's least painful at the beginning of the project instead of when you are late and over budget.

Requirements triage is a requirement prioritization process that limits the scope of an application to something that can be realistically delivered with the available resources.

3.3 Solution: Project Tasks

In this section I will discuss project task issues pertinent to the Define and Validate Requirements stage.

3.3.1 Managing the Define and Validate Initial Requirements Stage

There are several management issues that you must address that are specific to the definition and validation of the initial requirements for an application which are all based on taking the time to do things right and to build a solid foundation for the project. This is a straightforward stage to manage, where most of the effort is spent scheduling experts to work with the analysts to define and validate the requirements. To gain support for this process, you will find that you need to communicate how important it is to do this work, and that it will help to ensure an application that meets the needs of its users.

A key to the success of this stage is putting together an effective requirements team. Harrison (1996) with the Diversity of Membership organizational pattern shows that teams composed of people with a wide range of skills consistently outperform homogenous teams. He points out that to provide a diverse range of skills and views, requirements teams should include at least one developer, one subject matter expert, and one system tester.

DEFINITION

organizational pattern A pattern that describes a common management technique or a structure appropriate to a software organization.

3.3.2 Training and Education

Analysts need training and education in the modeling techniques and the communications skills used in this stage. This means training in interviewing (most likely from the local journalism

TIP

You Cannot Teach Communication and Modeling Skills Overnight

Do not expect to be able to send a programmer to a couple of training courses and have them come back an expert analyst. Although communication skills come easily to many people, you still have to work on them if you want to be able to define and validate requirements successfully. Modeling skills are also difficult to learn, taking years of experience to gain fully.

school), in meeting facilitation (most likely from the local school of business management), and in OO modeling techniques (most likely from an OO consulting firm). The key is to ensure that your analysts have sufficient communication skills and understand the object-oriented paradigm well enough to gather and validate requirements.

3.3.3 Quality Assurance

A large part of this stage is the validation of requirements, in many ways a quality assurance task. It is not enough to define your requirements; you must also validate them. Walk through your requirements. Walk through your prototypes. Perform use-case scenario testing. You cannot build a system that will meet the needs of its users unless you first understand those needs, and you cannot be sure that you truly understand those needs until you have verified the requirements that you have identified. You'll be amazed at what you have missed, and misunderstood, when you invest the time to validate the initial requirements. If you get it wrong at this stage all of your future development efforts will be based on incorrect requirements and will be wasted.

3.3.4 Potential Risks While Defining and Validating Requirements

The greatest risk during this stage is that nobody wants to do it. The users and experts each have their usual jobs to do and do not have the time to invest; the developers want to get into the "real work" of coding; and senior management wants to see some progress on the project, which usually means code. You have to communicate with everyone involved that their efforts will pay off in the long run, that this work is critical to the success of the project.

During the validation of requirements you should strive to determine which ones are going to be hard to achieve or that rely on nonexistent or questionable resources and technologies. These requirements increase the risk of the project, and should either be dropped from the project or flagged for special attention later. You often have a very good idea at the beginning of a project what things might go wrong, and it's better to deal with them sooner than later.

3.3.5 Opportunities for Reuse

There are some opportunities for reuse during this stage. The easiest one is achieve template reuse by creating documentation templates for documenting use cases and requirements. Furthermore, you may find that you may be able to achieve artifact reuse of previously defined requirements and use cases from other projects, particularly when you're working on a new release for an existing application. We also saw that the prototyping of the user interface of your application can be enhanced via component and framework reuse.

3.3.6 Metrics

You may choose to gather several metrics specific to the Define and Validate Requirements stage. These metrics are:

DEFINITIONS

artifact reuse The reuse of previously created development artifacts: use cases, standards documents, domain-specific models, procedures and guidelines, and other applications.

component reuse The reuse of prebuilt, fully encapsulated components in the development of your application.

framework A reusable, almost-complete application that can be extended to produce custom applications.

framework reuse The reuse of collections of classes that together implement the basic functionality of a common technical or business domain.

template reuse The reuse of a common set of layouts for key development artifacts—documents, models, and source code—within your organization.

1. **Number of use cases.** A count of the number of use cases to be implemented by your application provides valuable information for your estimation effort (Chapter 4). My experience is that you will want to count the number of simple, medium-complexity, and complex use cases to get a better understanding of the size of your application. This metric should be collected for several projects performed by your organization before you use it to estimate the size of new projects—you need to first determine how much effort each of the three types of use case take for your organization to implement before this metric is useful.
2. **Function/feature points.** Function points (Albrecht, 1979) and feature points (Jones, 1995) are metrics used for estimating the size of an application. The basic idea of function points is that you count five items: the inputs to the application, the outputs from it, inquiries by users, the data files that would be updated by the application, and the interfaces to other applications. Once you have these figures, you multiply by the following figures: 4, 5, 4, 10, and 7, respectively, then add the results to get your function point estimate. Function points worked reasonably well for simple management information system (MIS) applications, but unfortunately they often proved to be inadequate for estimating complex applications—the types of applications that object-oriented development is well suited for. Therefore, there exists the need for feature points (Jones, 1995), a superset of function points, to correct this problem. Feature points introduces a new measurement, algorithms, giving it a weighting of 3. Additionally, the data file weighting from is decreased from 10 to 7.

DEFINITIONS

feature points A metric that is the superset of function points, adding a count of the algorithmic complexities within your software.

function points A metric used for estimating software size that is calculated by counting five items: the inputs to the software, the outputs from it, inquiries by users, the data files that would be updated by the software, and the interfaces to other software.

3.4 Resulting Context: Exit Conditions for Defining and Validating Initial Requirements

You are not finished defining and validating the initial requirements of an application until you can show others that you understand the problem domain well enough to begin construction, and that you have defined the scope of the project. To show this, you must complete two deliverables:

1. **A validated requirements document.** This document is potentially a collection of the CRC cards you defined, the user interface prototypes you built, the use cases you created, and the user requirements which they generated. Very often this document includes the description of the project scope, the high-level use cases for the application, and a collection of well documented requirements in its body. The appendix of this document often includes the prototypes and CRC cards that were used as input into the definition of the requirements, as well as any interview notes or minutes of JAD sessions. The requirements document, once it is validated, should be complete enough so that it convinces others that you understand the problem domain well enough that you can begin the Construct phase.

A validated requirements document shows that you understand the problem domain well enough to begin the Construct phase.

2. **A project scope.** This is a statement, perhaps several paragraphs in length, which describes what the project will deliver, and more important what it will not deliver. In many ways a summarization of the initial requirements, this statement puts boundaries around the project and defines the success criteria for the project.

The project scope puts boundaries around the project.

3.5 Secrets of Success

The following pointers should help to improve your efforts at defining and validating the initial requirements for your application:

1. **Distribute agendas for all meetings.** Everyone involved in JAD sessions, in CRC modeling sessions, and in meetings where use cases are defined should have an agenda for the

session or meeting given to them several days before so that they can prepare for it.

2. **Communicate what it is you're doing and why.** In the agenda, describe the rules of a JAD session, or the process to create a CRC model. When you explain the process you are using and why it helps to build a strong foundation for your project, people will be more willing to invest their valuable time in it.
3. **Facilitate meetings.** Facilitators help to keep a meeting focused on the task at hand, increasing the productivity of those in the meeting.
4. **Involve the real experts.** When defining use cases and CRC models, you should strive to get the people who best know the problem domain involved. This very often means getting front-line workers, not just their managers, involved in the process.
5. **Document the source of each requirement.** The source of a requirement is often just as important as the requirement itself, as it helps to verify the credibility of the requirement. Furthermore, it indicates a source of information that can be used during modeling (covered in Chapter 8) to expand on the requirement.
6. **Realize that user requirements definition is a start at modeling.** In many ways this phase is merely a start at the modeling process, with the requirements document a major deliverable into that stage. The work that you do now will directly affect how much work will be needed to model the application. The more detailed and thorough the requirements are defined now, the less work will be needed later during modeling.
7. **Perform requirements triage early.** Recognize the fact that you aren't going to be able to deliver every single requirement requested by your users; therefore, you need to prioritize and deliver the most important requirements that you can identify.
8. **Have a technical writer aid in the documentation process.** A significant portion of requirements definition is the documentation of requirements. Because technical writers specialize in documentation, and because they are often paid significantly less than analysts, it makes sense to have them document requirements, allowing your analysts to concen-

trate on what they are good at: identifying requirements. The act of including a technical writer on your team is often referred to as the Mercenary Analyst (Coplien, 1995) organizational pattern.

9. **Get official acceptance.** Senior management must review and endorse both the scope definition for your project and the initial requirements for it. This will help to eliminate feature/scope creep.

3.6 Process Checklist

The following process checklist can be used to verify that you have completed the Define and Validate Initial Requirements stage.

DEFINE AND VALIDATE INITIAL REQUIREMENTS STAGE PROCESS CHECKLIST

Fulfillment of Entrance Conditions:

✔ A vision for the project has been defined and agreed to.
✔ The user community is committed to the project.
✔ Your information system (IS) department is committed to the project.
✔ Senior management is committed to the project.
✔ Everyone is committed to defining and validating the initial requirements.
✔ A thorough understanding of the legacy systems being replaced/extended is in place.
✔ The feasibility study, a key deliverable of the Justify stage, has started.
✔ Appropriate maintenance changes for previous versions have been identified.
✔ Team members have been given the appropriate training for their part in this stage.

Processes Performed:

✔ A use-case model has been developed and validated (if appropriate).
✔ A CRC model has been developed and validated (if appropriate).

✔ A user-interface prototype has been developed and validated (if appropriate).
✔ Appropriate technical requirements have been documented and validated.
✔ Appropriate operation and support requirements have been documented and validated.
✔ Requirements have been prioritized.
✔ The requirements of all appropriate stakeholders have been identified and considered.
✔ Artifacts that are potentially reusable by your project team during this stage have been identified and used where appropriate.
✔ Your risk assessment document has been updated where appropriate.
✔ Decisions made, and decisions forgone, have been documented in your group memory.
✔ Metrics have been collected.

Fulfillment of Exit Conditions:
✔ The requirements document has been validated and accepted by both the user community and by senior management.
✔ The scope of the project has been defined and accepted.

3.7 What You Have Learned in This Chapter

In this chapter you covered the process of defining and validating the initial requirements for an application. You saw that there are many techniques for defining requirements—CRC modeling, use case definition, prototyping, interviews, and JAD sessions—as well as several techniques for validating requirements, including walkthroughs and use-case scenario testing. The major deliverables of this stage are a definition of the project scope and the documentation of the initial requirements themselves. When this stage is done properly, you are left with the assurance that you understand the underlying problem domain that the application supports and that you have defined what, and what will not, be delivered by the project.

3.8 References and Recommended Reading

Albrecht, A. J. 1979. *Measuring Application Development Productivity*. Proceedings, IBM Applications Development Symposium, Guide International and Share, Inc., IBM Corporation.

Ambler, S. W. 1995. *The Object Primer: The Application Developer's Guide To Object Orientation*. New York: SIGS Books/Cambridge University Press.

Ambler, S. W. 1998. *Building Object Applications That Work—Your Step-By-Step Handbook for Developing Robust Systems With Object Technology*. New York: SIGS Books/Cambridge University Press.

Beck, K., and Cunningham, W. 1989. *A Laboratory for Teaching Object-Oriented Thinking*. Proceedings of OOPSLA'89, 1–6.

Booch, G., Jacobson, I., and Rumbaugh, J. 1996. *The Unified Modeling Language for Object-Oriented Development Documentation Set v1.0*. Monterey, California: Rational Software Corporation.

Coplien, J.O. (1995). *A Generative Development-Process Pattern Language*. Pattern Languages of Program Design, eds. Coplien, J.O. and Schmidt, D.C., Addison-Wesley Longman, Inc., pp. 183–237.

Harrison, N.B. (1996). *Organizational Patterns for Teams*. Pattern Languages of Program Design 2, eds. Vlissides, J.M., Coplien, J.O., and Kerth, N.L., Addison-Wesley Publishing Company., pp. 345–352.

Jacobson, I., Christerson, M., Jonsson, P., and Overgaard, G. 1992. *Object-Oriented Software Engineering—A Use Case Driven Approach*. New York: ACM Press.

Jones, C. 1995. What Are Function Points? http://204.96.51.2/library/funcmet.htm [Internet]. Software Productivity Research.

Lorenz, M. and Kidd, J. 1994. *Object-Oriented Software Metrics*. Englewood Cliffs, New Jersey: Prentice-Hall, Inc.

Wirfs-Brock, R., Wilkerson, B., and Wiener, L. 1990. *Designing Object-Oriented Software*. Englewood Cliffs, New Jersey: Prentice Hall, Inc.

Weir, C. (1998). *Patterns for Designing in Teams*. Pattern Languages of Program Design 3, eds. Martin, R.C., Riehle, D., and Buschmann, F., Addison Wesley Longman, Inc., pp. 487-501.

Yourdon, E. (1997). *Death March: The Complete Software Developer's Guide to Surviving "Mission Impossible" Projects*. Upper Saddle River, New Jersey: Prentice-Hall PTR.

Chapter 4

The Define Initial Management Documents Stage

MANY critical documents that are needed throughout a project to properly manage it, such as the project plan and project risk assessment, must be started at the beginning of the project and then maintained throughout its life. This chapter describes the Define Initial Management Documents stage, whose purpose is to initiate these documents. This stage goes hand-in-hand with the Justify stage and Define Infrastructure stage, described in Chapters 5 and 6 respectively. The key deliverables of this stage are the management documents themselves, which often have titles such as "Initial Risk Assessment" and "Initial Project Plan."

I'd like to start by sharing my belief that project management is both an art and a science. This chapter describes the foundation for the "science" of project management—estimates, schedules, and risk assessments—and the issues involved in developing and maintaining them. The art of project management is described throughout this book, explicitly in the sections that describe project management issues and implicitly in the tips and war stories that I share with you throughout the book. Anyway, the goal of this chapter is to identify and describe the fundamental deliver-

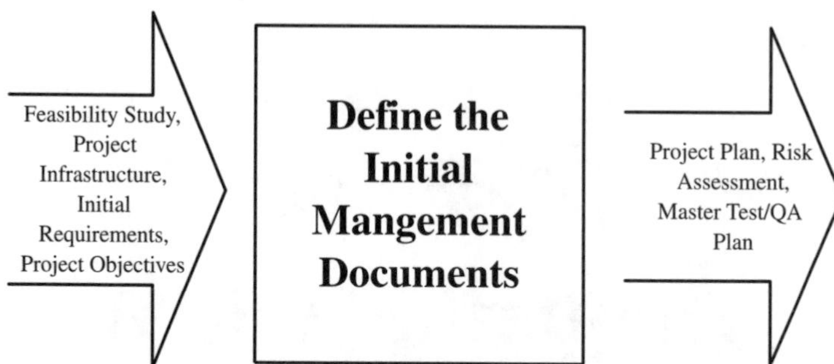

Figure 4.1. The Define Initial Management Documents stage

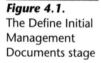

ables that project managers use to help them manage a software project.

Figure 4.1 shows that the major inputs into this stage are the project feasibility study developed by the Justify stage, described in Chapter 5, and the project infrastructure defined by the Define Infrastructure stage of Chapter 6. The deliverables of this stage include a project plan (which encompasses documents such as the estimate, schedule, charter, and scope) the initial risk assessment and the initial master test/quality assurance plan.

4.1 Initial Context: Entry Conditions for Defining Initial Management Documents

Several important entry conditions should be met before the Define Initial Management Documents stage begins:

1. **Project infrastructure.** The project infrastructure—the tools, people, and processes—that will be used on your project is a critical input for defining your project plan. The project infrastructure, defined in Chapter 5, and your project plan are ideally developed in parallel because of their integral nature: the choices you make for your project infrastructure directly impact your schedule and estimate (different infrastructures offer different capabilities) and needs defined by your project plan will drive decisions as to what infrastructure combination is selected by your project team.
2. **Feasibility study.** The feasibility study includes a cost/benefit analysis as well as a recommendation for which approach should be taken by your project team. The project plan and feasibility study will be developed in parallel, as they are so closely related.

DEFINITIONS

master test/quality assurance (QA) plan A document that describes your testing and quality assurance policies and procedures, as well as the detailed test plans for each portion of your application.

project charter A document issued by senior management that provides the project manager the authority to apply organizational resources to project activities.

project estimate An appraisal of how long a project will take and how much it will cost, given a specific environment and a specific team. Change the environment and/or change the team and your estimate should change. Project estimates are a deliverable of the Initiate phase and are updated regularly throughout a project.

project plan A collection of several project management deliverables, including, but not limited to, a project overview, a project schedule, a project estimate, a team definition, and a risk assessment. Project plans are a deliverable of the Initiate phase and are updated regularly throughout a project.

project schedule A project schedule indicates what will be done, when things will be done, and who will do them. A major component of a project schedule is a Gantt chart with its corresponding descriptions of tasks and resources. Project schedules are a deliverable of the Initiate phase and are updated regularly throughout a project.

project scope A definition of the functionality that will, and will not, be implemented by an application.

risk assessment A document indicating potential factors, called risks, that if they were to occur would harm the project. A risk assessment is used to identify risks so that they may be dealt with appropriately. Risk assessments are a deliverable of the Initiate phase and are updated regularly throughout a project.

3. **Project objectives.** The goals for the project should be explicitly documented, including a strategy for measuring and validating progress against them. Project objectives may include an indication of time and resource constraints and/or the desires of various project stakeholders. The objectives of your project will likely be not well defined, and will therefore be part of defining the scope of the project (see below). The important thing is that the project objectives should be recognized but not necessarily accepted, as they may not be consistent or even realistic. We have all heard horror stories (chances are good that you have lived through a few your-

DEFINITIONS

feasibility study A document that addresses three main issues: can the system be built; can you afford to build the system; and once the system is in place. can you maintain and support it? In other words, is the system technically feasible, is it economically feasible, and is it operationally feasible? Feasibility studies are a deliverable of the Justify stage.

project infrastructure The team, tools, and processes that will be used on a given project.

requirements document A document, also called a System Requirements Specification (SRS), which describes the user, technical, and environmental requirements for an application. This document potentially contains the major use cases for the application, detailed use-case scenarios for the application, and traditional requirements for the application as well. Requirements documents are a deliverable of the Initiate phase and are updated regularly during modeling. Requirements documents are also updated during the Maintain and Support phase as bugs and enhancements are identified.

self) of projects that have been given delivery dates that couldn't possibly have been met. Just because you're given an objective doesn't mean you're going to be able to meet it.

4. **Initial requirements document.** The initial requirements document describes, at least at a high level, the potential functionality that your application is to deliver. This information is critical input for planning your project.

4.2 Solution: Defining the Initial Management Documents

Figure 4.2 depicts the process pattern for defining initial management documents, showing that it is an iterative process that includes creating a project plan, creating an initial risk assessment, and creating an initial master test and quality assurance plan. The creation of a project plan is itself an iterative process, including the definition of the project scope and tasks to be performed, the creation of the initial schedule and estimate, and the securing of an approved project charter.

Although it isn't shown in Figure 4.2, an important input into the definition of the initial management documents is an under-

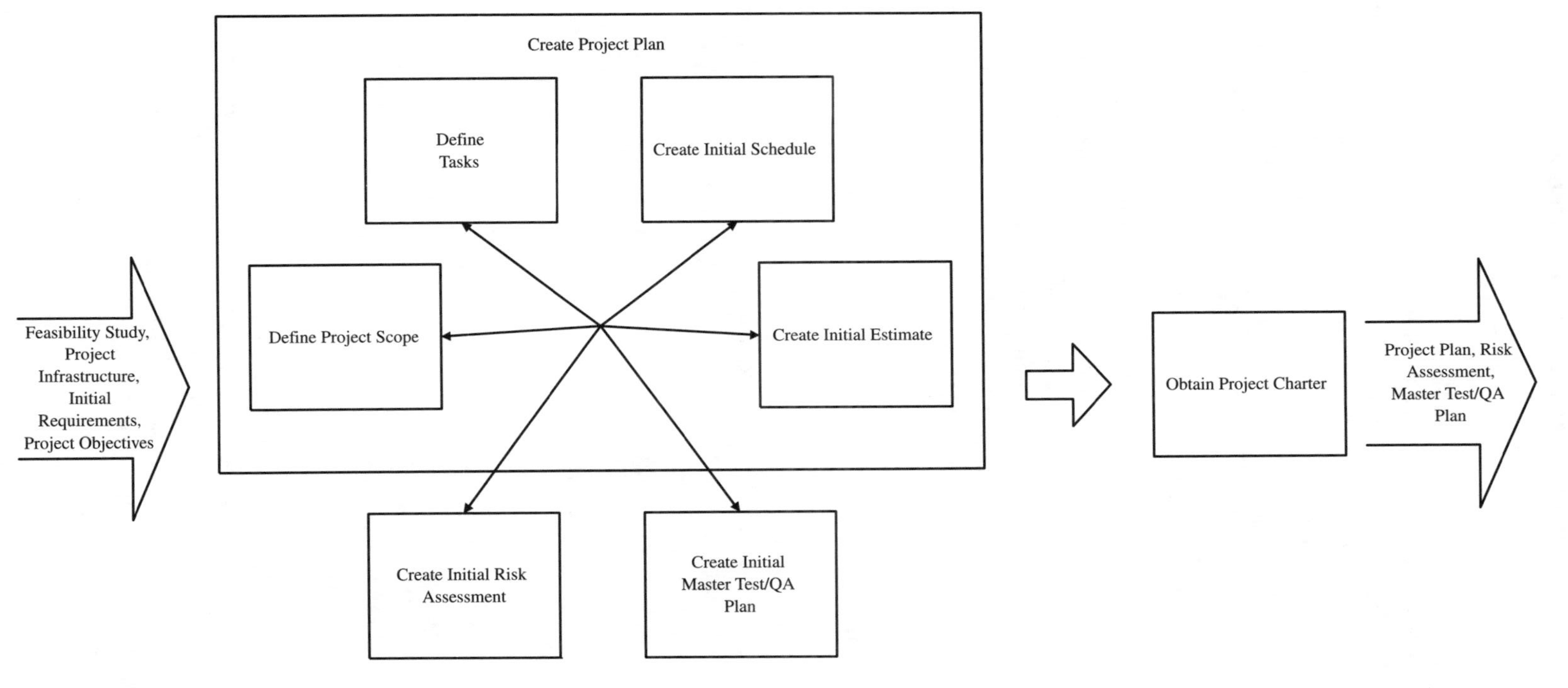

Figure 4.2.
The Define Initial Management Documents process pattern

standing of the "political landscape" of your organization. Understanding the priorities of the people who fund your project, who will support your project, and, more importantly, those who will not support your project is critical to the development of your project plans. It is also important for the development of your risk assessment, at least to the development of your internal/private risk assessment which we'll discuss later in this chapter.

4.2.1 Planning a Project

A project plan is a formal, approved document used to guide, control, and execute a project. Project plans are used to document your planning assumptions and decisions, to facilitate communication, and to document the approved scope, vision, cost, and schedule baselines. A project plan defines the commitments made by your project team to your organization and provides a mechanism against which you can measure your project.

To fail to plan is to plan to fail.

Why should you plan your project? Humphrey (1997) correctly argues that plans allow you to organize the efforts of your project team, avoid last-minute crises, reduce the chance of making mistakes, and generally produce better products. In other words, project plans increase the chance for successfully delivering your project. There is an old saying in the project management world: To fail to plan is to plan to fail.

Figure 4.3 shows that a project plan includes several components: a project scope, an estimate, a schedule, and assumptions and constraints. Therefore, there are several activities for creating a project plan:

- Define the project scope
- Define the project tasks
- Estimate the effort
- Create a viable schedule
- Document assumptions and constraints

4.2.1.1 Defining the Project Scope

A project scope, which is often simply a section of the project plan, defines what the project both will and will not deliver. In other words, the project scope defines the boundaries of the project. Putting boundaries around what your project team will deliver is important because it helps to avoid scope creep, the

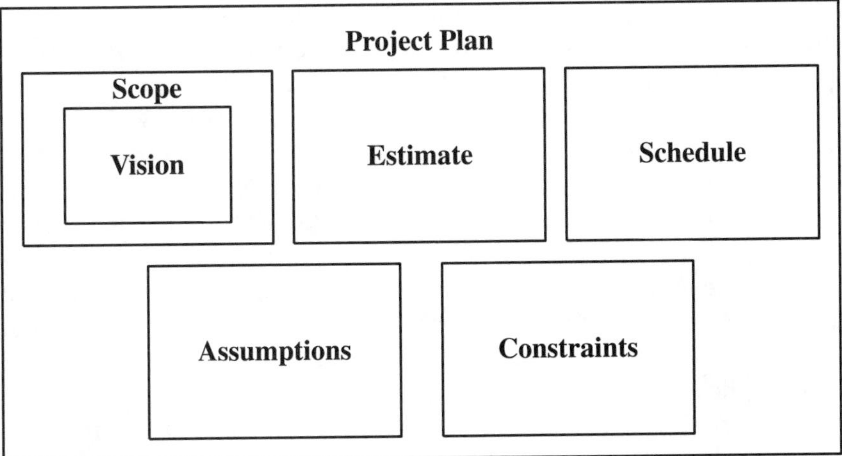

Figure 4.3. The components of a project plan

addition of new requirements as the project progresses. A project scope document enables you to negotiate whether you are responsible for delivering a "new" requirement, to justify why a new requirement will increase the delivery time/cost, and/or to argue that the requirement should be delivered in a later release.

The project scope defines what the project team will and will not deliver.

An important component of the project scope is the project vision: several paragraphs that define the purpose, goals, priorities, and expectations for the project. The vision defines what is important to users—for example, lower operating costs, increased market share, improved information quality, being seen as technologically advanced, and so on—and the order in which they are important. This is important information that helps both to guide the definition of the project scope and to enable a common understanding of the project among the developer and user communities.

The project vision defines the purpose, goals, priorities, and expectations for the project.

The act of defining the scope of a project is part of a larger process called system analysis. System analysis is the process of determining what projects will be undertaken, the order in which they will be undertaken, how they will be developed, and their scope. System analysis is effectively the act of strategic project planning, enabling your organization to develop applications in the most appropriate order possible. This is important because resources—funds, people, and time—are scarce; therefore, you need to plan how you expend those resources to gain the maximal benefit from them.

System analysis is the act of strategic project planning.

The task process pattern depicted in Figure 4.4 shows that there are several inputs into system analysis. Your organization's enterprise model, a product of the Model stage (Chapter 8), is an important source of information for system analysis because it defines what your organization does and how it fits into its external environment. Organizational priorities—for example, the strategic plans and goals of your organization—provide guidance as to the order in which projects should be developed. Environmental demands, government regulations and customer needs also provide input into both the order in which projects should be undertaken and what should be delivered by each project. Finally, the existing technical and application infrastructure is an important consideration during system analysis because some applications are easier to fit into the existing infrastructure due to dependencies between proposed applications (a reporting application needs to have the applications that provide the information being reported on in place first). Also, understanding the existing system infrastructure is important because you may realize that you need to rewrite an existing application or purchase a system from another organization and either use it directly or modify it and then use it. It is during system analysis that build-versus-buy decisions are made.

Build-versus-buy decisions are made during system analysis.

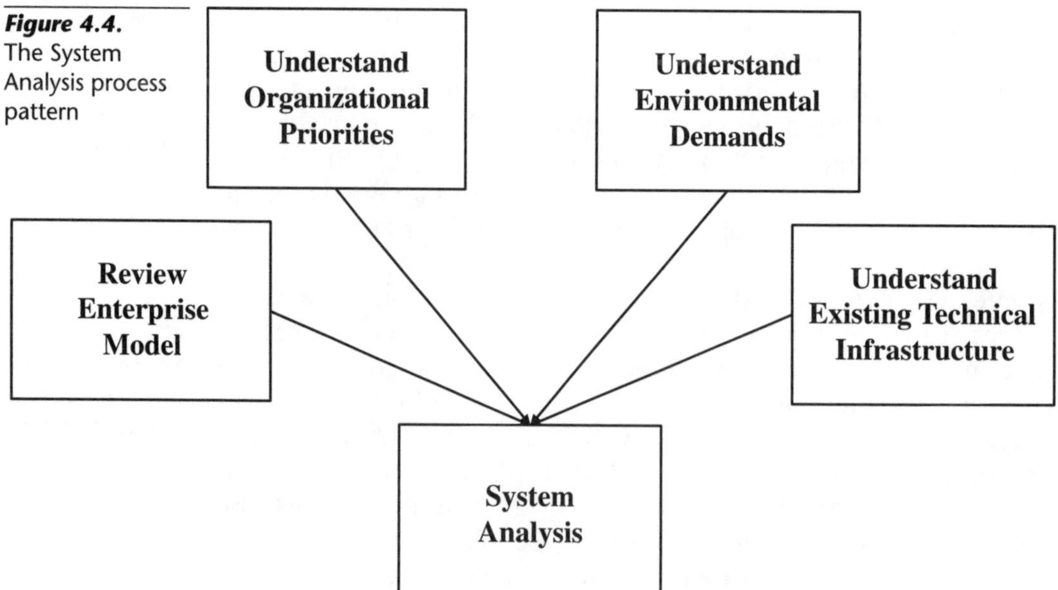

Figure 4.4. The System Analysis process pattern

DEFINITIONS

application release schedule A schedule indicating the dates of the incremental releases of your application.

project scope A definition of the functionality that will, and will not, be implemented by an application.

system analysis The process of determining what projects will be undertaken, the order in which they will be undertaken, how they will be developed, and the scope of each project.

The steps that you use to create the application will vary depending on the approach chosen to developing the application. A system rewrite is different from building an application new from scratch, which in turn is different from purchasing an application from another organization, which in turn is different from integrating an existing legacy application. It is important to note, however, that although the steps your project team will follow may vary, the process patterns that encapsulate the steps will likely not. Process tailoring—the selection of the appropriate approaches, standards, and guidelines for your project—is a significant portion of the Define Infrastructure stage described in Chapter 6.

Different types of projects will require different steps to develop them, although will follow the same process patterns.

A related task to your scoping effort is the development of an application release schedule, which describes the incremental releases of your application that your project team will develop. In Chapter 1 we saw that the incremental approach is a common way to develop object-oriented applications.

4.2.1.2 Defining the Tasks for the Project

An important part of project planning is to identify the tasks that will be performed by the project team. These tasks should be traceable to the project scope; in other words, the tasks to be performed should fall within the defined boundaries of the project. Because project planning is an iterative process, the project scope is used to identify the proposed tasks to be performed, and the proposed tasks to be performed provide insight into what the scope of the project should be.

Boehm (1981) suggests that it is useful to organize the tasks to be addressed by a project into a hierarchical structure called a work-breakdown structure (WBS). A WBS shows the tasks that must be performed on a project, but not necessarily the order in which they will be performed. Although WBSs were originally developed for the planning of structured development projects, my experience is that they can also be applied to the planning of object-oriented projects.

Figure 4.5 shows the beginning of a WBS for a new development project. When creating a WBS for a project, the first thing that you should do is look at the tailored process for your project, developed during the Define Infrastructure stage (Chapter 6), which defines the processes and procedures that will be followed by your project team. This information provides key input into the major tasks that need to be performed. For example, Figure 4.5 shows that the high-level tasks that need to be performed conform exactly to the three development phases of our object-oriented software process (OOSP); that the Construct task further decomposes into tasks corresponding to the stages of the Construct phase; that those tasks are further decomposed; and so on.

Leaf tasks can be estimated accurately.

Each task in a WBS will be decomposed until its cost and duration can be estimated accurately. For example, in Figure 4.5 you

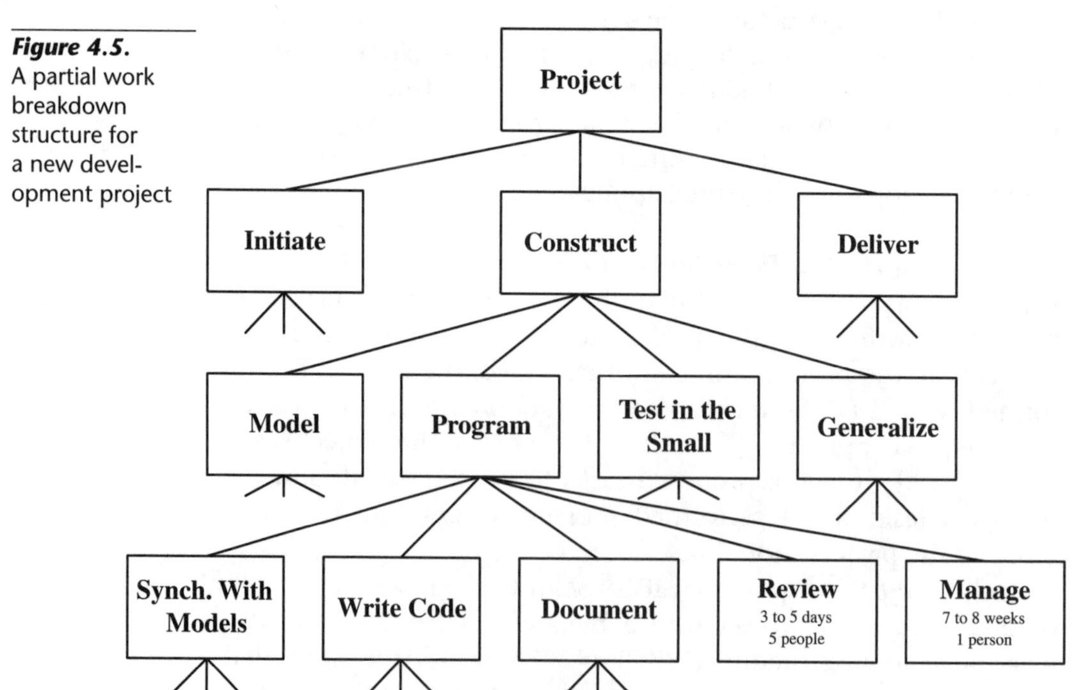

Figure 4.5. A partial work breakdown structure for a new development project

DEFINITION

work breakdown structure (WBS) A deliverable-oriented grouping of project elements which organizes and defines the total scope of the project. Each descending level represents an increasingly detailed definition of a project component.

see that most of the tasks still need to be further decomposed (that is what the lines beneath them represent) although the Review and Manage subtasks of Program are not. These subtasks are called leaf tasks: tasks that are not decomposed further. Leaf tasks should have estimates of the number of people required to perform them as well as the length of time that it will take to do so. If you find it difficult to make these estimates, it is an indication that you need to further decompose the task.

A WBS is a major input into both estimating the cost and effort required to complete a project and setting the schedule for the work to be performed.

4.2.1.3 Estimating the Effort Required

Estimating is the process of determining the cost and time to develop an application. Six fundamental factors affect the estimate of a project: scope, cost, people, tools/techniques, quality, and time. The scope refers to the functionality that will be delivered by the application and cost refers to the amount of money invested to deliver the application. The people assigned to a project affect its estimate because different people have different skillsets and different levels of productivity. Similarly, the tools and techniques employed by the project team will provide varying levels of productivity. The level of quality that your organization is willing to accept also affects your estimate, because the greater the desired quality, the more work that needs to be performed to achieve it. Finally, the desired delivery date of the project has a major impact on your estimate because it will drive your decisions as to who will work on the project, what will be accomplished, and/or the tools/techniques you will employ.

The desired resources, quality, and time to deliver are all important considerations for estimating a project.

Figure 4.6 shows the relationship between these estimating factors, indicating that you cannot change one factor without affecting the others. For example, if you want to reduce the time that it takes to deliver an application, you will need to make a corresponding change in the people assigned to the project, reduce the scope of the project, use different tools and techniques, or reduce the quality of the application. Similarly, if you wish to increase the quality, you will need to make a change in one or more of the other five estimating factors to support that increase.

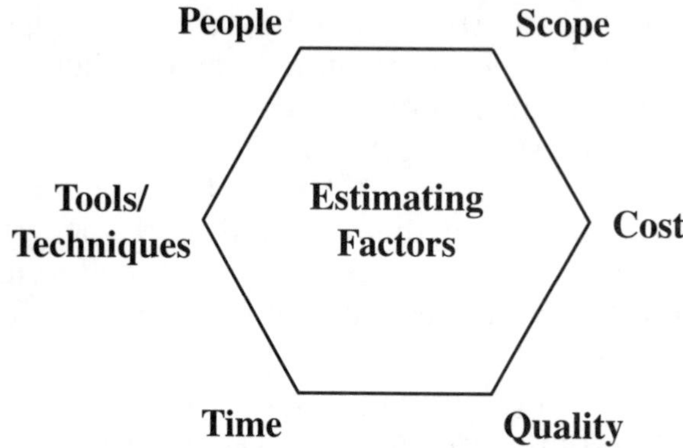

Figure 4.6. The interrelated factors of estimating

Yourdon (1997) states that a change of more than ten percent in any one factor will have an inverse-square change effect on a combination of the other factors. In other words, if you double the scope of your project and hold all other factors constant except for the number of people on your project, you will need roughly four times as many (2 squared). However, if you half the scope of the project and keep the other factors constant you would only need roughly one quarter of the people on the project (½ squared). Although Yourdon's inverse-square effect is only a rule of thumb, it matches closely with my own experience, although I know of no hard evidence proving it to be true or false; so take it for what it is worth.

Changes in one factor have an inverse-square effect on a combination of other estimating factors.

Estimators will often use metrics collected during the Define Initial Requirements stage (Chapter 3) to estimate the size of your project. Counts of the use cases to be implemented by your application and the function/feature points to be implemented provide insight into how large your project is.

There are several sources of information to determine the estimating factors. The people who will work on the project, as well as the tools and techniques that they will use, are defined by your project infrastructure. Because changes in each estimating factor result in changes to other factors, you will want to work closely with the team defining the project infrastructure to ensure that your estimate and infrastructure remain consistent. The project scope and the work breakdown structure (WBS) define the desired scope of your application; therefore, you will also need to work closely with the team defining the project's scope. Information about the desired quality of your project will be included in your project scope,

You will need to use several sources of information to determine the desired values of the six estimating factors.

TIP

There Are 212 Work Days in a Year

Quick, tell me how many working days that you can reasonably expect to get out of an average staff member in a year? Was your answer 212? No? If you thought there was more, you had better think again. Here is how I determined the 212 figure:

260	possible working days (52 weeks * 5 working days)
– 15	days of vacation (assume an average of 3 weeks of vacation time)
– 10	days of sick leave
– 13	days of statutory holidays
– 10	days of training
212	

TIP

Stick to Your Guns

Project managers will often be browbeaten by senior management and/or their users into committing to an unrealistic estimate—perhaps they will insist on delivering a project in six months instead of the twelve months that you initially estimated. Do not give in. If you think that there is no way you can do the project in anything less than twelve months, at least without a significant reduction in scope or a significant increase in resources, then committing to deliver it in six months is folly. Yourdon (1997) suggests several strategies for negotiating a reasonable estimate:

- Offer to deliver the critical twenty percent of the application that gives eighty percent of the value.
- Everybody wants an application delivered fast, cheap, and of high quality; ask which two of these three they would like.
- Try to identify other possible delivery strategies and attempt to make your detractors appear unreasonable for not accepting one of them.

as it should include any quality factors desired by your user community as well as your project infrastructure, which defines the chosen quality standards and processes that will be used on your project. The delivery date of your project will be

DEFINITIONS

feature points A metric that is the superset of function points, adding a count of the algorithmic complexities within your software.

function points A metric used for estimating software size that is calculated by counting five items: the inputs to the software, the outputs from it, inquiries by users, the data files that would be updated by the software, and the interfaces to other software.

project estimate An appraisal of how long a project will take, and how much it will cost, given a specific environment and a specific team. Change the environment and/or change the team and your estimate should change. Project estimates are a deliverable of the Initiate phase and are updated regularly throughout a project.

use case A description of a high-level user requirement that an application may or may not be expected to handle.

defined by your project schedule, which we'll discuss in detail later in this chapter.

4.2.1.3.1 The Value of a Work Month

Most organizations quote estimates in terms of work months, also called staff months or man months, which represent an organizational standard amount of time. A work month can be correlated to a specific monetary value to estimate the actual cost of the project. Quoting estimates in work months is important, because work months are a unit of measure that people can use to understand the size of a project. For example, if you say that a project will take eighteen work months to complete, I have a feel for the size and duration of the project. If you tell me that the project will cost $200,000, it is harder for me to comprehend the level of effort needed to complete the project. Because it is important to estimate both the expected duration and cost of a project, you need to be able to convert between work months and monetary values. Luckily, this is very straightforward.

Work months provide a common unit of measure from which duration, size, and cost can be determined.

To define the value of a work month, you must calculate the number of work days in a work month, define the number of hours in a work day, and then assign a monetary value to the average cost of a hour. For example, to calculate the number of work days in a work month, you take the number of actually

DEFINITIONS

work day A standard amount of time, measured in hours, that your organization considers a day. Most organizations define a standard work day as being seven, seven-and-a-half, or eight hours.

work month A standard amount of time corresponding to the average number of work days in an average month. Also known as a man month, person month, staff month, or engineering month.

working days in a year, excluding weekends and statutory holidays, and divide by 12. Therefore, if there are 270 work days in a year, your average work month is comprised of 22.5 work days (270/12). Next, take the number of hours in a day (in our case we'll assume 8) to determine that there are 180 hours in a work month. Finally, to determine the cost of a work month to your organization, you take the fully burdened cost of the average hour for developers (calculated by taking total annual human resources costs for your systems department and dividing by the total number of hours for the year) and multiply it by the number of hours in the month. Therefore, if the average hour is valued at $60, then the average work month should be valued at $10,800.

4.2.1.3.2 Estimating Tips and Techniques

The following tips will help you to improve your estimating efforts:

1. **It is easier to estimate small things than large things.** It is very easy to estimate how long it will take you to paint a room, but much more difficult to estimate how long it will take to paint an entire apartment building. That's because a room is much smaller than an apartment building, making it easier to estimate the effort required to paint it. This is why a work breakdown structure (WBS) is an important input into estimating: it takes a large project and decomposes it into a collection of small tasks.
2. **Use several techniques and compare the results.** When estimating each task, you have several ways to estimate the effort required to do it. You can ask somebody else who's performed the task before how long they think it will take. You can use measurements, also called metrics, collected by other

projects in the past for similar tasks and use them for your estimate. You can also make a rough guess based on what you feel it should take. The point to be made is that you have several estimating options to choose from, each of which will likely produce a different result. Therefore, to increase the accuracy of your estimate you should try to use several techniques and then average the results to increase the confidence level of your estimate.

3. **Get someone who has done it before.** The best estimates are often those made by people who have performed the task before, because they understand all of the issues and nuances involved in the task. This approach to estimating is encapsulated in Cunningham's (1996) Comparable Work task process pattern. Unfortunately, you may not have access to someone within your organization who has similar experience, or perhaps they only have partial experience in what your project is attempting. For example, you may have access to someone who has developed similar software using a structured development approach but not an object-oriented one, or perhaps you have access to object expertise but not domain expertise. The implication is that you may need to involve several people to accurately form an experience-based estimate, and you may even need to go outside of your organization to obtain the correct expertise.
4. **Pessimists are often closer to the truth than optimists.** With the abysmal record within the systems industry for estimating (the vast majority of projects are either late or over budget), it should be obvious that optimistic estimates have a much lower probability of being correct than pessimistic ones. In fact, my experience has been that the most pessimistic estimates often prove to be wildly optimistic most of the time.
5. **Do not reduce your estimate without a good reason.** You will often be pressured to reduce your estimate, to show that the project will cost less or will be delivered faster than expected. There's nothing wrong with reducing your estimate, as long as one or more estimating factors are modified appropriately. Do not forget that a change to one estimating factor will affect one or more of the other five factors.
6. **Base your estimate on existing metrics.** Whenever possible, try to use existing measurements, collected either by your

organization or within the industry, as input into your estimates. As you'll see in *More Process Patterns* (Ambler, 1998b), it is common to collect metrics for a single development process as well as for specific tools and procedures used within a development process. Existing metrics provide an indication as to the accuracy and validity of your estimate for a given task. If previous projects within your organization took ten work weeks to justify and you have estimated two work weeks, then you know that you have probably made a mistake, although if you feel that it will only take you eight work weeks, then perhaps your estimate is accurate.

7. **Quote your estimate in terms of ranges.** Yourdon (1997) states that it is crucial to state your estimates in terms of confidence levels or ranges because to build a realistic expectation by the audience of your estimate. An estimate that a project will take between five and seven months is more palatable to most senior managers than an estimate of exactly six months. Estimating isn't an exact science; therefore, an exact estimate should be considered with suspicion.
8. **Estimate each activity in terms of ranges.** Not only should your overall estimate be made in terms of confidence levels (ranges), so should the estimates for each task. Because some tasks will be late and some early (Humphrey, 1997), the range of your overall project will be much smaller than the total ranges of all subtasks. For example, even though your project is comprised of ten tasks that each take between one and three weeks, your estimate for the entire project may be that it will take between eighteen and twenty two weeks—not between ten and thirty weeks, which is what you would get by simply adding up the low and high ends of the ranges for each task.
9. **Document your assumptions.** Although we'll discuss this issue in detail later in the chapter, it is critical that you document the assumptions you made when developing an estimate. If you assume that a given toolset will be used, document it. If you assume that the team will reuse existing classes and components, document it. If you assume that the team is already trained and educated on the tools, techniques, and processes to be employed, then document it. By documenting your assumptions, you define the context in

which your estimate was developed—valuable information for anyone who is basing decisions based on your estimate.

10. **Recognize that others may not be interested in your estimates.** The software industry as a very poor track record in estimating, which has led to complete ambivalence towards estimates by many software professionals and users. However, this doesn't mean that you shouldn't invest the time to create an estimate for your project; instead, it means that you need to ensure that your estimate is as accurate as possible.
11. **Do not give off-the-cuff estimates.** A good estimate is well thought-out, not created as a spur-of-the-moment activity. Furthermore, wherever possible an estimate should be supported by a combination of data and experience, data and experience that takes time to gather and summarize.
12. **Estimate future activities with greater ranges.** The further in the future a task is, the less likely you are able to predict it accurately. Future tasks often depend on the result of other tasks being completed first. For example, programming depends on modeling; therefore, until the preceding tasks are completed or nearly completed, you often do not have sufficient information to accurately estimate the future task. Because your estimate is less accurate, you should give it a greater range of values to reflect the lower accuracy.

Because your estimate should indicate both the expected cost and time it will take to develop your project, scheduling goes hand-in-hand with estimating.

4.2.1.4 Scheduling the Project

Scheduling is the process of assigning people to tasks and to the time periods when they are going to perform their assigned tasks. Traditionally, the main deliverable of scheduling is a Gantt chart that shows tasks, when they will be performed, who will perform them, and the interrelationships between tasks. Figure 4.7 shows an example of a high-level Gantt chart for a project. This chart shows the main stages that a project will go through, but does not (yet) show the detailed tasks to be undertaken within each stage. The tasks to be performed are shown in the leftmost column; the people or groups who have been assigned those tasks are shown

Gantt charts are used to represent project schedules.

in the second column; an indication of the dates when the tasks will be performed is shown across the top of the chart; and within the body of the chart are horizontal bars indicating the period of time during which the tasks are to be performed.

War Story

Off-the-Cuff Estimates Are Taken Seriously

I once got cornered by the CIO of a client that I was working for and was asked for a quick estimate for the development of a project that he was considering. Thinking about it for about ten seconds, I said that I thought it could be done by four people in six (plus or minus one) months. He asked me for a quick estimate and I gave him one. What a mistake on my part!

Several days later I heard that the project was starting with four people assigned to it and that they would take six months. The first problem was that although I had given a range—I originally felt the project would take between five and seven months—it was ignored. The second problem is that my estimate was based on the premise that four experienced people would be assigned to the project, not the one experienced person and three novices that were assigned. Realizing that this assigned team didn't have a very good chance to deliver the project in the given time, I spoke to the CIO and revised my estimate to ten (plus or minus two) months for the chosen team. The third problem was that my new estimate was ignored and the CIO stuck with his perception of the original estimate, that of six months. When the team finally delivered the product, it took them thirteen months, one month outside the range of my second estimate (they were unable to get the novices trained when they needed to and ran into unanticipated scheduling problems with subject matter experts).

What can we learn from this experience? First, even though you give a range for your estimate, it will often be ignored in favor of the median number. Second, by not sharing with the CIO the assumptions that I made while estimating (that of an experienced team), I induced him to make an uninformed decision when putting the team together. Third, very often the first estimate that you give is the one that people will hold you to, so your first estimate had better be well thought-out. Fourth, it was foolish of me to give an off-the-cuff estimate; I should have asked for sufficient time to think about it, and then gotten back to the CIO after investing the time to put together a higher-quality estimate.

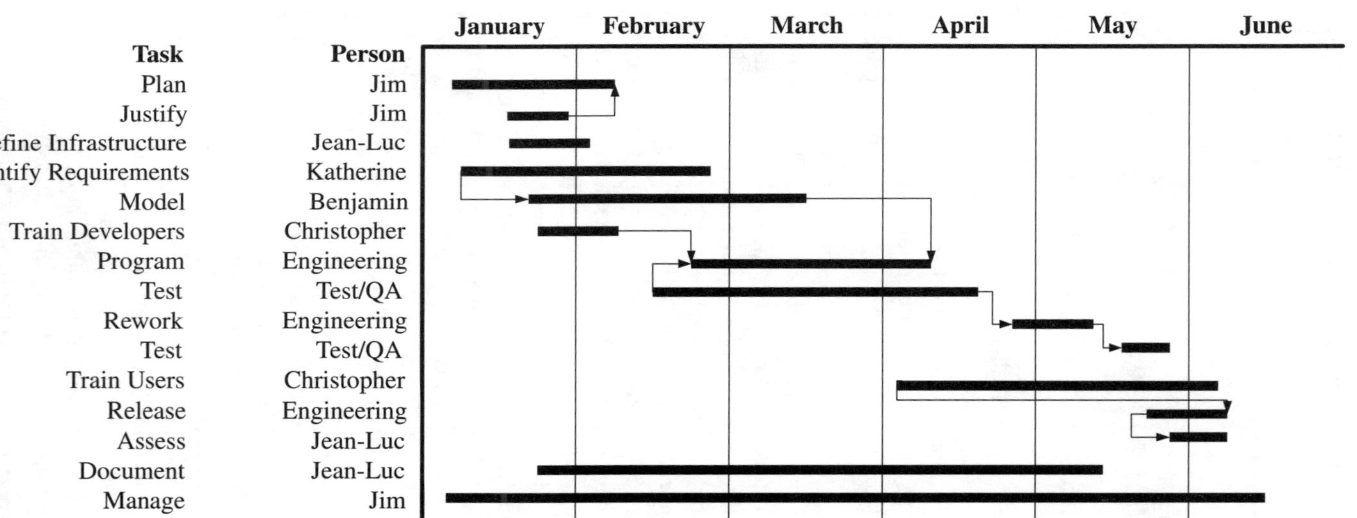

Figure 4.7.
A high-level Gantt chart for a project

Several of the task bars in Figure 4.7 are connected by arrows that represent relationships between those tasks. Five types of relationships may exist between tasks:

- A task must complete before another may begin.
- A task must complete before another may complete.
- A task must begin before another may begin.
- A task must begin before another may complete.
- A task has no relationship with another task.

In Figure 4.7 we have examples of each type of relationship between tasks. The Train Developers task must complete before the Program task may begin; the Justify task must complete before the Plan task may complete; the Identify Requirements task must begin before the Model task may begin; and the Train Users task must begin before the Release task may complete.

Scheduling is a very iterative process that takes as input the tasks defined by the work breakdown structure (WBS), the potential team members defined in the project infrastructure (Chapter 6), the skills assessments of the team members (Ambler, 1998b), and their personal vacation/training schedules. Because people have different skills and abilities, the person(s) assigned to a task have a direct impact on how long that task will take. As a result, scheduling and team definition are highly coupled and are often performed in parallel in an iterative manner. In Chapter 6 I will discuss team definition in greater detail.

The following iterative steps are performed to create a project schedule:

- Identify the tasks to be completed on the project (documented by the WBS).
- Order the tasks in the general order in which they are to start.
- Identify milestones.
- Identify the potential candidates for working on your project, including project team members (documented by the project infrastructure) and other teams/subcontractors to which you have access.

- For each task:
  - Identify the skillset needed to perform it.
  - Identify the amount of effort needed to perform it.
  - Identify potential candidates to perform it.

    - Identify relationships with other tasks.
    - Assign candidates to the task based on their skills and availability.

- For each candidate:
    - Identify their skillset.
    - Identify their career goals and aspirations.
    - Identify their availability.

- Review the schedule with:
    - Other project managers to verify that everything is covered.
    - Candidates to verify their availability and willingness to work on the project.
- Senior management to get the schedule approved.

The following tips will help you to improve your scheduling efforts:

1. **Schedule in the large and in the small.** The Gantt chart in Figure 4.7 showed very little detail with respect to the individual tasks to be performed on the project and there was a valid rea-

DEFINITIONS

Gantt chart A graphic display of schedule-related information, listing the activities to be completed down the left-hand side of the diagram, dates shown across the top, and horizontal bars showing activity duration between given dates within the diagram. Resources (teams, positions/roles, individuals) allocated to the activities are often shown on the bars, and dependencies between activities are shown as arrows connecting the horizontal bars. Relationships between tasks (for example, task A must complete before task B starts) can also be indicated.

milestone A significant event in a project, usually the completion of a major deliverable, a point where upper management is traditionally informed of the status of the project. Because the OOSP is serial in the large and iterative in the small, the only clear milestones occur at the completion of project phases.

project schedule A schedule that indicates what will be done, when things will be done, and who will do them. A major component of a project schedule is a Gantt chart with its corresponding descriptions of tasks and resources. Project schedules are a deliverable of the Initiate phase and are updated regularly throughout a project.

son for this: With a six-month time frame, it isn't appropriate to be scheduling tasks of a few hours or a few days duration. An effective technique for scheduling is to maintain a less-detailed "schedule in the large" that shows the main tasks to be performed, such as the one in Figure 4.7, and a detailed schedule "schedule in the small" for the next month or two that shows the detailed subtasks to be performed. This allows you to manage the project long-term, yet still be flexible enough to modify your short-term schedule as your situation warrants.

2. **Aggressive deadlines reduce quality, reusability, and extensibility.** We discussed earlier that a change to any one of the six estimating factors—time, people, tools/techniques, cost, quality, and scope—will impact at least one of the other five factors. When you allow your project to be completely calendar-driven, you will need to sacrifice one or more of the other factors to compensate. Constantine (1995) believes that you must be realistic about deadlines and act accordingly. If you know that a project schedule is unreasonable then cutting corners in modeling and/or testing will not help because sooner or later you're going to take the hit.
3. **Indicate accountability in the schedule.** Assigning people to tasks, and making them accountable for their successful completion, is a fundamental part of scheduling.
4. **Review the schedule with its stakeholders.** Humphrey (1997) suggests that you review the proposed schedule with everyone to ensure that there are no conflicts, disagreements, or misunderstandings.
5. **Schedule every OOSP stage and project task.** The very first thing that you should do when defining the tasks to be performed on a project is to list the stages and project tasks of the object-oriented software process (OOSP) to ensure that you cover everything that needs to be accomplished. There are valid reasons why each stage and project task exists; therefore, you need to consider including them in your schedule. One of the reasons why stages like Generalize (Chapter 10) and Rework (Ambler, 1998b) are included in the life cycle is to put them in your face to force you to include them in your schedule.
6. **Schedule for a longer modeling phase.** Modeling (Chapter 8) is a much larger part of the Construct phase with the object-oriented paradigm than with the structured paradigm, and you need to schedule accordingly.

TIP

Plan Your Metrics Program

Grady (1992) believes that a key to success for your metrics program is to plan for it. He suggests that at the beginning of your project you should select key metrics that you wish to collect (metrics are covered in detail in Chapter 10 of *More Process Patterns*) and include the time that it will take to collect them in your schedule. If you do not plan for metrics, you will not be able to collect and act on them effectively.

7. **Do not forget the "do not forgets."** There are many tasks and events which occur that reduce the time that developers can directly work on a project. We all know from experience that a significant portion of people's time is spent in training, supporting previous project teams, meetings, presentations, vacations, statutory holidays, system down time, and staying at home due to illness. Although this list isn't complete, it is enough to make it clear that you cannot count on people spending one hundred percent of their time on your project. Some of these things, such as training, vacations, and holidays, can be directly scheduled, whereas others, such as illness and downtime, must be accounted for via a "fudge factor" in your schedule.
8. **Create a schedule template.** Many organizations find it effective to create a high-level schedule template for projects and reuse it on many projects. This is possible only for organizations that have a well-defined OOSP that they follow because with the exception of specific process tailoring (see Chapter 6) all object-oriented development projects go through the same development process.
9. **Distant deadlines breed complacency.** When a deadline is far enough away, perhaps six to twelve months, nobody has to face up to the reality that the objectives are impossible (Yourdon, 1997). Techniques such as timeboxing, which decomposes a large project into smaller portions, each of which has a well-defined set of deliverables, can be used to give project teams a series of near-term deadlines to meet, instead of a single one sometime in the distant future. Timeboxing is discussed in Chapter 7 as a management technique of the Construct phase.
10. **Recognize that schedules are not exact.** Schedules often predict the best-case date, not the actual ship date for your application (Maguire, 1994).

TIP

State How You Will Eliminate Unknowns

You will often make an assumption because you do not have full access to the information that you need to complete your project plan. For example, during planning you might make the assumption that it is possible to schedule developers for training "just in time"—in other words, when it is most convenient for your project. It is quite common to include time in a project schedule for training, even when you do not know what that training will be. If this is the case, then you should document your assumption and document that once the appropriate training has been determined, the best possible training dates will be selected and the schedule updated accordingly.

11. **Maintain an internal and external schedule.** Coplien's (1995) Size the Schedule task process pattern suggests that two schedules be maintained, one that your development team works to and one that you "advertise" to your customers. He suggests that there be a several week difference between the two schedules, providing lag time for your team to catch up if it slips its internal schedule.
12. **Update your schedule throughout your project.** Your project team will sometimes be ahead of schedule, sometimes on schedule, and sometimes behind schedule. Throughout your project you should update your schedule to reflect your actual status.

4.2.1.5 Documenting Assumptions and Constraints

To put your planning into the proper context you should document the assumptions that you have made as well as the constraints which were placed on the project. If you do not document your assumptions and constraints, and portions of your plan prove to be mistaken, then you have nothing to help justify your the work. A list of your assumptions and constraints should at least be documented as an appendix to your project plan.

Documenting assumptions and constraints puts your project into the proper context.

The Software Engineering Institute (1995) suggests that the definition of quality goals for the deliverables produced by your project team should be included in your project plan. I believe in documenting these quality goals with the assumptions and constraints for your project. Defining quality goals for your project is an aspect of the level-four Software Quality Management key process area (KPA) of the Capability Maturity Model (CMM).

DEFINITIONS

Capability Maturity Model (CMM) A strategy, defined by the Software Engineering Institute (SEI), that describes the key elements of an effective software process.

key process area (KPA) An issue that must be addressed to achieve a specific Capability Maturity Model (CMM) maturity level.

4.2.1.6 Planning Tips and Techniques

The following tips and techniques will improve your planning process:

1. **Create a realistic plan.** A project manager must believe in the project goals, estimate, and schedule, and he or she must be able to convince the staff of the same (Yourdon, 1997). Goldberg & Rubin (1995) state that the implication is that you must plan truthfully and avoid planning beyond the limits of your understanding. They believe that ignorance can be tolerated if you plan to investigate the unknown.
2. **A project plan must reflect the overall plan of your organization.** The reason why an application is developed in the first place is to support the organization that is having it built. Furthermore, the development of the application itself must fit into the context of your organization; therefore, your project plan must reflect your organization's overall plan.
3. **Confidence comes from the planning process, not the plan itself.** Creating a project plan forces you to think about how you will build your application long before a single line of code is written, reducing your project's risk because you have worked through various strategies and approaches and chosen the one the makes the most sense. Your goal shouldn't be to simply go through the motions to produce a plan; it should be to produce a realistic plan against which you can manage your project successfully (Goldberg & Rubin, 1995).
4. **Learn from your planning mistakes.** To make more accurate plans, check where your previous plans were in error and make the appropriate modifications to your planning process (Humphrey, 1997).
5. **The doers should be the planners.** The best person to create a project plan is the person who is responsible for working that plan. When a project is planned is by one person and worked by another, the person working the plan is less likely to believe in it and more likely to blame the plan if the project becomes late or overbudget.
6. **Plan for reuse.** The only way you will get reuse is if you plan for it; you need to allocate the time and resources necessary to make your work reusable. If you do not step back and take

the time to generalize your work, then it will never happen; project pressures will motivate you to put that work aside until you have the time to do it. The bottom line is that if reuse management is not part of your development process, then reuse likely will not happen.

DEFINITION

Reuse management The process of organizing, monitoring, and directing the efforts of a project team that lead to reuse on a project, either reuse of existing or purchased items.

4.2.2 Assessing Risk

All software projects have risks—technical, schedule, and cost risks. A risk assessment identifies project risks, rates their impact and priority, and suggests possible courses of action (perhaps even just accepting the risk and hoping for the best) to be taken to alleviate the risk. The goal of risk management is to identify and alleviate risks as early as possible when they have had a minimal impact on the project and the team of professionals working on it.

Risk assessments identify risks, their impact and their priority, and suggest possible courses of action.

Technical risks focus on the functionality, quality, reliability, usability, timeliness, maintainability, and reusability of the software being delivered (Karolak, 1995). Anything that can negatively impact one or more of these factors is considered a technical risk. Technical risk is often the result of the use and/or pioneering of unfamiliar technology or techniques. Examples of technical risk include depending on a new release of a software or hardware product or package, the use of unfamiliar technology, the pioneering of new technology, the use of new development techniques (perhaps large scale, object-oriented development is new to your organization), and the use of new development tools.

Technical risk is often the result of new and/or unfamiliar technology or techniques.

Projects are often canceled because of cost overruns; therefore, you need to manage cost risks closely.

Cost risks focus on your project budget, non-recurring costs, recurring costs, fixed costs, variable costs, profit/loss margin, and the accuracy of the cost estimate (Karolak, 1995). Projects run the risk of being canceled if they incur cost overruns, and may not even begin if the cost is too great. By assessing and mitigating cost risks on your project you increase its chance of success.

Schedule risks focus on the flexibility of the schedule, the ability of the team to meet established milestones, and the ability of the schedule to accurately reflect the expectations of all project stakeholders (Karolak, 1995). An example of schedule risk is the reliance on a single vendor or person to deliver a key component of your project because if they run into trouble your project runs the risk of being late. A second example of schedule risk is the

TIP

Invest the Time to Learn the Basics of Finance

Senior management expects that people understand the fundamentals of business. This means that you need to understand the difference between the different types of costs, as there are corresponding types of revenue (one person's cost is another's revenue), especially if you are involved in assessing the risk of your project. A non-recurring cost is one that you incur once—for example, the initial purchase price of your development tools—and a recurring cost is one that you incur many times, often on a regular basis—for example the annual support fee for your persistence mechanism. A fixed cost is one that you will incur regardless of the project—such as the rental cost of your office—whereas a variable cost changes with the size of the project—such as the cost of hourly programming contractors working on the project. As you would expect, you can combine these two types of costs to have fixed recurring costs, fixed non-recurring costs, variable recurring costs and variable non-recurring costs.

promise of being able to deliver all or part of an application under a very aggressive schedule. Every software developer is an optimist who is willing to quote an aggressive delivery date predicated on the assumption that everything will go right, regardless of past project experiences where many things actually went wrong.

Create a risk assessment as early in a project as possible.

The earlier that you begin managing risk in a project the lower the overall cost of development will be because your project runs into fewer difficulties. Therefore you want to start a risk assessment document as early as possible, often before construction begins. This is why the creation of a risk assessment document during project initiation is crucial.

If you do not manage risk it will manage you.

At this point in a project, risk management typically entails the identification and assessment of potential risks. Your goal is to start a risk assessment document that will be updated continuously throughout the project. This document should list the identified risks, identify their likelihood of occurring, identify their impact if they do occur, and suggest a strategy for mitigating each risk. Risk mitigation strategies are often referred to as contingency plans. Although you will not be able to identify all risks at the beginning of your project, you should still attempt to identify and assess as many as possible so that you are in a position to manage them; otherwise, they will manage you.

To identify risks, Karolak (1995) suggests that there are three main determinants of risk that you should look for: lack of control, lack of information, and lack of time. Look for areas where you have little or no control, perhaps over the release date of critical software from a third-party vendor or new regulations pending approval of the government. Look for areas where you lack information: perhaps senior management has suggested the use of a certain technology based simply on a business magazine article that they have read; therefore, your project is potentially at risk because the technology may not be as good as the article made it out to be. Look for portions of your schedule that have aggressive deadlines, people that have many tasks to perform, and deliverables that are on the critical path of your schedule to find risks resulting from a lack of time.

When developing a risk assessment, you should involve people with various backgrounds to ensure a thorough job. This is important because Karolak (1995) observes that when software risk is defined by developers, it is in terms of technologies; however, when it is defined by management it is in terms of performance and profit. In other words, technologists focus on technical risks whereas managers focus on schedule and cost risks. The implication is that you need to include both developers and managers when assessing risk to increase the number or risks identified.

Risk management is an important part of software development, and a risk assessment document is the key to this task. In *More*

TIP

Maintain Both Public and Private Risk Assessments

I make it a habit to maintain both a public and a private risk assessment. The public risk assessment, which I make available to all project stakeholders, describes technical and managerial risks that need to be addressed. For example, a public risk assessment would include issues such as the project relying on *PraxisSoft's GloryBound v2* to be released by a given date and capacity problems experienced with the persistence mechanism. The private risk assessment, which I maintain for myself, describes risks associated with personnel on the project and/or politically sensitive issues. This would include issues like other project managers attempting to scuttle my project or the suspicion that a developer is looking for another job. The private risk assessment documents issues that you need to actively manage but cannot publicly acknowledge as risks to your project.

DEFINITION

Risk management The process of identifying, monitoring, and mitigating the risks faced by a project team. These risks may typically be strategic, technical, and/or political.

Process Patterns (Ambler, 1998b) I'll discuss risk management in greater detail. Until that time, I'll leave you with the observation of Booch (1995) that the failure of any one aspect of a development project can cause the entire project to fail. Personally, I take risk management seriously.

4.2.3 Creating a Master Test/Quality Assurance Plan

As we will discuss in Chapters 11, the cost of fixing errors increases exponentially the later in the development process they are found. The implication is that you want to test as early as possible on a development project; therefore, you need to plan to test as early as possible. A master test/quality assurance (QA) plan describes the testing policies and procedures of your organization, and provides a common repository of the individual test plans for the portions of your application.

Create a testing and quality assurance plan as early as possible in the development of a project.

To create a master test/QA plan, you first need to identify the techniques and procedures that you will employ for testing and quality assurance activities. Chapter 11 describes a wide range of testing and QA techniques. You should then produce a test/review schedule for the project. This should be a subset of the overall project schedule so that test/QA experts can be assigned to the appropriate tasks. Finally, the appropriate placeholders for the detailed test plans for each testing activity should be added to the master test/QA plan so that it can be updated later in the project as needed.

To ensure that testing and quality assurance are an integral part of the entire development process, you need to plan for it, otherwise it will fall to the wayside as the project progresses. By starting a master test/QA plan at the beginning of the project, you indicate that your team is serious about delivery of a product that works.

DEFINITION

Master test/quality assurance(QA) plan A document that describes your testing and quality assurance policies and procedures, as well as the detailed test plans for each portion of your application.

4.2.4 Establishing a Project Charter

A project charter is a document issued by senior management that provides your project team with the authority to apply organizational resources to project activities. A charter is effectively the blessing of senior management to proceed; therefore, it is key to the success of your project. A project charter is typically obtained by presenting your project plan and feasibility study, a product of the Justify stage (Chapter 5), to senior management so that it may be reviewed and, you hope, accepted. The funny thing about projects that have been

War Story

Project Charters Aren't Big Sticks

Many years ago I worked on the development of a management information system. This was the pet project of the Vice President of the group that I worked in, and the project charter that he defined for the project was to summarize and report information that was needed by managers within the department to perform their jobs. This meant that we needed to consolidate and report on data that was "owned" by several stovepipe systems, and in an organization rife with political infighting this would normally be a difficult but not insurmountable task. Luckily we had the best possible charter that a project of this kind could hope for, and unfortunately we used it whenever we could.

Our mistake was that whenever we needed access to system documentation, instead of negotiating with the owners of it we instead chose to use our project charter to take it from them. The Vice President had chartered us to work with any data that we felt necessary, and whenever one of the owners of that data was unwilling to give us the access that we demanded we simply pushed the decision up the management chain until we got our way. Because we used our charter to force people to do things quickly that we otherwise would have had to negotiate for, we made a lot of enemies on that project. We had used our project charter as a big stick to get our way on the current project; to our detriment, we learned that people will hold grudges for years.

shown to be viable by a fair feasibility study is that people will often fight to be involved with them; in an industry with an 85% failure rate for large projects, it is always good for your career to work on a project that has a reasonable chance at being in the 15% of projects that actually succeed. The acceptance of your project is signified by the awarding of a charter to your project team.

DEFINITION

Project charter A document issued by senior management that provides the project manager with the authority to apply organizational resources to project activities.

The way in which you obtain your project charter depends on your organization's culture. Perhaps you need to present your project plan and feasibility study to a management oversight committee that decides how your organization invests in projects. Perhaps you need to present your study to the chief information officer (CIO) of your organization so he or she can decide. Perhaps you work for a collective and your project must be put to a vote by all staff, or perhaps you merely need to send an email to your boss including your feasibility study as an attachment. Different organizations, different ways of doing things.

4.3 Solution: Project Tasks

In this section I will discuss project task issues that are pertinent to the Define Initial Management Documents stage.

4.3.1 Managing the Define Initial Management Documents Stage

Although this stage is itself a project management function, it still needs to be managed. The development of the project plan, master test/QA plan, and initial risk assessment can be performed either in parallel or in serial. Furthermore, because the development of the project plan and risk assessment are performed iteratively with the development of the project infrastructure (Chapter 6) and the feasibility study (Chapter 5) it is critical that the people involved with these efforts are working together and keeping their work synchronized. This requires a method for intergroup coordination to be established, perhaps an internal newsgroup where the teams post shared documents and status information, or perhaps regular synchronized meetings will be required. Regardless, it is the responsibility of the project manager to ensure that the team members are working together toward successfully developing the initial management documents, feasibility study, and project infrastructure.

4.3.2 Training and Education

Many people believe that project management is an art, not a science, and they're probably right. Creating the key documents needed by project managers, on the other hand, is definitely a science that can be taught. The skills for developing schedules and estimates are commonly taught in introductory project management courses at both colleges and corporate training organizations. Risk assessment courses are usually offered by training firms and consulting companies specializing in risk management and in university MBA programs.

Mentoring and apprenticeship programs, usually informal ones, are common in most organizations. Experienced project managers will often be assigned less-experienced staff that they are to groom to become project managers. Very often the first step of this process is to involve the trainee in the development of the initial management documents—in part because it is a lot of work, and in part because novice project managers first need to learn the basics of estimating, scheduling, and planning before they can use them on the job.

4.3.3 Quality Assurance

Any document worth creating is worth reviewing; this is true of user documents, technical documents, operations documents, and management documents. Walk through the project plan and initial risk assessment with experienced people, including both users and developers, to validate that it they are both reasonable and complete.

Any document worth creating is worth reviewing.

4.3.4 Potential Risks While Defining the Initial Management Documents

There are several risks that need to be mitigated to successfully define the initial management documents for a project.

1. **Unreasonable estimates and/or schedules.** The political reality of most organizations is that you will often be forced to accept an "unreasonable" project estimate and/or schedule based not on logic but instead on the desires/demands of senior management, who often do not take into account the technical and operational realities of software development. My advice is to not accept a schedule/estimate that you know you cannot meet—advice that is difficult to follow in the short term, but in the longer term will often help you to avoid being involved in a failed project. Never forget, eighty-five percent of all large projects fail; so why knowingly start out at a disadvantage?
2. **Inaccurate estimates.** A fundamental risk with estimating is getting it wrong. You can mitigate this risk by using several estimating techniques, perhaps combining the gut-feel estimate of an experienced developer with a rigorous subtask definition/estimation process, and by defining your estimate in terms of a range of likely figures as opposed to a single, exact figure.

3. **Lack of management support.** Many organizations, once they have decided to start a project, want to start doing the "real work," construction, as soon as possible. Many project managers are often pushed by senior management to begin construction before a realistic plan and risk assessment are in place. Creating the initial management documents at the beginning of your project provides you with the tools that you need to successfully manage it, and you need to convince senior management to allow you to invest the time that you need to do this.

You have to choose to be successful, a choice that is often the most difficult one to make.

DEFINITION

template reuse The reuse of a common set of layouts for key development artifacts—documents, models, and source code—within your organization.

4.3.5 Opportunities for Reuse

Every project is different; as a result, every project plan, test plan, and risk assessment is different. Nevertheless, it is still possible to obtain template reuse through the use of document templates. The tasks that you perform on a project are in part defined by your software process; because you're using a consistent process, doesn't it make sense that you should be able to create a template for your project plan based on your process? Furthermore, although the risks associated with each project may be different, the basic information that you define doesn't change: a description of the risk, a priority, a likelihood that the risk will occur, and a description of your risk mitigation strategy. Therefore, you should also be able to create a reusable template for your risk assessment.

You can develop and reuse document templates for plans and risk assessments.

4.3.6 Metrics

You may choose to gather metrics that are specific to the Define Initial Management Documents stage. These metrics are:

1. **Level of risk.** The risk assessment for your project is created during this stage. An interesting metric, and one that is easy to calculate, is a simple indicator of the level of risk for your project. This metric can be calculated by taking the number of low, medium, and high risks and applying appropriate multipliers to them—perhaps 1, 3, and 7 respectively. Knowing the level of risk for your project and tracking how it changes over time provides management with an indication of the likelihood of your project succeeding.
2. **Project size.** The size of your project, perhaps measured in feature points or work months, should be included in your pro-

ject estimate. This metric should be recorded and prominently and publicly shared so that everyone has an understanding of the amount of work to be performed by your project team.

4.4 Resulting Context: Exit Conditions for Defining Initial Management Documents

You haven't finished the Define Initial Management Documents stage until the initial versions of key management documents, such as the project plan, are defined and accepted by senior management and your development team. The exit conditions for this stage are:

1. **The initial versions of key management documents are defined.** Several key documents are required to manage a project, including the project plan, the risk assessment, and the master test/QA plan. These documents need to be started at the beginning of the project, both to obtain support from senior management for your project and to start your project off properly by developing a realistic strategy for delivering your application.
2. **The development team accepts the project plan.** A good plan is aggressive but realistic, and should be perceived as achievable by the people tasked to work it.
3. **The project has been chartered by senior management.** To proceed with your project, you need the support of senior management, and this support should be in the form of a project charter that indicates that the project team has the authority, funding, and ability to develop the application.

4.5 Secrets of Success

The following pointers should help to improve your efforts at defining the initial management documents for your project:

1. **Do not lose sight of the project.** The important thing is the success of the project, not the successful management of the project. Always remember that the ultimate goal of any software project is to develop a system that meets the needs of its

users in a timely and cost-effective manner. Management documents are merely tools that help you to achieve your goal; they are not the goal itself.

2. **Maintain and update your plan.** Project plan tracking is a fundamental part of project management. Humphrey (1997) makes the following suggestions for successfully maintaining and updating your project plan: do not change your schedule until you make a new plan; when posting status against the plan, do not change the plan; when showing new estimated completion dates, leave the original schedule in place and note the new dates with dotted lines; keep copies of the original schedule and all updates; and document why the schedule has changed so that you are able to justify your decisions if needed. The rule is this: estimated costs and delivery dates are nice to know, but it is nicer yet to know the actual costs and delivery date.
3. **Document your assumptions and constraints.** Every project has to operate under constraints, and everybody needs to make assumptions when they do not have ready access to the information that they need. This is the reality of management. By documenting your assumptions and constraints you put your project plan into context.
4. **Make your project plan public.** Yourdon (1997) suggests that if possible, you should post your schedule in a public place, either on a wall or on an internal Web site, where all project stakeholders can view it. This makes it clear to everyone exactly what their commitments and responsibilities are, and provides them with an opportunity to track your project's progress.
5. **Avoid death by planning.** The Death By Planning (Brown, Maveau, McCormick, Mowbray, 1998) antipattern warns of a common planning mistake: planning a project in minute detail and thereby giving yourself a false impression that your project is under control. Plans are a mechanism for controlling a project, but just because you have a plan doesn't mean you have control.

4.6 Process Checklist

The following process checklist can be used to verify that you have completed the Define Initial Management Documents stage.

DEFINE INITIAL MANAGEMENT DOCUMENTS STAGE PROCESS CHECKLIST

Fulfillment of Entrance Conditions:

✔ The project infrastructure has been selected, or at least selection has begun.
✔ A feasibility study for your project has been started.
✔ The project objectives have been identified and agreed to.
✔ The initial requirements have been defined, or at least their definition has begun.

Processes Performed:

✔ Your application has been scoped.
✔ Appropriate build-versus-buy decisions have been made for each portion of your application.
✔ The application release schedule has been defined and updated.
✔ The project tasks defined and estimated.
✔ A project work-breakdown structure (WBS) has been developed, if appropriate.
✔ A project estimate has been developed and accepted.
✔ A schedule has been developed and accepted.
✔ A plan for your metrics program has been developed and accepted.
✔ A plan for your project has been developed and accepted.
✔ Assumptions and constraints have been identified and documented.
✔ An initial risk assessment has been started.
✔ A master test/QA plan has been developed and accepted.
✔ A project charter has been developed and accepted.
✔ A method for intergroup coordination has been established.
✔ Artifacts that are potentially reusable by your project team during this stage have been identified and used where appropriate.
✔ Your risk assessment document has been updated where appropriate.

- ✔ Decisions made, and decisions forgone, have been documented in your group memory.
- ✔ Metrics have been collected.

Fulfillment of Exit Conditions:

- ✔ The initial version of the project plan has been accepted by senior management.
- ✔ The initial version of the project plan has been accepted by the development team.
- ✔ The initial version of the risk assessment has been accepted by senior management.
- ✔ The project has been chartered by senior management.

4.7 What You Have Learned in This Chapter

Many critical documents—the project plan, the testing and quality assurance plan, and the project risk assessment—are used in the management of a project. These documents must be started early in the life of a project to put the project on a solid footing. In this chapter you discovered how to create a work breakdown structure (WBS), a management artifact that is used to identify the project tasks to be accomplished, key input into the project schedule and estimate. You also learned the importance of obtaining a charter for your project, and saw how to do so. Finally, you learned the need to create an initial risk assessment for your project, the key document for managing and mitigating the risks associated with software development.

4.8 References and Recommended Reading

Ambler, S. W. 1998a. *Building Object Applications That Work—Your Step-by-Step Handbook for Developing Robust Systems with Object Technology*. New York: SIGS Books/Cambridge University Press.

Ambler, S. W. 1998b. *More Process Patterns—Delivering Large-Scale Systems Using Object Technology.* New York: SIGS Books/ Cambridge University Press.

Barbour, D. 1996. What Makes a Good Project Fail? *Object Magazine* 6(September), 60–62.

Baudoin, C. and Hollowell, G. 1996. *Realizing the Object-oriented Life Cycle.* Upper Saddle River, New Jersey: Prentice Hall PTR.

Boehm, B. W. 1981. *Software Engineering Economics.* Upper Saddle River, New Jersey: Prentice-Hall, Inc.

Booch, G. 1995. Practical Objects: A Question of Balance. *Object Magazine* 5 (July-August) 95–96.

Booch, G. 1996. *Object Solutions—Managing the Object-Oriented Project.* Menlo Park, California: Addison Wesley Publishing Company, Inc.

Brown, W., Malveau, R, McCormick, H., Mowbray, T. (1998). *AntiPatterns: Refactoring Software, Architectures, and Projects in Crisis.* New York: John Wiley & Sons.

Constantine, L. L. 1995. *Constantine on Peopleware.* Englewood Cliffs, New Jersey: Yourdon Press.

Coplien, J.O. (1995). *A Generative Development-Process Pattern Language.* Pattern Languages of Program Design, eds. Coplien, J.O. and Schmidt, D.C., Addison Wesley Longman, Inc., pp. 183– 237.

Cunningham, W. (1996). *EPISODES: A Pattern Language of Competitive Development.* Pattern Languages of Program Design 2, eds. Vlissides, J.M., Coplien, J.O., and Kerth, N.L., Addison-Wesley Publishing Company., pp. 371–388.

Goldberg, A. and Rubin, K. S. 1995. *Succeeding With Objects: Decision Frameworks for Project Management.* Reading, Massachusetts: Addison-Wesley Publishing Company, Inc.

Grady, R. B. 1992. *Practical Software Metrics For Project Management and Process Improvement.* Englewood Cliffs, New Jersey: Prentice-Hall, Inc.

Hetzel, B. 1988. *The Complete Guide to Software Testing.* 2d ed. New York: Wiley-QED.

Humphrey, W. S. 1997. *Introduction to the Personal Software Process.* Reading, Massachusetts: Addison-Wesley Longman, Inc.

Karolak, D. W. 1996. *Software Engineering Risk Management.* Los Alamitos, California: IEEE Computer Society Press.

Maguire, S. 1994. *Debugging the Development Process.* Redmond, Washington: Microsoft Press.

PMI Standards Committee. 1996. *A Guide to the Project Management Book of Knowledge.* Upper Darby, Pennsylvania: Project Management Institute.

Schofield, C. and Sheeperd, M. 1997. Estimating Software Project Effort Using Analogies. *IEEE Transactions on Software Engineering* 23(11), 736–743.

Software Engineering Institute. 1995. *The Capability Maturity Model: Guidelines for Improving the Software Process*. Reading Massachusetts: Addison-Wesley Publishing Company, Inc.

Yourdon, E. (1997). *Death March: The Complete Software Developer's Guide to Surviving "Mission Impossible" Projects*. Upper Saddle River, New Jersey: Prentice-Hall, Inc.

Chapter 5

The Justify Stage

THE purpose of the Justify stage is to determine whether or not an application should be built. This stage is potentially the most important part of the Initiate phase, as it is a reality check to determine whether or not a project makes sense. Unfortunately it is usually the most poorly done stage, generally because of either an unwillingness by senior management to invest the necessary resources to justify a project or simply due to a lack of understanding by developers of how to justify a software project. Because upwards of eighty-five percent of all large projects fail (Jones, 1996), the implication is that most projects should end at this stage, long before a large investment has been made (and then lost) attempting to build them. The main goal of the Justify stage is to define the best implementation solution for your project, if any, and justify why it is best.

As you can see in Figure 5.1, a key deliverable of this stage is a feasibility study that addresses the economic feasibility (does the project make financial sense?), the technical feasibility (can it actually be built?), and the operational feasibility (can you maintain and support the application?). A feasibility study is important because it drives the development of your project proposal, which is presented to senior management to gain their commitment to the project and to obtain project funding. Furthermore, during the creation of the feasibility study you will often identify risks associated with the project, providing valuable input into your risk assessment.

A feasibility study is a key component of a project proposal, which in turn is used to gain funding and management commitment.

Figure 5.1.
The Justify stage

Many projects tend to skip this stage, either because you are too rushed for time or because competition within your market segment places demands on your organization to create the application. Nevertheless, even if you know that you are going to do the project, it is still worth your while to attempt to justify it. If the project makes sense, then you have the ammunition that you need to argue your case when your project is called into question. If your project does not make sense—in other words, it looks like it is going to fail—then it is a very good indication that you should consider other alternatives (you do not have to automate everything) that may in fact make sense. Regardless, a side benefit of your justification effort is that you may come to the realization that portions of your application do make sense; therefore, you should nurture them to ensure that they succeed.

You should attempt to justify every project, even those that "absolutely must" be done.

DEFINITIONS

economic feasibility An assessment of whether an application or system will pay for itself.

feasibility study A document that addresses three main issues: can the system be built; can you afford to build the system; and once the system is in place, can you maintain and support it? In other words, is the system technically feasible, is it economically feasible, and is it operationally feasible? Feasibility studies are a deliverable of the Justify stage.

operational feasibility An assessment of whether your organization can maintain and support an application or system once it is deployed.

technical feasibility An assessment of whether an application or system can be built with a defined set of tools and technologies.

5.1 Initial Context: Entry Conditions for Justifying the Project

Several important entry conditions should be met before the Justify stage begins:

1. **Requirements document.** You need to have an understanding of the functionality of what will and will not be delivered to the user community to determine whether the project can be built. This implies that the requirements for the application, defined in the Define and Validate Initial Requirements stage (Chapter 3), should at least be well along if not fully documented.
2. **Project documents have been started.** To determine the economic feasibility of an application, you need to compare its expected costs to its expected impact on your organization's net profit. This information, at least the expected costs, is contained in the project plans in the form of schedules and estimates. Because riskier projects should have a higher expected payback to justify taking the risk, you also need to have the initial risk assessment to determine the economic feasibility of your project. The project plan and risk assessment are both deliverables of the Define Initial Management Documents stage described in Chapter 4.
3. **Project infrastructure selection has begun.** The project infrastructure defines the tools, processes, and people that will be used to develop your application. This is key information for determining both the technical and operational feasibility of your project. The project infrastructure is a deliverable of the Define Infrastructure stage of Chapter 6.
4. **Access to key information system (IS) and operations people.** The people who work with technology day-in and day-out are often the best people to talk to when attempting to assess the technical and operational feasibility of a technology to be used in an application.

5.2 Solution: Justifying a Project

As you can see in Figure 5.2, there are three aspects to justifying a project—determining its economic, technical, and operational

> **DEFINITIONS**
>
> **Project infrastructure** The team, tools, and processes that will be used on a given project.
>
> **Requirements document** A document, also called a System Requirements Specification (SRS), that describes the user, technical, and environmental requirements for an application. This document potentially contains the major use cases for the application, detailed use-case scenarios for the application, and traditional requirements for the application as well. Requirements documents are a deliverable of the Initiate phase and are updated regularly during modeling. Requirements documents are also updated during the Maintain and Support phase as bugs and enhancements are identified.

feasibility—and while this is happening, potential project risks are being identified. The main deliverables of this effort are a feasibility study and an updated risk assessment for the project, information that is used to obtain organizational support for the project in the form of funding and internal commitment to the project.

5.2.1 Performing a Feasibility Study

To justify a project, you need to perform a feasibility study that compares the various implementation alternatives based on their economic, technical, and operational feasibility. Based on the results of the study, you make a recommendation to accept one of the alternatives. The steps of creating a feasibility study are:

1. Determine implementation alternatives.
2. Assess the economic feasibility for each alternative.
3. Assess the technical feasibility for each alternative.
4. Assess the operational feasibility for each alternative.
5. Choose an alternative.

5.2.1.1 Determining Implementation Alternatives

The first stage of performing a feasibility study is to identify potential implementation alternatives for your project. Contrary to popular opinion, there are always several options for implementing an application. Potential alternatives include:

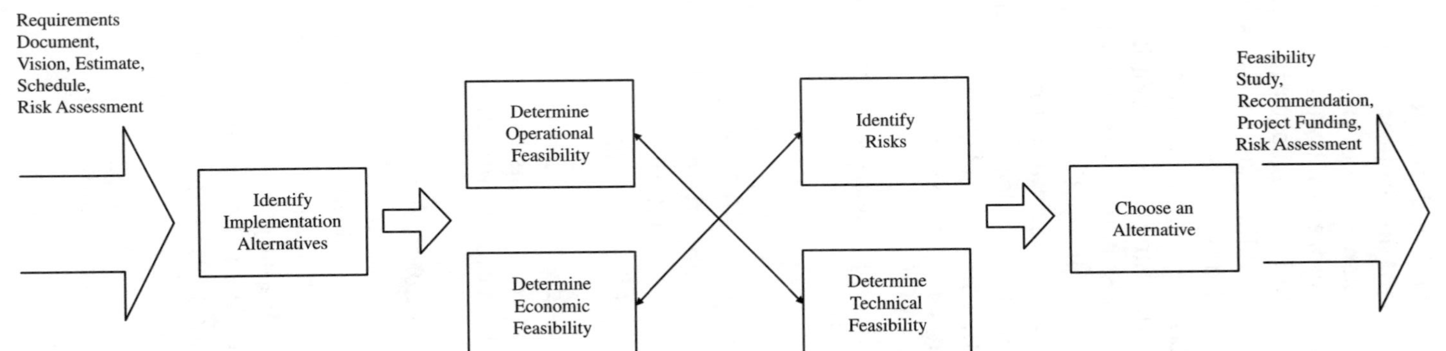

Figure 5.2. The Justify process pattern

1. **Do nothing.** A valid option is to remain with the status quo and not implement an application at all. Remember, you do not have to automate everything.
2. **Build it in one or more languages.** There are many object-oriented implementation languages that you can choose from, including Java, Smalltalk, and C++, among others. Furthermore, you can choose to work with several languages on a single project. For example, many organizations choose to use Java on client machines, because of its portability and ease of distribution, and Smalltalk on application servers due to its high development productivity and proven class libraries.
3. **Build it using one of several technical architectures.** You have several potential technical architectures to choose from (Ambler, 1998) using object technology. You may choose a two-tier client/server (C/S) architecture, taking either a fat-client or thin-client approach; an *n*-tier C/S approach; a distributed objects approach; or a full-fledged mobile objects/agents approach.
4. **Buy a package and integrate.** Perhaps your best alternative is to choose one or more packages developed by a software company that specializes in the problem domain that you are attempting to automate. Excellent packages for human resources, manufacturing, distribution, insurance, and banking exist, to name a few.

The important thing is to identify several viable alternatives for your project so that you may assess and then compare them to select the best one for your organization.

5.2.1.2 Assessing Economic Feasibility

When assessing the economic feasibility of an implementation alternative, the basic question that you are trying to answer is "How well will the application pay for itself?" You do this by performing a cost/benefit analysis, which, as its name suggests, compares the full/real costs of the application to its full/real financial benefits. Strassmann (1997) points out that alternatives should be evaluated on the basis of their contribution to net cash flow (the amount by which the benefits exceed the costs) because the primary objective of all investments is to improve overall organizational performance.

Economic feasibility addresses the question, "How well will the application pay for itself?"

DEFINITIONS

cost/benefit breakpoint The point at which the investment you make in your project is exactly the same as its expected return.

qualitative factor A cost or benefit that is subjective in nature, for which it is very difficult to identify a monetary value.

quantitative factor A cost or benefit for which a monetary value can easily be identified.

Table 5.1 lists some of the potential costs and benefits that may be accrued by a software project. Although the list is not comprehensive, it does provide an indication of the range of factors that you should take into consideration when assessing the economic feasibility of an application. The table includes both qualitative factors (costs or benefits that are subjective in nature) and quantitative factors (costs or benefits for which monetary values can easily be identified). I will discuss the need to take both kinds of factors into account when performing a cost/benefit analysis.

5.2.1.2.1 Quantitative Cost/Benefit Analysis

To perform a quantitative cost/benefit analysis, you need to identify the initial monetary costs of development, the expected monetary costs of operating and supporting the application, and the expected future monetary benefits of using the application. Because these costs and benefits are accrued at different times, some immediately and some in the future, you need to convert the costs to present-day values so that you can compare them fairly.

Present-day value allows you to compare monetary figures from different time periods fairly.

A present-day value is an amount of money into which inflation has been taken into account to determine its value in today's terms. For example, at an inflation rate of five percent per annum (per year) the value of one dollar four years from today is worth seventy-one cents ($\$1/(1.05)^4$) in today's terms. Another way to look at it: if I had seventy-one cents today and invested it at five percent per annum, I would have one dollar four years from now. By converting all figures to their present-day value, you are able to fairly compare them.

It is not enough to look at the net benefit of an alternative, you must also look at its internal rate of return (IRR). The IRR is an indication of the payback of the alternative as a percentage of its cost (Bergeron, 1991). Not only does a system have to pay for

TABLE 5.1. Potential Costs and Benefits of a Software Project

Type	Potential Costs	Potential Benefits
Quantitative	• Hardware/software upgrades • Fully-burdened cost of labor (salary plus benefits) • Support costs for the application • Expected operational costs • Training costs for users to learn the application • Training costs to train developers in new/updated technologies	• Reduced operating costs • Reduced personnel costs from a reduction in staff • Increased revenue from additional sales of your organizations products/services
Qualitative	• Increased employee dissatisfaction from fear of change • Negative public perception from layoffs as the result of automation	• Improved decisions as the result of access to accurate and timely information • Raising of existing, or introduction of a new, barrier to entry within your industry to keep competition out of your market • Positive public perception that your organization is an innovator

itself, it also has to provide a certain level of profitability to make it worthwhile for your organization. IRRs are important because your organization can often invest its money in several projects at any given time; therefore, they want to choose the ones that provide the best payback for their investment (i.e., the ones with the greatest IRRs).

Organizations want to invest their money in software projects that provide the best rate of return.

For example, if alternative A and B both have a net annual benefit of $50,000 in present-day terms, which is a better project? With this information both alternatives appear equal. Knowing that I invested $1,000,000 in alternative A and $100,000 in alternative B, which is the better one now? Alternative B is superior because it has an IRR of fifty percent, whereas alternative A only has an IRR of five percent. Bergeron (1991) points out that IRR is an important economic measure because it allows you to compare investments of different scope and size. Constantine (1995) concurs, stating that the rate of return is the deciding factor in determining whether or not a project should be undertaken.

Internal rates of return allow you to compare projects of different size and scope.

Internal rate of return is also important from a risk management point of view—high-risk alternatives should have a greater IRR than low-risk alternatives. For example, if alternatives C and D both have IRRs of ten percent, which is a better one to undertake? You cannot tell. However, if C has a lower risk than D, then it is the better one, because its risk-to-return ratio is superior. A small minority of organizations have defined desired IRRs for various levels of risk—perhaps low-risk projects must have an IRR of twenty percent, whereas high-risk projects must have an IRR of fifty percent, that must be exceeded in order for a project to be considered feasible. You should look into whether or not your organization has defined expected IRRs, and if it hasn't then you should consider suggesting that it should.

The higher the risk of the project, the greater the IRR it should have in order to justify that risk.

DEFINITIONS

internal rate of return (IRR) The interest rate that equates the cost of an investment to the present value of the respected returns from the investment.

present-day value An amount of money into which inflation has been taken into account to determine its value in today's terms.

5.2.1.2.2 Qualitative Cost/Benefit Analysis

To be able to fairly compare a collection of qualitative factors you need to quantify them, otherwise you will never truly be able to say which alternative is better than another. For example, you could argue all day with another person over whether or not it is better to buy a blue shirt or a pair of red running shoes, and both of you would be right—assuming, of course, that you cannot fairly rate and then compare the two alternatives.

To quantify the qualitative factors of the various alternatives for implementing an application, follow these steps:

1. Determine the qualitative factors.
2. Quantify the importance of each factor to your organization.
3. Rate each alternative for each qualitative factor on a scale of zero to ten.
4. Multiply the importance weighting by the rating for each alternative.
5. Calculate the overall score for each alternative by summing the individual scores.

Figure 5.3 shows a chart that was created to compare the alternatives in a decision to purchase a new type of media player that can be used for either video entertainment or a computer as an information storage device. The organization in question has money to invest in this technology and wants to determine which alternative to take. Notice that there is an alternative called "Status Quo," which is to do nothing and leave the money in the bank. Doing nothing is always a valid option in software development, and considering the high rate of failure in our industry, it apparently is often a very good one to consider.

Figure 5.3. Quantifying qualitative factors

Factor	Weight	Status Quo		Video		Computer	
Information access	15	0	0	0	0	10	150
Stress relief	5	0	0	10	50	2	10
Bragging rights	10	0	0	10	100	7	70
Compatibility	12	0	0	7	84	10	120
Investment potential	10	10	100	0	0	0	0
	Total:		**100**		**234**		**350**

To create this chart, we first identified the qualitative factors associated with the decision. The ability to access the information stored on the type of media, stress relief from the entertainment potential provided by games and/or videos released on the media, the bragging rights of owning interesting new technology, compatibility with the rest of the industry, and the investment potential of the purchase were all considered important factors. We then defined weightings for each factor; the actual numbers are not important, but the ratio between numbers is. For example, investment potential is twice as important than stress relief. Each alternative is given a rating between zero and ten for each qualitative factor, and a score for that alternative/factor combination is calculated by multiplying the weighting with the rating. The scores are then added up for each alternative, showing that the best way to spend this money is to purchase the computer version of the given technology.

The advantage of this approach is that it provides a mechanism for you to rationally compare competing alternatives. The disadvantage, however, as pointed out by Strassmann (1997), is that this approach relies entirely on consensus of subjective opinions. You have to determine a fair set of weights for each factor, then fair ratings for each alternative, ratings that are subjective at best. A good rule of thumb is that if you go back and reevaluate the weightings and/or ratings to obtain a different answer then you have failed.

5.2.1.2.3 Important Factors To Consider

When determining the economic feasibility of an alternative, you may want to take into account several important issues:

1. **Allocate costs fairly.** If your project requires hardware/software upgrades that other applications also need, then you should not have to bear the full cost of the upgrade. You will need to negotiate your portion of the upgrade with senior management.
2. **Allocate benefits fairly.** Many benefits can be achieved through the improvement of business processes without the need for additional automation. Because they still could have been achieved without writing a single line of code you cannot fairly attribute them to your project. The only benefits

that you can claim are those that are the *direct* result of automation (Strassmann, 1997).

3. **Work with developer salaries accurately.** Two fundamental realities of software development make estimating the cost of a software project unique: eighty percent of the cost is developer salaries, and developer salaries grow at a rate greater than inflation. The implication is that although a junior programmer earns $50,000 today, the same position next year may pay $55,000, a ten percent increase, even though the rate of inflation was only two percent. The implication is that the net present value (NPV) of a developer tomorrow is greater than that of one today, something that rarely happens in any other industry.
4. **Look for the benefits first.** Strassmann (1997) advises that you should first look for the benefits of a software project and then determine if you can afford the required IT spending to obtain them. It is an issue of perspective: if you know the benefits first, then you are able to decide quickly whether or not the project even has a chance of making sense; whereas if you start by looking at the costs, you are more likely to buy into the project, therefore more motivated to falsely justify the project, as a result of the planning that you need to do to estimate those costs. The short story is that if the project offers very little in the way of benefits, you can stop it right there.

Investing without verifiable benefits is gambling, not managing.* —*Paul A. Strassmann

5.2.1.3 Assessing Technical Feasibility

In addition to economic feasibility, you need to determine the technical feasibility of each implementation alternative. The basic question that you are trying to answer is, "Is it possible to build this application?" To do this you must investigate the technologies to be used on the project. Some of them will be defined by the tool selection process performed in the Define Infrastructure stage (Chapter 6), as well as an assessment of whether or not they will work together. Note that the technological assessments made during this stage will be used as input into the Define Infrastructure stage as factors into decisions pertaining to tools, standards, and guidelines. Remember, the stages of the Initiate phase are performed in an iterative manner.

The problem with technology is that everything works perfectly on marketing slides, but when you get the technology in house, it is often a very different story. As a result, alternatives for each technology, if any, should be identified. Note that to do a reasonable assessment, you may need to do a mini-project and build a proof-of-concept (technical) prototype that verifies that the technologies work together (see Chapter 8 for details). This effort may take several weeks or months but will pay for itself because it verifies how well your technology choices work.

For each technology alternative that you assess, you should

War Story

Relying on New Releases of Technology Is Highly Risky

I once worked on a project where everything was in beta release: the CASE tool, the development environment, the operating system, and the persistence mechanism (an object/relational database). We chose to work with beta copies of these technologies because their expected release dates were long before the expected release date for our project and we wanted to ensure that we had the most up-to-date technology for our project. We were also working closely with all but one vendor, the one for the operating system, but were not worried about that because the current release of the operating system was acceptable to our user community if we had to fall back to it. We scheduled extra time for unanticipated problems with the technology (you always run into bugs), and felt that we had properly mitigated the associated risk of using unproved software.

Were we ever wrong. Except for the operating system, which was completely out of our control anyway, nothing worked. Once the models reached a given size, the CASE tool randomly erased documentation (unbeknownst to the modelers). The development environment introduced bugs into the application as part of the packaging (compilation) process and the database had problems reading and writing data. Any one of these problems would have been bad, but at least manageable; all of them together were devastating. By relying on unproven technology that was still in beta, and without producing proof-of-concept prototypes for them (see Chapter 8), we had put the project at risk of failure. The end result was that we were extremely overbudget and almost a year late when we finally recovered from our mistake.

document the advantages and disadvantages of it, even if you are not going to use it on your project. This way you will not be second-guessed at some point in the future, and other projects can reuse your work so that they do not reevaluate the same technology again. Because technologies evolve quickly, you should document what needs to occur for a technology to be reconsidered at a later date. For example, a database may fail your technical assessment because the current version does not scale large enough for your organization, but you might indicate that if it was able to process 5,000 transactions per minute (or more) then it should be looked at again.

Table 5.2 describes two basic categories of issues that should be addressed by a technical assessment. The first category addresses hard-core technology issues, such as the scalability of the technology, while the second category addresses market issues with the technology, such as the viability of the vendor. Both categories are important to assess the technical feasibility of a project adequately.

TABLE 5.2. Issues That Should Be Addressed when Assessing a Technology

Technology Issues	Market Issues
• Performance • Ease of learning • Ease of deployment • Ease of support • Operational characteristics (in other words, can it run seven days a week, twenty-four hours a day?) • Interoperability with your other key technologies • Scalability	• Vendor viability (in other words, is it likely that they will be in business in two years? In five?) • Alternate sources for the technology, if any • Third-party support for related products and services • Level of support provided by the vendor • Industry mindshare of the product (in other words, is the market gravitating toward or away from this technology?)

TIP

Beware Technical Solutions to Management Problems

There is no point picking the latest technologies if the problem is curable by changing management practices (Strassmann, 1997). This is related to the fact that you shouldn't attribute all of the benefits associated with changing a business process to the software project that supports those changes; if you can still achieve the benefit without new software or hardware, then it is not a valid benefit of your software project.

A common mistake within the information industry, one that is constantly being repeated, is the identification of a technical solution to a non-technical problem. This occurs often enough to rate its own antipattern (Brown, Malveau, McCormick, Mowbray, 1998) called *Apply Technical Solution to Non-Technical Problem*. The lesson to be learned is that technical solutions are only appropriate when used to solve technical problems. For example, at the time of this writing the concept of a "Network Computer" is a hot fad in the computer industry. The basic idea is that by replacing personal computers with network computers, organizations can dramatically reduce their cost for supporting computer hardware and software. Studies have shown that the average annual cost of supporting a personal computer is somewhere between $5,000 and $30,000, depending on the study, once you include the costs of training and support for those PCs. Network computers, also called Java terminals because some only run programs that have been packaged as Java bytecode, will theoretically reduce these costs because of their simplicity to maintain and to support. For all the hype surrounding network computers, the fact is that to date they have sold very poorly and probably will for some time. On the surface the problem that network computers attempt to address looks like a technical one, but when you think about it the problem is really a management one. The reason why some organizations experience a $30,000 a year support cost is not because of personal computers; rather, it is because of their misuse of personal computers! By letting users choose and install their own software, instead of having a common configuration installed by a qualified information professional, the cost to the organization skyrockets when users run into difficulties. There is also the issue of incompatible file formats—without a common software suite, users waste time converting files back and forth between different versions of software from the same vendor or between software from different vendors. Hardware support becomes more difficult when users are purchasing their own equipment for similar reasons, and training and support becomes chaotic at best. The real issue is one of management, not technology.

5.2.1.4 *Assessing Operational Feasibility*

Just because you can build an application does not mean that you can keep it running.

Not only must an application make economic and technical sense, it must also make operational sense. The basic question that you are trying to answer is, "Is it possible to maintain and support this application once it is in production?" Building an application is decidedly different from operating it; therefore, you need to determine whether or not you can effectively operate and support it.

Very often you will need to improve the existing operations, maintenance, and support infrastructure to support the operation of the new application that you intend to develop. To determine what the impact will be, you will need to understand both the current operations and support infrastructure of your organization and the operations and support characteristics of your new application. If the existing operations and support infrastructure can handle your application, albeit with the appropriate training of the affected staff, then your project is operationally feasible. However, you may determine that you need to modify the existing operations and support process to make your application operationally feasible—something that you will need to take into account during the Define Infrastructure stage (Chapter 6).

5.2.1.5 *Choosing an Alternative*

Once you have assessed the economic, technical, and operational feasibility of each implementation alternative, you need to choose one. Remember, the goal of a feasibility study is to compare and contrast the various implementation alternatives *and* to suggest

Table 5.3. Issues to Consider when Determining the Operational Feasibility of a Project

Operations Issues	Support Issues
• What tools are needed to support operations? • What skills will operators need to be trained in? • What processes need to be created and/or updated? • What documentation does operations need?	• What documentation will users be given? • What training will users be given? • How will change requests be managed?

the best one. To do this, the first step is to remove any alternative that is not economically, technically, or operationally feasible. This might mean that you have no alternatives left; even doing nothing might not be feasible, which implies that you need to go back and identify more alternatives. If you have one alternative remaining, then your decision is easy, but if you have more than one alternative remaining, you have to choose the best one based on the values of your organization. You may also choose to simply identify the viable alternatives and leave it to senior management to make the decision.

5.2.2 Identifying Risks

During the Justify stage you will identify and define many potential risks while determining the technical and operational feasibility of your project. It is critical that they are added to your risk assessment document so that they may be dealt with appropriately during the project. Although risk management is a task that is applicable to all project phases and stages, the creation of a risk assessment document is addressed by the Define Initial Management Documents stage in Chapter 4.

DEFINITION

risk assessment A document indicating potential factors, called risks, that would harm the project if they were to occur. A risk assessment is used to identify risks so that they may be dealt with appropriately. Risk assessments are a deliverable of the Initiate phase and are updated regularly throughout a project.

Here are some of the potential risks that you may identify:

- The use of unproven (new and/or beta) technology on the project.
- Waiting for vaporware (software products that have been promised but not yet released).
- Inexperience of your organization with a given technology or process.
- Nobody else having attempted a project of this size with the given technology.
- The use of several unfamiliar technologies or processes.
- Potential inability to support and operate the application once in production.

5.3 Solution: Project Tasks

In this section I will discuss project task issues pertinent to the Justify stage.

5.3.1 *Managing the Justify Stage*

The Justify stage is reasonably straightforward: you determine the feasibility of your project and then, if appropriate, obtain support for it. As a result, the management issues for this stage are also reasonably straightforward. The main issue with managing the Justify stage is to ensure that the right people are involved with the assessment processes. Get people that understand the fundamentals of finance and development to determine the economic feasibility of the project. Get people that understand the proposed technologies to work the technical feasibility. Get people that understand your operations and support teams to determine the operational feasibility. In other words, get skilled people.

Get the right people.

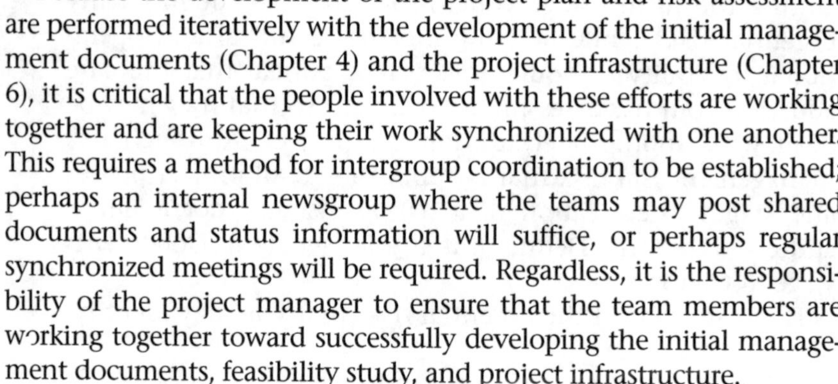

Because the development of the project plan and risk assessment are performed iteratively with the development of the initial management documents (Chapter 4) and the project infrastructure (Chapter 6), it is critical that the people involved with these efforts are working together and are keeping their work synchronized with one another. This requires a method for intergroup coordination to be established; perhaps an internal newsgroup where the teams may post shared documents and status information will suffice, or perhaps regular synchronized meetings will be required. Regardless, it is the responsibility of the project manager to ensure that the team members are working together toward successfully developing the initial management documents, feasibility study, and project infrastructure.

5.3.2 *Training and Education*

The skills needed to justify a project are often not taught to information professionals while they are in school. As a result, many technical people often do not have the fundamental skills needed to create a feasibility study, if they even know what one is. Most information professionals have the basic skills to perform technical and operational assessments; however, financial assessments are a different matter. The best way to gain these skills is to take a college-level management accounting course that covers how to perform a cost/benefit analysis, the major component of an economic feasibility assessment.

5.3.3 *Quality Assurance*

If possible, you should review the technical feasibility assessment of your feasibility study with other technical staff who have worked with similar technology on similar projects before. You should also do the same with the operational feasibility assessment, naturally working with operations and support personnel, and if you are not sure about the economic feasibility, then review it with a management accountant who has experience performing cost/benefit analyses.

Review the feasibility study.

You will find it hard to get an unrealistic economic feasibility assessment past senior management; many of them will understand the basics of finance, but because few have a technical or operations background, they will not have the ability to determine the quality of these portions of your feasibility study. The implication is that you'd better get these portions right, otherwise your project risks being accepted when it really shouldn't be. Although this often sounds like a good idea, when you need to actually deliver a working, operational application you may change your mind.

Senior management usually does not have the background to fully understand your technical assessment. Therefore you'd better get it right.

5.3.4 Potential Risks While Justifying the Project

Several potential risks should be managed during the Justify stage:

1. **Politics.** Your project can make total sense, yet still not be accepted by senior management for political instead of logical reasons. A good project manager will be cognizant of the political landscape and present the feasibility study appropriately.
2. **Skipping the stage.** Many projects are started with very little justification at all. Perhaps it is completely obvious to everyone involved that the project should go ahead, but the effort of performing a feasibility study will provide benefit in that you are forced to consider several implementation alternatives for the project. One of two things will happen: either you will determine a better way to implement your project, or you will prove that the way you initially intended to take was in fact the best alternative.
3. **Not looking at all three aspects of feasibility.** The need to prove economic feasibility will be a requirement of senior management to obtain funding, and technical feasibility is something that technical people will do naturally. Operational feasibility, however, is often forgotten in the rush to get the project started, often because operations and support

DEFINITIONS

artifact reuse The reuse of previously created development artifacts: use cases, standards documents, domain-specific models, procedures and guidelines, and other applications.

template reuse The reuse of a common set of layouts for key development artifacts documents, models, and source code—within your organization.

people are typically involved in a project just before its release, not at its initiation.

4. **Unqualified people perform the assessment.** Management is putting their trust in you, believing that your assessment is fair and accurate. This means that you need to staff this effort with people who will do a fair and accurate job; otherwise, you put your project at risk.

5.3.5 Opportunities for Reuse

There are two opportunities for artifact reuse at this stage. First, the information gathered about various technologies can be reused by other projects considering them for use. Second, the information gathered about the existing operations and support environment can be reused by other teams when they are performing operations feasibility assessments. Template reuse can also be achieved through the development of a documentation template for your feasibility study.

5.3.6 Metrics

There is one key metric to be taken during the Justify stage, that of the cost/benefit breakpoint. This is a measure, calculated when determining the economic feasibility of your project, of the point at which the investment you make in your project is exactly the same as the expected return provided by it. This is an important metric because it indicates the point at which it is no longer advisable to continue your project—information that enables you to make an intelligent decision later in the project of whether your organization should continue the project if its costs appear as if they are increasing or if the expected return appears to be decreasing.

5.4 Resulting Context: Exit Conditions for Justifying the Project

You have finished the Justify stage when:

1. **A feasible implementation alternative has been selected.** This is why you perform a feasibility study in the first place: to identify an approach to your project that will actually work.
2. **The project risk assessment has been started.** If the risk assessment had not already been started before the Justify stage began, then it certainly should be by now. During the assessment process you are guaranteed to identify technical and operational risks (there are always risks with software projects) and you should record them so that they can be dealt with appropriately.

5.5 Secrets of Success

The following pointers should help to improve your efforts for justifying your project:

1. **Actually do it.** This should not have to be said, but...
2. **Document your assumptions.** If you make any assumptions during the feasibility study, then document them because this is important information that senior management needs to judge the validity of your work. If an alternative hinges on the database from a given vendor to be used consistently on all database servers, then management needs to know this; perhaps they are considering changing vendors.
3. **Obtain management support for the justification process.** Senior management has to believe that it is a good investment for them to have you perform a feasibility study. The easiest way is to refer to previous projects that ran into problems that may have been avoided if they had attempted to justify their project first.

5.6 Process Checklist

The following process checklist can be used to verify that you have completed the Justify stage.

JUSTIFY STAGE PROCESS CHECKLIST

Fulfillment of Entrance Conditions:

✔ Development of the requirements document has begun.
✔ Development of the project plan has begun.
✔ Development of the initial risk assessment has begun.
✔ Selection/definition of the project infrastructure has begun.
✔ Access to key users, technical experts, and financial experts has been obtained.

Processes Performed:

✔ Several implementation alternatives were identified and considered.
✔ The economic feasibility of each alternative was determined.
✔ A cost/benefit analysis was performed.
✔ The technical feasibility of each alternative was determined.
✔ The operational feasibility of each alternative was determined.
✔ An alternative was suggested to senior management for approval.
✔ Artifacts that are potentially reusable by your project team during this stage have been identified and used where appropriate.
✔ Your risk assessment document has been updated where appropriate.
✔ Decisions made, and decisions forgone, have been documented in your group memory.
✔ Metrics have been collected.

Fulfillment of Exit Conditions:

✔ A feasible implementation alternative has been accepted by senior management.

✔ The initial risk assessment has updated.

5.7 What You Have Learned in This Chapter

When upwards of eighty-five percent of all large projects fail (Jones, 1996), doesn't it make sense to invest the time to determine whether or not a new project even has a chance of succeeding? In this chapter you saw that performing a feasibility study that looks at the economic, technical, and operational feasibility of a project is an effective way not only to determine whether a project makes sense, but also to identify the best implementation alternative for it. Given a fair and accurate feasibility assessment, you will find it that much easier to obtain the funding that you need for your project.

5.8 References and Recommended Reading

Ambler, S. W. 1998. *Building Object Applications That Work—Your Step-by-Step Handbook for Developing Robust Systems with Object Technology*. New York: SIGS Books/Cambridge University Press.

Bergeron, P. G. 1991. *Finance for Non-Financial Managers: The Quickest Way to the Bottom Line*. Scarborough, Ontario: Nelson Canada.

Brown, W., Malveau, R., McCormick, H., Mowbray, T. 1998. *Anti-Patterns: Refactoring Software, Architectures, and Projects in Crisis*. New York: John Wiley & Sons.

Boehm, B. W. 1981. *Software Engineering Economics*. Upper Saddle River, New Jersey: Prentice-Hall, Inc.

Constantine, L. L. 1995. *Constantine on Peopleware*. Englewood Cliffs, New Jersey: Yourdon Press.

Jones, C. 1996. *Patterns of Software Systems Failure and Success*. Boston, Massachusetts: International Thomson Computer Press.

Strassmann, P. A. 1997. *The Squandered Computer: Evaluating the Business Alignment of Information Technologies*. New Canaan, Connecticut: The Information Economics Press.

Chapter 6

The Define Infrastructure Stage

FOR a project to be successful, you need to define a firm foundation: a project infrastructure. The project infrastructure is made up of the project team, the tools that they will use, and a tailored version of your organization's software process that the team will follow. To define the project infrastructure you begin with what you already have—existing staff, existing tools, existing standards and guidelines, your standard software process—to select the most appropriate combination from your internal resources and then, if necessary, look outside for further resources. Many organizations refer to their processes, standards, guidelines, and tools as infrastructure artifacts.

Defining the project infrastructure before construction begins increases the probability of project success by choosing the appropriate people, tools, and processes.

As you can see in Figure 6.1, the key deliverables of this stage include a definition of the team members and their roles and responsibilities on the project, a description of the development toolset, a group memory where you record what you have accomplished and lessons learned, and a tailored software process that the project team will follow. The definition of your project infrastructure needs to be done as early in the project as possible so that construction can get underway. If you are starting your first object-oriented (OO) project, at least your first large OO project, you often will not have the experience needed to initially define the

SCOTT'S SOAPBOX

Doesn't Play Well with Other Children

A key issue/force that you will need to address with this stage is a general lack of support among developers for processes, standards, guidelines, and common tools: most developers prefer to do things their own way, suggesting the existence of a "Doesn't Play Well with Other Children" antipattern. The solution to this antipattern is of course the education and mentoring of developers who don't support your project/organization's infrastructure, the definition of which I will concentrate on in this chapter.

complete infrastructure needed for your projects. This is why this stage overlaps into construction: you will learn from experience what you're missing from your project infrastructure. In many ways this stage helps to define how the development team will interact internally with themselves and externally with their users.

Your first OO projects will need to spend significant effort defining the infrastructure for your organization, with subsequent projects benefiting from these efforts.

The first several large-scale projects will expend significant effort to define their project infrastructures because they have little to reuse from previous projects. In other words, your initial projects have the additional burden of defining the majority of the object-oriented infrastructure for your organization. This means that you need to plan for additional research into tools and processes, potentially bringing in consultants experienced in large-scale OO development to aid you in this process.

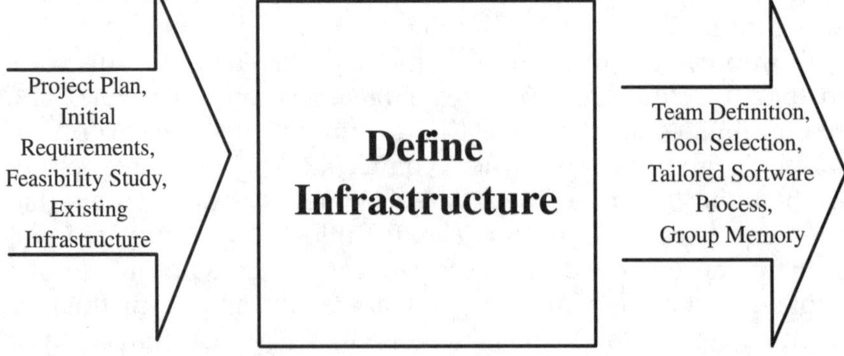

Figure 6.1. The Define Infrastructure stage

War Story

Use Qualified People to Define Your Infrastructure

I once worked with a large software organization, one that had several hundred developers, that invested the time and money to define a sophisticated project infrastructure. Unfortunately, they did it with people who had never been involved in an OO project. These people, who were actually quite good at structured development, did not have the necessary background to determine the needs of an OO project. The short story is that they made some very basic mistakes in the infrastructure that they put in place. They assumed that because class diagrams looked like data diagrams with methods, and that because their data modelers already had experience at modeling large scale databases, that their data modelers should be the ones to define the modeling process. This resulted in a data-centric view of the world that had very little to do with objects, using an enterprise data model as the basis for their modeling efforts (in Chapter 8 I'll discuss an OO modeling process that does work). Realizing that objects have both data and functionality, they decided that they also needed an enterprise process model to model the functionality. Yes, they basically took their existing structured modeling process and tried to force fit it for OO development. This mistake in turn affected their tool selection, choosing a structured CASE tool and a fourth generation language (4GL) instead of an OO CASE tool and OO language. Their standards and procedures for development and testing were in turn affected by this, which in turn negatively affected their overall management process.

Not realizing the infrastructure mistakes that they had made, their first several OO projects, at least what they mistakenly thought were OO, were "challenged." Realizing that something was wrong, they brought in an OO consulting company, one that specialized in OO and that had a proven software process, to help them out. One of the tasks given to the OO consultants, of which I was one, was to choose the appropriate tools and to define the processes that would take their organization into the future. They learned the hard way that the best people to define infrastructure are those who understand and have experience with what is being defined.

DEFINITIONS

group memory A record of what your project team accomplished, decisions made by your team and the reasoning behind them, deferred decisions, and the lessons learned on your project. A group memory provides a mechanism to record this information when it is first recognized so that it is not lost.

guideline A description, ideally with an example provided, of how something should be done. It is recommended, but not required, that you follow guidelines (unlike standards, which are mandatory).

infrastructure artifact An item, such as your organization's software process, a standard, a guideline, or a chosen tool that is common between project teams to build applications to support your organization.

project infrastructure The team, tools, and processes that will be used on a given project.

standard A description, ideally with an example provided, of how something must be done. It is required that you follow standards (unlike guidelines, which are optional).

tailored software process A software process that has been modified to meet the needs of a specific project.

team definition A document describing who will be involved with a project, what their roles on the project will be, and when they will be involved. This document should also provide a reporting structure, or organization chart, for the team.

6.1 Initial Context: Entry Conditions for Defining the Project Infrastructure

There are several important entry conditions that should be met before the Define Infrastructure stage begins:

1. **The initial project requirements have been (partially) defined.** To define the tools to be used on a project, you need to know the technical requirements, such as the hardware platform your application will be deployed on and the persistence mechanism to be used, to which the project must conform. Other requirements, such as regulatory ones, will also affect your choice of deliverables, standards, and guidelines.
2. **The project plan has been started.** You need to understand the scope of the project and the proposed project schedule

DEFINITIONS

feasibility study A document that addresses three main issues: can the system be built, can you afford to build the system, and once the system is in place can you maintain and support it? In other words, is the system technically feasible, is it economically feasible, and is it operationally feasible? Feasibility studies are a deliverable of the Justify stage?

project plan A project plan is a collection of several project management deliverables, including but not limited to a project overview, a project schedule, a project estimate, a team definition, and a risk assessment. Project plans are a deliverable of the Initiate phase and are updated regularly throughout a project.

project schedule A project schedule indicates what will be done, when things will be done, and who will do them. A major component of a project schedule is a Gantt chart with its corresponding descriptions of tasks and resources. Project schedules are a deliverable of the Initiate phase and are updated regularly throughout a project.

project scope A definition of the functionality that will, and will not, be implemented by an application.

(what is to be delivered in what amount of time) to determine who should be on the team and when they should be on it.

3. **The existing infrastructure, if any, is available.** When defining the infrastructure for a project, the first thing you should do is to attempt to reuse as much of the existing infrastructure as possible. Your organization may have applicable standards and guidelines in place, or perhaps ones exist in the industry already. Your organization may already have chosen a standard set of development tools, or may have a preferred subcontractor or personnel agency from which it hires developers. If you aren't sure what exists within your organization, then try to identify people who have been involved with other OO projects and determine what their infrastructure was.

Do not reinvent the infrastructure wheel; instead, reuse it.

4. **The feasibility study has been started.** The majority of the work for defining the project infrastructure should wait until the feasibility study is well underway, and ideally until the project has been justified and approved by management. Note that it is likely during the development of the feasibility study (a deliverable of the Justify stage, described in Chapter 5) that you will need to provide information pertaining to the existing infrastructure, if any, available to your project. This

implies that you will need to perform initial research into tools and techniques available in the industry as input into determining the technical and operational feasibility of your project.

6.2 Solution: Defining the Project Infrastructure

As you can see in Figure 6.2, the definition of your project infrastructure is an iterative process that involves tailoring your existing organizational software process to meet the specific needs of your project, the definition of your project team, the creation of a group memory, and the selection of the tools that you will use on your project. Process tailoring is comprised of three parts: the definition and/or selection of procedures and methodologies, the definition and/or selection of the standards and guidelines that you will follow, and the negotiation of the deliverables that your project will produce.

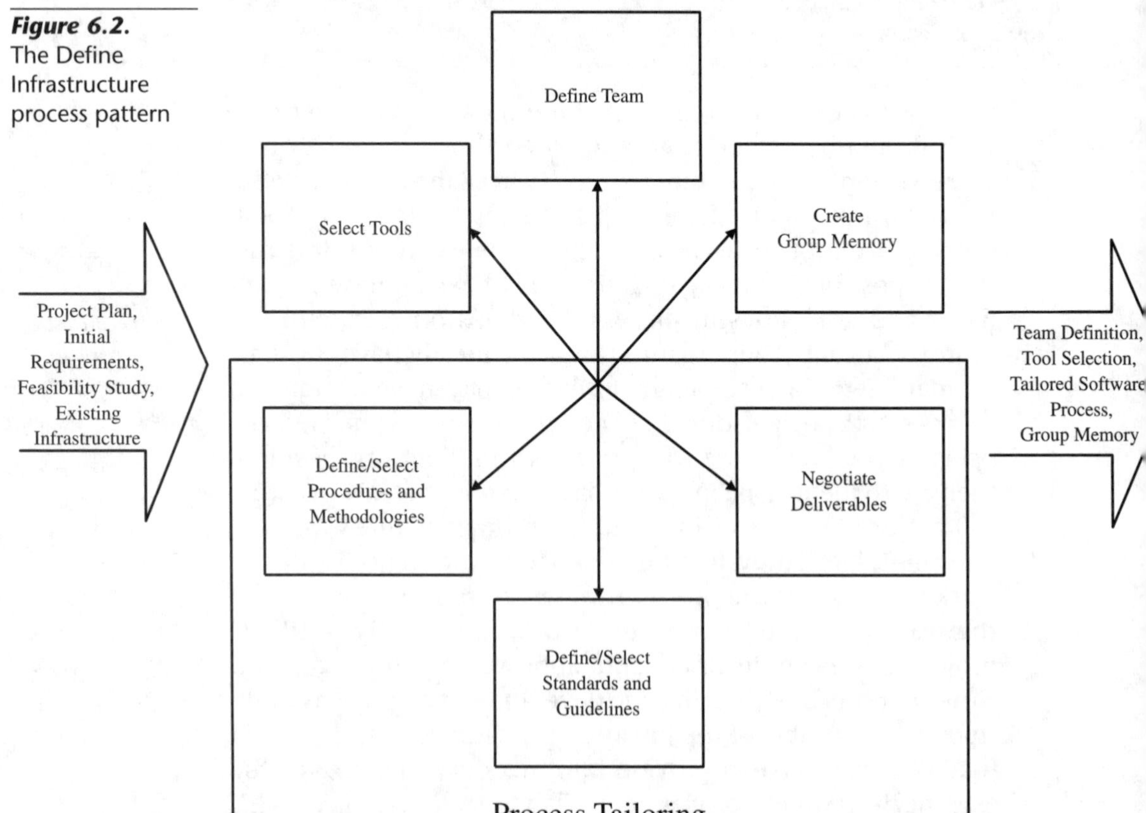

Figure 6.2. The Define Infrastructure process pattern

6.2.1 Defining the Project Team

It is critical that you define who will be on your development team, their roles and responsibilities, and when they will join and leave the team. It is important that you include both developers and key users, the subject matter experts, in your team definition because both of these groups are actively involved in the development of applications. The Domain Expertise in Roles (Coplien, 1995) organizational pattern suggests that you should hire domain experts with proven track records because local gurus are good, in all areas from business to technical expertise. Coplien correctly points out that any given person may fill several roles on a team, or that any given role may be filled by several people.

Project teams include both developers and subject matter experts.

A skills assessment of each potential team member should be performed before the project begins to help determine whether or not they should be on your team. A skills assessment is useful because it provides input into the potential role on your team that the person may take, and it is used to develop a training plan so that everyone can receive the training that they need to be productive team members. Note that a skills assessment and training plan should have been created for anybody transferring from an existing project (skills assessments are part of the Assess stage, covered in *More Process Patterns* [Ambler, 1998b]).

Skills assessments provide valuable input for choosing team members and developing training plans.

Your project schedule is the main input for defining the structure of your team, which in turn is a major input into the definition of your schedule. What your project needs to accomplish will help guide you in defining the positions that will need to be filled, and the people that you choose to fill those positions will help to determine the project schedule. Team and schedule definition are a

DEFINITIONS

organizational pattern A pattern that describes a common management technique or a structure appropriate to a software organization.

skills assessment (deliverable) A summary of the proficiencies of an individual, used for the purpose of developing a training plan for the individual and for identifying projects where their skills are needed.

skills assessment (process) A process in which the skills—both technical skills, such as C++ programming, and people skills, such as eliciting requirements from users—of an individual are determined/measured.

highly coupled, iterative process. Scheduling is part of the Define Initial Management Documents stage, covered in Chapter 4.

6.2.1.1 Organizing The Project Team

A team is more than just a group of people; it is a group of people who each have roles and responsibilities that come together to meet the overall goals of your project. Harrison's (1996) Unity of Purpose organizational pattern underscores the need for the leader of a team to instill a common vision for the project in all team members. Harrison suggests that you can do so by discussing as a group what the software is supposed to do, who the customer is, and how the software will help them. It is important that all team members be given the opportunity to express their views to help build rapport within the team.

DEFINITION

exit date The date that a person leaves, or is scheduled to leave, a project.

Teams have reporting structures and reporting procedures, and these will need to be defined for your team. Furthermore, a schedule for when people will join your team (you do not need everybody at once) and when they will leave your team needs to be defined.

Whenever possible you should take into account the career aspirations of your team members when defining their roles and responsibilities. Sometimes the best person for a position is one who can grow into the role; this provides them with an opportunity to learn new skills, increasing the chance that they will remain with your organization. This approach is enhanced by having an experienced person on your team mentor the less experienced person.

Try to grow people into a position.

TIP

Do Not Tie Exit Dates To The Calendar

An exit date, the date that a person leaves a project, should be tied to the successful delivery of a major project deliverable, not to a specific date. The reality of software development is that schedules often slip, and that means that you will need key members of your team longer than originally planned. It is wise to plan for some breathing space after your project has been delivered in case something goes wrong and your team needs to make "emergency repairs." Therefore you should negotiate exit dates that occur a month or so after a given deliverable.

6.2.1.2 Developing a Project Skills Matrix

One technique for determining who should be on a development team, and what roles and responsibilities they should hold, is to develop a project skills matrix (Raynor, 1995). To develop a project skills matrix, you list the skills needed on the project—technical skills, management skills, problem domain skills, and so on—down the vertical axis and all (potential) team members along the horizontal axis. You then rate each person on each skill, rating them as expert, skilled, familiar, or unskilled. You should then reorder the skills and people, putting the most important/critical skills to the top of the list and the most likely people to be on the team on the left-hand side of the matrix, making it easier for you to see who the key people are. You should consider distributing the matrix and/or reviewing it with others to get a second opinion, and maybe even having each person rate themselves on each skill to compare with your rating.

A project skills matrix is a working project deliverable; you will not submit it to your users, but you will use it internally to help manage your project. You should consider developing a skills database so you can reuse your ratings within and between projects, decreasing the effort it takes to develop a skills matrix, you simply pull the information out of the skills database and review it for accuracy. This also decreases the effort to reevaluate team members during the Assess stage (Ambler, 1998b) at the end of the project.

It is important to understand that a project skills matrix will not provide all of the information that you need to develop your team. First, it doesn't take into account the availability of people; someone might be ideal for one aspect of your project but not available when you actually need them. Second, it doesn't indicate whether or not the people will work together well. For example, Jim and Catherine might both be excellent candidates for

Skills matrices are useful, but they are only part of the picture.

DEFINITIONS

project skills matrix A chart that relates the skills needed on a project to the skills of the people (potentially) on a project team.

skills database A database which records the skills and experiences of people within your organization. This information is both the input and the output of a skills assessment.

your project, but because they'll fight like cats and dogs, you shouldn't have both of them on the same project.

6.2.1.3 Managing Subcontractors

Very often you will find that you are unable to fully staff a project with internal resources. This is due either to a shortage of people with the requisite skills (this is often called a skills shortage) or simply to a shortage of people. Either way, you need to subcontract all or a portion of your project to an external vendor. There are four basic steps to the subcontracting process (Software Engineering Institute, 1995):

1. **Select a subcontractor.** The first thing that you need to do is identify one or more subcontractors who can meet your requirements. Your organization may have a formal search process that involves sending out requests for proposals to a list of "approved" subcontractors, or it may have no process whatsoever, requiring you to do all the footwork yourself. Regardless, there are several things that you should be looking for in a subcontractor. First, they should actually have relevant experience and expertise in what you're trying to accomplish. Second, they should have a software process in place that they understand and follow—a process is more than a collection of binders that sit on a shelf gathering dust. If they do not have a process, then they're hacking—so why pay a premium price for low-quality work? Third, they should be able to provide relevant references of successful and not-so-successful accounts that are similar to your own. Yes, it is nice to hear good things about the subcontractor, but because nobody's perfect I also want to find out where they've made mistakes in the past and how they rectified them. If a subcontractor is unable to be honest with you up front, then you shouldn't be doing business with them.
2. **Define the commitments.** The work that your subcontractor is doing is effectively a miniature project; therefore, there should be a project plan that defines the scope, estimate, and schedule for their work. Furthermore, to maintain control of the subcontractor, you need to define how and when you will communicate. You also need to come to a mutual agreement as to what each side will deliver to the other—they are pro-

War Story

Subcontracting to India

Several years ago I was providing advice to a client who had just embarked on their first large-scale OO project. Trying to reduce the cost of their project, they decided to outsource a significant portion of the programming work, to be done in Smalltalk, to a subcontractor in India. At first this looked to be a viable option; Indian Smalltalk programmers were being billed out at $10 an hour, compared to $100 an hour or more for U.S. Smalltalk programmers. The interesting thing, something that I certainly did not predict, was that the deal eventually fell apart because it was not economically viable. The Indian firm rightfully demanded that my client perform all of the requirements definition and the bulk of the modeling to define adequate specifications. The problem is that with object-oriented development, the bulk of the effort is in requirements definition and modeling (see Chapters 7 through 11 for a description of the Construct phase); therefore, there was not much work to outsource. By the time the management overhead was included in the plan, there was very little economic reason to justify the risk of subcontracting the programming to a third party.

ducing something for you, but at the same time they need to have your requirements for what they are building and a definition of your technical environment and processes so that their work will fit into what you're doing. You will increase your project's chance of success by defining the commitments for both your organization and the subcontractor.

3. **Maintain ongoing, regular communications.** You need to manage the subcontractor, and the way that you do this is by maintaining contact with them. Demand regular, at least weekly, status reports from them that describe what they have accomplished to date, what is still in progress, and what has not been started yet. These figures should be measured in work days or work weeks, something that you can convert into money. Do not accept percentages as a unit of measure—a project can be ninety percent done for months or even years.

   Do not get caught waiting for some mythical deliverable several months in the future; instead, actively manage the subcontractor through status reports and inspections of work

TIP

Watch Out for Subcontractor Tricks

As an independent contractor who works with larger consulting firms that specialize in object-oriented development, I am regularly involved in the bidding process for new contracts. The following list describes some tricks that I've seen pulled by other consulting firms (because I have a low tolerance for dishonesty, and am in a position where I can be choosy about the work I do, I strictly work with ethical organizations) during the contract negotiation process:

1. **Bait-and-switch tactics.** With this trick a very good, or at least very presentable, negotiator works closely with senior management to secure the contract. Once the contract is in place, the project is staffed with one or two good people managing and directing a large group of significantly less experienced developers. There's nothing wrong with this approach as long as you know that it is being done and are being charged accordingly. I have seen companies unknowingly pay $125 an hour for programmers who had graduated from college only six months earlier. To avoid this problem, define the various positions to be held by the subcontractors and a sliding pay scale based on experience. Also, ensure accurate assessments of all staff by interviewing subcontractor personnel.
2. **Off-site development.** One way that subcontractors get away with a bait-and-switch approach is by doing all of the work at their own site, usually under the guise of reducing the expense to you. Typically what happens is they're hiding what they're doing, using inexperienced developers without your knowledge, knowing that you probably aren't going to find out about it. Off-site development works well as long as you have some of your own people at their site and/or perform regular inspections of the subcontractor. An alternative is to interview and accept or reject the people that the subcontractor will use on your project.
3. **Accounting firms who do development.** You should hire companies for their expertise. Accounting firms should be used when you need accountants, legal firms should be used when you need lawyers, and software development firms should be used when you need developers.
4. **Magical claims.** Beware of subcontractors who claim that their process or toolset can dramatically reduce the need for fundamental parts of the software process. Claims of a reduced need for testing often indicate that the subcontractor doesn't understand the testing process, not that they are experts at it. Claims of a reduced need for requirements definition, modeling, or an understanding of the technical domain should also be regarded with similar skepticism. Demand to see proof of their claims from their existing clients.

5. **Low-balling the estimate.** In the software industry, the lowest estimate usually ends up costing the most. Whenever you see a low estimate in comparison to others, one of several things has likely happened:

   - The subcontractor is not very good at estimating and has made an honest mistake.
   - The subcontractor intends to reduce the quality of what they will deliver (see Chapter 4 for a detailed discussion of estimating).
   - The subcontractor has knowingly produced a low initial estimate, knowing that when you realize that the project will take longer than originally estimated, it will be too late and that you will be forced to renegotiate the contract to finish the work.
   - The subcontractor is desperate for work.
   - The subcontractor truly is superior to the other bidders. If this is true, then they can provide you with several reference accounts that can attest to this fact.

   The best way to deal with low-ballers is to insist on fixed-price contracts.

6. **Relying on their company name.** I'm often amazed that organizations will hire a subcontractor simply because of their name. The name Kirk, Picard & Janeway may sound impressive, but are they any good? Just because you have heard of them, that doesn't mean that they're good at developing software; it just means that they're good at marketing. This is the equivalent of paying $250 instead of $40 for a pair of jeans because of the label on them. Are you looking for a good subcontractor or a fashionable contractor? The real issues are whether the subcontractor has a process with a proven track record of success and can provide you with an experienced team that knows and follows it.

7. **Increasing your dependency on them.** Good subcontractors make themselves obsolete. They come in, do a quality job, and ensure that their work can be operated effectively within your organization. These are the kind of subcontractors that I like to work with, because the only reason why you will continue to do business with them is because you want to, not because you have to. Other subcontractors will instead try to increase your dependency on them; they do not transfer the necessary skills to your staff, forcing you to continue and potentially even grow your relationship with them because it is too painful to do otherwise.

TIP

Good Subcontractors Take My Advice To Heart

Good subcontracting organizations will take the advice that I presented in the previous tip and turn it around to their advantage by:

- Admitting that they are using less experienced staff in some places and offer to let you interview them to ensure they meet your standards.
- Offering to include your staff in key positions for off-site development work.
- Proving their magical claims with reference accounts that have "magically" delivered software.
- Providing realistic estimates that include a realistic range of values.
- Relying on their track record of success, not the names of their founders.
- Including a training and mentoring plan to transfer their skills to your staff.

done. Your quality assurance (QA) group should be in regular contact with the QA group of the subcontractor so that you are fully aware of the actual status of the subcontractor's work. Yes, this is overhead, but it is an overhead that dramatically reduces the risk of subcontracting and is therefore money well spent.

4. **Analyze the effectiveness of the subcontractor.** Throughout the process of managing the subcontractor, you should keep track of actual results versus the original plan. This information will be needed in the future to determine whether or not you want to continue doing business with a given subcontractor and will prove to be useful information if legal action is to be taken.

DEFINITION

infrastructure engineer A person who is responsible for defining and supporting the project infrastructure (processes, guidelines, standards, and tools). The role is applicable to the Define Infrastructure stage and all stages of the Construct phase.

6.2.2 Tailoring Your Software Process

At the beginning of a project you must define the software process that you will follow—ideally a process that is modified from the common software process adopted by your organization. Every software project is unique; therefore, you need to tailor your software process to meet its unique needs. DeMarco (1997) observes that the danger of a standard process is that people will miss chances to take important

TIP

Different Types of Projects Have Different Life Cycles

A system rewrite is different from building an application from scratch, which in turn is different from purchasing an application from another organization, which in turn is different from integrating an existing legacy application. Each of these project categories—new development, rewrites, integration of purchased systems, and integration of legacy applications—have their own general project life cycles. Yes, every system rewrite is different, but you still perform similar tasks such as analysis of the current system, determination of how to integrate it with the new system infrastructure, and the construction of the new application. The point to be made is that your organization should consider developing "generic" tailored processes for each category of project that can be used as the basis for the process of specific projects. In other words you should strive to reuse tailored processes.

shortcuts, implying that you want to tailor your process to meet the specific needs of your project. Infrastructure engineers (in conjunction with the project manager) who understand your organization's standard object-oriented software process (OOSP) will perform the majority of this work.

You need to do three things to tailor your software process for a project:

- Define/select procedures and methodologies
- Define/select standards and guidelines
- Negotiate project deliverables

6.2.2.1 Defining and Selecting Procedures and Methodologies

Before construction begins, you must first identify the procedures and methodologies that you will follow so that team members know what they are to do and how they are to do it. This is

TIP

You May Need to Modify Your Operations Procedures

Very often your technical feasibility study, performed in the Justify stage (Chapter 5), indicates that you will need to modify your operations procedures to support a new technology being used for your project.

TABLE 6.1. Procedures and Methodologies that Need to Be Selected or Defined for a Project

Procedure/ Methodology	Purpose	Relevant Phases/Stages
Methodology for requirements	A definition of the techniques and processes that you will follow to define and validate requirements for your project.	Define and Validate Initial Requirements stage (Chapter 3)
Methodology for modeling	The approach that you will follow to model your application, including both the process and the modeling techniques to be used.	Model stage (Chapter 8)
Methodology for testing	This is the definition of your approach to testing your application.	Test in the Small stage (Chapter 11) Test in the Large stage (Ambler, 1998b)
Methodology for collecting metrics	This defines the measurements, also called metrics, that you will collect during the life of the application and how they will be used.	All project phases and stages
Build procedures	The process by which the code of individual programmers will be integrated to form a testable, working application or component.	Program stage (Chapter 9)
Release procedures	The process by which an application will be made available to the user, operations, and support communities.	Program stage (Chapter 9) Deliver stage (Ambler, 1998b)

(continued)

TABLE 6.1. *(continued)*

Procedure/ Methodology	Purpose	Relevant Phases/Stages
Operations procedures	The processes that the operations staff will follow to keep your application in production.	Deliver stage (Ambler, 1998b)
Software configuration management (SCM) procedures	The process that will be followed by developers throughout the project to manage the deliverables that they produce.	All stages, but critical to the Construct phase
Configuration control board (CCB) procedures	The processes that will be followed to identify new features and or defect fixes to be supported by a future release of the application.	Identify Defects and Enhancements stage (Ambler, 1998b)

important because a consistent approach to development will increase the effectiveness of your project team. If possible, reuse existing procedures and methodologies from the common software process adopted by your organization; otherwise, look to existing process artifacts from industry and adopt them (if applicable). A few hours invested in research on the Internet, or by simply walking around your local computer book store, can result in significant savings; you do not need to reinvent proven procedures and/or methodologies. Table 6.1 describes many of the procedures and methodologies that you need for your project.

In addition to the procedures and methodologies for your project, you must also define and select the applicable standards and guidelines to which you will build.

6.2.2.2 Defining and Selecting Standards and Guidelines

You need to define and select the standards and guidelines that will be applied to your project to ensure consistency and main-

DEFINITIONS

configuration control board (CCB) The group responsible for approving proposed software changes. Also called a change-control board or software configuration review board (SCRB).

methodology In the context of systems development, it is the collection of techniques and approaches that you take when creating systems.

procedure A series of steps to be followed to perform a given task.

software configuration management (SCM) A set of engineering procedures for tracking and documenting software and its related deliverables throughout their life cycles to ensure that all changes are recorded and the current state of the software is known and reproducible.

TIP

Learn from Your Process Tailoring Efforts

You are tailoring your organization's object-oriented software process (OOSP) for a reason, sometimes because your project is atypical and other times because your OOSP is deficient. An excellent way to improve your OOSP is to determine the reason why you are tailoring it for your project, and then to incorporate necessary changes to improve it for future projects.

tainability. Standards and guidelines can be set at various levels: industry standards that should be followed by all organizations, organizational standards and guidelines that are followed by all projects in your organization, and project-level standards and guidelines that are followed only on your project.

Ambler's Law of Standards: Industry standards > organizational standards > project standards > personal standards > no standards.

The greater the scope of the standards and guidelines, the more desirable they are; industry standards are more desirable than organizational standards, which in turn are more desirable than project standards. Projects aren't developed in a vacuum and organizations do not operate in a vacuum, either; therefore, the greater the scope of the standard, the greater the chance that somebody else is also following it, making it that much easier for you to work together with them.

It is critical to set standards and guidelines before construction begins to ensure consistency in the work between developers, and to provide a basis for the quality factors that will be looked for dur-

WAR STORY

A Mediocre Standard Followed Consistently Is Better Than a Perfect Standard Followed Inconsistently

In the spring of 1997 I was involved with the identification and documentation of a set of standards and guidelines for Java programming. One of the rules that we set for this process was that we would adopt industry standards wherever possible. If we couldn't identify an industry-accepted standard, we would identify potential alternatives, determine their strengths and weaknesses, and then choose one and stick to it. We produced our draft document and presented it to the other Java developers in the company.

We ran into problems right away, because some of our coders did not want to follow the standards no matter what the standards were. When they realized they did not have a chance at winning that battle they switched gears and wanted to set their own set of personal standards, typically those they followed previously for different languages. Instead of accepting perfectly good standards followed by many others in the industry, including several of the tools and class libraries that they were using, they instead wanted to reinvent the wheel and introduce their own unique set of standards.

The short story is that not only did they not have the maturity to initially recognize the value of standards and guidelines, they also were unwilling to reuse the good work of others who had gone before them. Granted, I was not completely satisfied with some of the existing standards for Java development, but I was willing to accept them because I recognized the fact that it was more effective to follow a not-so-perfect industry standard consistently than it was to try to develop a "perfect" set of standards that only we would follow. With industry standards there is a good chance that other developers that you hire will know and follow them, that tools and libraries that you purchase will follow them, and that courses and books you use in your training program will follow them. With home-grown standards this is not even a consideration.

The standards document can be downloaded free of charge from http://www.ambysoft.com/javaCodingStandards.html

Table 6.2. Standards and Guidelines that Need To Be Selected or Defined for a Project

Standard/ Guideline	Purpose	Relevant Stages/Phases
Documentation conventions	Describe how the deliverables will be internally and externally documented and may include common templates to be used for the various project deliverables	All phases and stages
Modeling standards	Define the modeling notation that will be followed by the modeling team. Common modeling notations include the Unified Modeling Language (UML) (Booch, Jacobson, Rumbaugh, 1997) and the Open Modeling Language (OML) (Firesmith, Henderson-Sellers, & Graham, 1997).	Model stage (Chapter 8)
Naming conventions	Describe how deliverables and components of deliverables will be named.	Construct phase (Chapters 7 to 11)

(continued)

ing peer reviews and inspections (a key component of the Test in the Small stage, covered in Chapter 11). Grady (1992) reports that a common set of terminology and standards improves the productivity of the peer review process because everyone understands the products that they are reviewing. Standards and guidelines increase the consistency, understandability, maintainability, and enhanceability of your application by defining a common basis from which all developers work. Table 6.2 describes the key standards and guidelines that you should set before construction begins.

When you're selecting and/or defining standards and guide-

TABLE 6.2. *(continued)*

Standard/ Guideline	Purpose	Relevant Stages/Phases
Testing approach	Describes how to define test models, test cases, test scripts, and test suites (collections of test scripts). Your testing approach document is used to define your master test/QA plan, which drives your testing efforts.	Test in the Small stage (Chapter 11) Test in the Large stage (Ambler, 1998b)
User interface design standards	Define the standards for designing the user interface, including screens, reports, and forms, that make up the application. Industry standards exist for most common operating systems.	Model stage (Chapter 8) Program stage (Chapter 9)
Programming standards	Define the naming conventions, documentation conventions, and development guidelines to be followed by programmers when writing source code.	Program stage (Chapter 9)

lines for your organization, make sure this effort is performed by people who are qualified to do it. For example, do not have a C programmer or COBOL programmer without OO experience set your Java coding standards. If they do not know the paradigm and the language then they cannot do a good job. You must have people involved who understand both the small picture, the immediate needs of development, as well as the big picture, the long-term needs of maintaining and supporting the application. This means that professional software engineers should be involved in the development of your organization's standards and guidelines.

Software engineers should be involved in the setting of organizational standards.

TIP

Make Standards and Guidelines an Integral Part of Quality Assurance

Standards and guidelines are effective only if they are followed consistently, and the only way to ensure that they are followed consistently is if your peer reviews and inspections look for compliance to them.

Landsbaum and Glass (1992) correctly point out that everyone is in favor of standards and guidelines as long as the standards and guidelines are their own. The reality is that developers are going to have to accept that the overall needs of your organization, needs that take into account both the short term and the long term, are more important than their own immediate needs. In other words, they will have to change the ways they do things for the greater good.

6.2.2.3 Negotiating Project Deliverables

The third part of tailoring your software process is to negotiate the deliverables that your project will produce. Many deliverables are mandatory, such as a class model (discussed in detail in Chapter 8), a project plan, and the application itself. Other deliverables, depending on the application, are optional. For example, if your application doesn't use a relational database for its persistence mechanism, then you do not need to produce a data diagram. The main point to be made is that you should create only the deliverables that are needed

DEFINITIONS

deliverable Any document or system component that is produced during the development of a system. Some deliverables are used internally on a project, whereas others are produced specifically for users of the application. Examples of deliverables include user requirements, models, plans, assessments, or other documents.

master test/quality assurance (QA) plan A document that describes your testing and quality assurance policies and procedures, as well as the detailed test plans for each portion of your application.

quality assurance (QA) The process of ensuring that the efforts of a project meet or exceed the standards expected of them.

TIP

Different Deliverables, Different Receivers

Some deliverables, such as the application itself and the corresponding user documentation, are presented to the user community. Other deliverables, such as operations procedures, are presented to the operations and support staff responsible for the application. Still other deliverables, such as source code and models, are presented to the developers who will be maintaining and enhancing the application in the future.

to maintain, support, and enhance the application once it is in production. Because every project is unique, you may not need to develop every single deliverable described by your software process.

6.2.3 Selecting Tools

Before construction begins you need to select the tool set that you will use. This includes modeling tools, documentation tools, project management tools, programming environments, configuration management environments, support tools, and testing tools. Try to choose tools that integrate easily, that support team development, and that are well supported in the industry.

When choosing between tools that you are unfamiliar with, you should first evaluate them to see if they are right for you. Start by defining the criteria that you will use to judge them, then evaluate them against that criteria. Do not accept the studies and white papers provided by the tool vendors at face value—everybody's tools look good on marketing slides. Determine what is important to you, not to the vendor, and evaluate the tools yourself.

TIP

Bring in a Consultant to Help Select Tools

The problem with tool selection is that there are a lot of tools to choose from; many of them aren't what you need, but the marketing literature looks really good. One way to cut through the chaff is to hire a consultant who has experience in several development tools and ask them to prepare a study for you of the tools that are potentially the best suited for your environment.

WAR STORY

Consider the Viability of Your Tool Vendor

An important issue that must be considered when selecting tools is the viability of the vendor. If it is likely that the tool vendor may go out of business, drop support for the tool, or simply be unable to provide the level of support that you require, then you shouldn't purchase their tool. In the late 1980s I worked for an organization that was forced to take over the maintenance of their repository tool when the software company that built it went out of business. Overnight they went from being a financial institution to a maintainer of software development tools, a situation that they did not relish.

A fool with a tool is still a fool.

Regardless of the tools chosen, you should ensure that each team member who will be using them has the appropriate access (perhaps your organization will need to purchase more licenses for existing tools) and that the tools have been properly installed at their workstation. You should also ensure that everyone has been trained to use both the tools and the techniques that the tools support. Just because you have a CASE tool at your disposal, that doesn't mean you have the ability to model a system; it just means you have access to a CASE tool.

Some of the tools that you should consider for a software project include:

- Modeling (CASE) tool
- Configuration management tool
- Programming language
- Project management software
- Time recording software
- Support knowledge base
- Automatic call distribution (ACD) system (for support)
- Change-management system
- Requirements tracking system
- User interface testing tool
- Data dictionary
- Word processor
- Spreadsheet
- Code editor

TIP

Some Tools Are Hardware

I suggest that, when choosing tools to support modeling, you choose a CASE (computer-aided software engineering) tool that supports your chosen modeling standards, a word processor, and a simple drawing tool for the diagrams not supported by your CASE tool. I highly suggest a full-page scanner to capture hand-drawn models that you want to keep but do not want to invest the time needed to draw using a drawing or CASE tool. My experience has been that a $300 scanner pays for itself in saved time in less than a week.

- Software delivery/distribution/installation system
- Computer aided training development and deployment environment
- Intranet development environments

6.2.4 Creating a Group Memory

Constantine (1995) suggests that you create a "group memory" for your project, which is a record of what your project team accomplished, decisions made by your team and the reasoning behind them, deferred decisions, and the lessons learned on your project. A group memory provides a mechanism to record this information when it is first recognized so that it is not lost. This information is a key input into the Assess stage, described in *More Process Patterns* (Ambler, 1998b), where you evaluate the effectiveness of the tools, techniques, and people used on your project so that you can improve your overall software process.

For each type of information—accomplishments, decisions made, decisions deferred, and lessons learned—you will want to track different data. For example, for accomplishments, you will want to track a description of the accomplishment, related deliverables (if any), and when the accomplishment was achieved. For decisions made, you should track the decision itself, when it was made, who made it, the alternatives considered, and the reasoning behind the decision. A deferred decision should have a description of the issue, potential alternatives, a reason why the decision has been deferred, and an indication of when the decision needs to be reconsidered. Finally, for a lesson learned, you should have a description of the lesson, an indication of what

TIP

Create a Common Library

Part of your infrastructure should be a common library of journals, magazines, books, papers, and Web sites to which all team members have access. This library should include material about developing software, industry standards, reference manuals, company standards, and relevant domain publications that describe your organization's business. For a few thousand dollars your team members can have the information at their fingertips that is critical to the success of your project and that will help them gain valuable insight into their jobs.

happened that lead to the lesson learned, and an indication of how your organization should act to institutionalize the lesson learned. By acting on lessons learned you are able to learn from your experiences and improve your software process.

A group memory may be as simple as a shared word processing document or as complex as a repository that records each decision, accomplishment, and lessons learned as its own unique document.

The advantages of a group memory are that you will not go over ground that you have already covered—the decisions that you have made and the decisions that you have deferred until later—and that you have an accurate record of what happened on the project in case things go wrong.

6.3 Solution: Project Tasks

In this section I will discuss project task issues that are pertinent to the Define Infrastructure stage.

6.3.1 Managing the Define Infrastructure Stage

Get the right people to define your infrastructure.

The key management issue with the Define Infrastructure stage is to assign the appropriate people to the task. These are people who are experienced with large-scale object-oriented projects, who understand your existing software process, and understand the existing tools. They should be able to see the big picture, understanding that there is more to the software process than simply developing software.

Ideally, the project infrastructure should be defined before con-

TIP

Object Technology Centers Should Support Infrastructure Efforts

An object technology center (OTC) is a technology transfer group that specializes in the rapid development and deployment of the infrastructure necessary to use object-oriented software development techniques successfully on a corporate scale (Korson, & Vaishnavi, 1995). In large organizations, OTCs should be your first source for many of the infrastructure deliverables described in this chapter. If they do not already have a chosen standard, guideline, tool, and so on that meets your specific needs, then they should help to identify what you need. OTCs are discussed in greater detail in *More Process Patterns* (Ambler, 1998b).

DEFINITION

object technology center (OTC) A technology transfer group that specializes in the rapid development and deployment of the infrastructure necessary to successfully use object-oriented software development techniques on a corporate scale.

struction begins, but because you will discover a need for better tools or more or different people during the Construct phase, you often will not be able to completely define your infrastructure when you would like it.

Because the development of the project plan and risk assessment are performed iteratively with the development of the initial management documents (Chapter 4) and the feasibility study (Chapter 5), it is critical that the people involved with these efforts are working together and are keeping their work synchronized with one another. This requires a method for intergroup communication to be established—perhaps an internal newsgroup where the teams may post shared documents and status information will suffice, or perhaps regular synchronized meetings will be required. Regardless, it is the responsibility of the project manager to ensure that the team members are working together toward successfully developing the initial management documents, feasibility study, and project infrastructure.

6.3.2 *Training and Education*

Every team member should at least be familiar with the tools, standards, methodologies, and so on that make up your project's infrastructure. For the portions of the infrastructure that are pertinent to their roles and responsibilities, each team member should be fully trained on those portions.

On a larger scale you may find that you need to train and educate

non-team members about your project's infrastructure so that they understand what you intend to accomplish and how. This is especially true of the first few OO projects attempted by your organization, as it is likely that these projects are being used as the test cases to determine whether OO is appropriate for your organization. This training and education will probably consist of formal presentations and informal bag-lunch sessions whose goals are to share lessons learned and to teach "new" OO techniques and technologies.

6.3.3 Quality Assurance

The project infrastructure should be peer-reviewed before it is submitted for approval to senior management. If possible, include managers from previous OO projects in the review as well as key developers such as architects, lead programmers, and test managers. Key issues to look for include:

- Are any deviations from your organization's software process justified?
- Are industry standards and guidelines being used, and if not why?
- Will the chosen tools work together?
- Are the tool vendors viable?
- Have issues like maintainability and extensibility been accounted for in the infrastructure?
- Are the deliverables that have been negotiated sufficient?
- Is the project team viable?

6.3.4 Potential Risks While Defining the Project Infrastructure

There is one fundamental type of risk during this stage, that of making the wrong choice. You might pick the wrong subcontractor, a technology that gets canceled three months after you implement, procedures that sounded good in principle but proved deficient in practice, or a set of deliverables that are not sufficient to maintain your system appropriately. To actively manage these risks you need to:

- Involve qualified, experienced people who understand the "big picture."
- Validate technology decisions with proof-of-concept prototyping (see Chapter 8).

- Contact other firms who used the same technology/standards/... and ask them what their experience was.
- Define your requirements first, then look for infrastructure items that fulfill your requirements.

DEFINITION

artifact reuse The reuse of previously created development artifacts: use cases, standards documents, domain-specific models, procedures and guidelines, and other applications.

6.3.5 Opportunities for Reuse

Almost every single deliverable produced by this stage should be reusable, and in fact should have been reused from other projects. Standards, guidelines, procedures, and methodologies are all things that you should be able to pick up off the shelf and modify if necessary. The tool evaluations that are done while defining the project infrastructure should be saved for future reference, and the skills evaluations of potential project members can also be reused in the future, at least as the basis for another skills evaluation. The bottom line is that a common infrastructure should be defined for your organization and tailored where necessary for specific projects, enabling a high-level of artifact reuse.

You do not need to reinvent the infrastructure wheel.

6.3.6 Metrics

You may choose to gather metrics specific to the Define Infrastructure stage. These metrics are:

1. **Number of reused infrastructure artifacts.** This is a count of the number of items (processes, standards, guidelines, and tools) that your project was able to reuse from other projects or from industry. This metric provides an indication of the commonality between projects and of your project team's attitude toward reuse (there are always infrastructure artifacts available within industry to reuse; you just have to choose to do so).
2. **Number of introduced infrastructure artifacts.** This is a count of the number of new infrastructure artifacts introduced by your project team. When this count is high, especially when compared to the number of reused infrastructure artifacts, it provides an indication that either your project team is not taking advantage of the existing infrastructure available to it, or if no infrastructure exists that the project is at risk because it is working with too many new things at once.

6.4 Resulting Context: Exit Conditions for Defining the Project Infrastructure

You have not finished defining the infrastructure for your project until you have selected the tools that will be used, defined the project team, and tailored your software process to meet the unique needs of the project. The deliverables of the Define Infrastructure stage are:

1. **An accepted set of tools.** You want a set of tools to work together efficiently that have been accepted by the developers who will be using them. These tools, wherever possible, should be the standard tools used throughout your company, and if not, then your use of them should be justified and accepted by senior management. If you do not have a good reason for using different tools, then do not use them.
2. **An accepted project team.** The project team members, the time period that they will be involved on the project, and their roles and responsibilities need to be defined and then accepted by senior management.
3. **An accepted, tailored software process.** The tailoring of your software process includes the definition and selection of the standards, procedures, guidelines, and methodologies that the team will follow and the deliverables that it will produce. Your tailored software process must be accepted by senior management, your quality assurance (QA) department, your project team, and your user community.
4. **A group memory has been initiated.** A group memory provides a mechanism to record and track team accomplishments, decisions made, decisions deferred, and lessons learned.

6.5 Secrets of Success

The following pointers should help to improve your efforts at defining an infrastructure for your project and/or organization:

1. **Reuse existing infrastructure.** You do not need to reinvent the infrastructure wheel. Look for existing infrastructure

components within your organization or better yet within the industry. Your job is to develop applications, not develop standards and guidelines.

2. **Let standards drive your tool selection.** A common mistake made during infrastructure definition is to choose tools first and then get stuck with their proprietary approach to development. If you want your destiny to be defined by your tool vendor, that's your business; I'd rather determine what I want to do and then find tools that best match my vision. Therefore, you should choose your modeling standards before selecting a CASE tool and set your user interface design guidelines before picking a development tool that supports them.
3. **Define the infrastructure early.** Your project infrastructure defines the development environment and rules for the Construct phase (Chapters 7 though 11), providing the guidance that the team needs to do their jobs properly. When the project infrastructure is not defined in time for construction you risk a false start to your project; the use of the improper tools, guidelines, standards, and so on can require the development team to do rework later in the project.
4. **Do not conform to anti-establishment trends.** The information technology industry moves at a very fast rate, providing the opportunity for opposing views to surface regarding many of the infrastructure components discussed in this chapter. A perfect example is in object-oriented modeling notations, where we're starting to see a shakeout of over 40 common notations[1] from the early 1990s to a small handful today. Although there several viable modeling notations available to you, the one with the greatest mind share is the Unified Modeling Language (UML). The UML has its faults, but it should be obvious that it is the clear winner in the market place. Yes, you could choose one of the other nota-

---

[1]In my second book, *Building Object Applications That Work,* I adopted the Unified Modeling Language (UML) instead of my original OO modeling notation that I introduced in my first book, *The Object Primer.* I was the first OO methodologist not directly associated with the UML to publicly accept the UML in favor of his own notation.

tions, which also have their faults, but what does it benefit you to buck the industry trend? Absolutely nothing, so do not do it.

5. **Train developers in the infrastructure.** If people do not understand your infrastructure they will not be able to use it properly.

6.6 Process Checklist

The following process checklist can be used to verify that you have completed the Define Infrastructure stage.

DEFINE INFRASTRUCTURE STAGE
PROCESS CHECKLIST

Fulfillment of Entrance Conditions:

✔ Development of the initial requirements has begun.
✔ Development of the project plan has begun.
✔ The existing infrastructure, if any, is available.
✔ Development of the feasibility study has begun.

Processes Performed:

✔ The project team has been defined.
✔ A skills assessment for each project team member has been updated.
✔ Training, if appropriate, has been identified for each project team member.
✔ A project/skills matrix was developed.
✔ Potential subcontractors have been identified and appropriate contracts have been ratified.
✔ Your organization's software process has been tailored appropriately for your project.
✔ Appropriate standards have been selected/developed for your project.
✔ Appropriate guidelines have been selected/developed for your project.
✔ Appropriate methodologies have been selected/developed for your project.

- ✔ Project deliverables have been negotiated with upper management and agreed to.
- ✔ Tools have been identified.
- ✔ Project team members have been trained on the tools.
- ✔ The tools have been installed.
- ✔ A group memory has been organized.
- ✔ A shared library of books and magazines is available.
- ✔ Artifacts that are potentially reusable by your project team during this stage have been identified and used where appropriate.
- ✔ Your risk assessment document has been updated where appropriate.
- ✔ Decisions made, and decisions forgone, have been documented in your group memory.
- ✔ Metrics have been collected.

Fulfillment of Exit Conditions:

- ✔ The set of tools has been accepted by the team and by senior management.
- ✔ The team has been accepted by senior management.
- ✔ The tailored software process has been accepted by the team and by senior management.
- ✔ A group memory has been initiated.

6.7 Exit Conditions for Justifying the Project

You have finished the Justify stage when:

1. **A feasible implementation alternative has been selected.** This is why you perform a feasibility study in the first place: to identify an approach to your project that will actually work.
2. **The project risk assessment has been started.** If the risk assessment had not already been started before the Justify stage began, then it certainly should be by now. During the assessment process you are guaranteed to identify technical and operational risks (there are always risks with software projects) and you should record them so that they can be dealt with appropriately.

6.8 What You Have Learned in This Chapter

In this chapter you saw that to make a project successful, you need to define the infrastructure—the team, the tools, and a tailored version of your organization's software process—that will be used on the project. You saw that you begin with what you already have—existing staff, existing tools, existing standards and guidelines, your existing software process—and look outside your organization for additional resources to select the most appropriate combination for your project. With a defined, accepted project infrastructure you increase the chance of success for your project, because everyone works from a common base.

6.9 References and Recommended Reading

Ambler, S. W. 1998. *More Process Patterns: Delivering Large-Scale Systems Using Object Technology.* New York: SIGS Books/ Cambridge University Press.

Booch, G., Jacobson, I., and Rumbaugh, J. 1997. *The Unified Modeling Language for Object-Oriented Development Documentation 1.1.* Monterey California: Rational Software Corporation.

Constantine, L. L. 1995. *Constantine on Peopleware.* Englewood Cliffs, New Jersey: Yourdon Press.

Coplien, J.O. (1995). *A Generative Development-Process Pattern Language.* Pattern Languages of Program Design, eds. Coplien, J.O. and Schmidt, D.C., Addison Wesley Longman, Inc., pp. 183–237.

Cunningham, W. (1996). *EPISODES: A Pattern Language of Competitive Development.* Pattern Languages of Program Design 2, eds. Vlissides, J.M., Coplien, J.O., and Kerth, N.L., Addison-Wesley Publishing Company., pp. 371–388.

DeMarco, T. 1997. *The Deadline: A Novel About Project Management.* New York: Dorset House Publishing.

Firesmith, D., Henderson-Sellers, B., and Graham, I. 1997. *Open Modeling Language (OML) Manual.* New York: SIGS Books.

Grady, R. B. 1992. *Practical Software Metrics For Project Management and Process Improvement.* Englewood Cliffs, New Jersey: Prentice-Hall, Inc.

Harrison, N.B. (1996). *Organizational Patterns for Teams.* Pattern Languages of Program Design 2, eds. Vlissides, J.M., Coplien, J.O., and Kerth, N.L., Addison-Wesley Publishing Company., pp. 345–352.

Humphrey, W. S. 1997. *Introduction to the Personal Software Process.* Reading, Massachusetts: Addison-Wesley Longman, Inc.

Korson, T. D. and Vaishnavi, V.K. 1995. *The Object Technology Center. Object Magazine* 5(October), 31–38.

Landsbaum, J. B. and Glass, R. L. 1992. *Measuring & Motivating Maintenance Programmers.* Englewood Cliffs, New Jersey: Prentice-Hall Inc.

Raynor, D. A. 1995. Get the Most from Training Dollars. *Datamation,* April 15, 1995.

Software Engineering Institute 1995. *The Capability Maturity Model: Guidelines for Improving the Software Process.* Reading, Massachusetts: Addison-Wesley Publishing Company.

Part 2

Construct

THE SECOND SERIAL PHASE of the OOSP is the Construct phase, commonly referred to as the development phase or the construction phase in the structured world. In the minds of most developers, this is where the "real" work begins. This is where you build the application by:

- Modeling the application, both from an analysis and a design point of view, so that you know what you're building and how you're going to build it.
- Programming the application using OO development tools.
- Testing in the small, a greatly expanded version of unit testing from the structured world, to verify that your modeling and programming efforts work.
- Generalizing your construction efforts so that you can reuse them on this project and on others.

Chapter 7

The Construct Phase

THE main goal of the Construct phase, the second serial phase of the Object-Oriented Software Process (OOSP), is to build working software that is ready to be tested and delivered to your user community. This software will be accompanied by the models and source code that was used to develop it, a test plan to verify that the software works, any reusable artifacts that can be used on future projects, and the initial documentation and training plans supporting the software. Unfortunately there are several forces arrayed against the success of the Construct phase, including a lack of understanding of how to work the phase by both senior management and by developers; an unwarranted focus on programming to the neglect of modeling, testing, and generalization; and a penchant by everyone involved to cut corners and take shortcuts that more often than not result in poor quality software that is late and over budget anyway.

But it is easy to understand why people believe so firmly that there is no single, solid basis for the difference between good building and bad. It happens because the single central quality which makes the difference cannot be named.

—Christopher Alexander

As you can see in Figure 7.1 the major deliverables of the Initiate phase, covered in Chapters 2 through 6, are the main inputs into the Construct phase, as are maintenance changes allocated to your application from the Maintain and Support phase (Ambler, 1998b). Remember that object-oriented development is incremental—previous releases of your application may already be in production, and as a result, maintenance changes, either fixes or new features, applicable to/for the previous versions may have been assigned to your project team by the Identify Defects and Enhancements stage

Figure 7.1.
The Construct process pattern

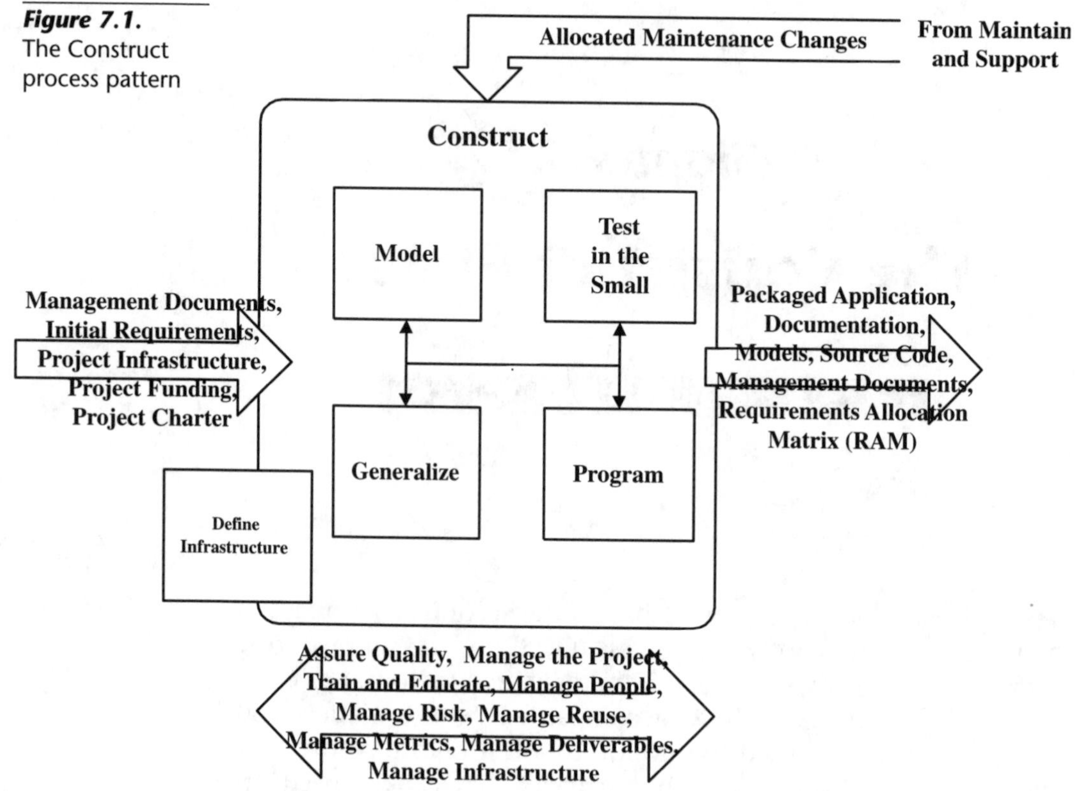

(Ambler, 1998b). Furthermore, because all of the tools to be used on the project may not yet be selected, the Define Infrastructure stage (Chapter 6) overlaps into the Construct phase.

An important implication of Figure 7.1 is that you are not starting from scratch when you enter the Construct phase; important management documents such as the project plan and initial risk assessment have been defined, the initial requirements for your application should have been defined, the project infrastructure is (mostly) defined, and the funding and charter for the project have been obtained. Furthermore, as you will see in the Model stage (Chapter 8), there may be existing models developed within your organization that define your technical and business/domain architectures, architectures that ease your development efforts.

The four iterative stages of the Construct phase are highly interrelated. The Model stage (Chapter 8) concentrates on the abstraction of the technical and/or problem domain via the use of diagrams, documents, and prototypes. The Program stage (Chap-

DEFINITIONS

code inspection A form of technical review in which the deliverable being reviewed is source code.

hacking A development approach where little or no effort is spent on analysis and design before coding begins.

maintenance change A description of a modification to be made to one or more existing configuration items (CIs).

opportunistic reuse A reuse approach in which reusable items are harvested from project deliverables after the fact.

systematic reuse An approach to reuse which involves modeling techniques whose purpose is to define high-leverage, reusable components.

technical review A testing technique in which the design of your application is examined critically by a group of your peers. A review will typically focus on accuracy, quality, usability, and completeness. This process is often referred to as a walkthrough or a peer review.

unit testing The act of testing small components of a system to ensure that they work. In the object world this is both method and class testing.

ter 9) focuses on the development and documentation of program source code. The Generalize stage (Chapter 10) is critical to your organization's reuse efforts, as it focuses on identifying reusable items, or items that may become reusable once modified, from a software project. This is effectively "opportunistic reuse" because you attempt to develop reusable items by harvesting your work after the fact, instead of "systematic reuse" in which you design software during modeling to be reusable. The goal of the Test in the Small stage (Chapter 11) is to verify and validate the deliverables developed by the other stages of the Construct phase. In many ways this stage is the equivalent of unit testing from the structured world combined with quality assurance techniques such as code inspections and technical reviews.

Just because the Construct phase is iterative in nature, it does not imply that your developers are allowed to start hacking. The reality of software development is that you must first identify and understand the requirements for something, then you must model them, and then code them. If you have not defined the requirements, then why are you building something? Do you honestly believe that it is more productive for you to start writing code before investing the time to think about and to model what you are building? Truly top-notch developers also know that they must verify their work before moving on to the next task. There is no value in modeling requirements that are invalid, or writing source code based on an incorrect model. This means that you need to test your work as you develop it, not at the end when it is often too late to fix discovered problems. I'm not saying that you have to define all of the requirements first, then do all of the modeling, then write all of the code. What I am saying is that any code that you write should be based on a validated model, and that any modeling you do should be based on one or more validated requirements.

Fundamentally, you must first identify requirements, then model them, then code them, verifying all of your work along the way.

7.1 Initial Context: Entry Conditions to the Construct Phase

The Construct phase can be entered two different ways, either from the Initiate phase or from the Maintain and Support phase. Regardless, there are several conditions that must be met before the Construct phase may begin:

1. **Key project management documents exist and are up-to-date.** Project management documents—the project plan, estimate, schedule, and risk assessment—are needed to manage and track progress during the Construct phase.
2. **The project infrastructure is defined.** The project infrastructure—team definition, standards and guidelines, methods, tools, and processes—should be either completely defined or very close to it. The project infrastructure provides the foundation upon which you build your application.
3. **High-level requirements are in place.** The requirements document should document most or all high-level requirements, with the project scope identified and agreed to by all appropriate parties. Furthermore, the high-level requirements should be validated and approved before construction begins.
4. **The project charter is in place.** A project charter summarizes many of the key project management documents, but more importantly it indicates that the project is funded and supported by senior management.

5. **Maintenance changes allocated to your application's release are identified.** Maintenance changes to address the repair of defects or the enhancement of a previous release of your application may have been assigned to your project team. Depending on your organizational policy and how far along in the project you are, these changes will either be assigned to the release of your application during the Initiate phase (Chapter 2), where they are used to drive initial require-

DEFINITIONS

project estimate An appraisal of how long a project will take, and how much it will cost, given a specific environment and a specific team. Change the environment and/or change the team, and your estimate should change. Project estimates are a deliverable of the Initiate phase and are updated regularly throughout a project.

project infrastructure The team, tools, and processes that will be used on a given project.

project schedule A project schedule indicates what will be done, when things will be done, and who will do them. A major component of a project schedule is a Gantt chart with its corresponding descriptions of tasks and resources. Project schedules are a deliverable of the Initiate phase and are updated regularly throughout a project.

requirements document A document, also called a System Requirements Specification (SRS), which describes the user, technical, and environmental requirements for an application. This document potentially contains the major use cases for the application, detailed use-case scenarios for the application, and traditional requirements for the application as well. Requirements documents are a deliverable of the Initiate phase and are updated regularly during modeling. Requirements documents are also updated during the Maintain and Support phase as bugs and enhancements are identified.

risk assessment A document indicating potential factors, called risks, that if they were to occur would harm the project. A risk assessment is used to identify risks so that they may be dealt with appropriately. Risk assessments are a deliverable of the Initiate phase and are updated regularly throughout a project.

software change request (SCR) A description of a potential improvement to a software deliverable, often identified by users of that deliverable.

software problem report (SPR) A description of a potential software defect identified by someone who is not directly responsible for a given software deliverable.

ments, or during the Construct phase, where they are incorporated into the design of your application. These maintenance changes will be accompanied by the original software change request (SCR) or software problem report (SPR) that initiated the required change to provide your team with the information required to make the given change.

7.2 Solution: How Work Generally Proceeds During the Construct Phase

The Construct phase should always begin with modeling, because you must first understand a problem before you attempt to solve it. Figure 7.2 shows that with the object-oriented approach to development, modeling is between thirty and fifty percent of the construction effort, whereas programming is between ten and thirty percent. Take this to heart: if you find that you are spending a significant amount of your time coding, then chances are very good that you short-changed your modeling effort. When developers do not think about the solution first, they tend to write far more code than they need to.

Modeling should be the largest single portion of the Construct phase.

Figure 7.2 also shows that the generalization of your work to make it reusable, and that testing in the small to verify that your work is correct should begin long before programming starts. In Chapter 10 we will discuss techniques to help make existing work reusable after the fact, and in Chapter 11 we cover testing techniques that are used to validate your analysis and design efforts to ensure that you correctly understand the problem domain before you attempt to implement a solution for it. As you would expect, tasks such as risk management, project management, and deliverables management occur throughout the Construct phase and comprise a significant portion of your efforts.

Figure 7.3 provides a more detailed look at how the work proceeds during the Construct phase. First, notice how the Define Infrastructure stage (Chapter 6) has overlapped into this phase, mainly because you may not always have your entire toolset defined when construction begins. Figure 7.3 also shows that enterprise/architectural modeling occurs constantly; in fact, you will see in Chapter 8 that many organizations have a separate modeling group that develops, maintains, and supports this effort. Notice how there is more to programming than just writing

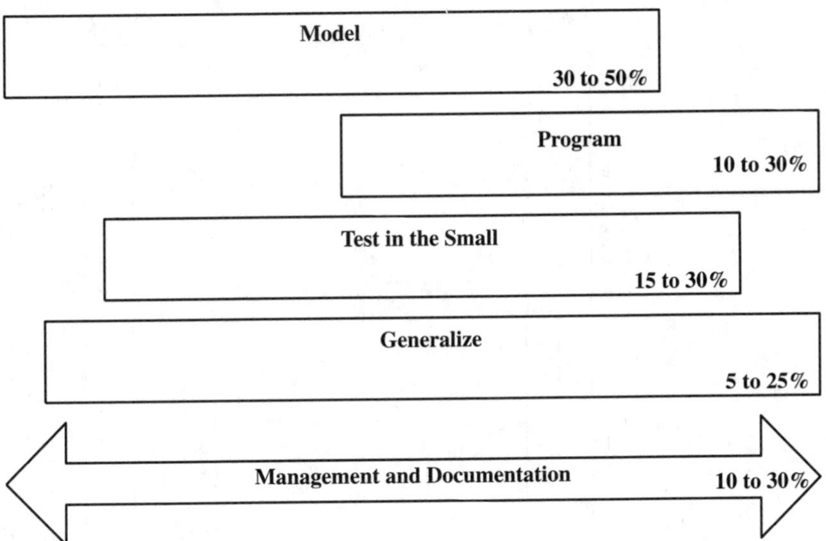

Figure 7.2. Organizing the Construct phase

code; coders must first invest the time to understand the models that they are developing to, then write and document the code, and then prepare their work for inspection and testing. At the end of the Program stage, the code and documentation is packaged and integrated to prepare the product baseline, the version of the application to be delivered to the user community (assuming the application passes testing in the large). Testing in the small occurs throughout the entire Construct phase to ensure that your work is accurate and to reduce the cost of fixing defects by finding those defects as early as possible. Regression testing, ensuring that existing behaviors still work in a new release of your application, as well as model reviews and code reviews and testing are important aspects of testing in the small. Generalization of your work to make it reusable is also an important aspect of the Construct phase, and as we see in Figure 7.3 you often hold joint application development (JAD) sessions with key experts to identify opportunities for reuse, then refactor and document your work, finally releasing it so that it is available to others.

Figure 7.3 shows that you need to prepare for the Deliver phase during the Construct phase. Developing and/or updating the master test/QA plan is critical for the Test in the Large stage (Ambler, 1998b), as is the release plan for the Release stage (Ambler, 1998b). The release plan will include the data conversion plan which describes the effort, often a project in itself, to convert your legacy

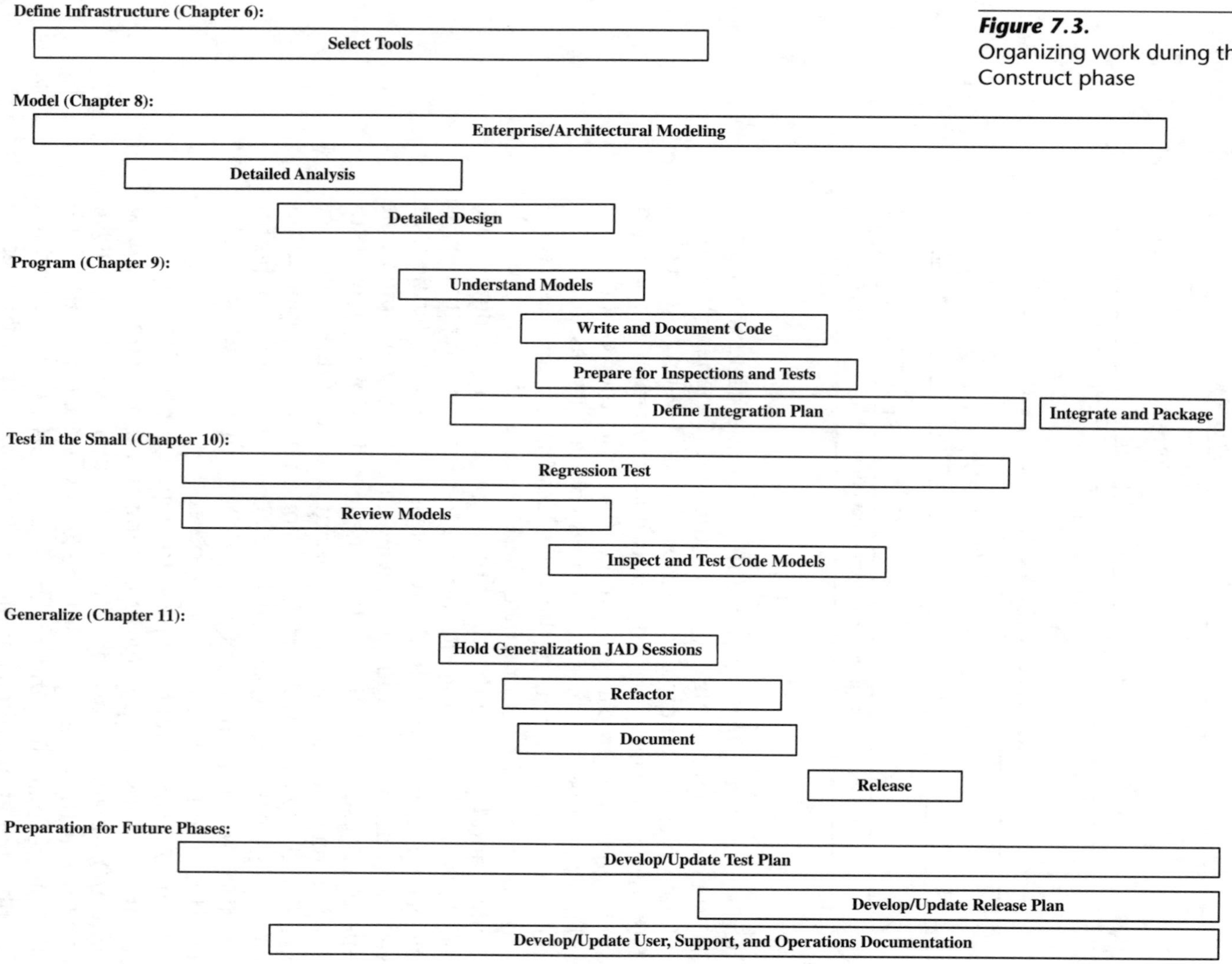

Define Infrastructure (Chapter 6):

Select Tools

Model (Chapter 8):

Enterprise/Architectural Modeling

Detailed Analysis

Detailed Design

Program (Chapter 9):

Understand Models

Write and Document Code

Prepare for Inspections and Tests

Define Integration Plan

Integrate and Package

Test in the Small (Chapter 10):

Regression Test

Review Models

Inspect and Test Code Models

Generalize (Chapter 11):

Hold Generalization JAD Sessions

Refactor

Document

Release

Preparation for Future Phases:

Develop/Update Test Plan

Develop/Update Release Plan

Develop/Update User, Support, and Operations Documentation

Figure 7.3.
Organizing work during the Construct phase

data into something usable for your object-oriented application. Part of your deliverables management efforts during the Construct phase is the development of the user, support, and operations documentation that will be packaged and released with the application during the Program stage (Chapter 9). These deliverables are distributed to the appropriate sources during the Release stage (Ambler, 1998b).

7.3 Solution: Project Tasks

In this section I will discuss the specific issues involved with project management, people management, and risk management that are pertinent to the Construct phase.

7.3.1 Managing the Construct Phase

The construction of software is a complex task, a task that can easily devolve into chaos inevitably leading to project failure. To avoid devolving into chaos during the Construct phase, or to rescue your project once it has, you need to consider the following:

- Planning and risk management
- Timeboxing
- Parallel development
- Reuse first, buy second, build last
- Infrastructure first, application second
- Software configuration management (SCM)
- Rescuing a project from chaos

7.3.1.1 Planning and Risk Management

Having a realistic plan in place is critical to the success of the Construct phase. The surest way to get into trouble is to start work without a complete plan in place—novice project managers often assume that they can finish the plan part way through the project. The reality is that the project manager will spend more and more of their time dealing with unexpected problems, moving from one crisis to another, and never find the time to get the project organized. Without a plan your project will quickly run into trouble.

Projects without a plan quickly devolve into chaos.

Having an active risk management process in place is also critical to the success of the Construct phase; if you do not manage

DEFINITIONS

data conversion plan A plan describing how a legacy data schema will be reworked to meet the new needs of your organization. A data conversion plan will likely refer to data models for both the existing and new data schema as well as the data access maps associated with both models.

joint application development (JAD) A structured, facilitated meeting in which modeling is performed by both users and developers together. JADs are often held for gathering user requirements.

master test/quality assurance (QA) plan A document that describes your testing and quality assurance policies and procedures, as well as the detailed test plans for each portion of your application.

operations documentation The documentation this is deployed to your operations department, including backup procedures, batch job and printing requirements, data extraction/sharing requirements, installation procedures for your application, resource requirements for your application, and the version description document (VDD) describing the product baseline for your application.

refactoring The act of reorganizing OO development efforts. For source code and models, refactoring will often comprise the renaming of methods, attributes, or classes; the redefinition of methods, attributes, or classes; or the complete rework or methods, attributes, or classes. For other project deliverables, refactoring may simply be the renaming or reorganization of sections of the deliverable.

release plan A plan which describes when your release procedures will be applied, and by whom, to release your application.

support documentation The documentation that is deployed to your support department, including your support call recording process, applicable call escalation procedures, relevant points of contact within your development and operations departments, and all user documentation for your application.

support documentation The documentation that is deployed to your support department, including your support call recording process, applicable call escalation procedures, relevant points of contact within your development and operations departments, and all user documentation for your application.

user documentation The documentation that is deployed to the user community, potentially including a user manual, tutorial manual, reference manual, and support user's guide.

risks your risks will manage you. Many projects fail because the unknowns, the risks, are left until the end of the project. How many projects have you seen run aground because the promised release of the new database or operating system did not get delivered in time? How about projects that get into trouble after the discovery that they do not operate with existing software the users are currently using? The bottom line is that you need to formulate and then work your risk management process before you can safely begin construction.

If you do not manage risk, it will manage you.

7.3.1.2 Timeboxing

A timebox is a defined period of time, from several days to several months, in which a team of developers are assigned to produce a given deliverable. With a timebox the end date is actually a fixed deadline; if the team needs to, it will cut features out of the deliverable but it will not extend the delivery date. According to McConnell (1996), timeboxing is a technique best used during the Construct phase to infuse a development team with a sense of urgency to help keep them focused on the most important features. Successful timeboxing keeps a project on schedule by reducing the delivered feature set without sacrificing the quality of the work delivered. It is better to have a small, working system on time than a large system that is late and does not work properly.

Timeboxing keeps the project on schedule by focusing on critical behavior, sacrificing low-priority features instead of product quality to meet a strict deadline.

With timeboxing you select an appropriate task, perhaps the development of a prototype or the programming of a portion of an application, and set a time period to work that task. Table 7.1 shows several deliverables that can be timeboxed and the sug-

TABLE 7.1. Potential Timebox Periods for Common Tasks

Deliverable	Timebox Period
Develop a error handling facility	5 to 15 days
Develop a user manual	5 to 20 days
Develop a persistence layer	2 to 4 months
Program a release of an application	3 to 6 months
Develop a proof-of-concept prototype	10 to 20 days

DEFINITIONS

persistence layer The collection of classes that provide business objects the ability to be persistent. A persistence layer effectively wraps access to your persistence mechanisms.

persistence mechanism The permanent storage facility used to make objects persistent. Examples include relational databases, object databases, flat files, and object/relational databases.

proof-of-concept prototype Software written to prove/test the viability a technology, language, or environment.

prototype A mock-up of all or a portion of your application.

timebox A defined period of time, from several days to several months, in which a team of developers is assigned to produced a given deliverable. With a timebox the end date is actually a fixed deadline, if the team needs to it will cut features out of the deliverable, it will not extend the delivery date.

gested periods of time in which the deliverable would be built. It is important to understand that although a range of suggested times is presented timeboxes actually have firm deadlines. For example, a timebox for developing an error-handling facility might have a firm date of 12 days to develop it.

The interesting thing about Table 7.1 is what it does not contain: development of a project plan, development of a requirements document, or development of your application design. These are all tasks that depend on the vagaries of the schedules of

WAR STORY

Timeboxing Often Misses the Big-Picture

Timeboxing is an excellent management strategy for getting things done, but are you getting the things done that you really want over the long term? Timeboxing, because of its focus on short-term goals, often concentrates on the details of a small portion of the application and misses the big picture. One way to avoid this problem is to work from an architectural model, covered in detail in Chapter 8, to put the efforts of the developers into context. Development standards, especially user interface and coding standards, also help to ensure that timeboxed deliverables work together and contribute positively to the overall application.

your user community and senior management. The good news is that timeboxing is applicable to the management of straightforward tasks such as the programming of applications whose design has been validated, and development of technical things like error-handling facilities or persistence layers. These are all tasks that you can control and manage yourself.

For timeboxing to be successful, you must be willing to cut product features, not product quality, to meet your given deadline. For the task that you are timeboxing you should have a well-defined set of prioritized requirements, a realistic schedule defined by the timebox team, a task that is appropriate to timeboxing, and sufficient end-user involvement to validate your work in progress (McConnell, 1996).

7.3.1.3 Software Configuration Management (SCM)

A critical issue for the successful management of a project is its use of software configuration management (SCM) techniques. Compton and Conner (1994) define SCM as a set of engineering procedures for tracking and documenting software, including its related deliverables, throughout their life cycles to ensure that all changes are recorded and the current state of the software is known and reproducible. As you would expect, SCM is a major component of deliverable management covered in Chapter 20. My experience is that any deliverable worth creating is worth putting under SCM control—if I'm going to invest my time building something then I should also invest the time to ensure that it is accurately tracked and documented.

Any deliverable worth creating is worth putting under SCM control.

To understand SCM we must start by learning the differences between revisions, versions, and baselines. A revision is any change to a deliverable, a version encompasses one or more revisions, and a baseline is a tested and certified version. As shown in Figure 7.4 there are four types of baseline: a functional baseline that represents the requirements and associated test criteria for the application; an allocated baseline that includes the software requirements, models, and an allocation of requirements to configuration items; a developmental baseline that represents the incremental software builds created during the Program stage; and a product baseline is the exact version of the software that is released to the user community. Figure 7.4 shows that there is one functional baseline that is developed during the Define and Validate

Initial Requirements stage (Chapter 3), one allocated baseline that is developed during the Model stage (Chapter 8), several developmental baselines created during the Program stage (Chapter 9), and one product baseline defined during the Release stage (Ambler, 1998b). Coplien's (1995) Named Stable Bases task process pattern suggests that you should seek to stabilize the system interfaces, the design, of your software no more than once a week, although other portions of your effort can be baselined more often. This provides developers with known, stable designs to work to.

SCM is comprised of four major activities (Compton and Conner, 1994):

- Configuration identification
- Configuration control
- Configuration auditing
- Configuration status accounting

7.3.1.3.1 Configuration Identification

Configuration identification is the process of designating configuration items (CIs), any deliverable or portion of a deliverable subject to SCM procedures, and the components of CIs. For the most part, CIs are identified during the stages of the Construct phase—Model, Program, Generalize, and Test in the Small—although many organizations will choose to place management documents such as risk assessments and project plans under configuration control as well, documents that are applicable through the Initiate, Construct, and Deliver phases. For each CI an audit trail, also called a modification log or revision history, is established so that changes can be recorded and managed.

In the object-oriented world a configuration item is any deliverable or portion of a deliverable that encompasses a single, cohe-

Figure 7.4. The various types of baselines

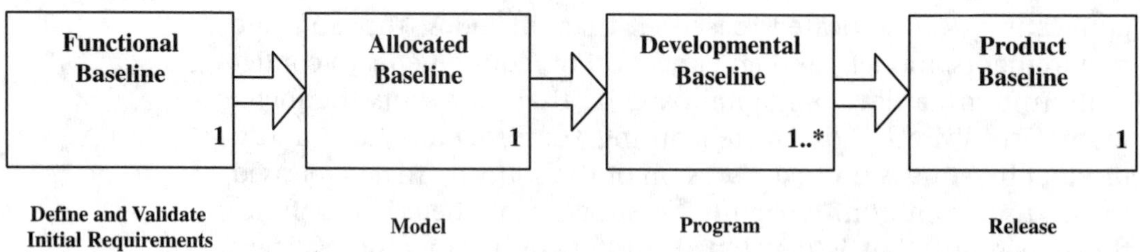

sive concept. This means that a class diagram is a potential configuration item, as is a class that appears on that class diagram, and potentially even the methods and attributes of that class. Stop and think about it—a class diagram encapsulates the static design of your application, therefore it needs to be placed under SCM control. A class encapsulates a single, cohesive concept (assuming that it was well designed) therefore it should be placed under SCM control. Furthermore, well-designed attributes and methods also encapsulate a single concept and therefore should potentially be placed under SCM control. Unfortunately few tools support this level of SCM sophistication, and the burden of manual configuration management at this level often proves to be too great a burden for the developers, resulting in single classes and/or files being the common unit of configuration management. A signifi-

Configuration items are potentially anything encapsulating a single, cohesive concept.

DEFINITIONS

allocated baseline A baseline where all requirements defined by the functional baseline are assigned/mapped to classes within your design.

baseline A tested and certified version of a deliverable representing a conceptual milestone which thereafter serves as the basis for further development and that can be modified only through formal change control procedures. A particular version becomes a baseline when a responsible group decides to designate it as such.

developmental baseline This represents the incremental software builds needed to develop the application. Developmental baselines are major deliverables of the Program stage.

functional baseline The application requirements, and related test criteria, that are defined in such a manner that software development can be performed. The requirements are typically in the form of a requirements document or System Requirements Specification (SRS).

product baseline The exact version of the software that is released to the user community.

revision A change to a deliverable.

software configuration management (SCM) A set of engineering procedures for tracking and documenting software and its related deliverables throughout their life cycles to ensure that all changes are recorded and the current state of the software is known and reproducible.

version One or more revisions to a deliverable results in a new version.

DEFINITIONS

class diagram Class diagrams show the classes of a system and their associations. Class diagrams are often mistakenly referred to as object models.

cohesion A measure of how much something makes sense. Cohesive items have a single purpose.

configuration control The management of changes to configuration items.

configuration identification The process of designating configuration items and their components.

configuration item (CI) Any deliverable, or portion of a deliverable, that is subject to SCM procedures.

deliverable Any document or system component that is produced during the development of a system. Some deliverables are used internally on a project whereas others are produced specifically for users of the application. Examples of deliverables include user requirements, models, plans, assessments, or other documents.

Changes should be made to configuration items only if the changes make sense.

To work on a configuration item you must check it out, work on it, then check it back in.

cant benefit of CIs is that everyone knows what the developer(s) will manage and deliver to their customers.

7.3.1.3.2 Configuration Control

Configuration control is the management of changes to CIs. The basic idea is that you should not make changes to software just because somebody asked for the changes, instead you should make changes because it makes sense to do so. Developers should be willing to accept constructive criticism, but at the same time be prepared to stand up and fight for the integrity of their work.

A critical component of configuration control is the prioritization of requested changes. By working on changes in priority order you ensure that the most important modifications are performed first and that you do not attempt to take on too much work at once and become overwhelmed. Prioritization techniques are discussed in detail in the Identify Bugs and Enhancements stage (Ambler, 1998b).

Another fundamental of configuration control is that no two developers should work on the same CI at once. This is one of the reasons why you want configuration items to be reasonably fine-grained, potentially down to the class or even method/ attribute level. To ensure that any given CI is worked on by one person at a

TIP

Developers Must Understand What a Baseline Is

A baseline is a tested and certified version of a deliverable. Baselines are effectively "official versions" of a deliverable, and because they are official you do not make modifications to them. Instead, you create a new version and modify it. This new version is now a working copy that will be updated as necessary and at some point possibly tested and certified to become the new baseline for that deliverable. Professional developers realize that other people will rely on a baseline remaining constant so that they can work on their own deliverables, therefore, they do not modify the baseline because to do so will negatively impact the work of their teammates.

time the configuration manager is responsible for defining a process to check in/check out CIs. When a developer wants to make a modification to a CI they must check it out of the configuration management tool that it is being stored in; make, document, and test the change; and then check the CI back in so that the new version is available to other developers.

Configuration auditing verifies and validates that configurations are complete and consistent.

7.3.1.3.3 Configuration Auditing

Configuration auditing is the process of verifying and validating the fact that a proposed configuration is complete and consistent. The main goals are to verify that a deliverable exists, is complete, is accurate, and contains an up-to-date revision history. When maintaining the revision history of a configuration item never assume that minor details are unimportant; you never know what information will be key to understanding the implications of a future change request or bug fix. Inexperienced developers will often fight the necessity of maintaining a revision history for their deliverables until a defect in their work is discovered and they need to go back and fix it.

DEFINITIONS

Configuration auditing The process of verifying and validating that a proposed configuration is complete and consistent.

configuration status accounting The process of keeping records of the other three configuration management activities—configuration identification, configuration control, and configuration auditing—for use in the CM process.

7.3.1.3.4 Configuration Status Accounting

Configuration status accounting is the process of keeping records of the other three SCM activities: configuration identification, configuration control, and configuration auditing. The goal is to develop and maintain key status reports about

DEFINITION

configuration control board (CCB) The group responsible for approving proposed software changes. Also called a change control board or software configuration review board (SCRB).

the SCM process, including information such as proposed changes, approved changes, and problem reports sorted in priority order. These reports are used by the configuration control board of your project.

7.3.1.3.5 The Configuration Control Board (CCB)

The configuration control board authorizes changes to configuration items.

The configuration control board (CCB), also called a change control board, is the group of people with the highest level of authority to make changes to configuration items. The CCB holds regularly scheduled meetings where they review the status of approved change requests and problem fixes; consider for approval new change requests and problem reports; and plan future baselines. The individuals on the board should have a stake in the project outcome and want to ensure that your organization's standards and guidelines are neither ignored nor applied so strictly that no revenue-producing product is ever fielded.

The CCB authorizes "high-level" changes but does not get involved with the minutiae of day-to-day development.

The important thing to keep in mind is that the CCB is only concerned with changes to the baseline product—they do not get involved with the managing of day-to-day revisions to CIs during construction. For example, the CCB may authorize a change to an existing report, which in turn may require revisions to several existing classes to support that change. The key is that the CCB authorized the team to make the change to the report, but did not get involved in the detailed revisions which were better left to be managed by the project manager or team lead responsible for that change.

7.3.1.3.6 SCM Tips and Techniques

The following tips and techniques should help you to improve your SCM process:

1. **Configuration items should encapsulate a single, cohesive concept.** The purpose of a configuration item is to provide a manageable thing against which you can easily identify changes for and then make those changes. If your CIs are not cohesive, if they do not have clearly defined purposes, then it will be very difficult to identify the impact of a proposed change to your application and then make that change. In other words, your application will be difficult to maintain and enhance.
2. **Record every problem and change request.** No matter how unimportant a change or bug fix may seem at the time you

need to maintain a record of it so that when a complex change or problem is identified you can readily determine the current state of your application.

3. **Close important changes/problems first.** By prioritizing changes and then acting on the most important ones first you maximize your effectiveness by concentrating on the modifications that matter the most.
4. **Put all deliverables under SCM control, not just code.** Many developers use SCM techniques just for source code. Yes, putting source code under SCM control is important but it is not sufficient. You need to place your models, plans, test cases, and documents under configuration management control as well as your source code.
5. **All developers must be subject to SCM procedures.** The best developers insist on configuration control: they do not want their quality work to be accidentally compromised by ill-considered changes. I wouldn't trust the work of somebody who is not willing to take simple, basic measures to protect it, would you? If you are burdened with cowboy programmers who are unwilling to follow your configuration management procedures then restrict and/or remove their access to your source code to prevent the inevitable damage that they will cause.

Why do you want to perform software configuration management? The answer is simple: change is a risky business, and risk must be managed. The risk is that one irresponsible developer can destroy the integrity of the work of others, and can even compromise the integrity of your application. Furthermore, by managing and tracking the deliverables produced during construction successful SCM results in reduced workloads for the development team because nobody's stepping on your toes or overwriting your work, as well as an improved build process because you know where your code is and what makes up a given version. Finally, SCM provides developers with the ability to easily roll back to a previous version of a deliverable, enabling them to experiment and try different approaches without fear of losing previous work.

7.3.1.4 Managing Parallel Development

Timeboxing is often used on projects that want to develop work in parallel—to have several development efforts occur simultane-

Parallel development reduces the calendar time required to produce an application but must be carefully managed.

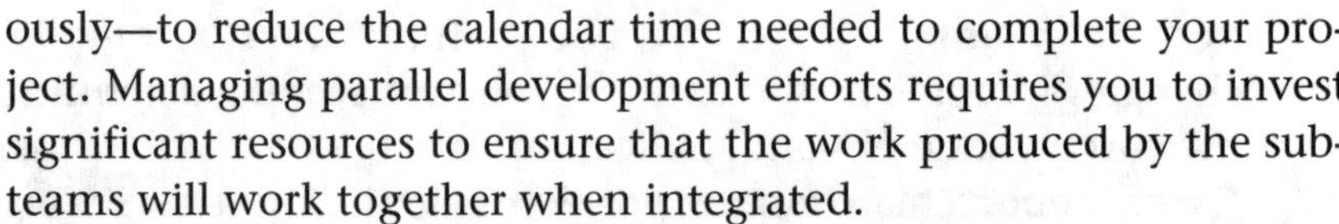

ously—to reduce the calendar time needed to complete your project. Managing parallel development efforts requires you to invest significant resources to ensure that the work produced by the subteams will work together when integrated.

Figure 7.5 depicts a parallel approach to software development, indicating that you start parallel development efforts by performing basic initiation work, including: the development of a design describing exactly what is to be built and how it will be built; an accepted set of development standards and guidelines to be followed by the subteams to ensure consistency between their deliverables; a realistic plan for the teams to follow; a defined software configuration management (SCM) process; and a strategy for synchronizing the efforts of the teams. For parallel development to be successful the subteams must work toward a common vision and must regularly communicate with one another to nurture and grow that vision. Without intergroup coordination, a key process area (KPA) of the capability maturity model (CMM), parallel development will quickly devolve into chaos.

Synchronization will often occur following a top-down approach: the architects will synchronize their efforts with the application/detailed modelers, the modelers and team leads will then synchronize with the programmers of their subteam. The Synchronizing Parallel Construction process pattern shown in Figure 7.6 indicates that you will need to synchronize frequently at the beginning of your project so that your subteams get into a

Initiate | **Manage and Sychronize Parallel Development Efforts**

Development Effort 1

Development Effort 2

•
•
•

Development Effort *n*

Figure 7.5. Taking a parallel approach to software development

Support Manager	Operations Manager	Configuration Control Board Manager
Support Engineer	Operations Engineer	Configuration Item Owner

Figure 7.6. The Synchronizing Parallel Construction task process pattern

rhythm for working together effectively. Later during construction you can meet less frequently, but as construction nears the end you need to synchronize more frequently to ensure that everything integrates well.

The key to synchronization is to define regular points of contact where the team gets together to keep each other updated. There are several ways to do this: you can get the teams together for regular meetings; the team leads can get together in regular meetings; a common internal newsgroup can be defined which all the developers access and use regularly; and email can be used to share electronic information. The point to be made is that the subteams must actively communicate with one another for parallel development to be successful. Most projects will have several types of synchronization points, employing both physical meetings and electronic communication technologies where appropriate.

You can employ several strategies for synchronizing parallel development efforts.

Some of the things that need to occur during the synchronization points include: the architect(s) must communicate and support their vision of the overall environment, the application modeler(s) must communicate and support their vision of the application; the programmers must communicate what they are doing; the project manager must communicate the status of the project; and the appropriate team members must discuss and debate issues that are important to the project.

7.3.1.5 Reuse First, Buy Second, Build Last

Figure 7.7 depicts the Reuse First task process pattern, a fundamental pattern that is applicable to all stages of the Construct phase, although to be truly accurate this process pattern is applicable to all stages of the Object-Oriented Software Process (OOSP). The Reuse First process pattern shows the basic steps of achieving reuse throughout your project: you determine the requirements

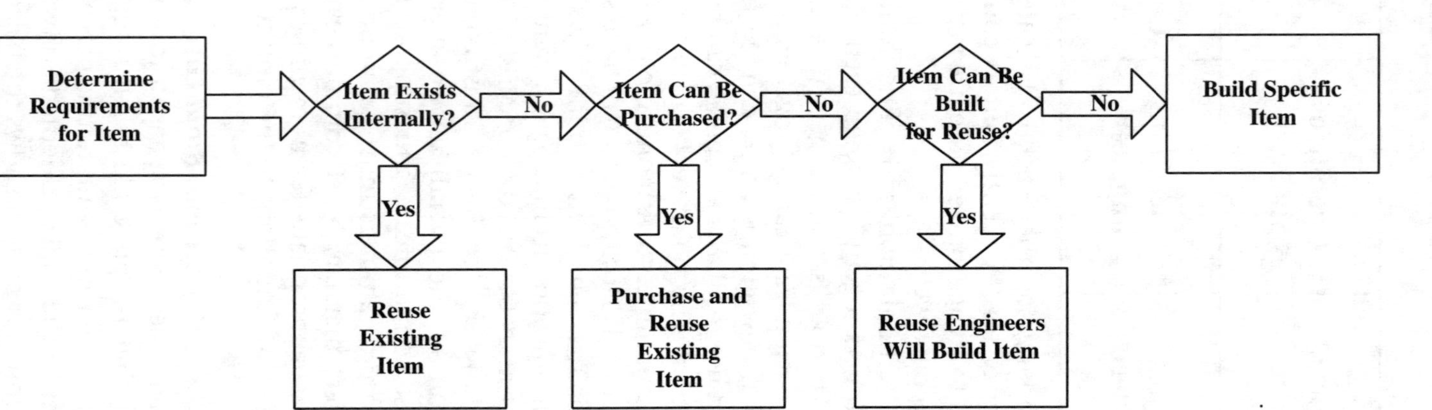

Figure 7.7. The Reuse First process pattern

for the item that you need, you determine if the item already exists within your organization, if not you attempt to purchase the item, if this fails attempt to build the item to be as reusable as possible if resources permit, or at worst build a version of the item that is specific to the task at hand. The advantages of this process pattern are that it reduces both the development time and cost for the software that you are building, and that it is applicable to any type of deliverable; this process pattern can be applied to the reuse of standards, of documentation, of models, and of source code. The only way that your organization will achieve high levels of reuse is to actively attempt to reuse or purchase items instead of building them.

Build things only as a last resort.

7.3.1.6 Infrastructure First, Application Second

The Infrastructure First organizational pattern, shown in Figure 7.8, applies the Reuse First with a parallel approach to development. The basic idea is that your project will often find that it needs several key infrastructure artifacts, such as a user interface framework, a persistence layer, or coding standards, in place before the Program stage (Chapter 9) may begin. If the required infrastructure artifacts were not procured during the Define Infrastructure stage (Chapter 6) then your project team will need to build one or more of them before they begin coding your application. Your goal is to develop one or more key artifacts so that they will be reusable, or at least can be made reusable during the Generalize stage (Chapter 10), for future projects. This work, if man-

You can develop key infrastructure items in parallel to modeling your application.

TIP

Perform Risk Management at Synchronization Points

Parallel development increases the risk to your project as it offers more opportunities for your project to devolve in chaos—subteams arguing about how to proceed, several subteams working on the same product, and the inability to integrate the deliverables of each team to name a few. Furthermore, because you have multiple streams of development occurring simultaneously the probability is that your project will run into problems that much sooner.

The best way to manage the risks of parallel development is to identify and investigate risks during your synchronization meetings. Ask your team members about any potential problems they see and have the entire team discuss the issue and formulate a solution.

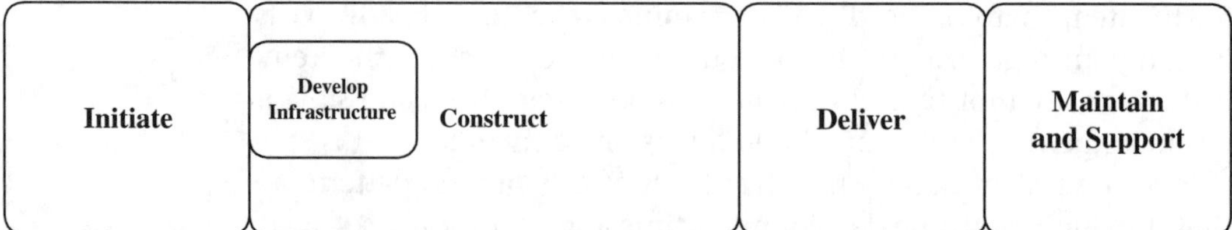

Figure 7.8. The Infrastructure First organizational pattern

aged appropriately, can be performed in parallel to your modeling efforts for your application.

The Infrastructure First organizational pattern is effective only when you are able to identify the requirements for the infrastructure artifacts that you require, a task that can be aided by experienced infrastructure engineers, you are able to manage the complexity of parallel development efforts, and you have experienced reuse and component engineers available to aid in the development of your infrastructure artifacts. It is virtually impossible for novice object-oriented developers to create items that are reusable from the start, very often they develop reuseless artifacts, not reusable artifacts. Experienced developers, however, are often able to develop reusable infrastructure artifacts because they have likely developed non-reusable versions of the artifacts in the past. This should be expected—Brooks (1995) states that "you should always plan to throw the first one away," which could be reworded to be "you know what you are doing the second time around." The Infrastructure First process pattern is a key enabler of infrastructure management.

7.3.1.7 Rescuing a Project From Chaos

The reality is that a project will often devolve in chaos and will need to be rescued from itself. It is possible to rescue a project from chaos, to bring it back from the brink of failure, if you are willing to make a few difficult decisions. My experience is that it is possible to rescue troubled projects by following the steps below.

7.3.1.7.1 Step One: Deal With Reality

To rescue a project from chaos you must start by dealing with the reality that the project has in fact devolved into chaos. This means that you need to:

1. **Accept the fact that you are in trouble.** You cannot rescue a project until you recognize that it needs to be rescued. There are several clear warning signs that your project needs help: everyone is

DEFINITIONS

component engineer A person who builds and then supports reusable components. Component engineers will often act as internal consultants to project teams to ensure that the teams are gaining the greatest benefits from reusable components. This is a key role for both the Program and Generalize stages.

infrastructure artifact An item, such as your organization's software process, a standard, a guideline, or a chosen tool that is common between project teams to build applications to support your organization.

infrastructure engineer A person who is responsible for defining and supporting the project infrastructure (processes, guidelines, standards, and tools). The role is applicable to the Define Infrastructure stage all stages of the Construct phase.

infrastructure management A cross-project effort which includes your organization's architectural and enterprise modeling efforts, as well as the definition and support of your organization's processes, standards, guidelines, and chosen toolsets.

organizational pattern A pattern that describes a common management technique or a structure appropriate to a software organization.

reuse engineer A senior, experienced developer who is responsible for supporting and enhancing the reuse process within your organization. This person works closely with component engineers and infrastructure engineers, and is a key role in all stages of the Construct phase.

reuseless An item that has been promoted as reusable but in practice is found to be too specific or of low quality.

coding-like-mad to make a deadline; you are several weeks/months behind but believe that if everything goes your way (they never do) that you just might make it; everyone is putting in heroic efforts working twelve-, fourteen-, even sixteen-hour days; and your user community is either up-in-arms against you or is completely ambivalent to your project. Any one of these issues is an indication that your project is in trouble, if your project exhibits several of them then you are clearly in bad shape.

2. **Do not panic.** It is rarely as bad as you think it is. Okay, sometimes it is as bad or even worse than you think, but without a positive attitude you are in even bigger trouble. Stop, calm yourself, and approach the problem with a clear and open mind.

3. **Recognize that it is likely a management problem.** Maguire (1994) believes that when one person is behind then they need to change the way that they are working, but that when an entire team is behind it is likely a management problem. By identifying the likely source of the problem, management, you are more likely to identify a workable solution. Perhaps your project does not have a realistic plan, perhaps your team is not following a realistic software process, perhaps your team is not working well together, or perhaps ill-considered decisions have been made regarding technologies employed by your team.
4. **Assess the work to date.** You need to honestly evaluate what work has been performed and what its status is to identify what you want to keep and what you need to throw away. This is probably the most difficult part of rescuing a project—realizing that some or all of the work you have done needs to be scrapped. You will often find that the code that was developed without the benefit of developing a model first needs to be rewritten as it will be a patchwork of approaches and ill-thought concepts. It is also common to see projects run aground when technology that was chosen for them, often by senior management or members of the user community, does not work as described in the business article they read.
5. **Communicate that the project is in trouble.** Your project team needs to be informed that the project is in trouble, as does senior management and your user community. Convincing the project team that you are in trouble is incredibly easy to do—they probably knew it long before you decided to tell them about it. The problem will be with senior management and your users, two groups of people who rarely like to hear bad news. If you truly are in trouble and likely to be over budget and/or late then the earlier you let everyone know the better. It is the responsibility of the project manager to set realistic expectations as to the state of the project. Both groups need to know what's happening so that they can make an informed decision about how to, or whether to, proceed with the project.
6. **Put together a realistic plan.** Once everyone recognizes that the project is in trouble, and an honest assessment of the situation has been performed, you are in a position to put together a revised plan to deliver your application. Maguire (1994) points out that the key ingredients to success are to first set a clear and consistent goal and then to develop a

realistic plan to reach that goal. This means that you must consider reducing the scope of your project and/or set a new realistic deadline for it. Once you have a plan in place you must then work the plan to get yourself out of trouble.

7.3.1.7.2 Step Two: Get Yourself Out of Trouble

You now have a plan in place and are ready to work it. The secret is to avoid past mistakes and to instead do what it takes to deliver the software successfully. This means that you need to:

1. **Rethink the project team.** Brooks's law (Brooks, 1995) states that if you add people to a late project you will make it later. My experience is that the opposite also holds true: if you remove the right people from a late project you will deliver it sooner. By removing your less-experienced developers from the project you enable your experienced developers to work faster as they are no longer being held back mentoring and supporting the novices. Unfortunately this strategy assumes that you know who your less-experienced people are. I've often seen projects go astray because the lead developer is a hack who's gotten in over his head, and removing this one person can often dramatically improve your project's chance of success. You can always identify the hacks by their reputations: these are the developers who work extraordinary hours producing code that only they can understand. Does it make sense to you that your "best" people need to work overtime to get their work done, and then produce something that is incomprehensible to everyone else?
2. **Work smarter, not harder.** Working long hours will not bring a troubled project under control, but working smarter will. Maguire (1994) points out that if you were on a sinking ship, would you get people to work harder bailing water or would you start looking for the leaks? In system development, where thinking is the critical input, working longer hours is not going to help much; you need to determine where the problem is and deal with it directly.
3. **Ensure that the up-front work has been performed.** Are the requirements well-defined, accurate, and accepted by the user community? Are the models up-to-date, accurate, and traceable back to the requirements? Many projects get them-

selves into trouble by starting to code before the requirements and models are in place, and if you are going to rescue the project, you need to ensure that you have a solid foundation from which to continue. The problem of not having the up-front work in place is that it inevitably goes hand-in-hand with having a hack coder for a team lead.

4. **Take daily action toward your goal.** Everything that is done should be directly related to delivering a quality product to your user community. If you are doing something that does not add direct value to the end product then stop doing it and focus on something that does add value.
5. **Timebox your deliverables.** Timeboxing, discussed previously, is an excellent technique for ensuring that your project meets its deadlines.

By following the advice above, you will eventually, most likely painfully, deliver your application to your user community. Now it is time to finish the recovery process.

7.3.1.7.3 Step Three: Recover From Your Mistakes
Rescuing the project from chaos is only part of what you need to do, although obviously it is your first priority. Once you have delivered the application to your user community, you must:

1. **Recognize that you will lose good people if you do not act quickly.** Although your project team has stuck it out and delivered the application, it does not mean that they intend to stay with your organization. When projects get into trouble many developers decide to start looking for another job once the project ends: they recognize the fact that they are obligated to finish their existing work, but at the same time they do not want to work for you anymore. This means that you need to invest the time to talk with each developer once the application is delivered, let them know that they are valuable to your organization and that the project was an aberration that you hope not to repeat. Consider giving raises and promotions to key staff at this point, as well as vacations disguised as training in interesting, out of town locales (as a Canadian I love going on courses held in California). Recognize that your staff has just been through a very stressful experience and have likely made personal sacrifices to make your project successful. Now is the time to reward them for it.

2. **Assess what happened.** At the end of every project you should assess what went right and what went wrong, which is why the object-oriented software process (OOSP) includes the Assess stage (Ambler, 1998b). Because you learn far more from your mistakes than from your successes it is critical that you invest the time to assess projects that needed to be rescued from chaos. By learning from your mistakes you are less likely to make them again, and the easiest way to manage a project in trouble is to not get into trouble in the first place.

7.3.2 People Management

In this section I will first describe the various roles filled by team members during the Construct phase and then discuss issues which are unique to this phase.

7.3.2.1 Roles During the Construct Phase

Figure 7.9 shows the critical roles, described in Table 7.2, that are performed by team members during the Construct phase. Because there is far more to developing software than programming there are many non-programming roles that must be filled during this phase.

As you would expect, the project manager and team lead are required throughout the entire Construct phase to manage the team. During the Model stage subject matter experts (SMEs) are needed to provide their expertise to the architectural and domain

Project Manager	**Team Lead**	**Software Configuration Manager**	**Test Manager**
Architectural Modeler	**Domain Programmer**	**Subject Matter Expert**	**Quality Assurance Engineer**
Domain Modeler	**Component Engineer**	**Reuse Engineer**	**Test Engineer**
Mentor	**Infrastructure Engineer**	**Technical Writer**	**R&D/Proof -of-Concept Engineer**

Figure 7.9. Potential roles on a construction team

TABLE 7.2. Common Roles Held During the Construct Phase

Role	Description
Architectural modeler	A person who is involved in understanding and modeling the enterprise, business architecture, and/or technical architecture for your organization.
Component engineer	A person who builds and then supports reusable components. Component engineers will often act as internal consultants to project teams to ensure that the teams are gaining the greatest benefits from reusable components.
Domain modeler	A person who is actively involved in modeling the problem domain for an application and/or for a reusable large-scale domain component.
Domain programmer	A developer who writes, documents, and unit tests program source code for an application.
Infrastructure engineer	A person who is responsible for supporting the project infrastructure (processes, guidelines, standards, and tools) during construction.
Mentor	An experienced developer who transfers their skills to less experienced developers to aid in their education experience.
Project manager	This person is responsible for obtaining funding and authorization for the project from senior management.
Quality assurance engineer	This person is responsible for validating that the deliverables produced by the development team meet or exceed the agreed-to standards and guidelines for the project.
R&D/proof-of-concept engineer	A developer who creates technical prototypes, also called proof-of-concept prototypes, to determine how to solve a given technical issue.
Reuse engineer	A senior, experienced developer who is responsible for supporting and enhancing the reuse process within your organization.

(continued)

TABLE 7.2. *(continued)*

Role	Description
Software configuration manager	The person responsible for ensuring that software, and related deliverables, are managed appropriately under configuration control as well as to communicate all SCM policies and procedures to developers. The greater the complexity of the software being developed the greater the need for a software configuration manager.
Team lead	This is the developer who is responsible for ensuring the overall technical integrity of the project and for working together with the project manager to aid and support the other developers on the team. A main responsibility of team leads is to ruthlessly eliminate any obstacles that keep the developers away from working to improve the application.
Technical writer	This person is responsible for writing, updating, and/or improving the technical documentation produced on the project, potentially including the requirements, models, standards, guidelines, and project plans.
Test engineer	This person is responsible for verifying that the application works as defined by the requirements for the application.

modelers who in turn are supported by technical writers to help document their models. The Program stage requires that the domain programmers be mentored and supported by the domain modelers, component engineers, and infrastructure engineers who understand the application model, domain components, and your project's chosen infrastructure respectively. The Test in the Small stage requires that the test manager, test engineers, and quality assurance engineers work closely with the developers (modelers and programmers) on your team. Finally, during the Generalize stage your reuse engineers work with your developers to make their application-specific deliverables reusable by future project teams.

7.3.2.2 People Management Issues Unique to the Construct Phase

There a several issues unique to the Construct phase with regards to people management. In this section we explore them in detail.

1. **The "I am superior to everyone else" attitude of developers.** Software development is a complex field that requires a certain mindset to be successful. You know what, the exact same thing can be said of marketing, medicine, accounting, law, manufacturing, support, and a myriad of other careers. Too many developers think that they are superior to their users just because they understand technology and their users do not. It is people with this arrogant attitude that are the most likely to fail, and the most likely to blame others for their shortcomings with comments like "the users do not know what they want" and "the users are too stupid to understand how to use the system properly." More likely the real problem was that the arrogant developer did not invest enough time to determine the requirements or to develop a usable user interface.
2. **The "bring me a solution, not a problem" mindset of project managers.** Maguire (1994) points out that it is unreasonable to expect everyone to be able to determine a solution to a problem, but if they identify the problem and share it with the team, then perhaps someone else will identify a solution. This is what teamwork is all about. Project managers who only want solutions brought to them will often find they are managing projects that get sidelined by problems that they did not hear about until it was too late.
3. **The "developers are just like every other employee" attitude of senior management.** In some organizations this may be true, knowledge-intensive ones, but in most it simply is not. By definition developers are knowledge workers, people who are hired for their thinking ability. Knowledge workers need their own private workspaces where they can think and do their work. Open-air cubicles may work for the accounting and marketing departments, which I personally doubt, but it certainly does not work for the system department.
4. **The "they will just have to share" mindset of senior management.** Software project teams often need greater physical resources than other employees, a perfect example being the

full-time use of a project workroom. Constantine (1995) suggests that each development project have its own meeting room that it uses exclusively as a workroom. Team members need access to a room where they can quickly get together, discuss an idea, and work on it without having to worry about booking it or losing whatever work they leave behind on the whiteboards. My experience is that the best workrooms have a lot of whiteboard space; I'm always willing to trade a window for a whiteboard, and somewhere to post printed models.

5. **The "we are only here to work" mindset of project managers.** The best development teams are those that gel together, and to do that you need to build team morale by holding non-work related events such as barbecues, movie outings, and boat cruises, to name a few. One of the hardest-working teams that I ever met was a small object-oriented consulting company in São Paulo, Brazil that played networked video games together after work (when I played against them I naturally let them win, yeah, that's it). Remember the saying: the teams that play together stay together.
6. **The "let's start coding" mindset of developers.** Constantine (1995) notes that developers are constantly getting ahead of themselves. Give them a user requirements document and they are instantly thinking about code. Mention a new piece of hardware and they are instantly thinking about code. Give them a diagram and they are instantly thinking about code. Give them some code and they are instantly thinking about code. You get the picture. Constantine suggests that one way to get developers to focus on the task at hand is that whenever a future development issue arises that it be tabled for discussion when it is appropriate to do so. This type of information should go into your group memory, which was started in the Define Initial Management Documents stage (Chapter 4).

DEFINITION

group memory A record of what your project team accomplished, decisions made by your team and the reasoning behind them, deferred decisions, and the lessons learned on your project. A group memory provides a mechanism to record this information when it is first recognized so that it is not lost.

7.3.3 Potential Risks During the Construct Phase

There are several risks pertinent to the Construct phase that you need to be aware of:

1. **Without a software configuration management process (SCM) in place your project is likely in trouble.** You have to be able to control the deliverables that you are producing, otherwise work will quickly get out of synch and will often be lost due to accidents. You need to put your SCM process into place before construction begins.
2. **"Changing requirements" often result in project failure.** When a project is beset by a deluge of new or changed requirements

Scott's Soapbox

Hacking Isn't Just for Programmers Anymore

Hackers come in all shapes and sizes. For the purpose of our discussion a hacker is someone who refuses to consider all of the relevant issues when developing their portion of an application. Hackers usually have limited experience and often only look at the small picture, usually run-time efficiency concerns, and as a result do not take the full life cycle viewpoint needed of a professional software engineer. Having said that, you do not want to confuse inexperience with hacking—a hacker is often missing key experience but does not recognize the fact, whereas a professional developer will recognize where he or she needs to improve and actively seeks to do so.

Who are likely candidates for hackers? First, a primary candidate is a programmer who has been working in the computer industry for several years but who has never been involved in the maintenance of an existing system. Maintenance is an important part of the life cycle, so any programmer who does not have maintenance experience does not have a complete understanding of the development process. Second, data modelers who have never worked closely with either process modelers or programmers also have a tendency to be hackers. The problem is that they tend to look at only half the picture, the data half, and ignore the behavior half that is equally as important. The result is that they tend to create models that are wonderful from a data point of view but often flawed from an object point of view. This becomes a problem on projects that use a relational database as their persistence mechanism, because the data modelers, a group of people who in the past often provided a key model for the development process, mistakenly think that data models should now drive OO development projects too. The point to be made is that it is possible for both programmers and modelers to be hackers, it is just that they hack in different ways.

during the Construct phase, the result is that the project will often be rethought, potentially resulting in a scope change or even the cancellation of the project. I have indicated "changing requirements" in quotations because my experience is that requirements rarely change; just the understanding of those requirements by the project team. Have you ever noticed that project teams that do not invest adequately in modeling their application experience high levels of changing requirements? Or that organizations that do not invest in architectural modeling, a topic covered by the Model stage (Chapter 8), often get blindsided by changes in their business or technical environments? Yes, requirements do evolve over time, but nowhere near the rate that many developers believe.

Very often what changes is your understanding of requirements, not the requirements themselves.

3. **Silver bullets rarely deliver.** A silver bullet is any product or technique that promises order-of-magnitude improvements in your

War Story

Everyone Should Have Their Own Plate

I once worked as a team member of a project where the manager insisted that everyone maintain what he called a "plate document"—a textual description of what each person was currently working on, what their time commitments were, and what their planned training and vacation schedule was. By requiring that everyone place their plates in a shared directory accessible by everyone on the team it was easy for people to determine who might need some help and more importantly who you could draw on for help. Everyone kept their plates up-to-date, which allowed us to plan among ourselves and to work together effectively.

Although this concept worked well for that team, a reasonably large team of people who had worked together for several years, it did not work very well when I tried to introduce it to the next team that I worked with. There were several problems: first, the team wasn't accustomed to working together and included several cowboy programmers who preferred to work alone. Second, the people who were inclined to work together were able to keep track of each other's status in their heads and did not need to use plate documents to do so.

Anyway, take the plate concept for what it is: one technique to help manage a team of developers.

development productivity. Examples of silver bullets include the structured paradigm, the object-oriented paradigm (to be brutally honest), computer-aided software engineering (CASE) tools, fourth-generation (4GL) languages, data warehouses, and client/server (C/S) architecture. All of these silver bullets do in fact help to improve the productivity of developers, but often by 10 to 50 percent, not 10 to 20 times as was often promised.

4. **Future releases of critical software will likely be late.** If you are depending on software from other organizations, perhaps a new release of your operating system or database, you are probably in trouble. The reality in this industry is that the vast majority of software is delivered late, and if your application depends on releases of other products it will likely become late waiting for the other software.
5. **Avoid too many new things at once.** Project teams that attempt to do too many new things at once usually get into trouble. This is a significant risk with object-oriented development because the first OO project often needs to use a completely different toolset, follow a completely different methodology, a new programming language, a new operating system, and for a new business domain that your organization has never tackled before. Projects that deal with a large number of new issues—effectively, a large number of relative unknowns—are at risk of failure if any one of these issues proves insurmountable. A good rule of thumb is to attempt projects where less than twenty percent of it is new to you, implying that you may need to reorganize your project into smaller releases to tackle each issue one release at a time.
6. **Protect your developers from politics.** Politics are, unfortunately, a necessary evil. That does not mean, however, that your developers need to get sidelined by the political machinations of others. I've seen project teams get distracted for several weeks based on a single rumor, a rumor which usually proves to be mistaken. At a minimum, the project manager should be politically adept, and it does not hurt if your senior staff, such as the architect, are politically savvy too. Yourdon (1997) advises that all developers be made aware of who the key players are to minimize the chance that they let any politically-sensitive information slip. It is critical that everyone know who their friends and who their foes are.
7. **Avoid a calendar-driven schedule.** Target delivery dates are often pulled from thin air by management and marketing

people, and not from a reasonable planning process. Rapid development of applications is often real, but the deadlines under which projects operate often aren't. Booch (1996) correctly observes that shortcuts taken during development often result in software that is rarely scalable, extensible, portable, or reusable—software that may meet its delivery date, but that fails to meet its other obligations to your organization. Your schedule should be based on reality, not on a whim.

8. **Communicate regularly to senior management.** Assuming that your team is reasonably on schedule and within budget a really easy way to get your project canceled is to keep senior management in the dark as to your progress. Management typically likes to see regular status reports, often weekly or monthly, to gauge how well your project is doing.
9. **Use timeboxing only where appropriate.** Timeboxing is best suited for well-understood construction tasks, such as developing an application once it has been designed, but not for doing the actual design itself. Many activities, such as requirements definition and design, are too vague to be held to a defined schedule, and therefore should not be put into a timebox (McConnell, 1996).

DEFINITIONS

architectural modeling High-level modeling, either of the business or technical domain, whose goal is to provide a common, overall vision of your domain. Architectural models provide a base from which detailed modeling will begin.

client/server (C/S) architecture A computing environment that satisfies the business need by appropriately allocating the application processing between the client and the server processes.

computer-aided system engineering (CASE) tool A tool that supports the creation of software.

data warehouse A large database, almost always relational, that is used to store data for reporting purposes.

fourth-generation language (4GL) A category of computer languages in which the development environment include tools which generate some or all of the source code for your application.

silver bullet Any product or technique that (unrealistically) promises order-of-magnitude improvements in your development productivity.

WAR STORY

Technology Doesn't Always Scale

I live near Toronto, Canada, and in the summer of 1997 a new, fully automated toll-highway north of the city was opened. Instead of toll booths with people collecting money, the new highway relied on computer technology to track the cars entering and exiting the highway. Although the identification of cars by the license plates (tags) worked (the part that I thought was sure to fail), the real problem ended up being that the database couldn't handle the number of transactions created by the toll equipment. The good news is that I got to drive for free for nearly five months until they reworked their database strategy. There's always a silver lining.

10. **The developers must see the product as the user does.** A sure way for a project to fail is for it to not meet the needs of its users. The implication is that developers must make the effort to understand the needs of its users, to work closely with their user community, and to recognize that sometimes the important issues to users are actually quite trivial from a technology point of view.
11. **Putting off the unknown for later.** Leaving all the hard decisions, all of the technological unknowns, for later in the project is always a recipe for disaster. "Later" always comes and you find that you are in trouble because what you thought would be a simple issue actually proves to be a show-stopper for your project. I've seen project teams assume that their database would scale to the actual needs of production, only to find out that it does not when they go to install it. One of the fundamentals of risk management is that once an unknown is identified that it be recognized as a risk to be alleviated, the sooner the better. Putting off unknowns increases your project's chance of failure.

7.3.4 Training and Education Issues

The following training and education issues are pertinent to the Construct phase:

1. **Everyone needs to be trained on your project infrastructure.** Everyone on your team must understand the tools that they are working with, the processes that they are following, and the standards and guidelines that are applicable to what they are producing. In other words they need to be trained on your project infrastructure.
2. **Everyone needs to understand the basics of their job.** Object-orientation is new to many developers; as a result, you may have to invest significantly in retraining your existing staff to give them the skills that they need to work on your OO projects.
3. **Make books, magazines, and journals available to your development team.** The least expensive and often most effective way for people to gain new skills is to first read about them. When you make reading material available to developers, they are able to expand their horizons and identify areas in which they feel that they need to improve. Many organizations will allow employees to subscribe to a magazine: when the issue arrives, the names of the subscribers are printed and stapled to the cover of the magazine, which is then passed around between the people on the list until everyone has read it. Also, a library of shared books and magazines can be a valuable project resource.
4. **You need to have a firm understanding of everyone's skills.** You need to identify everyone's strengths and weaknesses (skills assessments are a part of the team definition delivered by the

DEFINITIONS

class library A collection of classes, typically purchased off-the-shelf, that you can reuse and extend via inheritance.

design pattern A modeling pattern that describes a solution to a design problem.

mentor An experienced developer who transfers skills to less experienced developers to aid in their education experience. This is a key role during all phases, but specifically during the Construct phase.

pattern The description of a general solution to a common problem or issue from which a detailed solution to a specific problem may be determined. Software development patterns come in many flavors, including but not limited to analysis patterns, design patterns, and process patterns.

Infrastructure stage, described in Chapter 6) so that you can target specific training and mentoring for each developer. You also want to identify potential mentors among your staff (experts who can transfer their skills to others) to be assigned to novice developers to aid them in their education process.

5. **Ensure that your developers gain the long-term skills that they need.** Every developer should be learning something new every two months; otherwise, their skills go stale and they are no longer challenged by their work. Maguire (1994) points out that having people with a wide skill base provides greater flexibility for your organization. When training developers, focus first on skills that are beneficial to your organization and second on skills that are beneficial to your project.
6. **Hold bag-lunch training sessions.** My experience has been that the most effective training is done by developers themselves during regular lunch sessions, often weekly, where each developer takes their turn presenting a topic to the group. The basic idea is that your team gets together in a meeting or training room and eats their lunch while one of them presents a topic of interest to the group. The topics could range from a demo of the new version of a tool, to coding tricks, to a newly discovered design pattern, to a book report, or to an overview of a new class library. The advantage of this approach is that it provides an opportunity for developers to learn about new things going on outside of their project and to gain valuable experience giving presentations to groups of people.

7.4 Resulting Context: Exit Conditions from the Construct Phase

The Construct phase effectively ends when a code/development freeze has been declared. For a code/development freeze to be official, the following deliverables *must* be in place:

1. **Models and requirements allocation matrix (RAM).** The models for your application must be properly documented, validated, and placed under configuration control. The requirements allocation matrix (RAM) that maps the requirements for your application to the portions of your model

DEFINITIONS

requirements allocation matrix (RAM) A mapping of requirements defined in your requirements document to the portions of your model(s) that implement them.

use case A description of a high-level business process that an application may or may not be expected to support.

that implement them is needed by the Rework stage (Ambler, 1998b) to determine where fixes to defects need to be made, and by the Identify Defects and Enhancements stage (Ambler, 1998b) to allocate maintenance changes appropriately.

2. **Source code.** Your source code must be baselined and traceable to the appropriate portions of your models that describe them.
3. **Master test/QA plan.** Your test plan, needed for the Test in the Large stage (Ambler, 1998b), should at least be started and, ideally, should be complete so that testing may begin immediately.
4. **User documentation.** The user documentation for your application should at least be started; once you have use cases and your user interface design in place, you can start writing your user documentation. Ideally, the user documentation will be finished.
5. **Operations documentation.** The documentation needed by your operations staff to run your application should have been started during this phase and ideally should be finished.
6. **Support documentation.** The documentation needed by your support staff for your application should have been started during this phase and ideally should be finished.
7. **The application is packaged.** The software and corresponding user, operations, and support documentation should be integrated and packaged for testing in the large and eventually product release.

8. **Training plan.** The training plan, including training schedules for operations staff, support staff, and your user community, should be started and, ideally, finished so that training, an important part of the Release stage (Ambler, 1998b), may begin.
9. **Release plan.** The release plan, which includes your data conversion plans, your plans to release the application to operations and support, and your plans to release the application to your user community, should be started and, ideally, finished so that the Release stage (Ambler, 1998b) may begin.

10. **Lessons learned.** At the end of the Construct phase you should take the time to consider the processes that could be improved, what processes need to be added, and what processes could be removed. By identifying lessons learned at the end of the phase, you discover opportunities to improve your software process, and provide valuable input for the Assess stage (Ambler, 1998b).

7.5 Secrets of Success

I would like to share with you some of my secrets of success for the Construct phase:

1. **Follow your object-oriented software process (OOSP).** The Software Engineering Institute (1995) points out that a key to success during construction is to perform the engineering tasks to build and maintain your application in accordance with the project's defined software process and appropriate methods and tools. This is an important part of the level 2 key process area (KPA) Software Product Engineering of the Capability Maturity Model (CMM).
2. **Project managers must focus on more than the budget and delivery date.** There are many more factors to the success of a project than just getting it in on time and under budget. For example, your application must be usable, meet the needs of its users, and be easy to maintain and enhance.
3. **Plan ahead.** A plan is more than just a schedule; it is a collection of strategies. For example, what will you do to encourage productivity? What will you do when productivity exceeds expectations or when it falls short? How will your subteams communicate with one another? Will there be several teams in different locations, and will people be allowed to work from home or even from different time zones? These are all critical issues for which you need to plan.
4. **Get the best equipment for developers.** The easiest way to increase the productivity of developers is to give them access to good computer equipment with large screens, lots of memory, and lots of disk space. Development tools require better machinery than do typical business applications; therefore, your developers should have better equipment than the average user.

5. **Manage to your critical path and to your critical resources.** Managing to your critical path—the series of activities which determines the earliest completion of a project—is not sufficient. You must also manage to your critical resources—key developers that are needed for several project tasks; people such as quality assurance engineers and technical writers shared by several project teams; testing facilities; and training facilities, to name a few—to ensure that you have the resources your project needs when it needs them.
6. **Make everyone responsible for testing and documenting their work.** Goldberg and Rubin (1995) note that everyone should test and document their work to the best of their ability. In other words, everyone is responsible for the quality of their own work.
7. **Inspect and review all development work.** Each deliverable should have a "quality gate" defined for it: a set of conditions that it must pass to be considered usable by other developers. Anything worthy of being built is worthy of inspection and review.
8. **Start documentation early.** Key documentation, such as support, operations, and user documentation, should be started as early as possible; otherwise, you run the risk of it not getting done. Do not underestimate the effort that it takes to create these documents: you do not want to find out two weeks before you have to release your application that it will take you another two months to write the necessary documentation.
9. **Integrate your best people into your team.** Constantine (1995) believes that keeping your crack developers isolated from the rest of the organization may seem like a good idea at the time because it allows them to get a lot of work done, but it often proves to be a high-risk, high-payoff strategy because their final work may not be accepted by the rest of your development community. My experience is that the best use of your crack developers is to have them lead your teams, to have them share their insights with your less experienced developers, to mentor their teammates. The short-term pain of having your best developers transfer their skills to others will pay off in the long term through an overall increase in productivity among your staff.
10. **Expect to make mistakes.** You cannot always get it right the first time, so you need to be able to change without starting

DEFINITION

quality gate An objectively identifiable point in a project when a review is performed to validate one or more project deliverables. To meet a milestone, your project will usually need to "pass through" a quality gate successfully.

over (Goldberg and Rubin, 1995). The good news is that by regularly reviewing your work—by not waiting until the end of the project to test—you can detect and fix mistakes before they get out of hand. This is what the Test in the Small stage (Chapter 11) is all about.

11. **Perform regular mini-assessments of your project.** Yourdon (1997) suggests that you make the effort to perform regular mini-assessments of your project to learn from your experiences while they are fresh in your mind. This is in support of your efforts during the Assess stage, when you formerly assess your project and the members on your project team to aid in your effort to improve your software process. The results of the mini-assessments should be stored in the group memory of your project so that the knowledge is retained for future use.
12. **Perform user system upgrades during construction.** To streamline the deployment of your application to your user community (a major portion of the Release stage, described in *More Process Patterns* [Ambler, 1998b]), in parallel with the Construct phase you should evaluate the current hardware/software configurations of your users and make the necessary upgrades required by your application before you deploy it.

7.6 Process Checklist

The following process checklist can be used to verify that you have completed the Construct phase.

CONSTRUCT PHASE PROCESS CHECKLIST

Fulfillment of Entrance Conditions:

✔ The project plan has been accepted by senior management.

✔ The project schedule has been accepted by senior management.

✔ The initial risk assessment has been performed.

✔ The initial requirements have been accepted by senior management.

- ✔ Appropriate standards and guidelines have been identified.
- ✔ The software process has been tailored to meet the specific needs for your project.
- ✔ The appropriate tools have been identified, purchased if necessary, and installed.
- ✔ Funding for the project has been obtained.
- ✔ The project charter has been defined and accepted.
- ✔ The project team has been assembled.
- ✔ The maintenance changes allocated to the current release are identified.

Processes Performed:

- ✔ The models for the application have been developed and validated.
- ✔ The source code for the application has been developed and validated.
- ✔ Potential artifacts to be reused have been identified.
- ✔ Potential artifacts to be generalized for reuse have been identified and potentially generalized.
- ✔ User documentation has been developed.
- ✔ Risk management has been performed regularly.
- ✔ Decisions made, and forgone, have been documented in your project's group memory.

Fulfillment of Exit Conditions:

- ✔ The requirements allocation matrix (RAM) has been updated for your application.
- ✔ The project plan was updated appropriately
- ✔ The models, source code, and documentation have been baselined.
- ✔ The master test/QA plan has been updated for the Test in the Large stage.
- ✔ The user, support, and operations documentation is ready for testing.
- ✔ The application has been packaged for testing.
- ✔ The training, release, and project plans have been updated appropriately.

7.7 What You Have Learned in This Chapter

In this chapter you saw that the Construct phase is an iterative process made up of the following stages: Model, Program, Generalize, and Test in the Small. The Model stage (Chapter 8) concentrates on the abstraction of the technical and/or problem domain via the use of diagrams, documents, and prototypes. The Program stage (Chapter 9) focuses on the development and documentation of program source code. The Generalize stage (Chapter 10) is critical to your organization's reuse efforts as it focuses on identifying reusable items, or items that may become reusable once modified, from a software project. The goal of the Test in the Small stage (Chapter 11) is to verify and validate the deliverables developed during the Construct phase. You also saw that techniques such as software configuration management (SCM), parallel development, and timeboxing are critical to the success of this phase.

7.8 References and Recommended Reading

Ambler, S. W. 1998a. *Building Object Applications That Work—Your Step-By-Step Handbook for Developing Robust Systems with Object Technology.* New York: SIGS Books/Cambridge University Press.

Ambler, S. W. 1998b. *More Process Patterns: Delivering Large-Scale Systems Using Object Technology.* New York: SIGS Books/Cambridge University Press.

Booch, G. 1996. *Object Solutions—Managing the Object-Oriented Project.* Menlo Park, California: Addison Wesley Publishing Company, Inc.

Brooks, F. P 1995. *The Mythical Man Month—Anniversary Edition.* Reading, Massachusetts: Addison-Wesley Publishing Company, Inc.

Compton, S. B. and Conner, G. R. 1994. *Configuration Management for Software.* New York: Van Nostrand Reinhold.

Constantine, L. L. (1995). *Constantine on Peopleware.* Englewood Cliffs, New Jersey: Yourdon Press.

Coplien, J.O. (1995). *A Generative Development-Process Pattern Language.* Pattern Languages of Program Design, eds. Coplien, J.O. and Schmidt, D.C., Addison Wesley Longman, Inc., pp. 183–237.

Cunningham, W. (1996). *EPISODES: A Pattern Language of Competitive Development.* Pattern Languages of Program Design 2, eds. Vlissides, J.M., Coplien, J.O., and Kerth, N.L., Addison-Wesley Publishing Company., pp. 371–388.

Goldberg, A. and Rubin, K. S. 1995. *Succeeding With Objects: Decision Frameworks for Project Management.* Reading, Massachusetts: Addison-Wesley Publishing Company, Inc.

Humphrey, W. S. 1997. *Introduction to the Personal Software Process.* Reading, Massachusetts: Addison-Wesley Longman, Inc.

Maguire, S. (1994). *Debugging the Development Process.* Redmond, WA: Microsoft Press.

McConnell, S. 1996. *Rapid Development: Taming Wild Software Schedules.* Redmond, Washington: Microsoft Press.

Software Engineering Institute. 1995. *The Capability Maturity Model: Guidelines for Improving the Software Process.* Reading Massachusetts: Addison-Wesley Publishing Company, Inc.

Weir, C. (1998). *Patterns for Designing in Teams.* Pattern Languages of Program Design 3, eds. Martin, R.C., Riehle, D., and Buschmann, F., Addison Wesley Longman, Inc., pp. 487–501.

Yourdon, E. 1997. *Death March: The Complete Software Developer's Guide to Surviving "Mission Impossible" Projects.* Upper Saddle River, New Jersey: Prentice-Hall, Inc.

Chapter 8

The Model Stage

ONE of the fundamentals of software development is that you first need to understand what you are supposed to build, then you determine how you are going to build it, then you build it. In other words, you must first analyze, then design, then program. Having said that, you do not need to do all of the analysis, then do all of the design, then do all of the coding: you can work iteratively. But at the same time you just cannot start coding without first understanding the problem domain (actually you could, but most of your work will need to be redone in the long run). This chapter focuses on the analysis and design portion of construction, which we will refer to as modeling.

The object-oriented modeling process is based on the development of many interrelated models—diagrams, CRC (class responsibility collaborator) models, documents, and prototypes—which describe all or part of an application from a specific point of view. It is important to understand that no one single model captures the entirety of an application. A class diagram shows the static relationships between classes, whereas sequence diagrams show the dynamic interactions between objects. User interface prototypes model the design of screens and reports, whereas use cases model the user requirements for an application. Different models, different points of view. To be successful at object-oriented (OO) modeling, you need to understand each model, when each model should and shouldn't be used, how each model relates to the

There are many interrelated models available for describing an object-oriented application.

other models, and how to approach the modeling process for large-scale mission-critical projects. It is important to understand that a common force arrayed against the Model Stage is the lack of support of both senior management and your developers for modeling, often because they mistakenly believe that the only "real work" of software development is programming.

Models are the equivalent of a blueprint for software; they show how an application is to be built. Figure 8.1 shows that requirements and modeling standards, deliverables of the Initiate phase, are inputs into the Model stage. In other words, they should be in place before modeling starts. Although this sounds like a nice theory, what typically happens is that you have high-level requirements at best, because most projects typically skimp on the Define Initial Requirements stage (Chapter 3), and the modeling standards are usually in the form of an off-the-shelf OO analysis and design book because the Define Infrastructure stage (Chapter 6) was also short-changed. You'll pay for these mistakes in spades during modeling. Because construction is an iterative process, during detailed modeling you will use source code as an input into your efforts to reality-check your model against your code (programming is covered in Chapter 9).

The main deliverables of the Model stage are models and the start of a test plan, including test cases, to be used by both the Test in the Small stage (Chapter 11) and the Test in the Large stage (Ambler, 1998b).

8.1 Initial Context: Entry Conditions for Modeling

Several important entry conditions must be met for work to proceed during this stage, all of them deliverables of the Initiate phase.

1. **Initial requirements.** The most important thing you need is a requirements document, which give the requirements for the application that you are building; otherwise, you must first define the requirements as part of your modeling efforts. To do so you will be applying the requirements definition techniques described in Chapter 3 in combination with some of the analysis-oriented techniques described in this chapter.

Initial Context: Entry Conditions

279

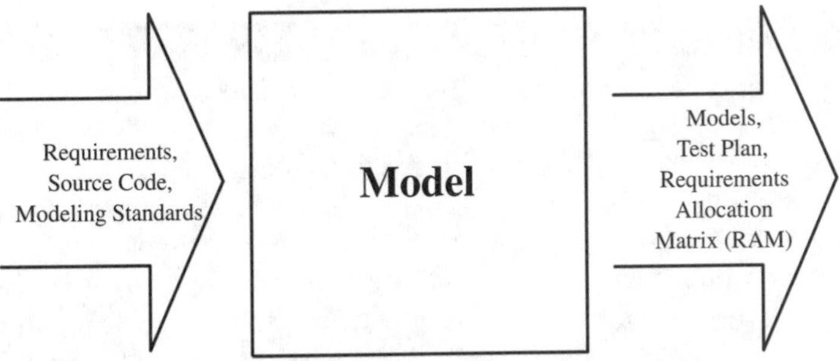

Figure 8.1. The Model stage

DEFINITIONS

class diagram Class diagrams show the classes of a system and their associations. Class diagrams are often mistakenly referred to as object models.

Class Responsibility Collaborator (CRC) card A standard index card divided into three sections that show the name of the class, the responsibilities of the class, and the collaborators of the class.

Class Responsibility Collaborator (CRC) model A collection of CRC cards that describe the classes that make up an application or a component of an application.

diagram A visual representation of a problem or solution to a problem.

model An abstraction describing a problem domain and/or a solution to a problem domain. Traditionally models are thought of as diagrams plus their corresponding documentation, although non-diagrams such as interview results, requirement documents, and collections of CRC cards are also considered to be models.

prototype A mock-up of all or a portion of your application.

sequence diagram A diagram that shows the types of objects involved in a use-case scenario, including the messages they send to one another and the values that they return. Also referred to as an object interaction diagram or simply an interaction diagram.

use case A description of a high-level business process that an application may or may not be expected to support.

DEFINITIONS

requirements document A document, also called a System Requirements Specification (SRS), which describes the user, technical, and environmental requirements for an application. This document potentially contains the major use cases for the application, detailed use-case scenarios for the application, and traditional requirements for the application as well. Requirements documents are a deliverable of the Initiate phase and are updated regularly during modeling. Requirements documents are also updated during the Maintain and Support phase as bugs and enhancements are identified.

standard A description, ideally with an example provided, of how something must be done. It is required that you follow standards (unlike guidelines, which are optional).

2. **Tool standards.** You need tools to aid in the modeling process, and a tool standards document defines exactly what tools you will use on your project. For modeling, you need to choose a CASE (computer aided system engineering) tool that supports your chosen modeling standards, a word processor, and a simple drawing tool for the diagrams not supported by your CASE tool at a bare minimum. I highly suggest a full-page scanner to capture hand-drawn models that you want to keep but do not want to invest the time needed to draw using a drawing or CASE tool. My experience has been that a $300 scanner pays for itself in saved time in less than a week. Tool standards should have been set in the Define Infrastructure stage (Chapter 6); if they weren't, you must start setting them now.

TIP

Avoid Tool Wars

When it comes to CASE tools everybody thinks they know better than everybody else, but the fact is that they usually do not. No tool is perfect, especially CASE tools, and at best all you can do is choose a tool with a set of acceptable features (and bugs that you can live with) for your organization. This is one of the reasons why I suggest supplementing a CASE tool with a drawing tool and word processor; you are not going to find a CASE tool that supports all of the models that you need. My advice is to choose several tools that work together to meet your modeling needs, and use them consistently.

3. **Modeling notation standards.** The Define Infrastructure stage (Chapter 6) should have chosen and/or defined the modeling notation that will be used to model your application. The modeling notation should be an industry standard, typically the Unified Modeling Language (UML) (Rational, 1997) or the Open Modeling Language (OML) (Firesmith, Henderson-Sellers, and Graham, 1997).
4. **Documentation standards.** Your documentation standards will define the layout of key modeling deliverables such as use cases and user requirements. It is important to have a standard approach to documentation, as the greater consistency in your work leads to increased understandability and usability. Documentation standards should have been set in the Define Infrastructure stage (Chapter 6).

8.2 Solution: The Object-Oriented Modeling Process

When tackling a large problem domain, you should organize your modeling efforts into smaller sections and attack the problem one piece at a time, making your project easier to manage and increasing its probability of success. An effective way to do so is called the 'T' approach to modeling (Taylor, 1995), a detailed version of which is shown in Figure 8.2, in which the first portion of modeling takes a breadth-first approach and models the entire problem domain at a high level. This modeling consists of three types of modeling: enterprise modeling, which explores your organization and its environment; domain architectural modeling, which explores the main domain components within your organization and their interrelationships; and technical architectural modeling, which defines the technical components and their interrelationships that are used to support your organization. Subsequent modeling efforts explore portions of the problem domain in detail, going into depth for each portion of the overall modeling. In this book the breadth approach to modeling will be referred to as architectural modeling (which includes enterprise modeling) and the depth approach to modeling will be referred to as detailed modeling. The overall modeling strategy is called the 'T' approach because the architectural modeling effort, in combination with one of the detailed modeling efforts (at least a middle one), forms the shape of the letter 'T.'

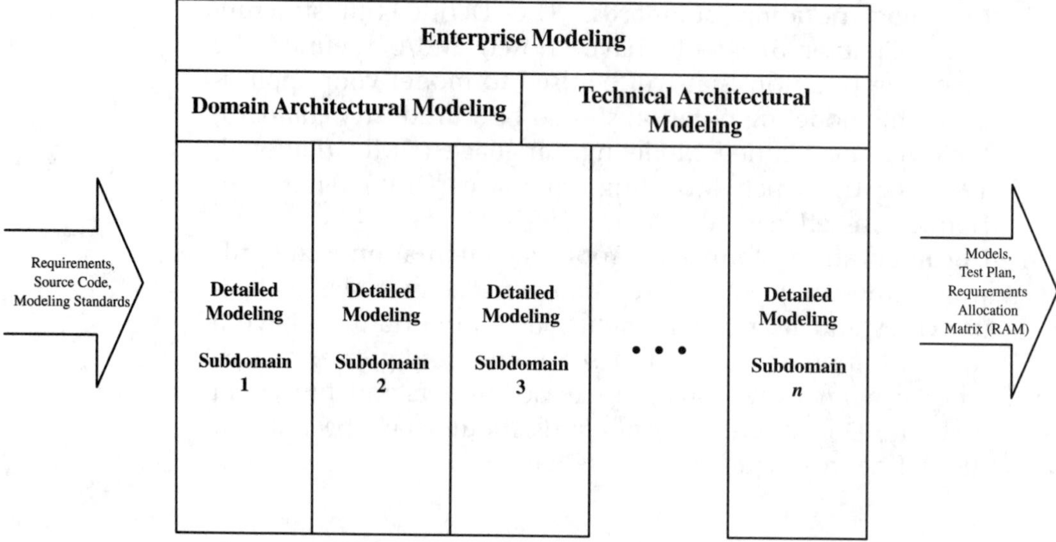

Figure 8.2. The 'T' approach to object-oriented modeling

Architectural models provide a high-level view of what your organization does, how it will do it, and how it fits into its environment.

Architectural modeling is a separate effort from project development.

The goal of architectural models is to describe both where your organization is today and where it is going in the future. For example, the architectural model for a bank would reflect the business needs of today, that of banking, but would also include the necessary "hooks" to add other financial services such as insurance and stock brokerage at some time in the future. A small investment of time in thinking about potential future requirements makes architecture models much more robust.

In large organizations architectural modeling is performed by a specific architecture group that is responsible for developing and maintaining the architectural models as well as for supporting the project teams responsible for developing the detailed models that describe their subset of the software within your organization. Any organization with one or more development teams should invest in a separate architecture group, or at least have the project teams pool their resources and work together to define a common architecture. Small organizations that have a single development team, often only a single developer, should still invest in the time to develop architectural models to gain the understanding of their environment that is needed for successful software development.

The purpose of detailed models is to provide a better understanding of a specific subdomain, perhaps an application or reusable subsystem, of the architectural model. For example, Fig-

TIP

Architectural Modeling Supports Systematic Reuse

Architectural modeling supports the concept of systematic reuse—the development of large-scale, components that are reused by several applications. These reusable components may be either problem-domain components or technical components, which is why there are two kinds of architectural models. Planned reuse occurs because you first consider the needs of your entire organization, looking for commonality between applications before you start building them. By thinking before you act, before you develop, you can achieve very high levels of reuse.

ure 8.3 shows several possible problem subdomains within a telecommunications firm: Customer Management, Billing, Transaction Rating, Service Offerings, Hardware Offerings, and Network Management. The Customer Management subdomain includes customer service and the management of customer and account information; Billing deals with the invoicing of customers; Transaction Rating deals with the calculation of what to bill for the services rendered; Service Offerings covers the various calling, Internet, and broadcast television services that the customer may subscribe to; and Product Offerings deals with the various physical products such as cellular phones and television descramblers that the company sells, rents, or leases. Network Management includes all of the systems and processes needed to keep the telecommunications network operating.

Detailed modeling provides a more thorough picture of one portion of the systems that support your organization.

In Figure 8.3 the architectural models would describe the organization and its external environment, define the various subdomains and how they relate to one another (including their public interfaces), and the hardware and software components used to support the business. The detailed models for the subdomains, on the other hand, describe how each subdomain should be built within the confines of the given architecture. When taking the 'T' approach your first release starts with the architectural model and a detailed model of at least one subset of the domain. The modeling for subsequent releases concentrates on detailed modeling of other domains, updating the architectural model to reflect the new knowledge gained in the detailed modeling effort. This is an important point: the architectural model provides a basis from

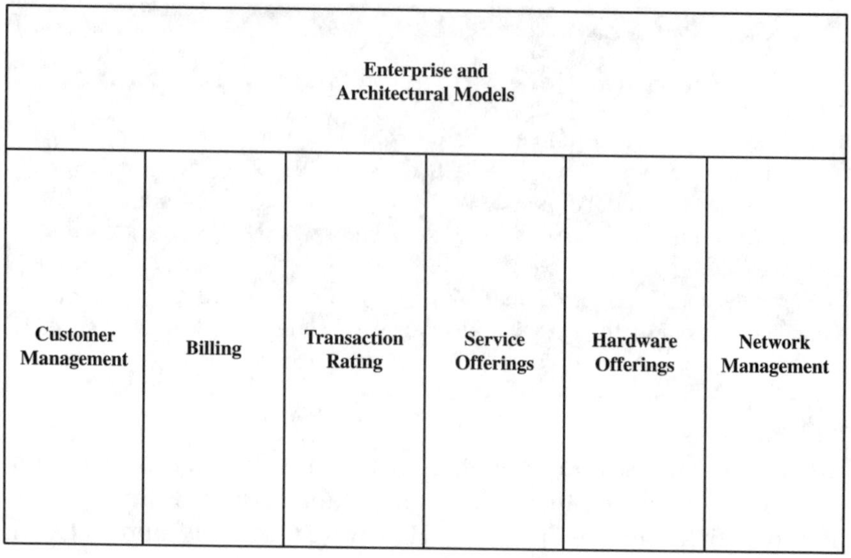

Figure 8.3. Taking a 'T' approach for modeling a financial institution

Enterprise and Architectural Models					
Customer Management	Billing	Transaction Rating	Service Offerings	Hardware Offerings	Network Management

The architectural models provide guidance for how the detailed subdomains should be modeled, ensuring that they work together effectively.

which to start detailed modeling, and the detailed modeling in turn drives changes to the architectural model. The detailed models should conform to the existing architecture, but at the same time the architectural model is shaped and evolved over time by the detailed models.

Because few project teams have the advantage of starting with a clean slate, your first release will likely need to interact with existing legacy applications. If this is the case, you will need to "wrap" existing legacy applications, a process in which you develop object-oriented code that encapsulates access to the legacy application to make it appear like an object-oriented subdomain. In fact, your first release might simply be the development of the architectural model and a set of facades (Buschmann, Meunier, Rohnert, Sommerlad, Stal, 1996) that access the wrapped features of your legacy applications.

I'd like to point out right away that the "T" approach is not appropriate for small pilot projects where you are simply trying to learn object technology. It is however a very effective strategy for developing mission-critical applications that will need to coexist with other systems within your organization for a long period of time. The initial focus on architectural modeling assures that you understand the environment in which your application will exist.

TIP

Do Not Use an Enterprise Data Model as the Basis for Your OO Enterprise Model

Data models only take into account half of the picture—data—whereas object-oriented models take into account the entire picture—data and behavior. Although it is tempting to use your enterprise data model as input into your OO enterprise model, this approach actually proves highly detrimental to your development efforts. Data models often do not take behavior and object-oriented concepts such as inheritance into account in their design. Furthermore, data models often include many assumptions derived from classic relational theory (keys can have business meaning, composite keys are a good idea, and centralized databases make sense) that prove to be undesirable from an object-oriented and/or software engineering point of view. Using data models to drive the development of object-oriented models is a common process antipattern that many organizations follow. The solution is to base your data model on your class model, not the other way around.

As we'll see below, architectural modeling and detailed modeling share a common set of models. The techniques used for both types of modeling are basically the same; the only thing that differs is your point of view while modeling. Before we discuss how to create architectural and detailed models, we must first understand the various object-oriented modeling techniques we have at our disposal.

TIP

Publicly Display Your Models on Both Sides of the Wall

A really easy win on a development project is to post your models on the wall, in both your modeling room(s) and in a public place where others can see them. Having your models on the wall of your modeling room provides a focal point for conversations about the application which is important during construction. Having your models posted in a public place helps to confirm to the rest of the world that you are making progress, shows that you are following a professional approach, and helps to generate ideas and suggestions from people outside of your project team.

DEFINITIONS

antipattern The description of a common approach to solving a common problem, an approach that in time proves to be wrong or highly ineffective.

detailed design A style of modeling that focuses on the design of a single piece of software.

domain architecture A collection of high-level models that describe the problem domain. Domain architectures are typically documented by high-level use cases, use-case diagrams, and class models that describe the various sub domains and the relationships between them.

enterprise modeling The act of modeling an organization and its external environment from a business, not an information system, viewpoint.

process antipattern An antipattern that describes an approach and/or series of actions for developing software that is proven to be ineffective and often detrimental to your organization.

systematic reuse An approach to reuse that involves modeling techniques whose purpose is to define high-leverage, reusable components.

technical architecture A set of models and documents that describe the technical components of an application, including but not limited to the hardware, software, middleware, persistence mechanisms, and operating systems to be deployed.

DEFINITION

Unified Modeling Language (UML) The industry standard OO modeling notation proposed by Rational Corporation of Santa Clara, California. The UML has been accepted by the Object Management Group (OMG) to make it the industry standard.

8.2.1 Understanding Your Modeling Options

In this section I will briefly review the major modeling techniques and diagrams used on object-oriented development projects. Some of these techniques were covered in Chapter 3 so they are only mentioned here, whereas many others are new to us. The goal of this section is to describe each modeling approach, provide an example where appropriate, and indicate when the approach should be used. I'm not going to go into enough detail to teach you how to actually model with them; there are many good books written about OO analysis and design. I instead direct you to the best sources for each modeling approach. I also go beyond the modeling techniques described by the Unified Modeling Language (UML) (Rational, 1997), although I stick to the UML notation for the diagrams that they do include. Yes, it is my opinion the UML is not complete, as you will see in this chapter, and as a result will need to be supplemented with extra diagrams to fill it out for mission-critical development needs.

TIP

How to Document Diagrams

My experience has been that the following rules of thumb for documentation apply to all types of diagrams:

1. Bubbles require at least a paragraph to describe them, and often are documented by a more detailed diagram.
2. Lines require a least a sentence to describe them and often a full paragraph.
3. Always reference pertinent business rules directly where they apply.
4. Always provide references (traces) to other documents or models where applicable.
5. Document all assumptions made at the point(s) where they apply.
6. Document any alternative choices that you considered to show that you did a thorough job and so that others, including yourself, are not tempted to second guess your decisions.

The modeling techniques that we will cover in this section include:

- User requirement gathering techniques
- Class responsibility collaborator (CRC) modeling
- Use cases and use-case scenarios
- Use-case diagrams
- Interviewing
- Joint application design (JAD)
- Interface flow diagrams
- Class diagrams
- Activity diagrams
- Data diagrams
- Sequence diagrams
- Component diagrams
- Deployment diagrams
- Statechart diagrams
- Collaboration diagrams

8.2.1.1 Modeling Techniques for Gathering User Requirements

Please refer to Chapter 3, The Define and Validate Initial Requirements Stage, for descriptions of the following modeling techniques:

TIP

Work Closely With Technical Writers

One of the easiest ways to improve the productivity of a modeling team is to have one or more technical writers available to aid in documentation. The technical writers do not need to be experts at OO development, although a basic understanding of the modeling approaches and how they fit together helps, but they do need to attend the modeling sessions whose results they are to document. The main advantages of technical writers are that they enable your modelers to concentrate on modeling, not documentation, and that they provide a higher quality and more thorough level of documentation than you would usually achieve. Technical writers help you make better use of one of your most valuable resources: OO modelers.

- CRC modeling
- Use cases and use-case scenarios
- Use-case diagrams
- Interviewing
- Joint application development (JAD)

8.2.1.2 Interface-Flow Diagrams

To your users, the user interface is the system. It is as simple as that. Does it not make sense that you should have some sort of mechanism to help you design a user interface? User interface prototypes are one means of describing your user interface, although with prototypes you can often get bogged down in the

DEFINITIONS

joint application development (JAD) A structured, facilitated meeting in which modeling is performed by both users and developers together. JADs are often held for gathering user requirements.

use case A description of a high-level business process that an application may or may not be expected to support.

use-case diagram A diagram that shows the use cases and actors for the application that you are developing.

use-case scenario A description of a specific, detailed user requirement that an application may or may not be expected to handle. A use-case scenario is a detailed example of a use case.

details of how the interface will actually work. As a result you often miss high-level relationships and interactions between the interface objects (usually screens) of your application. Interface-flow diagrams (Page-Jones, 1995; Ambler, 1998a) allow you to model these high-level relationships.

Interface-flow diagrams show the relationships between the user interface components, screens and reports, that make up your application.

In Figure 8.4 we see an example of an interface-flow diagram for an order-entry system. The boxes represent user interface objects (screens, reports, or forms) and the arrows represent the possible flow between screens. For example, when you are on the main menu screen you can go to either the customer search

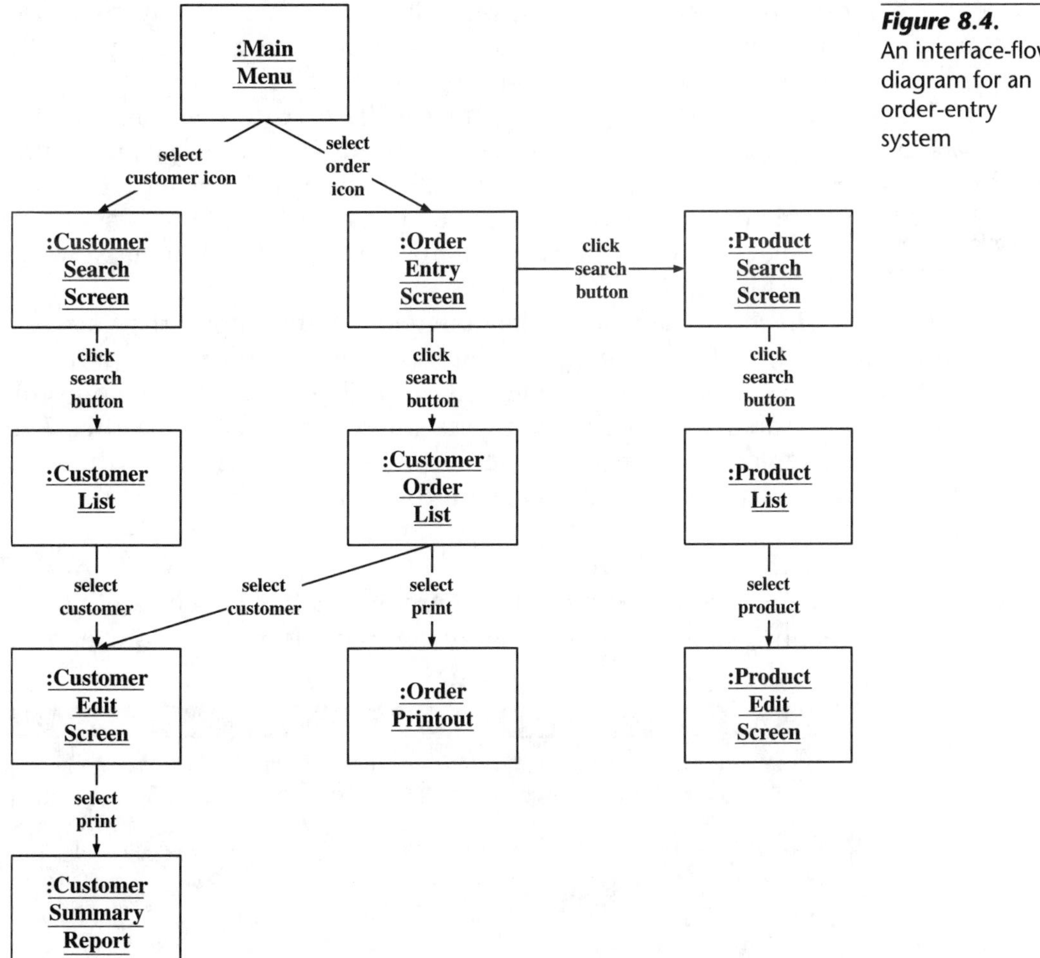

Figure 8.4. An interface-flow diagram for an order-entry system

screen or to the order-entry screen. Once you are on the order-entry screen you can go to the product search screen or to the customer order list. Interface-flow diagrams allow you to easily gain a high-level overview of the interface for your application.

Because interface-flow diagrams offer a high-level view of the interface of a system, you can quickly gain an understanding of how the system is expected to work. It puts you into a position where you can validate the overall flow of your application's user interface. For example, does the screen flow make sense? I'm not so sure. Why can I not get from the customer edit screen to the customer order list, which is a list of all the orders that a customer has ever made? Furthermore, why cannot I get the same sort of list from the point of view of a product? In some cases it might be interesting to find out which orders include a certain product, especially when the product is back-ordered or no longer available.

Interface-flow diagrams enable you to validate the design of your user interface.

Also, interface-flow diagrams can be used to determine if the user interface has been design consistently; for example, in Figure 8.4 you see that to create the customer summary report and a printed order that you select the print command. It appears from the diagram that the user interface is consistent, at least with respect to printing.

The boxes are often documented by the appropriate screen, report, or form designs as well as a description of their purpose. Arrows should be documented with an indication of the event associated with going from one interface object to another. For example, to move from the customer search screen to the customer list the user must click on the search button.

8.2.1.3 Class Diagrams

Class diagrams (Rational, 1997; Ambler, 1998a; Booch 1994; Rumbaugh, Blaha, Premerlani, Eddy, and Lorenson, 1991; Shlaer and

DEFINITIONS

interface-flow diagram A diagram that models the interface objects of your system and the relationships between them.

user-interface object An object displayed as part of the user interface for an application. This includes simple objects such as buttons and list boxes, icons, screens, and reports as well as complex objects such as editing screens and reports.

Mellor 1992), formerly called *object models*, show the classes of the system and their intrarelationships (including inheritance, aggregation, and associations). Figure 8.5 shows an example class diagram (using the UML notation) that models the Contact-Point analysis pattern (Ambler, 1998a). Class diagrams are the mainstay of OO modeling and are used to show both what the system will be able to do (analysis) and how it will be built (design).

Class diagrams (object models) are the mainstay of OO modeling.

Class diagrams are typically drawn by a team of people led by an experienced OO modeler. Depending on what is being modeled the team will be composed of subject matter experts who supply the business knowledge captured by the model, and/or other developers who provide input into how the application should be designed. The information contained in a class diagram directly maps to the source code that will be written to implement the application and therefore a class diagram must always be drawn for an OO application.

Classes are documented with a description of what they do, methods are documented with a description of their logic, and

Figure 8.5. A class diagram representing the Contact-Point analysis pattern

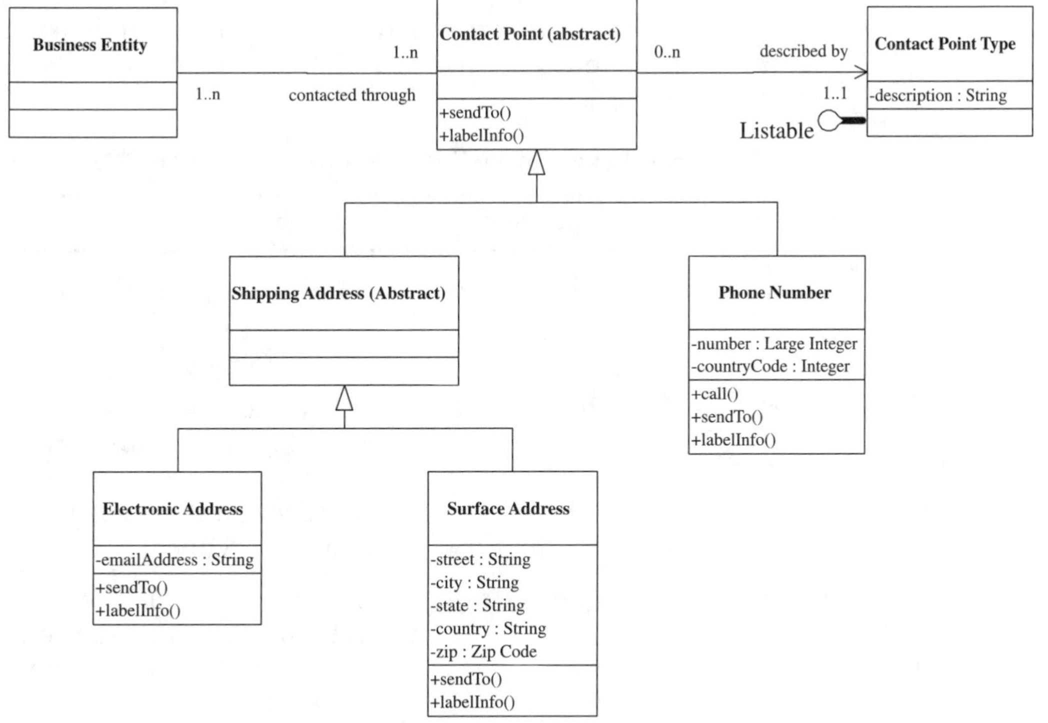

TIP

Modeling Interfaces is Important, Regardless of Language

In Figure 8.5 the class Contact Point Type supports an interface called Listable. Interfaces are a construct of the Java programming language that indicate that a class implements a specific set of methods (with specific signatures). Although not all languages directly support interfaces (at the time of this writing C++ and Smalltalk do not) you can still benefit from modeling them, as they supports a common, reusable, set of signatures among common classes.

attributes are documented with a description of what they contain, their type, and an indication of a range of values if applicable. Statechart diagrams, see below, are used to describe complex classes. Relationships between classes are documented with a description of their purpose and an indication of their cardinality (how many objects are involved in the relationship) and their optionality (whether or not an object must be involved in the relationship).

An interesting point about Figure 8.5 is the indication of the visibility of the attributes and methods; the three visibility levels that the Unified Modeling Language (UML) currently supports are described in Table 8.1.

TABLE 8.1. Levels of Visibility Supported by the UML.

Visibility	UML Symbol	Description
Public	+ (plus sign)	The attribute or method is accessible by all objects within your application.
Protected	# (number sign)	The attribute or method is accessible only by instances of the class, or its subclasses, in which the attribute or method is defined.
Private	- (minus sign)	The attribute or method is accessible only by instances of the class, but not the subclasses, in which it is defined.

DEFINITIONS

analysis pattern A modeling pattern that describes a solution to a business/domain problem.

cardinality A indication of how many.

optionality An indication of whether something is required.

statechart diagram A diagram that describes the states that an object may be in, as well as the transitions between states. Also called a "state diagram" or "state-transition diagram."

visibility A technique that is used to indicate the level of encapsulation of a class, method, or attribute.

8.2.1.4 Activity Diagrams

Activity diagrams (Rational, 1997) are used to document the logic of a single operation/method or the flow of logic of a business process. In many ways activity diagrams are the object-oriented equivalent of flow charts and data flow diagrams (DFDs) from structured development (Gane and Sarson, 1978). The activity diagram of Figure 8.6 shows the business logic for using a credit-card operated pump for filling your car with gasoline/petrol. The rounded rectangles represent processes to perform, the diamonds represent decision points, the arrows represent transitions between processes, the thick bars represent the start and end of potentially parallel processes, the filled circle represents the starting point of the activity, and the filled circle with a border represents the ending point.

DEFINITIONS

activity diagram A UML diagram which can be used to model a high-level business process or the transitions between states of a class (in this respect activity diagrams are effectively specializations of statechart diagrams).

data flow diagram (DFD) A diagram that shows the movement of data within a system between processes, entities, and data stores. Called a process diagram for OO development.

flow chart A diagram depicting the logic flow of a single process.

statechart diagram A diagram that describes the states that an object may be in, as well as the transitions between states. Also called a "state diagram" or "state-transition diagram."

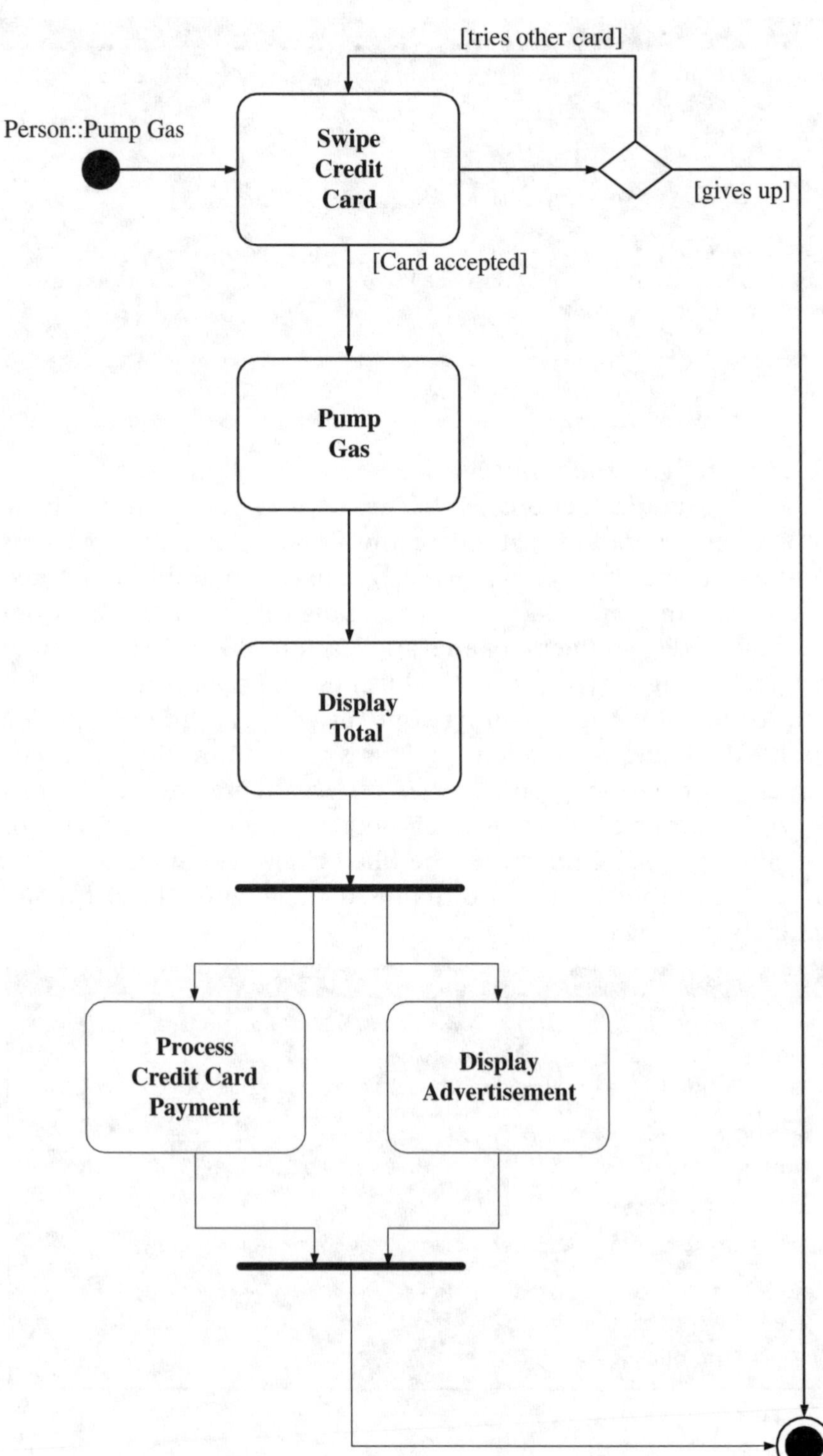

Figure 8.6. An activity diagram for using an automated gasoline/petrol pump

Activity diagrams are usually documented, if at all, with a brief description of the activity and an indication of any actions taken during a process. In fact, processes can be described with more detailed activity diagrams or with a brief description. In many ways activity diagrams are simply a variation of statechart diagrams, described in detail in section 8.2.1.6.

8.2.1.5 Data Diagrams/Models

Relational databases are often used as the primary storage mechanism to make your objects persistent. Because relational databases do not completely support OO concepts, the physical design of your database is often different from the design of your class diagram. Data diagrams (Hay, 1996; Ambler, 1998a) are used to communicate the physical design of a relational database. Class diagrams are typically used to model the design of an object/relational database.

Because relational databases are the most common type of persistence mechanism we need a diagram that describes how we will use them, and that is a data diagram.

In Figure 8.7 we see an example of a data diagram for the design of a simple human resources system. In the diagram we have four data entities—Position, Employee, Task, and Benefit—which in many ways are simply classes that have data but no functionality. The entities are connected by relationships. Relationships in a data diagram are identical in concept to associations in a class diagram. One interesting thing to note is the

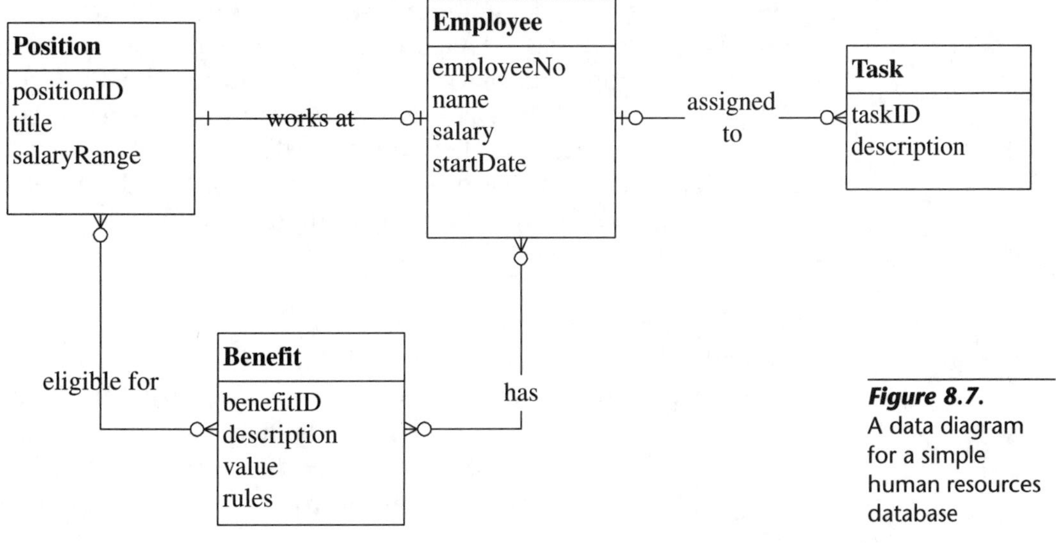

Figure 8.7. A data diagram for a simple human resources database

concept of a key: a key is one or more attributes that uniquely identify an entity. On data diagrams keys are indicated by underlining the attribute(s) that define them.

The strength of data diagrams is that data entities are conceptually the same as the tables of a relational database and that attributes are the same as table columns, providing a one-to-one mapping. Although often tempted to use data diagrams to drive the development of class diagrams, I tend to shy away from this approach. It is my experience that to use relational technology for object-oriented applications successfully, you should let your class diagram drive the design of your data diagram, because the class diagram models the full picture—data and behavior—needed by your OO application. In other words create the class diagram that is right for your application and then use it to derive the database design for that application. Mapping objects to relational databases is covered in detail by the Program stage (Chapter 10).

Data entities are described by a paragraph and their attributes, like those of classes, are documented with a description of what they contain, their type, and an indication of a range of values if applicable. Relationships between entities are documented with a description of their purpose and an indication of their cardinality and their optionality.

If your application requires the conversion of existing legacy data, then data models will be a key component of your data conversion plan. A data model is the combination of a data diagram and its corresponding documentation. You will need to develop a data model of your legacy database schema and one for your new, object-oriented application to provide the information that you need to formulate a strategy for either converting the legacy data or for having your new application coexist with existing, legacy applications. Data conversion is an important part of the Release stage (Ambler, 1998b) and often, due to the complexity of the task, is treated as a project in itself.

8.2.1.6 Sequence Diagrams

A sequence diagram (Rational, 1997; Jacobson, Christerson, Jonsson, and Overgaard, 1992; Ambler, 1998a) is often used to define the logic for a use-case scenario rigorously. Because sequence diagrams look at the use case from a different direction from which it was originally developed, it is common to use sequence diagrams

DEFINITIONS

data conversion plan A plan describing how a legacy data schema will be reworked to meet the new needs of your organization. A data conversion plan will likely refer to data models for both the existing and new data schema as well as the data access maps associated with both models.

data diagram A diagram used to communicate the design of a (typically relational) database. Data diagrams are often referred to as entity-relationship (ER) diagrams.

data model A data diagram and its corresponding documentation.

object-oriented database management system (OODBMS) A persistence mechanism, also known as an objectbase or object database, that fully supports the storage and manipulation of objects.

persistence mechanism The permanent storage facility used to make objects persistent. Examples include relational databases, object databases, flat files, and object/relational databases.

relational database (RDB) A type of persistence mechanism, based on relational theory, that stores data in tables. The rows of data within tables are related to one another; hence the term relational database.

to validate your use cases. Figure 8.8 shows an example (using the UML notation) of a sequence diagram. Sequence diagrams are a design construct that are typically drawn by a group of developers, often the programmers responsible for implementing the scenario, led by the designer or architect for the project.

Sequence diagrams are used to rigorously document and verify the logic contained within use cases.

Traditional sequence diagrams show the types of objects involved in the use case, the messages that they send each other, and any return values associated with the messages. For large applications it is quite common to show the components and use cases in addition to objects across the top of the diagram. The basic idea is that a sequence diagram shows the flow of logic of a use case in a visual manner, allowing you to both document and reality-check your application design at the same time. The boxes on the vertical lines are called method-invocation boxes and they represent the running of a method in that object.

Sequence diagrams are a great way to review your work as they force you to walk through the logic to fulfill a use-case scenario. Second, they document your design, at least from the point of view of use cases. Third, by looking at what messages are being sent to an object/component/use case, and by looking at roughly

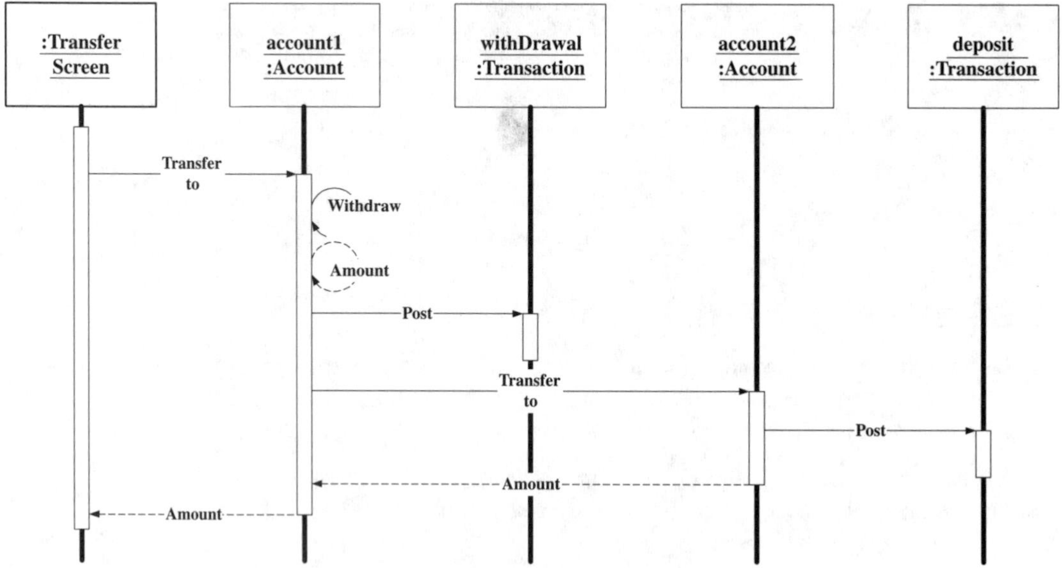

Figure 8.8. A sequence diagram for transferring funds from one account to another

how long it takes to run the invoked method, you quickly get an understanding of potential bottlenecks, allowing you to rework your design to avoid them.

When documenting a sequence diagram it is important to maintain traceability to the appropriate methods in your class diagram(s). The methods should already have their internal logic described as well as their return values (if they do not, take the time to document them).

8.2.1.7 Component Diagrams

Component diagrams (Rational, 1997; Booch, 1994) show the software components that make up a larger piece of software, their interfaces, and their interrelationships. For the sake of our

DEFINITIONS

method-invocation box The long, thin vertical boxes that appear on sequence diagrams that represent a method invocation in an object.

sequence diagram A diagram that shows the types of objects involved in a use-case scenario, including the messages they send to one another and the values that they return. Also referred to as an event-trace diagram or simply an interaction diagram.

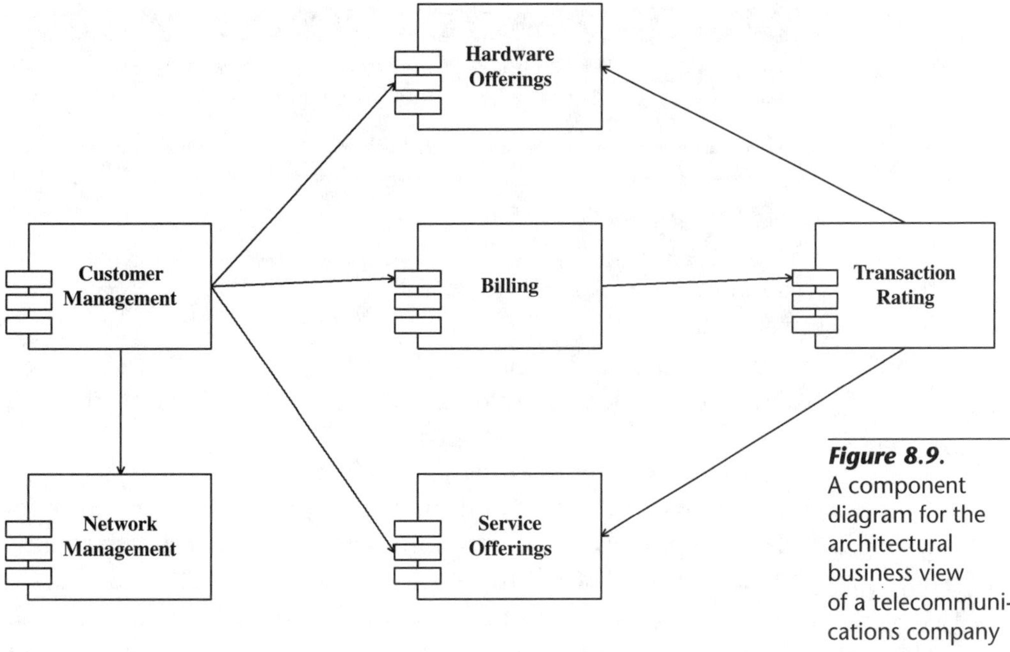

Figure 8.9. A component diagram for the architectural business view of a telecommunications company

discussion, a component may be any large-grain item—such as a common subsystem, a commercial off-the-shelf (COTS) system, an OO application, or a wrapped legacy application—that is used in the day-to-day operations of your business. In many ways a component diagram is simply a class diagram at a larger, albeit less detailed, scale.

Component diagrams show software components, their interfaces, and their interrelationships.

Figure 8.9 shows an example of a component diagram being used to model the architectural business view of a telecommunications company. The boxes represent components, in this case either applications or internal subsystems, and the dotted lines represent dependencies between components. One of the main goals of architectural modeling is to partition a system into cohesive components that have stable interfaces, creating a core that need not change in response to subsystem-level changes (Mowbray, 1997). Component diagrams are ideal for this purpose.

Each component within the diagram will be documented either by a more detailed component diagram, a use-case diagram, or a class diagram. In the example presented in Figure 8.9, it is likely that you would want to develop a set of detailed models for the component Customer Management because it is a reasonably well-defined subset. At the same time you would draw a more detailed

DEFINITIONS

commercial-off-the-shelf (COTS) system A system produced by a third-party vendor that is available for commercial purchase.

component diagram A diagram that shows the software components, their interrelationships, interactions, and their public interfaces that comprise an application, system, or enterprise.

legacy application Any application or system that is difficult, if not impossible, to maintain and enhance.

component diagram for Network Management because it is a large and complex domain that needs to be broken down further.

8.2.1.8 Deployment Diagrams

Deployment diagrams show the run-time configuration of hardware and software components.

Deployment diagrams (Rational, 1997) show the configuration of run-time processing components and the software that runs on them. Figure 8.10 shows an example of a deployment diagram, using the UML notation, which models the configuration of a customer service application that takes a three-tier client server approach. Deployment diagrams are reasonably simple models that are used to show how the hardware and software components will be configured and deployed for an application.

Deployment diagrams reflect decisions that have been made by the technical architecture group. In Figure 8.10 a three-tier client/server architecture has been chosen, as well as those within the detailed models developed for the application. The message flow between components is often analyzed to determine which software components should be deployed to which hardware devices. The idea is that you want to utilize the hardware at your

DEFINITIONS

client/server (C/S) architecture A computing environment that satisfies the business need by appropriately allocating the application processing between the client and the server processes.

deployment diagram A diagram showing the hardware, software, and middleware configuration for a given system.

middleware The technology that allows computer hardware to communicate with one another. This includes the network itself, its operating system, and anything needed to connect computers to the network.

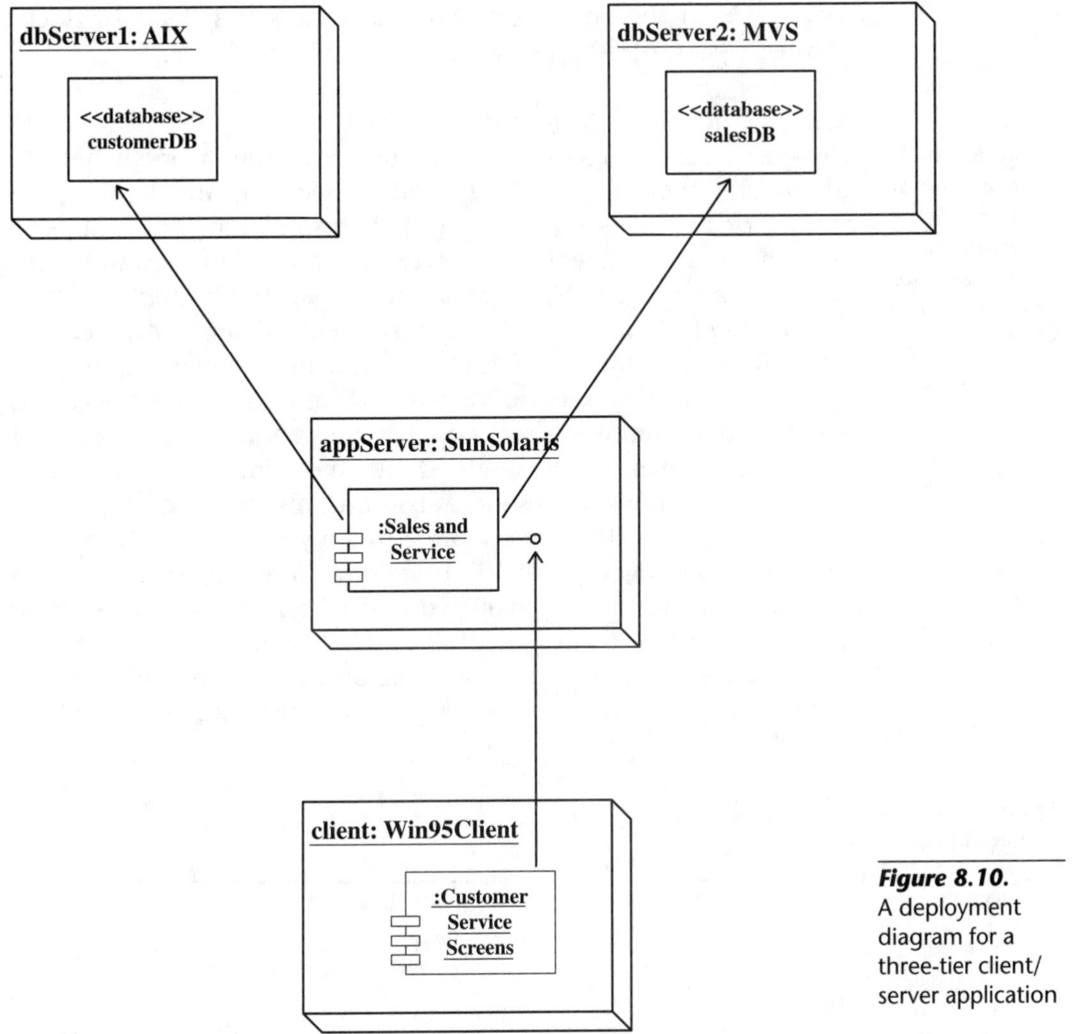

Figure 8.10. A deployment diagram for a three-tier client/server application

disposal in the best way possible to meet the requirements for your application.

For each component of a deployment diagram, you will want to document the applicable technical issues, such as the required transaction volume, the expected network traffic, and the required response time. Furthermore, each component will be documented by a set of appropriate models. For example, the databases will be described with data models, the application server will be described with a component diagram and/or class diagram, and the customer service screens will at least be documented by an interface-flow diagram and a prototype.

8.2.1.9 Statechart Diagrams

Statechart diagrams show the various states, and the transitions between those states, of an object.

Objects have both behavior and state; in other words, they do things and they know things. Some objects do and know more things, or at least more complicated things, than other objects. Some objects are incredibly complex, so to better understand them we often draw a statechart diagram (Rational, 1997; Ambler, 1998a; Booch, 1994; Rumbaugh, Blaha, Premerlani, Eddy, and Lorenson, 1991; Shlaer and Mellor, 1992) to describe how they work.

In Figure 8.11 we see the statechart diagram for a bank account. The rectangles represent *states,* which are stages in the behavior of an object. States are represented by the attribute values of an object. The arrows represent transitions, progressions from one state to another that are represented by the invocation of a method on an object. Transitions are often a reflection of our business rules. In Figure 8.11 you see that when an account is active you can withdraw from it, deposit to it, query it, and close it.

States are documented by a paragraph describing them and a indication of the range of values that applicable attributes take in

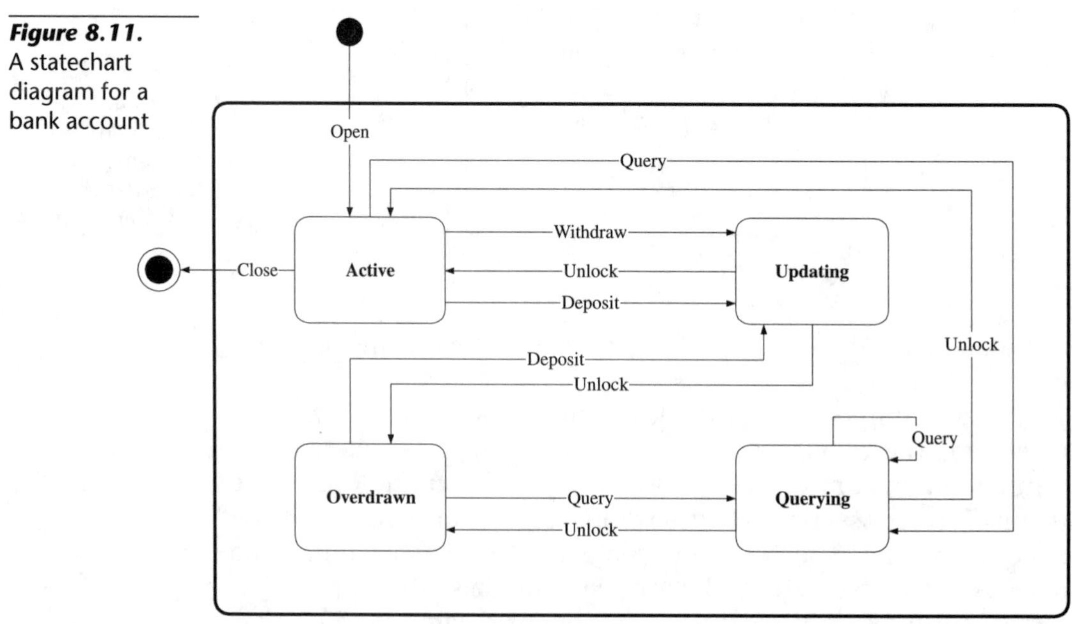

Figure 8.11. A statechart diagram for a bank account

the state, for example when an account is overdrawn the balance is negative. It is also appropriate to document any actions that are taken when an object enters a state, for example when an account becomes overdrawn a twenty-five dollar fine is charged to it. Transitions are documented with an indication of the event that triggers them. Where statechart diagrams are used to document the internal complexities of a class, collaboration diagrams are used to document the external interactions between objects.

8.2.1.10 Collaboration Diagrams

Unlike some notations (Coad and Yourdon, 1991; Ambler, 1995a) that show both state and behavior on class diagrams, UML separates out behavior into collaboration diagrams (Rational, 1997; Ambler, 1998). The basic difference between the two approaches is that UML class diagrams do not include messages, which makes sense because messages tend to clutter your class diagram and make them difficult to read. Because UML class diagrams do not show the message flow between classes a separate diagram, the collaboration diagram, was created to do so. Collaboration diagrams show the message flow between objects in an OO application and imply the basic associations (relationships) between classes.

Collaboration diagrams show the collaborations (messages), but not necessarily their order, between objects.

Figure 8.12 presents a simplified collaboration diagram for a university application. The rectangles represent the various classes that make up the application, and the lines between the classes represent the relationships/associations between them. Messages are shown as a label followed by an arrow indicating the flow of

DEFINITIONS

state A state represents a stage in the behavior pattern of an object. A state can also be said to represent a condition of an object to which a defined set of policies, regulations, and physical laws apply. On statechart diagrams a state is shown as a horizontal rectangle.

statechart diagram A diagram that describes the states that an object may be in, as well as the transitions between states. Also called a "state diagram" or "state-transition diagram."

transition A transition is a progression from one state to another. A transition will be triggered by an event (either internal or external to the object). A transition is shown on a statechart diagram as an arrow leading from one state to another.

DEFINITION

collaboration diagram Collaboration diagrams show instances of classes, their interrelationships, and the message flow between them. The order of the messaging is not indicated.

the message and return values are shown as labels with arrow-circles beside them. In the figure, Seminar and Enrollment are both classes, open and display info are both messages, and seats is a return value (presumably the result of sending the message max seats to Course).

Collaboration diagrams are usually drawn in parallel with class diagrams and sequence diagrams. Class diagrams provide input into the basic relationships between objects, and sequence diagrams provide an indication of the message flow between objects. The basic idea is that you identify the objects, the associations between the objects, and the messages that are passed between the objects. Collaboration diagrams are used to get a big picture outlook for the system, incorporating the message flow of many use case scenarios, but do not indicate the order of message invocations.

Now that we understand the various modeling techniques and diagrams that we have available to us, let's see how they can be used for both architectural and detailed modeling.

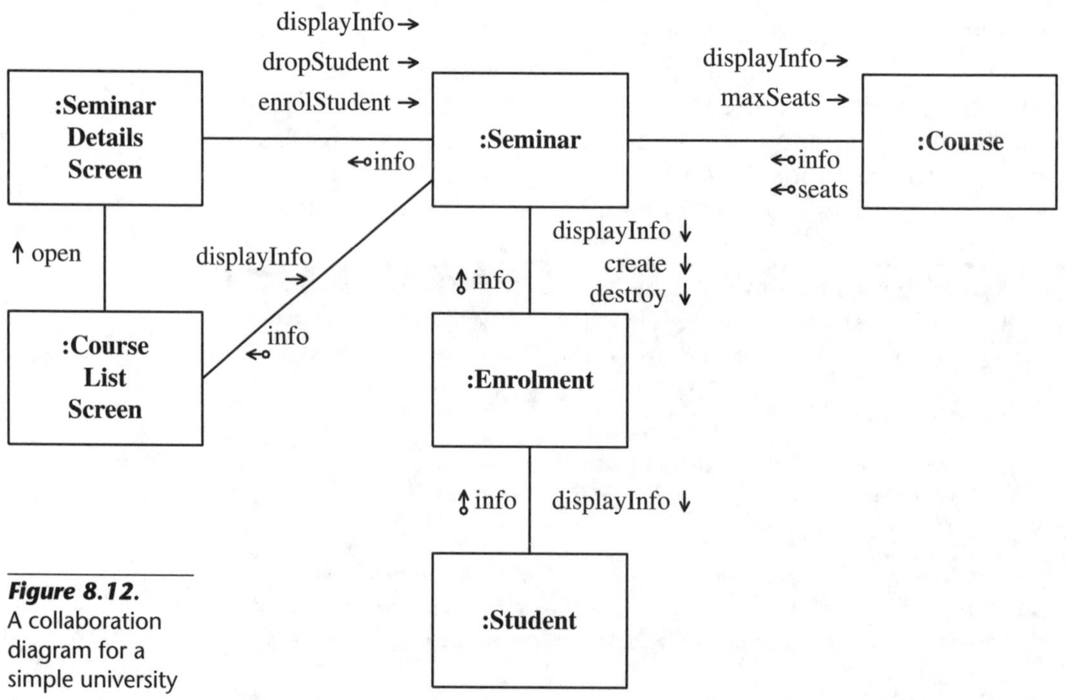

Figure 8.12. A collaboration diagram for a simple university

TIP

You Do Not Always Need a CASE Tool

Just because UML defines many different types of models and diagrams, it does not mean you need a CASE (Computer Aided System Engineering) tool to draw all of them. At a minimum, you need a CASE tool to develop class models and data models. Because class models map directly to code, you want a CASE tool that can synchronize your class models with your source code, and there are several data modeling tools on the market that will generate your DDL (data definition language) code for tables and triggers. This is a huge time saver during development.

For the other techniques, a word processor works just fine for use cases and use-case scenarios, and many of the other diagrams you can simply draw by hand and then scan if you want an electronic copy. I often draw activity diagrams on a whiteboard and then redraw them on paper (assuming the whiteboard does not print) for a permanent copy. I work with sequence and collaboration diagrams the same way, the real value of those diagrams are the hours of debate that went into them, not how pretty they look. For interface-flow diagrams and use-case diagrams, I will use a drawing tool because you often show those to users and/or senior management.

In an ideal world I would love to have a fully integrated CASE tool that meets all of my development needs, but we are years away from that; and frankly, I doubt if I will see it in my lifetime. Before I get email from CASE tool salespeople, here is my list of real-world needs:

- Full support for the complete UML notation plus the additional diagrams discussed in this chapter
- Full integration of those diagrams (in other words, changes in one diagram are reflected in all other related diagrams)
- Full configuration control down to the modeling unit (methods, attributes, classes, messages, relationships, . . .)
- Full support for multi-location, multi–time zone development
- Multiple development language support (Smalltalk and Java) within the *same* model
- Code generation and reengineering
- Full traceability of requirements and test cases throughout the model

This list reflects the realities of mission-critical development. Few CASE tools meet even one of these requirements fully; none to my knowledge meet two or more. Yet.

8.2.2 Architectural Modeling

Architecture is politics.
—Mitch Kapor

The reality is that without a common architecture the various project teams within your organization will develop OO versions of stove-pipe systems that are difficult and expensive to integrate in the future. The interesting thing is that everybody knows that this will happen, but nobody does anything about it. It is easier to point the finger at other teams than it is to work together to arrive at a common vision. My general rule of thumb is that if you know that your work will get scrapped sometime in the future when you introduce a new application or subsystem, then you need to invest the time in architectural modeling.

The goal of architectural modeling, also commonly referred to as high-level modeling or global modeling, is to define a robust framework within which applications and component subsystems may be developed. Architectural models provide the context for defining how applications and subsystems interact with one another to meet the needs of your organization. Architectural models increase the reusability on your OO development projects by providing a common base from which all project teams work.

Figure 8.13, modified from Gossain (1996), shows a process pattern for creating and maintaining architectural models. The initial inputs into an architectural model are technical and/or organizational constraints (perhaps senior management has decreed that the target hardware platform for all software applications will be

TIP

Good Architects Write Code

When somebody tells you that they only model and do not write any code, often because they believe that they're beyond that, then you should be wary of them. Coplien (1995) provides similar advice with his Architect Also Implements organizational pattern. Coding helps to keep modeler's feet on the ground, giving them an understanding of what can and cannot be built. I'm not saying that modelers have to spend a lot of time coding, but if they do not spend at least some of their time dabbling with code, then they have a tendency to lose touch with reality. Granted, enterprise modelers probably do not need any programming experience because they are modeling the business, not an information system. Any other modeler, including domain architects, should at least have a basic understanding of programming.

Java terminals), any initial requirements identified during the Define and Validate Initial Requirements stage (Chapter 3), the experiences and ideas of the architectural modeling team, and the architectural vision and principles that the team will follow. Later in the life of the application the discoveries that are made by

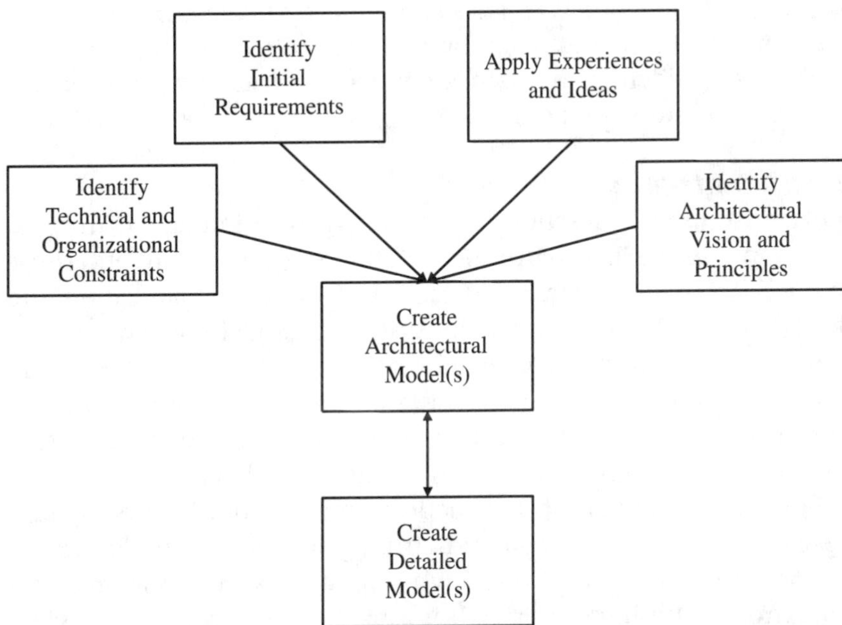

Figure 8.13. The Architectural Modeling process pattern

TIP

Everyone Should Own the Architecture

Developing an architectural model is easier said than done. Yourdon (1997) points out that architectural modeling is usually an order of magnitude more difficult than detailed modeling simply because of the politics and communications problems inherent in cross-functional activities of any kind. To increase your chances of success, you should consider including as many of the "players" within your organization as possible, naturally concentrating on the people with the applicable domain expertise. By doing so you increase both the quality of your architectural models as well as the acceptance of your work, because many people were involved in its definition (Whitenack and Bounds, 1995). It is crucial that everyone at all levels, including developers, users, and executives, understand and accept the architecture.

DEFINITION

organizational pattern A pattern that describes a common management technique or a structure appropriate to a software organization.

detailed modeling teams will be used as input to update and enhance the architectural model.

A quality OO architecture is the product of careful study, decision making, and experimentation. To be successful you want to avoid making hasty decisions, often due to schedule-related stress, that lead to compromises in architecture quality (Mowbray, 1997). Let's explore the architectural modeling process in greater detail by looking at its three flavors: enterprise modeling, domain architecture modeling, and technical architecture modeling.

8.2.2.1 Enterprise Modeling

Enterprise models describe your business and the environment in which your organization operates.

Enterprise models describe both your organization and your organization's external environment. The purpose of an enterprise model is to increase your understanding of your organization and how it fits into the world around it. The model concentrates on what your organization does, not how it does it, allowing you to consider both the present-day situation and likely future possibilities. The greater understanding of your complete environment that results from enterprise modeling reduces the likelihood that you will be taken off guard by the actions of your competitors, by new legislation, or by new demands from your customers. Enterprise models are effectively a very high-level analysis of your organization from a business, not an information system, point of view.

As you see in Figure 8.14 the Enterprise Modeling process pattern, a task process pattern, depicts the concept that object-oriented enterprise modeling focuses on the high-level behaviors, capturing this information in a use-case diagram and its corresponding use cases, that are pertinent to your organization. The boxes represent the main techniques/diagrams of OO modeling

TIP

Expect to Use the Same Kind of Model for Multiple Purposes

One concept that developers new to object orientation sometimes have trouble grasping is the fact that the same type of model is used at different points during the modeling process. For example, use-case models are used to model the enterprise and to model the behavioral requirements for a single application. One type of model, two different uses.

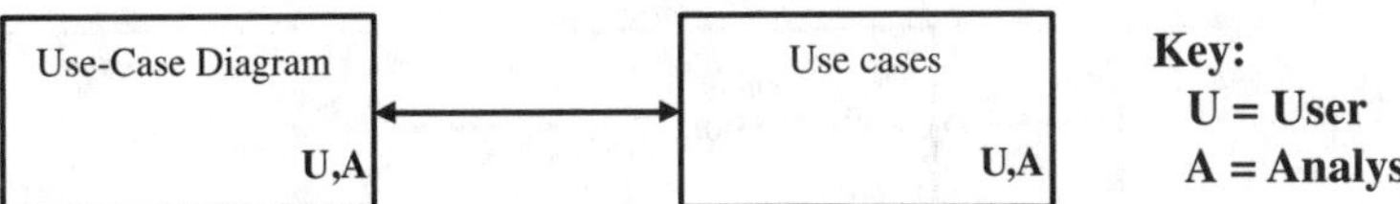

Figure 8.14. The Enterprise Modeling process pattern

and the arrows show the relationships between them, with the arrowheads indicating an "input into" relationship; in our case the two modeling techniques provide input into each other. In the bottom right-hand corner of each box are letters that indicate who is typically involved in working on that technique/diagram; in this case both users (subject matter experts) and analysts play key roles in the development of an enterprise model.

Let us consider an example. The enterprise model for a telecommunications firm (telecom) would be a use-case diagram likely showing twenty to thirty high-level use cases and the external actors with which the telecom interacts. Example use cases would include Manage Customer Accounts, Bill Customer, Run Marketing Campaign, Lobby Regulating Bodies, and Negotiate Carrier Agreements. Example actors would include Customer, Regulating Body, and Other Telecoms. The enterprise model for the telecom would define what it does and how it interacts with the outside world—information that is documented by the high-level use cases and the relationships with the external actors respectively.

8.2.2.2 Domain Architecture Modeling

Domain architectural modeling takes the enterprise model one step further by identifying the high-level deliverables (either applications or reusable subsystem components) that need to exist to support the high-level requirements of your organization. Figure 8.15 depicts the Domain Architecture Modeling process pattern, a task process pattern, indicating the deliverables used and/or created during object-oriented domain architectural modeling—the enterprise model, sequence diagrams, and a high-level component diagram—as well as their interrelationships and the people involved in developing them. Notice how the designers, people who determine how something should be built, are involved in the development of the sequence diagrams and the component diagram. This is because domain architectural modeling goes beyond enterprise modeling in that it starts to organize

Domain architecture models describe the components, their interfaces, their interactions, and their interrelationships that are needed to support your organization.

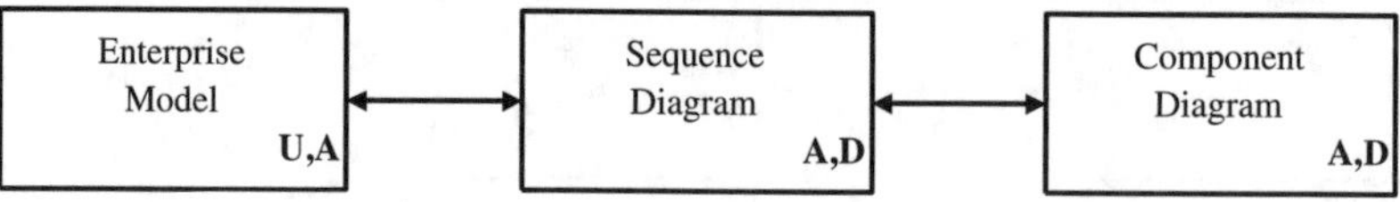

Figure 8.15. The Domain Architecture Modeling process pattern

the behaviors needed by your organization into large-scale, cohesive components: applications and/or reusable subsystems.

The main deliverable of domain architectural modeling is the high-level component diagram that shows the applications/subsystems that support your organization, their public interfaces, and the interactions and interrelationships between them. Figure 8.9 shows a high-level component diagram for a telecommunications firm. A component diagram is developed by first creating sequence diagrams for the high-level use cases defined in the enterprise model, analyzing them for common features, and then identifying components that encapsulate cohesive sets of these features. This is a highly iterative process that often involves updating the uses cases contained in the enterprise model, usually because the development of the sequence diagrams reveals holes in your original documentation.

A good domain architecture is intuitively understandable by the people who will be working with it and should be created with both the present and future in mind. Furthermore, a good domain architecture is developed with reuse as a top priority; large-scale reuse should be driven top-down from your architecture, not after the fact in a haphazard, bottom-up manner. This approach to reuse is called "systematic reuse" because you systematically develop reusable components by purposely modeling them that way. "Opportunistic reuse," the focus of the Generalize stage (Chapter 10), is based on the concept of harvesting reusable items from your existing work.

8.2.2.3 Technical Architecture Modeling

Technical architectural modeling focuses on the technologies and how they will work together to support your organization. It takes into account both the technical needs of your organization and the technological constraints imposed on you by your environ-

TIP

Challenge Assumptions

Architectural modeling, or any form of modeling in general, often reveals the underlying assumptions that govern the way that your organization operates. Your goal is to challenge even the most fundamental assumptions. For example, I once did some work with a very successful restaurant chain. They were in the process of reworking their systems infrastructure and were looking for new ways of doing things. In the process of all of this they came to the realization that their main area of expertise wasn't in the managing of restaurants, but instead in the distribution of perishable items to those restaurants. They challenged the assumption that they were a restaurant management company and in doing so realized that they were really a distribution company. This realization prompted them to successfully grow their distribution business and greatly increase their profitability.

Challenging assumptions is very hard to do because people tend to prefer the status quo—this is the way it is and has always been, therefore this is the way that it has to be. To challenge assumptions successfully, you need to use techniques such as brainstorming that promote thinking outside of the box. A focus on what should be done, instead of what is being done and/or how it is being done, is also crucial. Finally, you also need to be very patient and persistent.

ment. Figure 8.16 depicts the Technical Architecture Modeling task process pattern, showing the various modeling techniques, their relationships, and the people involved in creating them, for developing a technical architectural model.

Technical architectural models show the technologies and how they will work together to support your organization.

Although the main deliverable of technical architectural modeling is a deployment diagram that shows your hardware, operating system, middleware, and software configuration selections, the most important thing that you do is technical prototyping. Technical prototyping (Mowbray, 1997), also called proof-of-concept prototyping, is a process where small systems are created to test the capabilities of a given technology, with the main goal being to identify both the features of the technology and, more importantly, where the technology breaks. Technical prototyping will either prove or disprove that a given technology will work for you—it is very nice to argue that approach X to distributed computing is better than approach Y, but it is much better to prove that it is actually so. Note that it is important to define the priorities/goals for the technical prototyping effort so that you get the

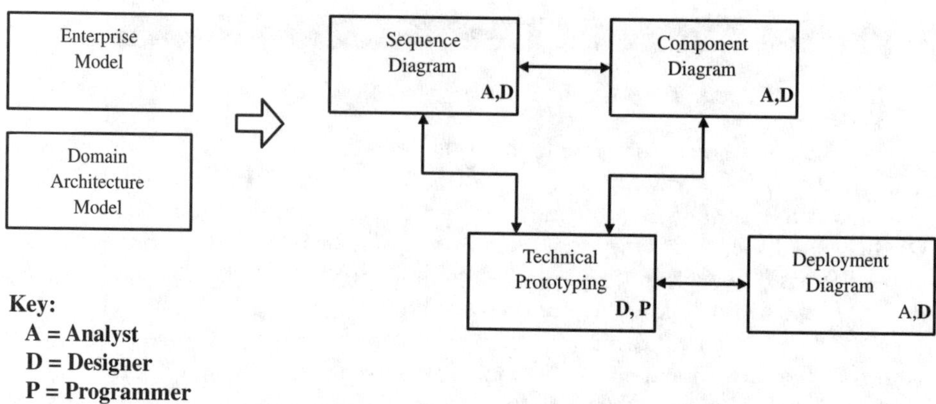

Figure 8.16. The Technical Architecture Modeling process pattern

answers to questions that are important to you; otherwise, you run the risk of becoming distracted by features that are not important to your organization. Stress testing, a technique of the Test in the Large stage (Ambler, 1998b), a process where you determine the volume of users, transactions, and so on that an application or prototype can handle is an important part of technical prototyping.

The creation of a technical architecture early in a project helps to avoid costly mistakes later because technical prototyping will test for critical robustness issues such as scalability, extensibility, and maintainability, as well as operational issues, such as whether or not the technology will work in a seven/twenty-four (seven days a week, twenty-four hours a day) environment. Technical prototyping can also help you to avoid the Vendor Lock-In (Brown, Malveau, McCormick, Mowbray, 1998) antipattern in which your organization becomes completely dependent on a single vendor's implementation. (By developing a technical prototype, you quickly understand the implications of using certain technologies, implications that aren't always obvious from the vendor's marketing literature and technical white papers.)

A key success factor for technical architectural models is that they are understood and accepted by both project managers and by developers. This is achieved by doing fair and honest proof-of-concept prototypes that examine all of the issues that are critical to your organization, and by publishing the results of that prototyping. When you provide people with the results of your work and with a description of your decision making process, they are much more willing to accept it, even when they disagree with some of your decisions. Technical architectural modeling and prototyping is one way of supporting the Level Five key process area (KPA) Technology Change Management of the Capability Maturity Model (CMM) (Software Engineering Institute, 1995).

The willingness to invest in the creation of proof-of-concept prototypes is a key factor in avoiding what I call the "Hook, Line, and Sinker" process antipattern, in which organizations fall prey to the exaggerated marketing claims of software/hardware vendors. Very few technologies work as advertised, or if they do there are usually unadvertised side-effects, also known as undocumented features. This process antipattern often begins with a senior manager reading an article in a business magazine about the amazing features of a new technology, or with a software developer reading a white paper posted on the Internet about a new development tool, language, or reusable component. Proof-of-concept prototypes combat this antipattern by verifying and validating the technology.

Proof-of-concept prototypes combat the Hook, Line, and Sinker process antipattern.

When creating architectural models, it is important to consider both the existing domain, including legacy applications, and the projected future needs of the organization. This is important because you need to determine the gap between what you currently have and what you are going to need in the future, information that drives your decision of what you can keep, what you need to replace/rebuild, and what you need to develop from scratch. At the same time you also need to determine what

TIP

The Features of a Good Architecture

Good architectures have the following characteristics (Mowbray, 1995):

- **Simplicity** If it is simple, it will be easy to understand, document, learn, reuse, and maintain.
- **Functionality** This is the main purpose of an architecture, but it needs to be balanced by extensibility.
- **Extensibility** Architectures must adapt to changing requirements and evolving technologies.
- **Isolation** Good architectures have interfaces that are independent of commercial products and legacy implementations.

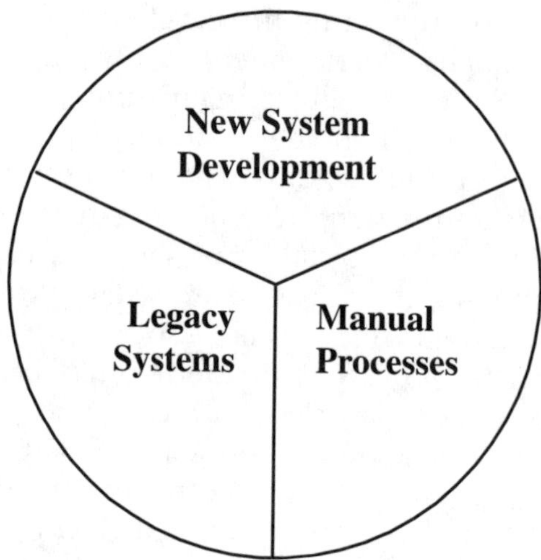

Figure 8.17. Determining what to automate

processes will be manual, what will be automated, and what will be a combination of the two. These decisions are used to determine the scope and nature of the system components and applications that together make up your overall architecture. Figure 8.17 describes the three types of systems that need to be taken into account in an architectural model.

Just as too many cooks spoil the broth, too many modelers spoil the application. One of the dangers of iterative and incremental development is that people think they can go off and do their own thing and it will all work together. This rarely happens, even when everyone does a very good job on their portion. When you try to integrate everything, it does not fit together well because there wasn't a consistent vision from which everything was built. An architectural model provides the consistent vision needed to provide direction for detailed modeling efforts.

8.2.3 Detailed Modeling

Detailed modeling—also called component modeling, application modeling, or subsystem modeling—concentrates on the modeling of one application or subsystem. Where the architectural models define the components needed to support your organization, a detailed model defines the inner workings of a single component.

Figure 8.18 depicts the Detailed Modeling process pattern, in which the boxes represent the main techniques/diagrams of OO modeling and the arrows show the relationships between them,

Scott's Soapbox

Does a Lack of Architecture Result in Feature Creep?

For years now the lament of developers has been that projects are often late because of feature creep, the inclusion of new requirements by users during construction, which increases the scope of the project and thereby the time it takes to deliver it. What I find interesting is that nobody ever questions why feature creep occurs in the first place. Yes, sometimes there is in fact a brand new requirement nobody ever thought of before, but more often than not the requirement already existed in the first place, but the modelers missed it. Therefore, the problem is not with users; it is really with developers who are not doing their job properly.

I have also noticed that firms that do not have architectures in place suffer the most from feature creep. For these firms a new requirement often throws them for a loop. Because they did not invest the time to create an architecture that supports likely future needs, a requirement that seems straightforward to users often cannot easily be added to legacy applications or to the new applications being built. Developers will often claim that the problem is that users do not understand how the system is built, but the real problem is that the developers do not understand how the business works. If they did, then their architecture would reflect this and the new requirement would be easy to add.

DEFINITIONS

Capability Maturity Model (CMM) A strategy, defined by the Software Engineering Institute (SEI), that describes the key elements of an effective software process.

key process area (KPA) An issue that must be addressed to achieve a specific Capability Maturity Model (CMM) maturity level.

proof-of-concept prototype Software written to prove/test the viability a technology, language, or environment. Also called a technical prototype.

stress testing The act of ensuring that the system performs as expected under high volumes of transactions, high numbers of users, and so on.

technical architecture A set of models and documents that describe the technical components of an application, including but not limited to the hardware, software, middleware, persistence mechanisms, and operating systems to be deployed.

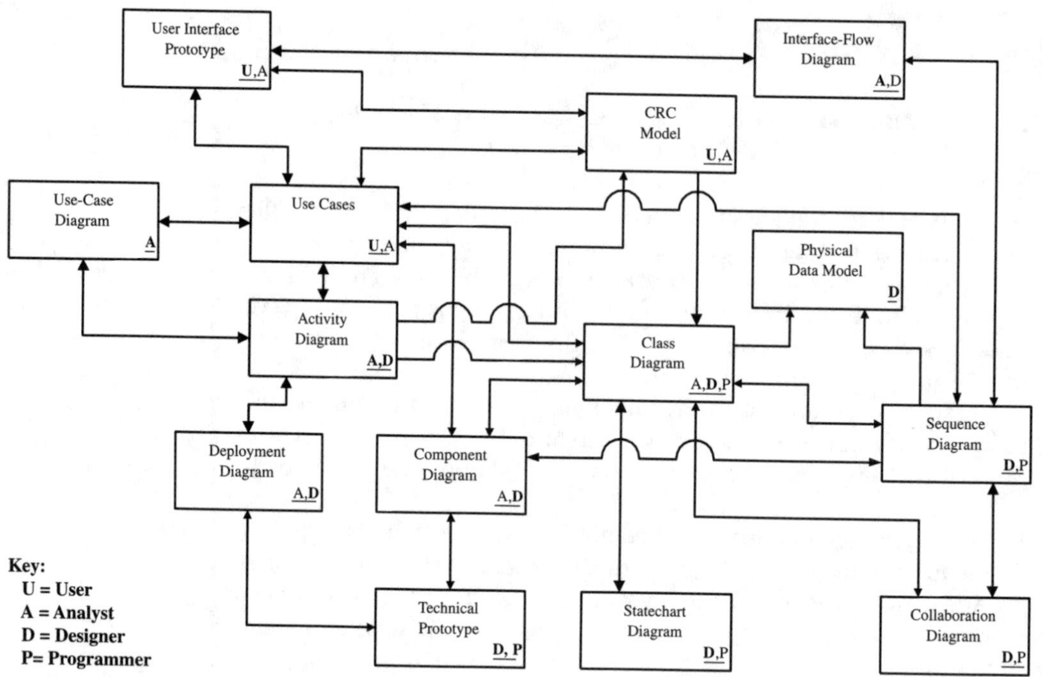

Figure 8.18. The Detailed Modeling process pattern

with the arrowheads indicating an "input into" relationship. For example, we see that an activity diagram is an input into a class diagram. In the bottom right-hand corner of each box are letters that indicate who is typically involved in working on that technique/diagram. The key is straightforward: U=User, A=Analyst, D=Designer, and P=Programmer. The underlined letter indicates the group that performs the majority of the work for that diagram. For example, we see that users form the majority of the people involved in developing a CRC model and designers form the majority of those creating statechart diagrams.

An interesting feature of Figure 8.18 is that it illustrates that the object-oriented modeling process is both serial in the large and iterative in the small. The serial nature is exemplified when you look from the top-left corner to the bottom right corner: the techniques move from requirements gathering to analysis to design. You see the iterative nature of OO modeling from the fact that each technique drives, and is driven by, other techniques. In other words, you iterate back and forth between models.

From a serial perspective, Figure 8.19 depicts the Deliverables Drive Deliverables approach process pattern, indicating the general

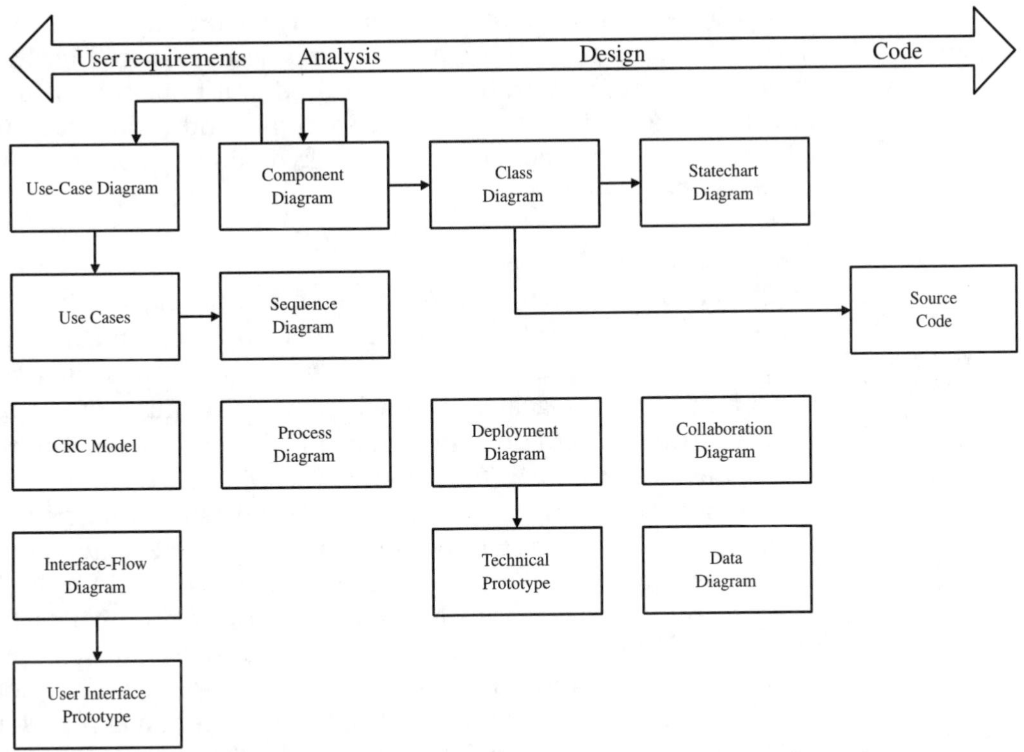

Figure 8.19. The Deliverables Document Deliverables process pattern

order in which you will work on deliverables during the Construct phase. It is important to point out that the views in Figures 8.18 and 8.19 are complementary, not contradictory. In Figure 8.19 we see that we generally start modeling with techniques such as use cases and CRC models that focus on user requirements, moving into analysis-oriented techniques such as sequence and component diagrams, then into design techniques, and finally to code.

The arrows in Figure 8.19 represent a documents relationship. For example, a use-case diagram is documented by use cases, which in turn are documented by sequence diagrams. Component diagrams are interesting in that a component within a component diagram is often documented by either another component diagram, a class diagram, and/or a use-case diagram.

As an aside, in UML (Rational, 1997) the *traces* stereotype is used to connect related pieces of information in separate models to maintain traceability throughout your work. Traceability is an important concept in testing that we will discuss in detail in Chapter 11.

In Figure 8.18 it is obvious that many of the modeling techniques can be used for both analysis and design. There's nothing wrong with this; in fact, this is quite good; but to be successful at OO modeling, you always need to keep in mind what your purpose is when using each technique. Are you doing detailed analysis or detailed design?

8.2.3.1 Detailed Analysis

Detailed analysis focuses on what needs to built, not how.

Analysis addresses what needs to be built, but not how to build it. Your detailed analysis effort should be driven by your domain architecture, because it provides the basic framework from which you begin modeling. The goal of detailed analysis is to fill out the work started by the problem domain architecture, to delve down into the requirements so that you fully understand what needs to be built.

The most common mistake made during detailed analysis is to slip into detailed design without realizing it—you are doing design as soon as you start talking about how something should be built. There's nothing wrong with doing design, as long as that's what you mean to do. You should always strive to understand a problem fully before you determine how you intend to solve it. That does not mean that you should do all of the analysis for an application, then all of the design; but you should attempt to do all of the analysis for a logical, cohesive portion of an application before you do the design for it. OO modeling is an iterative process, but that does not mean that you cannot use your common sense when you are doing it. It is common sense to understand as much about a problem as you can before you attempt to solve it.

DEFINITIONS

analysis An approach to modeling where the goal is understanding the problem domain.

public interface The collection of public methods and attributes of a class or component.

An important goal of detailed analysis is to define and stabilize the public interface for your classes as soon as possible so that other developers know what you intend to deliver and can make decisions accordingly. One technique that supports this concept is called "design by contract" (Meyer, 1995). The idea is that for every public method (the collection of public methods that a class implements is called its public interface) you should define:

- What the method will do.
- What the method will return.
- What the method must be passed.

- The preconditions that must be true before the method can be invoked.
- The post-conditions that will be true after the method completes.

This is the minimal information needed by other developers to understand how to properly use your work. As an aside, the design-by-contract approach to development has the side benefit of reducing the number of bugs in a system because most bugs occur at the boundaries between modules. By thoroughly defining the public interface of a class you minimize the opportunities for boundary errors to occur.

During analysis you want to ensure that you are implementing all of the requirements defined in your functional baseline, often documented in the form of a requirements document. The easiest way to do this is to maintain a requirements allocation matrix (RAM) that maps your requirements to the portions of your models that implement those requirements. In the OO world a RAM is often a simple spreadsheet comprised of three columns: Requirement Number, Implementing Class, and Implementing Method. The requirement number is the unique number assigned to the requirement within the requirements document, and the implementing class and method indicate where in your application the requirement is supported. The RAM provides a mechanism by which you are able to prove that the application your team has built meets the requirements defined for it and provides the primary traceability mechanism so that changes to the application can be easily made based on new/modified requirements.

DEFINITION

requirements allocation matrix (RAM) A mapping of requirements, defined in your requirements document, to the portions of your model(s) that implement them.

The requirements allocation matrix proves that you implemented the assigned requirements and provides the main traceability mechanism to support future changes to the application.

8.2.3.2 Detailed Design

Detailed design is driven both by your detailed analysis and by your technical architecture, focusing on how something should be built. It is during design that modelers take into consideration issues such as sizing, transaction volume, resource utilization, programming language, and platform.

Modelers who are responsible for creating the detailed design of a component or application must work within the constraints of the public interfaces defined by the detailed analysis model. The analysis model shows the outside view of the components and

Detailed design focuses on how to build something.

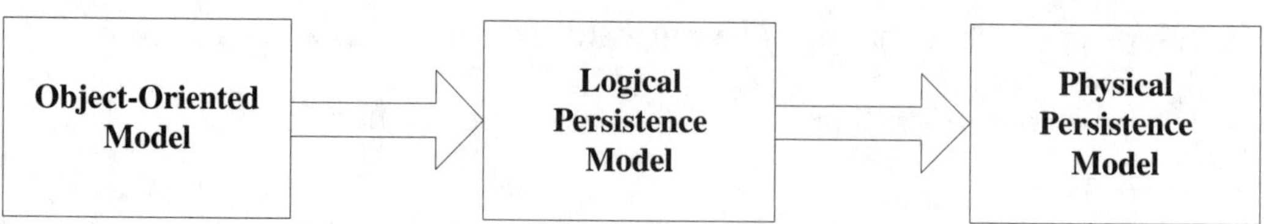

Figure 8.20. The Persistence Modeling process pattern

classes that make up your information systems, whereas the detailed model concentrates on the inner workings of those classes and components.

Your lead programmer(s) should also be part of the design team for two reasons: First, programmers often have a better understanding what can and cannot be done by your chosen development tools—important considerations to be taken into account during design. Second, their active involvement increases the chance that they will accept and follow the design model during the Program stage (Chapter 9). If your programmers are not willing to work from the design model, then why create it in the first place?

Figure 8.20 depicts the Persistence Modeling task process pattern, which indicates the process for modeling the persistence aspects of your object-oriented application. This process pattern shows that your Object-Oriented Model, the key to which is your Class Model, should drive the development of your Logical Persistence Model, which in turn drives the development of your Physical Persistence Model. The Persistence Modeling process pattern indicates that there exists two types of Persistence Model: a Logical Persistence Model and a Physical Persistence Model. A Logical Persistence Model is used to show what you want to build (in effect, it is an analysis model) and a Physical Persistence Model is used to show how you intend to build your persistence schema (in effect it is a design model). As indicated in Section 8.2, data models are typically used to model the schema for your persistence mechanism, at least when you use a relational database to store your objects.

8.2.4 How the Modeling Techniques Fit Together

OO modeling is ideally an architecture-driven, iterative process.

Figure 8.21 depicts the task process pattern for the object-oriented modeling process, showing the relationships between the types of modeling approaches that we have described in this chapter. Your enterprise model should drive the development of your domain and technical architecture. At the same time your domain archi-

WAR STORY

Simplify, Simplify, Simplify

I was once involved with the redesign of a customer service application. The existing system was a nightmare, and a previous modeling team had put together a proposal that took the existing system design as is and converted it to a nice, point-and-click graphical user interface (GUI). The client liked the proposal, not knowing any better, but luckily wanted a second opinion. My team was brought in to give that second opinion, and the prototype that we developed was an order of magnitude easier to use. Instead of reimplementing what was already there, we instead choose to model what needed to be done and then built a prototype that reflected this. To replace an application consisting of over a hundred screens and forms, we proposed an application consisting of eighteen simple-to-intermediate screens. We invested the time to simplify our design, which got us the contract and reduced our development effort substantially.

The lesson to be learned is that you should always strive to simplify a process; otherwise, you will automate chaos. Good modelers always attempt to simplify something so that it is easier to understand, to build, to test, and to maintain.

tecture drives detailed analysis, which provides feedback from which your domain architecture and eventually your enterprise model are updated. Your technical architecture and detailed analysis are used as the basis for detailed modeling, which in turn drives your coding efforts. Coding provides feedback to detailed design, which in turn provides feedback up the modeling chain. The point to be made is that object-oriented modeling is an architecture-driven, iterative process.

Figure 8.21 illustrates three important development concepts. First, source code is driven by your modeling efforts, not the other way around. Yes, during coding you will discover information that wasn't taken into account in your original design, information that should be fed back up to the modelers so they can improve their models. Second, it implies that your architects should have an influence over

DEFINITIONS

design A style of modeling with the goal of describing how a system will be built based on the defined requirements.

detailed design A style of modeling which focuses on the design of a single piece of software.

graphical user interface (GUI) A style of user interface design in which graphical components, as opposed to text-based components, are used.

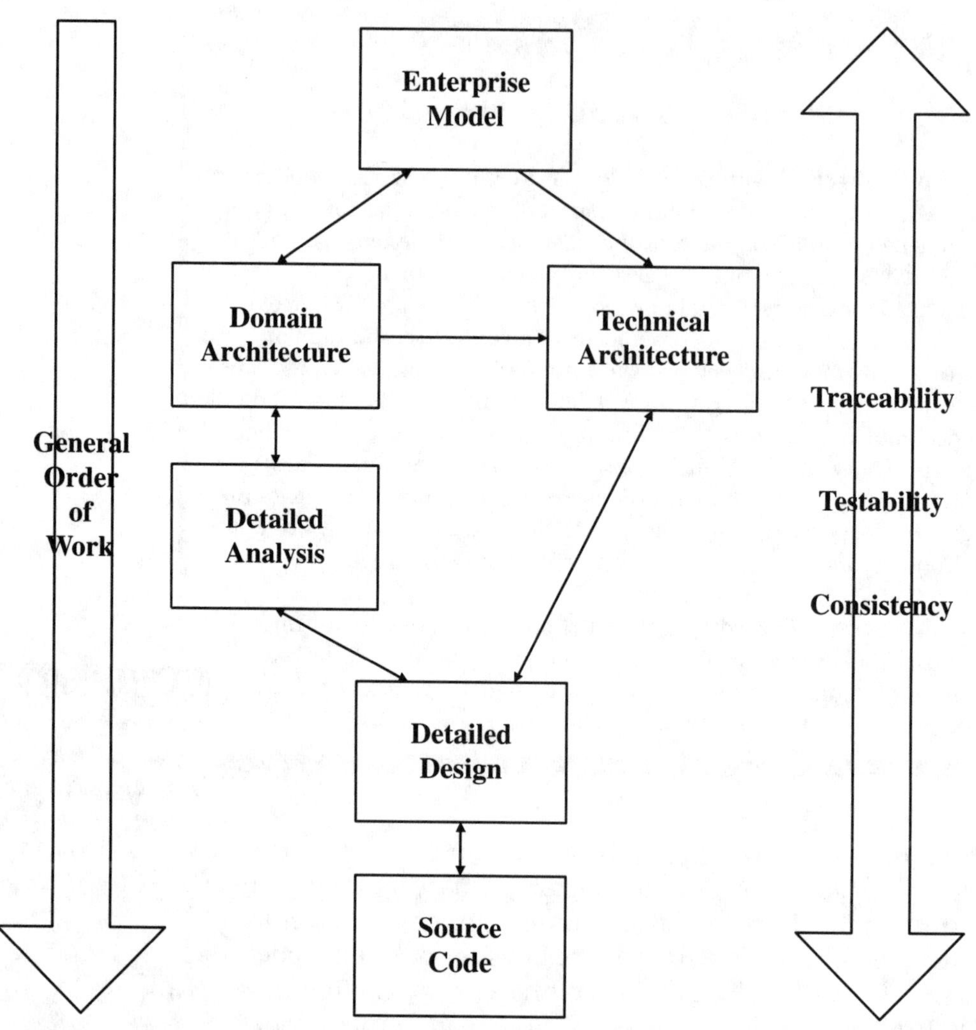

Figure 8.21. The Top-Down Development process pattern

the modeling and development efforts of your project teams, exemplified by Coplien's (1995) Architect Controls Product organizational pattern. This pattern suggests that your architects should advise and control your developers, as well as with your customers, to ensure a common focus in the software development efforts of your organization. Third, it is important to maintain traceability, testability, and consistency throughout your development deliverables. Traceability refers to the ability to show how a requirement can be tracked through your models to your source code; testability refers to how easy it is to verify that your

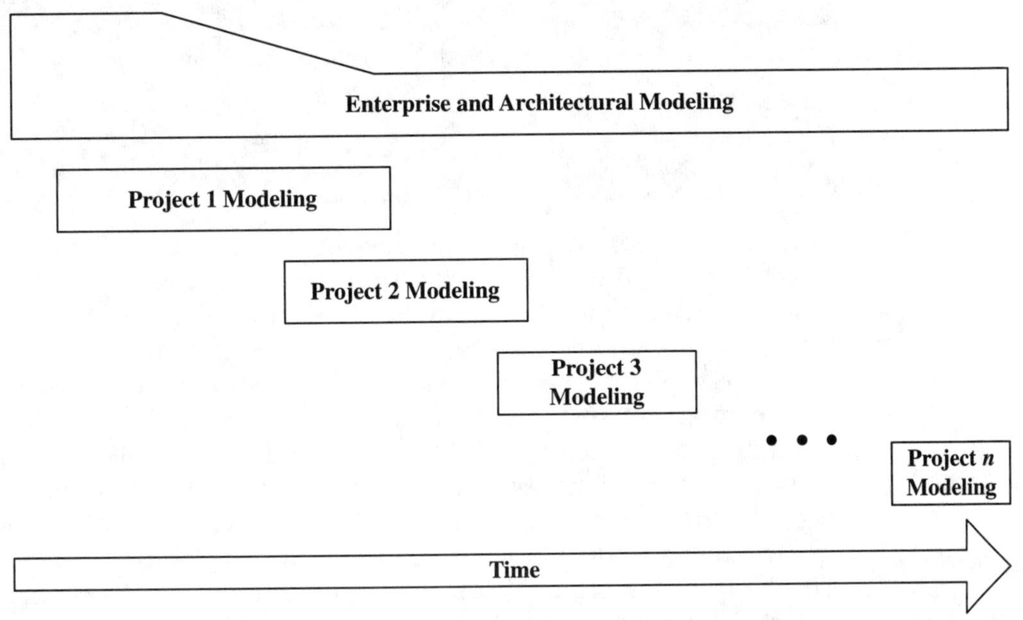

Figure 8.22. The Modeling Management process pattern

models and code are correct; and consistency refers to the lack of difference between similar information in different portions of your development efforts.

In Figure 8.22 you see a process pattern depicting a timeline view of how architecture-driven modeling is performed. You begin by creating the initial versions of your enterprise and architectural models, and once you have initial versions in place, you may begin detailed modeling for your first project. As time progresses, the enterprise and architectural models are continuously updated to reflect new knowledge gained from detailed project modeling. Also, the effort that you expend on detailed modeling for your projects decreases over time; as the domain components in your business become more robust, you have more and more to reuse, therefore less and less to model. An important lesson derived from Figure 8.22 is that enterprise and architectural modeling, although they support the efforts of your project team, actually occur outside the scope of a single project and effectively are a project in their own right.

At the moment when a person is faced with an act of design, he does not have the time to think about it from scratch.
—Christopher Alexander

Enterprise and architectural model occur outside the scope of a single project.

8.2.5 Styles of Modeling Sessions

One of the most important lessons, and one of the most difficult

DEFINITIONS

testability The measure of ease with which a product may be tested.

traceability The ease with which the features of one deliverable—a document, model, or source code—can be related and/or traced to the features of another.

ones to get across to hard-core developers, is that users can be directly involved in the modeling process. In fact, several of the modeling techniques, use cases and CRC modeling in particular, are often dominated by users and/or subject matter experts. There are several very good reasons why users should be involved in the modeling process. First, they're the ones that you are building the system for, and they have the final say as to whether or not what you have built is correct. Second, the users are the people who have the domain expertise, so when you are modeling the domain, does not it make sense to involve the experts? Third, the desperate shortage of information professionals demands that we share as much of our work with the user community as possible. The bottom line is that some modeling sessions will be dominated by users (facilitated by experienced modelers, of course) where requirements are defined and high-level analysis modeling takes place.

Users can and should actively participate in the modeling effort.

A second style of modeling session is one dominated by modelers, typically facilitated by an experienced architect. The goal of these modeling sessions is to perform detailed analysis modeling and/or high-level design modeling. The initial class diagrams and prototypes will be developed, along with interface-flow diagrams, activity models, and data models. These modeling sessions take the user requirements and add structure and detail to them, enough that developers can gain an understanding of how the overall application will be built. It is common to have coders involved in these modeling sessions to help to communicate the architectural vision to them and to train them in modeling skills.

The goal in many modeling sessions is both to get the work done and to train programmers in modeling.

A third style of modeling session is one dominated by programmers, facilitated by an experienced designer or by an architect. In these sessions detailed design is undertaken, typically via the use of class diagrams, sequence diagrams, statechart diagrams, and collaboration diagrams. This is where the designer ensures that

WAR STORY

Getting Programmer Acceptance Is Important

A few years back I was involved in a project where I was the lead modeler. Although the model was well underway before the first programmer came onto the project, as circumstance would have it the lead programmer did not accept the model that had been created. There were several reasons why this happened, but the main problem was that he was the type of developer who thought that code was the only thing that was important on a project and that everything else was superfluous. This strategy had worked well for him in the past on small, technical problems but unfortunately his vast inexperience hadn't prepared him for a large, mission-critical business application.

The short story is that he decided to do things his way, and lead many of the other programmers down the path to oblivion. Unfortunately, neither I nor the project manager knew what was going on before it was too late, and by then the entire programming team, or should I say hacking team, was in serious trouble. Because they did not follow the existing model, or develop one of their own, they ended up working sixteen-hour days seven days a week writing code that, for the most part, needed to be rewritten, often several times, before they finally got it right. The project was almost a year late and more than a million dollars over budget.

The truly unfortunate thing was that the programming team was eventually rewarded for their hard work. Because every other project at this company was also extremely late and overbudget, senior management had no idea that things did not have to be that way.

the programmers understand what they are building, and the programmers ensure that the model reflects what can actually be built. It also promotes acceptance by the developers for the model, because they were active participants in its creation. It does not matter how good your model is if your coders are not willing to follow it.

Programmers should be actively involved in the development of detailed design models.

One way to look at it is that user-dominated modeling sessions are at the 50,000-foot level, modeler-dominated sessions are at the 20,000-foot level, programmer-dominated modeling sessions are at the 5,000-foot level, and that coding is at ground level.

8.2.6 Patterns, Patterns Everywhere

A modeling pattern is a model of several classes that work together to solve a common problem in your problem or technical domain. There is a lot of exciting work going on right now in patterns; design patterns (Coad, 1992; Coad, North, and Mayfield, 1995; Gamma, Helm, Johnson, and Vlissides, 1995; Buschmann et. al. 1996) have shown very promising benefits, as have analysis patterns (Fowler, 1997; Ambler, 1998a). Design patterns describe solutions to common design problems, and analysis patterns describe solutions to common analysis problems.

Analysis patterns are often a little more specific than design patterns because they describe a solution for a portion of a problem domain. The concept of analysis patterns is fairly new, and I believe that they will prove to be of the greatest benefit in the long-term. Don't get me wrong: design patterns are very useful. It is just that analysis patterns provide insight into solutions to business problems, and solving business problems is what systems development is all about.

Modeling patterns are being used by thousands of developers to improve both their productivity and the quality of the systems that they create. Just as the achievements of great scientists are built on the shoulders of other scientists, the achievements of great developers are built on the shoulders of other developers.

8.2.6.1 Applying Modeling Patterns to Your Modeling Efforts

The following four steps describe how to use object-oriented modeling patterns effectively:

1. **Study the modeling patterns to which you already have access.** There are a lot of good books out there that describe

DEFINITIONS

analysis pattern A modeling pattern that describes a solution to a business/domain problem.

design pattern A modeling pattern that describes a solution to a design problem.

modeling pattern A pattern depicting a solution, typically in the form of a class model, to a common modeling problem.

object-oriented patterns, some interesting WWW (World-Wide Web) sites on the Internet, as well as some interesting magazine and journal articles. Reuse the work of others.

2. **Look for similar underlying concepts.** When you are studying existing object-oriented patterns, ask yourself what underlying concept is being modeled. Then try to find portions of your problem domain that are based on the same underlying concept and match the pattern to the problem.
3. **Apply the modeling pattern.** Once you have identified a pattern that describes a portion of your model, you should apply it.
4. **Do not expect that everything can be solved by modeling patterns.** The most common mistake that people make when they first start using modeling patterns is that they try to solve all problems with patterns. Unfortunately it does not work that way. Although there are many common problems between systems, there are also lots of times when portions of them are unique. Modeling patterns present solutions to common problems, not to unique problems.

Each pattern helps to sustain other patterns.
—Christopher Alexander

8.2.6.2 Discovering New Modeling Patterns

Although there are a lot of well-documented and interesting modeling patterns available to you, there are still many others waiting to be discovered. Here is some advice for discovering new patterns:

1. **Think in general terms.** When you are modeling a problem, attempt to step back and generalize what you are modeling. Does the problem occur in more than one context? Have you seen it before? Have you seen something similar before? The goal is to try to develop the forest pattern from the tree instances.
2. **Can the modeling pattern be used elsewhere?** Every so often, as you are modeling you get the suspicion that you have discovered a collection of classes that can be used elsewhere. Whenever this happens, ask yourself where the potential modeling pattern can be used and how it would be used. If you come up with a good answer or perhaps several good answers to these questions, then you should consider discussing your pattern with other people. If you think your

Discover and then develop the forest pattern from the tree instances.

modeling pattern could be used to solve a marketing problem, then discuss it with some marketing experts. If you think you have found a solution to a networking problem, discuss your pattern with some networking experts. Do not fall into the trap of assuming that your potential pattern is useful without reviewing it with others first.

3. **Use the modeling pattern several times.** The best test to determine if you have discovered a modeling pattern is to actually use it on other projects. A good rule of thumb that I use is that something is not considered reusable until it has been reused three times, and preferably used by three different development teams on three different projects. By the time the third team has used and potentially modified your pattern, you know you have something that's pretty solid.
4. **Expect to change your class diagram.** As other teams reuse your modeling pattern, chances are very good that they'll change it in the process. That's only natural. Each problem domain has its own set of requirements, some of which will be common and some of which will be unique. You may have left out, or perhaps ignored, something that is critical to another team. If you want to take advantage of the changes that other teams make, or at least remain consistent with them, then you should plan on updating both your class diagram and your source code to reflect those changes.
5. **Publish the pattern.** If you believe that you have identified a new pattern, share it with the rest of the world, ideally by posting it on the Web.

8.2.6.3 The Advantages and Disadvantages of Modeling Patterns

There are several advantages and disadvantages to working with object-oriented modeling patterns that you need to be aware of.

Advantages:

1. **Modeling patterns increase developer productivity.** By documenting solutions to common problems, modeling patterns promote reuse of development efforts. Increased reuse within your organization improves the productivity of your developers.
2. **Modeling patterns increase the consistency between applications.** By using the same modeling patterns over and over

again, you increase the consistency between applications, making them easier to understand and maintain. When your applications are developed in a consistent manner, it makes it that much easier to do technical walkthroughs that enable you to improve quality.

3. **Modeling patterns are typically more reusable than code.** Modeling patterns can be applied on any system platform because they are not environment-specific, whereas code often is.
4. **Modeling patterns can be used in combination to solve difficult problems.** Modeling patterns are solutions to small, cohesive problems and can be used as building blocks to create solutions to larger problems.
5. **More modeling patterns are being developed every day.** There is a lot of exciting work going on in patterns, with new patterns being introduced every day. This allows you to take advantage of the development efforts of thousands of people, often for the mere cost of a book, magazine, or Internet connection.

Disadvantages:

1. **You need to learn a large number of modeling patterns.** Although there is an advantage to having access to a large number of modeling patterns, the disadvantage is that you have to learn a large number of them, or at least know that they exist.
2. **Modeling patterns are not code.** Hard-core technical people are often unwilling to accept that anything other than code can be considered reusable.
3. **"Pattern" is quickly becoming a buzzword.** As more and more people realize the value of patterns more and more marketing people will begin to exploit it to increase the sales of whatever product or service they are pushing. Just as in the mid-1990s we saw the term *object-oriented* used as an adjective to describe products that had almost nothing to do with objects, we are seeing the same sort of thing happen with the term *pattern*. By writing a book about process patterns, am I guilty of promulgating this problem? Perhaps. You be the judge. Hmmm . . . a Judge pattern, not a bad idea.

The secret to using patterns successfully is to understand when and when not to use them.

8.3 Solution: Project Tasks

In this section I will discuss project task issues pertinent to the Model stage.

8.3.1 Managing the Modeling Stage

You must address several management issues that are specific to the modeling effort. They are all based on taking the time to do things right so that you create an accurate and valid model. Just like a house with a poor foundation eventually falls over and costs much more to repair in the long run, source code without the foundation of a good model also breaks in time and costs you significantly more than if you had done it right.

The secret to managing the modeling process is scheduling: you need to get the right people into the right room at the right time. This is a lot easier said than done, because the exploratory nature of modeling makes it difficult for you to plan what expertise on which you need to draw. I prefer to plan my modeling schedule about two weeks in advance—any less and it becomes difficult to find participants on short notice; any more and your schedule becomes inaccurate and requires constant revision.

TIP

Schedule Modeling in the Small and Large

As discussed in Chapter 4, I am a strong believer in scheduling in the large and small; I do detailed scheduling for near-term activities, such as modeling sessions, and general scheduling, such as what domains I will model, in the large. This means that for modeling I will have a fairly accurate meeting schedule, defining what specific topics will be modeled by whom, for the next week or two, and a general indication of which broad problem domain I wish to model past that. This scheduling strategy allows me to schedule the people for near-term modeling, while at the same time, it allows me to change my long-term schedule based on new knowledge gained during modeling (for example, I may realize that I need to rearrange the order of what I want to model over the long term, or that a given domain will take shorter or longer than originally anticipated). The main goal is to ensure that you always have domain experts available to you, you do not want to lose time because you cannot get domain experts in your modeling sessions when you need them.

Table 8.2 presents an organizational pattern for scheduling the efforts of a single modeling team, typically because there is only one modeler available. For the single stream of modeling I have found that on Monday through Thursday, modeling in the morning with documentation of results and preparation for the next modeling session works well, with Friday being reserved for other activities such as planning, communicating progress, and mentoring of junior team members. At first glance you would hope that you wouldn't "lose" one day a week to these kinds of tasks, but the reality is that this schedule is actually very aggressive and is hard to maintain over a long period of time without careful management.

Table 8.3 presents an organizational pattern for scheduling several streams of simultaneous modeling. The thing to notice is that you now lose a day and a half a week to other activities due to the increased overhead of managing several streams of simultaneous effort, but this is still an aggressive schedule. The big difference is that individual modelers work on their portion of the model in the mornings, potentially leading their own teams, and in the afternoons the modelers work together to synchronize their efforts and to work on joint modeling issues. The extra team

TABLE 8.2. The Single-Team Scheduling Organizational Pattern

	Monday	Tuesday	Wednesday	Thursday	Friday
Morning	Modeling	Modeling	Modeling	Modeling	Other
Afternoon	Document and prepare	Document and prepare	Document and prepare	Document and prepare	Other

TABLE 8.3. The Multiple-Team Scheduling Organizational Pattern

	Monday	Tuesday	Wednesday	Thursday	Friday
Morning	Other	Individual modeling	Individual modeling	Individual modeling	Other
Afternoon	Team modeling	Team modeling	Team modeling	Team modeling	Other

modeling session on Monday afternoon is used to increase the consistency in the model and to grow the overall modeling vision within the team.

The goal of the team modeling effort is to ensure consistency within the model, both from a content issue and from a modeling style issue—given the opportunity, everyone will follow their own personal style of modeling and documentation, which leads to arguments and wasted time during modeling. Unless a single documentation format is accepted among modelers (documentation formats should really have been developed by the Define Infrastructure stage, described in Chapter 6), it eventually leads to confusion and lower productivity during development. Unless otherwise scheduled for, documentation of the model is done mostly during individual modeling, with improvements to it during team modeling. Preparation for the next modeling session is often done at the end of the team modeling session for that day.

Harrison (1996) suggests with the Lock'em Up Together organizational pattern to gather everyone together to work out your architecture and literally put them in the same room to do so. He believes that everyone should commit to total participation until the architecture is complete (enough).

To get access to the right subject matter experts, I have always found it useful to have at least one or two general domain experts, often from the systems department, who understand the problem domain at a high level and who have contacts who are experts at specific portions of the problem domain. It is also crucial that you build a rapport with your users as you model (your goal being to have people that you can verify information) whom you can call on for further explanation and who support your project.

During modeling you will make important design decisions, a key aspect of modeling, and identify decisions that should be deferred for future consideration. You'll also learn which techniques and approaches work for your organization and which do not. This sort of information should be captured in your project's group memory (discussed in Chapter 6) so that you do not lose this valuable information.

8.3.2 Training and Education

The good news is that there are many sources of training and education available to you; the bad news is that there are many sources of training and education available to you. The first thing that you need to understand is that there is much more to object-oriented modeling than understanding the modeling notation and knowing how to use a CASE tool—two good things to know, but they simply are not enough. Second, it is also important to recognize that a five day course in OO modeling, or even a five-week intensive OO university program is not going to be enough. Good modelers became good modelers after years of experience, not after weeks of training.

You become a good modeler after years of experience, not weeks of training.

My advice:

1. **Read, read, read.** Give people access to good books, magazines, and journals about object-oriented modeling. Many people learn by reading and are willing to do so on their own time as long as you are willing to supply the reading material.
2. **Train in the notation.** Selecting a set of modeling notations like UML is a good start, but as you have seen in this chapter, they are not complete, and you must train people in their use. You should be able to find a two or three-day course that concentrates on each model, its use, and its notation.
3. **Train in modeling.** Send people on modeling courses, preferably ones that use your chosen notation, so that they gain at least an academic understanding of the models. Try to schedule several rounds of one week of training followed by three or four weeks of real-world work that uses what everyone learned in the course.
4. **Train in the CASE tool.** I'm a firm believer that CASE tool companies are the best source of training for their tools and the absolute worst source of training for understanding how to model. The reason for this is simple: although they know their tool very well, they rarely understand the development process outside what their tool implements (my experience is that most CASE tool vendors have a myopic view of the modeling process). I also believe that training in modeling should come before training in the tool; otherwise, people have a tendency to concentrate only on the techniques supported by your chosen CASE tool and not on all available techniques.
5. **Train in patterns.** Patterns are an important source of potential reuse and consistency within models, and a lot of very good patterns have been identified that you can use immedi-

ately. Get your modelers trained on the fundamentals of patterns and their usage.

6. **Get good instructors.** Ensure that the instructors have actually built real-world systems using object technology. The best instructors are usually consultants who give training courses one week a month and do development work the rest of the time. Because the best modelers also write a little code, the best modeling instructors should also spend some of their time coding too.
7. **Train in communication skills.** Train your modelers in communication skills, such as meeting facilitation, giving presentations, and interviewing. Professional management training schools are good sources for this kind of training, as are university business management programs. College journalism programs are good at least for interviewing.
8. **Get good mentors.** A mentor is an expert who also has the ability to transfer skills. A good modeling mentor has several years of OO modeling experience, is constantly learning new approaches and techniques, and has the patience needed to work with and grow novice modelers.

DEFINITION

mentor An experienced developer who transfers her or his skills to less experienced developers to aid in their educational experience. This is a key role during all phases, but specifically during the Construct phase.

8.3.3 Quality Assurance Issues

Every single deliverable on a project, including models, can be tested. In Chapter 11 we will discuss several techniques for validating your modeling efforts, in particular modeling walkthroughs. Things to look for:

1. **Traceability.** When information in one model is related to information in another, there should be some sort of link or trace connecting them so that the models can remain consistent as they evolve over time.
2. **Consistency.** Are the same notation and documentation styles being used throughout the model? Is the information contained in the model internally consistent?
3. **Simplicity.** Could the model be made simpler while still providing the same functionality? Models that are unnecessarily complex are more difficult to understand, develop, and maintain.

8.3.4 Potential Risks During Modeling

You should address several risks common to the modeling process:

1. **Myopia.** Technical people have a tendency to either ignore or underestimate business issues, and business people often do the same with technical issues. This is because people usually concentrate on what they know best. Unfortunately, your modeling efforts need to take both business and technological factors into account; therefore, you need a multi-dimensional team consisting of both technical and subject matter experts.
2. **Lack of a common architecture.** The most efficient way you can develop, at least in the long run, is to work top-down from a common architecture. Sometimes this is not an option for you, at least not immediately, because of time constraints on a mission-critical application. Or perhaps work has already begun, or even completed, on other OO applications within your organization before you realized that you really needed a common architecture first. So be it. The fact remains that without an architecture, you reduce the opportunities for reuse, you increase your development costs, you increase the time it takes to deliver new functionality, and you increase your maintenance costs. This is a simple reality of system development; there are no special cases where this rule does not apply. At some point your organization needs to accept the fact that it has to take the time and do it right; otherwise, it will continue doing it wrong.
3. **Coding starts too soon.** There's a word for starting to code before you have understood the problem that you are trying to solve and the solution to it: hacking. It is a lot easier and a lot more efficient to first draw some diagrams representing your solution than it is to write the code for it (when you make a mistake in a diagram it only affects a couple of bubbles and lines, instead of a couple thousand lines of code).

If you do not have time to model you surely do not have time to code.

8.3.5 Opportunities for Reuse

Figure 8.23 compares the productivity of each approach to reuse, showing that code reuse is the least productive, although still beneficial, and that domain-component reuse is the most productive.

War Story

Distributed Systems Have Distributed Risks

When designing a distributed application, never forget that there are some very specific risks associated with doing so (Neumann, 1996). For example, failures of isolated components, perhaps a critical network router, can result in severe and/or global outages. The issue is one of trying to build a dependable application from undependable components: if you do not control all of the distributed components, and even if you do, your application is at risk from the weakest link in the chain. I once saw an organization that could not serve their customers for several hours because of a failure in a five dollar network connector. This company lost thousands of dollars and angered many of their clients because their weakest link failed them.

The forms of reuse that can be applied during the Model stage are shown with an asterisk, and the forms that are supported (to be taken advantage of by other stages) by the Model stage are shown with a double asterisk. I compare and contrast these approaches to reuse in *More Process Patterns* (Ambler, 1998b).

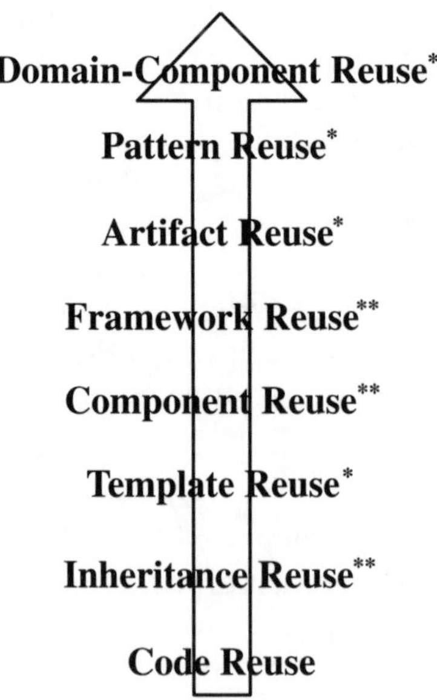

Figure 8.23. The increasing effectiveness of reuse techniques

During the Model stage, object-oriented modelers benefit from pattern reuse every time they apply a pattern within their models. Artifact reuse is achieved through the reuse of modeling standards and procedures, and template reuse is achieved by using common documentation templates when describing the models produced.

Object-oriented modelers benefit from pattern reuse, artifact reuse, and template reuse.

Domain-component reuse is supported by domain architecture modeling, which is the main purpose of this style of modeling. Framework and component reuse are supported by detailed analysis and design modeling by identifying the use of existing frameworks components on those models. These two approaches to reuse are also supported by the identification and modeling of reusable frameworks and components during detailed design. Finally, inheritance reuse is supported by the Model stage through the use of inheritance in the models.

8.3.6 Metrics

There are several metrics applicable to the Model stage that you may choose to gather. These metrics are:

DEFINITIONS

artifact reuse The reuse of previously created development artifacts: use cases, standards documents, domain-specific models, procedures and guidelines, and other applications.

code reuse The reuse of source code within sections of an application and potentially across multiple applications.

component reuse The reuse of pre-built, fully encapsulated components in the development of your application.

domain-component reuse The reuse of prebuilt, large-scale domain components that encapsulate cohesive portions of your business domain.

framework reuse The reuse of collections of classes that together implement the basic functionality of a common technical or business domain.

inheritance reuse The use of inheritance in your application to take advantage of behavior implemented in existing classes.

pattern reuse The reuse of publicly documented approaches, called patterns, to solving common problems.

template reuse The reuse of a common set of layouts for key development artifacts—documents, models, and source code—within your organization.

1. **Requirements instability.** This metric is calculated by taking the number of requirements changed during a given time period, typically a work month, and dividing it by the total number of requirements for your application. This metric provides an estimate of the quality of your efforts during the Define and Validate Initial Requirements stage (Chapter 3); a high figure indicates that your requirements were not well defined during the Initiate phase. It is common to have a high requirements instability at the beginning of the Model stage, because your analysis efforts should quickly identify missing or misunderstood requirements. Projects that experience changing requirements during the Construct phase have a high chance of failing.
2. **Method count of a class.** One metric that is very easy to collect and often proves useful is the method count of a class (Chidamber and Kemerer, 1991). Classes with large numbers of methods are most likely to be application-specific, whereas classes with fewer methods have a tendency to be more reusable. Although this is not always true, I find it worthwhile to get a method count for all the classes in my application, and then take a look at the ones that appear to have an unusually high count as compared to the other ones. Considering these classes, I then ask myself whether or not they might be applicable to another project in the future. If so, then I rethink their design to make them more reusable, if possible.
3. **Number of instance attributes of a class.** This metric indicates whether you are using inheritance effectively by counting the number of instance attributes in a class (Lorenz and Kidd, 1994). Whenever you have a lot of instance attributes in a single class, say, more than ten, there is a good chance that you have modeled more than one concept in that class. This is very common when you have what should be two classes that have a one-to-one relationship between them.
4. **Inheritance tree depth.** The metric indicates potential difficulties with the way that you have used the concept of inheritance is the depth of your inheritance trees (Chidamber and Kemerer, 1991). The depth of an inheritance hierarchy is defined as the maximum number of classes from the root of their hierarchy to its lowest leaf class, including the root class. The basic problem is that deeper trees constitute greater

design complexity. The lower down the tree a class is, the more it inherits, and the more it inherits, the harder it is to understand. If it is harder to understand, then it is harder to maintain and enhance. The general feeling in the object community is that if the depth of an inheritance tree is greater than five, at least within a domain/business model, then you need to revisit its design.

5. **Number of children of a class.** A metric that is related to the inheritance tree depth, and which partially contradicts it, is the number of children of a class (Chidamber and Kemerer, 1991). Although we want to avoid the complexity that results from inheritance tree depth, it is generally better to have depth than breadth, because it promotes reusability through inheritance. One way that the number of children can be used to evaluate the quality of your use of inheritance is to look at where in the class hierarchy your classes are. You see, classes higher up usually have more subclasses than those lower down because they have less application-specific code (and hence are more reusable). Whenever you create classes that are specific to the application that you are working on, you typically inherit from the existing class hierarchy at your disposal. This usually results in application-specific classes being lower down in the class hierarchy—classes that are often the only children of their superclass.
6. **Number of class attributes.** By counting the number of class attributes of a class(Lorenz and Kidd, 1994) you obtain an indication of the quality of your design. Classes with more than three or four class attributes are often masking a coupling problem in your application. Class attributes can be used as global variables within an application, and the use of global variables increases coupling. The only valid use of a class variable is to share common information among the instances of that class. If you are using class variables in some sort of scheme to speed up the processing of your application, then chances are good that you are abusing the concept. The CPU (central processing unit) cycles that you are saving had better be incredibly critical to your application to justify the increase in coupling.
7. **Number of ignored methods within a subclass.** This metric (Ambler, 1998a) is a measure of your lack of use of pure

inheritance in your design. Although there is nothing wrong with overriding a method to expand its functionality, there is a problem when you override a method to remove its functionality. In other words, you have effectively ignored it. Ignored methods within a class are an indication that it is not inheriting all of the methods of its superclass, or in other words it violates the principle of pure inheritance. You should aim for having no ignored methods in your classes, although you will not always be able to achieve this.

8.4 Resulting Context: Exit Conditions for Modeling

Several conditions should be met before you can consider modeling to be finished. These conditions are:

1. **The models have been validated.** The models should be validated using the appropriate testing techniques described in Chapter 11. After all, the fundamental goal of modeling is to produce accurate models that can be used by developers to create an application.
2. **The models have been placed under software configuration**

DEFINITIONS

application-specific class Any class that is used in a single application.

ignored method An inherited method that is overridden to remove its functionality.

inheritance tree depth The maximum number of classes from the root of a class hierarchy to its lowest node, including the root class.

leaf class A class within an inheritance hierarchy that does not have other classes inheriting from it.

override The redefinition of a method or attribute in a subclass.

pure inheritance When a subclass inherits everything from its superclass(es).

requirements instability A metric calculated by taking the number of changed requirements in a given time frame by the total number of requirements.

root class The top class in an inheritance hierarchy.

management (SCM) control. For the Model stage to be complete, your models need to be baselined and put under SCM control so that everyone knows what the "official" models are. As you saw in Chapter 1, SCM is a Level Two key process area (KPA) of the Capability Maturity Model (CMM) (Software Engineering Institute, 1995).

3. **The test plan and test cases are current.** You must update your test plan and test cases to accurately reflect the information contained in your models. This means that for a new project, you start the creation of a test plan and update your existing plan for an existing system. You need an accurate test plan for testing in the large, covered in *More Process Patterns* (Ambler, 1998b), as well as for regression testing of future releases of your application. Regression testing is covered in Chapter 11.
4. **You have support for the model.** The programmers who are working from your models must accept that they are valid, which is one of the reasons why they are involved in the development of many of them. Furthermore, senior management and other development teams must also accept that your mod-

baseline A tested and certified version of a deliverable representing a conceptual milestone which thereafter serves as the basis for further development and that can be modified only through formal change control procedures. A particular version becomes a baseline when a responsible group decides to designate it as such.

Capability Maturity Model (CMM) A strategy, defined by the Software Engineering Institute (SEI), that describes the key elements of an effective software process.

key process area (KPA) An issue that must be addressed to achieve a specific Capability Maturity Model (CMM) maturity level.

software configuration management (SCM) A set of engineering procedures for tracking and documenting software and its related deliverables throughout their life cycles to ensure that all changes are recorded and the current state of the software is known and reproducible.

test case A description, often documented as a series of steps, of a situation that a software item must support.

test plan A document that prescribes the approach to be taken during the testing process.

els truly present an accurate picture of the problem domain and of a valid solution to it, otherwise they will not give you the support that you need to successfully complete your project.

5. **You have improved the lot of your users.** Successful modeling efforts result in an improved understanding of the problem domain, which in turn provides you with the opportunity to create applications that truly reflect the needs of your user community.
6. **You have improved the lot of your programmers.** The best models describe a solution that meets the needs of the problem domain in the easiest possible manner, making it easier for the programmers who have to build applications based on the models.

8.5 Secrets of Success

The following pointers will help you to improve your object-oriented modeling efforts:

If you do not have time to model, you do not have time to code.

1. **Do not focus on implementation issues too early.** Understand the problem, then define the solution, then build it. Remember the saying: if you do not have time to model, you surely do not have time to code.
2. **There must be one vision.** There must be one common vision produced by the architectural modeling team. Yes, many people should be involved in coming to that common vision, but in the end everyone must come to a consensus about a single architecture.
3. **The architect(s) and the project manager(s) must work closely together.** On a small project the architect and the project manager should work closely together. On larger projects the same holds true, the only difference being that the architecture group works closely with the project managers.
4. **The modelers must understand the technical and business environments.** Fundamentally you need to understand the environment you are modeling for, and that means that a good modeler even does a little coding now and again.
5. **Do not reverse-engineer your model.** A fatal mistake that many projects make is to take existing source code and read

it into their modeling tool to automatically generate a model from it. This process is called reverse engineering, and is often promoted as a technique for reducing your modeling. The reality is that this actually increases your modeling time because of the typical low quality of the resulting model. Call it like it is: source code that wasn't developed from a well-thought out model is a hack job, and the reverse-engineered model based on that code will also be a hack job.

6. **Challenge assumptions.** How does the saying go: when you assume something you make an a** of "u" and me? Real increases in productivity from new systems occur when the existing rules, the existing way of doing things, are called into question so that the underlying process may be reengineered. Challenge as many assumptions as you can.
7. **Simplify, simplify, simplify.** If you can make something simpler yet still deliver the same or increased functionality, then do it. The simpler something is, the easier it is to understand, build, maintain, and enhance.
8. **Validate, validate, validate.** Every single deliverable, including models, must be tested and verified. It should be the goal of every developer to produce high-quality work that they know is correct, and to do so means that you need to validate everything that you produce.
9. **Put your best people on the architectural team.** Your architectural model is the foundation upon which all other modeling efforts are built; therefore, you should put your best and brightest on that team.
10. **Recognize that architecture is an ongoing process.** Your architectural models drive the development of your detailed models and vice versa. As your understanding of the problem domain evolves, as the problem domain itself evolves, and as technology evolves your architecture must also.
11. **Have a technical writer aid in the documentation process.** A significant portion of modeling is writing documentation describing the models. Because technical writers specialize in documentation, and because they often cost significantly less than modelers, it makes sense to have them write documentation, which enables your modelers to concentrate on modeling.
12. **Manage your tools; otherwise, they will manage you.** You need to choose one set of tools that are hopefully well inte-

grated and ensure that everyone uses them. A lot of organizations lose valuable time and money wasting time fighting internal tool wars. A word to the wise: no tool is perfect; therefore, pick the ones with the features and bugs that you can live with so that you can get on with the real work, the development of software.

13. **Train and educate everyone appropriately.** Modelers need training in more than just tools. They need to understand the modeling process, the modeling notation, and the proper use of object-oriented patterns, as well as have a strong set of communication skills. Provide them with the training and education to build the knowledge that they need.
14. **Do not allow politics to derail your architecture.** Your architecture defines the basis from which the information systems for your organization are developed. As a result, your architecture becomes the focal point for many political battles, with the likeliest casualty being the architecture itself. Although the winners may support you, the losers will often do whatever they can to see your work, your architecture, fail.
15. **A fool with a tool is still a fool.** Computer aided system engineering (CASE) tools provide little benefit if your modelers do not understand the underlying concepts that they automate.

8.6 Process Checklist

The following process checklist can be used to verify that you have completed the Model stage.

MODEL STAGE PROCESS CHECKLIST

Fulfillment of Entrance Conditions:

✔ The initial requirements have been documented and accepted.
✔ Modeling standards and guidelines, including the notation, have been selected/defined.
✔ The modeling tool(s) have been selected and installed.
✔ Documentation standards have been selected/defined.
✔ Subject matter experts (SMEs) have been scheduled and prepared appropriately.

✔ Team members have been given the appropriate training for their part in this stage.

Processes Performed:

✔ The enterprise, domain architecture, and technical architecture models were reviewed prior to detailed modeling to determine where the current project efforts fit in.

✔ The enterprise, domain architecture, and technical architecture models were updated appropriately based on new knowledge gained during detailed modeling.

✔ A user interface prototype was developed and validated.

✔ An interface-flow diagram was developed and validated to model the user interface prototype.

✔ A class diagram has been developed and validated to model the classes of your software.

✔ Activity diagrams were developed and validated where appropriate.

✔ A data diagram was developed and validated (if a relational database is used to persist objects).

✔ Sequence diagrams were developed and validated to model the logic of use cases.

✔ A deployment diagram was developed and validated.

✔ Statechart diagrams were developed and validated for complex classes.

✔ Collaboration diagrams were developed and validated to model the interaction between objects.

✔ Assumptions made during modeling were challenged and documented appropriately.

✔ Manual processes, legacy applications, and new system development was identified and modeled accordingly.

✔ The requirements allocation matrix (RAM) was updated/developed.

✔ Patterns were applied appropriately.

✔ Artifacts that are potentially reusable by your project team during this stage have been identified and used where appropriate.

✔ Your risk assessment document has been updated where appropriate.

✔ Decisions made, and decisions forgone, have been documented in your group memory.

✔ Metrics have been collected.

Fulfillment of Exit Conditions:
✔ The models have been appropriately documented.
✔ The models have been put under software configuration management (SCM) control.
✔ The models have been validated.
✔ The test plan and test cases are current, based on the models.
✔ The models have been accepted by the team and by senior management.

8.7 What You Have Learned in This Chapter

In this chapter we covered the fundamentals of object-oriented modeling. We saw that the modeling process should be architecture driven, where the architecture includes an enterprise model that describes your organization and its business environment, a domain architectural model that shows the high-level software components that will support your organization, and a technical architecture that describes the technologies that will be used to build your applications. We also discussed a collection of modeling techniques and discovered when to use them effectively, information that is summarized in Table 8.4 below.

8.8 References and Recommended Reading

Ambler, S. W. 1995. *The Object Primer: The Application Developer's Guide to Object-Orientation.* New York: SIGS Books/Cambridge University Press.

Ambler, S. W. 1998a. *Building Object Applications That Work: Your Step-by-Step Handbook for Developing Robust Systems with Object Technology.* New York: SIGS Books/Cambridge University Press.

Ambler, S. W. 1998b. *More Process Patterns: Delivering Large-Scale Systems Using Object Technology.* New York: SIGS Books/Cambridge University Press.

Booch, G. 1994. *Object-Oriented Analysis and Design with Applications,* 2d ed. Redwood City, California: The Benjamin/Cummings Publishing Company, Inc.

Brown, W., Malveau, R, McCormick, H., Mowbray, T. (1998). *AntiPatterns: Refactoring Software, Architectures, and Projects in Crisis.* New York:John Wiley & Sons.

TABLE 8.4. When to Use Each Modeling Technique

Modeling Technique	User Requirement Definition	Enterprise Modeling	Domain Arch.	Technical Arch.	Detailed Analysis	Detailed Design
Activity diagrams					X	X
Class diagrams					X	X
Collaboration diagrams						X
Component diagrams			X	X	X	X
CRC modeling	X				X	
Data models						X
Deployment diagrams				X		X
Interface flow diagrams					X	
Interviewing	X	X	X	X	X	X
Joint application design (JAD)	X	X	X	X	X	X
Sequence diagrams						X
Statechart diagrams				X		X
Technical prototypes	X	X			X	
Use cases and scenarios	X	X			X	
Use-case diagrams					X	X
User interface prototypes						

Buschmann, F., Meunier, R., Rohnert, H., Sommerlad, P., and Stal, M. 1996. *A System of Patterns: Pattern-Oriented Software Architecture*. New York: John Wiley and Sons Ltd.

Chidamber S. R. and Kemerer C. F. 1991. Towards a Suite of Metrics for Object-Oriented Design. *OOPSLA'91 Conference Proceedings,* 197–211.

Coad, P. 1992. Object-Oriented Patterns. *Communications of the ACM* 35(9), 152–159.

Coad, P., North, D., and Mayfield, M. 1995. *Object Models—Strategies, Patterns, and Applications*. Englewood Cliffs, New Jersey: Yourdon Press.

Coad, P., Yourdon, E. 1991. *Object-Oriented Analysis,* 2d ed. Englewood Cliffs, New Jersey: Yourdon Press.

Coplien, J.O. (1995). *A Generative Development-Process Pattern Language.* Pattern Languages of Program Design, Addison Wesley Longman, Inc., pp. 183--237.

Coplien, J.O., and Schmidt, D. C., eds. 1995. *Pattern Languages of Program Design.* Reading, Massachusetts: Addison-Wesley Publishing Company, Inc.

Firesmith, D., Henderson-Sellers, B., and Graham, I. 1997. *Open Modeling Language (OML) Manual.* New York: SIGS Books.

Fowler, M. 1997. *Analysis Patterns: Reusable Object Models.* Menlo Park, California: Addison Wesley Longman Inc.

Gamma, E., Helm, R., Johnson, R., Vlissides, J. 1995. *Design Patterns—Elements of Reusable Object-Oriented Software.* Reading, Massachusetts: Addison-Wesley Publishing Company, Inc.

Gane, C. and Sarson, T. 1978. *Structured Systems Analysis: Tools and Techniques.* Englewood Cliffs, New Jersey: Prentice Hall, Inc.

Gossain, S. 1996. *System Architecture: Designing Architectures.* Surrey, UK: SIGS Conferences Ltd., Object Expert July–August, 1996, 1(5), pp. 14–17,58.

Hay, D. C. 1996. *Data Model Patterns: Conventions of Thought.* New York: Dorset House Publishing.

Harrison, N.B. (1996). *Organizational Patterns for Teams.* Pattern Languages of Program Design 2, Addison-Wesley Publishing Company., pp. 345–352.

Jacobson, I., Christerson, M., Jonsson, P., and Overgaard, G. (1992). *Object-Oriented Software Engineering—A Use Case Driven Approach.* New York: ACM Press.

Jacobson, I., Griss, M., and Jonsson, P. 1997. *Software Reuse: Architecture, Process, and Organization for Business Success.* New York: ACM Press.

Lorenz, M. and Kidd, J. 1994. *Object-Oriented Software Metrics.* Englewood Cliffs, New Jersey: Prentice-Hall, Inc.

Meyer, B. 1995. *Object Success: A Manager's Guide to Object Orientation, its Impact on the Corporation and its Use For Engineering the Software Process.* Englewood Cliffs, New Jersey: Prentice Hall Inc.

Mowbray, T. 1995. Architectures: Essentials of Object-Oriented Architecture. *Object Magazine* 5(September), 28–32.

Mowbray, T. 1997. Architectures: The Seven Deadly Sins of OO Architecture. *Object Magazine* 7(April) 22–24.

Neumann, P.G. 1996. Distributed Systems Have Distributed Risks. *Communications of the ACM* 39(11), 130.

Page-Jones, M. 1995. *What Every Programmer Should Know About Object-Oriented Design*. New York: Dorset-House Publishing.

Rational Software Corporation. 1997. *The Unified Modeling Language for Object-Oriented Development Documentation v1.1*. Monterey, California: Rational Software Corporation.

Rumbaugh, J., Blaha, M., Premerlani, W., Eddy, F., and Lorensen, W. 1991. *Object-Oriented Modeling and Design*. Englewood Cliffs, New Jersey: Prentice Hall, Inc.

Shlaer, S. and Mellor, S. 1992. *Object Life Cycles—Modeling the World in States*. Englewood Cliffs, New Jersey: Yourdon Press.

Software Engineering Institute. 1995. *The Capability Maturity Model: Guidelines for Improving the Software Process*. Reading Massachusetts: Addison-Wesley Publishing Company, Inc.

Taylor, D. A. 1995. *Business Engineering With Object Technology*. New York: John Wiley & Sons, Inc.

Vlissides, J. M., Coplien, J. O., and Kerth, N. L. 1996. *Pattern Languages of Program Design 2*. Reading, Massachusetts: Addison-Wesley Publishing Company, Inc.

Weir, C. (1998). *Patterns for Designing in Teams*. Pattern Languages of Program Design 3, Addison Wesley Longman, Inc., pp. 487–501.

Whitenack, B. and Bounds, B. B. 1995. The Keys to a Truly Successful Smalltalk Project. *Object Magazine* 5(June), 76–78.

Yourdon, E. 1997. *Death March: The Complete Software Developer's Guide to Surviving "Mission Impossible" Projects*. Upper Saddle River, New Jersey: Prentice-Hall, Inc.

Chapter 9

The Program Stage

DURING the Program stage the source code for your application is documented, written, reviewed, tested, and packaged for delivery. For this stage to be successful, your models must drive the development of your source code. The most important lesson that you should learn from this chapter is that there is far more to programming than writing source code. You need to understand the models, then seek out reusable artifacts to reduce your work load, then document what you are going to write, then write the code, then inspect and improve it, then test and fix it, and then finally package it. In this chapter I discuss these tasks in detail as well as provide tips and techniques for improving the quality and robustness of the code that you develop.

There is more to programming than writing code.

As you see in Figure 9.1, the main inputs into the Program stage are the models produced by the Model stage (Chapter 8) and the project infrastructure developed during the Define Infrastructure stage, (Chapter 6) which defines the tools, standards, and procedures to be used by your project team. The main outputs of the Program stage are a packaged application ready for testing in the large, and an updated master test/QA plan so that the application can be tested.

My experience is that the vast majority of programmers have a far too narrow focus in their approach to programming and will unknowingly produce work that is difficult to maintain and to

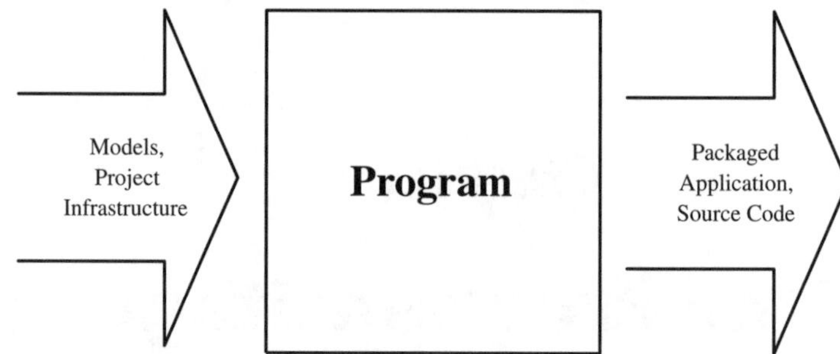

Figure 9.1. The Program stage

extend. There are several reasons why this happens. First, because few organizations choose to define their development priorities, most programmers set their own, almost always putting performance first even when it is not appropriate. My personal coding priorities, in order, are correctness, robustness, usability, and performance a distant last. Don't worry, I will discuss optimization issues later in the chapter. Second, the education system, including both colleges and professional training organizations, tend to concentrate on technical issues such as language features and optimization, not on professional software engineering issues such as maintainability and robustness. Third, the vast majority of programming books also concentrate on technical issues and not quality issues, such as how to document your source code properly or organize your programming logic based on class type, and as a result programmers do not learn coding habits that will make them truly effective. Finally, many programmers have never had the experience of maintaining someone else's code and have never seen the damage caused by developers who did not follow standards, did not document their code properly, and did not base their work on sound modeling and software engineering principles. Whenever I talk with a programmer who has never been in a maintenance role, I discount everything that they say; in my mind they do not yet have the experience necessary to truly understand the development process.

Most programmers do not have the training or experience necessary to write robust, quality code.

9.1 Initial Context: Entry Conditions for Programming

Several conditions must be met before programming may begin:

1. **The models must be in place.** You should never write a single

DEFINITIONS

extensibility A measure of how easy it is to add new features to a system. The easier it is to add new features, the more extensible we say the system is.

master test/quality assurance(QA) plan A document that describes your testing and quality assurance policies and procedures, as well as the detailed test plans for each portion of your application.

robustness A measure of the quality of a product. Robust software products continue to operate once an error occurs, and are relatively easy to maintain and to enhance.

line of code, with the exception of prototype code, without a model in place first. I am not saying that the model for the entire application needs to be in place before you begin coding, but the portion of the model that you want to code should be complete. Fundamentally, it is far more efficient to draw some bubbles and lines to model your thinking than it is to simply start writing code. Think about it first, then code it.

2. **The project infrastructure must be defined.** Before coding begins, your project infrastructure (at least the portion of it that pertains to programming) needs to be in place. This means that your software configuration management (SCM) tools and processes should be available to coders, that coding standards should be documented and accepted by the team, that user interface design standards should be documented and accepted, and that your development tools should be available to all programmers. If you start programming without this infrastructure in place, your development team will quickly devolve into chaos and inconsistency.
3. **Professional programmers must be available.** A professional programmer is someone who is willing to work as part of a larger team, who is willing to learn new techniques, who is willing to follow the accepted standards and guidelines of your organization, and who is willing to work closely with your modelers to ensure that their code fits into the overall whole. Unprofessional programmers, often called cowboy coders or hacks, believe that they know everything, that their way is the only way, and that they are better off working by themselves

DEFINITION

software configuration management (SCM) A set of engineering procedures for tracking and documenting software and its related deliverables throughout their life cycles to ensure that all changes are recorded and the current state of the software is known and reproducible.

instead of as part of a team. When you compare the productivity of these two groups of programmers over the complete software process, taking in the costs of both development and maintenance, I believe that you will find that professional programmers are far more productive.

9.2 Solution: Programming Object-Oriented Code

Figure 9.2 depicts the process pattern for the Program stage, showing that there is more to this stage than simply writing source code. Although programming is an iterative process, I will present the tasks of programming in the order that they generally occur.

The iterative tasks of the Program stage are:

- Understanding the model(s)
- Reusing existing code and components
- Documenting source code
- Writing source code
- Synchronizing source code with models
- Preparing code for inspections

Figure 9.2. The Program process pattern

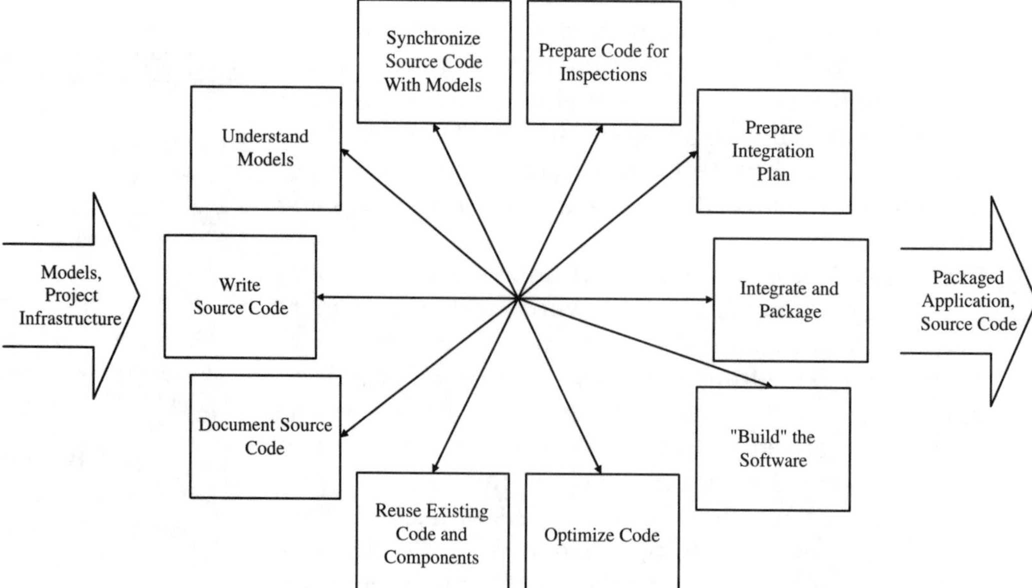

- Optimizing your code
- Preparing the integration plan
- Integrating and packaging your code

9.2.1 Understanding the Models

The very first thing that must occur before coding begins is that programmers must take the time to understand the models that define what they are to build. Although this sounds straightforward and obvious, it very often is not done. If programmers do not take the time to understand the model before they begin coding, then why bother creating the models in the first place? The goal is for programmers to understand the design issues and trade-offs involved, and how their code will fit into the overall application. They must invest the time to understand both the problem and the solution before they write the code.

Programmers must invest the time to understand the models before they begin coding.

A very effective way to ensure that programmers understand the models that they are building to is to have them actively involved in the modeling process to begin with. Not only does this increase their understanding of the models, it also brings their experience to the table as to what can actually be built—injecting a dose of reality into your modeling efforts—and provides them with opportunities to expand their skillsets and increase their value to your organization.

Although some programmers will bridle at taking the time to understand the design of your application, DeMarco (1997) points out that successful project teams spend the majority of their time in modeling, not in coding. With a direct correlation between success and modeling, it makes a lot of sense to invest the time in understanding your application model before coding begins.

9.2.2 Reusing Existing Code and Components

Once your programmers have taken the time to review the models and to understand what needs to be built, they should then look to see what has already been built. One of the promises of object-oriented development is that of increased reuse, but you need to recognize the fact that you can only increase reuse on your projects if you choose to do so. This means that somebody has to make an effort to reuse existing artifacts, and the best way to do so is to look for reusable artifacts before you start writing code.

You must choose to reuse the work of others.

Your design models should already define how your application interacts with the large-scale domain components described by your domain architecture model(s) and with technical components described in technical architecture model(s). Your design models will also describe how your application classes will interact with each other, indicating reuse of classes developed by your own team. What your design models will not describe is the reuse of construction level components—user interface widgets such as tool bars and system components such as file access classes—that can also be reused by your programming team.

Your design models will point out opportunities for large-scale reuse.

There are several common approaches for obtaining reuse during the Program stage. These approaches are:

- Artifact reuse
- Code reuse
- Component reuse
- Inheritance reuse
- Framework reuse

9.2.2.1 Artifact Reuse

Artifact reuse, an approach to reuse in which items developed on previous projects are reused by your development team, can be achieved through the reuse of coding standards and software configuration management (SCM) procedures.

9.2.2.2 Code Reuse

Code reuse, the most common kind of reuse, refers to the reuse of source code within sections of an application and potentially across multiple applications. At its best, code reuse is accomplished through the sharing of common classes and/or collections of functions and procedures (this is possible in C++, but not in Smalltalk or Java). At worst, code reuse is accomplished by copying and then modifying existing code. A sad reality of our industry is that code copying is often the only form of reuse practiced by developers.

A key requirement of code reuse is that you have access to the source code; if necessary, you either modify it yourself or have someone else modify it for you. This is both good and bad; by looking at the code, you can determine, albeit often slowly, whether or not you want to use it. At the same time, by releasing the full source code to you, the original developer is less motivated to document it properly (see below), increasing the time

DEFINITIONS

artifact reuse The reuse of previously created development artifacts: use cases, standards documents, domain-specific models, procedures and guidelines, and other applications.

class A person, place, thing, event, concept, screen, or report.

code reuse The reuse of source code within sections of an application and potentially across multiple applications.

component reuse The reuse of pre-built, fully encapsulated components in the development of your application.

domain architecture A collection of high-level models that describe the problem domain. Domain architectures are typically documented by high-level use cases, use-case diagrams, and class models that describe the various sub domains and the relationships between them.

domain-component reuse The reuse of pre-built, large-scale domain components that encapsulate cohesive portions of your business domain.

framework reuse The reuse of collections of classes that together implement the basic functionality of a common technical or business domain.

inheritance reuse The use of inheritance in your application to take advantage of behavior implemented in existing classes.

opportunistic reuse A reuse approach in which reusable items are harvested from project deliverables after the fact.

pattern reuse The reuse of publicly documented approaches, called patterns, to solving common problems.

reuse repository A tool used to store reusable items.

systematic reuse An approach to reuse that involves modeling techniques whose purpose is to define high-leverage, reusable components.

technical architecture A set of models and documents that describe the technical components of an application, including, but not limited to, the hardware, software, middleware, persistence mechanisms, and operating systems to be deployed.

template reuse The reuse of a common set of layouts for key development artifacts—documents, models, and source code—within your organization.

that it takes you to understand it and consequently decreasing the benefit of it to you. The main advantage of code reuse is that it reduces the amount of actual source code that you need to write, *potentially* decreasing both development and maintenance costs.

The disadvantages are that its scope of effect is limited to programming and that it often increases the coupling within an application.

Brown, Malveau, McCormick, and Mowbray (1998) describe the Cut-and-Paste Programming antipattern, a common approach to programming where source code is copied and then modified slightly to meet some new needs. This is in effect the worst-case approach to code reuse, often resulting in defects propagating throughout your software and a greater maintenance burden due to having multiple copies of relatively the same code.

9.2.2.3 Inheritance Reuse

Inheritance reuse refers to the use of inheritance in your application to take advantage of behavior implemented in existing classes. Inheritance is one of the fundamental concepts of object orientation, allowing you to model *is a, is like,* and/or *is a kind of* relationships. For example, to develop a CheckingAccount class you start by having it inherit from SavingsAccount, directly reusing all of the behavior implemented in that class.

The advantage of inheritance reuse is that you take advantage of previously developed behavior, decreasing both the development time and cost of your application. Unfortunately, there are several disadvantages to inheritance reuse. First, the misuse of inheritance will often result in developers missing an opportunity for component reuse, which, as we'll see, offers a much higher level of reuse. Second, novice developers will often skimp on inheritance regression testing (the running of superclass test cases on a subclass), resulting in a fragile class hierarchy that is difficult to maintain and enhance. As you can see, this is reuse, but at a prohibitive cost.

9.2.2.4 Component Reuse

Component reuse refers to the use of pre-built, fully encapsulated components in the development of your application. Components are typically self sufficient and encapsulate only one concept. Component reuse differs from code reuse in that you do not have access to the source code, and it differs from inheritance reuse in that it does not use subclassing. Common examples of components are Java beans and ActiveX components.

Component reuse has several advantages. First, component reuse offers a greater scope of reusability than either code or inheritance reuse because components are self-sufficient: you literally plug them in and they work. Second, the widespread use of common platforms such as the Win32 operating system and the Java virtual machine provide a market that is large enough for third-party vendors to create and sell components at a low cost. The main disadvantage to component reuse is that because components are small and encapsulate only one concept, you need a large library of them.

To get going with components, the easiest way is to start out with user interface widgets—slide bars, graphing components, and graphical buttons, to name a few. But do not forget that there is more to an application than the user interface; you can get components that encapsulate operating system features such as network access and persistence features such as access components to a relational database. If you are building your own components, make sure they do one thing only. For example, a user interface component for editing surface addresses is very reusable; you can use that on many editing screens. A component that edits a surface address, an email address, and a phone number is not as reusable; there aren't as many opportunities where you'll want all three of those features simultaneously. Instead it would be better to build three reusable components and reuse each one where it is needed. When a component encapsulates one concept, we say that it is cohesive.

9.2.2.5 Framework Reuse

Framework reuse refers to the use of collections of classes that together implement the basic functionality of a common technical or business domain. Developers use frameworks as the foundation from which they build an application: the common eighty percent is in place already; they just need to add the remaining twenty percent that is specific to their application. Frameworks that implement the basic components of a graphical user interface are very common, and there are now frameworks for insurance, human resources, manufacturing, banking, and electronic commerce available. Framework reuse represents a high level of reuse at the problem domain level.

The main advantages of frameworks are that they provide a good start at developing a solution for a problem domain and often encapsulate complex logic that would take years to develop from scratch. Unfortunately, framework reuse suffers from several disadvantages. The complexity of frameworks makes them difficult to master, requiring a lengthy learning process on the part of

> **DEFINITION**
> **framework** A reusable, almost-complete application that can be extended to produce custom applications.

developers. Frameworks are often platform-specific and tie you into a single vendor, increasing the risk for your application. Although frameworks implement eighty percent of the required logic, it is often the easiest eighty percent; and the hard stuff, the business logic and processes that are unique to your organization, is still left for you to do. Frameworks rarely work together unless they come from a common vendor or consortium of vendors, and often require you to change your business to fit the framework instead of the other way around.

9.2.2.6 Comparing the Techniques

In this section we have seen that there are several reuse techniques applicable to the Program stage, and as we'll discover throughout the book, there are several more approaches to reuse that we discuss elsewhere. Figure 9.3 compares the productivity of each approach to reuse, showing that code reuse is the least productive, although still beneficial, and that domain-component reuse is the most productive. In Figure 9.3 the forms of reuse that are used by the Program stage are shown with an asterisk to set them apart. We'll compare and contrast these approaches to reuse in Chapter 20.

9.2.2.7 Supporting Reuse During the Program Stage

McClure (1997) points out that developers need access to a repository that contains high-quality components and/or artifacts that they can reuse. Your reuse repository will contain items that were developed in-house and items purchased off-the-shelf from a third-party vendor. To find reusable components, your developers need a search tool that accesses a catalog describing the items stored in your repository.

> **DEFINITIONS**
>
> **component** Small-scale, cohesive items such as user interface widgets that programmers reuse when building applications.
>
> **domain component** A large-scale component which encapsulates cohesive portions of your business domain. Domain components are identified by architectural modeling.
>
> **pattern** The description of a general solution to a common problem or issue from which a detailed solution to a specific problem may be determined. Software development patterns come in many flavors, including but not limited to analysis patterns, design patterns, and process patterns.

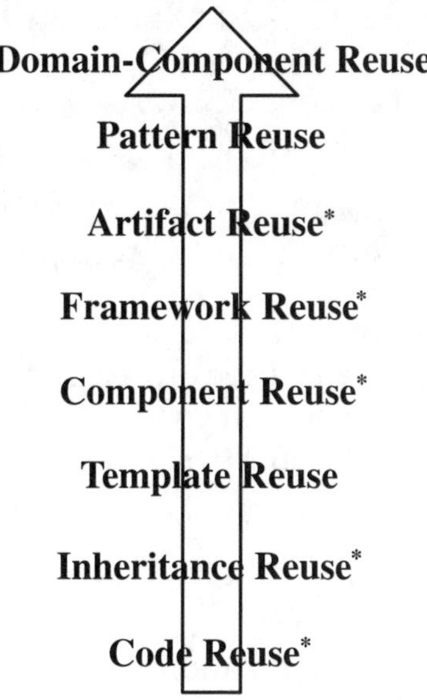

Figure 9.3. The increasing effectiveness of reuse techniques

Programmers will often be aided by reuse engineers who specialize in the development and support of reusable components. As we will see in the Generalize stage (Chapter 10) reuse engineers are actively involved in the identification of potentially reusable components created by application developers; components that will be harvested, generalized, and made available to all developers within your organization. This style of reuse is called opportunistic reuse, because you make an artifact reusable after the fact; whereas systematic reuse creates items that are reusable because they are designed to be so from the very start. Reuse engineers are also responsible for supporting the efforts of developers to reuse the items within the reuse repository.

A clever person solves a problem. A wise person avoids it.
—Einstein.

9.2.3 Documenting Source Code

Before you write your source code, you should first document it. Although this seems non-intuitive at first, experience shows that programmers who start by writing brief comments that describe their coding logic are significantly more productive than programmers who do not. The reason for this is simple: the hard part about programming is getting the logic right, not writing the actual code that implements that logic. Writing source code before documenting it is a common process antipattern, one that you want to avoid if possible. By documenting your logic first in the form of brief comments, also called pseudocode, you invest

DEFINITIONS

antipattern The description of a common approach to solving a common problem, an approach that in time proves to be wrong or highly ineffective.

process antipattern An antipattern that describes an approach and/or series of actions for developing software that is proven to be ineffective and often detrimental to your organization.

Programmers who document their code before they write it are significantly more productive than those who do not.

the time to get your logic in place, avoiding the problem of writing a lot of code that later needs to be scrapped because it does not work right. Think first, then code.

To understand how to effectively document source code programmers need to write:

- Class documentation
- Method header documentation
- Internal method documentation
- Attribute documentation

9.2.3.1 Documenting a Class

The following information should appear in the comments immediately preceding the definition of a class:

1. **The purpose of the class.** Developers need to know the general purpose of a class to determine whether it meets their needs. I also make it a habit to document any good things to know about a class; for example, is it part of a pattern, or are there any interesting limitations/constraints to using it (Ambler, 1998)? Although this information is contained within your class model, it must also appear in your source code so that programmers have ready access to it.
2. **Known bugs**[1]. All outstanding problems should be documented so that other developers understand the weaknesses/difficulties with your code. Furthermore, the reason for not fixing the bug should also be documented.

[1]Yes, it is better to fix bugs. However, sometimes you do not have the time to do so, or it is not important to your work at the moment. For example, you might know that a method that, when passed a negative number, does not work properly; but it does work properly for positive numbers. Your application only passes it positive numbers, so you can live with the bug. Please be polite and document that the problem exists.

DEFINITIONS

concurrency The issues involved with allowing multiple people simultaneous access to your persistence mechanism.

concurrency strategy The approach taken by the developer of a class to support concurrent access to instances of that class. Common concurrency strategies include the following: Synchronized objects, balking objects, guarded objects, versioned objects, concurrency policy controllers, and acceptors.

invariant A set of assertions about an instance or class that must be true at all "stable" times, where a stable time is the period before a method is invoked on the object or class and immediately after a method is invoked.

3. **The development/maintenance history of the class.** It is common practice to include a history table listing dates, authors, and summaries of changes made to a class. One advantage of a change log is that it gives maintenance programmers insight into the past modifications made to a class. Note that this information should be maintained in your software configuration management (SCM) tool instead of the actual code itself.
4. **Applicable invariants.** An invariant is a set of assertions about an instance or class that must be true at all "stable" times, where a stable time is defined as the period before a method is invoked on the object or class and immediately after a method is invoked (Meyer, 1997). By documenting the invariants of a class, you provide valuable insight to other developers as to how a class can be used.
5. **The concurrency strategy.** Concurrent programming is a complex topic that is new to many programmers; therefore, it is important to document your concurrency strategy and why you chose that strategy over others.

9.2.3.2 Writing Method Header Documentation

Every method should include some sort of header, called method documentation, at the top of the method source code that documents all of the information that is critical to understanding it. This information includes, but is not limited to the following:

1. **What and why the method does what it does.** By documenting what a method does, you make it easier for others to

determine if they can reuse your code. Documenting why it does something makes it easier for others to put your code into context. You also make it easier for others to determine whether a new change should actually be made to a piece of code (perhaps the reason for the new change conflicts with the reason why the code was written in the first place).

2. **What a method must be passed as parameters.** You also need to indicate what parameters, if any, must be passed to a method, how they will be used, and what type of class of which they are an instance. This information is needed so that other programmers know what information to pass to a method.
3. **What a method returns.** You need to document what, if anything, a method returns so that other programmers can use the return value or object appropriately.
4. **Known bugs.** Any outstanding problems with a method should be documented so that other developers understand the weaknesses/difficulties with the method. If a given bug is applicable to more than one method within a class, then it should be documented for the class instead.
5. **Any exceptions or error messages that a method throws or returns.** You should document any and all exceptions or error messages that a method throws or returns so that other programmers know what their code will need to catch.
6. **Visibility decisions.** If you feel that your choice of visibility for a method will be questioned by other developers (perhaps you have made a method public even though no other objects invoke the method yet), then you should document your decision. This will help to make your thinking clear to other developers so that they do not waste time worrying about why you did something.
7. **How a method changes the object.** If a method changes an object, for example the **withdraw** method of a bank account modifies the account balance, then this needs to be indicated. This information is needed so that other programmers know exactly how a method invocation will affect the target object.
8. **Include a history of any code changes.** Whenever a change is made to a method, you should document when the change was made, who made it, why it was made, who requested the change, who tested the change, and when it was tested and approved to be put into production. This history information

is critical for developers who are responsible for modifying and enhancing the code.

9. **Examples of how to invoke the method, if appropriate.** One of the easiest ways to determine how a method works is to look at an example. Consider including an example or two of how to invoke a method.
10. **Applicable preconditions and post-conditions.** A precondition is a constraint under which a method will function properly, and a post-condition is a property or assertion that will be true after a method is finished running (Meyer, 1997). In many ways preconditions and postconditions describe the assumptions that you have made when writing a method (Ambler, 1998), exactly defining the boundaries of how a method is used.
11. **All concurrency issues.** Concurrency is a new and complex concept for many developers, and at best it is an old and complex topic for experienced concurrent programmers. Help other programmers to understand your thinking by documenting your approach to concurrency.

DEFINITION

visibility An indication of the level of access to a class, method, or attribute.

9.2.3.3 Writing Internal Method Documentation

Internally, within your method code you should document:

1. **Control structures.** Document every control structure, such as comparison statements and loops, to improve the clarity of your code. It should be possible to look at a one- or two-line comment immediately preceding a control structure to determine what the code does.
2. **Why, as well as what, the code does.** You can always look at a piece of code and figure out what it does, but for code that is

TIP

Documentation Should Add to the Clarity of Your Code

The important thing is that you should document something only when it adds to the clarity of your code. You wouldn't document all of the factors described above for each and every method because not all of them are applicable. You would, however, document several factors for each method that you write.

not obvious, you can rarely determine why it is done that way. For example, you can look at a line of code and easily determine that a five percent discount is being applied to the total of an order. That's easy. What is not easy is figuring out *why* that discount is being applied. Obviously there is some sort of business rule that says to apply the discount, so that business rule should at least be referred to in your code so that other developers can understand why your code does what it does.

3. **Local variables.** Each local variable defined in a method should be declared on its own line of code and should usually have a comment describing its use.
4. **Difficult or complex code.** If you find that either you cannot rewrite complex code, or you do not have the time, then you must document it thoroughly. My general rule of thumb is that if your code is not obvious then you need to document it.
5. **The processing order.** If there are statements in your code that must be executed in a defined order, then you should ensure that this fact gets documented (Ambler, 1998). There's nothing worse than making a simple modification to a piece of code only to find that it no longer works, then spending hours or days looking for the problem only to find that you have gotten things out of order.

9.2.3.4 Documenting an Attribute

Every attribute should be documented well enough so that other developers can understand it. To be effective, you need to document:

1. **Description.** You need to describe an attribute so that people know how to use it.
2. **The type of an attribute.** Other developers need to know whether an attribute is a number or a string; whether it is another object, such as a customer or bank account, or if it is a boolean. By documenting the type of an attribute, you provide valuable information to other developers of how it is to be used.
3. **Document all applicable invariants.** The invariants of an attribute are the conditions that are always true about it. For example, an invariant about the attribute dayOfMonth might be that its value is between 1 and 31 (obviously you could get far more complex with this invariant, restricting the value of the attribute based on the month and the year). By documenting

the restrictions on the value of an attribute, you help to define important business rules, making it easier to understand how your code works (or at least should work).

4. **Examples.** For attributes that have complex business rules associated with them, you should provide several example values to make them easier to understand. An example is often like a picture: it is worth a thousand words.
5. **Visibility decisions.** If you have declared an attribute to be anything but private, then you should document why you have done so. The use of accessor methods to support encapsulation is discussed later in this chapter. The bottom line is that you better have a really good reason for not declaring a variable as private.

DEFINITION

private visibility An indication that a method or attribute is accessible only by instances of a class.

9.2.4 Writing Object-Oriented Source Code

Once programmers have invested the time to understand the models that they are implementing, searched for reusable components to reduce their workload, and then written at least initial documentation for their code, they are ready to actually begin writing object-oriented source code. The code that is written should conform to the standards and guidelines defined and selected for your project—conformance that will be verified by code reviews.

To understand how to write robust object-oriented source code, you need to consider the following issues:

- Class-type architecture
- Mapping objects to relational databases
- User-interface design
- Programming by contract
- Accessor methods
- The development/maintenance trade-off
- The Law of Demeter
- Programming tips and techniques

9.2.4.1 The Class-Type Architecture

Figure 9.4 shows a class-type architecture (Ambler, 1998) that your programmers should follow when coding their applications. The class-type architecture is based on the Layer pattern (Buschmann,

War Story

What Is Really Important when Programming?

My experience is that for ninety-five percent of large-scale development projects, the following programming priorities are applicable:

1. **Correctness.** If your code does not work properly, then nothing else matters. Code is correct when it fulfills its requirements as defined in your models.
2. **Robustness.** Source code will be around long after the original programmer has moved on, source code that needs to be maintained and extended; therefore, you must invest the effort required to make that code robust. As organizations found out the hard way with the Year 2000 problem (ensuring that legacy software handles dates after December 31, 1999 properly), source code that was written in the 1960s and 1970s was still in use and needed to be enhanced. Learn from the mistakes of the past.
3. **Efficiency.** The run-time efficiency of source code is a distant third to correctness and robustness. Yes, it is important to ensure that your code runs fast enough, which is why you will find that you need to optimize sections of it once it is written. Experience shows that you rarely know where the bottlenecks in your application are until it is built and running. The implication is that there is little value in optimizing your code early in the programming process; instead you first want to get your code working and write it so that it is easy to optimize once you know what needs to be tweaked. In other words, the most efficient way to write code is to get it correct, then make it robust, and then optimize it.

Layering your application code dramatically increases its robustness.

Meunier, Rohnert, Sommerlad, and Stal, 1996): the basic idea that a class within a given layer may interact with other classes in that layer or with classes in an adjacent layer. By layering your source code in this manner, you make it easier to maintain and enhance because the coupling within your application is greatly reduced.

Figure 9.4 shows that users of your application interact directly with the User Interface Layer of your application. The User Interface Layer is generally made up of classes that implement screens and

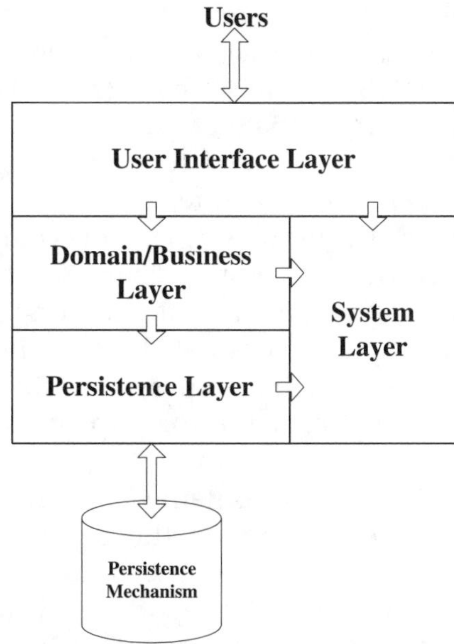

Figure 9.4. The class-type architecture

reports. User interface classes are allowed to send messages to classes within the Domain/Business Layer and the System Layer. The Domain/Business Layer implements the domain/business classes of your application; for example, the Business Layer for a telecommunications company would include classes such as Customer and Phone Call, and the System Layer implements classes that provide access to operating system functionality such as printing and electronic mail. Domain/business classes are allowed to send messages to classes within the System Layer and the Persistence Layer. The persistence layer encapsulates the behavior needed to store objects in persistence mechanisms such as object databases, files, and relational databases. I will discuss the issues associated with mapping objects to relational databases in the next section.

By conforming to this class-type architecture, your source code increases dramatically in robustness due to reduced coupling within your application. Figure 9.4 shows that for the User Interface Layer to obtain information it must interact with objects in the Domain/Business Layer, which in turn interact with the Persistence Layer to obtain the objects stored in your persistence mechanisms. This is an important feature of the class-type architecture: by not allowing the user interface of your application to access information stored in your persistence mechanism directly, you effectively de-couple the user interface from the persistence schema. The implication is that you are now in a position to change the way that objects are stored (perhaps you want to reorganize the tables of a relational database or port from the persistence mechanism of one vendor to that of another) without having to rewrite your screens and reports.

User interface classes should not directly access your persistence mechanisms.

By encapsulating the business logic of your application in domain/business classes, and not in your user interface, you are able to use that business logic in more than one place. For example, you could develop a screen that displays the total produced by an instance of the domain/business class Invoice as well as a report that does the same. If the logic for calculating the total changes (perhaps complex discounting logic is added), then you only need to update the code contained within Invoice and both the screen and report will display the correct value. Had you implemented totaling logic in the user interface, it would have been in both the screen and the report and you would need to modify the source code in two places, not just one.

Domain/business classes should not directly access your persistence mechanisms.

Just as you do not want to allow user interface classes to directly access information contained in your persistence mechanism, neither do you want to allow domain/business classes to do so. We'll see in the next section that a good persistence layer protects your application code from persistence mechanism changes. If a database administrator decides to reorganize the schema of a persistence mechanism, it does not make sense that you should have to rewrite your source code to reflect those changes. I will discuss persistence layers in the next section.

The class-type architecture is orthogonal to your hardware/network architecture.

An important thing to understand about the class-type architecture is that it is completely orthogonal to your hardware/network architecture. Table 9.1 shows how the various class types would be implemented on common hardware/network architectures. For example, we see that with the thin-client approach to client/server computing, user interface and system classes are implemented on the client and domain/business, persistence, and system classes are implemented on the server. Because system classes wrap access to network communication protocols, you are guaranteed that some system classes will reside on each computer.

9.2.4.2 Mapping Objects To Relational Databases

In the early 1990s a common misconception held among object-oriented developers was that it was inappropriate to store objects

TABLE 9.1. Deployment Strategies for Class Types for Various Hardware/Network Architectures

Class Type	Stand Alone	Thin-Client	Fat-Client	Distributed *n*-Tier	Objects
User interface	Client	Client	Client	Client	Client
Domain/business	Client	Server	Client	Application server	Do not care
Persistence	Client	Server	Server	Database server	Do not care
System	Client	All machines	All machines	All machines	All machines

DEFINITIONS

application server A server on which business logic is deployed. Application servers are key to an *n*-tier client/server architecture.

client A single-user PC or workstation that provides presentation services and appropriate computing, connectivity, and interfaces relevant to the business need. A client is also commonly referred to as a "front end."

client/server (C/S) architecture A computing environment that satisfies the business need by appropriately allocating the application processing between the client and the server processes.

coupling A measure of how connected two items are.

database server A server that has a database installed on it.

distributed objects An object-oriented architecture in which objects running in separate memory spaces (i.e. different computers) interact with one another transparently.

domain/business classes Classes that model the business domain. Business classes are usually found during analysis, examples of which include the classes Customer and Account.

fat client A two-tiered C/S architecture in which client machines implement both the user interface and the business logic of an application. Servers typically only supply data to client machines with little or no processing done to it.

DEFINITIONS

***n*-tier client/server** A client/server architecture in which client machines interact with application servers, which in turn interact with other application servers and/or database servers.

persistence classes Persistence classes provide the ability to permanently store objects. By encapsulating the storage and retrieval of objects via persistence classes, you are able to use various storage technologies interchangeably without affecting your applications.

persistence mechanism The permanent storage facility used to make objects persistent. Examples include relational databases, object databases, flat files, and object/relational databases.

server One or more multiuser processors with shared memory that provides computing connectivity, database services, and interfaces relevant to the business need. A server is also commonly referred to as a "back end."

system layer The collection of classes that provide operating-system-specific functionality for your applications, or that wrap functionality provided by non-OO applications, hardware devices, and/or non-OO code libraries.

thin client A two-tiered client/server architecture in which client machines implement only the user interface of an application.

user interface classes User interface classes provide the ability for users to interact with the system. User interface classes typically define a graphical user interface for an application, although other interface styles, such as voice command or handwritten input, are also implemented via user interface classes.

wrapping The act of encapsulating non-OO functionality within a class, making it look and feel like any other object within the system.

Mapping objects to relational databases is the norm, not the exception.

in relational databases. Later, in the mid-to-late 1990s after a few false starts, the OO development community began to realize that the multi-billion-dollar relational database market wasn't going away after all, and that using relational databases to store objects was the norm among application developers and not the exception. The techniques to map objects to relational databases are not completely obvious, so I'd like to take the opportunity to share my experiences with you. In Chapter 10 I overview the design of a persistence layer that supports the mapping techniques presented in this section.

The object paradigm is based on building applications out of objects that have both data and behavior, whereas the relational

DEFINITIONS

Object/relational impedance mismatch The difference resulting from the fact that relational theory is based on relationships between tuples (records) that are queried, whereas the object paradigm is based on relationships between objects that are traversed.

Persistence layer The collection of classes that provide business objects the ability to be persistent. A persistence layer effectively wraps access to your persistence mechanisms.

Relational database A type of persistence mechanism, based on relational theory, that stores data in tables. The rows of data within tables are related to one another; hence the term relational database.

paradigm is based on storing data in the rows of tables. The "object/relational impedance mismatch" comes into play when you look at the preferred approach to access: with the object paradigm you traverse objects via their relationships, whereas with the relational paradigm you join the rows in tables via their relationships. This fundamental difference results in a non-ideal combination of the two paradigms; but when have you ever used two different technologies together without a few hitches? One of the secrets of success for mapping objects to relational databases is to understand both paradigms and their differences, and then make intelligent tradeoffs based on that knowledge.

To reduce the impact of the object/relational impedance mismatch, you need to:

- Use object identifiers
- Understand the basics of mapping
- Avoid stored procedures
- Understand the realities of mapping objects to relational databases

9.2.4.2.1 Object Identifiers

To map objects to relational databases, we need to assign unique identifiers to our objects so that we can identify them. In relational terminology a unique identifier is called a key; in object terminology it is called an object identifier (OID). OIDs are typically implemented as full-fledged objects in your OO applications and as large integers in your relational schema.

An object identifier (OID) uniquely identifies an object.

A critical feature of an OID is that it should have absolutely no business meaning whatsoever. In the relational world this is called a surrogate key. The reason for this is simple: any column with a business meaning can potentially change, and if there is one thing that we learned over the years in the relational world, it is that it is a fatal mistake to give your keys meaning. Consider a customer number, a classic example of a key with a business meaning. If your users decide to change the business meaning (perhaps they want to add some digits or make the number alphanumeric), you need to make changes to your database in every single spot where you use that information. Anything that is used as a primary key in one table is virtually guaranteed to be used in other tables as a foreign key. What should be a simple change, adding a digit to your customer number, can be a huge maintenance nightmare if it is used as a key.

OIDs should have no business meaning.

OIDs allow us to simplify our key strategy within a relational database. Although OIDs do not completely solve our navigation issue between objects (fundamentally, relational databases simply aren't set up this way), they do make it easier. You still need to perform table joins, assuming you do not intend to traverse, to read in an aggregate of objects such as an invoice and all of its line items, but at least it is doable. Another advantage is that the use of OIDs puts you into a position in which it is fairly easy to automate the maintenance of relationships between objects. When all of your tables are keyed on the same type of table column(s) (in this case, OIDs), it becomes very easy to write generic code to take advantage of this fact.

DEFINITIONS

foreign key A column in a relational table that identifies a row within another relational table.

key A column, or several columns when combined, within a relational database table whose value(s) uniquely identifies a row.

object identifier (OID) An attribute that uniquely identifies an object. The object-oriented equivalent of a key.

primary key The column(s) of a table that have been chosen as the primary means of uniquely identifying rows in that column.

table join A relational database concept in which information from two or more tables is accessed. Tables are joined by selecting rows from each table that contain identical values in one or more common columns.

9.2.4.2.2 Understanding The Basics of Mapping
A strategy for keys is just the beginning; we must also have a strategy for mapping objects to relational databases. This means that we need to understand how to map:

- Attributes
- Inheritance relationships
- Associations
- Aggregation relationships

9.2.4.2.2.1 Mapping Attributes to Table Columns
First, the attribute of a class will map to zero or more columns in a relational database. Remember, not all attributes are persistent. For example, an Invoice class may have a grandTotal attribute that is used by instances for calculation purposes, but that is not saved to the database. Furthermore, because some attributes of an object are objects in their own right, a Customer object has an Address object as an attribute; sometimes a single OO attribute will map to several columns in the database (actually, chances are that the Address class will map to one or more columns). The important thing is that this is a recursive definition: at some point any given attribute will be mapped to zero or more columns.

Attributes are mapped to table columns.

9.2.4.2.2.2 Mapping Inheritance
Now let's consider inheritance, the relationship that introduces interesting twists for saving objects into a relational database. The problem basically boils down to, "How do you organize the inherited attributes within the database?" The way in which you answer this question can have a major impact on your system design.

There are three fundamental solutions for mapping inheritance into a relational database:

1. **Use one table for an entire class hierarchy.** Map an entire class hierarchy into one table, where all the attributes of all the classes in the hierarchy are stored in it. The advantage of this approach are, first, that it is simple: polymorphism is supported when a person either changes roles or has multiple roles (in other words, the person is both a customer and an employee). Second, ad-hoc reporting is straightforward with this approach, because all of the data you need about a person is found in one table. The disadvantages are that every

time a new attribute is added anywhere in the class hierarchy, a new table column needs to be added. This increases the coupling within the class hierarchy: if a mistake is made when adding a single attribute, it could affect all the classes within the hierarchy and not just the subclasses of whatever class got the new attribute. It also wastes space in the database, because not every column is applicable to every object stored in the table.

2. **Use one table per concrete class.** Each table includes both the attributes and the inherited attributes of the class that it represents. The main advantage of this approach is that it is still fairly easy to do ad-hoc reporting, as all the data you need about a single class is stored in only one table. There are several disadvantages, however. First, when we modify a class, we need to modify its table and the table of any of its subclasses. For example if we were to add height and weight attributes to the Person class, we would need to add it in all three of our tables (Person, Customer, and Employee)—a lot of work. Second, whenever an object changes its role (perhaps we hire one of our customers), we need to copy the data into the appropriate table and assign it a new OID—once again, a lot of work. Third, it is difficult to support multiple roles and still maintain data integrity (it is possible, just harder than it needs to be).
3. **Use one table per class.** Create one table per class, the attributes of which are the OID and the attributes that are specific to that class. The main advantage of this approach is that it conforms to object-oriented concepts the best. It supports polymorphism because you merely need to have records in the appropriate tables for each role that an object might have. It is also very easy to modify superclasses and add new subclasses, as you only need to modify/add one table. There are several disadvantages to this approach, however. First, there are many tables in the database, one for every class (plus tables to maintain relationships). Second, it takes longer to read and write data using this technique, because you need to access multiple tables because the inherited attributes of an object are stored in the tables of the superclasses. This problem can be alleviated if you organize your database intelligently by putting each table within a class

TABLE 9.2. Comparing the Three Approaches to Mapping Inheritance

Factors to Consider	One table per hierarchy	One table per concrete class	One table per class
Ease of implementation	Simple	Medium	Difficult
Ease of data access	Simple	Simple	Medium/Simple
Coupling	Very high	High	Low
Ad-hoc reporting	Simple	Medium	Medium/Difficult
Speed of data access	Fast	Fast	Medium/Fast
Support for polymorphism	Medium	Low	High

hierarchy on different physical disk drives. Third, ad-hoc reporting on your database is difficult unless you add views to simulate the desired tables.

Table 9.2 shows a comparison of the three inheritance-mapping strategies. It is important to understand the trade-offs between each strategy because, as you can see, none of them is perfect for all situations. For the development of large applications you will find that you will need to use each technique at some point based on the specific access needs of the class hierarchies within your application.

Large applications often require the use of all three inheritance-mapping strategies.

9.2.4.2.2.3 Mapping Association and Aggregation

From a database perspective the only difference between association and aggregation is how tightly the objects are bound to each other. From a database point of view aggregation and association

DEFINITIONS

abstract class A class from which objects are not instantiated, but that are instead used to implement common behavior inherited by other classes.

ad-hoc reporting Reporting performed for the specific purposes of a small group of users where it is common that the report(s) were written by the users themselves.

concrete class A class from which objects are instantiated.

From a database point of view, objects are more tightly bound by aggregation than by association.

are different in that with aggregation, you usually want to read in the part when you read in the whole, whereas with an association it is not always as obvious what you need to do. The same goes for saving objects to the database and deleting objects from the database. Granted, this is usually specific to the business domain, but this rule of thumb seems to hold up in most circumstances.

Relationships in relational databases are maintained through the use of foreign keys. A foreign key is a table column that appears in one table but that is also used as the primary key of another table. Foreign keys allow you to relate a record in one table with a record in another. To implement one-to-one and one-to-many relationships, you merely have to include the key of one table in the other table. To implement many-to-many relationships, we need to introduce the concept of an associative table—a table whose sole purpose is to maintain the relationship between two or more tables in a relational database. In Figure 9.5 we see that there is a many-to-many relationship between instances of Customer and Account. In Figure 9.6 we see how to use an associative table to implement a many-to-many relationship within a relational database. In relational databases the attributes contained in an associative table are traditionally the combination of the keys in the tables involved in the relationship. It is common to indicate primary keys in a data diagram with an underline and foreign keys with a dotted underline. It has been my experience, however, that it is easier to implement associative tables if you treat them as just another type of table: you assign them their own key field, in our case OID, and then add the necessary foreign keys to maintain the relationship.

DEFINITIONS

aggregation Represents "is-part-of" relationships between objects.

association A relationship between two or more objects or classes. For example, students *take* courses.

9.2.4.2.3 Avoid Stored Procedures

Stored procedures were introduced to meet the needs of structured developers, not OO developers.

A very common mistake made by developers who are mapping objects to relational databases is the use of stored procedures. A stored procedure is a function that runs on a relational database server. Stored procedures were introduced in the mid-1980s to support the need of structured developers building two-tier client/server applications. This is the mistake that people make: they assume that because stored procedures may have been a good idea for structured development, they are still a good idea for object-oriented development.

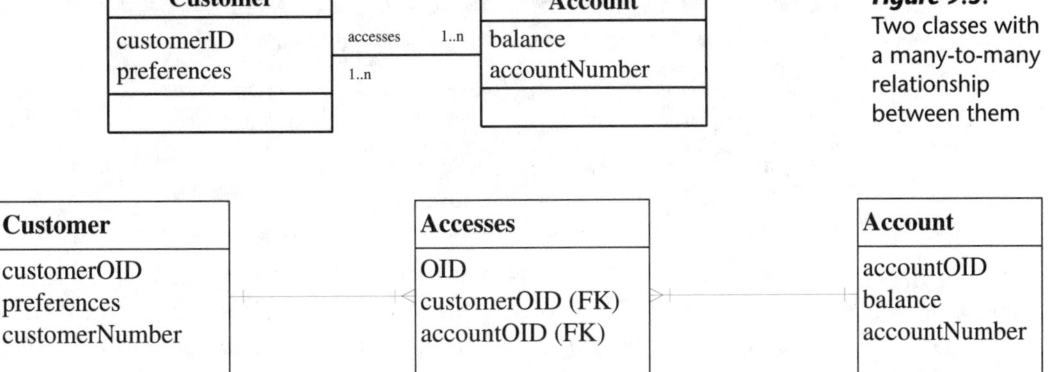

Figure 9.5. Two classes with a many-to-many relationship between them

Figure 9.6. Implementing a many-to-many relationship in a relational database

You do not want to use stored procedures when mapping objects to relational databases for several reasons. First, the server can quickly become a bottleneck using this approach. You really need to have your act together when moving functionality onto your server: a simple stored procedure can bring the server to it knees if it is invoked often. Second, stored procedures are written in a proprietary language, and as anyone knows who has ever ported between database vendors, or even between database versions from the same vendor, this can be a show-stopper. The one thing that you can count on in this industry is change, and your database is guaranteed to at least be upgraded over time. Third, you dramatically increase the coupling within your database, because stored procedures directly access tables, coupling the tables to the stored procedures. This increased coupling reduces the flexibility of your database administrators (when they want to reorganize the database they need to rewrite stored procedures), and increases the maintenance burden of developers because they have to deal with the stored procedure code.

Stored procedures are proprietary and increase the coupling within your database.

When mapping objects to relational databases, using stored procedures makes sense in two situations. The first is when you are building a prototype that you intend to throw away; assuming that you do not have a solid persistence layer already built, this may be the quickest way to get your prototype working. The second situation is when you are mapping to a legacy database whose design is completely inappropriate for objects and you aren't able to rework it for your specific needs. You can create stored procedures to read and write records that look like the objects that you want. Note

DEFINITIONS

stored procedure A function implemented within a relational database.

Structured Query Language (SQL) A standard mechanism used to create, retrieve, update and/or delete records in a relational database.

two-tiered client/server An approach to client/server architectures in which client machines directly interact with server machines.

At best, stored procedures are a quick hack used to solve your short-term mapping problems.

that you do not need to write this code using stored procedures; instead, you could do it in your language of choice and run it outside of your database (although perhaps still on your server machine to avoid unnecessary network traffic).

9.2.4.2.4 The Realities of Mapping Objects to Relational Databases

This section describes and expands on several mapping issues that I described in the October 1997 issue of *Software Development* (Ambler, 1997). These issues are:

1. **Objects and relational databases are the norm.** For years, object gurus claimed that you shouldn't use relational databases to store objects because of the "object/relational impedance mismatch." Yes, the object paradigm is different from the relational paradigm, but for ninety-five percent of us, the reality is that your development environment is object-oriented and your persistence mechanism is a relational database.
2. **ODBC and JDBC classes aren't enough.** Although most development environments come with rudimentary access mechanisms to relational databases, they are at best a good start. Common "generic" mechanisms include Microsoft's Open Database Connectivity (ODBC) and JavaSoft's Java Database Connectivity (JDBC). Most object development environments include class libraries that wrap one of these standard approaches. The fundamental problem with these class libraries, as well as those that wrap access to native database drivers, are that they are too complex. In a well-designed library, I should only have to send objects messages like **delete**, **save**, and **retrieve** to handle basic persistence functionality. The interface for working with multiple objects in the database is not much more complicated. The bottom line is that the database access classes provided with your develop-

ment environment are only a start, and a minimal one at that.

3. **You need a persistence layer.** A persistence layer encapsulates access to databases, allowing application programmers to focus on the business problem itself. This means that the database access classes are encapsulated, providing a simple yet complete interface for application programmers. Furthermore, the database design should be encapsulated so that programmers do not need to know the intimate details of the database layout: that's what database administrators (DBAs) are for. A persistence layer completely encapsulates your permanent storage mechanism(s), sheltering you from changes. The implication is that your persistence layer needs to use a data dictionary that provides the information needed to map objects to tables. When the business domain changes (and it always does), you shouldn't have to change any code in your persistence layer. Furthermore, if the database changes (perhaps a new version is installed or the DBA rearranges some tables), the only thing that should change is the information in the data dictionary. Simple database changes should not require changes to your application code, and data dictionaries are critical if you want to have a maintainable persistence approach. In Chapter 10 I overview the design of a robust persistence layer.
4. **Embedded SQL is an incredibly bad idea.** A related issue is one of including Structured Query Language (SQL) code in your object application. By doing so, you effectively couple your application to the database design, which reduces both maintainability and enhanceability. The problem is that whenever basic changes are made in the database (perhaps tables or columns are moved or renamed), you have to make corresponding changes in your application code. A better approach is for the persistence layer to generate dynamic SQL based on the information in the data dictionary. Yes, dynamic SQL is a little slower, but the increased maintainability more than makes up for it.
5. **You have to map to legacy data.** Although the design of legacy databases rarely meets the needs of an object-oriented application, the reality is that your legacy databases are there to stay. The push for centralized databases in the 1980s has now left us with a centralized disaster: database schemas are difficult to modify because of the multitude of applications

coupled to them. The implication is that few developers can truly start fresh with a relational database design that reflects their object-oriented design; instead, they must make do with a legacy database.

6. **The data model does not drive your class diagram.** Just because you need to map to legacy data, that does not mean that you should bastardize your object design. I have seen several projects crash in flames because a legacy data model was used as the basis for the class diagram. The original database designers did not use concepts like inheritance or polymorphism in their design, nor did they consider improved relational design techniques (see below) that become apparent when mapping objects. Successful projects model the business using object-oriented techniques, model the legacy database with a data model, and then introduce a "legacy mapping layer" that encapsulates the logic needed to map your current object design to your ancient data design. You'll sometimes find it easier to rework portions of your database than to write the corresponding mapping code, code that is convoluted because of either poor or outdated decisions made during data modeling. As you saw in Chapter 8, allowing your data model to drive the development of your OO models is a common process antipattern.
7. **Table joins are slow.** You often need to obtain data from several tables to build a complex object or set of objects. Relational theory tells you to join tables to get the data that you need, an approach that often proves to be slow and untenable for live applications. Therefore, do not do table joins! Because several small accesses are usually more efficient than one big join, you should instead traverse tables to get the data. Part of overcoming the object/relational impedance mismatch is to traverse instead of join where it makes sense.
8. **Keys with business meaning are a bad idea.** Experience with mapping objects to relational databases leads to the observation that keys shouldn't have business meaning, which goes directly against one of the basic tenets of relational theory. The basic idea is that any field that has business meaning is out of the scope of your control, and therefore you risk having its value or its layout change. In the end I believe that it simply does not make sense for a technical concept, a unique key, to be dependent on business rules.

9. **Avoid composite keys.** While I am attacking the sacred values of DBAs everywhere, composite keys (keys made up of more than one column) are also a bad idea. Composite keys increase the overhead in your database as foreign keys, increase the complexity of your database design, and often incur additional processing requirements when many fields are involved. My experience is that an object id (OID), a single column attribute that has no business meaning and which uniquely identifies the object, is the best kind of key.
10. **You need several inheritance strategies.** There are three fundamental solutions for implementing inheritance in a relational database: use one table for an entire class hierarchy; use one table per concrete class; or use one table per class. Although all three approaches work well, none of them are ideal for all situations. The end result is that your persistence layer will need to support all three approaches at some point, although implementing one table per concrete class at first is the easiest way to start.
11. **Stored procedures are a bad idea.** Stored procedures are proprietary solutions that increase the coupling within your database, consequently reducing the robustness of your application.

9.2.4.3 User Interface Design

A fundamental reality of application development is that the user interface is the system to the users. What users want is for developers to build applications that meet their needs and that are easy to use. Too many developers think that they are artistic geniuses. They do not bother to follow user interface design standards or invest the

TIP

You Need to Understand Mapping Issues to Convert Legacy Data Effectively

If your application must coexist with existing legacy applications, then you need to develop a data conversion plan for doing so. Part of your data conversion effort is to determine how your new object-oriented applications will share data with your existing legacy applications. To do so you must understand the data access needs of both your new and legacy applications; and to understand the access needs of your new application, you need to understand how to map objects to relational databases.

DEFINITIONS

antipattern The description of a common approach to solving a common problem, an approach that in time proves to be wrong or highly ineffective.

data conversion plan A plan describing how a legacy data schema will be reworked to meet the new needs of your organization. A data conversion plan will likely refer to data models for both the existing and new data schema as well as the data access maps associated with both models.

data dictionary A repository of information about the layout of a database, the layout of a flat file, the layout of a class, and any mappings among the three.

database administrator (DBA) A person responsible for administering and maintaining the schema of a database.

dynamic SQL A Structured Query Language (SQL) statement that is generated, often by a persistence layer, based on information describing the mapping between your objects and the schema of the persistence mechanisms in which they are stored.

embedded SQL An SQL statement that is written directly in the code of your application. When the schema of your persistence mechanism changes, or the schema of your application, then this code will need to be updated to reflect those changes. Embedded SQL increases the coupling between your application and your persistence mechanisms.

process antipattern An antipattern that describes an approach and/or series of actions for developing software that is proven to be ineffective and often detrimental to your organization.

table join A relational database concept in which information from two or more tables are accessed. Tables are joined by selecting rows from each table that contain identical values in one or more common columns.

effort to make their applications usable; instead, they mistakenly believe that the important thing is to make the code clever or to use a really interesting color scheme. Constantine (1995) points out that the reality is that a good user interface enables people who understand the problem domain to work with the application without having to read the manuals or receive training.

In this section we will cover a series of user interface design tips that will help you to improve the object-oriented interfaces that you create.

1. **Consistency, consistency, consistency.** The most important thing that you can possibly do is to make sure that your user

interface works consistently. If you can double-click on items in one list and have something happen, then you should be able to double-click on items in any other list and have the same sort of thing happen. Put your buttons in consistent places on all of your windows, use the same wording in labels and messages, and use a consistent color scheme throughout. Consistency in your user interface enables your users to build an accurate mental model of the way that it works, and accurate mental models lead to lower training and support costs.

2. **Set standards and stick to them.** The only way that you'll be able to ensure consistency within your application is to set design standards and then stick to them. The best approach is to adopt an industry standard and then fill any missing guidelines that are specific to your needs. Industry standards, such as the ones set by IBM (1993) and Microsoft (1995), will often define ninety-five to ninety-nine percent of what you need. By adopting industry standards, you not only take advantage of the work of others; you also increase the chance that your application will look and feel like other applications that your users purchase or have built. User interface design standards should be set during the Define Infrastructure stage (Chapter 6).
3. **Explain the rules.** Your users need to know how to work with the application that you built for them. When an application works consistently, that means you only have to explain the rules once. This is a lot easier than explaining in detail exactly how to use each and every feature in an application step by step.
4. **Support both novices and experts.** Although a library catalog metaphor might be appropriate for casual users of a library system (library patrons), it probably is not all that effective for expert users (librarians). Librarians are highly trained people who are able to use complex search systems to find information in a library; therefore, you should consider building a set of search screens to support their unique needs.
5. **Navigation between screens is important.** If it is difficult to get from one screen to another, then your users will quickly become frustrated and give up. When the flow between screens matches the flow of the work that the user is trying to accomplish, then your application will make sense to your

users. Because different users work in different ways, your system will need to be flexible enough to support their various approaches. Interface-flow diagrams can be used during the Model stage (Chapter 8) to model the flow between screens.

6. **Navigation within a screen is important.** In Western societies people read left to right and top to bottom. Because people are used to this, you should design screens that are also organized left to right and top to bottom. You want to organize navigation between widgets on your screen in a manner that users will find familiar to them.
7. **Word your messages and labels appropriately.** The text that you display on your screens is a primary source of information for your users. If your text is worded poorly, then your interface will be perceived as poor by your users. Using full words and sentences as opposed to abbreviations and codes makes your text easier to understand. Your messages should be worded positively, imply that the user is in control, and provide insight into how to use the application properly. For example, which message do you find more appealing: "You have input the wrong information" or "An account number should be 8 digits in length"? Furthermore, your messages should be worded consistently and displayed in a consistent place on the screen. Although the messages "The person's first name must be input" and "An account number should be input" are separately worded well, together they are inconsistent. In light of the first message, a better wording of the second message would be "The account number must be input" to make the two messages consistent.
8. **Understand your widgets.** You should use the right widget for the right task, helping to increase the consistency in your application and probably making it easier to build the application in the first place. The only way that you can learn how to use widgets properly is to read and understand the user interface standards and guidelines that your organization has adopted.
9. **Look at other applications with a grain of salt.** Unless you know that another application follows the user interface standards and guidelines of your organization, you must not assume that the application is doing things right. Although it is always a good idea to look at the work of others to get ideas,

until you know how to distinguish between good user-interface design and bad user-interface design, you have to be careful. Too many developers make the mistake of imitating the user interface of another application that was poorly designed.

Do not assume that the user interfaces of other applications are designed well.

10. **Use color appropriately.** Color should be used sparingly in your applications, and if you do use it, you must also use a secondary indicator. The problem is that some of your users may be color blind; if you are using color to highlight something on a screen, then you need to do something else to make it stand out if you want these people to notice it, such as display a symbol beside it. You also want to use colors in your application consistently so that you have a common look and feel throughout your application. Also, color generally does not port well between platforms—what looks good on one system often looks poor on another system. We have all been to presentations where the presenter said "it looks good on my machine at home."
11. **Follow the contrast rule.** If you are going to use color in your application, you need to ensure that your screens are still readable. The best way to do this is to follow the contrast rule: Use dark text on light backgrounds and light text on dark backgrounds. It is very easy to read blue text on a white background, but very difficult to read blue text on a red background. The problem is that there is not enough contrast between blue and red to make it easy to read, whereas there is a lot of contrast between blue and white.
12. **Use fonts appropriately.** Old English fonts might look good on the covers of William Shakespeare's plays, but they are really hard to read on a screen. Use fonts that are easy to read, such as serif fonts like Times Roman. Furthermore, use your fonts consistently and sparingly. A screen using two or three fonts effectively looks a lot better than a screen that uses five or six. Never forget that you are using a different font every time you change the size, style (bold, italics, underlining, ...), typeface, or color.
13. **Gray things out, do not remove them.** You often find that at certain times it is not applicable to give your users access to all the functionality of an application. You need to select an object before you can delete it, so to reinforce your mental model the application should do something with the Delete button and/or menu item. Should the button be removed or grayed

out? Gray it out, never remove it. By graying things out when they shouldn't be used, you enable people to start building an accurate mental model of how your application works. If you simply remove a widget or menu item instead of graying it out, then it is much more difficult for your users to build an accurate mental model, because they only know what is currently available to them and not what isn't available. The old adage that out of sight is out of mind is directly applicable here.

14. **Use nondestructive default buttons.** It is quite common to define a default button on every screen, the button that gets invoked if the user presses the Return/Enter key. The problem is that sometimes people will accidentally hit the Enter/Return key when they do not mean to, consequently invoking the default button. Your default button shouldn't be something that is potentially destructive, such as delete or save (perhaps your user really did not want to save the object at that moment).
15. **Align fields.** When a screen has more than one editing field, you want to organize the fields in a way that is both visually appealing and efficient. As shown in Figure 9.7, I have always found that the best way to do so is to left-justify edit fields, or in other words make the left-hand side of each edit field line up in a straight line, one over the other. The corresponding labels should be right-justified and placed immediately beside the field. This is a clean and efficient way to organize the fields on a screen.
16. **Justify data appropriately.** For columns of data it is common practice to right-justify integers, decimal align floating point numbers, and left justify strings.
17. **Do not create busy screens.** Crowded screens are difficult to understand and hence are difficult to use. Experimental results (Mayhew, 1992) show that the overall density of the screen should not exceed forty percent, whereas local density within groupings shouldn't exceed sixty-two percent.
18. **Group things on the screen effectively.** Items that are logically connected should be grouped together on the screen to communicate that they are connected, whereas items that have nothing to do with each other should be separated. You can use whitespace between collections of items to group them and/or you can put boxes around them to accomplish the same thing.

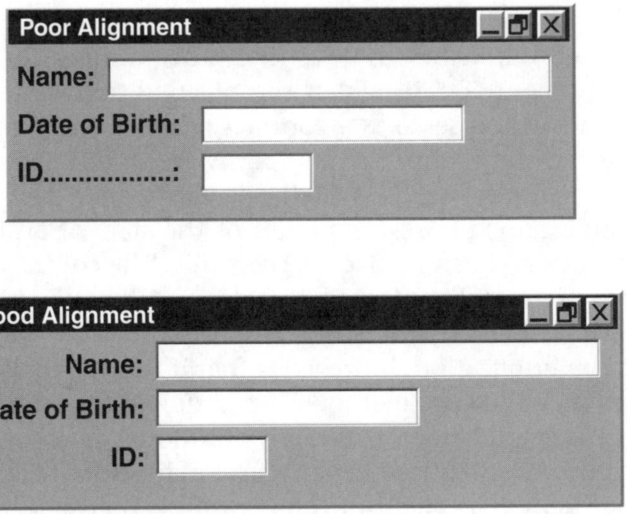

Figure 9.7. Alignment of fields is critical.

19. **Open windows in the center of the action.** When your user double-clicks on an object to display its edit/detail screen then his or her attention is on that spot. Therefore it makes sense to open the window in that spot, not somewhere else.
20. **Pop-up menus should not be the only source of functionality.** Your users cannot learn how to use your application if you hide major functionality from them. One of the most frustrating practices of developers is to misuse pop-up, also called context-sensitive, menus. Typically there is a way to use the mouse on your computer to display a hidden pop-up menu that provides access to functionality specific to the area of the screen that you are currently working in.

Everybody follows rules of thumb.
—Christopher Alexander

DEFINITIONS

interface-flow diagram A diagram that models the interface objects of your system and the relationships between them.

mental model An internal representation of a person's conceptualization and understanding of a system.

pop-up menu A style of menu, often tailored depending on the context in which it is invoked, which is displayed when requested by a user. A common GUI design standard is to display a pop-up menu when the user clicks the secondary mouse button. Also called a context-sensitive menu or hidden menu.

widget A user interface component such as a list, button, or window.

9.2.4.4 *Programming by Contract*

The preconditions and postconditions of a method define a contract between the supplier of the method and the client of the method.

Meyer (1997) describes an advanced programming concept called "design by contract" in which the preconditions and postconditions of a method serve as a contract between the supplier of the method and the client of a method. A precondition expresses the constraints under which a method will operate properly and a post-condition expresses properties of the state of an object after the method has been invoked successfully. The contract effectively becomes: if you satisfy the preconditions defined for the method, then the post-conditions will hold true once the method completes. The implication, however, is that if the preconditions aren't properly met, then the method is not required to perform properly.

Like any good contract, the preconditions and post-conditions for a method define both benefits and obligations for the supplier and the client. The client of the method is obligated to meet the preconditions, benefiting from the knowledge that the method will perform as defined. The supplier of the method is obligated to fulfill the post-conditions, and benefits because the method can be written under the assumption that the preconditions have been met.

As an example, consider the withdraw method of the Account class. There would be one precondition for this method: the amount to be withdrawn is expected to be an instance of the class Currency whose value is positive. There would be two post-conditions: the corresponding amount would be withdrawn from the instance of Account and an instance of BankingTransaction would be created to record the withdrawal. The contract would be that if the client supplies a Currency object whose value is positive, the amount will be withdrawn from the account and the withdrawal will be recorded appropriately.

You have significantly less code to write when programming by contract.

What is the benefit of design and programming by contract? The answer is simple: you have less code to write because the developers of a method do not have to write additional code to verify that preconditions have been met, and the client of a method does not have to write additional code to verify that the method ran properly. This is the antithesis of defensive programming, an approach in which additional code is written to verify that the proper input to a method has been received and that when a method was invoked that it worked properly. Defensive programming is based on the belief that you cannot trust your coworkers.

TIP

Programming by Contract Does Not Alleviate the Need for Error Checking

Very often a method will return an error message or will throw an exception, requiring the invoker of a method to check for that error message or exception. The return value of a method effectively becomes a post-condition in this case if an error message or exception is returned, then it is expected that the invoker of a method handles it appropriately.

There are two drawbacks to programming by contract. First, you have to document your preconditions and postconditions, something that we saw you need to do anyway in Section 9.2.3.2. Second, everybody has to follow this approach; otherwise, a defect will quickly propagate through your application. My experience is that programming by contract only works for teams comprised of experienced object-oriented developers who understand how to develop high-quality, maintainable code.

Programming by contract should only be attempted by experienced, professional developers.

9.2.4.5 Accessor Methods

An easy way to improve the robustness of your code is to use accessor methods—methods that provide the functionality to either update an attribute or to access its value. Accessor methods come in two flavors: setters and getters. A setter method modifies the value of a variable, whereas a getter method obtains it for you. Although accessor methods add minor processing overhead, they help to hide

DEFINITIONS

defensive programming An approach in which additional code is written to verify that the proper input to a method has been received and that when a method was invoked that it worked properly.

exception handling The act of identifying and acting on run-time problems (exceptions) in an application.

postcondition An expression of the properties of the state of an object after a method has been invoked successfully.

precondition An expression of the constraints under which a method will operate properly.

Accessor methods increase the maintainability of your code.

the implementation details of your class. By having at most two control points from which a variable is accessed, one setter and one getter, you are able to increase the maintainability of your classes by minimizing the points at which changes need to be made when you decide to change the implementation of an attribute.

Attributes should always be declared private.

Several languages, such as C++ and Java, allow you to define the visibility of attributes. The visibility of an attribute defines how it can be accessed. For example, in C++ an attribute declared public can be modified by any object in your application; an attribute declared protected may only be accessed within a class hierarchy; and an attribute that is declared private may only be accessed by the object itself. My approach, based on years of experience developing object-oriented applications, is to declare all attributes private and to implement accessor methods for them. This approach provides for greater encapsulation and greater control over how an attribute is accessed; for example, the getter method for an attribute may be public, but the setter method is protected.

The only place that an attribute should be directly manipulated is in its two accessor methods.

A key concept with the appropriate use of accessor methods is that the only methods that are allowed to work directly with an attribute are the accessor methods themselves. Yes, it is possible to access a private attribute directly within the methods of the class in which the attribute is defined, but you do not want to do so because you would increase the coupling within your class.

9.2.4.6 The Development/Maintenance Trade-off

An issue that is important for all developers to understand is something called the *development/ maintenance trade-off*—decisions that speed up the development process often harm you during maintenance, whereas decisions that improve the maintainability

DEFINITIONS

accessor method A method that is used to either modify or retrieve a single attribute.

coupling A measure of how connected two items are.

getter method An accessor method that retrieves the value of an attribute.

setter method An accessor method that modifies the value of an attribute.

visibility A technique that is used to indicate the level of encapsulation of a class, method, or attribute.

TIP

Use Getters for Constants

I always use getter methods to provide the value of a constant within my code. The reason for this is simple: you want to encapsulate a constant so that its implementation is hidden from other developers. This makes your code more robust and protects you from changes to business rules.

Consider the following example: The Archon Bank of Cardassia has always insisted that an account must have a minimum balance of $500 to earn interest. To implement this, we could add a static attribute named MINIMUM_BALANCE to the class Account that would be used in the methods that calculate interest. Although this would work, it is not flexible. What happens if the business rules change and different kinds of accounts have different minimum balances—perhaps $500 for savings accounts, but only $200 for checking accounts? What would happen if the business rule were to change to a $500 minimum balance in the first year, $400 in the second, $300 in the third, and so on? Perhaps the rule will be changed to $500 in the summer but only $250 in the winter? Perhaps a combination of all of these rules will need to be implemented in the future. By implementing this "constant" as a getter method, perhaps called getMinimumBalance(), we make our application flexible enough to easily handle changes to the business rules surrounding the minimum balance.

of your system can often increase the time that it originally takes you to develop it, at least in the short term. You see, code that is more maintainable is much more likely to be reused than code that is not. If it is hard to maintain, it is hard to reuse.

The things that make your code maintainable—documentation, indenting, intelligent naming strategies, good design—many of the things that we talk about in this chapter all take time and money during the development process. Although they will pay for themselves many times over during maintenance, the short-term pain is often enough to motivate you to put them off for a later date, a date that more often than not never comes. Your real trade-off is this: do you invest a little bit of time and effort during development to greatly reduce your future maintenance efforts? I think that the answer is yes; how about you?

9.2.4.7 The Law of Demeter

Demeter was an OO research project in the late 1980s and early 1990s, and out of that project came the Law of Demeter, which suggests restrictions of where objects can send messages in order to make them more maintainable. The Law of Demeter states that objects should only send messages to:

- Themselves
- Their direct or indirect superclasses
- Other objects returned directly from their own methods
- An object passed to them as a parameter to a method
- Their class

The important thing to understand is that objects shouldn't send messages to objects that have been returned by invoking a method in an object other than themselves. This restriction helps to reduce coupling in a system by reducing the knowledge that objects have of each other. Let's consider an example.

In Figures 9.8 and 9.9 we see two approaches for building a screen that displays the total of a series of transactions posted to an account. In the first approach the screen object sends a message to an account object requesting the transactions for a given period of time. Once it has them, it then sends messages to each transaction requesting the amount. In the second approach the summary screen sends a message to the savings account requesting the total transaction amount for a given period of time; the account then gets the amount of each transaction, adds them up, and passes the result back to the summary screen. Which approach is better?

The Law of Demeter reduces coupling between classes, increasing the maintainability of your code.

According to the Law of Demeter, the second approach is better because the summary screen sends a message only to an object that is returned by one of its methods (the savings account would be returned by an accessor method within the screen object), and then this object does the necessary work. The advantage of this approach is that the coupling within the system is minimized. Summary screen objects only need to know that they have to send a single message to a savings account to get the job done, whereas in the first approach it has to know to send a message to an account to get the transactions, then it has to know to send a message to each transaction. Taking the first approach, the class SummaryScreen is coupled to both SavingsAccount and Transaction, whereas with the second approach it is coupled only to SavingsAccount.

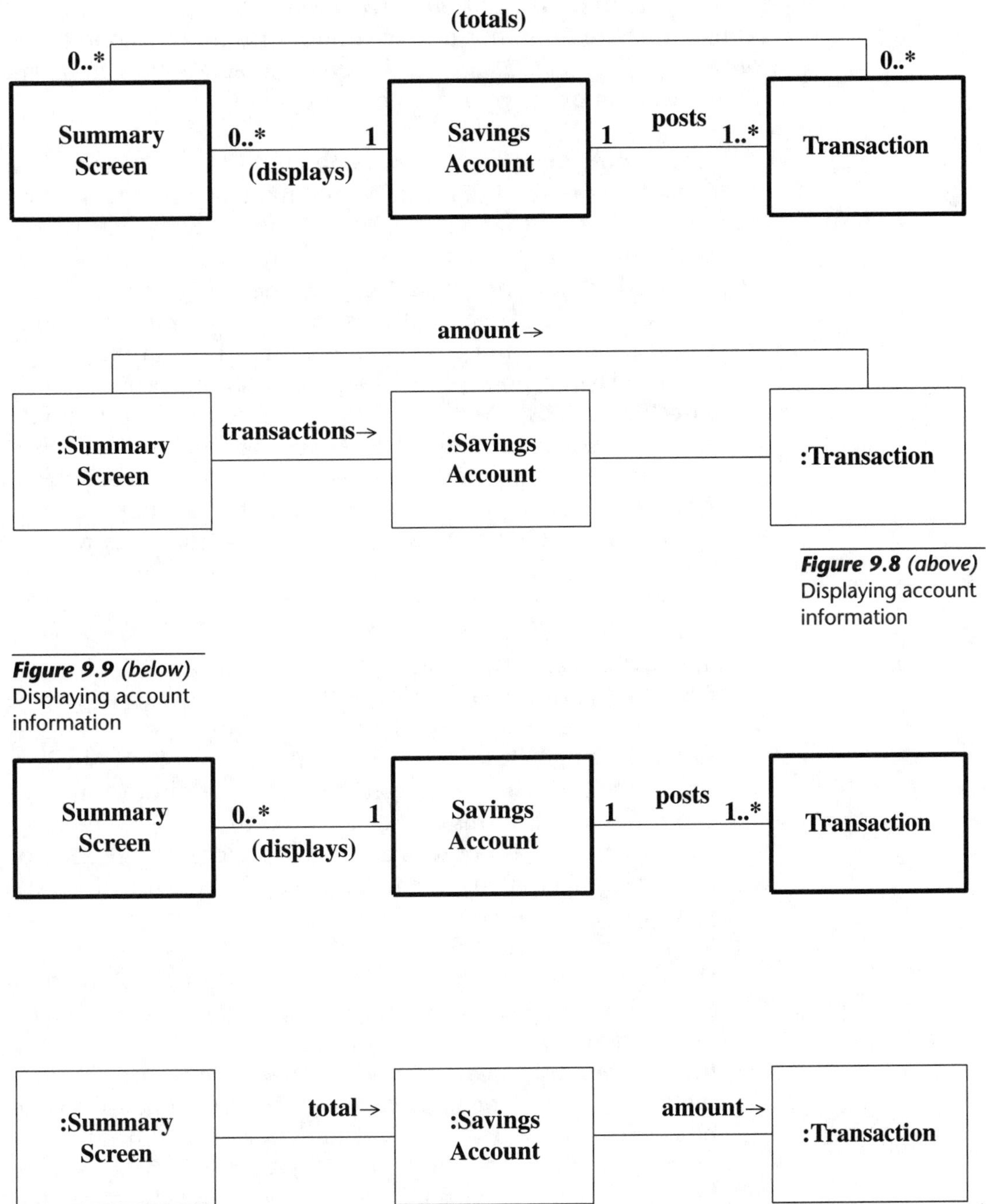

***Figure 9.8** (above)*
Displaying account information

***Figure 9.9** (below)*
Displaying account information

9.2.4.8 Programming Tips and Techniques

I'd like to share some tips and techniques from my second book, *Building Object Applications That Work* (Ambler, 1998), that will dramatically improve your coding productivity.

1. **Document your code.** It is not enough just to write code; you have to write code that can be maintained and enhanced by someone other than yourself. The easiest way to increase the maintainability of your code is to document it properly.
2. **Methods should do one thing and one thing only.** This is a cohesion issue in that methods that do one thing are much easier to understand than methods that do multiple things.
3. **Encapsulate vendor-proprietary application programming interfaces (APIs).** Mowbray (1997) argues that you should not use vendor-proprietary interfaces without proper layering and wrapping for isolation to protect yourself from changes to that interface. If you want to use the Microsoft Open Database Connectivity (ODBC) API to access data in relational databases, that's fine; just make sure that you develop a set of classes that wrap the details of that API so that when it changes, as it has several times already, your applications are not impacted by those changes.
4. **Do one thing per line of code.** Back in the days of punch cards it made sense to try to get as much functionality as possible on a single line of code, but considering it has been over fifteen years since I have even seen a punch card, I think we can safely rethink this approach to writing code. Whenever you attempt to do more than one thing on a single line of code, you make it harder to understand. Why do this? We want to make our code easier to understand so that it is easier to maintain and enhance. Just as a method should do one thing and one thing only, you should only do one thing on a single line of code—assuming, of course, you aren't using punch cards.
5. **Indent your code.** One way to improve the readability of a method is to indent your code within the scope of a code block. For C++ and Java, any code within braces, the { and } characters, forms a block; and for Smalltalk it is square braces, the [and] characters. The code within a block should be uniformly indented one unit, typically a horizontal tab character or three or four spaces.

6. **Develop in small steps.** I have always found that developing in small steps, writing a few methods, testing them, and then writing a few more methods is often far more effective than writing a whole bunch of code all at once and then trying to fix it. It is much easier to test and fix ten lines of code than a hundred, in fact, I would safely say that you could program, test, and fix a hundred lines of code in ten ten-line increments in less than half the time than you could write a single one-hundred line block of code that did the same work. The reason for this is simple. Whenever you are testing your code and you find a bug, you almost always find that bug in the new code that you just wrote; assuming, of course, that the rest of the code was pretty solid to begin with. You can hunt down a bug a lot faster in a small section of code than in a big one. By developing in small incremental steps, you reduce the average time that it takes to find a bug, which in turn reduces your overall development time.

   There's a small caveat that I'd like to point out. Developing in small, incremental steps is faster only in interpreted environments like Smalltalk that allow you to see the effects of changes to your code instantly, or on small applications that can be compiled quickly in environments like C++ that do not support interpreted development. When your application takes several hours to compile, you probably cannot afford to write a few lines, compile it, then test it.
7. **Use whitespace effectively.** There are two different types of whitespace: blank lines between sections of code and spaces within a single line of code. Blank lines make your code much more readable by breaking it up into small, easy-to-digest sections. Also, single spaces between keywords, separators, parameters, and parentheses increase the readability of a single line of code: for example, withoutspacesthissentenceishardtoread. The addition of whitespace in your code makes it much easier to read and to understand.
8. **Follow the thirty-second rule.** Another programmer should be able to look at a method and be able to understand fully what it does, why it does it, and how it does it in less than thirty seconds. If he or she cannot, then the code is too difficult to maintain and should be improved. Thirty seconds, that's it. A good rule of thumb

> **DEFINITIONS**
>
> **cohesion** A measure of how much something makes sense. Cohesive items have a single purpose.
>
> **wrapping** Wrapping is the act of encapsulating non-OO functionality within a class, making it look and feel like any other object within the system.

is that if a method is more than a screen, then it is probably too large.

9. **Specify order of operations.** A really easy way to improve the understandability of your code is to use parentheses, also called "round brackets," to specify the exact order of operations in your code. If I have to know the order of operations for a language to understand your source code then something is seriously wrong. This is mostly an issue for logical comparisons where you AND and OR several other comparisons together. Note that if you use short, single command lines as suggested above then this really shouldn't crop up as an issue.

Perhaps today is a good day to code. —A Klingon programming proverb

9.2.5 Synchronizing Source Code with Models

Earlier I stated that the first thing that programmers must do is invest the time to understand the model to which they are coding. While this is a good start, it is not enough. Throughout the coding process programmers must constantly take the time to synchronize their source code with the model. During coding it often becomes clear that the models/documentation doe not include all of the information needed by the coder. If this is the case, then the coder should first talk to the modeler to determine a solution, and then both the model(s) and the code should be updated to reflect the solution. The important thing is that the code reflects the information contained in the models and vice versa.

9.2.6 Preparing Code for Inspections

Programmers must occasionally prepare their work to be inspected.

The source code produced by a development team will be inspected, in whole or in part, as part of the Test in the Small stage (Chapter 11). To prepare for a code review, a programmer should be reasonably assured that their code will pass inspection. This means that the code satisfies the design, follows standards, is well documented, is easy to understand, and is well written. If they have been following the advice presented in this chapter, that should be no problem.

Part of the code review process is to distribute copies of the code and supporting models and documentation to the reviewers several days ahead of time. To do this the programmer will need to work closely with the inspection facilitator to put together the appropriate package.

9.2.7 Optimizing Code

I have left my discussion of code optimization toward the end of this chapter for a reason: optimizing your code is one of the last things that programmers should be thinking about, not one of the first. My experience is that you want to leave optimization to the end because you want to optimize only the code that needs it: very often a small percentage of your code results in the vast majority of the processing time, and this is the code that you

WAR STORY

Inspect First, Test Second

I was first introduced to the concept of code inspections in the late 1980s while working as a junior programmer on a medium-sized development team. We would get together regularly and inspect the code of someone on the team, pointing out its strengths and weaknesses and learning from what we discussed. Code reviews were very effective for this team because they used them both to improve the quality of their work products and to transfer skills among team members.

The next team I worked on that attempted to use code reviews failed miserably at it. Instead of doing code reviews throughout development, they chose to do one large code review after the code had been tested, but before it was delivered to the user. The idea was that the team should only review working, functional code so that they wouldn't improve code during development that might be removed later. This proved to be a bad idea for several reasons. First, because the project was late, the code review period was cut by two-thirds. Second, because the code was tested and accepted, the programmers weren't motivated to review it; why bother improving code that was proven to work, running the risk of introducing new bugs? Third, mistakes that could have been caught early in the development process weren't caught and instead were propagated throughout the code, making them much more difficult to fix at the end of the project, so difficult in fact that most problems weren't dealt with. The lesson to be learned is that you want to inspect your code early and often, long before it is tested.

Do not waste your time optimizing code that nobody cares about.

should be optimizing. A classic mistake made by inexperienced programmers it to try to optimize all of their code, even code that already runs fast enough. Personally, I prefer to optimize the code that needs it and then move on to more interesting things than trying to squeeze out every single CPU cycle.

What should you look for when optimizing code? Koenig (1997) points out that the most important factors are fixed overhead and performance on large inputs. The reason for this is simple: fixed overhead dominates the run-time speed for small inputs, while the algorithm dominates for large inputs. His rule of thumb is that a program that works well for both small and large inputs will likely work well for medium-sized inputs.

Developers who have to write software that works on several hardware platforms and/or operating systems need to be aware of idiosyncrasies in the various platforms. Operations that might appear to take a particular amount of time, such as the way that memory and buffers are handled, can show substantial variations between platforms. It is common to find that you need to optimize your code differently depending on the platform.

You do not always need to make your code run faster to optimize it in the eyes of your users.

Another issue to be aware of when optimizing code is the priorities of your users, because depending on the context, people will be sensitive to particular delays. For example, your users will likely be happier with a screen that draws itself immediately and then takes eight seconds to load data than with a screen that draws itself after taking five seconds to load data. In other words, most users are willing to wait a little longer as long as they're given immediate feedback—important knowledge to have when optimizing your code.

TIP

Define Your Project's Development Priorities

Everybody has their own idea about what is important, and software developers are no different. The issue is that your project, and your organization, needs to define what its development priorities are so that all team members are working to the same vision. Maguire (1994) believes that your organization needs to establish a ranking order for the following factors: size, speed, robustness, safety, testability, maintainability, simplicity, reusability, and portability. These factors define the quality of the software that you produce, and by prioritizing them you will help to define the development goals for your team and will reduce the opportunities for disagreement between your developers.

Why bother investing the time to optimize your code? First, the contract that you have with your users might define run-time characteristics that your application must exhibit. Second, making a program faster now may mean the difference between people using it immediately or having to wait for the next generation of hardware. Yes, improvements in hardware will often resolve run-time deficiencies in software, but sometimes you do not have the opportunity to wait for these improvements and you need to optimize your code.

Although optimization may mean the difference between the success and failure of your application, never forget that it is far more important to get your code to work properly. Never forget that slow software that works is always preferable to fast software that does not.

Get it right, then get it fast.

9.2.8 Creating a "Build"

Creating a build is the act of compiling and linking your source code in compiled languages such as Java and C++, or packaging your code in languages like Smalltalk. As you would expect, you use tools called compilers, linkers, and packagers to create a build, which I will refer to as "builders" for the sake of our discussion. Successful builds produce software that can be run and tested, whereas unsuccessful builds produce an indication of what your builder did not like about your code. Builds are important because they help to find integration problems in your code; if your code does not integrate well, it will likely break your build, and the build shows that your code does in fact compile—often an incredible morale booster for your programming team.

Creating a build is the act of compiling and linking your software.

How often should you create a build? The answer depends on where you are in the programming stage. At the start of your project you might not be able to produce a build for the first week or two of programming. My advice is to insist on your first build to be the first Friday afternoon, or sooner if the team requests it, and then follow with daily builds from then on. The advantage of daily builds is that you always have a working version of your code that you can show to users and management.

Software configuration management (SCM) tools, specifically version control tools, are critical for managing the build process. Individual developers must be able to check their work in and out

TIP

Create Builds in Isolation

Running software will access memory on your computer, and if it is not well written it could potentially modify information stored in memory locations that it shouldn't have access to—memory locations "owned" by other running software. For this reason you want to create a build in isolation on a machine that is running only the builder software; you do not want to run the risk of another program introducing random errors into the software that you are building. I once wasted several days trying to track down a bug in an application that was apparently introduced by the email program that I had running in the background during the build. My advice: before creating a build, reboot your machine and run the build isolated in a fresh memory space.

of your version control tool, as well as be able to define which version of their code is ready to be added to the official build. At any given time you should be able to extract the current version of your application's code so that you can create a build of it, and the easiest way to do this is to have a version control tool that supports this ability (all the good ones do) and to have your developers responsible for ensuring that they have indicated the "buildable" versions of their code.

You need SCM tools.

The build process is fairly straightforward and should have been defined during the Define Infrastructure stage (Chapter 6). You begin by extracting the source code for what you want to build from your version control tool and installing it onto your build machine/environment. Reboot the build machine to ensure that you have a clean memory space, then use your builder tool to create the build. If the build fails, you need to fix the indicated errors, often recorded in an error log file and/or error log display screen, and try again. If the build is successful, then you need to "smoke test"' it to verify that your application actually works. A smoke test is a collection of tests, often automated, that are designed to verify that the build application works. Your smoke test naturally needs to evolve as your application evolves because you want to test new functionality as you add it to your software.

To increase the chance that your build is successful, McConnell (1996) advises that code should be added to the build only when coders believe that it works. This implies that each programmer is

War Story

Invest in a Good Build Machine

I once audited a large C++ project (it was 750,000 lines of code) that took between six and seven hours to build. Because they were doing a daily build, actually a nightly build, they had little opportunity to fix a mistake in a build if it broke toward the end. I suggested that they immediately purchase a faster build machine with more memory, which they did, cutting their build time down to about three hours. A small investment in a good build machine had a large impact on their productivity. As you would expect, they further invested the time to split the build down into portions, many of which could be built in parallel, to reduce the build time further.

responsible for extracting the buildable code of their coworkers, creating a private build of their own, testing their code, fixing it where necessary, and then checking in the newest version of their code so that it can be included in the official build for your application. The main difficulty with this approach is that although everyone's private build may work, nobody is working with the latest version of all the code until the official build is attempted, because several programmers may submit new versions of their code for any given build. The implication is that it is possible that your build may still break.

Programmers are responsible for ensuring that their code works with the rest of the build.

McConnell (1996) suggests that the person's code who broke the build be the one who is responsible for running the build until someone else's code in turn breaks it. Running builds can be a grueling job: if the build works, you have to wait while it runs (depending on your project, this could be anywhere from several minutes to several hours), and if it does not work you have to determine what the problem is and what section of code is responsible for it, and then report the problem(s) to the appropriate developers.

Daily builds increases your chance of success because you always know whether your application works. Yourdon (1997) suggests posting the results of the daily build in a visible place so that everyone knows the status of your project; good advice for

DEFINITIONS

build The process by which a software product is created from its base source code. This is the act of compiling and linking source code in compiled languages such as Java and C++, or packaging code in languages like Smalltalk.

builder A tool that developers use to build software, such as compilers, linkers, and packagers.

software configuration management (SCM) A set of engineering procedures for tracking and documenting software and its related deliverables throughout their life cycles to ensure that all changes are recorded and the current state of the software is known and reproducible.

version control tool A software tool used to check in/out, define, and manage versions of project deliverables.

projects that are going well, not so good advice for projects that want to hide the fact that they are having problems. It's your call.

9.2.9 Preparing the Integration Plan

Long before you attempt to integrate and package your application you must first have a plan to do so. Three key deliverables are needed by the developers responsible for integrating and packaging your application: an integration plan that describes the schedule, resources, and approach to integrating the elements of an application, a version description document (VDD) that describes the elements of an application and their intrarelationships, and a deployment diagram that shows how the software will be deployed to the user community.

Portions of the VDD, deployment diagram, and integration plan should have been completed previously.

The good news is that if you are performing daily builds then a large portion of the information described by your VDD, the software elements of your application, is contained in your version control tool. To develop the VDD you simply extract the description of the software elements of your build and add to it descriptions of supporting documents, such as your user documentation and support documentation. Also, a deployment diagram should have been developed during the Model stage (Chapter 8). The only additional work that you need to perform is the development of a schedule and the assignation of resources to that schedule to perform the integration and packaging, information which may already be captured in your project plan.

DEFINITIONS

deployment diagram A diagram showing the hardware, software, and middleware configuration for a given system.

integration plan A plan that describes the schedule, resources, and approach to integrating the elements of an application.

project plan A project plan is a collection of several project management deliverables, including but not limited to a project overview, a project schedule, a project estimate, a team definition, and a risk assessment. Project plans are a deliverable of the Initiate phase and are updated regularly throughout a project.

version description document (VDD) A complete list of all items included in a product baseline release of software, including all configuration items and supporting deliverables. The VDD includes an indication of all changes made to the software from the previous version and a list of all applicable SPRs and SCRs implemented in the current version.

9.2.10 Integrating and Packaging Your Application

To integrate and package your application, you must build and smoke-test your software, produce the supporting documentation, and develop the installation process for your software. As noted previously, if you perform daily builds, then the first step is straightforward, as you merely need to follow your existing build procedure to gather and then build the source code files that make up your application.

The first step is to build and smoke test your application.

The second step, producing the supporting documentation is more complex: following your version design document (VDD) you must produce documents such as your user manual, training manual, user reference manual, support documentation, and operations documentation. These documents are discussed in detail in the Release stage (Chapter 5 in *More Process Patterns*). These documents should have been developed throughout the Construct phase; at this point you merely need to gather them in one single package for testing.

The second step is to gather/develop the supporting documentation for your application.

Third, you need to develop an installation procedure so that your application may be installed on your users' machines. Installation procedures may be as simple as a set of instructions for manually installing the software, to batch scripts that automatically install the software, to interactive software that the user will use to perform a custom installation of your application. Note that your installation procedures must reflect your project's

The third step is to develop an installation procedure for your application.

DEFINITION

Application package The software and supporting documentation that is deployed to your user community.

release procedures, defined and selected during the Define Infrastructure stage (Chapter 6), which describe the entire release process, including the proposed installation process. Installation utilities can be purchased from third-party vendors and modified for the unique needs of your software.

Once your application has been integrated and packaged it is ready to be passed on to the Deliver phase.

9.3 Solution: Project Tasks

In this section I will discuss several project task issues specific to the Program stage.

9.3.1 Managing the Program Stage

Shortcuts taken during the Program stage often results in the software taking longer to produce.

Management of the Program stage is critical to the success of your project. Many projects get into trouble during the Program stage, sometimes because rogue programmers aren't managed properly, but more often than not because management decides to take shortcuts in an effort to deliver the software at an earlier date, which often results in mistakes being made and the software taking longer to program.

Several tasks need to be performed during the Program stage to ensure that it is managed properly. Software configuration management (SCM) is key to the success of the Program stage; you need to manage the source code that your developers produce. Also, Maguire (1994) suggests that to keep your project on track, whenever there is the possibility that a feature may slip the team member responsible should inform the team lead and brainstorm a solution. Finally, to avoid going over the same decisions over and over and over and over again, your team should record all decisions made, decisions deferred, and lessons learned into your project's group memory. Keeping your group memory up-to-date increases the efficiency of your project team and provides a detailed description of your work that can be used in the future by maintenance developers tasked with the maintenance and enhancement of your application.

Keep your group memory up-to-date.

Traditional management tasks such as maintaining the project plan, reporting your project's status to senior management, and managing risk are naturally applicable during the Program stage.

DEFINITION

group memory A record of what your project team accomplished, decisions made by your team and the reasoning behind them, deferred decisions, and the lessons learned on your project. A group memory provides a mechanism to record this information when it is first recognized so that it is not lost.

9.3.2 People Management

The main challenge with respect to people management is to keep your programmers under control throughout the Program stage. At the beginning of the Program stage I believe in strict control of programmers via regular code reviews to ensure that the programmers are following the design produced by the Model stage (Chapter 8) and the coding standards and guidelines chosen during the Define Infrastructure stage (Chapter 6). Once the programmers on my team have proven themselves, I loosen up a bit, very often a lot, and allow them to expand their responsibilities beyond programming. My experience is that there are many good programmers out there, but significantly more bad programmers, and until I know who is who, I believe in keeping a close eye on them.

Keeping programmers under control and working together is the main challenge of the Program stage.

A common difficulty on many projects are cowboy/rogue programmers who think they know everything, that their way is best, and that they can do whatever they like. The reality is that nobody can know everything because software development is far too complex, and that developers who think they know everything are often so narrowly focused that they do not realize the true scope of the software process. The best developers are the ones who understand that they have much more to learn, that they can learn from their teammates by working with them cooperatively, and that they are part of a team that must work together to succeed.

It is not possible to know everything, regardless of what your "best" programmers think.

Although you need to keep your programmers under control, you must not do so in a detrimental way. Every member of your team is important; otherwise, why are they on it? Their work is valuable and must be recognized as such. Ensure that your programmers are working from the models and that they are following standards, but also ensure that within these constraints they are still empowered to produce high-quality work and that they are able to expand their knowledge and skills. Programming to a well-defined model and set of coding standards is still a complex

Management must appreciate that programming is a complex and challenging task.

and challenging task; ensure that your programmers understand that you appreciate this fact.

9.3.3 Training and Education

You become a good programmer after years of experience, not weeks of training.

The good news is that there are many sources of training and education available to you; the bad news is that there are many sources of training and education available to you. The first thing you need to understand is that there is much more to object-oriented programming than understanding the syntax of the language and the features of your development tool. Second, it is important to recognize that a five-day course in your language of choice, perhaps Java or C++, is not enough. Good programmers became good programmers after years of experience, not after weeks of training.

My advice:

1. **Read, read, read.** Give people access to good books, magazines, and journals about object-oriented modeling. Many people learn by reading and are willing to do so on their own time, so supply them with a lot of reading material.
2. **Educate programmers in software engineering concepts.** The best programmers understand the implications of concepts such as coupling and cohesion, understand that the software process includes far more than programming, and understand the needs of maintenance. In other words, programmers need to be educated in the principles of software engineering.
3. **Train in the tools.** Programmers need to understand the tools that they work with to use them efficiently.
4. **Get good instructors.** Ensure that the instructors have actually built real-world systems using object technology. The best instructors are usually consultants who give training

DEFINITIONS

cohesion A measure of how much something makes sense. Cohesive items have a single purpose.

coupling A measure of how connected two items are.

mentor An experienced developer who transfers skills to less experienced developers to aid in their education experience. This is a key role during all phases, but specifically during the Construct phase.

courses one week a month and do development work the rest of the time.

5. **Get good mentors.** A mentor is an expert who also has the ability to transfer skills. A good programming mentor has several years of experience in OO modeling and programming, is constantly learning new approaches and techniques, and has the patience needed to work with and grow novice programmers.

9.3.4 Quality Assurance

Quality assurance is an important issue during the Program stage, with code inspections being the primary mechanism for ensuring quality. Quality is everyone's job, and to ensure that your programmers produce quality code, you need to choose standards and guidelines and then enforce them on your project. Furthermore, you want to provide training and education to your programmers in writing quality code: the sad fact is that few programming courses include quality and software engineering material, and instead focus on technical issues of the language being taught. The result is that few programmers have been exposed to the techniques that improve the quality of their code (many of these techniques were discussed earlier in this chapter), and therefore need to be trained.

Code inspections are the primary mechanism for quality assurance during the Program stage.

TIP

Teach The Importance of Quality Assurance Through Code Swapping

One of the best approaches to teaching the importance of coding standards and documentation to programmers is to take two programmers and swap their coding responsibilities. If the two programmers are working from different standards, or from no standards at all, they will quickly see how difficult it is to pick up someone else's code. This is also a good way to test the quality of the code documentation, especially if you do not let the programmers communicate with each other.

I am a firm believer that the best job that a programmer can take when coming out of school is as a maintenance programmer. Ideally, they should maintain and enhance the code of several programmers so as to gain an appreciation of the effect of everyone doing their own thing.

9.3.5 *Potential Risks While Programming*

There are several risks unique to the Program stage:

1. **Cowboy coders.** Cowboy/rogue programmers believe that they know it all and that they do not have to work with their fellow teammates. This attitude is anathema to successful development of large-scale, mission-critical software.
2. **Lack of training in the infrastructure.** Programmers must understand the tools that they are working with and the standards and guidelines that they are expected to follow. Too many organizations fail to invest sufficiently in training their programming staff—you cannot place a Java development environment on someone's desk and expect them to start developing complex applications with graphical user interfaces.
3. **Premature release.** McConnell (1996) points out that a major drawback of a daily build is that senior management is tempted to release the application prematurely because they have a working version of it. Yes, the application may work, but that does not mean that it is complete.
4. **Not following your models.** Everyone knows that your model must drive your code, yet many projects fail to do so due to lack of time or tension between your modelers and programmers. My response to these excuses is this: if you do not have time to model you surely do not have time to code, and if you invested the time to model then why wouldn't you follow it? When your programmers refuse to use existing models, one of two things has happened: you are burdened with cowboy coders who need to be retrained, or you need to rethink your approach to modeling because it is not producing realistic models. Either way, it is a management problem.
5. **Lack of documentation.** The most effective way to develop code is to document it before you write it, forcing you to think through your logic before committing it to source code. If the code for your project is poorly documented, that is a sign that your programmers are not taking the most effective approach to their work.
6. **Overly focused on optimization issues.** Many programmers will waste time optimizing code that already works fast enough, sacrificing the time needed to write high-quality

code. Knight (1996) points out that no one cares how fast a list box updates if the code is not tested properly or is poorly documented.

9.3.6 Opportunities for Reuse

We saw in section 9.2.2 that there are several common approaches to obtaining reuse during the Program stage:

- Artifact reuse
- Code reuse
- Component reuse
- Inheritance reuse
- Framework reuse

9.3.7 Metrics

You may choose to collect several metrics applicable to the Program stage. These metrics are:

1. **Requirements instability.** This metric is calculated by taking the number of requirements changed during a given time period, typically a work month, and dividing it by the total number of requirements for your application. This metric provides an estimate of the quality of your efforts during the Define and Validate Initial Requirements stage (Chapter 3) and Model stage (Chapter 8). Projects that experience changing requirements during the Construct phase have a high chance of failing.
2. **Method size.** This metric is calculated by counting the number of statements of a method, providing an indication of the quality and maintainability of your code. Everything being equal, larger methods will be more difficult to understand, and therefore more difficult to maintain, than smaller methods. Lorenz and Kidd (1994) believe that if a method is large, it is a good indication that your code is actually function-oriented as opposed to object-oriented. Objects get things done by collaborating with each other and not by doing everything themselves. This results in short methods, not long ones. Although you'll occasionally run into long methods, they are few and far between. If your methods are long, it is an indication that there is a problem.

DEFINITIONS

method response A count of the total number of messages that are sent as a result of a method being invoked.

requirements instability A metric calculated by taking the number of changed requirements in a given time frame by the total number of requirements.

3. **Method response.** Method response (Chidamber and Kemerer, 1991) is a count of the total number of messages that are sent as a result of a method being invoked. The exact definition of method response is recursive: it is the count of all message sends within a method, plus the method response of each method invoked by those message sends. The reason why this is an important metric is that methods with high method-response values indicate that the method is difficult to test, as you have to test all the code that gets invoked. Another potential problem is the potential for high coupling. Remember, the only way an object can send a message to another object is when it knows about that other object, implying that there is some coupling between the two objects. The higher the method response, the greater the chance of coupling.
4. **Comments per method.** A very useful metric for estimating the quality of your code is the number of lines of comment per method (Lorenz and Kidd, 1994). My experience has been that good methods have more lines of comments than lines of code. Too few comments indicates that other programmers will have a difficult time trying to understand your code, and too many comments indicates that you are wasting too much time documenting it.
5. **Percentage of commented methods.** Although I instantly want to say that this metric (Lorenz and Kidd, 1994) should always be one hundred percent, the reality is that it does not have to be. This is because you do not really need to document setters—methods that set the value of attributes. Once you ignore setters, this metric should be one hundred percent, however, and if it is not then you have done a poor job.
6. **Global usage.** This metric (Lorenz and Kidd, 1994) is a count the number of global variables that you are using in the code for your application. You want to minimize the use of global variables because they increase the coupling within your application, making it harder to maintain and enhance. My rule of thumb is that if you have any global variables at all, then you are in trouble. Do not put them in your design and especially do not put them in your code.

9.4 Resulting Context: Exit Conditions for Programming

The following conditions must be met before the Program stage may be considered complete:

1. **The code has passed inspection.** Although you may choose to inspect only a portion of your source code, perhaps as little as ten percent, it must still pass the inspection(s) to be ready for release. It is important to understand, however, that the percentage of inspected code varies between programmers: mature programmers who have proven their ability to write maintainable, extensible code have their work trusted more than developers who have not proven their ability to write clean code. Yes, that means that both junior programmers and senior hackers will have their code inspected much more often than senior programmers.
2. **The code works.** Your application source code must pass the tests performed by the Test in the Small stage (Chapter 11).
3. **The code has been optimized sufficiently.** Your application must meet the performance requirements identified for it.
4. **The application is integrated and packaged for the Delivery phase.** The source code must be built, the installation process developed for your application, and the application documentation (user documentation, support documentation, and so on) be packaged in. All of these things for your application and need to be tested in the large and released to your user community.

9.5 Secrets of Success

Over the years I have discovered that by following the subsequent advice you will greatly improve your chance of success during the Program stage:

1. **Define your priorities.** Programmers need to understand the priorities of your organization and of your project; otherwise, they will set their own priorities that are usually not well

aligned with those of your organization. I typically make correctness my number-one priority, followed closely by robustness to make my work extensible and maintainable, with performance my third priority.

2. **The code should be based on the model.** Would you feel comfortable walking over a bridge that was put together without a plan, just with the hard work of a group of construction workers who felt they knew what they were doing? Of course you wouldn't: you'd be afraid that the bridge could fall down at any minute. Why should your users be comfortable working with software built by a group of programmers who felt they knew what they were doing? How comfortable would you be when you are taking a flight somewhere if you were to find out that the air-traffic-control system was written without first putting together, and then following, a really solid design? Think about it. Have you ever been in a situation where some of the code needs to be changed that your code relies on? Perhaps a new parameter needs to be passed to a method, or perhaps a class needs to be broken up into several classes. How much extra work did you have to do to make sure that your code works with the reconfigured version of the code that got changed? How happy were you? Did you ask yourself why somebody did not stop and think about it first when he or she originally wrote the code so that this did not need to happen? That they should have *designed* it first? Of course you did. If you take the time to determine how you are going to write your code before you actually start coding, you'll probably spend less time doing it and potentially reduce the impact of future changes on your code simply by thinking about them up front.
3. **Employ software configuration management (SCM).** Programmers need to store, version, and share their code with their teammates. SCM tools and techniques provide the mechanisms by which they do this.
4. **Follow coding standards and guidelines.** Standards and guidelines provide the information that programmers need to ensure that their code is consistent with each others and is of the quality expected by your organization.
5. **Be realistic when it comes to your tools.** Booch (1995) believes that programmers often become enamored with tools, forgetting that their job is to produce software that

supports the needs of their users. He suggests that you should not become intoxicated with in-vogue commercial tools or trends; instead, you should be realistic in your expectations of what you can or cannot accomplish with them.

6. **Source code must be documented thoroughly.** Many programmers balk at writing documentation, often because they do not realize that it is their job to write source code that not only works, but that can be maintained and extended over time. Code that is not worth documenting is not worth keeping.
7. **Programmers need to understand the big picture even while working on the little picture.** Everyone's work must coexist with the work of others, and the best way to ensure that is to follow the architecture and models defined during the Model stage (Chapter 8). You can write the best code in the world, but if it does not work with the rest of the systems used and/or developed by your organization, then your work is of little value.
8. **Work together as a team, not as individual superstars.** The development of large-scale, mission-critical software is a very complex endeavor, an endeavor that requires coordinated effort between groups of people.
9. **Programmers must realize that there is more to development than programming.** The point to be made is that good developers understand that there is more to development than coding; there is analysis, design, testing, and delivery, too. Until you understand the big picture and how you fit into it, you will never reach your full potential as a developer. Programmers do not need to be an expert at every part of the development process, but they at least need to understand the fundamentals.
10. **Developers must understand that there is more to development than development.** There's also maintenance and support, and in fact an application will spend the vast majority of its lifetime in maintenance (post development). The average computer program spends eighty to ninety percent of its lifetime being maintained, and only a very small portion being developed.
11. **Programmers should "own" their code.** The Code Ownership organizational pattern (Coplien, 1995) suggests that every code module in an application be "owned" by a single programmer who is responsible for its update. Coplien points out

DEFINITION

organizational pattern A pattern that describes a common management technique or a structure appropriate to a software organization.

that developers cannot keep up with a constantly changing base of source code, and that because not everyone can know everything all the time you need to organize the source code for your application so that any given code is the responsibility of one programmer. By having a portion of source code assigned to a specific programmer there is always someone available who understands that code, reducing your organization's cost of discovery during the update of that code.

9.6 Process Checklist

The following process checklist can be used to verify that you have completed the Program stage.

PROGRAM STAGE PROCESS CHECKLIST

Fulfillment of Entrance Conditions:

✔ The appropriate models are available.
✔ Software configuration management (SCM) tools and processes are in place.
✔ Coding standards have been selected/defined.
✔ User interface design standards have been selected/defined.
✔ The development tools are available and have been installed.
✔ Professional programmers are available.
✔ Team members have been given the appropriate training for their part in this stage.

Processes Performed:

✔ The programmers worked with the designers to understand the models they are developing to.
✔ The source code was documented, at least to the pseudocode level, before it was written.
✔ The source code was written and documented.
✔ The source code was layered according to the class-type architecture.
✔ Coding standards were followed.

- ✔ User interface design standards were followed.
- ✔ The source code was synchronized with the models.
- ✔ The source code was prepared for inspection during the Test in the Small stage.
- ✔ The source code was optimized where required.
- ✔ The integration plan was prepared.
- ✔ Artifacts that are potentially reusable by your project team during this stage have been identified and used where appropriate.
- ✔ Your risk assessment document has been updated where appropriate.
- ✔ Decisions made, and decisions forgone, have been documented in your group memory.
- ✔ Metrics have been collected.

Fulfillment of Exit Conditions:

- ✔ The source code has passed inspection (Test in the Small).
- ✔ The source code works.
- ✔ The source code was optimized appropriately
- ✔ The application has been packaged for the Deliver phase.

9.7 What You Have Learned in This Chapter

In this chapter you saw that you begin the Program stage by understanding the models for your application, then you seek out reusable artifacts to reduce your work load, then you document the code that you are going to write, then you write the code, then you inspect and improve it, then you test and fix it, and then you finally package it for delivery to your user community. As always, you do not need to write all of the documentation first, then write all of the code, the inspect all of the code, and so on, but this is the order in which you would develop a portion of the source code for your application.

There is more to the Program stage than writing source code.

In this chapter we also discussed several key topics for programmers, topics that are seldom covered by typical object-oriented programming books. These topics included the class-type architecture, mapping objects to relational databases, user interface design, programming by contract, the proper use of accessor methods, the development/maintenance trade-off, and the Law of Demeter. Object-oriented programming is a complex and diverse topic, one that takes years to master.

9.8 References and Recommended Reading

Ambler, S. W. 1997. The Realities of Mapping Objects To Relational Databases. *Software Development* 5(October), 71–74.

Ambler, S. W. 1998. *Building Object Applications That Work: Your Step-by-Step Handbook for Developing Robust Systems with Object Technology*. New York: SIGS Books/Cambridge University Press.

Booch, G. 1995. Practical Objects: A Question of Balance. *Object Magazine* 5(July–August), 95–96.

Brown, W., Malveau, R, McCormick, H., Mowbray, T. (1998). *AntiPatterns: Refactoring Software, Architectures, and Projects in Crisis*. New York: John Wiley & Sons.

Buschmann, F., Meunier, R., Rohnert, H., Sommerlad, P., and Stal, M. 1996. *A Systems of Patterns: Pattern-Oriented Software Architecture*. New York: John Wiley and Sons Ltd.

Chidamber, S. R. and Kemerer, C. F. 1991. Towards a Suite of Metrics for Object-Oriented Design. *OOPSLA'91 Conference Proceedings*. Reading, Massachusetts: Addison-Wesley Publishing Company, Inc. 197–211.

Compton, S. B. and Conner, G. R. 1994. *Configuration Management for Software*. New York: Van Nostrand Reinhold.

Constantine, L. L. 1995. *Constantine on Peopleware*. Englewood Cliffs, New Jersey: Yourdon Press.

Coplien, J.O. (1995). *A Generative Development-Process Pattern Language*. Pattern Languages of Program Design, eds. Coplien, J.O. and Schmidt, D.C., Addison Wesley Longman, Inc., pp. 183–237.

DeMarco, T. 1997. *The Deadline: A Novel About Project Management*. New York: Dorset House Publishing.

IBM. 1993. *Systems Application Architecture—Common User Access Guide to User Interface Design*. Cary, North Carolina: IBM Corporation.

Koenig, A. 1997. The Importance—and Hazards—of Performance

Measurement. *Journal of Object-Oriented Programming* 9(January), 58–60.

Knight, A. 1995. More Principles of OO Design. *Smalltalk Report* 5(March–April), 20–32.

Lorenz, M. and Kidd, J. 1994. *Object-Oriented Software Metrics.* Englewood Cliffs, New Jersey: Prentice-Hall, Inc.

Maguire, S. 1994. *Debugging the Development Process.* Redmond, Washington: Microsoft Press.

Mayhew, D. J. 1992. *Principles and Guidelines in Software User Interface Design.* Englewood Cliffs New Jersey: Prentice Hall.

McConnell, S. 1996. *Rapid Development: Taming Wild Software Schedules.* Redmond, Washington: Microsoft Press.

McClure, C. 1997. Harvesting Components for Reuse. *Object Magazine* 7(September), 59–64.

Meyer, B. 1997. *Object-Oriented Software Construction,* 2d ed. Upper Saddle River, New Jersey: Prentice-Hall, Inc.

Microsoft 1995. *The Windows Interface Guidelines for Software Design.* Redmond, Washington: Microsoft Press.

Mowbray, T. 1997. Architectures: The Seven Deadly Sins of OO Architecture. *Object Magazine* 7(April), 22–24.

Whitenack, B. and Bounds, B. B. (1995). The Keys to a Truly Successful Smalltalk Project. *Object Magazine* 5(June), 76–78.

Yourdon, E. 1997. *Death March: The Complete Software Developer's Guide to Surviving "Mission Impossible" Projects.* Upper Saddle River, New Jersey: Prentice-Hall, Inc.

Chapter 10

The Generalize Stage

THE Generalize stage is based on the idea that reusable artifacts can be rescued, or mined, from software projects after the fact; that application-specific items can identified and then reworked to be reusable by other project teams. The Generalize stage is the recognition that the short-term pressures of software development result in the temptation for developers to settle for specific, non-reusable solutions. Although developers often intend to go back later to make their work reusable, a common process antipattern called Make It Reusable Later, this rarely happens in practice—senior management is often tempted, once a solution is in place, to move developers on to the next task or the next project without making their previous work reusable (Meyer, 1995). The reality is that you need to include time and resources in your plan to make your work reusable; reuse doesn't just happen by itself.

The Generalize stage rescues potentially reusable deliverables from existing projects and improves them so that they can be reused.

As you see in Figure 10.1, the main inputs into this stage are project deliverables—planning documents, user manuals, source code, and models—that are potentially reusable by other project teams. The main output is reusable items, based on the original project deliverables input into this stage, that have been modified and properly documented so that they are in fact reusable.

This stage is based on the concept of opportunistic reuse, in which you harvest reusable items from projects after the fact; as opposed to systematic reuse, in which reusable artifacts are identi-

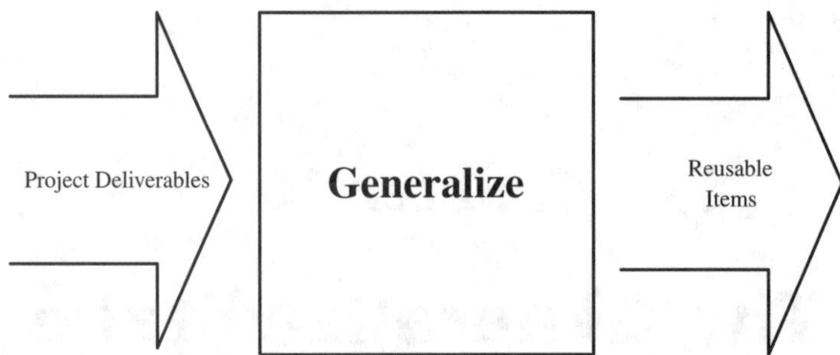

Figure 10.1. The Generalize Stage

fied via architectural and enterprise modeling (Chapter 8) and are designed to be reusable from the very start. The Develop Reusable Artifacts process pattern of Figure 10.2 shows that systematic reuse is a top-down approach to reuse, whereas opportunistic reuse is bottom-up. Both approaches to reuse are needed: systematic reuse to achieve reuse of large-scale domain components and common frameworks, opportunistic reuse to achieve reuse of smaller-scale artifacts such as class hierarchies, user interface widgets, and common documentation templates.

You need to take both systematic and opportunistic approaches to reuse.

DEFINITIONS

antipattern The description of a common approach to solving a common problem, an approach that in time proves to be wrong or highly ineffective.

opportunistic reuse A reuse approach where reusable items are harvested from project deliverables after the fact.

process antipattern An antipattern which describes an approach and/or series of actions for developing software that is proven to be ineffective and often detrimental to your organization.

repository A centralized database into/from which you can check-in and check-out versions of your development work, including documentation, models, and source code.

reuse engineer A senior, experienced developer who is responsible for supporting and enhancing the reuse process within your organization. This person works closely with component engineers and infrastructure engineers, and is a key role in all stages of the Construct phase.

systematic reuse An approach to reuse which involves modeling techniques whose purpose is to define high-leverage, reusable components.

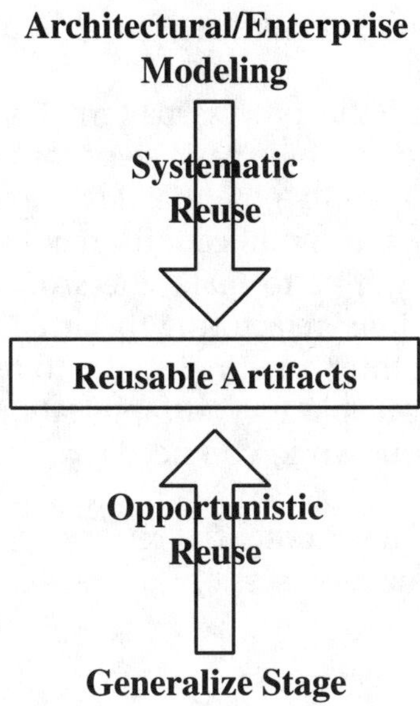

Figure 10.2. The Develop Reusable Artifacts process pattern

10.1 Initial Context: Entry Conditions for Generalizing Your Work

The following conditions must be met before you may begin the Generalize stage:

1. **Project deliverable(s) exist.** This stage begins when you have project deliverables that you believe should be evaluated for their potential to be made reusable.
2. **Reuse engineers are available.** As we will see in this chapter, it is a definite skill to make an artifact reusable. Developers with many years of experience are the best reuse engineers, because they understand what developers can and cannot reuse on a project. Because they have been reuse consumers in the past—developers who have reused the work of others—they understand what is important to their potential customers.
3. **Organizational support for reuse exists.** It takes time, effort, and money to make an artifact reusable, and your organization must be willing to invest the necessary resources to achieve significant levels of reuse.

DEFINITION

reuse consumer A developer who reuses the work of other developers.

10.2 Solution: Generalizing Your Work

Figure 10.3 depicts the process pattern for the Generalize stage, showing that there are three basic steps for generalizing your work. The first step is to identify potentially reusable artifacts—the project deliverables that, with modification, may be reused on other projects. The second step is to make the artifact reusable by holding generalization sessions, refactoring the artifact, and documenting it appropriately. The third and final step is to release the reusable artifact to make it available to your application development teams.

To generalize your work, you need to:

- Identify an item for potential reuse
- Hold a generalization session
- Refactor the item
- Document the item
- Release the item

10.2.1 Identifying Deliverables for Potential Reuse

One of the responsibilities of a reuse engineer is to identify and acquire project deliverables that can be modified to be made reusable. To understand how a reuse engineer identifies deliverables that may potentially be reused, you must (a) understand what approaches to reuse lend themselves to the Generalize stage, and (b) understand what to look for in a project deliverable that makes it a good candidate for reuse.

Figure 10.3. The Generalize process pattern

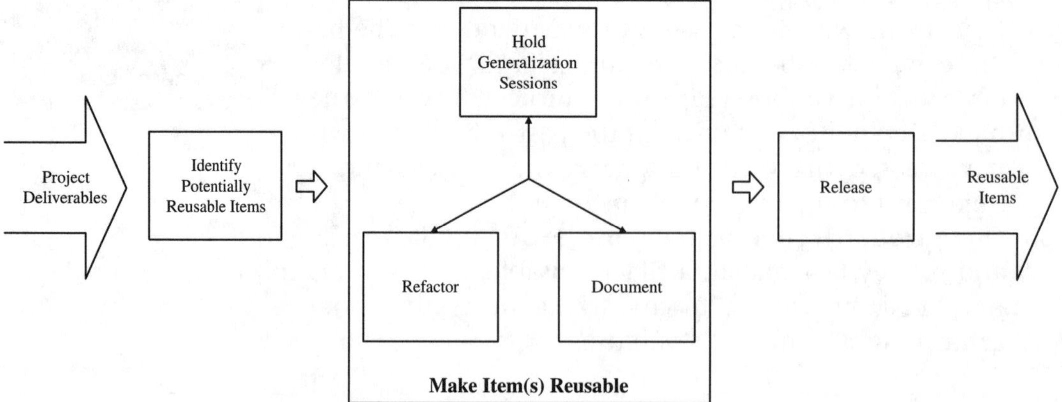

10.2.1.1 Approaches to Reuse

One of the skills of a reuse engineer is to understand what the various approaches to reuse are and which approaches are applied during a stage and/or are supported by a given stage. The Generalize stage supports several approaches to reuse—template reuse, component reuse, framework reuse, and artifact reuse—by identifying and developing the items that are reused by each approach. Figure 10.4 compares the productivity of each approach to reuse, showing that code reuse is the least productive, although still beneficial, and that domain-component reuse is the most productive. The forms of reuse that are supported by the Generalize stage are shown with a double asterisk to set them apart. We'll compare and contrast these approaches to reuse in *More Process Patterns* (Ambler, 1998b).

10.2.1.1.1 Template Reuse

Template reuse refers to the practice of using a common set of layouts for key deliverables—documents, models, and source code—within your organization. For example, it is quite common for organizations to adopt common documentation templates for use cases, status reports, developer time sheets, change requests, user requirements, class files, and method documentation headers. The main advantage of documentation templates is that they increase the consistency and quality of your development arti-

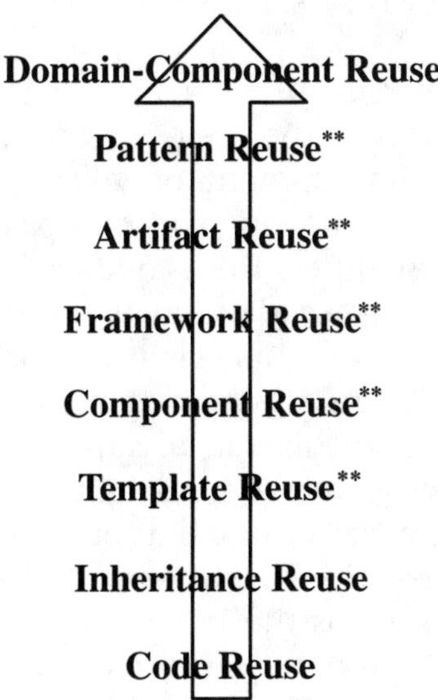

Figure 10.4. The increasing effectiveness of reuse techniques

DEFINITIONS

artifact reuse The reuse of previously created development artifacts: use cases, standards documents, domain-specific models, procedures and guidelines, and other applications.

code reuse The reuse of source code within sections of an application and potentially across multiple applications.

component reuse The reuse of prebuilt, fully encapsulated components in the development of your application.

domain-component reuse The reuse of prebuilt, large-scale domain components that encapsulate cohesive portions of your business domain.

framework reuse The reuse of collections of classes that together implement the basic functionality of a common technical or business domain.

inheritance reuse The use of inheritance in your application to take advantage of behavior implemented in existing classes.

pattern reuse The reuse of publicly documented approaches, called patterns, to solving common problems.

template reuse The reuse of a common set of layouts for key development artifacts—documents, models, and source code—within your organization.

The practice of reusing common layouts for deliverables is called template reuse.

facts, and the main disadvantage is that developers have a tendency to modify templates for their own use and not share their changes with their coworkers.

10.2.1.1.2 Component Reuse

Component reuse refers to the use of prebuilt, fully encapsulated components in the development of your application. Components are typically self-sufficient and encapsulate only one concept. Component reuse differs from code reuse in that you do not have access to the source code, and it differs from inheritance reuse in that it doesn't use subclassing. Common examples of components are Java Beans and ActiveX components.

Component reuse has several advantages. First, component reuse offers a greater scope of reusability than either code or inheritance reuse, because components are self-sufficient—you literally plug them in and they work. Second, the widespread use of common platforms, such as the Win32 operating system and the Java virtual machine, provides a market that is large enough for third-party vendors to create and sell components to you at a low cost. The main disadvantage to component reuse is that components are small and encapsulate only one concept, requiring you to have a large library of them to be effective.

10.2.1.1.3 Framework Reuse

Framework reuse refers to the use of collections of classes that together implement the basic functionality of a common technical or business domain. Developers use frameworks as the foundation from which they build an application; the common eighty percent is in place already, they just need to add the remaining twenty percent that is specific to their application. Frameworks that implement the basic components of a graphical user interface are very common, and there are now domain frameworks for insurance, human resources, manufacturing, banking, and electronic commerce available. Framework reuse represents a high level of reuse at the problem domain level.

The reuse of collections of classes that work together to fulfill a common domain is called framework reuse.

The main advantages of frameworks are that they provide a good start at developing a solution for a problem domain and often encapsulate complex logic that would take years to develop from scratch. Unfortunately, framework reuse suffers from several disadvantages. The complexity of frameworks makes them difficult to master, requiring a lengthy learning process on the part of developers. Frameworks are often platform-specific and tie you into a single vendor, increasing the risk for your application. Although frameworks implement eighty percent of the required logic, it is often the easiest eighty percent; and the hard stuff, the business logic and processes that are unique to your organization, is still left for you to do. Frameworks rarely work together, unless they come from a common vendor or consortium of vendors, and often require you to change your business to fit the framework instead of the other way around.

10.2.1.1.4 Artifact Reuse

Artifact reuse refers to the use of previously created development artifacts—use cases, standards documents, domain-specific models, procedures and guidelines, and other applications—to give you a kick start on a new project. There are several levels of artifact reuse, ranging from one-hundred-percent-pure reuse, in which you take the artifact as is and use it on a new project, to "example reuse" where you look at the artifact to give you an idea about how to proceed. For example, standards documents such as coding and user interface design standards are valuable artifacts to reuse between projects, as are modeling notation documents and methodology overview documents. I've also been able to reuse existing applications either via a common data interface or by putting an object-oriented "wrapper" around them to make them look like normal classes.

The reuse of deliverables from previous projects is called artifact reuse.

DEFINITION

wrapper A collection of one or more classes that encapsulates access to non-OO technology to make it appear as if it is OO.

Artifact reuse promotes consistency between projects and reduces the project management burden for your new project. Another advantage is that you can often purchase many artifacts or find them online: User interface standards are common for most platforms; coding standards for leading languages are often available; and standard object-oriented methodologies and modeling notations have been available for years. The main disadvantage of artifact reuse is that it is often perceived as "overhead reuse" by hard-core programmers—you simply move the standards and procedures binders from one desk to another. The bottom line is that artifact reuse is an important and viable technique that should not be ignored.

The reuse of documented solutions to common problems is called pattern reuse.

10.2.1.1.5 Pattern Reuse

Pattern reuse refers to the use of publicly documented approaches to solving common problems. Patterns are often documented by a single class diagram and are typically comprised of one to five classes. With pattern reuse, you are not reusing code; instead, you are reusing the thinking that goes behind the code. Patterns are a very high form of reuse that will prove to have a long life span, at least beyond the computer languages that you are currently using, and potentially even beyond the object-oriented paradigm itself.

DEFINITION

pattern The description of a general solution to a common problem or issue from which a detailed solution to a specific problem may be determined. Software development patterns come in many flavors, including but not limited to analysis patterns, design patterns, and process patterns.

Pattern reuse provides a high level of reuse that can be implemented across multiple languages and multiple platforms. Patterns encapsulate the most important aspect of development: the thinking that goes into the solution. Patterns increase the maintainability and enhanceability of your application by using common approaches to problems that are recognizable by any experienced object-oriented developer. The disadvantage of pattern reuse is that patterns do not provide an immediate solution: you still have to write the code that implements the pattern.

10.2.1.2 What to Look for in a Project Deliverable

To evaluate a project deliverable to determine if it can be generalized, the first question to ask is whether other projects need something similar to this deliverable. If the answer is yes, then ask if a reusable item similar to this one already exists. If one does in fact exist, you may still decide to generalize another, perhaps for a different computing platform or purpose. Once the decision has been made to generalize an item, the effort to do so must be justified; in fact, you would perform the actions of the Justify stage (Chapter 5) on a smaller scale to determine whether it makes sense to generalize the item. Part of the justification process is the determination of how the item will be generalized: you will need to decide if it will become an artifact, a template, a framework, or a component.

You must justify making an item reusable.

Consider an example. Your project team has developed a search screen that you believe could be generalized for use on other applications, so you submit it to your organization's reuse group for consideration. They evaluate the search screen and quickly determine that other applications could in fact use something like this. To justify the generalization of the search screen, the reuse engineers consider reusing it as one of: an artifact to provide an example to other developers, a component that can be reused within many applications; or as a portion of a framework. They quickly decide against creating a search screen component because every search screen has its own unique search criteria fields. They also decide against using the search screen as an artifact because they want more than just an example. Instead they choose to include the search screen within an application framework that they have been developing—although the search criteria fields differ between search screens, much of the basic behavior (the input of search criteria, the search for objects that meet that criteria, the display of those objects) is similar. Section 10.3.2 presents a high-level design for this framework.

10.2.2 Making an Item Reusable

To make an application-specific item reusable, you must iteratively perform the following three tasks:

- Hold generalization sessions
- Refactor the item
- Document the item

10.2.2.1 Holding Generalization Sessions

Once you have decided to generalize an item, you must then decide how to perform the work. The best way to accomplish this is to get a small group together, comprised of one or two reuse engineers, the creator of the item being generalized, and one or two potential customers of the item once it is ready for reuse. The reuse engineers provide the expertise for making the item reusable and provide guidance to the group. The creator of the item provides insight into how the item was developed, why it was developed, how it is currently being used, and any outstanding issues for improving the item. The goal of the potential customers is to ensure that the item does in fact become generalized in a way that they could actually reuse it.

DEFINITION

joint application development (JAD) A structured, facilitated meeting in which modeling is performed by both users and developers together. JADs are often held for gathering user requirements.

I prefer to run generalization sessions as I would a traditional JAD (Joint Application Development) session, which is a structured, facilitated meeting. The purpose of a generalization JAD is to review and rework an item to make it reusable. There are three steps to a generalization JAD:

1. **Plan the generalization JAD.** The facilitator, with the help of the reuse engineers, determines who will attend the JAD, defines the agenda, sets the location and date for the session, and distributes the agenda to the JAD participants. Some of the participants at a JAD will be there simply to observe the JAD as part of their training in the JAD process.
2. **Hold the generalization JAD.** Generalization JADs are held in large meeting rooms with a U-shaped table that faces a whiteboard and/or projection screen that the facilitator uses during the session. The observers do not participate directly in the JAD, whereas the other attendees follow a set of structured meeting rules: everyone is allowed to speak and share their ideas, everyone at the table is equal, and ideas are to be shared but not judged. There are usually one or two people who act as scribes so that the generation information is recorded.
3. **Follow-up.** The facilitator prepares the minutes of the generalization JAD session: a summary of the information that was generated as well as the details. The minutes are distributed to all attendees so that they may review the minutes and add any comments/corrections to ensure that the minutes are correct.

It is quite common to work on several items in a single generalization JAD, especially when they are fairly straightforward. The goal of a generalization JAD is to determine a strategy for refactoring an item so that it can be reused.

10.2.2.2 Refactoring for Reuse

From a construction point of view, refactoring refers to the reworking or reorganization of an OO design or OO source code. For our purposes we will expand the definition to include the rework/reorganization of all kinds of items. The specific way that an item is refactored is usually determined either by a generalization JAD or by one or more reuse engineers assigned to the task. However, as you would expect, there are common strategies for developing items to be reusable, based on the approach by which they are to be reused.

Items that will be reused as templates are easy to generalize: you simply take an existing project deliverable and remove its content while keeping the sections of which it is comprised. The best approach to creating templates is to gather several examples of the deliverable; if you are creating a project plan template, try to obtain several project plans developed in the past so that you have an understanding of the previous uses of that deliverable.

Reusable templates are creating by removing the content from existing deliverables and then generalizing the remaining headings and fields.

Components are a little more difficult to generalize than templates, although an easy way to get going with components is to start out with user interface widgets such as slide bars, graphing components, and graphical buttons. It is important to not forget that there is more to an application than the user interface and that you can obtain or build components that encapsulate operating system features such as network access and persistence features such as relational database access components.

If you are building your own components, make sure they do one thing only. For example a user interface component for editing surface addresses is very reusable; you can use that on many editing screens. A component that edits a surface address, an email address, and a phone number isn't as reusable; there are not as many opportunities where you'll want all three of those features simultaneously. Instead, it would be better to build three reusable components and reuse each one where it is needed. When a component encapsulates one concept, we say that it is cohesive.

Reusable components should be cohesive.

Frameworks are often developed when you have common behaviors that cannot be encapsulated by a component.

Because frameworks are very complex, they are significantly more difficult to generalize. Frameworks are generally created by experienced object-oriented developers who have recognized a common, large-scale need that cannot be fulfilled through simpler approaches to reuse. A good rule of thumb for determining that you need to create a reusable framework is that you have identified a set of behaviors that is common to many applications, but there are enough differences between those applications that you cannot develop a generic component to encapsulate those behaviors. This rule of thumb goes directly to the definition of a framework, which is a set of common behaviors that is extended by application developers to meet their specific needs.

Artifact reuse is the easiest form of reuse for the Generalize stage to support, because project artifacts are used as is on other projects. Some project artifacts can become institutionalized by your organization (for example, your project may be the first to develop and use a set of coding standards), whereas other project artifacts, such as a project plan, will only be used by other project teams as an example for how to create one.

Always remember that your main goal is to ensure that the refactored item reflects the general needs of many projects, not just the specific needs of a single project. In addition to refactoring an item for reuse, it must also be appropriately documented.

10.2.2.3 Documenting Reusable Items

Would you purchase a development tool that didn't include documentation? Of course not. Would you reuse something that didn't come with documentation, that required you to invest

TIP

Items Should Be Reusable, Not Reuseless

A common mistake that many organizations make is that they identify many items that nobody will ever reuse. I have seen organizations with hundreds of items in their reuse repository, but when I ask them how many of the items have actually been reused, the answer is only a small handful. This is what I call the Reuseless process antipattern, the identification of a large quantity of low-quality items that others will supposedly improve and reuse on future projects. An item that is of low quality almost always proves to be useless from a reuse point of view—it is reuseless. Quality, not quantity, is the secret to reuse.

DEFINITIONS

antipattern The description of a common approach to solving a common problem, an approach that in time proves to be wrong or highly ineffective.

process antipattern An antipattern that describes an approach and/or series of actions for developing software that is proven to be ineffective and often detrimental to your organization.

refactoring The act of reorganizing OO development efforts. For source code and models, refactoring will often comprise the renaming of methods, attributes, or classes; the redefinition of methods, attributes, or classes; or the complete rework or methods, attributes, or classes. For other project deliverables, refactoring may simply be the renaming or reorganization of sections of the deliverable.

reuseless An item that has been promoted as reusable but in practice is found to be too specific or of low quality.

significant time to learn how to work with the item? Of course not; instead, you would just build the item yourself. The implication is that an item needs to be well documented to make it attractive for reuse.

If an item isn't well documented, it will not be reused.

The documentation requirements of a reusable item are often more stringent than that of a component used on a single project. In your external documentation for a reusable item (documentation that is likely stored in your reuse repository), you will need to include a description of the item, its purpose, and how to reuse it. Furthermore, you will need to provide documented examples that reuse the item so that other developers may determine how to work with it.

TIP

Document when an Item Should (Not) Be Reused

One of the goals for documenting a reusable item is to put it into context for the developers who will consider reusing it. This implies that you need to document both when an item should be reused and when it shouldn't. For example, consider a reusable security component that controls a user's access to portions of an application. The documentation for this component may indicate that it should only be used for applications that require security clearance 5 or above; otherwise, the developer should use the "ANA security component," which is more appropriate for low-security applications.

DEFINITIONS

class model A class diagram and its associated documentation.

public interface The collection of public methods and attributes of a class or component.

reuse repository A tool used to store reusable items.

Reusable frameworks should include the appropriate models describing their design, which would be a class model and the appropriate statechart diagrams and sequence diagrams. These models and diagrams are described in detail in Chapter 8. A reusable component should by accompanied by documentation describing the public interface of the component, an excellent way to do this is to develop a class model containing a single class, the component itself. Artifacts are often documented by one or two pages of prose, except in the case of example source code which should be documented following the code documentation strategies described in Chapter 9.

10.2.3 Releasing Reusable Items

Generalized items are released into your reuse repository.

The generalized item, be it a model, a class, or a class library, needs to be made available to other developers so they can reuse it. Reusable items are stored in your reuse repository. To release an item to your reuse repository, it must be packaged with its accompanying documentation and examples, tested thoroughly, and described within the reuse repository so that other developers can find it.

To release the application framework that we discussed earlier, the framework, its documentation, and any examples would be submitted to your reuse repository. The framework would be described in the repository with a couple of paragraphs, and keywords describing the framework would be defined to support keyword searching by other developers.

10.3 Examples of Generalization

In this section I present the high-level designs of three common reusable items that I have generalized over the years. The first is a persistence layer that encapsulates the behaviors needed to map objects to relational databases; the second is an application framework that I use as the basis for all of the business applications that I develop; and the third is an error handling facility for tracking and solving errors encountered by users as they work with an application.

10.3.1 A Persistence Layer

A persistence layer encapsulates access to persistence mechanisms (relational databases, flat files, object-relational databases, and

TABLE 10.1. The Classes and Hierarchies of the Persistence Layer

Class	Description
ClassMap	A collection of classes that encapsulate the behavior needed to map classes to relational tables.
Cursor	This class encapsulates the concept of a database cursor.
PersistenceBroker	Maintains connections to persistence mechanisms, such as relational databases and flat files, and handles the communication between the object application and the persistence mechanisms.
PersistentCriteria	This class hierarchy encapsulates the behavior needed to retrieve, update, or delete collections of objects based on defined criteria.

(continued)

object bases), making objects independent of their storage strategy. A persistence layer increases the maintainability and extensibility of your object-oriented applications and is a required feature for the vast majority of business applications. The design[1] presented here represents my experiences building persistence layers for Java, C++, and Smalltalk applications within several problem domains for several different industries. This design works and has been proven in practice by a wide range of applications.

PersistentObject provides the fundamental behavior needed to make objects persistent.

Figure 10.5 presents a high-level design of a robust persistence layer, the classes for which are described in Table 10.1. Note that I use a dollar sign ($) to denote class methods and attributes, a UML standard. An interesting feature of the design is that an application programmer only needs to know about four classes to make their objects persistent: PersistentObject, the PersistentCriteria

[1]The detailed design of this persistence layer was presented in the January 1998 through to April 1998 issues of Software Development magazine. You can reach Software Development at http://www.sdmagazine.com.

Table 10.1. *(continued)*

Class	Description
PersistenceMechanism	A class hierarchy that encapsulates the access to flat files, relational databases, and object-relational databases. For relational databases this hierarchy wraps complex class libraries, such as Microsoft's ODBC (Open Oatabase Connectivity) or Java's JDBC (Java Database Connectivity), protecting your organization from changes to the class libraries.
PersistentObject	This class encapsulates the behavior needed to make single instances persistent and is the class that business/domain classes inherit from to become persistent.
PersistentTransaction	This class encapsulates the behavior needed to support transactions, both flat and nested, in the persistence mechanisms.
SqlStatement	This class hierarchy knows how to build insert, update, delete, and select SQL (structured query language) statements based on information encapsulated by ClassMap objects.

class hierarchy, PersistentTransaction, and Cursor. In fact, junior programmers only need to know about PersistentObject and PersistentCriteria to start. The other classes are not directly accessed by application development code, but will still need to be developed and maintained to support the "public" classes.

I would like to explain quickly the behaviors of the four classes that application programmers will work with. PersistentObject encapsulates the behavior needed to make a single object persistent and is the class from which all classes in your problem/business domain inherit from. For example, the business/domain class Customer will either directly or indirectly inherit from PersistentObject.

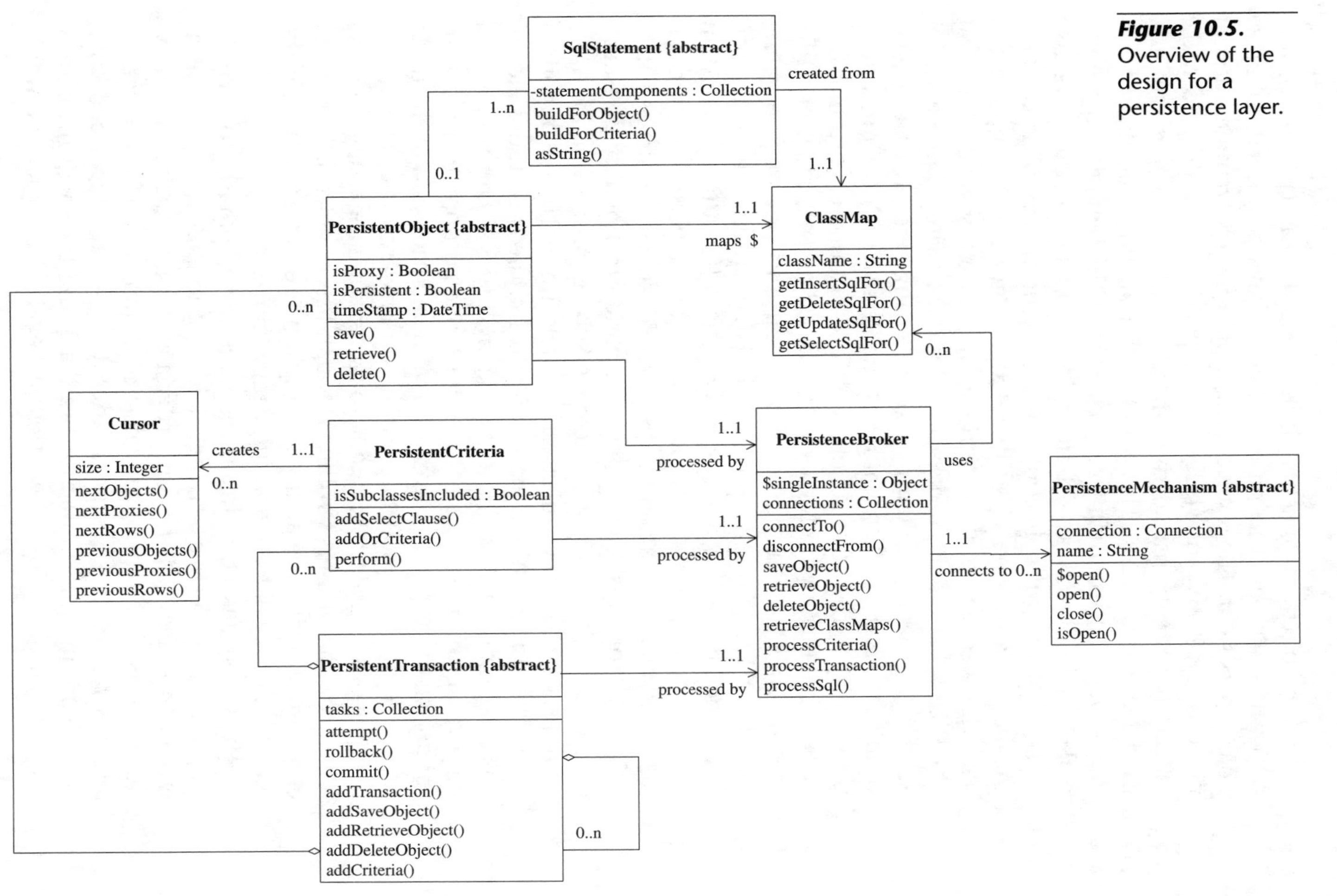

Figure 10.5. Overview of the design for a persistence layer.

PersistentCriteria allows programmers to interact with collections of persistent objects without any knowledge of how they are stored.

PersistentObject implements three methods—save(), delete(), and retrieve()—that are the fundamental behaviors needed to make objects persistent. The result is that application programmers do not need to have any knowledge of the persistence strategy to make objects persistent; instead they merely send objects messages and they do the right thing. This is what encapsulation is all about.

Although PersistentObject encapsulates the behavior needed to make single objects persistent, it isn't sufficient because we also need to work with collections of persistent objects. This is where the PersistentCriteria class hierarchy comes in: it supports the behavior needed to save, retrieve, and delete several objects at once. There are four subclasses of PersistentCriteria, one each for deleting, retrieving, updating, and inserting zero or more objects simultaneously. The key feature of the PersistentCriteria hierarchy is its ability to define selection criteria: for example, customer first names that begin with the letter "J," based on the values of attributes of objects within your application and not on the values stored in table columns. In short, PersistentCriteria allows application programmers to work directly with collections of persistent objects and does not require knowledge of the persistence mechanism schema. Once again the persistence strategy is encapsulated.

The Cursor class encapsulates the basic functionality of a database cursor, allowing you to retrieve subsets of information from your persistence mechanism at a single time. This is important because a single retrieve may result in hundreds or thousands of objects coming across the network; by using a cursor, you can retrieve this result set in small portions, one portion at a time. Cursor objects allow you to traverse forward and backward in the result set of a retrieval (most databases support forward traversal, but may not support reverse traversal due to server buffering issues), making it easy to support users scrolling through lists of objects. The Cursor class also supports the ability to work with rows (records) from the database, proxy objects, and full-fledged objects.

PersistentTransaction instances are made up of tasks to occur to single objects, such as saving, deleting, and retrieving them, as well as instances of PersistentCriteria and other PersistentTransaction objects. The typical life cycle of a transaction is to create it, add a series of tasks, send it the attempt() message, and then either commit the transaction, rollback the transaction, or retry the transaction by invoking attempt() again. Note that you would

PersistentTransaction encapsulates the concept of a database transaction.

commit the transaction, make the tasks of the transaction permanent, only if the attempt() method indicated that the transaction was successful. Otherwise, you would either roll back the transaction, or retry the transaction if it is likely that locks in your persistence mechanism have been removed (making it possible to successfully run the transaction). The ability to commit and roll back transactions is important, because transactions are atomic, either they succeed or they fail: you must be able either to completely back out of the transaction by rolling it back or completely finish the transaction by committing it.

To support the persistence layer, an administration application needs to be built to maintain the instances of the ClassMap classes, as shown in Figure 10.6. These objects encapsulate the behavior needed to map objects into the persistence mechanism, including the complex relationships between the objects that make up your application, and form the information that is stored in the data dictionary for your application. This is the secret to a successful persistence layer: the objects stored in the data dictionary provide the behaviors needed to map objects into the persistence mechanism(s) where they are stored. When the design of your application or persistence mechanism schema changes, you merely have to update the mapping objects within your data dictionary; you do not have to update your application source code.

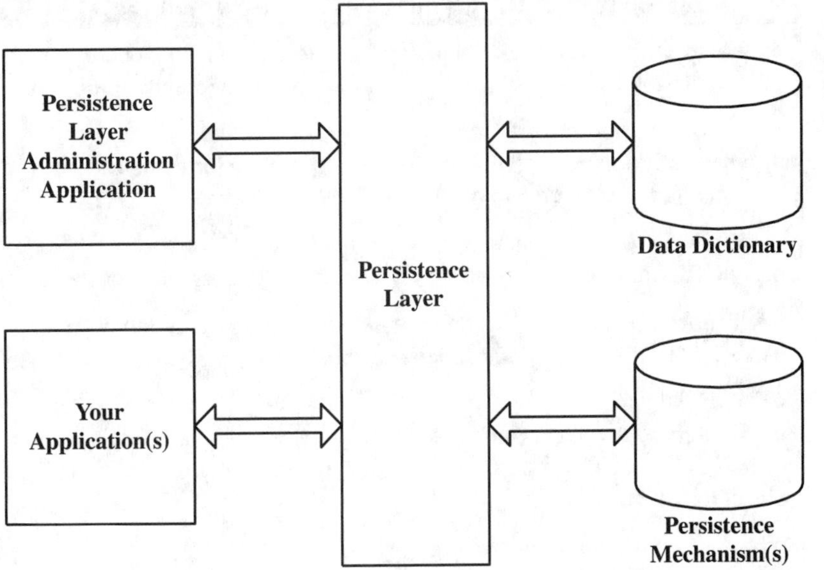

Figure 10.6. How the persistence mechanism works

This approach to persistence effectively allows your database administrators (DBAs) to do what they do best—administer databases—without forcing them to worry about what their changes will do to existing applications. As long as they keep the data dictionary up-to-date, they can make whatever changes they need to make to the persistence mechanism schema. Similarly, application programmers can refactor their objects without having to worry about updating the persistence mechanism schema, because they can map the new versions of their classes to the existing schema. Naturally when new classes or attributes are added or removed to/from an application, there will be a need for similar changes within the persistence mechanism schema.

Persistence layers protect application developers from changes made by database administrators and vice versa.

10.3.2 An Application Framework

A persistence layer is only part of the overall picture; you can also develop a reusable framework for the user interface of your applications. Although many development environments include user interface frameworks, my experience is that you still need to extend them to meet the needs of business application developers. In Figure 10.7 I present the design for an application framework that shows a collection of user interface classes interacting

DEFINITIONS

data dictionary A repository of information about the layout of a database, the layout of a flat file, the layout of a class, and any mappings among the three.

database administrator (DBA) A person responsible for administering and maintaining the schema of a database.

database cursor A connection, that was the result of a query, to a persistence mechanism that allows you to traverse the result set of the query.

persistence mechanism The permanent storage facility used to make objects persistent. Examples include relational databases, object databases, flat files, and object/relational databases.

proxy object lAn object that is used to represent another object. A common responsibility of a proxy object is to pass messages that it receives to the object for which it is a proxy.

schema The design of something.

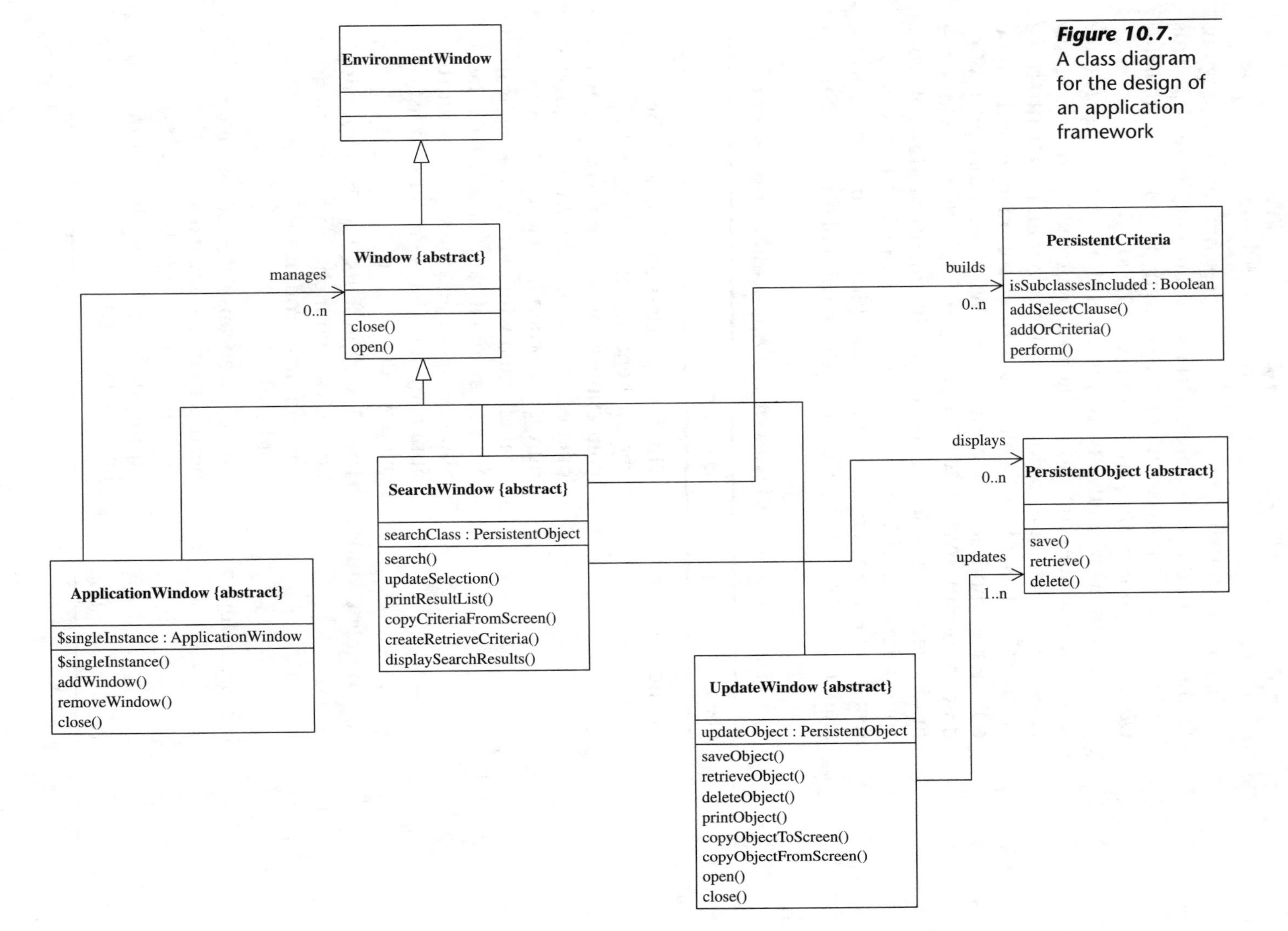

Figure 10.7. A class diagram for the design of an application framework

with portions of the persistence layer presented in the previous section. Table 10.2 describes the classes shown in Figure 10.7. This design is an improvement of the design presented in *Building Object Applications That Work* (Ambler, 1998a).

This framework, effectively an extension of the persistence layer that includes common behaviors exhibited by the user interface (UI) of an application, provides programmers with three abstract UI classes from which their UI classes may inherit. These classes are ApplicationWindow, SearchWindow, and UpdateWindow. ApplicationWindow is a singleton class that provides the fundamental behaviors needed by the main window of your application; SearchWindow provides the common behavior of a search screen by encapsulating the ability for users to specify search criteria and then display the results of that search; and

TABLE 10.2. The Classes of the Application Framework

Class	Description
ApplicationWindow	This abstract class encapsulates the generic behavior of the main window for your application. When this window is opened, it handles login/security procedures; and when it is closed, it ensures that all child windows for the application are also automatically closed. This class also manages the child windows for the application, perhaps providing a list of open windows.
EnvironmentWindow	This class represents the window/dialog box class of your chosen development environment. You buy this class—you do not build it.
PersistentObject	This class encapsulates the behavior needed to make single instances persistent, and is the class that business/domain classes inherit from to become persistent.

(continued)

UpdateWindow provides the fundamental behaviors of an editing/update screen.

The advantage of this framework is that it enables application programmers to concentrate specifically on the unique features of the application that they are developing, saving them from having to develop the common behaviors over and over again. My experience is that the UI portion of this framework increases the productivity of application programmers during construction by about twenty-five percent, a gut-feel estimate, and will reduce the maintenance burden even more due to programmers taking a common approach to developing the UI of their applications. One of the benefits of using frameworks is that programmers are developing to a common vision, that of the framework, making their work easier to maintain.

The application framework increases the productivity of application programmers and reduces the maintenance burden.

TABLE 10.2. *(continued)*

Class	Description
SearchWindow	This abstract class is inherited from to build specific search screens for your application. For example, your application may need a customer search screen that enables users to input search criteria such as the customer's name, address, phone number, or customer number.
UpdateWindow	This abstract class is inherited from to build specific editing/update screens for your application. For example, your application may need an editing screen to update and/or display customer information.
Window	The abstract class extends the behavior of the window class that comes with your development environment. It encapsulates the specific behavior to open and close windows within your application environment, which would include the necessary security/access control required by your organization.

DEFINITIONS

abstract class A class from which objects are not instantiated, but that is instead used to implement common behavior inherited by other classes.

framework A reusable, almost-complete application that can be extended to produce custom applications.

singleton A class that will have at most one instance.

10.3.3 An Error-Handling Component

Mistakes happen: no matter how good a system is, something always goes wrong. Your persistence mechanism goes down, portions of the network fail, code defects make it through testing, and users input the wrong information. In this section I present a component for effectively handling error in an object-oriented (OO) application.

Figure 10.8 presents the design of an error handling component, comprised of the classes ErrorMessageFactory and ErrorMessageDisplay, and the classes needed to support it. The classes are described in Table 10.3. The purpose of ErrorMessageFactory is to give application programmers the ability to create and post error messages automatically. ErrorMessageDisplay is a user interface class that displays error messages to users when they occur, informing them of what has happened.

Our design distinguishes between three types of error: run-time errors such as the network being unavailable, coding errors that made it through testing, and simple user errors such as improper input. It is important to distinguish error types because you deal with different types of errors in different ways. For example, run-time errors should be automatically brought to the attention of support people, perhaps by sending a message across the network to display information about the error on their screen. User errors, on the other hand, do not need to be brought to the attention of support people, although they might be recorded to enable you to detect problems with your user interface design (many user errors on a single screen indicate that the screen's design needs to be reworked). Code errors should be recorded (assuming that it is possible to automatically detect and recover from these kinds of errors while your application is running) so your application programmers can fix the error in a future maintenance release.

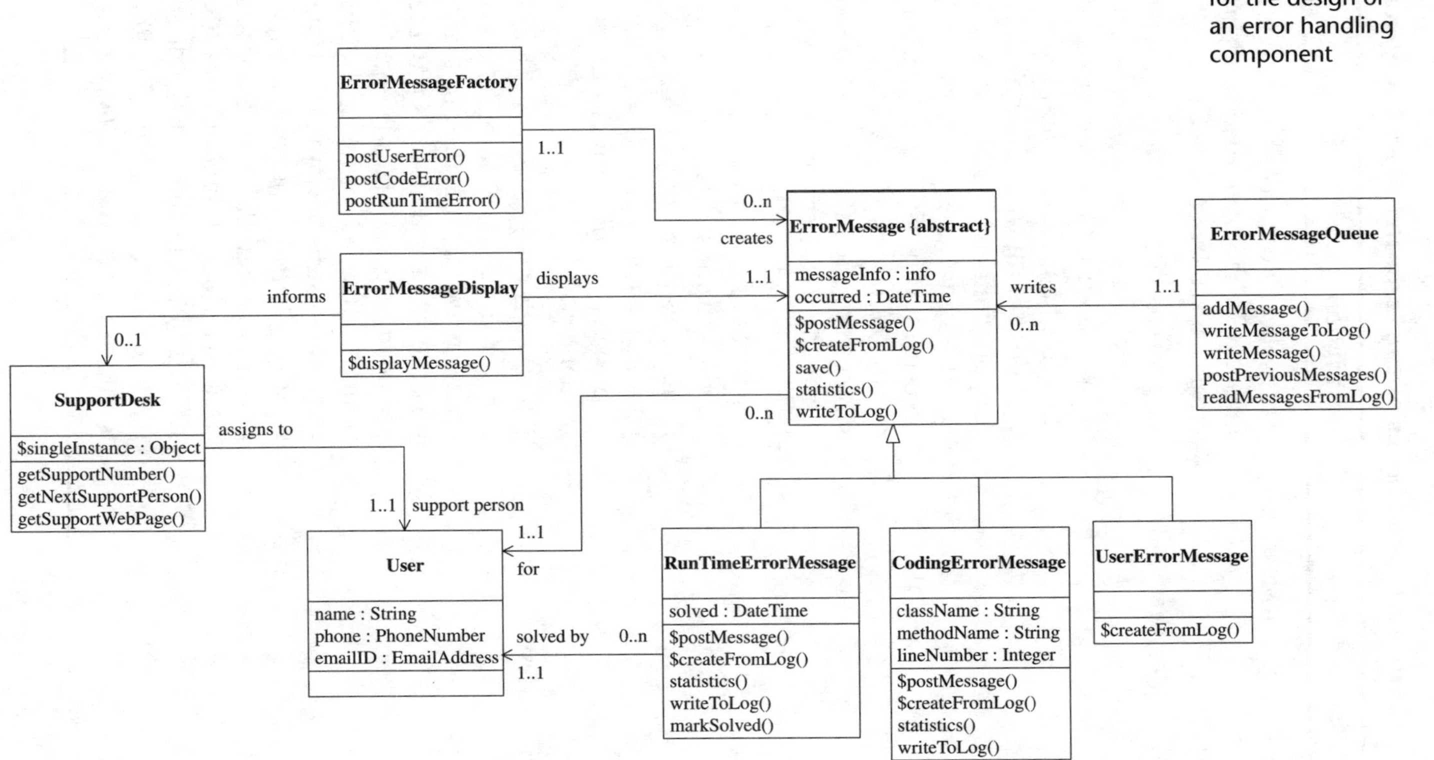

Figure 10.8.
A class diagram for the design of an error handling component

TABLE 10.3. The Classes of the Error Handling Component

Class	Description
CodingErrorMessage	This subclass of ErrorMessage encapsulates the behavior needed to record errors caused by code defects.
ErrorMessage	An abstract class which encapsulates the basic behavior of an error message. It knows when the error occurred, who the error happened to, and the information describing what the error was. To support the behavior of ErrorMessageQueue, all error message objects must be able to write themselves out to a temporary log and create themselves from the information contained in the log so that they may be written to permanent storage at a later time. Instances of ErrorMessage also know how to output statistics about themselves for reporting purposes. If you have a persistence layer, then ErrorMessage would inherit from PersistentObject.
ErrorMessageFactory	This class is the entire error-handling component, as far as application developers are concerned: they interact with no other classes. This class provides the public interface, or facade, for the component. This class provides the ability to handle user, code, and run-time error messages. This is a perfect example of both the Design Pattern design pattern (Gamma, Helm, Johnson, and Vlissides, 1995) and the Design Pattern design pattern (Buschmann, Meunier, Rohnert, Sommerlad, and Stal, 1996).

(continued)

TABLE 10.3. *(continued)*

Class	Description
ErrorMessageQueue	This class has the responsibility of ensuring that error messages are saved to permanent storage. Because the network or persistence mechanism may not be available (that's why there is an error), the error message may need to be written to a temporary log file until the connection to the persistence mechanism has been reestablished.
RunTimeErrorMessage	This subclass of ErrorMessage encapsulates the behavior needed to record errors caused by run-time problems, such as a lost network connection or errors in your persistence mechanism.
User	This class represents the person currently operating the application (the assumption is that the users have to log on and identify themselves), so that the person who experienced/fixed the error may be identified.
UserErrorMessage	This subclass of ErrorMessage encapsulates the behavior needed to record errors caused by mistakes made by users, such as improperly input information into an edit screen.

When an error occurs the application detects it, and ErrorMessageFactory is used to create, display, and record the error message. ErrorMessageFactory's postUserError(), postRunTimeError(), and postCodeError() methods perform the appropriate behavior for their corresponding error message types. The main idea is that application programmers do not need to know anything about the error-handling process supported by your organization. To provide superior service to your user community, ErrorMessageDisplay interacts with the SupportDesk class to obtain basic information about how to help correct the problem. Instead of displaying a message like "The database is not currently available." it will display something like "The database is not currently available. The problem has been assigned to support engineer Montgomery Scott at x1701." This latter message is much more comforting to your users because they know that the support desk has been informed of their problem and that someone is responsible for fixing it.

It is easy to provide superior customer service with this component.

The class ErrorMessageQueue is responsible for recording a permanent record of an error message. Assuming that the persistence mechanism where error messages are stored exists on a different machine than the user's, your ability to record the error message relies on both the network and the database being accessible to your application. The problem is that the majority of run-time errors are caused by lost connections to the network and/or persistence mechanism. The implication is that ErrorMessageQueue needs to be able to detect this problem and save the message to temporary storage until a connection is reestablished, at which point it would retrieve all of the error messages in the log and save them to permanent storage. Note that ErrorMessage simply has to inherit from PersistentObject to make it persistent.

DEFINITION

facade class A class that provides the interface for a component or domain component. A facade class is composed of a collection of public methods that route messages to the other classes within a component. A component may have multiple facade classes to provide different versions of its interface.

The way that you handle errors can often make or break your application; therefore, it makes sense to create a common component to do so. In this section I have described the design for such a component, one generalized from an error handling facility that I developed specifically for a single application.

10.4 Solution: Project Tasks

In this section I will discuss project task issues pertinent to the Generalize stage.

10.4.1 Managing the Generalize Stage

The Generalize stage needs to be scheduled and planned for; otherwise, it will be pushed aside when your project slips its schedule. A common problem within most organizations is that they do not recognize the fact that it takes time, effort, and money to make an

WAR STORY

Developing Reusable Items Takes Longer

In every project that I have ever worked on where reusable items were developed, my experience was the same: developing reusable items takes between two and three times longer than developing specific, non-reusable items. To make something reusable you need to do extra design work, extra documentation, and extra quality assurance.

When I originally developed the application framework described earlier in this chapter, I simply put it in my company's reuse repository as it was. Although a few people looked at it, nobody bothered to reuse it. The problem was that it was too much effort for them to understand it; I had only described it with a few paragraphs, because I required them to study the source code. Concerned that others weren't taking advantage of my work, I invested the time to document the design and improve the code; then I had it reviewed by several other developers that I worked with; and finally provided an example application that used the framework. After I resubmitted it to the reuse repository, other developers looked at it and started using it on their projects. As you would expect, the framework evolved over time as new features were added by other project teams.

item reusable. If you do not plan the required resources needed to generalize an item, it will never happen. Furthermore, you also need experienced reuse engineers whose sole purpose is the identification, development, and support of reusable items.

Your projects will experience short-term pain as you invest in your future by generalizing items for reuse.

A key issue during the Generalize stage is to gain management support for reuse. Senior management always wants increased reusability on their projects; they just do not want to pay for it. Part of gaining support for reuse is that senior management needs to understand that this stage will slow down the development of a specific project, but that having reusable components will speed up overall development within your organization.

10.4.2 Training and Education Issues

The skillset of a reuse engineer is typically very broad: they require hard-core technical skills such as object-oriented design and qual-

TIP

Only a Select Few Can Be Reuse Engineers

It is important to understand that not every developer can become a reuse engineer. Myers (1997) points out that not every developer conceptualizes reuse well, and that such skill is different from simply writing code. My experience is that the developers best suited to become reuse engineers are developers with several years of experience on a wide range of applications who have been reuse consumers on those projects. A reuse consumer is a developer who reuses existing items in their work: a developer who actively strives to avoid reinventing the wheel on every project. A wide range of development experience is required by reuse engineers so they will understand what is needed by application developers, as is experience as a reuse consumer so that they understand what makes an item reusable.

ity assurance, documentation skills, and people-oriented skills so they can interact effectively with other developers to both acquire new reusable items and to support the use of existing items. The result is that the training and education plan for reuse engineers must include a wide variety of courses and reading materials.

10.4.3 Quality Assurance

The quality assurance efforts for reusable items are exactly the same for items that are application-specific, the only difference being that they are applied more stringently. Peer reviews, a technique of the Test in the Small stage (Chapter 11), should be performed for all reusable items. This helps to assure that the items have been built properly and also advertises the fact, at least to the review participants, that the reusable item exists and is ready to be reused by other developers.

10.4.4 Potential Risks While Generalizing Your Work

Several risks are inherent to the Generalize stage:

1. **Leaving generalization to future projects.** One approach to generalization is to maintain a repository of candidate components that are generalized on future projects only when they are needed (Due and Henderson-Sellers, 1995). Although this approach sounds like it might be more produc-

tive because you wait to make something reusable "just in time," in practice this approach leads to very low levels of reuse. While developers are usually willing to reuse the work of others, they are often unwilling to make someone else's work reusable. The general principle is that if something is easy to reuse—if it has already been generalized—then it will be reused. If something is difficult to reuse—if it has not yet been generalized—then it will not be reused.

2. **Lack of management support.** As mentioned previously, senior management must be willing to invest the resources to generalize items for future reuse—short-term pain for long-term gain.
3. **Thinking that the Generalize stage is the sole reuse task.** There is far more to reuse than making something reusable. The Generalize stage is a perfect example of opportunistic reuse, but as we saw in the Model stage (Chapter 8), architectural and enterprise modeling support systematic reuse. Furthermore, you need to put together a reuse management program (Ambler, 1998b), which includes both the nurturing and support for reuse within your organization.

10.4.5 Metrics

You may choose to gather several metrics specific to the Generalize stage (metrics applicable to your reuse effort will be covered later in the book). These metrics are:

1. **Number of candidate items.** This is a count of the number of items submitted for consideration for generalization. A low count often indicates a lack of support for your reuse program, whereas a high count often indicates that project teams are not being sufficiently selective in what they are submitting.
2. **Percentage of items generalized.** This measurement is calculated by taking the number of candidate items generalized divided by the number of candidate items submitted to be generalized. A low percentage indicates that project teams are having difficulty determining what is potentially reusable.
3. **Effort required to generalize an item.** This is a measurement of the work effort to generalize an item for reuse. When compared with the work effort to originally develop the item, it

provides an indication of how many times that the item must be reused to recoup your investment. For example, if it takes an additional 250 work hours to generalize an item that originally took to 100 hours to develop, then the item must be reused at least three times (250/100 rounded up to the nearest integer) for your investment to pay for itself.

10.5 Resulting Context: Exit Conditions for Generalizing Your Work

The following conditions must be met before the Generalize stage is considered complete:

1. **The generalized item(s) has been submitted to the reuse repository.** The reusable item, its accompanying documentation, its test plan, and one or more examples must be placed in your organization's reuse repository so that other developers have access to it.
2. **An announcement has been made.** The appropriate developers who will potentially reuse the item(s) need to be informed, perhaps via email or by word of mouth, that the item(s) has been placed in the reuse repository. Yes, we saw in the Program stage (Chapter 9) that the first thing that developers should do is look in the reuse repository for reusable items; but it doesn't hurt to point out the existence of a new item.

10.6 Secrets of Success

I would like to share with you a few tips and techniques for making your generalization efforts successful:

1. **Recognize that you may still need to rework an item.** Although your generalization efforts will result in a product that is more likely to be reused, very often you will find that you will need to rework an item to make it truly fit the needs of another project. I aim to get ninety percent of the way toward a reusable item coming out of the Generalize stage, ninety-five percent the first time that the item is reused and subsequently reworked, and ninety-nine percent of the way

the next time the item is reused.

2. **Recognize that some items will never be reused.** It is difficult to predict the needs of future projects, and sometimes you will generalize an item that is never reused. When this happens, try to determine why nobody reused it so that you can learn from your mistakes.
3. **Organizational support for reuse is critical.** For the Generalize stage to be successful, your organization needs to take a long-term perspective with respect to software development. In an organization with a short-term focus, when an item works then it is satisfactory; in an organization with a long-term perspective, when an item works it may then be reworked so that other projects may use it.
4. **You need experienced developers.** It is incredibly difficult to be successful with this stage if you do not have experienced developers in the role of reuse engineer. Many organizations make the mistake of trying to produce reusable items before they have any experience reusing off-the-shelf items. Gain experience reusing things before you try to generalize items for reuse.
5. **Provide documentation and examples.** If it isn't easy to reuse something, then it will not be reused. Items in your reuse repository must be well documented and have one or more real-world examples of how to use them.
6. **Plan to generalize your work.** You need to allocate the time and resources necessary to make your work reusable; otherwise, project pressures will motivate you to put that work aside until you have the time to do it.

10.7 Process Checklist

The following process checklist can be used to verify that you have completed the Generalize stage.

GENERALIZE STAGE PROCESS CHECKLIST

Fulfillment of Entrance Conditions:

✔ Project deliverable that are potentially generalizable exist.

✔ Experienced reuse engineers are available.

- ✔ Organizational support for reuse exists.
- ✔ Team members have been given the appropriate training for their part in this stage.

Processes Performed:

- ✔ Items that are potentially reusable have been identified.
- ✔ Generalization session(s) were held.
- ✔ The potentially reusable items were refactored.
- ✔ The items were documented appropriately.
- ✔ Examples of how to reuse the items were documented/developed.
- ✔ The items were released into your reuse repository and made accessible to all developers.
- ✔ Artifacts that are potentially reusable by your project team during this stage have been identified and used where appropriate.
- ✔ Your risk assessment document has been updated where appropriate.
- ✔ Decisions made, and decisions forgone, have been documented in your group memory.
- ✔ Metrics have been collected.

Fulfillment of Exit Conditions:

- ✔ Generalized items have been submitted to the reuse repository.
- ✔ Developers have been made aware of new items.

10.8 What You Have Learned in This Chapter

Reuse doesn't happen automatically.

In this chapter I described the Generalize stage of the Construct phase, a stage that supports opportunistic reuse by generalizing existing project deliverables so that they may be reused by future project teams. This is an after-the-fact, bottom-up approach to reuse that identifies potentially reusable items that were not called out by your architectural and enterprise modeling efforts. You saw that to make an item reusable, you need to evaluate it, determine how it needs to be improved, improve it, document it, and then finally provide one or more examples of it being reused so that other developers understand how to take advantage of it.

10.9 References and Recommended Reading

Ambler, S. W. 1998a. *Building Object Applications That Work: Your Step-by-Step Handbook for Developing Robust Systems with Object Technology*. New York: SIGS Books/Cambridge University Press.

Ambler, S. W. 1998b. *More Process Patterns: Delivering Large-Scale Systems Using Object Technology*. New York: SIGS Books/Cambridge University Press.

Bassett, P. G. 1997. *Framing Software Reuse: Lessons From the Real World*. Upper Saddle River, New Jersey: Prentice-Hall, Inc.

Buschmann, F., Meunier, R., Rohnert, H., Sommerlad, P., and Stal, M. 1996. *A Systems of Patterns: Pattern-Oriented Software Architecture*. New York: John Wiley and Sons Ltd.

Constantine, L. L. 1995. *Constantine on Peopleware*. Englewood Cliffs, New Jersey: Yourdon Press.

Due, R. T. and Henderson-Sellers, B. 1995. The Changing Paradigm for Object Project Management. *Object Magazine* 5(July-August), 54–60,78.

Gamma, E., Helm, R., Johnson, R., and Vlissides, J. 1995. *Design Patterns: Elements of Reusable Object-Oriented Software*. Reading, Massachusetts: Addison-Wesley Publishing Company, Inc..

Jacobson, I., Griss, M., and Jonsson, P. 1997. *Software Reuse: Architecture, Process, and Organization for Business Success*. New York: ACM Press.

McClure, C. 1997. *Software Reuse Techniques: Adding Reuse to the Systems Development Process*. Upper Saddle River, New Jersey: Prentice-Hall, Inc.

Meyer, B. 1995. *Object Success—A Manager's Guide To Object Orientation, Its Impact On The Corporation And Its Use For Engineering The Software Process*. Englewood Cliffs, New Jersey: Prentice Hall Inc.

Myers, W. 1997. Software Reuse: Ostriches Beware. *Computer* 30(April), 119–120.

Reifer, D. J. 1997. *Practical Software Reuse: Strategies for Introducing Reuse Concepts in Your Organization*. New York: John Wiley and Sons, Inc.

Chapter 11

The Test in the Small Stage

THE Test in the Small stage focuses on the verification, validation, and testing of documents, models, and source code produced during the Construct phase. In many ways it is quality assurance techniques such as peer reviews and inspections combined with unit testing techniques for validating source code. Related to Testing in the Small, performed during construction, is the Test in the Large stage (Ambler, 1998b) which is performed during the Delivery Phase after construction is complete. The goal of testing in the small is to ensure that your application is ready to be delivered, whereas the goal of testing in the large is to prove that your application is ready to be deployed.

Testing in the small is conceptually the combination of quality assurance techniques and unit testing techniques.

Tasks performed during this stage, such as reviews and code tests, often focus on a subset of the overall application. For example, a technical walkthrough, also called a peer review, may focus on the design of a single class, or a code review may concentrate on the source code for several classes that work together. The point to be made is that the techniques of testing in the small will concentrate on a portion of your application, not on the entire application at once. The Test in the Large stage, on the other hand, focuses on testing an object-oriented application as a whole. Common forces applicable to this stage include a lack of knowledge by developers with respect to object-oriented testing techniques, a

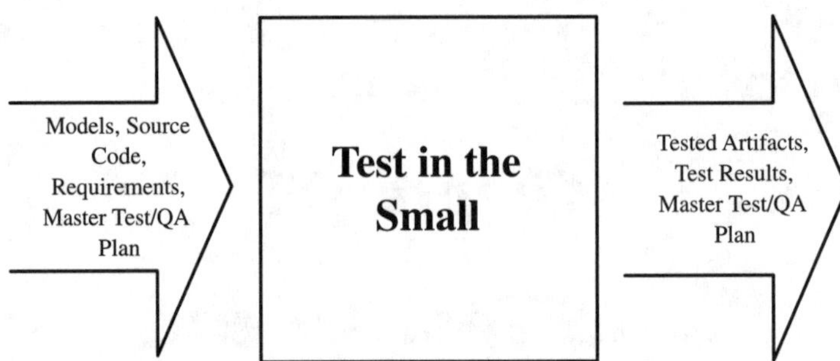

Figure 11.1. The Test in the Small stage

lack of understanding that more (not less) testing is required for OO software, and mere lip service instead of concrete support paid by senior management to testing and quality assurance.

As Figure 11.1 shows, the main inputs into the Test in the Small stage are the key deliverables of the Construct phase—models, source code, and requirements—as well as the initial version of the test plan, developed during the Define Initial Management Documents stage (Chapter 4). The main deliverables are tested and validated development artifacts (the models, etc.), the results of testing, and an updated version of the test plan. The test results and plan are important inputs into the Test in the Large stage (Ambler, 1998b).

The techniques of the Test in the Small Stage are a subset of those of the Full Life Cycle Object-Oriented Testing (FLOOT) techniques depicted in Figure 11.2, composed of the techniques for analysis testing, design testing, and code testing. This makes a lot of sense: the purpose of this stage is to verify and validate (V&V) the deliverables of the Construct phase as they evolve; therefore, the Test in the Small stage concentrates on model and code testing.

Why should we test during the Construct phase? Hunt (1996) describes the reasons for testing in the small: first, testing in the small permits developers to test portions of an application before the other parts are available, working, and integrated. This allows developers to find and fix defects, also referred to as bugs or faults, in their work as early as possible. Second, testing in the small limits the possible areas in which to search for defects because you are testing/validating only a portion of the application, perhaps a single class diagram or the source code for a subset of the classes within the application. Third, testing in the small enables the validation of internal conditions that are not easily reached by

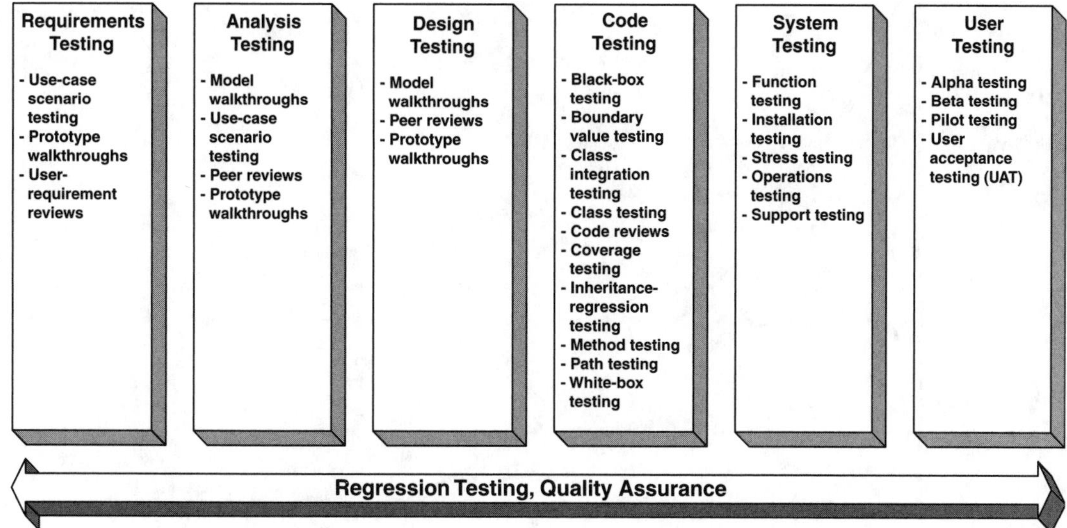

Figure 11.2. The Techniques of Full Life Cycle Object-Oriented Testing (FLOOT)

inputs to the complete, integrated system. Fourth, testing in the small avoids lengthy compile-build-debug cycles when fixing knotty problems in a subsystem because of its focus on portions of the overall application. Fifth, testing in the small aids the incorporation of simple regression tests for previously found defects to ensure that fixed defects stay fixed.

More important, testing in the small enables the identification and eradication of defects early in the development of software, a goal documented in DeLano and Rising's (1998) Get Involved Early organizational pattern. There are two reasons why we want to find and fix defects as early as possible: we make most of our mistakes early in the life of a project; and the cost of fixing defects increases exponentially the later they are found. Technical people are very good at technical things such as design and coding; that is why they are technical people. Unfortunately, technical people are often not as good at non-technical tasks such as gathering requirements and performing analysis—probably another reason why they are technical people. The end result, as shown in Figure 11.3, is that developers have a tendency to make more errors during requirements definition and analysis than during design and coding.

Most defects are introduced early in the development of an application.

The problem, as shown in Figure 11.4, is that the cost of fixing these defects rises the later they are found. This happens because of the nature of software development: work is performed based on

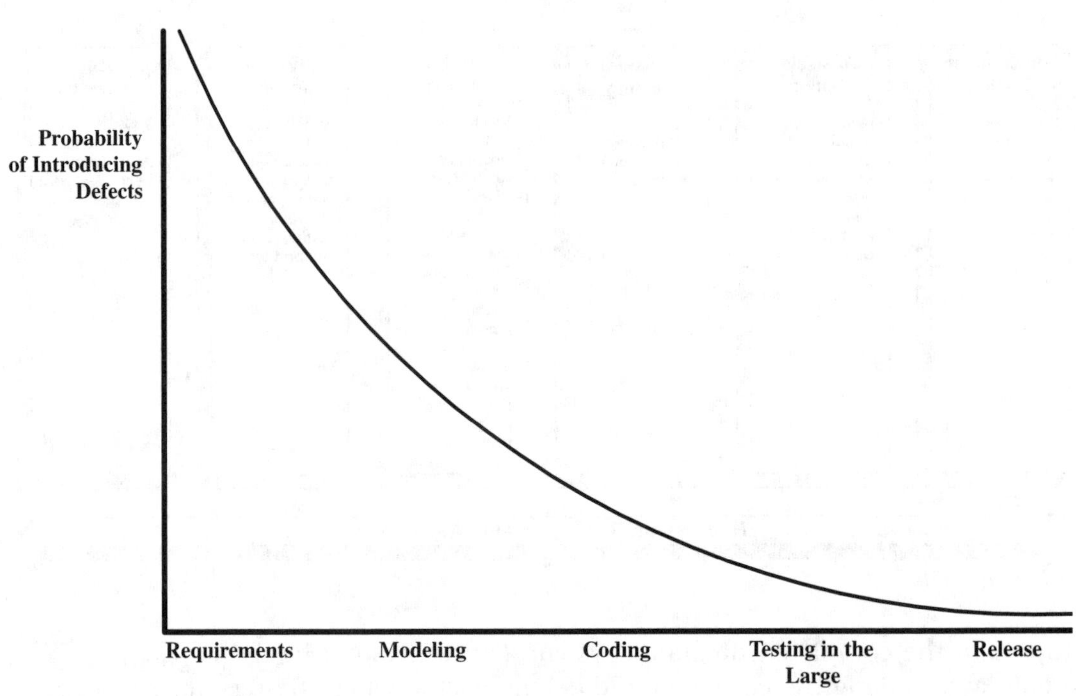

Figure 11.3. The decreasing probability of introducing defects

work performed previously. For example, modeling is performed based on the information gathered during the definition of requirements. Programming is done based on the models that were developed, and testing is performed on the written source code. If a requirement was misunderstood, all modeling decisions based on that requirement are potentially invalid, all code written based on the models is also in question, and the testing efforts are now verify-

The cost of fixing defects rises exponentially the later they are found during the development of an application.

DEFINITIONS

analysis error An error that occurs when a user requirement is missed or misunderstood.

defect Anything that detracts from your application's ability to meet your user's needs completely and effectively. Also known as a bug, fault, or feature.

organizational pattern A pattern that describes a common management technique or a structure appropriate to a software organization.

technical review A testing technique in which the design of your application is examined critically by a group of your peers. A review will typically focus on accuracy, quality, usability, and completeness. This process is often referred to as a walkthrough or a peer review.

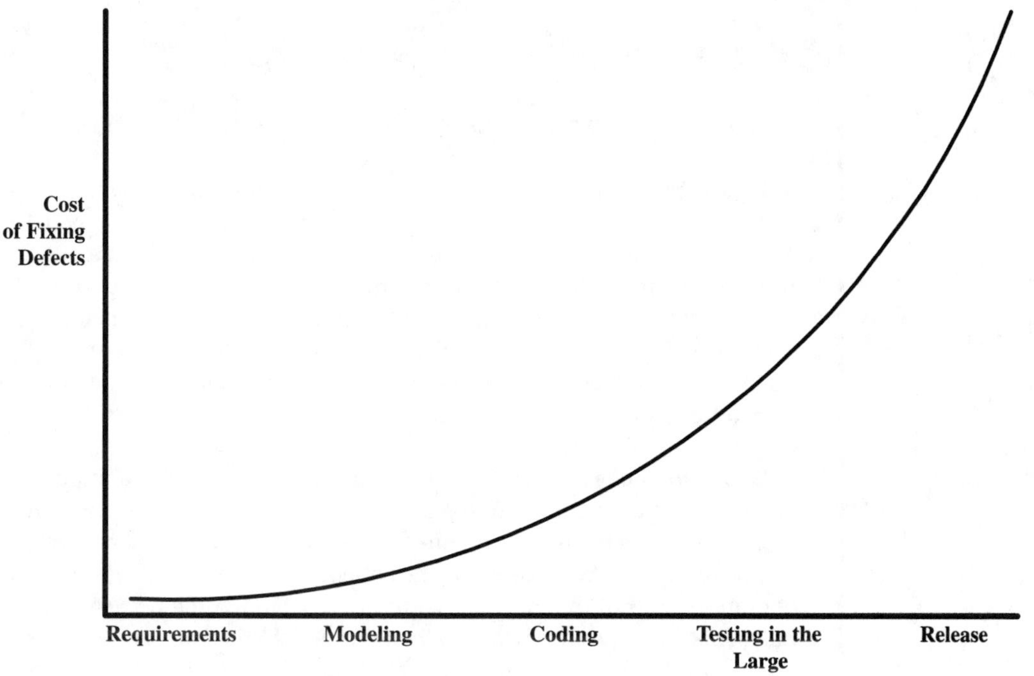

Figure 11.4. The rising costs of finding and fixing defects

ing the application against the wrong conditions. If errors are detected late in development, during testing in the large or after the application has been released, they are likely to be very expensive to fix. If they are detected during requirements definition, where they are likely to be made, then they are likely to be much less expensive to fix (you only have to update your requirements

In this chapter we will discuss a collection of testing and quality assurance techniques that are used early during the development of an application so they can be fixed as early and inexpensively as possible.

11.1 Initial Context: Entry Conditions for Testing in the Small

Several important entry conditions should be met before the Test in the Small stage begins:

1. **There are development artifacts to be tested.** Testing in the small focuses on the validation and testing of the deliverables of the Construct phase—object-oriented models, source

Scott's Soapbox

Debunking the Myths of Object-Oriented Testing

Developers may have several common misconceptions concerning object-oriented testing. This is in part due to a scarcity of research in OO testing in the early days of object-orientation—people were struggling with concepts, modeling, and programming practices—and in part due to the industry's tendency to focus on the front end of development, on modeling and programming, and not on the back end, on testing. I want to address these misconceptions so that you have an accurate understanding of object-oriented testing.

1. **With OO you do less testing.** This is the most dangerous misconception that a developer can have, a misconception that is often the result of an incomplete understanding of inheritance. Novice OO developers will often assume that because a class has already been tested, they can create subclasses that inherit from it, but not have to test the new subclass fully. This assumption is wrong. When a class inherits from another it is adding new behaviors, some of which may be completely new and some of which may be extensions of existing behaviors. A subclass will implement new, and often more complex, business rules than its superclass. These business rules may extend, or conflict with, the rules implemented in the existing classes. The result is that you need to rerun the appropriate test cases originally developed for the superclass on the new subclass to ensure that it still works, in addition to test cases associated with the new behaviors. In other words, you are doing more testing, not less. When you stop and think about it, this makes sense: one of the reasons why you move to OO in the first place is because you want to develop applications that are more complex than those you could have

DEFINITION

master test/quality assurance (QA) plan A document that describes your testing and quality assurance policies and procedures, as well as the detailed test plans for each portion of your application.

code, and supporting documents. These artifacts must exist, although may not yet be complete, and be available to the testing community for testing.

2. **A master test/quality assurance plan exists.** Your master test/QA plan, started during the Initiate phase, will include the procedures and guidelines to be followed during testing. These procedures and guidelines will encompass standard checklists of things to look for during

developed following a structured/procedural approach. Therefore, does it not make more sense that you would need to do more testing for a more complex application?

2. **Structured testing techniques can be used for OO testing.** The good news is that this misconception is in fact partly correct; the bad news is that this misconception is only partly correct. As we'll see in this chapter, many code testing techniques, such as boundary-value testing, are still applicable for testing OO code. In *More Process Patterns* (Ambler, 1998b) we'll see that many integration testing techniques, such as user acceptance testing, are applicable for testing in the large. However, in this chapter we'll see that some traditional testing techniques, such as coverage testing, are no longer as important in the OO world. Polymorphism, the ability of objects to change type, negates the value of coverage testing because your code might work today for a given object, but might fail tomorrow after the object changes type. Also, structured testing techniques do not take into consideration the fact that objects encapsulate both data and behavior; the development paradigm has changed, does it not make sense that the testing paradigm should also change?

3. **Testing the user interface is sufficient.** Because tool vendors have concentrated on building tools for testing the user interface of an application and spent less effort on other aspects of testing, it is easy for developers with little testing experience to assume that testing the user interface is sufficient. Yes, user interface testing is important, but there's more to an application than screens and reports. You have to test all aspects of your application, the ones that are visible in the user interface and the ones that are hidden from view.

technical walkthroughs and code reviews, as well as descriptions of the testing techniques described in this chapter that are to be employed by your project team.

3. **Requirements are documented.** To ensure that the right thing is being built, you need a definition of what needs to be built; therefore, the requirements for the application must be made available to the testers.

11.2 Solution: Testing in the Small

As you can see in Figure 11.5 the process pattern for testing in the small is quite complex. The important thing to understand is that these tasks occur in parallel, as shown in Figure 11.6, with the modeling and programming efforts described in chapters 8 and 9 respectively. Furthermore, because modeling and coding are performed iteratively, so is testing in the small.

The tasks of testing in the small can be organized into several broad categories:

- Developing/updating the test plan
- Regression testing
- Validating your modeling efforts
- Validating your coding efforts
- User-interface testing
- Recording defects

11.2.1 Developing/Updating the Master Test/QA Plan

In Figure 11.5 we see that the initial version of the master test/QA plan, developed during the Define Initial Management Documents stage (Chapter 4), must be updated to reflect the improved understanding of the application gained during construction. Assuming that a test plan has been started based on the initial requirements, you will need to add new test cases and improved review checklists before testing may begin. If a test plan was not started during the Initiate phase, then you will have to start one now; you cannot test effectively without a test plan to guide your efforts. Fundamentally, you first plan the testing that you will do, then you perform the tests and record the results.

First you plan to test, then you test.

The project test plan should describe the overall strategy that the project team will follow to ensure that the project deliverables are valid (McGregor, 1997). With respect to testing in the small, this means the models, documents, and source code produced during construction. The test plan should indicate what will be tested, who will do the testing, and when the testing will be performed. The point to be made is that before testing can begin, you must understand what you are going to test and how you will test it.

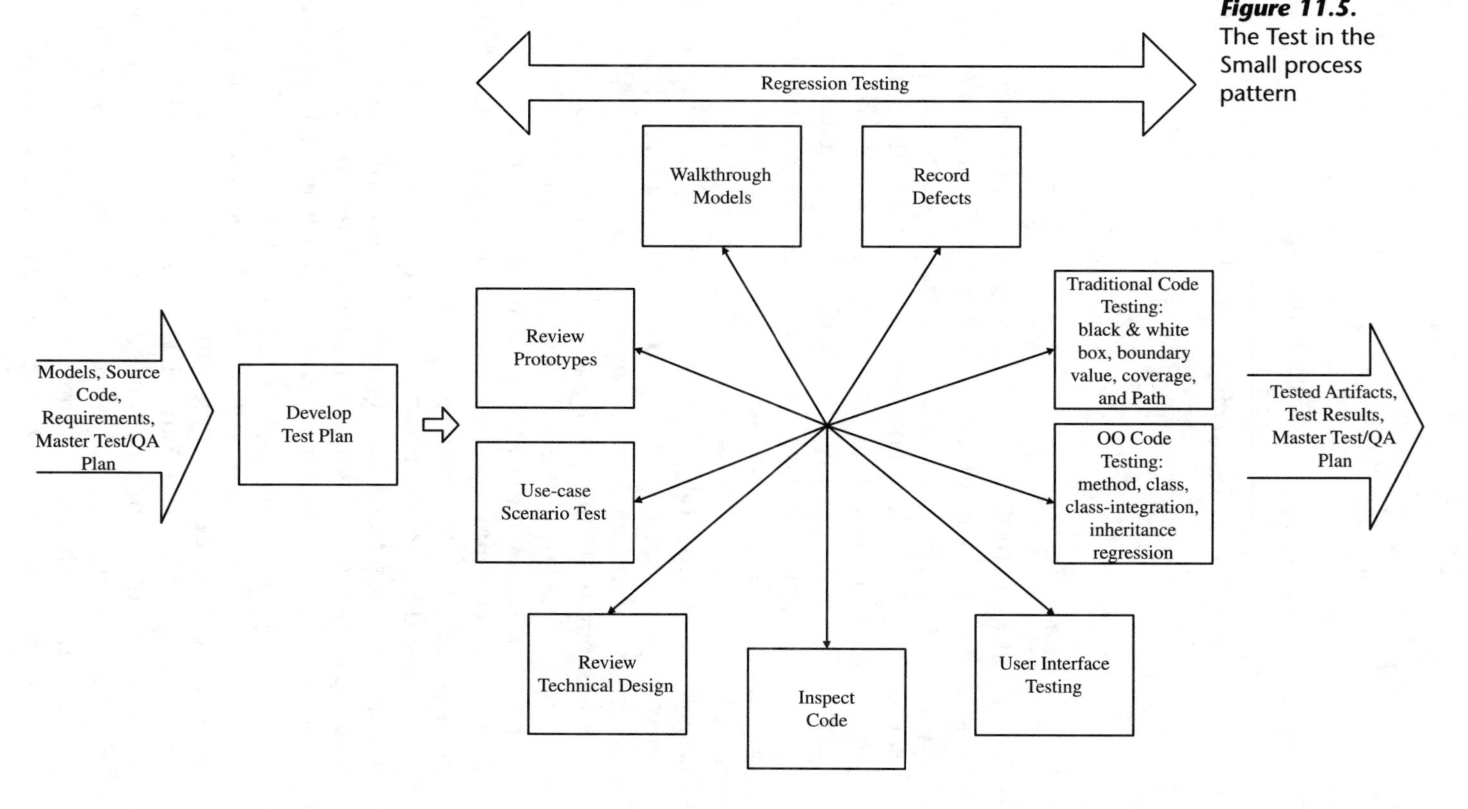

Figure 11.5. The Test in the Small process pattern

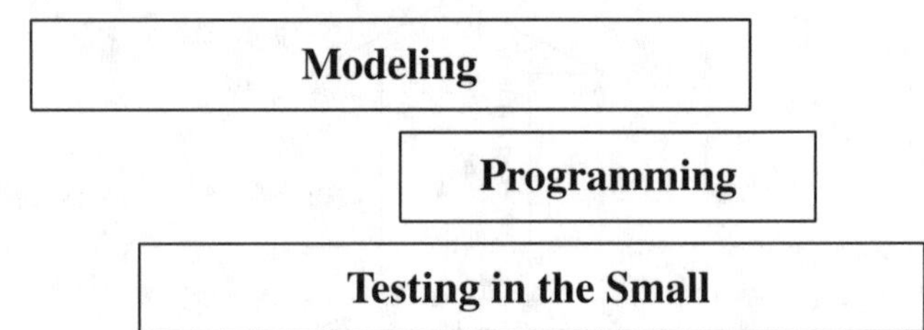

Figure 11.6. Testing in the small occurs in parallel with modeling and programming

11.2.2 Regression Testing

Regression testing is the act of ensuring that changes to an application have not adversely affected existing functionality. We've all had experiences where we made a small change to a program; we then successfully tested the change that we made, thinking that everything was fine; and then we put the program into production, only to see it fail because our small change affected another part of the program that we had completely forgotten about. Regression testing is all about avoiding problems like this.

The goal of regression testing is to ensure that existing functionality still works after changes have been made.

Users expect that all of the functionality they had in a previous version will either still exist or will be enhanced by new releases.

Regression testing is the very first thing that you should be thinking about when you begin testing your application. How angry would you get if you took your car into a garage to have a new stereo system installed just to discover afterward that the new stereo works but that the headlights do not? Pretty angry. How angry do you think your users would get when a new release of an application no longer allows them to fax information to other people because the new e-mail feature that you just added has affected it somehow? Pretty angry.

Changes in the design may result in changes to your old testing procedures.

How do you do regression testing? The quick answer is to run all of your previous test cases against the new version of your application. Although this sounds like a good idea, it often proves not to be realistic. First, you may have changed part of, or even all of, the design of your application. This will mean that you need to modify some of the previous test cases. Second, if the changes you have made truly affect only a component of the system, then potentially you only need to run the test cases that affect this single component. Although this approach is a little risky because your changes may have had a greater impact than you suspect, it does help to reduce both the time and cost of regression testing.

Regression testing is vitally important because developers tend

DEFINITION

regression testing The act of ensuring that previously tested behaviors still work as expected after changes have been made to an application.

to test only the new functionality that they added to a system, assuming that the old functionality that they didn't touch still works. You didn't touch the piece of code so you do not have to test it, right? Absolutely wrong. You have to put as much effort into testing the code that you didn't update to ensure that you still support all of your application's previous functionality. You probably will not like it, but that is the way it is.

Many developers assume that code they didn't change still works. Don't fall into this trap.

It is important to recognize that incremental development (remember, OO development is incremental in the small), makes regression testing critical. Whenever you release an application, you have to ensure that its previous functionality still works, and because you release applications more often when taking the incremental approach, that means that regression testing becomes that much more important.

Incremental development dramatically increases the importance of regression testing.

11.2.3 Validating Your Models

Long before you test your source code, you can validate that your models are accurate and that they reflect the needs of your user community. There are several testing and quality assurance techniques for validating models:

- Model reviews/walkthroughs
- Prototype reviews
- Use-case scenario testing

11.2.3.1 Model Reviews/Walkthroughs

A model review, also called a model walkthrough or model peer review, is a testing technique in which your modeling efforts are examined critically by a group of your peers. The basic idea is that a group of qualified people, both technical staff and subject matter experts, get together in a room and evaluate a model that

DEFINITIONS

model review A technical review in which a model is inspected.

peer review A style of technical review in which a project deliverable, or portion thereof, is inspected by a small group of people with expertise in the product being reviewed.

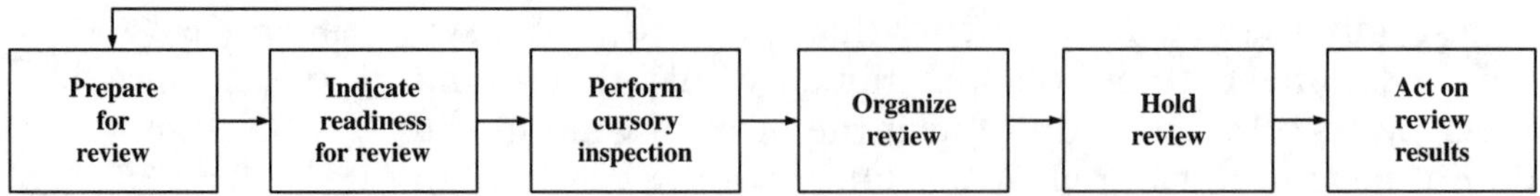

Figure 11.7. The Technical Review process pattern

Model reviews reveal defects early during development when they are reasonably inexpensive to fix.

describes all or part of the application that you are currently developing. The purpose of this evaluation is to determine whether the model not only fulfills the demands of the user community, but is also of sufficient quality to be easy to develop, maintain, and enhance. When model reviews are performed properly, they can have a big payoff because they often identify defects early in the project, reducing the cost of fixing them. In fact, Grady (1992) reports that fifty to seventy-five percent of all design errors can be found through technical reviews.

11.2.3.1.1 The Technical Review Process Pattern

Figure 11.7 shows that there are six basic steps to the Technical Review process pattern (model reviews, document reviews, and code inspections are all specific processes that follow the Technical Review process pattern). The steps of a technical review are as follows:

1. **The development team prepares for review.** The item(s) that are to be reviewed are gathered, organized appropriately, and packaged so that they may be presented to the reviewers.
2. **The development team indicates that they are ready for review.** The development team must inform the review manager, often a member of quality assurance, when they are ready to have their work reviewed as well as what they intend to have reviewed.
3. **The review manager performs a cursory review.** The first thing that the review manager must do is determine if the development team has produced work that is ready to be reviewed. The manager will probably discuss the development team's work with the team leader and do a quick rundown of what they have produced. The main goal is to ensure that the work to be reviewed is good enough to warrant getting a review team together.

War Story

Have Real Peers in Peer Reviews

Reviews only work when the people doing the review understand what they are reviewing and have worked with that kind of deliverable before. If you are reviewing Java source code, then you need Java programmers in the review. If you are reviewing a class diagram, then you need experienced OO modelers. If the reviewers are not experienced in what is being reviewed, then their comments will be of little value.

Several years ago I was on a Smalltalk development project and the client wanted to get an outsider's opinion of the quality of our work. I am a firm supporter of independent audits—they are a great way to prove that you are doing a good job—so I was eager to be reviewed. Then I met the reviewer. The person the client brought in, although he had sold himself as an OO development expert, only had experience in C++. After an intensive, several-day review of our work he presented a fairly negative review, something that I hadn't expected. Because of his lack of experience, his concerns focused on several inappropriate issues, such as our "refusal" to use multiple inheritance (Smalltalk is a single-inheritance language), our lack of type checking (Smalltalk is typeless, and we were following the program-by-contract approach, described in chapter 9), and our lack of memory management code (Smalltalk manages memory automatically). Once we removed the comments that weren't applicable to the environment we were working in, we were left only with a few minor, although still good, suggestions to improve our application. The point to be made was that because the reviewer had little experience in what he was reviewing, the review process wasn't very effective.

Not everyone in the review needs to be an expert at creating the deliverable being reviewed, but a couple of people should be. Sometimes people will be involved in a review who are there to be trained—perhaps they are going to be reviewed next week and need to see how a review works, or perhaps they need greater insight into how to produce the deliverable being reviewed. You may also have subject matter experts in the review who may not be conversant with the OO paradigm, but they are experts at the domain and should be able to recognize and comment on what has been developed.

4. **The review manager plans and organizes the review.** The review manager must schedule a review room and any equipment needed for the review, invite the proper people, and distribute any materials ahead of time that are needed for the review. The potential contents of a review package are discussed in the next section.
5. **The review takes place.** Technical reviews can take anywhere from several hours to several days, depending on the size of what is being reviewed, although the best reviews are less than two hours so as not to overwhelm the people involved. The entire development team should attend, or at least the people responsible for what is being reviewed, to answer questions and to explain/clarify their work. There are typically between three to five reviewers, as well as the review manager, all of whom are responsible for doing the review. It is important that all material is reviewed. It is too easy to look at something quickly and assume that it is right. It is the job of the review facilitator to ensure that everything is looked at, that everything is questioned.
6. **The review results are acted on.** A document is produced during the review describing both the strengths and weaknesses of the work being reviewed. This document should provide both a description of any weakness, why it is a weakness, and provide an indication of what needs to be addressed to fix the weakness. This document will be given to the development team so that they can act on it, and to the review manager to be used in follow-up reviews in which the work is inspected again to verify that the weaknesses were addressed.

11.2.3.1.2 Review Packages

Several items should be included in the package sent to the review participants:

- The deliverable (model, document, code, etc.) to be reviewed.
- A copy of the standards and guidelines that should have been followed by the developers who built the deliverable.
- The rules/procedures to be followed during the review.
- A checklist of features and/or potential problems that the deliverable may have.

TIP

Quality Comes from More than Just Inspections

Technical reviews and/or inspections are one of many ways to achieve quality, but when used alone they result in little or no quality improvement over the long run. In application development quality comes from developers who understand how to build software properly: developers who have learned from experience and/or have gained these skills from training and education. Inspections will help you to identify quality deficits, but they will not help you to build quality into your application from the outset. Reviews and inspections should be only a small portion of your overall quality strategy.

- An agenda indicating the location and time of the review, the objectives of the review, and an indication of everyone's role in the review.
- A description of the rationale for holding the review.

11.2.3.2 Reviewing Prototypes

A prototype walkthrough, covered in detail in Chapter 3, is an analysis-testing process in which your users work through a series of use cases to verify that the design of a prototype meets their needs. The basic idea is that your users pretend that the prototype is the real application and they try to use it to solve real business problems described by the scenarios. Granted, they will need to use their imaginations to fill in the functionality that the application is missing (such as reading and writing objects from/to permanent storage), but for the most part this is a fairly straightforward process. Your users simply sit down at the computer and begin to work through the use cases. It is your job to sit there and observe them, looking for places where the system is difficult to use or is missing features. In many ways

DEFINITIONS

prototype walkthrough A process in which your users work through a collection of use cases using a prototype as if it was the real thing. The main goal is to test whether or not the design of the prototype meets their needs.

user acceptance testing (UAT) A testing technique in which users verify that an application meets their needs.

WAR STORY

Reviewers Should Earn Their Way to the Table

I once worked for a client that had institutionalized peer reviews into their software process, a decision that I supported fully; but they had unfortunately run into troubles with the review process. Although they sent review packages out ahead of time, few people invested the time to work through the package to identify needed improvements. Instead, everyone came to the review unprepared and very little was accomplished. They also had a related problem in that several of the people involved with the review weren't familiar with the products that they were reviewing (frankly, they shouldn't have been in the review to begin with), so to "add value" they spent most of their time harping about trivial spelling and grammar errors, instead of reviewing the content of the deliverable. Something had to be done.

I suggested that people be required to earn their way to the table by providing insightful comments about the product before the review. This forced anyone who wanted to actively participate in the review to work through the review package ahead of time, document issues that they have with it, and submit them to the review facilitator before the review. The result was that the participants were prepared for the review, the facilitator had a better understanding of what the issues were, and the reviews became significantly more productive. People who didn't earn their way to the table were welcome to attend the review as observers but were not allowed to participate.

Prototype walkthroughs quickly verify that your prototype meets the needs of your users.

prototype walkthroughs are a lot like user acceptance tests, a technique of the Test in the Large stage (Ambler, 1998b); the only difference is that you are working with the prototype instead of the real system.

11.2.3.3 Use-Case Scenario Testing

Use-case scenario testing (Ambler, 1995; Ambler, 1998a), covered in detail in Chapter 3, is a testing process in which users are actively involved with ensuring that user requirements are accurate. The basic idea is that a group of subject matter experts (SMEs), with the aid of a facilitator, step through a series of defined use cases to verify that the CRC model or Class Diagram

TIP

Have a Review Checklist for Each Type of Deliverable

A generic review checklist should be maintained for each kind of deliverable. These generic checklists will be used as the basis against which a deliverable will be evaluated. For example, some of the items in a review checklist for a class diagram may be:

- Are the class names singular?
- Are the associations between classes labeled accurately?
- Do classes perform a single, cohesive set of behaviors?
- Are the classes loosely coupled?
- Do user interface classes perform business/domain related behavior?
- Is a class potentially reusable? If so, what needs to be improved to make it so?

As you gain greater experience developing large-scale object-oriented applications, and gain experience reviewing object-oriented deliverables, you will want to modify your checklists to reflect this experience. Sometimes you will discover new problems not yet covered by your existing checklists; therefore you will want to add new points. Sometimes you'll discover that some items on your checklists do not result in the discovery of problems; therefore, you will want to remove these items from your lists.

that they created accurately reflects the requirements defined by the use cases. In Figure 11.8 you see a process pattern, depicted as a traditional flow chart, representing the steps that a facilitator leads a group through to perform use-case scenario testing. The SMEs, typically the people who worked on the CRC model, work through each scenario one at a time and update the model(s) where appropriate. The advantage is that once use-case scenario

DEFINITIONS

flow chart A diagram depicting the logic flow of a single process.

subject matter expert (SME) A person who is responsible for providing pertinent information about the problem and/or technical domain, either from personal knowledge or from research. This is a key role during the Define and Validate Initial Requirements stage and the Model stage.

use-case scenario testing A testing process in which users work through use cases with the aid of a facilitator to verify that the user requirements are accurate.

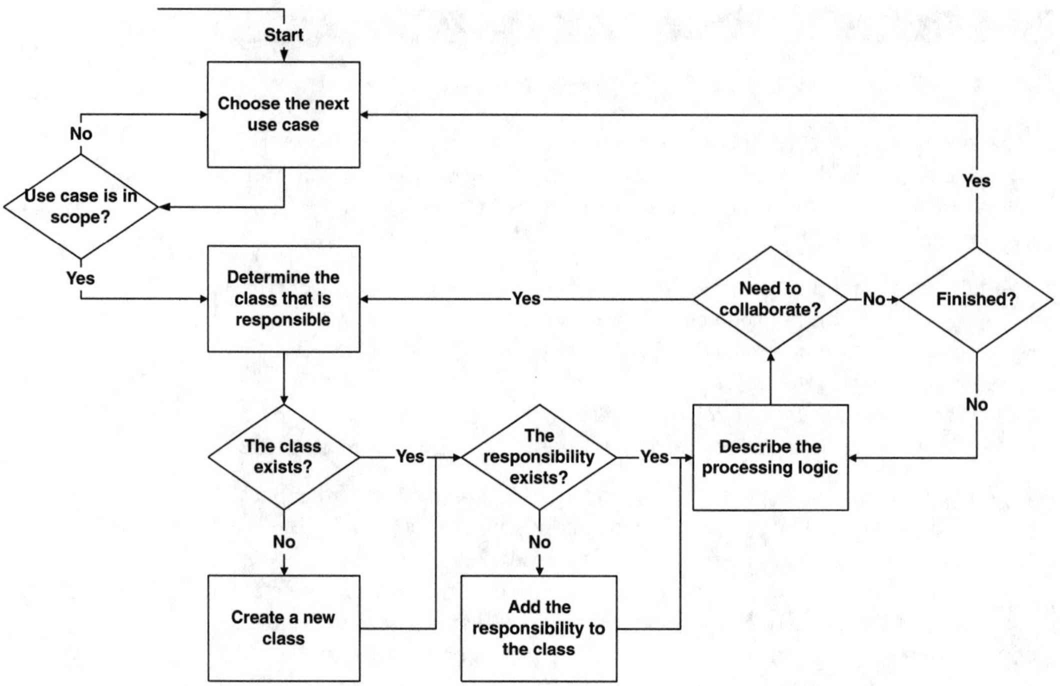

Figure 11.8. The Use-Case Scenario Testing process pattern

testing is finished, they will be assured that their model is complete and accurate.

Use-case scenario testing is also used by developers who want to verify that their component diagrams and/or their class diagrams support the requirements described by the use cases. Common use for this technique is to work through the logic of a set of use cases on several candidate designs to determine which design best supports the needs of the system, which is useful when you want to estimate the performance factors of several competing designs.

11.2.4 Validating Your Code

Source code must be tested. Period. In this section we will concentrate on three forms of code testing:

- Inspecting code
- Traditional code testing techniques
- Object-oriented code testing techniques

11.2.4.1 Inspecting Code

DEFINITION

code inspection A form of technical review in which the deliverable being reviewed is source code.

The Technical Review process pattern, depicted in Figure 11.8, can be used to review the quality of your code as well as the quality of your design. Code reviews often reveal problems that normal testing techniques do not; in particular, poor coding practices that make your application difficult to extend and maintain. My experience is that code reviews should be performed before testing, because once code has been tested and approved, developers are rarely motivated to have their code inspected. Their attitude is the code works so why bother looking at it again? The lesson is that you should first review your code, act on the recommendations from that review, then test it.

Code reviews should concentrate on quality issues such as:

- Making sure the code satisfies the design
- Naming conventions for your classes, methods, and attributes
- Code documentation standards and conventions:
- Have you documented what a method does?
- Have you documented what parameters must be passed?
- Have you documented what values are returned by a method?
- Have you documented both what and why a piece of code does what it does?
- Writing small methods that do one thing and one thing well
- Simplifying the code

Why do you want to do a code inspection? Code inspections verify that you built the code right and that you built code that will be easy to understand, to maintain, and to enhance. Code inspections can be an effective means of training developers in software engineering skills, because reviews reveal areas that they need to improve. Finally, code inspections are a great way to detect and fix problems as early in the coding process as possible: better to write 1,000 lines of code, review it, fix it, and move on than to write 100,000 lines of code and then find out that it is unintelligible to everyone but the people who wrote it.

Code inspections verify that you built the code right, aid in the training of developers, and detect potential problems early in the coding process.

11.2.4.2 Traditional Code Testing Techniques

In this section we will discuss several "traditional" techniques for testing source code whose origins are in structured testing from the mid-1970s. These techniques, arguably fundamental techniques, are:

- Black-box testing
- White/clear-box testing
- Boundary-value testing
- Path and coverage testing

11.2.4.2.1 Black-Box Testing

Black-box testing, also called interface testing, is a technique in which you create test cases based only on the expected functionality of a method, class, or application without any knowledge of its internal workings. One way to define black-box testing, as shown in Figure 11.9, is that given defined input A we should get the expected results B. The goal of black-box testing is to ensure that the system can do what it should be able to do, but not how it does it. For example, a black-box test for a word processor would be to verify that it is able to read a file in from disk and then write it back exactly as it was originally. It's a black-box test because we can run it without having any knowledge of how the word processor reads and writes files.

DEFINITION

black-box tests Test cases that verify that given input A the component/system being tested gives you expected results B.

The creation of black-box tests are often driven by the user requirements for the application, typically documented by use cases. The basic idea is that we look at the user requirement and ask ourselves, what needs to be done to show that the user requirement is met? The advantage of black-box tests is that they enable you to prove that your application fulfills the user requirements defined for it. Unfortunately, black-box testing does not allow you to show that extra, often technical, features not defined by your users also work. For this you need to create white/clear-box test cases.

11.2.4.2.2 White/Clear Box Testing

White-box testing, also called clear-box testing or detailed code testing, is based on the concept that your program code can drive the development of test cases. The basic idea is that you look at your

Figure 11.9.
Black-box testing

code and then create test cases that exercise it. In Figure 11.10 we see that with white-box testing we are able to see the internal workings of an application, and that with this knowledge we create test cases that will run specific sections of code.

> **DEFINITION**
> **white-box test** A test that verifies that specific lines of code work as defined. This is also referred to as a clear-box test.

For example, assume that we have access to the source code that reads in files for a word processor. When we look at it we see that there is an *if* statement that determines whether or not the file being read is a word-processing file or a simple text file, and then reads it in appropriately. This indicates that we need to run at least three tests on this source code: one to read in a word-processor file, one to read in a text file, and one to read in a file that is neither a word-processor file nor a text file. By looking at the code we were able to determine new test cases to exercise the different logic paths within it.

The main advantage of white-box testing is that it enables you to create tests that will exercise specific lines of code that may not have been tested by simple black-box test cases. Unfortunately, it does not allow you to confirm that all the user requirements have been met, as it only enables you to test the specific code that you have written.

11.2.4.2.3 Boundary-Value Testing

Boundary-value testing is based on the fact that you need to test your code to ensure that it can handle unusual and extreme situations. For example, boundary-value test cases for withdrawing funds from a bank account would include test cases such as attempting to withdraw \$0.00, \$0.01, -\$0.01, a very large amount of money, and perhaps even a large negative amount of money. Furthermore, if there is a daily limit of \$500 for withdrawals from automated teller machines, you would want to create tests that verify that you could withdraw \$500 on a single transaction but not \$500.01, and run the same tests for a collection of transactions that add up to the same amount.

> **DEFINITION**
> **boundary-value test** A test that tests unusual or extreme situations that your code should be able to handle.

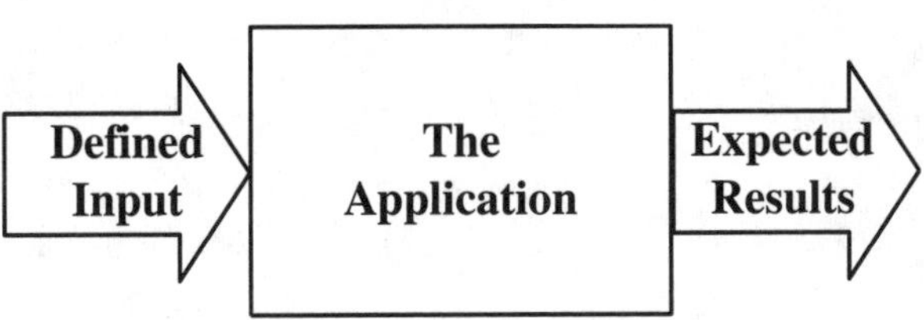

Figure 11.10
White-box testing

The idea is that you want to look for limits defined either by your business rules or by common sense, and then create test cases to test attribute values in and around those values. The main advantage of boundary-value testing is that it allows you to confirm that your program code is able to handle unusual or extreme cases. A serious disadvantage of boundary-value testing is that it is easy for developers to convince themselves that they only need to do boundary-value testing; after all, it discovers unusual errors, doesn't it? The reality is that you want to find both the usual and unusual errors.

11.2.4.2.4 Coverage and Path Testing

Coverage testing ensures that all lines of code were tested. Path testing ensures that all logic paths were tested.

Coverage testing is a technique in which you create a series of test cases designed to test all the code paths in your code. In a lot of ways coverage testing is simply a collection of white-box test cases that together exercise every line of code in your application at least once. Path testing is a superset of coverage testing that ensures that not only have all lines of code been tested, but all paths of logic have been tested as well. The main difference occurs when you have a method with more than one set of *case* statements or nested *if* statements: to determine the number of test cases with coverage testing, you would count the maximum number of paths between the sets of *case*/nested *if* statements, and with path testing you would multiply the number of logic paths.

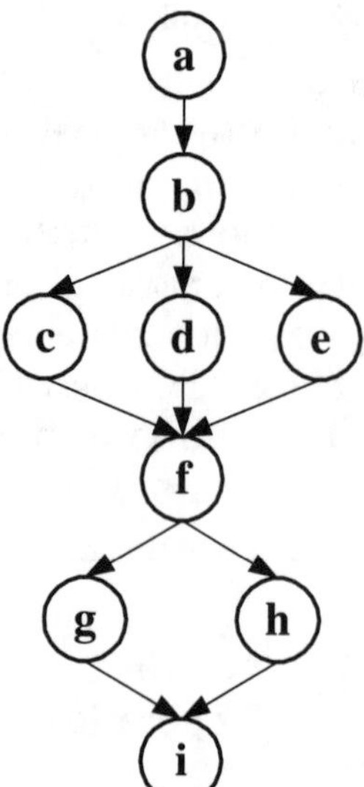

Figure 11.11. The flow of code in a method

TIP

Ask Questions when You Find a Bug

Van Vleck (1997) suggests that whenever you find a bug in your code that you should ask the following three questions:

1. **Is this mistake somewhere else also?** By asking this question you open the opportunity to fix several bugs at once. My advice is to first fix the bug that you found and verify that it works, then apply the solution to the other areas of your code where you made the same mistake.
2. **What next bug is hidden behind this one?** In other words, will the next statement work, are there combinations of features you didn't test, and can you invoke all possible error messages generated by your code?
3. **What should I do to prevent bugs like this in the future?** The goal here is to learn from your mistakes. How did the bug get into your code in the first place, how could you have detected this bug earlier, and how can you encapsulate common behavior so that you never have the opportunity to have this bug again?

Let's consider an example. In Figure 11.11 you see a code-logic diagram for a method. In this method we see that we have two sets of case statements: the combination of b, c, d, and e, and the combination of f, g, and h. When each case statement is considered alone, it has the following logic paths: bcf, bdf, and bef; fgi, and fhi respectively. To coverage test this code you would need only three test cases that would cover the following paths through the code: abcfgi, abdfhi, abefhi (or abefgi, it does not matter). Although coverage testing would ensure that all code is tested, it does not ensure that all combinations of the code would be tested. Path testing, on the other hand, would use six test cases to test all logic paths present in the code. These logic paths would be: abcfgi, abdfgi, adefgi, abcfhi, abdfhi, and adefhi.

DEFINITIONS

coverage testing The act of ensuring that all lines of code are exercised at least once.

path testing The act of ensuring that all logic paths within your code were exercised at least once. This is a superset of coverage testing.

The main advantage of coverage testing is that it helps to ensure that all lines of code within your application have been tested, although it does not ensure that all of the combinations of the code have been tested. Path testing, on the other hand, does test all combinations of the code, but requires significantly more effort to formulate and run the test cases.

11.2.4.3 Object-Oriented Code Testing Techniques

The development paradigm has changed; therefore, it is reasonable to expect that the testing paradigm must change, too. In this section we will discuss the following object-oriented code testing techniques:

- Method testing
- Class testing
- Class-integration testing
- Inheritance-regression testing

11.2.4.3.1 Method Testing

Method testing is the unit testing of the object world.

Method testing is the act of ensuring that your methods, called member functions in C++ and Java, perform as defined. The closest comparison to method testing in the structured world is the unit testing of functions and procedures. Although some people argue that class testing is really the object-oriented version of unit testing, my experience has been that the creation of test cases for specific methods often proves useful and should not be ignored. Hence the need for method testing.

Issues to address during method testing include:

- Ensuring that your accessor methods work.
- Ensuring that each method returns the proper values, including error messages and exceptions.
- Basic checking of the parameters being passed to each method.
- Ensuring that each method does what the documentation says it does.

11.2.4.3.2 Class Testing

Class testing is both unit testing and integration testing.

Class testing is both unit testing and traditional integration testing at the same time. It is unit testing because you are testing the class and its instances as single units in isolation; but at the same time, it is integration testing because you need to verify that the methods and attributes of the class work together. Class testing is an important component of the OO code-testing process.

The one assumption that you need to make during class testing is that all other classes in the system work. Although this may sound like an unreasonable assumption, it is basically what separates class testing from class-integration testing. The main purpose

DEFINITIONS

class testing The act of ensuring that a class and its instances (objects) perform as defined.

accessor method A method that is used to either modify or retrieve a single attribute.

integration testing A test that verifies that several portions of software work together.

method testing The act of ensuring that a method (member function) performs as defined.

unit testing The act of testing small components of a system to ensure that they work. In the object world this is both method and class testing.

of class testing is to test classes in isolation, which is difficult to do if you do not assume everything else works.

11.2.4.3.3 Class-Integration Testing

Class-integration testing addresses the issue of whether or not the classes in your system work together properly. We know that the only way classes, or to be more accurate the instances of classes, can work together is by sending each other messages. Therefore there must be some sort of relationship between those objects before they can send the message, implying that the relationships between classes can be used to drive the development of integration test cases. In other words, our strategy should be to look at the association, aggregation, and inheritance relationships that appear on our class diagram aid in formulating class-integration test cases.

Class-integration testing verifies that your classes work together appropriately.

Figure 11.12 shows a simple class diagram of a banking account class hierarchy and a Transaction class. Instances of Account and its subclasses post instances of Transaction; when a deposit is made to an account a deposit transaction is posted, and when a withdrawal is made, a withdraw transaction is posted. To properly test the class CheckingAccount you would need to verify, among other things, that its ability to charge a monthly fee works. This quickly becomes a class-integration testing issue because to charge a monthly fee a withdrawal is made by invoking the withdraw() method in Account which in turn invokes the postTransaction() method which creates

DEFINITION

class-integration testing The act of ensuring that the classes, and their instances, that form an application perform as defined.

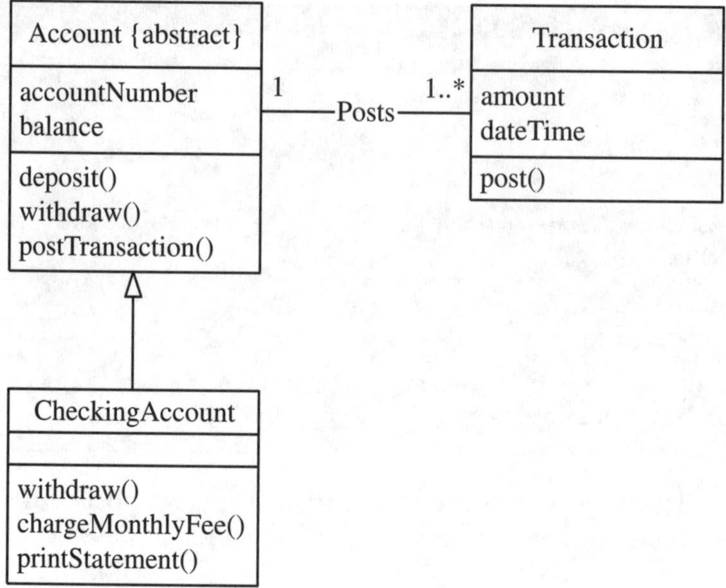

Figure 11.12. Posting banking transactions.

an instance of Transaction and invokes the post() message on it. To test this behavior we effectively need to verify that these three classes work together appropriately.

11.2.4.3.4 Inheritance-Regression Testing

Without a doubt the most important part of object-oriented testing is inheritance-regression testing—the running of the class and method test cases for all of the superclasses of the class being tested. The motivation behind inheritance-regression testing is simple: it is incredibly naive to expect that errors have not been introduced by a new subclass. New methods are added and existing methods are often redefined by subclasses, and these methods access and often change the value of the attributes defined in the superclass. It is very possible that a subclass may change the value of the attributes in a way that was never intended in the superclass, or at least was never expected. Personally, I would want to run the old test cases against my new subclass to verify that everything still works.

DEFINITION

inheritance-regression testing The act of running the test cases of all the super classes, both direct and indirect, on a given subclass.

11.2.4.4 User-Interface Testing

The user interface (UI) of an application is the portion that the user directly interacts with: screens, reports, documentation, and

DEFINITIONS

human-factors engineer (HFE) A person who is expert at the analysis and design of the user interface for an application and/or work environment for your users. This is a key role during the Define and Validate Initial Requirements stage, Model stage, and Program stage.

user interface (UI) The user interface of an application is the portion that the user directly interacts with, including the screens, reports, documentation, and software support (via telephone, electronic mail, and so on).

user-interface event An occurrence, often initiated by a user, such as keyboard input, a mouse action, or spoken input captured by a microphone, that causes action within your application.

user-interface testing The testing of the user interface (UI) to ensure that it follows accepted UI standards and meets the requirements defined for it. User-interface testing is often referred to as graphical user interface (GUI) testing.

your software support staff. User interface testing is the verification that the UI follows the accepted standards chosen by your organization, and that the UI meets the requirements defined for it. User interface testing is often referred to as graphical user interface (GUI) testing. User interface testing can be something as simple as verifying that your application "does the right thing" when subjected to a defined set of user interface events, such as keyboard input, or something as complex as a usability study where human-factors engineers verify that the software is intuitive and easy to use.

11.2.5 Recording Defects

There are two lines of thought regarding the recording of defects during testing in the small: that it is critical that defects are recorded, and that it isn't worth the effort. By recording key information about the defect, you have an accurate description of the problem for repairing it, and you have the data that you need to identify weak areas in your software process. The problem is that you introduce additional overhead to the construction process by requiring that defects are formally recorded. Software problem reports (SPRs) are used to record defect information.

Recording defect information provides the information needed to identify where your software process needs to be improved, but it adds additional overhead.

My experience is that during the Test in the Small stage, you do in fact need to record defect information, but not always. You

Scott's Soapbox

Automated Testing Tools Have Their Place, But . . .

I would like to share with you a few words of wisdom (Kaner, 1996) about automated testing tools.

- Early in development an application, even portions of the application, can only handle simple test cases. Automating simple test cases, especially ones that will need to be modified or even removed, may not be very efficient to start. Furthermore, regarding complexity, these test cases pale in comparison to those run manually later during construction.
- Automating user interface tests is problematic at best. When the user interface changes, which it does considerably during development, the effort to update your automated test cases can be substantial. Granted, many developers will wait until the user interface has "stabilized" until they start creating test scripts for it. Most user interface test tools have problems when you port your application to a new spoken language, such as from English to Spanish, which is a serious issue in today's world of electronic commerce and international applications.
- You need to plan for the development of automated tests. Nothing is free, and that includes the preparation time need to define, develop, and test your automated test suite. In many ways, the development of automated tests are a mini-project themselves; therefore, they should be treated as such.
- Many benefits of automated testing are realized in the next release. Automated testing tools can dramatically reduce the costs associated with regression testing, at least for the stable portions of your system. The implication, however, is that the benefit from the automated tests that you create today will be realized when you are regression testing future releases of your application.

want to record information about defects when one or more of the following situations occur:

- You are conducting a peer review of a deliverable. If it is important enough to have a peer review it is important enough to record the results of that review.
- Someone else other than the original developer(s) is doing the testing. SPRs provide the needed communication mechanism.
- The developer wishes to record the information on their own volition to improve their own skills.

DEFINITION

software problem report (SPR) A description of a potential software defect identified by someone who is not directly responsible for a given software deliverable.

Humphrey (1997) suggests that the following information be recorded about a defect:

- Description of the defect
- Date the defect was found
- Name of the person who found it
- Defect type (user interface bug, application crash, and so on)
- Stage the defect was found in
- Stage that the defect was introduced in
- Stage the defect was removed in
- Date the work was started
- Date the defect was fixed
- Steps to recreate the defect
- Effort, in hours or work days, to fix the defect
- Description of the solution

Collecting this information is important for several reasons. First, it provides an accurate description so that the defect may be fixed. Second, in provides the metrics (measurements) that you need to analyze and then improve your work practices. This data should be used to avoid defects in the first place, or at least to find defects sooner in the development process to reduce the cost of fixing them.

11.3 Solution: Project Tasks

In this section I will discuss project task issues pertinent to the Test in the Small stage.

11.3.1 Managing the Test in the Small Stage

The major management issue for the Test in the Small stage is to ensure that testing occurs continuously throughout the Construct phase. Many project managers make the mistake of assuming that testing in the small will manage itself, that programmers will test their own code and that modelers will produce models that accurately reflect the needs of their users. This belief is questionable at best; like every other stage, the Test in the Small stage needs to be actively managed for it to be successful.

Fix defects sooner rather than later.

The important thing is to keep testers actively involved throughout the entire construction effort. To do this, you need to schedule tests and reviews of all deliverables produced by the Construct phase, ensure that the tests and reviews are performed, and ensure that the results are acted upon immediately. Maguire (1994) points out that to maintain control of your project, do not allow outstanding defects to remain. Fixing one bug will inevitably expose latent bugs obscured by the original bug. Also, as you saw earlier in the chapter, the earlier that you fix defects, the less expensive they are to resolve.

It is critical that the master test/QA plan for the Test in the Large stage (Chapter 3 in *More Process Patterns*) is developed during this stage. The reason why the test plan should be developed, or at least started, during the Construct phase is to enable testing in the large to begin immediately after the Construct phase ends. If you wait to develop the test plan during the Test in the Large stage your project schedule will be impacted.

11.3.2 Training and Education

To provide for appropriate training and education of staff involved with testing in the small, which is all of your developers, you should consider the following issues:

1. **Review facilitators need meeting facilitation skills.** Peer reviews/walkthroughs are effectively facilitated meetings in which a deliverable is inspected, and the major skill requirement is to understand how to facilitate meetings. Many firms provide training courses in meeting facilitation, including both colleges and private management training firms.
2. **Modelers need to understand peer review process.** Because

the concept of reviewing models part way through modeling is new to many modelers, you may find that you need to provide them with a one- or two-day training course in peer reviews.

3. **Programmers need basic testing skills.** As you saw in this chapter testing object-oriented code is a complex process, a process in which your programmers are likely not proficient. My experience is that it is difficult to find good training courses in object-oriented testing. A good course will be taught by someone who is actively involved in the testing of object-oriented software, who understands that testing OO code is actually more difficult than testing structured code. Avoid courses taught by structured testers who have only read about OO.
4. **Programmers must understand that code reviews are critical.** Many programmers view code reviews as a waste of time, that the only important thing is that the code works. The problem with this attitude is that it ignores the fact that the vast majority of source code will be maintained and enhanced by someone who is not the original developer. This means that code must be reviewed to ensure that others can understand it.
5. **Management needs to understand that testing in the small is important.** The main justification for testing in the small is that the earlier you discover defects, the easier and less expensive they are to fix. By testing only at the end of construction, the traditional approach to testing, you increase the risk on your project and the cost to your organization. These are all important issues that senior management need to be aware of.

11.3.3 People Management

The main issue regarding people management is one of attitude, one that DeLano and Rising (1998) identify in the Designers Are Our Friends organizational pattern. Test engineers need to build a rapport with developers, to approach them with the attitude that they need to work together to identify and solve problems with the software. Developers, in the same light, must understand that defects, including shoddy work such as overly complex models or code that is difficult to understand, are simply unacceptable. Developers must understand that quality is the responsibility of everyone on the project, not just the quality assurance and test

Quality is an attitude, not a department.

TIP

Have Regular Informal Peer Reviews

One of the most effective techniques that you can do to ensure quality within your application is to hold regular, at least weekly, informal peer reviews of deliverables currently under construction. I prefer to keep informal reviews within the team, using the reviews to both inspect the products and to provide training to my staff. Novice developers benefit from the experience of senior staff who point out potential problems with their work, and the senior staff benefit because the questions they are asked force them to think about and explain how to do things. Everybody benefits from informal peer reviews.

A common process antipattern, called Only Peer Reviewing Milestones, is for organizations to hold peer reviews only at major milestones, typically the end of each project phase. The problem with this approach is that it is often too late to act on the results of the review; the team needs to move on to the next task, not clean up their previous work. A second problem is that there is too much to review, making it likely that many defects will not be detected.

DEFINITIONS

antipattern The description of an approach to solving a common problem, an approach that in time proves to be wrong or highly ineffective.

milestone A significant event in a project, usually the completion of a major deliverable, a point where upper management is traditionally informed of the status of the project. Because the OOSP is serial in the large and iterative in the small, the only clear milestones occur at the completion of project phases.

process antipattern An antipattern that describes an approach and/or series of actions for developing software that is proven to be ineffective and often detrimental to your organization.

project phase The large components of the OOSP, which are performed in a serial manner. The four project phases are Initiate, Construct, Deliver, and Maintain and Support. A project phase is depicted by a process pattern.

engineers. All developers must actively use techniques to detect and prevent defects.

DeLano and Rising (1998) describe The Tester's More Important Than the Test Cases organizational pattern which states that testing tasks should be assigned to test engineers based on their experience and talent, because no matter how effective the test cases are, the results of testing are highly dependent on the tester. The problem is that test engineers who become too familiar with an area often overlook problems by making assumptions, implying that the same test case in the hands of different test engineers will not necessarily produce the same results.

You can, and should, review the deliverables of your test engineers.

11.3.4 Quality Assurance

Quality assurance is an issue during all project stages, including the Test in the Small stage. The deliverables of your test engineers—test plans, test scripts, and test cases—can be peer-reviewed. Remember the golden rule of quality assurance: if you can create it you can review it.

11.3.5 Potential Risks While Testing in the Small

You need to be aware of several potential risks with respect to the Test in the Small stage:

1. **Lack of knowledge.** Few developers have received sufficient training in testing concepts, let alone in object-oriented testing. Because the average developer knows very little about testing, very few applications are tested properly. Get your developers the training they need.
2. **Testing in the small not seen as a continuous process.** One of the fundamentals of testing in the small is that it is performed continually throughout the Construct phase, not just at the end or at key points.
3. **Developers testing their own work.** It's everyone's responsibility to produce the best work that they can. At the same time, you need to recognize that because most people are convinced that their work is correct, they often miss errors that others will find. The best approach is to have developers initially test their own work to get the major defects out of it, and then have a professional test engineer take over the testing of the work to increase the chance of finding all of the bugs.
4. **Not performing code reviews.** The only way to ensure that source code is maintainable and extensible is to review it for understandability. Testing only shows that the code works; it does not show that the code is easy to understand. You have to review the source code of all programmers.
5. **No development standards or guidelines.** Your organization must come to a consensus on the standards and guidelines

that it will follow during development. These standards and guidelines should have been defined and selected during the Define Infrastructure stage (Chapter 6), and they are critical to ensuring that the work produced by your developers is of the quality that your organization requires. Developers should follow the standards and guidelines when working on your application, and reviews should ensure that they have done so.

6. **Lack of time.** Testing is often shortchanged during construction in favor of programming. I have never understood it, but the vast majority of developers apparently feel that it is more important to deliver a lot of functionality that may not work properly (they have not tested, so they do not know how good their work actually is) than it is to deliver something small that definitely works. Instead, developers should either take the extra time to ensure that their application works properly, or should reduce the functionality of what they are delivering to produce quality work within the same time frame. There is little value in delivering something on time that does not work.
7. **The "you can only test code" attitude.** You can test all deliverables, not just source code. At a minimum you can review models and documents, and by doing so you can find and fix defects long before they get into your code.
8. **The belief that object-oriented testing is just like structured testing.** Many structured testing techniques are still applicable for object-oriented testing, although, as you have seen, a few are not. Furthermore, because structured testing is based on the structured paradigm, not the object-oriented paradigm, you should expect that it does not fully meet the needs of testing object-oriented software. A sure sign that your project is in danger is the comment: "OO testing is the same as structured testing."
9. **Underestimating the importance of regression testing.** Taking either an incremental and iterative approach to development, both fundamental aspects of object orientation, requires that you regression-test your work effectively.
10. **Lack of management support.** There is a saying within the testing community: "Organizations that do not want to find defects will succeed (in not finding defects)."

11.3.6 *Opportunities for Reuse*

There are opportunities for reuse within and between projects during the Test in the Small stage:

1. **Standards, guidelines, and procedures.** Your organization should define and support a common set of standards, guidelines, and procedures for development that should be used across all projects. There should be procedures for review and testing activities, and standards and guidelines against which deliverables will be reviewed.
2. **Peer review checklists.** There should be a standard peer review checklist developed for every type of deliverable that your organization creates. This checklist should be used as the basis against which a deliverable of that type is reviewed. For example, to review a class diagram, you will take your generic review checklist for class diagrams which discuss naming and notational conventions and expand it to include issues specific to your project; perhaps you have a requirement to use an existing class library in your model. The point is that it is possible to develop reusable checklists to aid the peer review process.

11.3.7 *Metrics*

You should consider collecting several common metrics during the Test in the Small stage:

DEFINITIONS

class diagram A diagram that shows the classes of a system and their associations. Class diagrams are often mistakenly referred to as object models.

guideline A description, ideally with an example provided, of how something should be done. It is recommended, but not required, that you follow guidelines (unlike standards which are mandatory).

procedure A series of steps to be followed to perform a given task.

standard A description, ideally with an example provided, of how something must be done. It is required that you follow standards (unlike guidelines which are optional).

1. **Percentage of deliverables reviewed.** It is important to track the actual percentage of lines of code reviewed, the percentage of the portion of a model reviewed (you may not review an entire model), and the percentage of documents reviewed. Because reviews can be a time-consuming process, you often choose to review only a portion of someone's work under the assumption that they will make appropriate changes to all of their work. This metric is important because it provides an indication of how effective the review process is: if you are reviewing twenty percent of the source code and still finding that it is difficult to maintain, then you should consider reviewing thirty to forty percent on your next project.
2. **Time to fix defects.** The time to fix a defect is the difference between when it is first identified and when it fixed and verified to work by testing. This is an important metric because it indicates how serious defects are, information that you can use to determine whether or not you need to try to find defects earlier (the earlier a defect is found the easier it is to fix).
3. **Defect recurrence.** This is a count of the number of times that the same defect occurs in your work. This metric indicates the true effectiveness of your efforts to fix bugs: if you declare a defect to be fixed only to find the same bug again a few months later, then you know that it wasn't fixed the first time; instead it is likely that it was only patched.
4. **Defect type recurrence.** This is a count of the number of times that a given defect type occurs in your work. For example, if you find that your modelers are constantly indicating key attributes in their class diagrams—keys are indicated on data diagrams, not class diagrams—then it is clear that they need to be trained on class diagramming. This metric is an important means of determining whether your developers are improving their work processes over time.
5. **Defects per class.** This is a count of the number of defects found in each class, indicating the classes where you have the most rework to do.

11.4 Resulting Context: Exit Conditions for Testing in the Small

The Test in the Small stage effectively ends once your application is ready to be packaged, a part of the Program stage (Chapter 9), for testing in the large. For this to occur:

DEFINITION

configuration item (CI) Any deliverable, or portion of a deliverable, that is subject to SCM procedures.

1. **All configuration items are reviewed/tested.** All configuration items (CIs) from which your application is built must be reviewed and/or tested and accepted on an individual basis.
2. **The master test/QA plan is in place.** The master test/QA plan should be updated during the Construct phase so that the Test in the Large Stage (Ambler, 1998b) may begin immediately. Keeping this plan up to date is a management responsibility of the Test in the Small stage.

11.5 Secrets of Success

I'd like to share with you several thoughts that will improve your testing in the small efforts:

1. **Successful tests find errors.** The main goal of testing is to find problems in your application so that you are able to fix them. If your tests do not find any problems, then it is likely that you need to improve your testing efforts.
2. **A new development paradigm implies a new testing paradigm.** Object-oriented development is significantly different from structured/procedural development. Many of the techniques that we used in the past to test structured applications are either no longer applicable or need to be reworked to meet the new needs of OO development.
3. **Use software problem reports (SPRs) to drive testing.** The Use Old Problem Reports (DeLano and Rising, 1998) task process pattern suggests that test engineers should use SPRs to drive the development of new test cases to validate that the identified defects have in fact been resolved.
4. **The better your deliverable, the easier it is to test.** The time and effort that you invest up front to create a good model or write high-quality code will pay off in spades when you test. Do it right and do it once.
5. **Create a Software Quality Assurance (SQA) department.** Software quality assurance departments aid in creation of testing procedures, guidelines, and plans. They also aid in the

technical review process. SQA people are experts at ensuring that your applications meet the standards of quality expected by your user community, and can be an excellent resource during the testing process by providing advice and expertise. If you have an SQA department in your organization, take advantage of the fact and get them involved as early as possible in your projects.

6. **Provide feedback to developers about defects.** You will never be able to improve your work habits if you do not know that you are doing something wrong. By tracking defects found in the models and source code created by individual developers, and then providing them with feedback about those defects, you provide them with the opportunity to learn from their mistakes. Constantine (1995) reports that quality in one organization went up dramatically when they started providing such feedback to developers.
7. **Test to the risk of the artifact.** McGregor (1997) points out that the riskier something is, the more it needs to be reviewed and tested. In other words, I am going to invest significant effort testing an air traffic control system, but nowhere near as much effort testing a "Hello World" application.
8. **One test is worth a thousand opinions.** You can tell me that your application works, but until you show me the test results I will not believe you.
9. **You need a software configuration management (SCM) strategy.** SCM is critical to the testing effort, because there needs to be a planned and coordinated impound of software before it can be tested. Furthermore, SCM makes it easy to identify new features and modified areas with your code so that testing can be focused on those areas. Finally, because a configuration item (CI) has a status that cannot be both development and test at the same time, you effectively have a control mechanism with which you can "freeze" your code and declare it to be ready for test (Compton and Conner, 1994).
10. **Scratch and sniff.** DeLano and Rising (1998) identify in their Scratch 'n Sniff task process pattern that you should test areas where problems have already been found. Because defects tend to be clustered, the advantage is that problematic areas will be targeted and defects resolved earlier.
11. **Target strange behavior.** The Strange Behavior task process

DEFINITIONS

software configuration management (SCM) A set of engineering procedures for tracking and documenting software and its related deliverables throughout their life cycles to ensure that all changes are recorded and the current state of the software is known and reproducible.

software quality assurance (SQA) The process and techniques by which the development of software is verified, tested, and ensured to be of sufficient levels of excellence for your organization.

pattern (DeLano and Rising, 1998) suggests that test engineers should take any unusual behavior exhibited by software as an indication of a potential problem and to investigate it further. They suggest that this should be done even if the behavior is not related to the test currently being executed (for example the printer resets itself when you delete a customer object).

11.6 Process Checklist

The following process checklist can be used to verify that you have completed the Test in the Small stage.

TEST IN THE SMALL STAGE PROCESS CHECKLIST

Fulfillment of Entrance Conditions:

✔ There are development artifacts to be tested.
✔ The master test/QA plan exists.
✔ The requirements have been documented.
✔ Team members have been given the appropriate training for their part in this stage.

Processes Performed:

✔ The master test/QA plan was updated appropriately.
✔ Regression testing has been performed to show that existing behaviors still work.
✔ The models were reviewed and/or walked through and accepted.

✔ User-interface prototypes were reviewed and accepted.
✔ Use-case scenario testing was performed to verify that your classes fulfill the defined requirements.
✔ Source code was inspected and improved accordingly before being tested.
✔ Traditional testing techniques such as black-box, white/clear-box, boundary-value, path, and coverage testing were applied where appropriate.
✔ Object-oriented testing techniques such as method, class, class-integration, and inheritance-regression testing were applied were appropriate.
✔ User interface testing was performed to verify that the user interface works properly.
✔ Defects were recorded and analyzed accordingly.
✔ Artifacts that are potentially reusable by your project team during this stage have been identified and used where appropriate.
✔ Your risk assessment document has been updated where appropriate.
✔ Decisions made, and decisions forgone, have been documented in your group memory.
✔ Metrics have been collected.

Fulfillment of Exit Conditions:
✔ All configuration items have been reviewed/tested and updated accordingly.
✔ The master test/QA plan has been updated.

11.7 What You Have Learned in This Chapter

In this chapter you saw that testing in the small is a continuous process that is critical to the success of the Construct phase because it identifies defects early in the development process when they are the least expensive to fix. It is based on the concept that you can test all deliverables and that they should be tested as early as possible to minimize the impact of defects. I discussed testing and quality assurance techniques for validating your models and your code, covering structured testing techniques that are still applicable for object-oriented development and new techniques that are specific to the needs of the object-oriented paradigm.

11.8 References and Recommended Reading

Ambler, S. W. 1995. *The Object Primer: The Application Developer's Guide To Object Orientation*. New York: SIGS Books/Cambridge University Press.

Ambler, S. W. 1998a. *Building Object Applications That Work: Your Step-by-Step Handbook for Developing Robust Systems with Object Technology*. New York: SIGS Books/Cambridge University Press.

Ambler, S. W. 1998b. *More Process Patterns: Delivering Large-Scale Systems Using Object Technology*. New York: SIGS Books/Cambridge University Press.

Compton, S. B. and Conner, G. R. 1994. *Configuration Management for Software*. New York: Van Nostrand Reinhold.

Constantine, L. L. 1995. *Constantine on Peopleware*. Englewood Cliffs, New Jersey: Yourdon Press.

DeLano, D.E. & Rising, L. (1998). *Patterns for System Testing*. Pattern Languages of Program Design 3, eds. Martin, R.C., Riehle, D., and Buschmann, F., Addison Wesley Longman, Inc., pp. 503–525.Grady, R. B. 1992. *Practical Software Metrics For Project Management and Process Improvement*. Englewood Cliffs, New Jersey: Prentice-Hall, Inc.

Humphrey, W. S. 1997. *Introduction to the Personal Software Process*. Reading, Massachusetts: Addison-Wesley Longman, Inc.

Hunt, N. 1996. Testing Object-Oriented Code:Unit Testing. *Journal of Object-Oriented Programming* 8(February), 18–23.

Kaner, C. 1996. Pitfalls and Strategies in Automated Testing. *Computer* 30(April), 114–116.

Maguire, S. 1994. *Debugging the Development Process*. Redmond, Washington: Microsoft Press.

McGregor, J. D. 1997. Quality Assurance: Planning for Testing. *Journal of Object-Oriented Programming* 9(February), 8–12.

Siegel, S. 1996. *Object Oriented Software Testing: A Hierarchical Approach*. New York: John Wiley and Sons, Inc.

Van Vleck, T. 1997. *Three Questions*. http://www.best.com/~thvv/threeq.html.

Chapter 12

Toward More Process Patterns

IN THIS, the first of two books, I introduced you to the concept of process patterns and showed how the Software Engineering Institute Capability Maturity Model (SEI, 1995) can be used as the basis from which to develop an object-oriented software process (OOSP). Figure 12.1 presents the life cycle for a mature software process for developing large-scale, mission-critical software built from four serial phase process patterns, patterns which in turn are described by iterative stage process patterns. I spent the majority of this book discussing the Initiate and Construct phases of the OOSP pattern language, describing their stages in detail. In short, *Process Patterns* provides sufficient information from which your organization can tailor the first half of their software process for building software using object technology.

12.1 Coming Attractions in *More Process Patterns*

In *More Process Patterns* (Ambler 1998b) I continue to cover four main topics:

- The Deliver phase
- The Maintain and Support phase

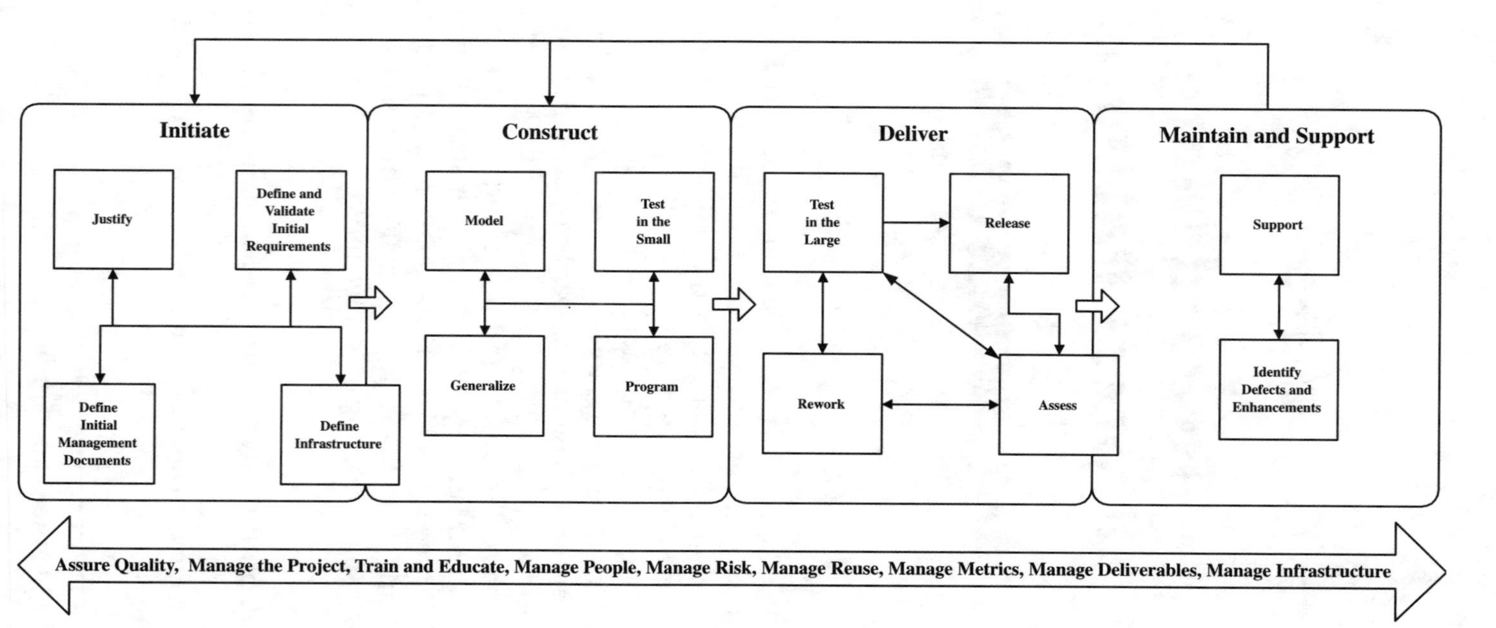

Figure 12.1. The Object-Oriented Software Process (OOSP)

- The project and cross-project tasks of the OOSP
- Introducing the OOSP into your organization

12.1.1 The Deliver Phase

The main goal of the Deliver phase, the third serial phase of the object-oriented software process (OOSP), is to deploy your application, including the appropriate documentation, to your user community. A major theme throughout the Deliver phase is that although your user community is the primary customer of your efforts you must never forget your secondary customers which are your organization's operations and support departments. As shown in Figure 12.2 the Deliver phase is made up of four iterative stages: Test In The Large, Rework, Release, and Assess. The inputs to the Deliver phase are the development deliverables of the Construct phase, comprised of the packaged application; the models and source code; the initial versions of the test, training, and release plans; and the user, operations, and support documentation which accompany the packaged application.

The Deliver phase puts your application and supporting documentation into the hands of your user community, operations department, and support department.

Figure 12.2. The Deliver process pattern

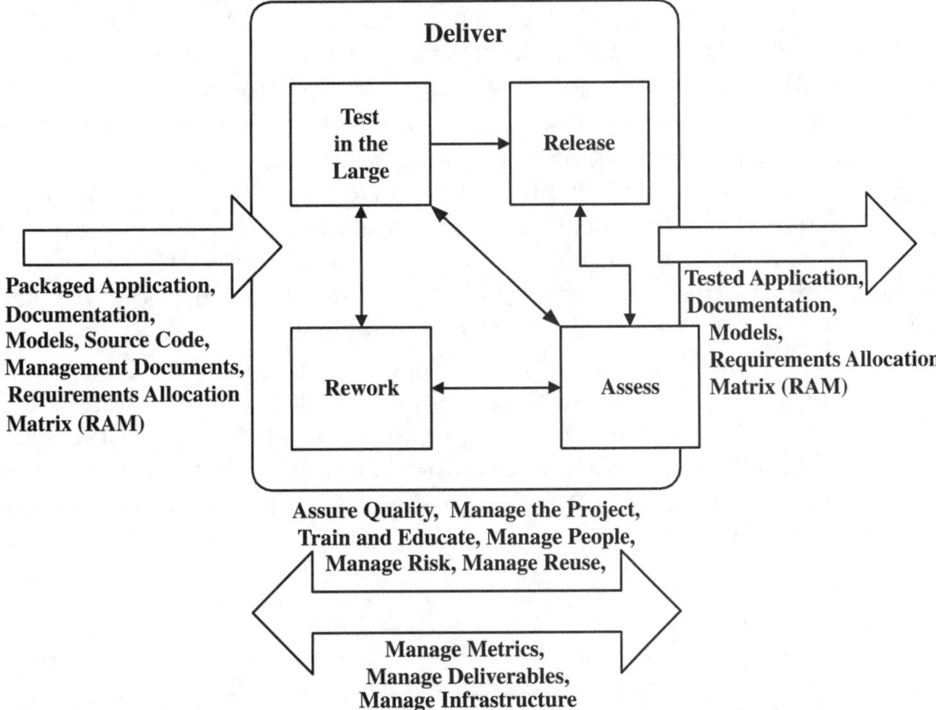

You need to freeze the code and test your application before putting it into production.

The Test In The Large stage is the traditional testing phase from structured development, with the caveat that we are now testing an OO application instead of a structured one. Testing in the large consists of testing techniques such as function testing, system testing, user acceptance testing (UAT), stress testing, operations testing, and alpha/beta/pilot testing. The key deliverables of this stage are a tested application and test results indicating whether or not the application can be released to the user community. Note that if the test results show that the application should not be released, then that release of the application must be reworked and then retested.

We almost always need to rework an application before it can be released.

Very often testing in the large shows that portions of an application need to be improved, or reworked, before it can be released to its users. Although you hope that something like this will not happen, it is unfortunately one of the realities of life – we aren't perfect and we cannot always do a perfect job. Another reality is that we are typically blind to the fact that we aren't perfect and that we make mistakes, the end result being that we forget that we often need to invest time reworking our applications before they can be released to our users. The OOSP includes an explicit Rework stage so that we do not forget to include the need to rework our applications in our schedules and estimates.

The Release stage is the point at which you put the application, and its corresponding documentation, into the hands of your users. It is also at this point that you train the users, operations staff, and support staff in the application. The key deliverable of this stage is the provision of an application that successfully supports users doing their work.

By assessing the project you can improve your development efforts the next time.

Part of the Deliver phase is to review the project to determine what went right as well as what went wrong. The main goal of the Assess stage is to learn from your experiences so that you may improve the development practices of your organization. The key deliverable here is a report indicating both best and worst practices that occurred on the project, as well as an action plan to improve your development efforts next time. In addition to assessing the project, you should also assess the people who worked on the project, rewarding them appropriately and defining a training plan for them to help them address any skills gap that they ma

12.1.2 The Maintain and Support Phase

The goal of the Maintain and Support phase, the fourth serial phase of the object-oriented software process (OOSP), is to keep your application running in production and to ensure that changes to the application are identified and acted on appropriately. The process pattern depicted in Figure 12.3 shows that the Maintain and Support phase is comprised of two stages, the Support Stage and the Identify Defects and Enhancements stage. The Maintain and Support phase begins for an application after it has been successfully delivered to your customers – your user, support, and operations communities. The main output of this phase is a series of maintenance changes that have been allocated to the configuration items (CIs) that make up your application, changes that are accompanied by the software problem reports (SPRs) and software change requests (SCRs) from which they were generated.

Because the OOSP is concerned with the entire life of an application, including efforts beyond development, the Support Stage

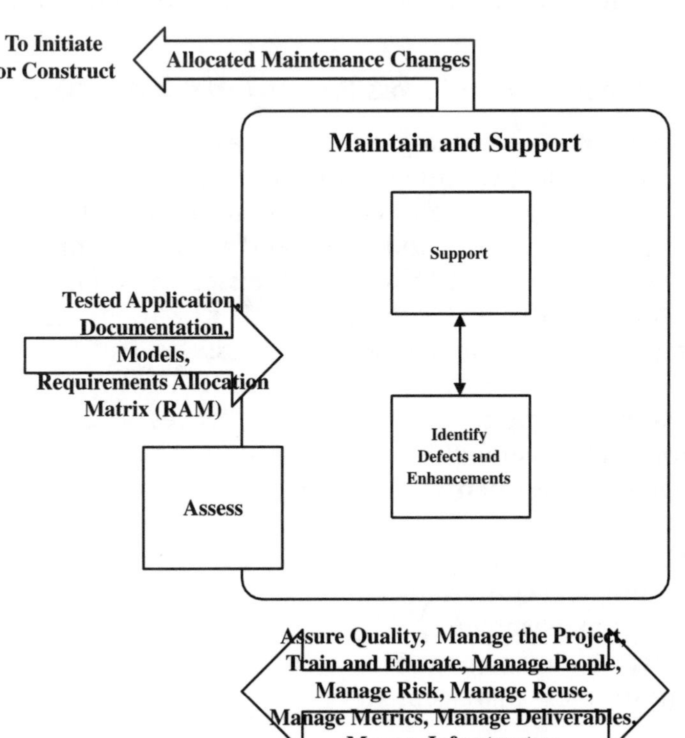

Figure 12.3. The Maintain and Support process pattern

is included in the OOSP. We are concerned with different levels of support: direct support for users of the application by the support desk (who may in fact be one of the application's developers), as well as technical support for the support people by the developers to help answer difficult questions. The key deliverable of this stage is the summary of collected metrics, such as the number of support calls taken and the average length of time to respond to a support call.

This stage defines and prioritizes new requirements for future releases of your application.

Because no application works perfectly or meets 100% of the needs of its users, we need the Identify Defects and Enhancements stage. A change control process is needed to track and verify these requests. This process should distinguish the differences between something that does not work, something that could work better, and something that simply is not there. If you do not have a process in place to actively manage the identification of defects and enhancements then the quality of the application will degrade over time because you are making changes to it on an ad hoc basis. The key deliverable of this stage is a series of verified and prioritized requirements for subsequent releases of the application.

12.1.3 The Project and Cross-Project Tasks of the OOSP

Chapter 10 of *More Process Patterns* focuses on the "big arrow" portion of the Object-Oriented Software Process (OOSP), shown in Figure 12.1, the project and cross-project tasks. These tasks apply across all project phases and stages and although I have touched on them in this book I have not addressed these tasks in detail. The following tasks make up the glue that hold projects together, helping to increase your chance of success:

- Quality assurance
- Project management
- People management
- Risk management
- Reuse management
- Training and education
- Metrics management
- Deliverable management
- Infrastructure management

Quality assurance is the process of ensuring that the efforts of a project meet or exceed the standards expected of them by the organization. Fundamentally, quality assurance attempts to answer the following questions: "Are you building the right thing?" and "Are you building it the right way?" Quality assurance is critical to the success of a project, and should be an integral part of all project stages. At all points in the OOSP you should be reviewing your work to ensure its quality.

Project management is the process of organizing, monitoring, and directing a project. Project management is planning. Project management is scheduling. Project management is estimating. Project management is people. Projects must be skillfully managed if they are to be successful.

People management is the process of organizing, monitoring, coaching, and motivating people in such a manner to ensure that they work together effectively and contribute to a project/organization positively. People develop software, therefore managing people must be part of the software development process.

Risk management is the process of identifying, monitoring, and mitigating the risks faced by a project team. These risks may come from a range of sources, and may be strategic, technical, and/or political. The key concept of risk management is that you want to identify and deal with them as soon as possible, and if you are unable to deal with them, or at least unwilling to deal with them, then you should at least keep an eye on them to ensure that they do not harm your project (at least not too badly). Risk management is one of the keys of success for system development projects, a task which must be performed throughout the project.

Reuse management is the process of organizing, monitoring, and directing the efforts of a project team that lead to reuse on project (or on subsequent projects); either reuse of existing or purchased items. It is possible to achieve reuse throughout the entire OOSP, but it is not free and it is not automatic. You have to work at it. Furthermore, although we have a project stage called Generalize (Chapter 10) that is dedicated specifically to building reusable components during the Construct Phase, this is only a start. You can reuse your project plans, your estimates, your risk analysis, your test strategies, your construction standards, and your documentation templates – but only if you put in the effort. Reuse management is key to reducing the overall cost of application development.

Training and education (T&E) are important to the success of a project. Training gives people the skills that they need to do their jobs, whereas education provides them with the knowledge that they need to understand their jobs. For example, people may take a course that teaches them the fundamentals of application development. This is education because it provides them with knowledge. The same people may attend a 5-day course to learn how to program in Java. This is training because it teaches them a specific skill. Education generally deals with knowledge that is useful for a long period of time, whereas training often has a much shorter shelf-life, often on the order of months or years. You want to distinguish between training and education because in many ways training is an investment that needs to pay for itself in the short term, perhaps over one or two projects, whereas education pays for itself over the long term, typically the employment of an individual. At some point most projects require the training and/or education of both developers and users, therefore T&E is an important part of the OOSP.

Metrics management is the process of collecting, summarizing, and acting on measurements (metrics) to potentially improve both the quality of the software that your organization develops and the actual software process of your organization. As the old saying goes "you cannot improve it if you cannot measure it." Metrics management provides the information that is critical to understanding the quality of the work that your project team has performed and how effectively that work was performed. Metrics range from simple measurements of work effort such as the number of hours invested to develop a model to code quality measurements such as the percentage of comments within your code.

Deliverable management is key to the management of a project, to the successful operation of an application, and to the successful maintenance and support of an application. A deliverable is any information, either printed or electronic, that describes all or part of an application or system such as models, documents, and plans. Deliverables may be internal, used only by members of the project team, or external, delivered as part of the application. Deliverables may be for developers, for users, for support staff, or for operations staff. The review and update of deliverables is a fundamental part of quality assurance, and the existence of accurate and complete documentation is a fundamental part of risk management. Deliverables are created and updated by all members of a project team throughout the entire project.

Infrastructure management is a cross-project effort which includes the architectural and enterprise modeling efforts of the Model Stage (Chapter 8), and the definition and support of your organization's processes, standards, guidelines, and chosen toolsets. The Define Infrastructure Stage (Chapter 6) is a key function of infrastructure management because it defines and/or selects the infrastructure for a single project. However, from the point of view of your organization the Define Infrastructure Stage is not sufficient to promote a common infrastructure between projects, hence the need for infrastructure management.

12.1.4 Introducing the OOSP Into Your Organization

Humphrey (1997) describes the Software Engineering Institute's (SEI's) SMIDEAL[1] (Initiating, Diagnosing, Establishing, Acting, and Leveraging) model for process improvement. The experience of the SEI, and my experience, is that process improvement should be performed iteratively over a long period of time, often years, and that it is in fact a task that is never truly finished. In other words, you can always improve. The five iterative steps of the IDEAL model are used as a basis from which to introduce, and then over time improve, a tailored version of the OOSP in your organization. My experience is that the most effective way to define and then introduce process patterns into your organization is to follow these steps:

- Initiate—Get your process improvement program started.
- Diagnose—Assess your situation and identify your goals.
- Establish—Organize your process improvement program.
- Act—Define process patterns for your organization.
- Act—Implement process patterns.
- Leverage—Assess and iterate.

12.2 What You Have Learned

You have seen that *More Process Patterns* describes in detail four topics that key to the success of your organization. First is how to successfully deliver working software to your user community, a

[1] SMIDEAL is a service mark of Carnegie Mellon University.

task that often proves to be quite difficult in practice. Second, processes for maintaining and supporting software once it is in production are presented in the second volume: not only must you put software into production you need to keep it there. Third, the project and cross-project tasks of the OOSP are described in detail. Fourth, *More Process Patterns* presents proven advice for tailoring a mature software process from the process patterns presented in these two volumes that meets your organizations unique needs for building and delivering large-scale systems using object technology.

12.3 References and Recommended Reading

Ambler, S.W. 1998a. *Building Object Applications That Work: Your Step-By-Step Handbook for Developing Robust Systems with Object Technology*. New York: SIGS Books.

Ambler, S.W. 1998b. *More Process Patterns: Delivering Large-Scale Systems Using Object Technology*. New York: SIGS Books/ Cambridge University Press.

Emam, K. E., Drouin J., Melo, W. 1998. *SPICE: The Theory and Practice of Software Process Improvement and Capability Determination*. Los Alamitos, CA IEEE Computer Society Press.

Humphrey, W.S. 1997. *Managing Technical People: Innovation, Teamwork, And The Software Process*. Reading, MA: Addison-Wesley Longman, Inc.

Maguire, S. 1994. *Debugging the Development Process*. Redmond, WA: Microsoft Press.

Software Engineering Institute 1995. *The Capability Maturity Model: Guidelines for Improving the Software Process*. Reading MA: Addison-Wesley Publishing Company.

Glossary

A

abstract class A class from which objects are not instantiated, but are instead used to implement common behavior inherited by other classes.

accessor method A method that is used to either modify or retrieve a single attribute.

ActiveX An approach to developing reusable components defined by Microsoft.

activity diagram A UML diagram that can be used to model a high-level business process or the transitions between states of a class (in this respect, activity diagrams are effectively specializations of statechart diagrams).

actor A role played by any person, organization, or system that interacts with an application but is external to it. Actors are modeled on use-case diagrams.

ad-hoc reporting Reporting performed for the specific purposes of a small group of users, in which it is common that the report(s) are written by the users themselves.

aggregation A structure that represents *is-part-of* relationships between objects.

allocated baseline A baseline in which all requirements defined by the functional baseline are assigned/mapped to classes within your design.

alpha testing A testing period in which pre-release versions of software products, products that are often buggy, are released to users who need access to the product before it is to be officially deployed. In return these users are willing to report back to the software developers any defects that they uncover. Alpha testing is typically followed by a period of beta testing.

analysis An approach to modeling in

which the goal is understanding the problem domain.

analysis error When a user requirement is missed or misunderstood.

analysis paralysis A derogatory term used by system professionals to describe the actions of a development team that spends too much time when modeling in trying to document every minute detail.

analysis pattern A modeling pattern that describes a solution to a business/domain problem.

analysis testing The testing of your analysis modeling efforts.

analyst A person responsible for defining and validating the initial requirements for the application via working closely with subject matter experts. This is a key role during the Define and Validate Initial Requirements stage and the Model stage.

antipattern The description of an approach to solving a common problem, an approach that in time proves to be wrong or highly ineffective.

application package The software and supporting documentation that is deployed to your user community.

application release A software release that delivers an application containing new, improved, and/or fixed functionality.

application release schedule A schedule indicating the dates of the incremental releases of your application.

application server A server on which business logic is deployed. Application servers are key to an *n*-tier client/server architecture.

application-specific class Any class that is used in a single application.

approach process pattern A process pattern that depicts a general approach to development; for example, serial development or parallel development.

architectural modeler A person who is involved in understanding and modeling the enterprise, business architecture, and/or technical architecture for your organization. This is a key role during the Model stage.

architectural modeling High-level modeling, either of the business or technical domain, whose goal is to provide a common, overall vision of your domain. Architectural models provide a base from which detailed modeling will begin.

artifact reuse The reuse of previously created development artifacts: use cases, standards documents, domain-specific models, procedures and guidelines, and other applications.

association A relationship between two or more objects or classes. For example, students TAKE courses.

audit trail A complete record of changes to a deliverable, also called a modification log or revision history.

automatic call distribution (ACD) system A phone system that distributes calls to support engineers in an efficient manner.

B

back end *See* Server

baseline A tested and certified version of a deliverable representing a conceptual milestone that thereafter serves as the basis for further development, and that can be modified only through formal change control procedures. A particular version becomes a baseline when a responsible group decides to designate it as such.

beta testing Similar to alpha testing, except that the software should be less buggy. This is typically used by software development companies who want to ensure that they meet as many of their client needs as possible.

big-bang development An approach to development in which an application is released all at once in one, single project.

black-box tests Test cases that verify that given input A, the component/system being tested gives you expected results B.

boundary-value test A test that checks unusual or extreme situations that your code should be able to handle.

bug *See* Defect

build The process by which a software product is created from its base source code. This is the act of compiling and linking source code in compiled languages such as Java and C++, or packaging code in languages like Smalltalk.

builder A tool that developers use to build software, such as a compiler, a linker, or a packager.

business-domain expert (BDE) Someone with intimate knowledge of all or a portion of a problem domain. Often referred to as a subject matter expert (SME).

C

calendar time The overall time that it takes to complete a project, measured from the start of a project to its end. A project that starts on May 1st which then ends on May 24th of the same year has a calendar time of twenty-four days.

Capability Maturity Model (CMM) A strategy, defined by the Software Engineering Institute (SEI), that describes the key elements of an effective software process.

cardinality An indication of how many.

change agent A person responsible for defining, implementing, and supporting change within your organization. This is a key role during software process improvement.

change request (CR) A formal document describing a potential modification to an application or system. Software problem reports (SPRs) and enhancement descriptions are specializations of change requests.

class A person, place, thing, event, concept, screen, or report.

class diagram Class diagrams show the classes of a system and the associations between them. Class diagrams are often mistakenly referred to as object models.

class library A collection of classes,

typically purchased off-the-shelf, which you can reuse and extend via inheritance.

class model A class diagram and its associated documentation.

Class Responsibility Collaborator (CRC) card A standard index card divided into three sections that show the name of the class, the responsibilities of the class, and the collaborators of the class.

Class Responsibility Collaborator (CRC) model A collection of CRC cards that describe the classes that make up an application or a component of an application.

class testing The act of ensuring that a class and its instances (objects) perform as defined.

class-integration testing The act of ensuring that the classes, and their instances, that form an application perform as defined.

client A single-user PC or workstation that provides presentation services and appropriate computing, connectivity, and interfaces relevant to the business need. A client is also commonly referred to as a *front end.*

client/server (C/S) architecture A computing environment that satisfies the business need by appropriately allocating the application processing between the client and the server processes.

code inspection A form of technical review in which the deliverable being reviewed is source code.

code reuse The reuse of source code within sections of an application and potentially across multiple applications.

cohesion A measure of how much something makes sense. Cohesive items have a single purpose.

collaboration diagram A diagram that shows instances of classes, their interrelationships, and the message flow between them. The order of the messaging is not indicated.

collaborator On a CRC card, a collaborator of a class is another class that it interacts with to fulfill one or more or its responsibilities.

commercial-off-the-shelf (COTS) system A system produced by a third-party vendor that is available for commercial purchase.

Common Object Request Broker Architecture (CORBA) An OMG specification defining a distributed-object architecture. CORBA specifies how to develop OO applications that are able to connect and communicate with other CORBA-compliant (and potentially non-OO) applications.

component Small-scale, cohesive items such as user interface widgets that programmers reuse when building applications.

component diagram A diagram that shows the software components, their interrelationships, interactions, and their public interfaces that comprise an application, system, or enterprise.

component engineer A person who builds and then supports reusable components. Component engineers will often act as internal consultants to project teams to ensure that the teams are gaining the greatest benefits from reusable components. This is a key role for both the Program and Generalize stages.

component reuse The reuse of prebuilt, fully encapsulated components in the development of your application.

computer-aided system engineering (CASE) tool A tool that supports the creation of software.

computer-based training (CBT) A program designed for the purpose of training users in a specific topic. CBT programs often use multimedia features such as animated graphics and sound.

concrete class A class from which objects are instantiated.

concurrency The issues involved with allowing multiple people simultaneous access to your persistence mechanism.

concurrency strategy The approach taken by the developer of a class to support concurrent access to instances of that class. Common concurrency strategies include the following: synchronized objects, balking objects, guarded objects, versioned objects, concurrency policy controllers, and acceptors.

configuration auditing The process of verifying and validating that a proposed configuration is complete and consistent.

configuration control The management of changes to configuration items.

configuration control board (CCB) The group responsible for approving proposed software changes. Also called a change control board or software configuration review board (SCRB).

configuration control board (CCB) manager The person responsible for managing the CCB. This is a key role during the Identify Defects and Enhancements stage.

configuration identification The process of designating configuration items and their components.

configuration item (CI) Any deliverable, or portion of a deliverable, that is subject to SCM procedures.

configuration item owner The person or group responsible for developing and updating a given configuration item. This is a key role during the Identify Defects and Enhancements stage.

configuration status accounting The process of keeping records of the other three configuration management activities (configuration identification, configuration control, and configuration auditing) for use in the CM process.

cost/benefit breakpoint The point at which the investment you make in your project is exactly the same as its expected return.

coupling A measure of how connected two items are.

coverage testing The act of ensuring that all lines of code are exercised at least once.

critical path In a project network diagram, it is the series of activities that determines the earliest completion of a project. The critical path for a project will change from time to time as activities are completed ahead of or behind schedule.

CRUD Abbreviation for create, retrieve/read, update, delete. The basic functionality that a persistence mechanism must support.

customer The customer of an application is your user community, your operations department, and your support department.

D

data access map A depiction of a query into a database, made by an application or report, showing the tables accessed and the order in which they are accessed.

data conversion plan A plan describing how a legacy data schema will be reworked to meet the new needs of your organization. A data conversion plan will likely refer to data models for both the existing and new data schema as well as the data access maps associated with both models.

data diagram A diagram used to communicate the design of a (typically relational) database. Data diagrams are often referred to as entity-relationship (ER) diagrams.

data dictionary A repository of information about the layout of a database, the layout of a flat file, the layout of a class, and any mappings among the three.

data flow In a process model a data flow represents the movement of information, either physical or electronic, from one source to another.

data model A data diagram and its corresponding documentation.

data store In a process model, a place where information is stored, such as a database or filing cabinet.

data warehouse A large database, almost always relational, that is used to store data for reporting purposes.

database administrator (DBA) A person responsible for administering and maintaining the schema of a database.

database cursor A connection to a persistence mechanism, that was the result of a query, that allows you to traverse the result set of the query.

database proxy An object that represents a business object stored in a database. To every other object in the system, a database proxy appears to be the object that it represents. When other objects send a proxy a message, it immediately fetches the object from the database and replaces itself with the fetched object, passing the message on to it.

database server A server that has a database installed on it.

data-flow diagram (DFD) A diagram that shows the movement of data within a system among processes, entities, and data stores. Called a process diagram for OO development.

defect Anything that detracts from your application's ability to completely and effectively meet your user's needs. Also known as a bug, fault, or feature.

defensive programming An approach in which additional code is written to verify that the proper input to a method has been received and that, when a method was invoked, it worked properly.

degenerate pattern A pattern that has been described without the use of a pattern template.

deliverable Any document or system component that is produced during the development of a system. Some deliverables are used internally on a project, whereas others are produced specifically for users of the application. Examples of deliverables include user requirements, models, plans, assessments, or other documents.

deliverable management The process of organizing, monitoring, and directing the deliverables of a project.

deployment diagram A diagram showing the hardware, software, and middleware configuration for a given system.

design A style of modeling with the goal of describing how a system will be built based on the defined requirements.

design pattern A modeling pattern that describes a solution to a design problem.

detailed design A style of modeling which focuses on the design of a single piece of software.

developer Any person directly responsible for the creation of software, including, but not limited to, modelers, programmers, and reuse engineers. This is a key role during the Construct and Deliver phases.

development/maintenance trade-off Development techniques that speed up the development process often have a negative impact on your maintenance efforts, whereas techniques that lead to greater maintainability will negatively impact your development efforts, at least in the short term.

developmental baseline This represents the incremental software builds needed to develop the application. Developmental baselines are major deliverables of the Program stage.

diagram A visual representation of a problem or solution to a problem.

distributed objects An object-oriented architecture in which objects running in separate memory spaces (such as in different computers) interact with one another transparently.

domain architecture A collection of high-level models that describe the problem domain. Domain architectures are typically documented by high-level use cases, use-case diagrams, and class models that describe the various sub domains and the relationships between them.

domain component A large-scale component that encapsulates cohesive portions of your business domain. Domain components are identified by architectural modeling.

domain modeler A person who is actively involved in modeling the problem domain for an application and/or for a reusable large-scale domain component. This is a key role during the Model stage.

domain programmer A developer who writes, documents, and tests program source code for an application. This is a key role in the Program stage.

domain/business classes Domain/business classes model the business domain. Business classes are usually found during analysis, examples of which include the classes Customer and Account.

domain-component reuse The reuse of prebuilt, large-scale domain components that encapsulate cohesive portions of your business domain.

dynamic SQL A structured query language (SQL) statement that is generated, often by a persistence layer, based on information describing the mapping between your objects and the schema of the persistence mechanisms in which they are stored.

E

economic feasibility An assessment of whether an application or system will pay for itself.

education The process by which people gain knowledge and understanding.

effort time The total time taken to develop an application, calculated by adding up all the time expended by each person contributing to development. A project that has two people working on it for four weeks each, and one person working on it for three, has an effort time of eleven weeks.

embedded SQL An SQL statement that is written directly in the code of your application. When the schema of your persistence mechanism changes, or the schema of your application, then this code will need to be updated to reflect those changes. Embedded SQL increases the coupling between your application and your persistence mechanisms.

engineering month *See* Work month

enhancement description A type of change request that specifies a new feature for an application or system.

enterprise modeling The act of modeling an organization and its external environment from a business, not an information system, viewpoint.

environmental requirement A nonfunctional requirement that deals with the environment in which the application will be used. This may be a politically motivated requirement, an ergonomic requirement, a requirement to follow specific standards or guidelines, or a requirement generated by the external business environment in which your firm operates.

escalation procedures The process by which difficult support calls are forwarded to people with greater expertise, within both your support organization and your development community.

estimator/planner This person(s) is responsible for activities such as initial project estimating, scheduling, and planning. This is a key role during the Define Initial Management Documents stage and Justify stage.

exception handling The act of identifying and acting on run-time problems (exceptions) in an application.

exit date The date that a person leaves, or is scheduled to leave, a project.

extensibility A measure of how easy it is to add new features to a system. The easier it is to add new features, the more extensible we say the system is.

external entity In a process model, the source or destination of data that is external to the system being modeled. In a class diagram we would call this an actor class.

F

facade class A class that provides the interface for a component or domain component. A facade class is composed of a collection of public methods that route messages to the other classes within a component. A component may have multiple facade classes to provide different versions of its interface.

fat-client A two-tiered client/server architecture in which client machines implement both the user interface and the business logic of an application. Typically, servers simply supply data to client machines with little or no processing done to it.

fault *See* Defect

feasibility study A document that addresses three main issues: can the system be built, can you afford to build the system, and, once the system is in place, can you maintain and support it? In other words, is the system technically feasible, is it economically feasible, and is it operationally feasible? Feasibility studies are a deliverable of the Justify stage.

feature *See* Defect

feature creep The addition, as development proceeds, of new features to an application that are above and beyond what the original specification called for. This is also called scope creep.

feature points A metric that is the superset of function points, adding a count of the algorithmic complexities within your software.

flow chart A diagram depicting the logic flow of a single process.

foreign key A column in a relational table that identifies a row within another relational table.

Fountain SDLC An iterative approach to application development first proposed by Brian Henderson-Sellers and Julian Edwards.

fourth-generation language (4GL) A category of computer languages in which the development environment includes tools that generate some or all of the source code for your application.

framework A reusable, almost-complete application that can be extended to produce custom applications.

framework reuse The reuse of collections of classes that together implement the basic functionality of a common technical or business domain.

front end *See* Client

Full Life Cycle Object-Oriented Testing (FLOOT) A testing methodology for object-oriented development that comprises testing techniques that taken together provide methods to verify that your application works correctly at each stage of development.

function points A metric used for estimating software size that is calculated by counting five items: the inputs to the software, the outputs from it, inquiries by users, the data files that would be updated by the software, and the interfaces to other software.

function testing A part of systems testing in which development staff confirm that their application meets the user requirements specified during analysis.

functional baseline The application requirements, and related test criteria, that are defined in such a manner that software development can be performed. The requirements are typically in the form of a requirements document or System Requirements Specification (SRS).

functional requirement A feature that describes a behavioral aspect of the business/problem domain.

G

Gantt chart A graphic display of schedule-related information, listing the activities to be completed down the left-hand side of the diagram, dates shown across the top, and horizontal bars showing activity duration between given dates within the diagram. Resources (teams, positions/roles, individuals) allocated to the activities are often shown on the bars, and dependencies between activities are shown as arrows connecting the horizontal bars. Relationships between tasks, for example task A must complete before task B starts, can also be indicated.

getter method An accessor method that retrieves the value of an attribute.

glossary A document that summarizes the business and technical terms being used by the development team. Glossaries help to facilitate communications and avoid misunderstandings.

graphical user interface (GUI) A style of user interface in which graphical components, as opposed to text-based components, are used.

group memory A record of what your project team accomplished, decisions made by your team and the reasoning behind them, deferred decisions, and the lessons learned on your project. A group memory provides a mechanism to record this information when it is first recognized so that it isn't lost.

groupware A form of software which allows several users to work together on common information, often simultaneously from different physical locations.

GUI testing *See* user interface testing

guideline A description, ideally with an example provided, of how something should be done. It is recommended, but not required, that you follow guidelines (unlike standards, which are mandatory).

H

hacking A development approach where little or no effort is spent on analysis and design before coding begins.

hierarchical organization A organization with a reporting structure where each person reports to a single manager.

human-factors engineer (HFE) A person who is expert at the analysis and design of the user interface for an application and/or work environment for your users. This is a key role during the Define and Validate Initial Requirements, Model, and Program stages.

I

ignored method An inherited method that is overridden to remove its functionality.

immature software organization A software organization that is reactionary, its managers usually focused on solving immediate crises. There is no objective basis for judging product quality or for solving product or process problems. There is little understanding of how the steps of the software process affect quality, and product quality is difficult to predict.

impact analysis A determination of how your application will be affected by a given change. Your analysis should describe the modifications that need to be made to your models, documentation, and source code and should provide an estimate of the work effort involved to make those changes.

incremental development An approach to development in which applications are released in several "mini-projects," each delivering a portion of the required functionality for the overall application.

infrastructure artifact An item, such as your organization's software process, a standard, a guideline, or a chosen tool, that is common between project teams to build applications to support your organization.

infrastructure engineer A person who is responsible for defining and supporting the project infrastructure (processes, guidelines, standards, and tools). The role is applicable to the Define Infrastructure stage and all stages of the Construct phase.

infrastructure management A cross-project effort that includes your organization's architectural and enterprise modeling efforts, as well as the definition and support of processes, standards, guidelines, and chosen toolsets.

inheritance The representation of an *is a*, *is like*, or *is kind of* relationship between two classes.

inheritance-regression testing The act of running the test cases of all the super classes, both direct and indirect, on a given subclass.

inheritance reuse The use of inheritance in your application to take advantage of behavior implemented in existing classes.

inheritance tree depth The maximum number of classes from the root of a class hierarchy to its lowest node, including the root class.

installation testing The act of ensuring that your application can be installed successfully.

instance Another word for *object*. We say that an object is an instance of a class.

integration testing A test that verifies that several portions of software work together.

integration plan A plan that describes the schedule, resources, and approach to integrating the elements of an application.

interaction diagram *See* Sequence diagram

interface-flow diagram A diagram that models the interface objects of your system and the relationships between them.

internal rate of return (IRR) The interest rate that equates the cost of an investment to the present value of the respected returns from the investment.

International Standards Organization (ISO) A non-profit organization promoting the development and support of internationally accepted standards.

invariant A set of assertions about an instance or class that must be true at all "stable" times, where a stable time is the period before a method is invoked on the object or class and immediately after a method is invoked.

ISO 9001 A standard, defined by the International Standards Organization (ISO), that defines how organizations should manage their quality-assurance programs.

ISO 9003 The standards defining how organizations should manage their software quality assurance programs.

iterative development An approach to development that occurs in a non-serial manner.

J

JAD/meeting facilitator This person(s) is responsible for organizing, running, and summarizing the results of joint application development (JAD) sessions in which requirement definition and validation is performed. This is a key role during the Define and Validate Initial Requirements stage.

Java An industry standard object-oriented programming language originally developed by Sun Microsystems.

Java applet A program written in Java that is commonly operated in a Web browser.

Java bean A well-defined approach to developing reusable components with the Java programming language.

joint application development (JAD) A structured, facilitated meeting in which modeling is performed by both users and developers together. JADs are often held for gathering user requirements.

K

key A column, or several columns when combined, within a relational database table whose value(s) uniquely identifies a row.

key process area (KPA) An issue that must be addressed to achieve a specific Capability Maturity Model (CMM) maturity level.

L

leaf class A class within an inheritance hierarchy that does not have other classes inheriting from it.

learning history A written narrative of an organization's recent critical experience; often, the experiences of a software development project team.

learning team A small group of people assigned the task of working together to learn a particular subject.

legacy application Any application or system currently in production. Legacy applications are often difficult, if not impossible, to maintain and enhance.

life cycle process pattern A process pattern that depicts a software life cycle process, often made up of a collection of phases, stages, and tasks.

maintenance The update of configuration items (CIs) based on prioritized software change requests (SCRs) allocated in such a way as to retain and/or enhance the reusability and robustness of said CIs.

maintenance change A description of a modification to be made to one or more existing configuration items (CIs).

maintenance release An application release that contains only bug fixes and does not contain new functionality.

man month *See* Work month

master test/quality assurance(QA) plan A document that describes your testing and quality assurance policies and procedures, as well as the detailed test plans for each portion of your application.

matrix organization An organization with a reporting structure wherein individuals potentially report to several managers: often, one manager for the project to which they are currently assigned, and another manager of a specialized group such as Modeling.

mature software organization A software organization in which the managers monitor the quality of the software products and the process that produces them. There is an objective, quantitative basis for judging product quality and analyzing problems with the product and process.

maturity level A well-defined evolutionary plateau toward achieving a mature software process. According to the Capability Maturity Model (CMM), for an organization to achieve a specific maturity level it must satisfy and institutionalize all of the key process areas (KPAs) for that level and the levels below.

member function *See* Method

mental model An internal representation of a person's conceptualization and understanding of a system.

mentor An experienced developer who transfers their skills to less experienced developers to aid in their education experience. This is a key role during all phases, but specifically during the Construct phase.

method The object-oriented equivalent of a function or procedure, with the exception that a method is specific to the class, and subclasses thereof, for which it is defined.

method-invocation box One of the long, thin vertical boxes appearing on sequence diagrams that represent a method invocation in an object.

method response A count of the total number of messages that are sent as a result of a method being invoked.

method testing The act of ensuring that a method (member function) performs as defined.

methodology In the context of systems development, it is the collection of techniques and approaches that you take when creating systems.

metric A measurement.

metrics management The process of collecting, summarizing, and acting on measurements (metrics) to potentially improve both quality of the software that your organization develops and the actual software process of your organization.

middleware The technology that allows computer hardware to communicate with one another. This includes the network itself, its operating system, and anything needed to connect computers to the network.

milestone A significant event in a project, usually the completion of a major deliverable; a point where upper management is traditionally informed of the status of the project. Because the OOSP is serial in the large and iterative in the small, the only clear milestones occur at the completion of project phases.

model An abstraction describing a problem domain and/or a solution to a problem domain. Traditionally, models are thought of as diagrams plus their corresponding documentation, although non-diagrams such as interview results, requirement documents, and collections of CRC cards are also considered to be models.

model review A technical review in which a model is inspected.

modeling The act of creating or updating one or more models.

modeling pattern A pattern depicting a solution, typically in the form of a class model, to a common modeling problem.

N

notation The set of symbols that are used in the drawing of diagrams. The Unified Modeling Language (UML) defines a defacto industry-standard modeling notation.

not-invented-here (NIH) syndrome A common myth in the information technology (IT) industry that states that developers are unwilling to reuse the work of others. The reality is that developers will only reuse high-quality work of other developers.

***n*-tier client/server** A client/server architecture in which client machines interact with application servers, which in turn interact with other application servers and/or database servers.

O

objectbase *See* Object-oriented database management system (OODBMS)

object database *See* Object-oriented database management system (OODBMS)

object identifier (OID) An attribute that uniquely identifies an object; the object-oriented equivalent of a key.

object-interaction diagram *See* Sequence diagram

OPEN modeling language (OML) A set of notations for OO modeling proposed by the OPEN Consortium.

object-oriented database management system (OODBMS) A persistence mechanism, also known as an objectbase or object database, that fully supports the storage and manipulation of objects.

Object-Oriented Software Process (OOSP) A collection of process patterns that together describe a complete process for developing, maintaining, and supporting software.

object-oriented test case A collection of: objects that are in states appropriate to what is being tested; message sends to those objects; and the expected results of those message sends that together verify that a specific feature within your application works properly.

object/relational impedance mismatch The difference resulting from the fact that relational theory is based on relationships between tuples that are queried, whereas the object paradigm is based on relationships between objects that are traversed.

object technology center (OTC) A technology transfer group that specializes in the rapid development and deployment of the infrastructure necessary to use object-oriented software development techniques successfully on a corporate scale.

OPEN Object-oriented Process, Environment, and Notation; a standard development method developed by the OPEN Consortium.

OPEN Consortium A group of individuals and organizations promoting and enhancing the use of object-oriented technology.

OPEN Process An object-oriented software process promoted by the OPEN Consortium.

operational feasibility An assessment of whether your organization can maintain and support an application or system once it is deployed.

operations documentation The documentation deployed to your operations department, including backup procedures, batch job and printing requirements, data extraction/sharing requirements, installation procedures for your application, resource requirements for your application, and the version description document (VDD) describing the product baseline for your application.

operations engineer A person responsible for operating one or more applications once they are placed in production. This is a key role during the Maintain and Support phase.

operations manager A person responsible for managing your organization's operations department and operations engineers. This is a key role during the Maintain and Support phase.

operations testing The act of ensuring that the needs of operations personnel who have to support and/or operate the application are met.

opportunistic reuse A reuse approach where reusable items are harvested from project deliverables after the fact.

optionality An indication of whether something is required.

organizational pattern A pattern that describes a common management technique or a potential organization structure.

override The redefinition of a method or attribute in a subclass.

P

paradigm A way of thinking about a given subject.

parallel development An approach to developing applications in which work on various sub-applications proceeds simultaneously in parallel.

patch release A software release that contains one or more bug fixes, replacing only a portion of the total application.

path testing The act of ensuring that all logic paths within your code were exercised at least once. This is a superset of coverage testing.

pattern The description of a general solution to a common problem or issue from which a detailed solution to a specific problem may be determined. Software development patterns come in many flavors, including but not limited to analysis patterns, design patterns, and process patterns.

pattern language A collection, or catalog, of related patterns. A pattern language for processes enables you to create an infinite variety of combinations, each one of which would be considered a tailored software process.

pattern template A predefined format for describing a pattern. There is currently an effort within the patterns community to describe a standard template for process patterns, but at the time of this writing one has not been finalized.

pattern reuse The reuse of publicly documented approaches, called patterns, to solving common problems.

peer review A style of technical review in which a project deliverable, or portion thereof, is inspected by a small group of people with expertise in the product being reviewed.

people management The process of organizing, monitoring, coaching, and motivating people in such a manner to ensure that they work together effectively and contribute to a project/organization positively.

performance requirement A requirement defining the speed at which a software feature is to operate.

persistence The issue of how to store objects to permanent storage. Objects need to be persistent if they are to be available to you and/or to others the next time your application is run.

persistence classes Classes that provide the ability to permanently store objects. By encapsulating the storage and retrieval of objects via persistence classes, you are able to use various storage technologies interchangeably without affecting your applications.

persistence layer The collection of classes that provides business objects the ability to be persistent. A persistence layer effectively wraps access to your persistence mechanisms.

persistence mechanism The permanent storage facility used to make objects persistent. Examples include relational databases, object databases, flat files, and object/relational databases.

person month *See* Work month

PERT chart *See* Project network diagram

phase *See* Project phase

phase process pattern A process pattern that depicts the interactions between the stage process patterns for a single project phase.

pilot project A small project whose purpose is to prove the viability of a new technology.

pilot testing A testing process equivalent to beta testing that is used by organizations to test applications they have developed for their own internal use.

planned reuse *See* systematic reuse

pop-up menu A style of menu, often tailored depending on the context in which it is invoked, that is displayed when requested by a user. A common GUI design standard is to display a pop-up menu when the user clicks the secondary mouse button. Also called a context-sensitive menu or hidden menu.

postcondition An expression of the properties of the state of an object after a method has been invoked successfully.

precondition An expression of the constraints under which a method will operate properly.

present-day value An amount of money into which inflation has been taken into account to determine its value in today's terms.

primary key The column(s) of a table that have been chosen as the primary means of uniquely identifying rows in that column.

private visibility An indication that a method or attribute is accessible only by instances of a class.

problem reproduction environment An environment in which a copy of your application runs in isolation. This environment is used by support engineers to simulate problems reported by your user community.

procedure A series of steps to be followed to perform a given task.

process A series of actions in which one or more inputs are used to produce one or more outputs.

process action team (PAT) A group of software professionals, often from different parts of your organization, who are given the responsibility to identify and define applicable process patterns for your organization.

process antipattern An antipattern that describes an approach and/or series of actions for developing software that is proven to be ineffective and often detrimental to your organization.

process checklist An indication of the tasks that should be completed while working a defined process.

process diagram A diagram that shows the movement of data within a system. Similar in concept to a data-flow diagram (DFD) but not as rigid and documentation-heavy.

process improvement plan A plan identifying potential improvements to your existing object-oriented software process (OOSP), including an estimate, schedule, and staff assignments for making the improvements.

process pattern A pattern that describes a proven, successful approach and/or series of actions for developing software.

process specialist A person who is responsible for choosing and/or defining the development processes to be used on the project, and who may act as an infrastructure consultant during later phases. This is a key role during the Define Infrastructure stage.

product baseline The exact version of the software that is released to the user community.

programme A collection of projects or releases of one or more applications.

project assessment A two- or three-page document that summarizes what occurred on a project. This document is often used as introductory material to your learning history for the given project, and for the process improvement plan that results from the lessons learned on the given project.

project auditor A professional who specializes in the review and assessment of projects. This is a key role during the Assess stage.

project charter A document issued by senior management that provides the project manager with the authority to apply organizational resources to project activities.

project-defined software process The process, tailored from your organization's standard software process, used for a given project.

project estimate An appraisal of how long a project will take and how much it will cost, given a specific environment and a specific team. Change the environment and/or change the team, and your estimate should change. Project estimates are a deliverable of the Initiate phase and are updated regularly throughout a project.

project funding The money and resources used to finance a project.

project infrastructure The team, tools, and processes that will be used on a given project.

project management The process of organizing, monitoring, and directing a project.

Project Management Institute (PMI) An organization dedicated to the research of, and dissemination of information about, project management techniques.

project manager A person who is responsible for obtaining funding and authorization for the project from upper management, as well as for day-to-day management of a project. This is a key role during all phases of the project.

project network diagram A schematic display of the logical relationships between project activities, always drawn left-to-right to reflect project chronology. Often incorrectly referred to as a PERT (Program Evaluation and Review Technique) chart.

project objectives A description of the criteria against which the success of a project will be measured. This potential includes clear, measurable definitions of goals for the cost of the project, desired delivery date, quality factors, and desires of the various project stakeholders.

project overview A description of the purpose of the project, the scope of the project, its advantages and disadvantages, the expected cost and delivery date(s), and the technical platform for which it will be developed. A project overview is effectively a summary of the other components the schedule, estimate, team definition, and risk assessment that comprise a project plan. Project overviews are a deliverable of the Initiate phase.

project phase The large components of the OOSP that are performed in a serial manner. The four project phases are Initiate, Construct, Deliver, and Maintain and Support. A project phase is depicted by a process pattern.

project plan A project plan is a collection of several project management deliverables, including, but not limited to, a project overview, a project schedule, a project estimate, a team definition, and a risk assessment. Project plans are a deliverable of the Initiate phase and are updated regularly throughout a project.

project schedule A project schedule indicates what will be done, when things will be done, and who will do them. A major component of a project schedule is a Gantt chart with its corresponding descriptions of tasks and resources. Project schedules are a deliverable of the Initiate phase and are updated regularly throughout a project.

project scope A definition of the functionality that will, and will not, be implemented by an application.

project skills matrix A chart that relates the skills needed on a project to the skills of the people (potentially) on a project team.

project sponsor A person who takes responsibility for supporting, nurturing, and protecting the project throughout its life, and who is crucial for starting the project successfully. This is a key role during the Justify stage.

project stage The components of a project phase, performed in an iterative manner, that make up a project phase. For example, the project stages that make up the Construct phase are

Model, , Program, Generalize, and Test in the Small. A project stage is depicted by a process pattern.

project stakeholder Any individual or organization that may be affected by project activities.

proof-of-concept prototype Software written to prove or test the viability of a technology, language, or environment. Also called a technical prototype.

protected visibility An indication that an attribute or method is accessible only to the instances of the class, and all subclasses of, that the method/attribute is defined in.

prototype A mock-up of all or a portion of your application.

prototype walkthrough A process by which your users work through a collection of use cases using a prototype as if it was the real thing. The main goal is to test whether or not the prototype design meets their needs.

prototyping An iterative analysis technique in which users are actively involved in the mocking up of the user interface for an application.

proxy object An object that is used to represent another object. A common responsibility of a proxy object is to pass messages that it receives to the object for which it is a proxy.

public interface The collection of public methods and attributes of a class or component.

public visibility An indication that a method, attribute, or class is accessible to all objects within your application.

pure inheritance When a subclass inherits everything from its superclass(es).

Q

qualitative factor A cost or benefit that is subjective in nature, against which it is very difficult to identify a monetary value.

quality assurance (QA) The process of ensuring that the efforts of a project meet or exceed the standards expected of them.

quality assurance (QA) engineer A person responsible for validating that the deliverables produced by the development team meet or exceed the agreed-to standards and guidelines for the project. This is a key role during all stages of the Construct phase, the Define and Validate Initial Requirements stage, and the Rework stage.

quality gate An objectively identifiable point in a project at which a review is performed to validate one or more project deliverables. To meet a milestone, your project will usually need to "pass through" a quality gate successfully.

quantitative factor A cost or benefit against which a monetary value can easily be identified.

R

R&D/proof-of-concept engineer A developer who creates technical prototypes, also called proof-of-concept prototypes, to determine how to solve a given technical issue. This role is applicable to the Model stage to verify decisions made during technical architectural modeling and detailed design.

refactoring The act of reorganizing OO development efforts. For source code and models, refactoring will often comprise the renaming of methods, attributes, or classes; the redefinition of methods, attributes, or classes; or the complete rework or methods, attributes, or classes. For other project deliverables refactoring may simply be the renaming or reorganization of sections of the deliverable.

reference manual A document, either paper or electronic, aimed at experts who need quick access to information.

regression testing The act of ensuring that previously tested behaviors still work as expected after changes have been made to an application.

regulatory requirement A requirement that you must fulfill by law. Regulatory requirements include the need to provide specific information to the government, perhaps for taxation or environmental reasons, or the use of a specific programming language or technique in the case of government contracts.

relational database (RDB) A type of persistence mechanism, based on relational theory, that stores data in tables. The rows of data within tables are related to one another; hence the term *relational database*.

release A version of an application or component that has been made available for use by its developers.

release plan A plan that describes when your release procedures will be applied, and by whom, to release your application.

release procedures A description of the tasks, and the order in which to take them, to release an application. Release procedures will refer to your data conversion plan and your training plan for your release.

repository A centralized database into/from which you can check in and check out versions of your development work, including documentation, models, and source code.

requirement Something that is essential, or perceived to be essential.

requirements allocation matrix (RAM) A mapping of requirements, defined in your requirements document, to the portions of your model(s) that implement them.

requirements document A document, also called a System Requirements Specification (SRS), that describes the user, technical, and environmental requirements for an application. This document potentially contains the major use cases for the application, detailed use-case scenarios for the application, and traditional requirements for the application as well. Requirements documents are a deliverable of the Initiate phase and are updated regularly during modeling. Requirements documents are also updated during the Maintain and Support phase as bugs and enhancements are identified.

requirements engineering The identification and validation of requirements.

requirements instability A metric calculated by taking the number of changed requirements in a given time frame by the total number of requirements.

requirements triage The act of prioritizing requirements for example, "must have," "nice to have," and "nonessential" to aid in the definition of an application that can be delivered with the limited resources at hand.

requirement-verification matrix A document that is used to relate use cases to the portions of your application that implement the requirements addressed by those use cases. For OO applications, the names of classes are listed across the top of the matrix, the use cases are listed along the left-hand axis of the matrix, and in the squares are listed the main method(s) involved in fulfilling each use case.

responsibility Behavior that a class is expected to be able to perform, either for its own use or in response to a request from another class. A responsibility may be for a class to know something, to have data, or to do something (to perform a function).

Reuse Capability Model (RCM) A model which describes five maturity levels at which your organization may operate with respect to reuse.

reuse consumer A developer that reuses the work of other developers.

reuse engineer A senior, experienced developer who is responsible for supporting and enhancing the reuse process within your organization. This person works closely with component engineers and infrastructure engineers, and plays a key role in all stages of the Construct phase.

reuseless An item that has been promoted as reusable but in practice is found to be too specific or of low quality.

reuse management The process of organizing, monitoring, and directing the efforts of a project team that lead to reuse on a project, either of existing or of purchased items.

reuse producer A developer that creates reusable items.

reuse repository A tool used to store reusable items.

revision A change to a deliverable.

risk assessment A document indicating potential factors, called risks, that if they were to occur would harm the project. A risk assessment is used to identify risks so they may be dealt with appropriately. Risk assessments are a deliverable of the Initiate phase and are updated regularly throughout a project.

risk assessor A person who is responsible for identifying and potentially addressing the initial risks associated with your project. This is a key role during the Define Initial Management Documents stage and Justify stage.

risk management The process of identifying, monitoring, and mitigating the risks faced by a project team. These risks may typically be strategic, technical, and/or political.

risk officer Someone in your organization who is responsible for supporting and overseeing risk management.

robustness A measure of the quality of a product. Robust software products continue to operate once an error occurs and are relatively easy to maintain and enhance.

root class The top class in an inheritance hierarchy.

S

schema The design of something.

scope creep *See* Feature creep

sequence diagram A diagram that shows the types of objects involved in a use-case scenario, including the messages they send to one another and the values that they return. Also referred to as an event trace diagram or simply an interaction diagram.

serial development An approach to development in which a series of tasks are performed in a defined, sequential order.

server One or more multiuser processors (with shared memory) that provide computing connectivity, database services, and interfaces relevant to the business need. A server is also commonly referred to as a "back end."

setter method An accessor method that modifies the value of an attribute.

silver bullet Any product or technique that (unrealistically) promises order-of-magnitude improvements in your development productivity.

singleton A class that will have at most one instance.

skills assessment (deliverable) A summary of the proficiencies of an individual, used for the purpose of developing a training plan for the individual and for identifying projects where their skills are needed.

skills assessment (process) A process in which the skills, both technical skills such as C++ programming and people skills such as eliciting requirements from users, of an individual are determined and measured.

skills database A database that records the skills and experiences of people within your organization. This information is both the input and the output of a skills assessment.

software change request (SCR) A description of a potential improvement to a software deliverable, often identified by users of that deliverable.

software configuration management (SCM) A set of engineering procedures for tracking and documenting software and its related deliverables throughout their life cycles to ensure that all changes are recorded and the current state of the software is known and reproducible.

software configuration manager A person responsible for ensuring that software and its related deliverables are managed appropriately under configuration control, as well as to communicate all SCM policies and procedures to developers. The greater the complexity of the software being developed, the greater the need for a software configuration manager. This is a key role throughout the Construct, Deliver, and Maintain and Support phases.

Software Engineering Institute (SEI) An organization within Carnegie Mellon University whose goal is to provide leadership in advancing the state of the practice of software engineering to improve the quality of systems that depend on software.

Software Engineering Process Group (SEPG) A group of dedicated professionals whose sole responsibility is to support the improvement of your organization's software process.

software maintenance The update of existing configuration items based on change requests allocated in such a way as to retain and/or enhance the reusability and robustness of said configuration items.

software problem report (SPR) A description of a potential software defect identified by someone who is not directly responsible for a given software deliverable.

software process A set of project phases, stages, methods, techniques, and practices that people employ to develop and maintain software and its associated products (plans, documents, models, code, test cases, and manuals).

software Process Improvement and Capability dEtermination (SPICE) An ISO software process improvement project.

software quality assurance (SQA) The process and techniques by which the development of software is verified, tested, and ensured to be of sufficient levels of excellence for your organization.

software unit An identifiable portion of software potentially an application, a file that is a portion of an application, a domain component, or a service supported by your technical architecture. Software units are one type of configuration item (CI).

Spiral SDLC An iterative approach to application development first proposed by Barry Boehm.

staff assessment A summary of the performance with your organization of a single staff member. An assessment of the staff member's skills is included, as is a training plan for maintaining and improving those skills.

staff month *See* Work month

stage *See* Project stage

stage process pattern A process pattern that depicts the steps, often performed iteratively, of a single project stage.

standard A description, ideally with an example provided, of how something must be done. You are required to follow standards (unlike guidelines, which are optional).

standards specialist A person responsible for choosing and/or defining the development standards to be used on a project, and who may act as an infrastructure engineer/consultant during later phases. This is a key role during the Define Infrastructure stage.

state A representation of a stage in the behavior pattern of an object. A state can also be said to represent a condition of an object to which a defined set of policies, regulations, and physical laws apply. On statechart diagrams a state is shown as a horizontal rectangle.

state diagram *See* Statechart diagram

statechart diagram A diagram that describes the states that an object may be in, as well as the transitions between states. Also called a "state diagram" or "state-transition diagram."

state-transition diagram *See* Statechart diagram

status report A two- or three-page document briefly summarizing the work performed on a project over a given period of time and any change in status of the project, including updates to your risk assessment.

stored procedure A function implemented within a relational database.

strategic reuse plan Your organization's plan for implementing its reuse management approach, including a description of its reuse goals, its schedule, and its commitment to supporting reuse management.

stress testing The act of ensuring that the system performs as expected under high volumes of transactions, high numbers of users, and so on.

stress-test plan The test plan that describes how you intend to go about stress-testing your application.

string of message sends A series of messages sent to the same object.

Structured Query Language (SQL) A standard mechanism used to CRUD records in a relational database.

subject matter expert (SME) A person who is responsible for providing pertinent information about the problem and/or technical domain either from personal knowledge or from research. This is a key role during the Define and Validate Initial Requirements stage and the Model stage.

support center A group of support engineers and their support tools.

support documentation The documentation deployed to your support department, including your support call recording process, applicable call escalation procedures, relevant points of contact within your development and operations departments, and all user documentation for your application.

support engineer A person whose job is to collaborate with users needing help to use your software. This is a key role during the Support stage and Test in the Large stage.

support flow The process through which support requests are received by support engineers from users, solutions are found, and answers are returned to the user.

support manager The person responsible for managing your organization's support center and support engineers. This is a key role during the Support stage.

support request A request for aid using an application made by a user. This may be in the form of a phone call, an electronic mail (e-mail) message, a fax, or an entry into a support request database (likely via a Web page).

support request database An application built for the specific purpose of recording support requests. This database may be accessible to your users to allow them to submit support requests, perhaps via a Web page data entry screen.

support request escalation A process in which a support request is passed from the support engineer who initially responded to it to another person, potentially a more senior support engineer or developer, to be resolved.

support testing The act of ensuring that the needs of support personnel who have to support the application are met.

support user's guide A brief document, usually a single page, that describes the support services for your application that are available to your user community. This guide will include support phone numbers, fax numbers, and Web site locations as well as hours of operations and tips for obtaining the best services.

system analysis The process of determining what projects will be undertaken, the order in which they will be undertaken, how they will be developed, and the scope of each project.

system classes System classes provide operating-system-specific functionality for your applications, or they wrap functionality provided by other tool/application vendors. System classes isolate you from the operating system, making your application portable between environments, by wrapping OS-specific features.

system development life cycle (SDLC) The process by which software is developed. An SDLC is comprised of interrelated techniques that are used to define, build, implement, support, and maintain software.

system layer The collection of classes that provide operating-system-specific functionality for your applications, or that wrap functionality provided by non-OO applications, hardware devices, and/or non-OO code libraries.

system requirement specification (SRS) *See* Requirements document

system testing A testing process in which you find and fix any known problems to prepare your application for user testing.

systematic reuse An approach to reuse that involves modeling techniques whose purpose is to define high-leverage, reusable components.

T

table join A relational database concept in which information from two or more tables are accessed. Tables are joined by selecting rows from each table that contain identical values in one or more common columns.

tailored software process A software process that has been modified to meet the needs of a specific project.

task list A list of activities that an individual or team is to perform in a defined period of time. Task lists are often defined to manage the creation of a project deliverable.

task process pattern A process pattern that depicts the detailed steps to perform a specific task, such as detailed modeling or performing a technical review.

team definition A document describing who will be involved with a project, what their roles on the project will be, and when they will be involved. This document should also provide a reporting structure, or organization chart, for the team.

team lead The developer who is responsible for ensuring the overall technical integrity of the project and for working together with the project manager to aid and support the other developers on the team. A main responsibility of team leads is to ruthlessly eliminate any obstacles that keep the developers away from working to improve the application. This is a key role during all stages of the Construct phase.

technical architecture A set of models and documents that describe the technical components of an application, including but not limited to the hardware, software, middleware, persistence mechanisms, and operating systems to be deployed.

technical feasibility An assessment of whether an application or system can be built with a defined set of tools and technologies.

technical prototype *See* Proof-of-concept prototype

technical requirement A description of a nonbehavioral feature, such as the required time for something to run in or the operating system that an application must work in.

technical review A testing technique in which the design of your application is examined critically by a group of your peers. A review will typically focus on accuracy, quality, usability, and completeness. This process is often referred to as a walkthrough or a peer review.

technical-review plan A document that describes the goal of a technical review, who is to attend and why, the information that the reviewers require before the review, and the records and documentation that will be produced by the review.

technical writer The person responsible for writing, updating, and/or improving the technical documentation produced on the project, potentially including the requirements, models, standards, guidelines, and project plans. This is a key role throughout all project phases.

template reuse The reuse of a common set of layouts for key development artifacts documents, models, and source code within your organization.

templated pattern A pattern that has been documented using a pattern template.

test case A description, often documented as a series of steps, of a situation that a software item must support.

test engineer This person is responsible for verifying that the application works as defined by the requirements for the application. This is a key role during all stages of the Construct phase and the Test in the Large stage.

test log A chronological tracking of your testing activities.

test manager The person responsible for managing the testing engineers and testing process within your organization. This person works closely with your organization's project managers to ensure that the testing of applications is being performed in an effective manner. This is a key role during all stages of the Construct phase and the Test in the Large stage.

test plan A document that prescribes the approach to be taken during the testing process.

test script The steps to be performed to run a test case. Test scripts will be implemented using a variety of techniques, from source code for code tests to written steps for function testing.

test suite A collection of test scripts.

testability The measure of ease of which a product may be tested.

testing The act of verifying that the "right" thing, as defined by its requirements, was built.

testing release A software release in which your application is released for alpha/beta/pilot testing.

test-procedure scripts The description of the steps that must be carried out to perform all or part of a test plan.

thin client A two-tiered client/server architecture in which client machines implement only the user interface of an application.

timebox A defined period of time, from several days to several months, in which a team of developers is assigned to produced a given deliverable. With a timebox the end date is actually a fixed deadline; if the team needs to, it will cut features out of the deliverable rather than extend the delivery date.

tools specialist A person who is responsible for evaluating and selecting the development tools to be used on the project, and who may act as an infrastructure engineer/consultant during later phases. This is a key role during the Define Infrastructure stage.

traceability The ease with which the features of one deliverable a document, model, or source code can be related or traced to the features of another.

trailblazer project A medium-sized project whose purpose is to prove the viability of a software process by developing software while following the given process.

trainer A person responsible for the delivery, and possibly development, of training courses. This is a key role during the Release stage.

training The process by which people gain tangible skills.

training manager The person responsible for managing your organization's training department. This person oversees your organization's internal trainers, if any, and is responsible for hiring outside training firms to deliver courses to your organization's employees. This is a key role during the Release stage.

training plan A plan that describes the training to be delivered, to whom it will be delivered, how it will be delivered, when it will be delivered, and where it will be delivered.

transition A transition is a progression from one state to another.

A transition will be triggered by an event (either internal or external to the object). A transition is shown on a statechart diagram as an arrow leading from one state to another.

tutorial manual A document, either paper or electronic, aimed at novice users who need to learn the fundamentals of an application.

two-tiered client/server An approach to client/server architectures in which client machines directly interact with server machines.

U

Unified Modeling Language (UML) The industry-standard OO modeling notation proposed by Rational Corporation of Santa Clara, California. The UML has been accepted by the Object Management Group (OMG) to make it the industry standard.

unit testing The act of testing small components of a system to ensure that they work. In the object world this is both method and class testing.

usability testing The verification, typically performed by human-factors engineers, that an application or system is as easy to use as it needs to be for its user community.

use case A description of a high-level business process that an application may or may not be expected to support.

use-case diagram A diagram that shows the use cases and actors for the application you are developing.

use-case scenario A description of a specific, detailed user requirement that an application may or may not be expected to handle. A use-case scenario is a detailed example of a use case.

use-case scenario testing A testing process in which users work through use cases with the aid of a facilitator to verify that the user requirements are accurate.

user acceptance testing (UAT) A testing technique in which users verify that an application meets their needs.

user documentation The documentation deployed to the user community, potentially including a user manual, tutorial manual, reference manual, and support user's guide.

user interface (UI) The portion of an application with which the user directly interacts, including the screens, reports, documentation, and software support (via telephone, electronic mail, and so on).

user interface classes User interface classes provide the ability for users to interact with the system. User interface classes typically define a graphical user interface for an application, although other interface styles, such as voice command or handwritten input, are also implemented via user-interface classes.

user interface event An occurrence (often) initiated by a user, such as keyboard input, a mouse action, or spoken input captured by a microphone, that causes action within your application.

user interface object An object displayed as part of the user interface for an application. This includes simple objects such as buttons and list boxes, icons, screens, and reports as well as complex objects such as editing screens and reports.

user interface testing The testing of the user interface (UI) to ensure that it follows accepted UI standards and meets the requirements defined for it. This is often referred to as graphical user interface (GUI) testing.

user manual A document, either paper or electronic, aimed at intermediate users who understand the basics of an application but may not know how to perform all applicable work tasks with the application.

user requirement A behavioral requirement for an application that describes the needs of all or part of the user community, and whose source either directly or indirectly came from the user community.

user requirement review A testing process in which a facilitated group of users verify and prioritize the user requirements gathered by a development team.

user testing Testing processes in which the user community, as opposed to developers, performs the tests. User testing techniques include user acceptance testing, alpha testing, beta testing, and pilot testing.

V

version One or more revisions to a deliverable results in a new version.

version control tool A software tool used to check in/out, define, and manage versions of project deliverables.

version description document (VDD) A complete list of all items included in a product baseline release of software, including all configuration items and supporting deliverables. The VDD includes an indication of all changes made to the software from the previous version and a list of all applicable SPRs and SCRs implemented in the current version.

virtual organization An organization with a reporting structure wherein professionals collaborate as equals to perform specific tasks.

visibility An indication of the level of access to a class, method, or attribute.

volume testing A subset of stress testing that deals specifically with determining how many transactions or database accesses an application can handle during a defined period of time.

W

waterfall SDLC An approach to building applications in which development efforts proceed in a serial manner from one project stage to another.

white-box test A test that verifies that specific lines of code work as defined. This is also referred to as a clear-box test.

widget A user interface component such as a list, button, or window.

work breakdown structure (WBS) A deliverable-oriented grouping of project elements which organizes and defines the total scope of the project. Each descending level represents an increasingly detailed definition of a project component.

work day A standard amount of time, measured in hours, which your organization considers a day. Most organizations define a standard work day as being seven, seven-and-a-half, or eight hours.

work month A standard amount of time corresponding to the average number of work days in an average month. Also known as a man month, person month, staff month, or engineering month.

wrapper A collection of one or more classes that encapsulates access to non-OO technology to make it appear as if it is OO.

wrapper class Any class that is part of a wrapper.

wrapping The act of encapsulating non-OO functionality within a class, making it look and feel like any other object within the system.

Y

year 2000 (Y2K) problem A common problem where dates within software, and databases, have been recorded with a two-digit year (for example 05), instead of a four-digit year (for example 2005). This problem results in software not recognizing dates on or after January 1st, 2000, believing that they represent dates on or after January 1st, 1900 instead.

Index

T